Montgomery
and
The Portsmouth

In Memory
of
Joseph P. Copley
1928-1990

This seventeenth book published by the Portsmouth Marine Society is dedicated to the memory of the Society's esteemed secretary, Joseph P. Copley.

One of the enthusiasts who was responsible for the reactivation of the Portsmouth Marine Society, originally chartered in 1808, Joseph P. Copley served as secretary of the society from its rechartering in 1981 until his death,

For many years the curator of the Portsmouth Athenaeum, and in recent years curator of the Portsmouth Historical Society and the John Paul Jones House Museum, Joseph P. Copley was a man of integrity who dedicated his life to the pursuit of excellence in every facet of his research and preservation of local history. His careful contributions to preserved history are within the covers of many books and can be found in the archives of the organizations he served.

Joseph P. Copley is now part of the history of the Port of Portsmouth, New Hampshire.

Republished by
The Portsmouth Marine Society
in cooperation with
The Portsmouth Historical Society
and
The John Paul Jones House Museum

Sponsors

The Accounting Firm—Purdy, Bornstein, Hamel & Burrell
Nancy Olice Morison Allis
Ferris G. Bavicchi
Blake Insurance Agency
Carl W. Brage
Mr. & Mrs. R. H. Brighton
Harry A. Buron
Charles B. Doleac
First National Bank of Portsmouth
William E. Gilmore, Jr.
Granite State Minerals, Inc.
Henley Corporation
Mr. & Mrs. George B. Horne
Mr. & Mrs. William White Howells
Paul & Shaun McEachern
N. H. Glass Corporation—Richard Seedner
Muriel Obrist
Olde Port Bank
Mark G. Phillips, Auctioneer
Sarah Sawtelle Patrick
Piscataqua Savings Bank
Peter E. Randall Publisher
Ricci Supply—Donald Hayes
Rockingham House
Joseph & Jean Sawtelle
Shearson, Lehman, Hutton—John J. Hebert
Mr. & Mrs. Cyrus B. Sweet III
Dorothy & Arthur Thornhill
Tyco Laboratories
Brian L. Van Allen
William & Kay Wagner
Mr. & Mrs. Alexander R. Warrick
Helen & Sumner Winebaum

Subscribers

John Belcher
Wyman Boynton
Peter C. Braseth
Mr. & Mrs. Anthony S. Brown
Virginia Cumings
Mr. & Mrs. William F. deRochemont
CDR Barbara Ellis USN (Ret.)
Richard Gallant
Bruce & Joanne Graves
Mrs. Daniel E. Hobbs
Henry C. Horner, Esq.
Jackson, Jackson & Wagner
I. R. Lebel, C. P. A.
Robert A. Lee
Attorney & Mrs. John P. McGee, Jr.
Mara Frost Marshall
Alexander V. Munton
Brian Nickerson & Susan Sawtelle
Donald & Virginia O'Connor
Regal Limousine Service—The Fords
Thomas & Suzanne Shevenell
Helen H. St. John
Andrew H. Sherburne
Jane & Peter Torrey
Charles L. Vaughn
John & Sheila Welch

John Berrien Montgomery
1794-1873
AS COMMANDER, U. S. NAVY

Montgomery
and
The Portsmouth

by
Fred Blackburn Rogers

The Portsmouth Marine Society
Publication Seventeen

1990

Published for the Society by
Peter E. Randall Publisher

Printed in the United States of America
The Portsmouth Marine Society
Box 147, Portsmouth, NH 03802

Produced by
Peter E. Randall Publisher
Box 4726, Portsmouth, NH 03801

Library of Congress Cataloging-in-Publication Data

Rogers, Fred Blackburn
Montgomery and the Portsmouth / by Fred Blackburn Rogers.
p. cm. -- (Publication / the Portsmouth Marine Society ; 17)
Reprint. Originally published: San Francisco : J. Howell, 1958.
Includes bibliographical references (p.) and index.
ISBN 0-915819-16-3 : $25.00
1, California--History--1846-1850. 2. Bear Flag Revolt, 1846.
3. Montgomery, John Berrien, b. 1794. 4. Portsmouth (Corvette)
I. Title. II. Series: Publication (Portsmouth Marine Society) ; 17.
F864.R73 1990
979.4'03'092--dc20
[B] *90-20215*
CIP

Other Portsmouth Marine Society Publications:

1. *John Haley Bellamy, Carver of Eagles*
2. *The Prescott Story*
3. *The Piscataqua Gundalow, Workhorse for a Tidal Basin Empire*
4. *The Checkered Career of Tobias Lear*
5. *Clippers of the Port of Portsmouth and the Men Who Built Them*
6. *Portsmouth-Built Submarines of the Portsmouth Naval Shipyard*
7. *Atlantic Heights, A World War I Shipbuilders' Community*
8. *There Are No Victors Here*
   A Local Perspective on the Treaty of Portsmouth
9. *The Diary of the Portsmouth, Kittery and York Electric Railroad*
10. *Port of Portsmouth Ships and the Cotton Trade*
11. *Port of Dover, Two Centuries of Shipping on the Cochecho*
12. *Wealth and Honour*
    Portsmouth During the Golden Age of Privateering, 1775-1815
13. *The Sarah Mildred Long Bridge*
    A History of the Maine-New Hampshire Interstate
    Bridge from Portsmouth, New Hampshire, to Kittery, Maine
14. *The Isles of Shoals, A Visual History*
15. *Tall Ships of the Piscataqua, 1830-1877*
16. *George Washington in New Hampshire*

Montgomery

AND

The Portsmouth

BY

FRED BLACKBURN ROGERS

PUBLISHED BY JOHN HOWELL—BOOKS

MCMLVIII

Preface

"That flag floated proudly up." DOWNEY

A PROUD DAY INDEED, that 9th of July, 1846, at Yerba Buena, Alta California. Certainly it was the high point in the combined service of the Commander and his ship, for then and there occurred the raising of the American flag, which gave to California two names important in its annals—Montgomery and the *Portsmouth*.

The name Montgomery was soon and appropriately attached to a street, then little more than a sandy path on the shore of San Francisco Bay, now a way through an awesome, man-made canyon at the financial center of the Pacific Coast of America. Now relatively overshadowed, but then more important, is the pleasant plaza soon called Portsmouth Square, for Montgomery's ship. One is now a place of employment, the other of relaxation. How many of those who use or see them know much of their historical import? Perhaps this work may change curiosity to a rewarding interest.

Here are the life stories, as they occurred in combination and separately, of a fine officer and a fine ship. Emphasis is on the California scene, but much is added regarding their other service.

In the early days a naval officer, acting under very general instructions, was often isolated by poor communications and thus denied live information. Necessarily he had to exercise a high degree of initiative and often diplomacy—sometimes under irksome conditions of neutrality. The Montgomery mission to California is a case at point.

From the age of seventeen to nearly seventy-five, Montgomery spent his life in the naval service. There is a dearth of strictly personal material pertaining to him, so it is necessary to depend largely on his official writings and acts to form an estimate of the man. Many such writings are quoted extensively here because of their historical importance. The quotations retain their original spelling and punctuation. This method retains a feeling of the time, the persons, and the places otherwise lacking in any paraphrase. Moreover, it makes available in one work scarce and scattered material, part of which has not been published before. Thus this work, in parts, takes on the nature of a source book. Montgomery's relations with Frémont, Gillespie, Sloat, and Stockton are set forth in detail. His doings at San Francisco Bay and Yerba Buena are emphasized.

An interesting group of uncommon illustrations has been assembled. Here we have reproductions of four extremely rare Yerba Buena imprints by Sam Brannan. Three bear his name as printer, and the other was certainly done by him. Only one has been reproduced, and that as an extra illustration in a few copies of Henry R. Wagner's *California Imprints*. The Montgomery portrait is first published here.

It is a pleasure to add the story of the *Portsmouth* to that of her first commander. She also has a long life of service—over seventy years on the Navy List.

Special credit for assistance in my research goes to John Montgomery Mahon, who furnished much information and allowed the reproduction of the portrait of his great-grandfather.

The cooperation of the heads and staffs of the following agencies is gratefully acknowledged: The National Archives; Division of Naval History, Department of the Navy; U.S. Naval Institute;

Commandant, Third Naval District; Commander, Portsmouth Naval Shipyard; U. S. Naval Observatory; U. S. Coast and Geodetic Survey; Western Americana Collection, Yale University Library; Library of Congress; Special Collections, University of California Library, Los Angeles; Bancroft Library; Huntington Library; California State Library and its Sutro Branch; Franklin D. Roosevelt Library; Boston Public Library; Los Angeles Public Library; Peabody Museum of Salem; California Historical Society; Society of California Pioneers; Bank of America; *Boston Globe; Boston Herald;* and the W. W. Norton Company.

Among the individuals who helped are: Mrs. James H. Beal, Alfred H. Bill, Mrs. Fred J. Buenzle, Victor U. Buenzle, Howard I. Chapelle, John W. Collier, Dr. William N. Davis, Jr., Dr. Clifford M. Drury, Rear Adm. E. M. Eller, the Galvin Family, Dr. Archibald Hanna, Dr. E. Kenneth Haviland, Dr. Boyd F. Huff, Dr. John A. Hussey, Dr. Robert E. Johnson, Dr. John H. Kemble, Mrs. Gerald D. Kennedy, Walter Loos, Dale L. Morgan, David F. Myrick, Allan R. Ottley, Earl C. Palmer, Henry Rusk, Col. George L. Smith, and Edward Rowe Snow. John Swingle read my manuscript and made very helpful suggestions.

This is my last participation directly in this series. In taking leave, I desire especially to thank my publisher, Warren R. Howell, who gave every encouragement from the inception of the series.

FRED B. ROGERS

TABLE OF CONTENTS

ILLUSTRATIONS

Beginnings

A TRADITION OF NAVAL SERVICE often has a dominant effect within a family. Therefore no one could have been surprised when, at the age of seventeen, John Berrien Montgomery became a midshipman, United States Navy, on June 4, 1812, only a fortnight before war was declared against Great Britain.

Already Montgomery's younger brother, Nathaniel Lawrence Montgomery, had become a midshipman on December 17, 1810, at the age of ten. He later lost an arm during the engagement between the *President* and the *Belvidera,* and as an aide to Commodore Macdonough was again wounded at the Battle of Lake Champlain in 1814. He was promoted to lieutenant the same year, said to be the youngest officer so commissioned in the American Navy. Montgomery's older brother, Alexander Maxwell Montgomery, became an acting surgeon's mate and was on the *Essex* with Porter at the fight off the Harbor of Valparaiso, March 28, 1814. Later he served as assistant surgeon and surgeon.

Montgomery's aunt, Eliza Berrien, had married Nathaniel Lawrence, son of Capt. Thomas Lawrence of "Don't give up the ship" fame, and his two sisters, Margaret and Maria, married respectively Purser John B. Shaw, and William Inman, who became a commodore.

Thus the Montgomerys were truly a Navy family.

The Montgomery family has been traced back over ten centuries to Count Roger de Montgomerie, who lived in northern

France before the coming of Rollo, the Northman chief, in 912. The family line is too extended for presentation here, but several useful reference works are cited in a note.[1] In 1701-1702 William of Brigend (Scotland), twenty-seventh of the line, crossed the ocean with his young family and came to Doctor's Creek, Monmouth County, East Jersey. In 1706 he bought 500 acres there, settled on the property, and called it "Eglinton," named after an estate in Scotland.

Thomas West Montgomery, grandson of William and son of Alexander Montgomery, was born in July 1764. By that time the spelling of the terminal *ry* in the surname had become well established. In 1787 Thomas was admitted to the practice of medicine, and in 1788 he married Mary Berrien, daughter of John Berrien, onetime Justice of the Supreme Court of New Jersey. Thomas practiced his profession at Allentown, New Jersey, and later at Princeton and New York.

John Berrien Montgomery, son of Thomas and Mary, was born November 17, 1794, at Allentown. Nothing is found regarding his boyhood life except the fact that he was educated at Allentown. It may be assumed that he had the privilege of much work and some play afield—rights of any small boy in any small, American town. With those rights probably came a sense of discipline and obligation, heightened by the fact of his father's public service. Only from portraits made much later is anything learned of his physical characteristics; early records of the Navy lacked such data. At his middle age his hair was a medium dark brown, his eyes grey green, complexion fair, and his height average, probably not exceeding five feet and nine inches.

Undoubtedly the Montgomery family made trips to the Berrien home, "Rockingham," at Rocky Hill near Princeton. There they must have heard that General George Washington had used the house as his last military field headquarters while the Congress was in session at Princeton, also that at the house he prepared and first delivered from its balcony his Farewell Address to the Armies. There too, the Montgomerys could see a pair of gaming tables of the Chippendale style, presented by General Washington as a personal memento to Margaret Eaton Berrien, wife of Judge Berrien. One of those tables later passed through John Montgomery Mahon to the Philadelphia Museum of Art.[2]

Soon after Montgomery was commissioned as a midshipman, President Madison signed the bill declaring that a state of war existed with Great Britain, and Montgomery was on his way via New York to Sacket (also called Sackett's) Harbor on Lake Ontario. There his service was on the schooner *Hamilton*, 9 guns; the sloop *Madison*, 20 guns; and the corvette *General Pike*, of 24 guns. He was at Kingston on November 10, when an attempt failed to cut out the British flagship *Royal George*. On April 27, 1813, he participated in the capture of Little York (present Toronto), and on May 27 he assisted in the capture of Fort George.

Meanwhile, early in 1813, Lieut. Oliver Hazard Perry had been ordered to Lake Erie, where, by reason of his seniority he became commodore. The building of a new American fleet at Presque Isle (now Erie) was pushed, under enormous difficulties, by Noah and Adam Brown. Built were the brigs *Lawrence* and *Niagara*, each of 20 guns, and the schooners *Ariel*, *Ohio*, and *Porcupine*. These, with a few additional small craft, constituted the force which Perry had ready by August to oppose the British fleet under Commodore Robert H. Barclay.[3]

The fourth of the same month a contingent of seven officers and one hundred seamen, Americans then at Lake Ontario, volunteered for service on Lake Erie. One of this group was Montgomery, who was then assigned to the *Niagara*, under Lieut. Jesse D. Elliott.

It was on September 10, 1813, that Perry met and defeated Barclay at the Battle of Lake Erie. It must have been a most memorable occasion for our young midshipman on the *Niagara* to view a scene famous in the annals of the United States Navy—that of Perry's movement in a small boat from the riddled *Lawrence* to the *Niagara* and to victory.

No description by Montgomery of this engagement appears to be extant; assiduous search has failed to locate any writing by him regarding his early naval service. It is not plain whether this is because of his reticence; or the loss, mislaying, or hoarding of such writings. It is to be hoped that such material may yet come to light. Fortunately, Gen. Theophilus F. Rodenbough, U.S. Army, a relative, devoted himself to the Montgomery story, and it is to him that we are indebted for much data which might otherwise have become lost.

Montgomery and the other midshipmen who served at the Battle of Lake Erie were awarded swords by act of the Congress.[4] He was also at the blockade and attack on Mackinac, Lake Huron, and assisted in the destruction of a blockhouse and of a gun brig. He aided in protecting the line of communications between Fort Erie and the hospitals at Buffalo, and in the transportation of troops across Lake Erie. When the campaign ended he returned to New York late in February 1815 in time to witness the general illumination of the city in honor of peace.

War with Algiers was declared March 2, 1815. Montgomery was ordered to the sloop of war *Ontario,* 16 guns, at Baltimore, and sailed in May in the first squadron for Algiers, under Commodore Decatur. The *Ontario* took part in the capture of the Algerian flagship *Mashuda,* 46 guns, and in the blockade of the port of Algiers. Commodore Bainbridge arrived with the second squadron. After an overpowering show of strength and the establishment of an uneasy peace, both squadrons sailed for home, leaving the *United States, Constellation, Erie,* and *Ontario*. Montgomery thus remained in the Mediterranean and did not return to the States until 1817.

Arriving at Norfolk, Virginia, in August, he was ordered to New York for service on the *Hornet*. In February 1818 he was assigned to the *Cyane,* and April 18, 1818, he was promoted to the rank of lieutenant. The *Cyane* sailed from Norfolk in 1819 for the coast of Africa to locate a settlement for liberated slaves. Again, in February 1820, she sailed from New York for the coast of Africa, from which Montgomery returned in December of that year.

Although no confirming statement is found, it is deduced that it was during a home stay between these two voyages, possibly as late as January 1820, that Lieut. Montgomery married Mary, daughter of William Henry of New York. Many years later Montgomery stated that their first son, William Henry, was born in October 1820.

In 1821 the *Cyane* was again back in the States. On November 16, 1821, from the home of his mother-in-law at Bellville, New Jersey, Montgomery wrote that Friday morning last Mrs. Montgomery presented him with a fine, healthy daughter (Julia Maria), that he intended to spend the winter at Bellville, and in the spring following would be keeping house in New York.[5] The next daughter, Delia Henry, was born March 6, 1823.

Then came a long tour of duty and Mediterranean service with the *Erie,* from which Montgomery returned November 1826 to receive a leave of absence, perhaps his longest to that time. Recruiting duty followed in 1828-1829 at Chambersburg, Pennsylvania; in 1830 he went to the West Indies and became executive officer of the *Peacock;* then served as captain of the *Erie;* flag lieutenant of the *Natchez* in 1831; had leave the same year; then recruiting duty in Philadelphia and New York from January 1833 to February 1835; he was executive officer of the *Constitution* (Old Ironsides) commencing the latter date; had command of the receiving ship *Columbus* at Boston, March 1837; was detached April 1839; promoted commander, December 9, 1839; and was on recruiting service at Boston, May 1841 to February 1844.

During the period 1830 to 1844, the following-named children had been born to the Montgomerys: John Elliott, 1830; Henry Edwards, 1831; David Edwards, 1835; Samuel Lawrence Ward, 1836; Mary Henry, 1839; and Helen Vredenberg, 1844. Of the nine children of the Montgomerys only two of those who married, Julia Maria and Delia Henry, seem to have had children.

With his length of service, combat experience, and varied assignments, Montgomery was well equipped for his next important naval duty in 1844.

The Building of the Ship

PORTSMOUTH, NEW HAMPSHIRE, rates as the cradle of naval shipbuilding in the United States, for it was there that the *Falkland* was built for the British Navy in 1690. Also built there under contract was the *America*, 44 guns, launched in 1749.[6]

Built for the Continental Navy at Portsmouth by James K. Hackett were *Raleigh*, 32, and *America*, 74, launched 1776 and 1782, respectively. The first *Portsmouth*, a 24 gun ship of 593 tons and a complement of 220 men, was built there by Hackett for the Federal Navy in 1798. Costing $59,560, she was sold at Baltimore in 1801 for $34,366, after but short service at sea. Hackett followed with *Congress* (3d) in 1799.[7]

With such a local tradition of experience and craftsmanship, it was logical that in 1800 the Government bought the 58-acre Dennets Island at Portsmouth Harbor, for use as a navy yard. Improvements came slowly, but progress accelerated with the outbreak of the War of 1812. In March 1814 the keel of the 74 gun ship, *Washington* (5th), was laid and the vessel launched in 1815. Then followed: *Alabama*, 1818; *Santee*, 1820; *Porpoise*, 1821; *Concord*, 1827; *Preble* (2d), 1839; *Congress* (4th), 1839; and *Saratoga* (3d), 1842. Chapelle states: "The Portsmouth Yard was much more consistent in time required to build sailing men-of-war than were most of the other navy yards."

Now comes the vessel of our principal concern, the sharer of the title of this book, *Portsmouth* (2d) of 20 guns. She was designed by Josiah Barker, plans by B. F. Delano, and was one of several big corvettes which had been authorized. Barker once said that *Portsmouth's* lines had been adapted from those of the *Union,* previously built by him based on the design of the French letter of marque, *Frolic,* both the latter very fast vessels. However, Chapelle states: "The accuracy of his [Barker's] statement is open to doubt; there is nothing in the design of this handsome ship that indicates an unusual model."

Chapelle continues: "Delano once stated that she was drawn as an improvement on the *Saratoga,* built in the same yard a year earlier. The *Portsmouth* had lower bilges and hollow floors, compared to the *Saratoga;* she was also a much larger ship. The *Portsmouth* measured 151 feet 10 inches between perpendiculars, 37 feet 3 inches moulded beam, and 16 feet 9 inches depth of hold; she was armed with 18 medium 32's and 2 Paixhans 8-inch shell guns, according to her design. Her plans were sent to Washington in May [1843] and were approved, and the ship was laid down at the Portsmouth Navy Yard on the 15th of June and launched on the 23rd of October of the same year." Her cost when ready for sea was $170,586.

The *New Hampshire Gazette* (Portsmouth) of October 24, 1843, told with pride of the launching: "Yesterday a few minutes before 11 o'clock this splendid vessel (being one of the largest class of sloops-of-war,) was launched from the spacious new ship-house, into the Piscataqua, accompanied with a salute of 13 guns. She is a rare beauty—and a fine specimen of the workmanship of our mechanics."

Again Chapelle: "The *Portsmouth* was a very sleek appearing vessel, as she had no mouldings and her side was unbroken between the rail cap and the water line. Her stern was almost round, with a very short overhang. After the Civil War she was fitted with a light spar deck, like many of her class; as built she had (like the *Saratoga)* a short, light top gallant forecastle, and a short poop, made of gratings at the level of the top of the hammock rail, for convenience in handling the anchor and in conning ship."

In October 1844, Commander John B. Montgomery was ordered to command of the ship and, on October 7, he reported at the Portsmouth Navy Yard. The log of the *Portsmouth,* preserved at the National Archives, commences with the entry of Sunday, Nov. 10, 1844: "At 9:45 [A.M.] the ship was put in commission by order of Captain George W. Stover. Called all hands and mustered the Ships Company." Then followed a list of the officers.

Included in the ship's complement as Captain's clerk was John Elliott Montgomery, son of Commander Montgomery. Another son, Samuel Lawrence Ward Montgomery, was allowed on board as a passenger, on approval of his father's request.[8] Montgomery's first son, William Henry Montgomery, was serving elsewhere, having been appointed midshipman December 21, 1837, and passed midshipman June 29, 1843. Mrs. Montgomery apparently remained in the vicinity of Boston, for a letter was addressed to her at Charlestown in 1846.[9]

The days following the commissioning were busy times for all aboard. Probably because no purser had yet been attached, the entries in the log were uncommonly detailed. Names of the Marine guard which reported November 13, and of the draft of men from Boston November 21, were listed, as were naval stores and individual issues of clothing, which ordinarily would have been recorded by a purser.

At 11 A.M., December 9, 1844, *Portsmouth* slipped her moorings "and stood down the Harbour under Topsails Jib and Spanker." At 1 P.M. she hove to and discharged the pilot. All hands were called to witness punishment by the lashing of offenders with the cat or colt.[10] The needs of discipline having been served, *Portsmouth* was soon on the first leg of a cruise which every man Jack knew was to take her to the Pacific.

Off for the Pacific

GOOD ADMINISTRATION dictated that ships assigned to distant squadrons be relieved every two or three years. This was desirable from the standpoint of health, morale, maintenance, and general economy. *Portsmouth,* then, was off on what might have been such a routine cruise.

The log of December 11, 1844, states that the ship was remarkably easy in motion and steered within ¾ of a point in a very heavy sea.[11] Hampton Roads was reached without incident, and at 2:30 P.M. while standing up for Norfolk on December 16, there was made out the enormous 120-gun *Pennsylvania* "bearing the broad pendant of Commodore Bolton." After firing the first salute of her career, *Portsmouth* moored in the same waters where old "Pennsy" was to meet her death, burned in 1861 to prevent her use by Confederates. Montgomery made several reports praising his ship as a "fine sailer" and a "fine and comfortable sea boat."[12]

In preparation for Christmas, twenty turkeys were received on the afternoon of December 24. Also coming aboard at the same time were ten men from the *Pennsylvania,* one of whom was the irrepressible Joseph T. Downey. His fascinating story of this cruise, *Odds and Ends,* is an interesting successor in its field to Herman Melville's *White Jacket.* That Downey story and his *Filings from an Old Saw* have been resurrected after more than a century of oblivion. Later we shall call on him for some brief quotations.

While at Norfolk, *Portsmouth* had some minor alterations made, and received more supplies. Finally, she and the *Jamestown* put to sea together and passed Cape Henry January 26. After sailing together over 2000 miles, with the *Portsmouth* consistently leading under varied sailing conditions, these ships became separated at night in squally weather. The *Portsmouth* continued alone to Rio de Janeiro, where she arrived February 27 and from which she sailed March 8.

Next came the run to and the passage of the Straits of Le Maire. For several days southwest squalls prevented the rounding of Cape Horn, but Valparaiso was reached April 6, 29 days actual run from Rio and 62 days from the United States. Montgomery, reporting by letter to his commodore, John D. Sloat, named many technical details of the ship's performance and gave its maximum rate as 13½ knots.

Callao, then the rendezvous of the U.S. Pacific Squadron, was made April 19, and Sloat there inspected the *Portsmouth*. Thence to Valparaiso June 1, and back to Callao June 19, where at anchor were the frigate *Brandywine,* the sloop *St. Louis,* and the brig *Perry,* en route from the East Indian Squadron to the United States.

As a matter of training, supply, and intelligence, Sloat kept his ships on the move. So *Portsmouth* was sent to the Hawaiian Islands, where she arrived at Hilo August 20 and at Honolulu on the 24th. There the newspaper *Polynesian* of August 30 duly noted her arrival, listed her officers, and gave a good description of the ship. Supplies, including thirty-four barrels of whiskey, were placed in the hold. After an all-too-short stay, the ship was off for California, already made famous in the minds of sailors and others by Dana's *Two Years Before the Mast.*

In describing this voyage, Downey, in his *Odds and Ends,* devotes a whole chapter to a description of "A Sabbath at Sea."

"It was our fortune however to have a Commander of whom it might be said, at least to outward show, 'he feared God and honored the Congress.' He never, from the first Sabbath we spent on board to the last (when weather permitted) failed to read Divine Service, or to check any man who uttered any profane or obscene language in his hearing. Sabbath was never with us looked upon as a mending day, but as one of entire rest. . . ."

There was the usual inspection, then "After a delay of a few moments to allow the Carpenters to rig the Capstan Bars, open shot boxes to form seats, and the Quarter Masters to throw a Jack over the Capstan, the loud call of the Boatswain and his mates summons all hands to muster. Upon arriving upon the Quarter Deck, we find it transformed into a Bethel and each and every one takes his seat as reverently as though he were in the most gorgeous Cathedral in America. . . . The Captain has assumed his post and opened the Book; look, every head is uncovered and every eye and ear bent upon him and a more orderly, serious and attentive lot of hearers, to my belief never listened to the word of God. The beautiful and impressive service of the Church of England is read, followed occasionally by a short and applicable sermon, and when the benediction is pronounced, every man silently and seemingly fearing to make the least noise, glides forward and the Crew are piped down—each one spending the balance of the Day to their own liking."[13]

On September 26 tells the log: "Read funeral service & committed to the deep the body of Jno. Whelan late (Sea)." Downey has a chapter on "The First Death," and says in part: "The Body, after being sewed up in a Hammock and having a 64 Pound shot lashed at the feet, was removed to the Quarter Deck and covered with a Jack. At noon the call of 'All Hands Bury the dead' summoned us on deck, where the crew were all assembled neatly in Blue. The Main Topsail was thrown aback, the colors half masted, and the body being lain upon a plank in the Lee Gangway, our Captain began the beautiful and impressive service of the Episcopal Church. Solemnity was stamped on the countenance of every one, and at the words 'we commit his body to the deep' the Jack was withdrawn, the inner end of the Plank raised, the body slid off a sullen plunge was heard, and the waters closed over the remains of poor Whelean."[14]

The following day anchor was dropped at Monterey, California, destined to be an important port of call for the *Portsmouth* for several years. The American Consul, Thomas O. Larkin, came aboard and was saluted with nine guns.

Here is the first of many excerpts from Montgomery's private journal to be used here.

"Monterey Sept. 28, 1845. Sent a boat with Lieut. [Washington A.] Bartlett to wait on the Consul, Mr. Larkin, who returned in the boat. Learned from him that American interests were perfectly secure, and little probability of their being interrupted in any way unless by a war with Mexico, which Mr. L. seemed to regard as a probable event, growing out of the Texas question in which he said that a Sloop of War would be greatly needed at Monterey, to protect from seizure whaling and trading vessels calling there. He further informed me that by a vessel from Acapulco information had been brought of the arrival of 2000 Mexican troops at that port, destined for the immediate occupation of California, to be paid by English individuals, under the sanction and countenance of the British government; in proof of which he had seen a letter from Mr. Barron, the English Consul at St. Blas, stating the fact that he was to be their Paymaster. The said troops are very soon expected to arrive here.... In a second interview with our Consul, Mr. Larkin, I was corrected in the matter of the letter from Mr. Barron, said (in my remarks above) to have been sent by him. There is, however, sufficient reason to believe that the troops intended for California are to be paid with English funds through Mr. Barron, from letters which have been received by English residents in Monterey."[15]

Montgomery left Monterey September 30, and wrote in his journal at Mazatlan, October 16, 1845: "Visited by a Mexican officer from shore with the Governor's compliments and congratulations on my arrival, etc. Sent my First Lieutenant to wait on the Consul, Mr. Parrott, who returned with information of the annexation and occupation of Texas by the United States; of the perfect quietude of Texas under this proceeding; that it was believed no war or difficulty would accrue from the event, and that the American interests, etc., were secured."

Written at Acapulco, Montgomery's entry of October 29, 1845, tells of the situation regarding the plan for Mexican troops for California: "Intelligence from Mexico, per last mail, altogether of a pacific character, and the prevalent impression on shore that there will be no hostilities with the United States. Five vessels in port awaiting the arrival of troops intended for California, a corps of artificers and several officers (subordinates) to make arrangements, etc., being all of the expedition yet arrived. The vessels having waited already two months, leads to the conclusion that the expedition, through the supineness of the government and want of funds, will wholly fall through; this is my impression. The belief is prevalent that California is prepared and determined to resist the introduction of Mexican troops."

After visiting all ports of importance on the west coast of Mexico, the *Portsmouth* by December 10, 1845, was again back at Mazatlan, where the U.S. Pacific Squadron was being concentrated.

On January 1, 1846, Commodore John D. Sloat's Pacific Squadron consisted of his flagship (the frigate *Savannah*), the sloops *Portsmouth*, *Warren*, and *Levant*, the schooner *Shark*, and the storeship *Erie*. The frigate *Congress* and the sloop *Cyane* were en route to relieve, respectively, the *Savannah* and *Levant*. The frigate *Constitution*, on the way home from the East India Station, arrived January 14, but was held by Sloat for over three months.

Also cruising the Mexican coast was the British Pacific Squadron, Admiral Sir George F. Seymour, consisting of the *Collingwood* (80), *Juno*, *America*, *Talbot*, *Frolic*, and *Spy*. Both squadrons kept a close watch on the other, and their components were quite constantly on the move.

The scope planned for this book does not permit of a detailed discussion of the relations of the United States, Mexico, and England with respect to California. Nevertheless, it is necessary to outline briefly the background of the mission destined for our commander and his ship.

War between the United States and Mexico seemed imminent. California, coveted by both the United States and England, was not united. Pío Pico, Governor of California, and José Castro, its Comandante General, were often engaged in controversy. Larkin, American Consul at Monterey, and secret agent, was working hard and with considerable success to obtain a favorable attitude toward the United States. James A. Forbes, British Vice-Consul, was less active or less effective, but Pico and some of his adherents favored the British if intervention must come.

For several years groups of emigrants from the United States had reached California either directly or by way of Oregon. Their reception varied between hospitality and distrust. A greater influx was expected in 1846.

In February of that year Capt. John C. Frémont, U. S. Topographical Engineers, concentrated the dispersed elements of his exploring party of about sixty in the Santa Clara Valley. Thence in disregard of California authorities he moved at will to the Santa Cruz Mountains, to the Salinas Valley, and then camped on the Gabilan Range, some twenty-five miles northeast of Monterey. There in March he raised the American flag and built a breastwork of logs. Castro moved troops to nearby San Juan. Their running battle of words, conducted partly through the apprehensive Larkin, ended without battle casualties when Frémont broke camp and was off for Oregon via Sutter's Fort.

Already, back at Washington, 1st Lieut. Archibald H. Gillespie, U. S. Marine Corps, on November 1, 1845, had been placed on special service with instructions to proceed to California and communicate with Frémont. Gillespie moved to New York, thence via Veracruz overland to Mazatlan, from which he was transported in the *Cyane* to Honolulu, en route to Monterey. He traveled under his own name, but in the role of a merchant, a guise which later did not deceive the Californians. At Honolulu he was received by the King, and his military rank was printed in the *Polynesian;* he had previously visited Honolulu and was probably quite well known there.[16]

Larkin, at Monterey, was highly disturbed by the danger of conflict between Castro and Frémont, so on March 9th, 1846, he sent messages to Consul Parrott and to the U. S. naval commander at Mazatlan, requesting that a man-of-war be sent to California without delay.

A Mission to California

DURING THE FIRST THREE MONTHS of 1846, *Portsmouth* received officer and enlisted replacements. [17] Among the officers were two whose writings have added interest to the California scene, Lieut. Joseph W. Revere, and Asst. Surg. Marius Duvall.

Boredom was somewhat alleviated by exchange of social amenities between squadron and squadron, ship and ship, ship and shore. Mrs. Isaac T. Mott, wife of the Mazatlan representative of the merchant house of Mott and Talbot, tells of a playmate of her daughter "Fan." "He is a son of Captain Montgomery of the Portsmouth and is precisely Fan's age. He comes on shore every afternoon to play an hour or two with her, and, as you may suppose, they make a fine racket."[18] It is to be supposed that the playmate was Samuel L. W. Montgomery, aged ten, rather than John Elliott Montgomery, who, at the age of sixteen, had to uphold the dignity of his position as ship's clerk for his father.

All such pleasures came to an end when Sloat, stated by Mrs. Mott to be "a nice rosy-faced old gentleman fond of talking," acted on Larkin's plea and on April 1, 1846, ordered Montgomery as follows:

"You will proceed with the U. S. Ship Portsmouth under your command to Monterey Coast of California where you will afford countenance and all proper protection to our citizens and their interests in that country, you will also visit the Bay of San Francisco and any ports on that Coast you may judge necessary for the same objects.

"When on that coast you will communicate frequently with our consul at Monterrey and will ascertain as exactly as you can the nature of the designs of the English and French in that region, the temper of the inhabitants—their disposition toward the U. States and their relations towards the central Government of Mexico. You will do every thing that is proper to conciliate towards our country the most friendly regard of the people of California.

"When at Monterrey and San Francisco you will distribute the accompanying constitutions of the State of Texas printed in Spanish.

"Should you meet Commo Stockton at Monterrey you will deliver to him the accompanying letters. Should he not have arrived you will leave one with the U. S. Consul at that place—the other you will leave at St Francisco should he not have been there: but in case he has been on that Coast and you can ascertain that he has gone South you will retain both letters.

"In addition to the above you will be governed in your general course by the instructions you have heretofore received."[19]

This letter calls for comment. It is in furtherance of the often repeated policy of conciliation of the Californians. It provides for close cooperation with Larkin, and for the gathering of further information on the California situation. Contact with Commodore Robert F. Stockton was greatly desired. He had sailed in the *Congress* in late October 1845 from Norfolk and was now in the Pacific, bound for Honolulu.

The provision for the dissemination to Californians of the printed copies of the Texas Constitution is a case of propaganda which apparently has escaped historical comment. It was designed to promote separatism in California either by secession or by support of American interests. There is a copy of the printed document at the Huntington Library, but no evidence is found that it was one of those distributed by Montgomery.

The *Portsmouth* sailed from Mazatlan on the date of Sloat's letter and reached Monterey on the evening of April 22. The following day the Mexican flag was saluted with 21 guns, returned by the fort on the hill above the Custom House. Larkin came aboard, and Montgomery wrote at length of the ensuing conversation. A few excerpts will suffice. "It is well understood that no real attack upon the camp of Captain Fremont was contemplated by General Castro when he directed this movement, but that it was done with the view only of furnishing materials for forming a high sounding, flaming despatch to the central government of Mexico. . . . The feeling is rife, that California is soon to be governed by England or the United States, predilections being divided. . . . In the event of war with Mexico, it is thought that no opposition would be offered to hoisting the flag of the United States either here or at San Francisco, and that such an occurrence would at once unite from five hundred to one thousand sturdy American and other foreign residents to sustain our banner."[20]

The *Cyane* had landed Gillespie at Monterey on April 17 and then departed for Mazatlan. Larkin consulted with Gillespie and gave him a letter of introduction to William A. Leidesdorff, the American Vice-consul at Yerba Buena, who facilitated Gillespie's departure to overtake Frémont. Hence Gillespie was well on his way before Montgomery arrived at Monterey. Receiving much help from Peter Lassen and others in the upper Sacramento Valley, Gillespie reached Frémont at Klamath Lake and delivered his messages. These were sufficient to cause Frémont to return to the Sacramento in California.

At Monterey several of the *Portsmouth's* officers went ashore for picnics, hunting, or short trips. Lieutenants Bartlett and Watson travelled as far as Santa Clara to visit the quicksilver mines in that vicinity. Castro objected that passports for them had not been requested; Larkin replied that such had not been required for other foreign officers. Bartlett and Watson returned on May 4 with "a most glowing description of the beauty and fertility of the country," and reported: "The residents of the district through which they passed are represented as principally from the United States, who, with many of the most intelligent Mexicans and Californians, express openly their desire for and expectation of a change of government which shall unite them to the United States."[21]

On May 5 Castro visited the *Portsmouth* and on leaving was given a salute of 15 guns as befitted his rank. He probably extended an invitation for an affair to be held May 9, mentioned by Montgomery: "Rode ten miles into the country in company with sixty persons, male and female, mounted on horseback to a picnic, by invitation of General Castro, the Commandant General of California. Seven of the officers of the ship were of the party. On our return visited the Mission house and convent of Carmello (or Carmel) now deserted and in a dilapidated condition."[22]

Portsmouth reciprocated in style, for, says Downey: "Commander Montgomery, it must be premised, was a very devout and religious man, eschewing all worldly amusements on the part of his officers and men, and yet he allowed them to give a grand ball in the Barracks to the officers of the Mexican army, and after lending all the flags and signals to decorate, and all the cooks and stewards to prepare and officiate, even attended himself in full uniform, and appeared particularly gracious to the doughty Governor [Comandante] and Staff."[23] Montgomery himself says under date of May 15, 1846: "A ball given on shore by the wardroom officers of the ship to the inhabitants of Monterey, which was very numerously attended. Among the guests were the commandant General Castro, with all the principal officers of government and their ladies. It passed off very satisfactorily, seemingly, as the dance was continued until daybreak, I am informed."

On May 31, Samuel Neal, already gaining fame as a courier, arrived at Monterey with information from Gillespie to Larkin regarding Frémont's movements and position. It was decided that *Portsmouth* should move to San Francisco Bay. This was an obvious strategical decision—indeed an essential one for the exercise of power should the need come. Aside from the great harbor advantages, the bay and its extensive system of tributary waterways afforded much mobility, and excellent communications to many points, including San Jose, Sonoma, and Sutter's Fort. So too, these waterways might be dominated and thus constitute obstacles to an enemy.

Larkin asked for and obtained passage for Neal on the *Portsmouth,* and the ship sailed June 1. Both Duvall and Downey tell of Neal. Says Duvall, "This courier is a very singular being—his costume is a white hat, ragged cloth jacket, tight breeches, and buckskin leggins and shoes of the same material. His hair seems as if it had never known the comb, and his face and hands are strangers to soap and water. He is as fearless as man can be. . . ." From Downey: "The masts, spars, sails and cordage were all sources of amusement to him, and when told to go below with his traps, he begged to be excused, for as he expressed it, 'he always rid on the outside of a horse.' . . . He soon learned the meaning of the Boatswain's pipe, and was never behind at the mess cloth, or the grog tub, because, as he said, 'whiskey came kinder natural to him.' "[24]

June 3, 1846, the *Portsmouth* moored at Sausalito, long known by whalers and merchantmen as a fine place for watering and wooding.[25] That afternoon Neal left for Frémont, and in the evening William A. Richardson, principal man at Sausalito and former captain of the port, dined in the wardroom.[26]

With Neal, Montgomery sent a letter to Frémont dated June 3. It is important as stating Montgomery's position.

"On the 31st ulto. the day previous to my sailing from Monterey a courier from Lieut. Gillespie to the U. States Consul arrived bringing the only definite intelligence of your movements & position since my arrival at that port on the 22d of April last. The instructions under which I am now serving & which may detain me until late in the fall, or longer upon this coast, have relation specifically to the objects of affording protection to the persons & property of citizens of the U. States & of maintaining a watchful care over the General interests of our Country. Without reference in any manner to the enterprise in which you are so actively engaged; the nature & subject of which, except, so far as I have been rightly informed by paragraphs casually met with in public prints I am totally ignorant.

"I beg leave however, (availing myself of the return of the Messenger [Neal]) to assure you Sir of the interest I feel in the successful prosecution & Issue of the public interests committed in your direction, and without desiring information further than you may deem necessary, to enable me to aid & facilitate your operations, to express my sincere desire and readiness to serve you in any manner consistent with other duties.

"Permit me to say Sir that if you should find it convenient to visit the U.S. Ship Portsmouth during her stay in this port, that I with the officers of the Ship—will be most happy to see you.

"I shall remain here probably three weeks unless unforseen circumstances requiring an earlier movement & my present intention is to return to Monterey."[27]

To be noted is Montgomery's lack of knowledge of any new Frémont mission, his determination not to ask for such information, and his promise of cooperation regardless.

By June 7, Gillespie had arrived with a request from Frémont to Montgomery for supplies. On the 8th at Yerba Buena Duvall met Gillespie "who narrated several interesting adventures and exhibited some Indian Curiosities, such as bears' claws, 'a lady's full dress,' bows and poisoned arrows, and a primitive cuirass, perforated by the ball which killed the wearer—this breastplate was saturated with the Indians blood." Duvall also learned from Gillespie of the attack on him and Frémont, made by Indians on the night 9-10 May.[28]

Soon came the task of loading the *Portsmouth's* launch with the requisitioned supplies, among which were: "5 Bbls Flour, one doz pork one box soap 2 boxes tobacco, 10 lbs candles, 3 dozen pair stockings, 100 Blue Flannel Shirts, one sack coarse Salt, one Breaker, 50 lbs Lead, 400 Purcussion Caps, 37 yards Russia Duck, 73 yards No. 6 cotton Canvass, 4 lbs. Twine, one Box Medicines 500 lbs Iron."[29]

The launch was of good size: 30′ length, 8′5″ beam, and 3′10″ depth.[30] When it departed June 11 it was deeply laden, for in addition to the supplies and the crew it carried Lieut. Ben F. B. Hunter (in charge), Gillespie and his colored servant, Purser James H. Watmough, Asst. Surg. Marius Duvall, Robert E. Russell, a pilot, and "a lawless Frenchman who had crossed the mountains with Capt. Fremont."[31]

With Hunter went this letter, dated June 10th, from Montgomery to Frémont.

"Since writing you by Neal on the 3d. Inst. I have been by Lieut. Gillespie informed of your present position and circumstances and made acquainted with your design soon to proceed South with your party as far as Santa Barbara before striking accross the country for the U. States. I am also informed by Lieut. G. of your having expressed a desire for the presence of a vessel of war at Santa Barbara, during the period of your temporary sojourn in the vicinity of that port.

"Now Sir I am happy to say that I feel myself at liberty to visit any or all ports upon this coast should the public interests require it & if on receipt of this you shall still think that the presence of a Ship of War at Santa Barbara may prove serviceable to you in carrying out the views of our Government & will do me the favor by the return boat to communicate your wishes with information as to the time you will probably reach that part of the coast I will not fail (Providence permitting) to meet you there with the Portsmouth.

"I feel gratified Sir in having it in my power to forward you by Lt. Hunter the amt. of funds asked for in your name by Lieut. Gillespie with most of the articles of Stores &c. required to meet the demand of your urgent necessity regretting only, my inability to furnish the whole. You will oblige me by signing the Requisitions & Receipts annexed to the several invoices transmitted by Lt. Hunter, & with a view to the settlement of Purser James H. Watmough's accts. at the Navy Department, be pleased to give an order or bill (in duplicate) on the proper Dept. of Government, payable to Purser Watmough's order to the 4t. Auditor of the Treasury for the aggregate amt. of money and Pursers Stores Supplied.

"Articles having no prices affixed need only be receipted for.

"Lieut. Gillespie informs me that you may find it convenient to visit the Portsmouth at Santa Barbara should we have occasion to go there. With this prospect in view I beg leave again to assure you that we shall all on board be most happy to see you."[32]

The launch progressed across the bay with a fair wind and tide.

The Bears Revolt

EVERYTHING IN THE SACRAMENTO COUNTRY centered around "Captain" John A. Sutter and his fort. Sutter came to California by sea in 1839. South of the American River near its junction with the Sacramento he commenced an establishment which was to increase in size to become the largest of its kind in Alta California, superseding in this respect the Russian Fort Ross on the coast. He became a Mexican citizen and in 1841 was granted by Alvarado eleven leagues, extending from a line south of the American, up the Sacramento and Feather Rivers to the Three Buttes near present Marysville. It was an ideal location for farming, trading, trapping ventures, and the exploitation of Indian labor. Of particular interest here was its favorable position with regard to the emigration from the United States, either by way of the Sierra Nevada or Oregon. The site of Sutter's large adobe fort is now within the limits of the city of Sacramento.

Sutter helped the emigrants, some of whom were almost destitute, and employed some. A few made their way to San Jose and Monterey, but most "settled" either in the Sonoma-Napa country, or along the Sacramento from Sutter's Fort northward. A very few obtained grants of land, but most were squatters. In April 1846 the latter were confronted with a serious situation. General Castro proclaimed that the purchase or acquisition of land by foreigners who had not become naturalized as Mexicans "will be null and void, and they will be subject (if they do not retire voluntarily from the country) to be expelled whenever the country may find it convenient."[33]

Then came rumors that it was planned soon to enforce Castro's edict, and that Indians had been encouraged to burn crops of the foreigners. Sutter began a campaign against the Moquelumne Indians on June 3; and the following day Samuel J. Hensley, who had returned from a trip to the bay for information, left to report to Frémont, camped near the Buttes. Neal soon joined Frémont.

The result of the rumors was a widely distributed summons for a meeting of the settlers, instigated by Frémont, says Ide. Aroused by hard riding couriers, representatives came from as far as the Napa Valley and from the Sacramento Valley. Several from the latter vicinity deserve special mention because of the importance of their forthcoming roles.

William Brown Ide, born 1796, a native of Massachusetts, lived in Vermont, New Hampshire and Ohio, before he arrived in Illinois in 1838. By 1844, if not earlier, he had embraced the Mormon faith, for he was delegate from Sangamon County, Illinois, at the Mormon convention which nominated Joseph Smith for President and Sidney Rigdon as Vice President. In the spring of 1845 he left overland for Oregon with his family, but changed his destination to California, where he arrived the same year and moved to the upper Sacramento.[34]

Henry L. Ford, true name Noah Eastman Ford, was born in 1822 at North Conway, New Hampshire. He enlisted in the Dragoons in 1841, but within a year he deserted, adopted the name of his brother Henry L., and arrived by whaler at Monterey, California, in 1843. For a while he hunted and trapped for Sutter and served with him during the revolt against Micheltorena. Ford then became associated with William C. Moon at the latter's ranch opposite Lassen's.[35]

Also frequently at Moon's, but as foot-loose as one could be, was one Ezekiel "Stuttering" Merritt, an old Rocky Mountain trapper of antecedents unknown. Of all these, Merritt had the least to lose and probably the most personal satisfaction to gain. He seems to have harbored an overpowering resentment against Salvador Vallejo, who was alleged to have struck Merritt when in the upper Napa Valley. Duvall says of Merritt: "He is a brawny, stern man of forty years of age; he is hard-featured has blood-shot eyes and a peculiar stuttering speech. His whole appearance and manner was that of a man moved by some revengeful intoxicating passion."[36]

Living at a farm on Cache Creek some twenty-five miles west of Sutter's Fort was William Levi Todd. He wintered there after coming overland from Illinois to California in 1845 with the Swasey party. He was born at Edwardsville, Illinois, in 1818, was a cousin of Mrs. Abraham Lincoln, and "was in youth raised as a Druggist & Apothecary."[37]

At the meeting, Frémont failed to promise assistance, but encouraged the settlers to resist. Already, events were moving toward the first decisive incident of what soon came to be known as the Bear Flag Revolt.

Early in June, General Mariano G. Vallejo at Sonoma promised some 170 horses for the use of Castro, then organizing at Santa Clara. The horses, with a small escort under Lieutenants Francisco Arce and José María Alviso, arrived June 8 at Sutter's Fort by way of the Sacramento crossing at William Knight's. The following day the party was at the Cosumnes River place of Martin Murphy.

Knight promptly notified Frémont of Arce's movement, and the settlers felt that the horses were intended as mounts for forces to be used against them. So, on the morning of June 9, a party of about ten men under Merritt left the vicinity of Frémont's camp, then on the Feather, and took up the pursuit of Arce. Gaining four more men en route, the party neared Murphy's, camped for the night, and at dawn surprised Arce with a charge. The Californians were not made prisoners by Merritt, but were released with mounts for each. The remaining captured horses were taken to Frémont's new camp at the Bear River. Arrival was on the morning of the eleventh. The round trip of about 120 miles had taken two days, but the party was not to be allowed to recuperate.[38]

Merritt increased his band to about twenty—Ide was a notable addition—and on the afternoon of June 11 departed on an expedition forever to be famed in the annals of California.

The objective? Sonoma.

At Sonoma were kept several hundred muskets, a few cannon, and some ammunition. The town was not garrisoned, but it was the home of the very influential Mariano G. Vallejo, Colonel in the Mexican Army, also called general because of his former service as Comandante General. There too, were Lieut. Col. Victor Prudon and Capt. Salvador Vallejo, brother of Mariano. Capture of Sonoma would serve to protect the Americans in that vicinity and gain their adherence. San Francisco Bay would constitute an obstacle to any Californian forces which might attempt retaliatory action. And Sutter was considered favorable to the American cause.

Merritt the hunter, now in quest of other game, crossed the Sacramento at Hardy's, led his party through rich bottom lands luxuriant with saddle-high oats, and by nightfall reached "Uncle" Billy Gordon's on Cache Creek. To gain secrecy he then took the more difficult route over Blue Ridge, thence via Elias Barnett's place in Pope Valley he arrived at the upper Napa Valley. There the party was increased to about thirty-three, including Todd and others who had joined along the way.

After some rest and a speech at Bale's mill by the loquacious Robert Semple, the party moved down Napa Valley during the night June 13-14 and approached Sonoma at dawn.

The surprise was complete. General Vallejo was awakened and made prisoner. Victor Prudon, Salvador Vallejo, and Jacob Leese soon appeared. Knight acted as interpreter for the negotiations held in the General's house. The two Vallejos and Prudon, as prisoners, signed a pledge of future neutrality. Merritt, Semple, William Fallon, and Samuel Kelsey signed for the revolters, promising respect for private property not required for their "immediate support," and respect for the persons of all "not in opposition to the cause."

Most of the revolters had remained outside, but they became impatient, elected John Grigsby as captain, and sent him in to ascertain the cause of the delay. A keg of brandy appeared outside and a celebration was under way. Then Ide was sent inside to investigate. Later he wrote this classic statement of his findings:

"The General's generous spirits gave proof of his usual hospitality, as the richest wines and brandies sparkled in the glasses, and those who had thus unceremoniously met soon became merry companions; more especially—the weary visitors. . . . There sat Dr. S. [Semple], just modifying a long string of articles of capitulation. There sat Merritt—his head fallen; there sat Knight, no longer able to interpret; and there sat the new-made Captain [Grigsby], as mute as the seat he sat upon. The bottles had well nigh vanquished the captors."[39]

Certainly there was some drinking, but probably not enough to interfere seriously with the important work to be done. Semple made another speech. Rather than release the prisoners on parole, it was determined that they should be escorted to the Sacramento, there to be held in protective custody. Ide's imprecations followed Merritt, Semple, and Grigsby when, for reasons never fully explained, all these former leaders left with the prisoners at about 11 A.M. Thus Ide and about two dozen others, including Ford, were left in command of the situation at Sonoma.

Gillespie, whom we left in the *Portsmouth's* launch en route with supplies for Frémont, reached Reading's fishing camp on the Sacramento on the night of June 11. That night several men from Sutter's arrived and told of the Arce affair at the Cosumnes and of the crop burning threat. By one of these men, Lazarus Everhart, Gillespie sent a pencil note to Montgomery, reporting the incidents. Montgomery received the note on the morning of June 14, the day Sonoma was taken.[40] About midnight June 12-13 the launch reached Sutter's embarcadero. On the 13th Gillespie left in search of Frémont and returned without success. The launch was moved several miles up the American River on the 14th, where messengers arrived to tell that Frémont would join the next day. Arrive he did with an earth-shaking mock charge, punctuated with rifle shots and cheers.

The supplies were distributed. "The head of the whiskey barrel was knocked in, a cup slung to the side, the fires re-kindled, and every one ordered, yes ordered to make themselves as happy as possible. This order was well obeyed, and kept in full force until broad daylight, or at least until there was not a soul left who had life enough to crawl to the barrel for his *tod*."[41]

At about 8 A.M. on the 16th, Merritt and Neal rode into Frémont's camp to tell of the success of the Americans at Sonoma. Sutter openly declared for the side of the foreigners. That evening the escort arrived with the prisoners from Sonoma, who were then taken to Sutter's Fort. By June 20 the *Portsmouth's* launch had returned without further incident to its ship at Sausalito.[42]

Hunter brought to Montgomery a long and rather cryptic letter from Frémont dated June 16, 1846. Frémont expressed thanks for the stores received and tells of the arrival of the Sonoma prisoners, who wished to surrender to him. He says that the hostile attitude of the military authorities of California and the advanced season of the year had frustrated his intention to examine the Colorado, that he expected to move eastward about the first of July, that he would meet or anticipate any hostile movements against him by Castro; and he asks that Montgomery "remain with the Portsmouth in the Bay of San Francisco."[43]

At Sonoma on the morning of June 14 we found Ide in command of the revolters after the departure of the erstwhile leaders and their prisoners. Of course it was necessary to design, make, and hoist a flag to replace that of Mexico. The source of the materials used is still a matter of controversy. The basic cloth was a piece of unbleached cotton, about three feet in height (hoist) by about five feet in length (fly). Along the bottom was sewn horizontally a stripe of red flannel about five inches in height.

On the flag's upper right (observer's left) was painted in red a large star. Henry Ford's suggestion, that the central feature of the flag be a grizzly bear, was adopted. It was painted solidly in red, facing the star and standing on all fours. The artist was William Levi Todd, who had joined the party on Cache Creek. His bear was the source of much fun, for the watchers thought it looked more like a hog.

Underneath the bear and above the red stripe were done in black capitals the words CALIFORNIA REPUBLIC. Todd made some errors, not easily erased, in the spelling of REPUBLIC. These very errors served to identify the original flag when it was returned to California after having been taken to the States. It was held for over a half-century by the Society of California Pioneers until destroyed in the San Francisco fire of 1906. Because of the bear on their flag, the insurgents immediately became known as Bears and their uprising is logically titled the Bear Flag Revolt.

Ford says that the Bear Flag was raised "amid the hurrahs of the little party who swore to defend it if need be with their lives." A military organization was effected. The two companies formed, riflemen and artillerymen, were of about ten men each, but other Americans soon joined. Ide remained in command, and Henry L. Ford was elected first lieutenant. At the sunrise flag raising on the 15th Ford told his men that they were at war with the Mexican nation and that discipline was necessary. All agreed.

During the night June 14-15 Ide completed a proclamation to which he gave the latter date. In it he stated the reasons for the revolt and outlined his policies. He also wrote a long letter to Stockton, dated the 15th, and carried by Todd, the flag maker. Since Stockton had not arrived in California, Montgomery received the letter at Sausalito. The arrival of Todd and another messenger from Sonoma, and the subsequent action are told by Montgomery.

"On Monday morning [June 15] Don Jose de la Rosa arrived on board from General Don Guadaloupa Vallejo, deputed to inform me that eighty Americans had taken forcible possession of Sonoma and made himself, General Vallejo, and several other Mexican officers of note, prisoners, who were on their way under strong escort to the Sacramento, and apprehending from a party that seemed to act without a head to direct or influence them, that acts of violence might be perpetrated upon their defenseless families and others in and about Sonoma, requested the interposition of any authority of [or?] influence I might have over them for their security.

"I replied to General Vallejo in effect that my position as an officer of the United States government precluded my interference between the conflicting parties, or with any political or popular movement of the people of California, disclaiming at the same time any previous knowledge of this rising of the people and all agency on the part of my government or by myself in producing it, which seemed to be called for by the implication embraced in General Vallejo's request for the exercise of authority with the insurgents. I expressed my readiness, however, to use my friendly endeavors to prevent the perpetration of violence upon the defenseless people of Sonoma, and at once directed the First Lieut. Missroon to be prepared to proceed in one of the ship's boats to Sonoma in the morning for that purpose.

"On Tuesday morning [16th], before Lt. Missroon had started on the mission assigned, a courier arrived on board from Sonoma bringing a letter from the insurgent chief at that place, confirming in part the statement of De la Rosa, but representing the number of their forces at Sonoma to have been thirty-five instead of eighty persons in the first instance, ten of whom were sent in charge of the prisoners to the Sacramento, leaving twenty-five only in charge of the place. The letter states the nine pieces of cannon, and stand of small arms, with ammunition and ball cartridges, etc., etc., in sufficient quantity for rifle and musket use, to sustain themselves against any attack which could be made upon them with small arms, but apprehended they should fall short if their artillery should be called into requisition, as was probable in case of an attack from the government troops, and requested a supply from the ship, which, of course, was refused on the ground of neutrality; my position and duty here compelling me to abstain (much in opposition to my sympathies, I confess) from rendering aid or facilities to either of the parties.

"I told Mr. Todd the insurgent messenger (a very intelligent and clever Kentuckian) [actually Todd was from Illinois] that I was about to dispatch a boat with an officer and General Vallejo's messenger to Sonoma, with a request to his chief in behalf of the terrified families of that place, to which he replied that he was happy to hear it, and would be glad to return with them, and send his horse back by another, which was assented to. He stated that a full and satisfactory guarantee for the security of the people from harm had been given by proclamation almost immediately after taking possession, and that it was well understood that condign punishment would promptly meet the transgressor; that if Vallejo had been less precipitate in sending to me, he would have seen no necessity for the trouble.

"I addressed a hasty communication in reply to the one received from Mr. Ide, and dispatched the boat at about 10 A.M. with Lieut. Missroon and the courier of both parties. I have no doubt of the honest motives and intentions of the insurgent party in this serious movement, which is in all probability, although small, the beginning to eventuate in their ruin or glorious triumph over their insidious enemies, who are charged with the design of cutting off by the hand of oppression, or driving from possession the American resident of the country. Their present leader, William E. [B.] Ide, although villified and abused by the Mexicans is represented to me by persons who know him as being one of the most wealthy and respectable men in California, and an exceedingly intelligent and judicious man, whose name and character cannot fail to inspire confidence and give weight to the cause he has espoused. Not the least important feature of their scheme, as presented in Mr. Ide's letter, is that of declaring the independence of California, and in due time annexing with the United States."

Montgomery's instructions for Missroon were in the form of a letter dated June 15 and a postscript of the 16th. Missroon, John E. Montgomery (captain's clerk), and the two messengers departed on the latter date and reached Sonoma the same day. Young Montgomery wrote a long letter to his mother on July 25, 1846, in which he said in part: "On arriving found a party of 24 men mostly dressed in Buckskins & we were met half way accross the Square by a plain man about fifty years old in his Shirt Sleeves, with a pair of pantaloons which certainly had seen better days to my eyes his Shoes looked as if they had not seen the outside of one of Day & Martin's blacking bottles for six months & his hat was somewhat more holy than rightous this man was Captain Ide he welcomed us to Sonoma & on Mr. Ms intimating to him that he would like to see him he called his 1st Lt. Mr. Ford a nephew of old Deacon Ford of Charlestown, & then retired after the business was settled Mr. M. & myself called on Mrs. Vallejo & he assured her of her husbands safety & she offered us beds in her house which we accepted she is a very pleasant woman indeed. . . ."[44]

At the meeting with Ide, Missroon handed him a Montgomery letter of June 16th, reading as follows:

"On the point of despatching an officer to Sonoma, to confer with you respecting the state of alarm and apprehension into which your sudden movement seems to have thrown the helpless people of Sonoma and country around, your Messenger Mr. Todd arrived, and handed me your communication of yesterday addressed to Commodore Stockton but designed, as Mr. Todd said for me. The circumstances stated therein, which has led to the hasty organization of the Foreign Population of this part of California; in opposition to the constituted authorities, had, in part previously reached me through irregular channels not entirely to be relied on; and in respect to which I would only observe as a general rule, without direct application or reference to the position in which you stand; that I hold it to be the privilege of all men everywhere, by such proper means as they possess, to counteract the sinister designs of treachery, and resist oppression in whatever form or manner they may be assailed by them, and that a right motive, and a just cause, will be always characterized by a mild, tender, and human regard, for the security of the happiness, proper interests, and privileges of others.

"I am most happy Sir, to understand from Mr. Todd that these (by Proclamation) have been guaranteed to your Prisoners and the defenceless people within your reach. And I sincerely hope, that whatever may be the future course of the popular movement in which you are engaged; that this policy may distinguish the conduct of your party, as well as that of your opposers.

"Permit me Sir, in response to your call for Powder for the use of your Party to say, that I am here as a representative of a Government at peace (as far as I know) with Mexico and the Province of California, having in charge the Interests, and security of the Commerce, and Citizens of the United States lawfully engaged in their peaceful pursuits; and have no right or authority to furnish Munitions of War, or in any manner to take sides, with any Political Party, or even indirectly to identify myself, or official name, with any popular movement (whether of Foreign or native residents) of the Country, and that Sir, must decline giving the required aid.

"Lieut. Missroon, the Executive Officer of the U. States Ship Portsmouth under my command who will hand you this, will explain more fully than the few moments allowed me to answer your Letter will permit me to do."

On the 17th, Ide executed the following pledge, a copy of which was delivered by Missroon to the alcalde of Sonoma.

"I pledge myself that I will use my utmost exertion, to restrain and prevent the Men in Arms under my command, (all of whom present acknowledge my authority and approve the measure of forbearance and humanity) from perpetrating any violence, or in any manner molesting the peacable inhabitants, in person or property, of California, while we continue in arms for the liberty of California."

His mission accomplished, mediator Missroon reported back to Montgomery "with the thanks of both parties," and a copy of Ide's proclamation of June 15.

The request made on Montgomery having failed, Lieut. Ford sent Thomas Cowie and one Fowler for a keg of powder at Fitch's rancho on the Russian River. These men were captured near Santa Rosa, tortured, mutilated, and killed by Californians. In the band which perpetrated the killings were Juan N. Padilla, Ramón Carrillo, and Bernardino García ("Three-fingered Jack"). Todd, on his way to Bodega with another man, was also captured. Ford sent Sergeant Samuel Gibson with four men to Fitch's to investigate. Gibson got the powder, captured a Mexican, and learned of the killings of Fowler and Cowie.

With a party of about eighteen men Ford left Sonoma June 23d to attempt the rescue of the remaining prisoners. Before his departure he sent a message to Merritt at the Sacramento, calling for help because of a report that Castro would cross the bay and attack Sonoma.

Frémont Acts

OVERLAPPING AND CONNECTED EVENTS now concerned Ford, Montgomery, Castro, and Frémont.

Ford, with his small party, moved to Santa Rosa and then followed the trail of the Mexicans to one of Padilla's houses near Two Rock. Indians there said that the Mexicans had left for the Laguna de San Antonio, about five miles southwest of Petaluma. The Bears followed, camped near the lagoon, and at daylight, June 24, 1846, took four prisoners. Ford and his men changed horses. A prisoner and horse guard was detailed, and the pursuit continued toward the rancho of Olompali, nearly four miles north of the present Novato.

Meanwhile, Castro had sent Joaquín de la Torre across the bay with a party of about fifty, which joined Padilla at Olompali, bringing the combined force to a strength of about seventy. Ford charged the place and was surprised to see the large force of the enemy. He ordered his men to dismount and to take cover among some near trees. Torre made a charge which encircled the Bears, who replied with rifle fire. For a while, firing at longer range continued and then Torre, says Ford, "dashed off at great speed in the direction of San Rafael and the fight was ended."

Todd rejoined his comrades and later stated that he had been threatened with death until he reminded his captors that a similar fate would meet the Sonoma prisoners. Ford returned to Sonoma without casualties; those of the enemy were at least one dead and several wounded.[45]

Now let us describe a controversy between Castro and Montgomery. In a letter dated June 17, 1846, Castro asked of Montgomery an explanation of the conduct of Frémont, charging the latter with taking possession of Sonoma and making prisoners of the two Vallejos, Prudon, and Leese. On the following day Montgomery replied:

"The undersigned, Commander of the United States Ship Portsmouth, has the honor to acknowledge the receipt of General Don Jose Castro's communication of yesterday which was handed to him late last evening, and in reply begs leave to assure General Castro of his entire conviction that Capt. J. C. Fremont, of the United States Topographical Engineers, whose visit to California has reference only, to scientific researches, is in no manner whatever, either by authority of the United States Government or otherwise, connected with the Political movement of residents of the country at Sonoma.

"The undersigned feels pleasure in communicating to General Don Jose Castro, that at the instance of General Mariano Guadalupa Vallejo, thru his Messenger, Don Jose de la Rosa, an officer of the United States Ship Portsmouth, was promptly despatched with overtures to the Chief of the Party in possession of Sonoma, in behalf of the families of the captured officers and other defenseless inhabitants; with a view to their protection from injury in their persons, property, and privileges; and is happy to inform General Castro, that on the arrival of the deputed officer at Sonoma, so far from the Anarchy and disorder which seemed to have been apprehended by General Vallejo; he found the most perfect order and quietude prevailing throughout the place, and that in no instance had there been on the part of the Captors a deviation from the most delicate regard for the happiness and protection of all.

"The undersigned feels constrained to avail himself of the opportunity now presented, to express to General Don Jose Castro, his unfeigned surprise that the Commanding General of Upper California, whose facilities for obtaining correct information concerning events, transpiring within the Department; under his own immediate observation is naturally inferred; should by any means, *this second time*, have fallen into error, respecting the designs and operations of a scientific party; whose approach to the vicinity of Monterey, in March last, had been preceded by a visit and explanation from Captain Fremont, to General Castro, and the authorities of Monterey (as I am credibly informed) which appeared at the time, perfectly satisfactory; illiciting a direct or implied assent on their part, to the prosecution of Captain Fremont's peaceful designs.

"The undersigned, Commander of the United States Ship Portsmouth, with all due respect for the high station of General Don Jose Castro, begs leave to remark, that under the circumstances above stated, he is constrained to regard the belligerent demonstration, made against the scientific party of Captain Fremont in March last, as wholly gratuitous on the part of General Castro; having no plea of necessity, or expediency even, for its justification. And furthermore, professes himself wholly at a loss to understand upon what ground the Commanding General of California, predicates the unqualified assumption of the co-operation of an Officer of the United States Army, in the recent transactions at Sonoma thereby impugning the integrity of the United States Government.

"The undersigned concludes by expressing the supposition, that General Castro may possibly have overlooked the implication named, in the next preceding paragraph; and regrets very much, that the tenor of his communication of yesterday, to which this is a reply; had not been restricted alone; to the simple inquiry, respecting the position of Captain Fremont in the premises. Leaving out the Slanderous imputations so copiously bestowed by the Commanding General of Upper California upon that Officer."[46]

The *Portsmouth* moved from Sausalito to Yerba Buena June 23. The same day Castro addressed a letter to Montgomery complaining that boats of the *Portsmouth* "go about the Bay armed, for the purpose of examining its trade," and calling for an explanation. Montgomery's reply was as follows:

"The undersigned, Commander of the U.S. Ship Portsmouth, has the honor to acknowledge the reception (this moment) of General Castro's communication of yesterday; and in reply has to inform him, that the Launch of the Portsmouth was despatched on the 10th instant in search of the Camp of Captain J. C. Fremont (whose neutral position in the country, and non-interference with its Political, or Military movements, the undersigned begs leave to reiterate) with supplies of which he stood in need, and a Second Boat was despatched a day or two since, for the purpose of communicating with Captain Fremont.

"The undersigned has the honor to assure General Castro; that the information he has received respecting the movements of the boats of the U.S. Ship Portsmouth under his command; is wholly erroneous, the neutral character of the Flag of the U. States having in no instance been violated by himself or those under his command.

"The undersigned with the view, and in full expectation of allaying and finally putting to rest, in the mind of the Commandant General; suspicions so injurious to the honor of the Flag of the U. States, as well as to the undersigned (being the representative of his Government), begs leave to assure General Castro of his established purpose, of strictly adhering to the principles involved in the obligations of his neutral position, within the waters, and Coast of California.

"The undersigned thinks it proper in the circumstances, to inform General Castro of his intention, to despatch a Third Boat to the camp of Captain Fremont, toward the close of the present week, with communications, previous to his (Captain Fremont's) final departure from California."[47]

On June 23 Montgomery had dispatched a boat, under Lieut. Joseph W. Revere, carrying Asst. Surg. Andrew A. Henderson from the *Portsmouth* with orders to report to Frémont for temporary duty. With the boat went a Montgomery letter to Frémont, stating in part:

"Although aware that the public mind in California was prepared for a change of Government, I little expected the movement to take place at this time or in the manner it has. The capture of the horses and surprise at Sonoma were master strokes, but should have been followed up by a rush on Santa Clara where Castro, with the residue of ordinance & munition in the country, might have been taken by thirty men at any time previous to Saturday evening. Castro must have felt sensibly the loss of the Vallejos & Prudon—as well as that of the arms & munitions taken at Sonoma.

"I have exchanged communications with the Commanders on both sides and others; preserving a strict neutrality and avowing my purpose of scrupulously adhering to this principle; while I confess my sympathies are wholly with the gallant little band in arms for mutual defence.

"An irregular band of one hundred and fifty are said to have joined Castro at Santa Clara on Saturday."[48]

On June 26 Montgomery prepared a letter to George Bancroft,

Secretary of the Navy, beginning as follows: "As I cannot but regard the intelligence of passing events in this country of sufficient importance to the Government, to justify its direct transmission by Captain J. C. Fremont; instead of waiting on opportunity; which may not offer for some time; of passing it through the Commodore (Sloat) now at Mazatlan."[49] Then followed an account of the Bear Flag Revolt. This letter and copies of supporting documents were made into a packet and dispatched to Frémont on the 27th by boat under Lieut. Washington A. Bartlett. With Bartlett also went several personal letters destined for the States and a letter, dated June 26, to Frémont from Montgomery, who tells of the Olompali fight, asks the return of Henderson, and requests that Frémont take charge of the packet to be handed him by Bartlett.[50] Montgomery also refers to extracts of a Larkin letter of June 20, and a confidential letter of Sloat to Larkin, May 18, 1846.

It was May 17, 1846, when Sloat had received through acting consul James R. Bolton news of the attack by Mexicans on a small American force north of the Rio Grande. The following day Sloat ordered Capt. William Mervine to proceed with the *Cyane* to Monterey. On the 18th Sloat wrote a confidential letter to Larkin, telling of the hostilities and stating his intention to move to California immediately and to arrive possibly as soon as the *Cyane*. But Sloat did not move immediately. He was in a fog, but he was not yet sure that it was the fog of war.

Larkin reported to Montgomery the arrival of the *Cyane* on June 19 and requested that Montgomery remain at his "present anchorage." Another Larkin letter of June 20, to Montgomery, told of Sloat's confidential letter of May 18, and stated that Sloat expected information not possessed by Larkin.[51] The Consul concluded: "You will see into the affair as you can as I can not explain it. I presume you will under the circumstances of the case remain where you are. as each port should have one of our Vessels there at least for a time or untill the arrival of the Congress—the Origon and Texas affairs remains as by our last dates. yet there is reason to believe the two encamped Armies on the Rio del Norte have met. should you be asked you will not admit it to be the case."

With Commodore and Consul confused, all that Montgomery could do was to remain at Yerba Buena and to inform Frémont as best he could. It is perfectly evident that as late as June 26 Montgomery and his officers believed that Frémont would soon be off for the United States. They were due for a surprise.

We have seen that Frémont, since his return from Oregon, had made several changes of his camp site, each bringing him closer to Sutter's Fort. His last move was to the American River, thus improving his supply situation and placing him in a better position of readiness for offensive action. Also to be remembered is the fact that Ford, before leaving Sonoma for the chase of Padilla, had sent a message to Merritt, requesting help for the Bears at Sonoma because of an impending Castro attack. Ide says that the message was for Frémont, informing him "that the men of the garrison had no confidence in the ability of Mr. Ide to manage matters at the fort at Sonoma."[52]

Spurred by Ford's note and other information that Castro intended an attack, Frémont threw off any remaining pretense of neutrality and left Sinclair's for Sonoma on June 23. In addition to most of his own explorer party, many settlers joined, bringing the force to about ninety. James W. Marshall, later of gold discovery fame, says: "There were Americans, French, English, Swiss, Poles, Russians, Prussians, Chilians, Germans, Greeks, Austrians,

Pawnees, native Indians, etc. . . . Well if they whip this crowd they can beat all the world, for Castro will whip all nations, languages and tongues!"[53]

Prominent among those who went with Frémont were Gillespie, Semple, and Samuel J. Hensley. Edward M. Kern, a Frémont man, was left at the Sacramento. Grigsby had previously rejoined at Sonoma. Merritt is not mentioned—he would remain in character if he stayed behind because of his interest in Salvador Vallejo.

Frémont arrived at Sonoma June 25, learned of the operations of Padilla and Torre, was joined by Ford and many others, and marched on the 26th on San Rafael with a force of about 130 men. Torre was found to have left the mission, and scouts were sent out to locate him.

On the 28th the twin brothers Ramón and Francisco de Haro crossed by boat from San Pablo to the vicinity of San Rafael. Accompanying was José de los Berryesa, father of the Sonoma alcalde. One of these carried a message for Torre concerning a planned crossing of the bay by more Castro forces. The three were shot to death when intercepted by members of Frémont's party. This was retaliation, without torture, for the killings of Cowie and Fowler. Duvall soon heard from John Sears one account of the fate of the three Californians and was convinced "that the blood of these men is on the conscience of Captain Fremont."[54]

The same day Montgomery confesses to his journal:

"At 6 P.M. a sailboat arrived bringing Lieut. Gillespie, who came immediately on board with information that he had separated from Captain Fremont at St. Raphael, twelve miles to the north of my anchorage, who at the head of 160 men was in pursuit of a Californian force under De la Force [Torre], having a day or two previously determined to change his course and assist the revolutionists, in consequence of hearing that Castro was proposing and had expressed the determination to drive him from the country.

"This course of Captain Fremont renders my position as a neutral peculiarly delicate and difficult. Having avowed, not only my own but Captain Fremont's entire neutrality and non-interference in the existing difficulties of the country, in which it can scarcely be supposed, under the circumstances, that I shall be regarded as having spoken in good faith and sincerity."

Torre now practiced a clever deception by writing a letter stating that he would attack Sonoma on the morning of the 29th. Frémont's scouts captured an Indian who carried the letter. This, with the intercepted Castro message for Torre, convinced Frémont that Sonoma was indeed in danger. Gillespie and Ford feared a ruse, but Frémont decided to return to Sonoma.

Ide tells a dramatic story of how he held the fire of the Sonoma garrison when Frémont charged into the pueblo before dawn.[55] Thus, possibly, a future Presidential candidate was saved for the Nation. The tricked Frémont soon set out for San Rafael only to learn that his quarry had escaped. Torre had commandeered a boat belonging to William A. Richardson and had crossed the bay to San Pablo.

Several entries in Montgomery's journal follow:

"July 1, 1846. At 9 A.M. a boat from Point St. Puebla [San Pablo] gave information of the retrograde march of the Californians under Castro towards Santa Clara yesterday on being rejoined by the retreating party under De la Torree from before Sonoma. At 10 A.M. received two notes from Lieut. Gillespie at San Solito [Sausalito], dated June 29th and 30th, and postcript of this morning informing me that Captain Fremont with a part of his camp had advanced to San Solito, Captain Fremont having crossed the passage to the Fort [the undefended Castillo de San Joaquín, on the south side of the bay entrance] to spike a number of brass guns mounted there; one of his men having been accidentally shot by his own rifle, he requested that I would receive him on board. Dispatched a boat to bring [him] and the gig with Lieut. Missroon to see Fremont."

"July 2, 1846. At 3 P.M. the gig with Lieut. Missroon returned bringing intelligence that Captain Fremont had succeeded in spiking seven brass guns in the Fort, and that he intended fitting a launch in his possession with two swivels and twelve trusty men to be employed in keeping open the narrows between the bays, and in intercepting or preventing all communication across on the part of the Californians; while with the main body of his force he would make a circuit round by the Sacramento, with the view of bringing Castro to battle in ten days, who, unsuspecting of any such design, it was believed would remain stationary at Santa Clara or the Pùebla [San Jose] above. At 10 A.M. Captain Fremont moved from San Solita, leaving a small guard to make prisoners, and follow him in boats to the Sacramento."

"July 3, 1846. Six of the insurgents passed from San Solito to Yerba Buena, and took Mr. [Robert] Ridley, Captain of the Port, prisoner, and sent him to the Sacramento. At 4 A.M. despatched the launch with Acting Master [Napoleon B.] Harrison to Monterey, all communication by land being intercepted. Omitted yesterday to mention the reception on board of George W. Brewer, one of Captain Fremont's company who had received, accidentally, a dangerous wound from his own rifle."

Brewer's arm was amputated, probably by Duvall, since Henderson had not returned from duty with Frémont. The leader of the party which took Ridley on July 2 has been stated as Semple; Ford says he placed Sgt. Samuel Gibson in charge. Alcalde William S. Hinckley, detested by Leidesdorff, was also sought by the insurgents but was not available. Duvall had been sent June 30 to administer to Hinckley, but found him dead, cause not stated.[56]

With Harrison in the launch went a long letter, dated July 2, from Montgomery to his superior officer, Capt. Mervine, commanding *Cyane* at Monterey. The letter begins:

"Informed by your letter of the 20th ulto. that you had a letter from Commdr Sloat for me which I have not received and impressed with the belief, (from the tenor of yours & Mr. Larkins letters received at the same time) that in the present crises it may be very important for me to get it; I have determined to despatch my Launch with the information I have to communicate, and to bring back the Commodores letters with any thing else you may have for the Ship. Should there be at this time a War with Mexico; or otherwise if it is intended to seize this fine country in the way of reprisal, which I strongly suspect By being notified of the fact, in the existing state of affairs, I should find opportunities of improving passing occurences, (the belligerents operating in my immediate vicinity) in such a manner probably as to facilitate the ultimate designs of our Government, which my present neutral positions necessarily forbid.

"You will readily imagine my dear Sir, that the inactivity; and apparent indifference, to the exciting & successful operations of our gallant countrymen around us, incident to the avowed neutrality of our Flag, is any thing but agreeable, and I cannot but feel a restless impatience to hear something of the actual state of affairs with Mexico, which disposes me at times to be *half angry* with my Old Friend [Mervine] for his seeming reservations when writing to me so briefly on the 20th Ulto."

Then followed a very complete report of events in Montgomery's area, ending with the plea: "Do not omit to give all matters of intelligence, bearing in mind that we have been cut off from all means of information since the 1st of April last."[57]

Frémont returned to Sonoma July 3, and the Fourth was celebrated "in old independent style." The Declaration of Independence was read by Lieut. Selim E. Woodworth, U.S. Navy, who arrived from the States via Oregon, after crossing the country with dispatches. Salutes were fired, and a fandango ended the day.

A military organization of a four-company battalion was effected. Ide was displaced by Frémont. One company consisted of Frémont's explorer group; the three others were commanded respectively by Ford, Granville P. Swift, and Grigsby. The latter's company remained at Sonoma; the remainder of the battalion, with Frémont in command, left for the Sacramento on July 6 and by the tenth was assembled at the American River.

At Yerba Buena, the *Portsmouth* fired a twenty-eight gun salute at noon on the Fourth. Montgomery had advised Leidesdorff, the Vice-consul, not to fly the American flag on that day. Leidesdorff agreed, since he had not hoisted the flag previously. Montgomery's journal has this entry for July 5:

"Informed by the Vice Consul of the United States that all the Spanish and Californian families having been removed from Yerba Buena as the instance of the Prefect [Pablo de la] Guerra, an attack upon the American and other foreign residents was apprehended during the night, by Guerra and Francisco Sanchez at the head of a number of Californians known to be hovering about in the vicinity. The brushwood and bushes in the rear and to windward of the town have been fired in a number of places by them, with a view of setting fire to the town, and at 6 o'clock P.M. intelligence was brought in that a party of sixteen had joined them at the Mission of —— [Dolores] in the neighborhood.

"Eighteen foreign residents have banded together to watch

during the night, and to act in defense if necessary, but poorly supplied with arms. At 9 P.M., at the earnest request of the Vice Consul, and receiving a message from Mr. Mellen [Mellus] that all property in the town belonged to Americans and foreigners, Lieut. Missroon with Lieut. [Henry B.] Watson, of Marines, and eighteen of the guard and three of the crew with their arms, were sent on shore to protect the Consulate and American citizens with their property from attack or violence. The night passed without disturbance, and the officers with marines returned on board at daylight."

On July 7th Bartlett, who had caught up with Frémont, returned with Henderson to the *Portsmouth*. Bartlett brought a letter of July 5 from Frémont, telling of his new organization and of his intention to move to Sutter's Fort.[58] Also on the 7th July, Agaton Ruiz, a Californian wounded at Olompali, was received on board "to be rationed by the Captain's orders."[59]

This is a proper place to pause and summarize the military situation in the northern part of Alta California to date, and to evaluate the services of Montgomery there.

The Bears, by action at the Cosumnes, Sonoma, and Olompali, had gained considerable control north of San Francisco Bay. Frémont's joining and the military organization at Sonoma assured that control. Grigsby was at Sonoma with fifty men. The Sonoma prisoners, with some additions, were safely at Sutter's Fort. Frémont was in that vicinity with a mobile force nearing one hundred and fifty and had definitely committed himself. Not so, the waiting naval officers, Montgomery at Yerba Buena and Mervine, whose *Cyane* had been joined by the *Levant* at Monterey on June 30. Castro had a sizable force near Santa Clara.

Montgomery, after arriving at Monterey April 22, had set

about his assigned mission of conciliating the Californians, beginning with Castro. Then he moved to San Francisco Bay and soon filled Frémont's request for supplies. He believed to the last possible moment Frémont's avowed intention of proceeding to the States. Considerably irked by Castro's complaints, he returned pointed answers, defending Frémont's neutrality. He helped in a tense situation by counselling and obtaining moderation by the Bears at Sonoma. He maintained his neutral position after Frémont's aggressive move. His sympathy was with the Bears and with Frémont, but there is found no valid evidence that he had been in collusion regarding their military actions. He did land a small force for a short time at Yerba Buena when so advised by Leidesdorff because of a real or fancied danger to Americans there. He commenced a policy, to be extended later, of medical aid to Californians. He conducted himself under the foregoing trying situations in a manner to reflect credit on his profession.

The stage was set for offensive action if justified by further news of the situation in Texas.

The American Flag Raised

Now that the *Portsmouth* had been anchored for several weeks at Yerba Buena, her complement had some opportunity to see and learn something of the little town and its people. Many works tell of Yerba Buena; among the good descriptions are those by John Henry Brown and by Joseph T. Downey.[60] Here is attempted only such brief statement as required by the present narrative. Published herewith is a reproduction of a lithograph by William F. Swasey, looking west from the cove, made years later from his own recollection and with the advice of several old timers. It is still the best for our purpose. In order to fix locations, present-day street names are used.

The place name "Yerba Buena" derived from the wild mint which grew profusely in the vicinity. Richard Henry Dana, Jr., a visitor in 1835, mentions as the only habitation then "a shanty of rough boards put up by a man named [William A.] Richardson, who was doing a little trading between the vessels and the Indians." Later Richardson improved his site with an adobe house at the corner of Grant Avenue and Clay Street. In 1836 came Jacob P. Leese, who built a frame house and store near Richardson. The only "street" at the time was in front of these houses and was named "Calle de la Fundacion" (Founding Street) by Richardson. Thence one trail wound about five miles west to the decrepit Presidio of San Francisco. The Castillo de San Joaquín was at an elevated point about one and one-half miles northwest of the Presidio. Another trail led for about three miles southwesterly to the Mission Dolores.

As the commerce of the Bay increased, so did the size of its port town. By July 1, 1846, the population was nearing 100, and the structures numbered about 25. Of all the buildings, the Custom House has to us the most historical interest. It faced east toward the Plaza, which can be noted in the Swasey view as an open space bounded on three sides by Kearny, Clay, and Washington streets. The Custom House, completed in 1845, was a long, one-story adobe with a tile roof. Immediately south was later built a calaboose. Several saloons bordered the square. Just east of present Montgomery Street was a beach where small boats could land at high tide only. But at Clark's Point, at about the junction of Broadway and Battery Street (right foreground of Swasey's view), was a landing practicable for small boats at any stage of the tide.[61] Swasey not only depicts the *Portsmouth* at Yerba Buena Cove, but also shows other vessels including transports, as of 1847. With this description of the setting at Yerba Buena we return to Mazatlan.

When, on May 17, Sloat had ordered the *Cyane* to Monterey, he planned to follow, but changed his mind. On May 31 he received news of the American victories at Palo Alto and Resaca de la Palma. He reported that he would "sail immediately," but again wavered and only ordered the *Levant* to Monterey. On June 5 he learned of the capture of Matamoros, but did not feel that his orders justified his "taking possession of any part of California." On June 7 he received news of the blockade of the east coast of Mexico. This strengthened his resolve, and he departed on June 8 in the *Savannah* for California. The *Warren* was left at Mazatlan to receive dispatches or information.

After arriving at Monterey on July 2, 1846, Sloat was briefed on the California situation, but formulated no final plan of action

View of San Francisco, Formerly Yerba Buena, in 1846-1847

A: U.S.S. *Portsmouth*. B: U. S. transports. C: *Vandalia,* merchantman. D: Coastal schooner.

until after the arrival on July 5 of Harrison in the *Portsmouth's* launch. Harrison delivered Montgomery's letter to Mervine and another to Larkin, both dated July 2 and both detailing Frémont's actions in concert with the Bears. Of course these letters were shown to Sloat. With Frémont in complete control north of the bay, no longer could Sloat remain irresolute. On July 6 Sloat wrote Montgomery:

"Since I wrote you last evening, I have determined to hoist the flag of the United States at this place to-morrow, as I would prefer being sacrificed for doing too much than too little.

"If you consider you have sufficient force, or if Frémont will join you, you will hoist the flag of the United States at Yerba Buena, or any other proper place, and take possession, in the name of the United States, of the fort and that portion of the country. I send you a copy of my summons to the military commandant of Monterey to surrender the place, and also my proclamation to the people of California, which you will have translated into Spanish, and promulgate many copies in both languages. I have sent a similar letter to General Castro, with an addition of an invitation for him to meet me at this place to enter into a capitulation.

"I will send you a duplicate copy of these documents to-morrow by land, which I hope will reach you before the boat can get up. You will secure the bay of San Francisco as soon as possible, at all events. It is my intention to go up to San Francisco as soon as I can leave this, which I hope will not be many days.

"Mr. Larkin advises that you should not send by courier anything that would do harm to make public; and should you have anything that you consider important for me to know, you can send the launch down again.

"I am very anxious to know if Captain Frémont will co-operate with us. Mr. Larkin is writing to him by the launch, and you will please put him in possession of his letter as soon as possible. . . ."[62]

Sloat landed a party and raised the American flag at the Monterey Custom House on July 7th. The same day he sent to Montgomery duplicate dispatches in the numerical code which deciphered as follows:

"Your launch left yesterday. I enclose you two documents, by which you will see what I have done.

"I hoisted the American flag here to-day at nine, A.M.

"You will immediately take possession of Y—— B—— [Yerba Buena], and hoist the American flag within range of your guns; post up the proclamation in both languages; notify Captain Frémont and others; put the fort and guns in order.

"I wish very much to see and hear from Captain F——, that we may understand each other and co-operate together."[63]

Separate sets of these papers were sent by couriers Henry F. Pitts and Job F. Dye. The former arrived at the *Portsmouth* at 7 P.M. on July 8th, the latter at 1 P.M. the following day.

Duvall records in his journal: "July 8th The weather as usual—a little before sunset, a great excitement on board. Bartlett put his head down the hatch and 'sung out' Watson, there is war—General Taylor has defeated the Mexican Army, and Commodore Sloat has taken Monterey. Soon afterwards the 'Proclamation' was brought down into the Wardroom and read with thrilling effect. . . ."

Montgomery's period of watchful waiting was over. Among his next actions was to send this letter to Vice-consul Leidesdorff at Yerba Buena:

"At ½ past seven oclock tomorrow morning I propose landing a considerable body of men under arms and to march them from the boats to the flagstaff in Yerba Buena, upon which, at 8 oclock

I shall hoist the flag of the U. States under a salute of twenty one guns from the Portsmouth, after which the proclamation of the Commander in Chief Commodore Sloat, will be read in both languages for the information of all classes.

"I will thank you therefore to have it translated and ready for that purpose at the appointed hour—and be pleased to present my compliments to the Alcaldy—and say if agreeable to him I shall be gratified to see him pleasant [present?] on the occasion, that I may, under the authority of the Proclamation, confirm him in his official position, until the pleasure of the Commander in Chief shall be known."[64]

A cutter left at 4 A.M., July 9, carrying Lieut. Joseph W. Revere with a flag to be raised at Sonoma and another to be sent to Sutter's Fort. "Breakfast was served at 6 A.M, and the word passed for all hands [sailors] to clean in white frocks, blue pants, black hats and shoes and prepare for muster." The officers and Marines donned full dress. Nearly all the officers, the Marines, and the carbineers constituted the *Portsmouth* party of about seventy which, says Downey, landed at Clark's Point.[65] The ship's log gives the time of the landing as 7 A.M. At that time the tide stage was so low as to render the use of the Montgomery Street beach impracticable. A scientific discussion of the tide situation appears in a note.[66]

The column was formed. James H. Crocker raised his fife, drummer William F. Steele his sticks, and all were off to the tune of "Yankee Doodle." The march was short: first to Montgomery Street, then up Clay, thence to the plaza, where a square was formed around the flagstaff in front of the Custom House.

At 8 A.M., July 9, 1846, the American flag was there raised to the peak. It is impossible to express adequately the feelings of a service man who sees the flag of his country raised on foreign soil in token of occupation. Downey says simply, "That flag floated proudly up, which has never yet been cowered to mortal foe."[67]

America had come to California to stay.

A twenty-one gun salute roared from the *Portsmouth,* echoed from the hills back of town, and punctuated the cheers from ship and shore. Montgomery then made this address:

"Fellow Citizens: I address all classes, whether native or foreign residents of California, who cordially assent to the transaction just witnessed. I have the pleasure to announce that the flag of the United States was, on the 7th instant, hoisted at Monterey, and will, I expect, this day be substituted for the revolutionary flag recently hoisted at Sonoma.

"The proclamation of the United States naval commander-in-chief now at Monterey, which is about to be read to you, has already been widely circulated in the country; and the advantages which cannot fail to accrue to the population of this fine country, as therein set forth, have, and will, undoubtedly, meet with a cordial reception by all classes of the people of California.

"It is earnestly recommended to all that they continue in the quiet pursuit of their proper occupations, in which, under the shadow of that glorious banner, there can be no fear of oppression, or undue interruption. After leaving this place, all persons who are disposed to unite in the formation of a local militia, to be held subject to drill and such military duty as the public security, under the new order of things, shall call for, are invited to attend at the house of William A. Leidesdorff, esq., where arrangements will be immediately entered into for such an organization."[68]

A reading of Sloat's proclamation followed. Second Lieut. Henry B. Watson, USMC, was detailed as Commandant of Yerba Buena, and to him were assigned fourteen of his Marines to be barracked at the Custom House. The remainder of the *Ports-*

mouth party was marched back to the landing "notwithstanding various and sundry wistful looks . . . cast toward the several rummeries," says Downey; and "without a man having left the ranks," proudly reports Montgomery.[69]

The ninth of July was a busy day for all. On returning to the ship, Montgomery prepared the following proclamation:

"Military possession having been this day taken of this place, and the flag of the United States displayed, in obedience to the orders of the commander-in-chief of the United States squadron, John D. Sloat, esq., now in possession of Monterey, I have the honor to call upon all the residents of this district, agreeably to laws of the United States of America regulating the militia, to enroll themselves into a military company, appoint their own officers, and observe such rules and regulations as shall be issued for the maintenance of order, and for the protection of property in Yerba Buena and its immediate neighborhood. A military guard has been stationed in possession of the custom-house, under Henry B. Watson, esq., whom I have appointed the military commandant (pro tem.) of all the marines and militia, to whom I require that reports shall be made, as soon as the militia shall be organized, and whose call upon the militia, I am confident, will be promptly and honorably complied with.

"In the event of an attack by the Mexicans or other forces upon Yerba Buena, all necessary assistance will be immediately landed from the United States ship Portsmouth; and, in the meantime, your country expects, and your best interests require, that every man will do his utmost to protect his home, and defend the flag of the United States."[70]

Later the same day, Watson was given written instructions, including the prescribing of the display of a rocket and blue lights as a signal to the ship in case of attack. Also he was furnished with a list of the militia, and thirteen muskets with bayonets and ammunition for their use.[71]

Missroon was sent on reconnaissance and returned with this report:

"I have the honor to report that, in obedience to your order, I proceeded to the forts at the entrance of the harbor, about four [later reported seven] miles distant from the town, accompanied by Purser Watmough, the late [!] Vice-consul Leidesdorff, and several volunteers, and displayed the flag of the United States upon its ramparts, calling on our way at the Presidio, where I had understood that one or more cannon were mounted; no cannon, however, were found there, and it is certain that they have been lately removed; nor were there any of the usual residents there.

"The walls of the fort [Castillo de San Joaquín] are badly rent in several places, yet they are capable of sustaining and rendering good service. It would be an improvement to dig a ditch in the rear, and to build a wall connecting the two terminating ends of the work. But, to render the fort tenable in case of approach to it by land, it is *indispensable* that a work be thrown up on the eminence which commands it, about four or five hundred yards immediately in its rear, otherwise it is at the mercy of an enemy on the land side. The platform is decayed, and should be renewed entirely.

"The barracks in the centre is in a dilapidated state.

"There are three brass guns, (12's and 18's), old Spanish pieces, made in 1623 [1673], 1628 and 1693, besides three long iron 42's, and four smaller iron guns. All of these iron guns have been lately spiked by Captain Frémont, except two unserviceable and dismounted iron pieces. New vents may be drilled in the brass pieces. The gun carriages are partially decayed, and several of them are totally unserviceable; but a portion of the iron work might be applied to new carriages.

"There is a quantity of round shot, of different calibers, in the fort, but *all* are more or less injured by rust.

"Our party was not molested on our route, nor did we see other than a few inoffensive Indians."[72]

Then Montgomery dispatched Purser James H. Watmough to Santa Clara, with a letter for Frémont, who was believed to be en route to that point. Frémont was told of the flag raisings at Monterey and Yerba Buena, and was informed that Sloat desired his presence at Monterey.[73]

Nothing is found to indicate whether an extra ration of grog was issued on board ship, but the ensuing celebration on shore was a lively one. It is doubtful whether many of the thirty-two militiamen enrolled were in condition that evening for immediate, effective service. Nevertheless the "Volunteer Guards of Yerba Buena" was the first militia organization formed under American rule in California. John H. Brown says that the officers elected were William D. M. Howard as Captain; William Smith, First Lieutenant; and John Rose, Second Lieutenant.[74] The two last named later participated in the Santa Clara campaign.

Before the momentous day ended, Montgomery prepared a report of his actions to Sloat. Included were copies of Montgomery's address, proclamation, and letter to Frémont, also Missroon's report on his reconnaissance. The bulk of the Montgomery report related to events already known to the reader. The captain did add a request for authority to move to Yerba Buena two brass 18's from Sonoma, and stated his intention to prepare a gallery and platform on an eminence to receive the pieces for the defense of the harbor.

The *Portsmouth's* log for July 10 tells, "Sent the Small gun on Shore, with 16 round of Grape and Cartridges." The gun was from the ship's launch, was called "Betsy Baker," and was placed in front of the flagstaff in the plaza.

Revere, having returned, made a written report to Montgomery on July 11. It is so important as a part of the annals of Sonoma that it is reproduced here:

"In obedience to your orders, I landed at the town of Sonoma from this ship on the 9th instant, having caused the troops of the garrison and the inhabitants of the place to be summoned to the public square. I then read the proclamation of Commodore Sloat to them, and then hoisted the United States flag upon the staff in front of the barracks, under a salute from the artillery of the garrison.

"I also caused the proclamation to be translated into Spanish, and posted up in the plaza. A notice to the people of California was also sent the next day to be forwarded to the country around, requesting the people to assemble at Sonoma on Saturday next, (the 11th,) to hear the news confirmed of the country having been taken possession of by the United States.

"An express, with a copy of the proclamation, and an United States flag, was also sent to the commander of the garrison at Sutter's fort, on the Sacramento, with a request to do the same there that had been done at Sonoma.

"The same was also done, with a request to the principal American citizen, (Mr. Stephen Smith,) at Bodega, with a demand for two field pieces of artillery, which I understand was there, to be removed to Sonoma, and placed under the custody and protection of the garrison there, by request of Captain John Grigsby, the commander of the port [post].

"I am happy to report that great satisfaction appeared to prevail in the community of Sonoma of all classes, and among both foreigners and natives, at the country having been taken possession of by the United States and their flag hoisted, more particularly after the general feeling of insecurity of life and property, caused by the recent events of the revolution in this part of California."[75]

At sunrise July 11 the American flag was raised at Sutter's Fort, having been delivered the evening before by William W. Scott, Revere's courier, from Sonoma. The ensuing twenty-one gun salute broke nearly all the glass in the fort.

At Yerba Buena, Missroon made a visit to the Mission Dolores and on his return reported that residents there who had fled, because of assumed danger, were beginning to return; that he assured the people of their safety; and that he collected some public documents and placed them under consulate seal at the Custom House in care of Watson.[76]

Less than a mile north of the plaza site rises a high hill, now known as Telegraph Hill, which affords an extensive view of San Francisco Bay and its entrance from the ocean. Of course this vantage point must have been used on occasion, early in the history of the town, to watch for expected ship arrivals. But it was on July 11, 1846, that there was initiated what probably was the first organized use of the hill as an equipped and manned signal station. The first record that has been found of such use appears in the *Portsmouth's* log: "Put up a signal pole on the hill off the point of Yerba Buena."

Doctor Duvall, in his journal entry of July 11, gives the reason for this action:

"Today about 1 P.M. it was reported that a Frigate was standing into the Bay—a great excitement was raised in consequence of it—a Midshipman was was sent to one of the highest hills to make signals—she soon came in and anchored at Sausalito—for a time her ensign was doubtful—soon made it out to be the blue flag of England. We made preparations for an engagement, having been directed and cautioned on this subject by the Commander-in-chief. Lieut. B. [Bartlett] was sent on board with the compliments of Capt. M. with the offer of any assistance in his power. At night, the officer returned, and reported that it was the British ship, Juno, 28 Guns, eight days from Santa Barbara. He received 'The Proclamation,' with apparent good grace, and supposed 'that the Commodore acted according to his instructions.'"[77]

Both Duvall and Downey tell of further use of the signal station for reporting ship arrivals while the *Portsmouth* was at Yerba Buena. Steady commercial use of the hill for signalling appears to date from the erection of a station house there in early 1849.

Thomas Fallon, known as "captain" because of his activities in raising foreign volunteers, wrote to Montgomery from San Jose July 12. He reported his arrival there with nineteen men in the expectation of joining Frémont. Since Frémont had not made his appearance, Fallon placed himself at Montgomery's command and offered to raise and protect the American flag. Six guns, pistols, and ammunition were requested, and the capture of Charles M. Weber by Castro was reported. Montgomery replied July 13, gladly accepted Fallon's offer; made the muskets and ammunition available on call at Yerba Buena; and recommended that Fallon organize his company.[78] Fallon received a flag from Sloat and on July 16 reported to Montgomery, "I am happy to inform you that I have hoisted the American Flag here on the 14 July."[79] This proves the date of the flag raising, erroneously stated by some writers as July 13 or 16.

On July 12 Frémont departed from Sutter's Fort with a force of about 160, leaving Edward M. Kern in charge of the prisoners and the fort. Crossing the San Joaquin near its junction with the

Merced, Frémont moved via Pacheco Pass and arrived at San Juan Bautista July 17. On the same day Purser Daingerfield Fauntleroy's troop joined, and the American flag was raised. This completed the American occupation of every place of any importance in northern California. At this time, or very soon thereafter, were recovered cannon, arms, and ammunition which had been hidden by Castro before he moved south. Frémont arrived at Monterey July 19 with his sizable force, which created quite a stir among the spectators, especially those from the British Admiral Seymour's *Collingwood,* recently in from Mazatlan.

Back at Yerba Buena, Montgomery was engaged in the establishment of the first American fortification on San Francisco Bay. The site selected was at the junction of present Battery and Green streets, at a place known before the later ground fills as "Montgomery Point." Work was commenced on the morning of July 15, 1846, when, reads the *Portsmouth's* log, "A gang of men on shore employed in putting up a battery." A "gallery" or terrace was to be cut at the rocky site, and a platform prepared upon which some of the captured guns were to be mounted. The progress of the work was as follows: July 16, received two guns from the fort [castillo]; July 18, party digging fort and unspiking guns; July 20, launch to Sonoma for guns; July 21, second cutter arrives bringing prize schooner *Sarmiento,* Mdn. Daniel C. Hugunin sent in *Sarmiento* to Sonoma for artillery, shot, etc.; July 23, Hugunin returns with three guns, 12, 6, and 4 pounders, with carriages and shot, other supplies listed; July 25, *Sarmiento* returns with more arms and munitions; August 5, supplies to the fort ashore.

Timbers and planks for the platform were salvaged at the Presidio or Mission. The sods were cut from the marsh grass at the Mission Creek flats, and when dried formed ready-made adobes for the parapet. They were carried up the slope on the heads of the members of the work party.

Of greatest interest, however, were the beautiful bronze guns, five of which were emplaced at the battery. Douglas S. Watson has written a fine monograph on "San Francisco's Ancient Cannon."[80] He proves that, of the five guns mounted at Fort Montgomery, two came from the Castillo de San Joaquín; two from Sonoma; and one from the Presidio, where it had been buried but had its location revealed by Francisco Sanchez. These five guns and a sixth, still spiked as it was by Frémont's party, have been preserved by the U. S. Army—four are now at the Presidio of San Francisco, two at Fort Mason.

Montgomery's battery was virtually complete about three weeks after its beginning. It came to be known as Fort Montgomery, but was also nicknamed by the sailors as "Missroon's Folly," for the officer in charge of its construction. Also, a long twelve on a pivot was mounted in a blockhouse, built southwest of Portsmouth Square.

So Montgomery was well prepared to hold Yerba Buena.

Comes Stockton

Commodore Robert F. Stockton arrived in the frigate *Congress* at Monterey on July 15, 1846. There he learned that Commodore Sloat intended to leave soon for the United States, because of failing health. When Frémont's battalion arrived at Monterey on July 19, Sloat refused to receive it in the service, deeming Frémont's recent campaign premature and without authority. On July 23 Sloat placed Stockton in command of the forces and operations on shore. Frémont and Gillespie now had a resolute champion in Stockton, by whom they were given battalion appointments as major and captain, respectively.

Plans were made immediately for an invasion of southern California. Frémont's battalion left in the *Cyane* on July 26 and arrived at San Diego, where the American flag was raised July 29. Sloat left Monterey for home in the *Levant* on the 29th, and the same day Stockton issued a lengthy address, outlining his policies and reasons therefor, and promising to march against Castro. On August 1 Stockton sailed in the *Congress*, raised the American flag at Santa Barbara and arrived at San Pedro August 6. His campaign in the south shall be summarized later.

Before leaving Montgomery, Stockton issued piecemeal orders for the release of the Sonoma prisoners at Sutter's Fort.[81] He also issued instructions for recruiting and defined Montgomery's command as including Yerba Buena, Sonoma, Sutter's Fort, San Jose, and their vicinities. This was called the Northern Department of California. Mervine, who remained at Monterey with the *Savan-*

nah, commanded the Monterey-San Juan Bautista area, the Central Department.

During military occupation of conquered territory it is highly desirable that the local governmental officials, if cooperative, be encouraged to continue their functions. In Montgomery's district such cooperation was not forthcoming from the prefects and alcaldes, with the exception of Sutter. Montgomery's troops did make arrests, but it was necessary that a system be set up to try civil offenders. It seems that the first such instance at Yerba Buena was on July 20, 1846, when Montgomery ordered Lieutenant Revere and Surgeon Henderson to investigate alleged offenses of prisoners at the guard house, hear witnesses under oath, make findings, and recommend punishment. To Francis Alias, a cook recently discharged from the *Portsmouth,* seems due the doubtful honor of having been found guilty by this tribunal. He was charged with attempting to take a horse from an Indian, and abusing and drawing a knife on Vice-consul Leidesdorff. Duvall says that Alias had declared, "There is no law here now, he would act as he pleased." The sentence approved by Montgomery on July 21 was of one month of hard labor on the public works. Four other prisoners were found not guilty, and released.[82] Again, on August 7, Lieutenant Bartlett and Surgeon Duvall were ordered by Montgomery to sit as a court at Yerba Buena.

From time to time Montgomery issued "laws" or "notices" prohibiting certain conduct and setting forth penalties. His letter book and other documents show the following such prohibitions issued for the government of Yerba Buena: July 16, 1846, plundering, maltreating of peaceable inhabitants; July 20, drunkenness, fighting, boisterous conduct; August 1, slaughtering cattle in the streets, failure to remove offal; August 6, discharge of firearms, drunkenness, seller of liquor punished; August 14, retail sales of liquor and any sales of less than one gallon prohibited; August 15, closing places of amusement on the Sabbath.

Yerba Buena had a large increase in population on July 31, 1846. Then there arrived the ship *Brooklyn,* from New York via Honolulu, carrying and soon landing some 230 Mormons and a few not of that faith. The passengers were taken to shore in boats, and most were sheltered in tents. A few, including the leader, Sam Brannan, found housing. Personal property, including farm implements, arms, a printing press, and stores was landed. Montgomery required that merchandise on the manifest be kept on the ship until custom regulations were known. The services of eighty Mormons, "completely armed, organized & drilled as a Military Company," were offered to Montgomery for use in an emergency.[83] Downey tells an interesting story of a divine service held on the *Portsmouth* for the Mormons, and of the favorable impression made by them.[84] Some of the Mormons became engaged in lumbering, some went to found a settlement on the Stanislaus, but most remained at Yerba Buena during 1846. Soon the *Brooklyn* was off for Honolulu via Bodega.

Although Montgomery confessed to Mervine "writing never was a favorite occupation of mine," his letter book was necessarily filled with scores of letters dealing with the organization, operations, supply, and intelligence of the enemy, for the posts in his district. On July 29 Grigsby was ordered to provide for the enlistment of fifty men at Sonoma, and to keep confined the prisoners under his charge until further orders. One of these prisoners was Bernardino García, known as "Three-fingered Jack" and accused of connection with the Cowie-Fowler murders. On August 3 Revere was placed in command at Sonoma and was ordered to complete the enlistments. The pay was to be near the army rate, but not to exceed $15 per month; the period to be for two or three months. Revere succeeded in his mission. He must have enjoyed his new station, for he soon went on hunting and exploring trips, and was finally admonished by Montgomery not to absent himself for a single day.[85]

Missroon, who had been ordered on August 1 to Sonoma to arrange preliminaries, then moved to New Helvetia, Sutter's rancho, to open articles of enlistment for emigrants from Oregon and the States. The plan was to complete the garrisons in Montgomery's district, including short-handed San Jose, and to send surplus enlistees to Mervine at Monterey. By letter of July 25, Stockton had appointed Edward M. Kern as first lieutenant, and Montgomery continued him in command at Sutter's Fort. Stockton also had directed Montgomery to release General Vallejo, and on July 29 Montgomery had ordered Kern to take such action. Vallejo was released on August third or fourth. Missroon carried orders for the release of the remaining prisoners, and by August 8 Salvador Vallejo, Leese, Prudon, and Robert Ridley were also free. A garrison was formed of some thirty men, of whom about twenty were Indians, and Sutter was appointed lieutenant under Kern. Montgomery asked Kern to send a letter from Stockton to Lieut. Neil M. Howison, commanding the *Shark*, directing the return of the schooner from the Columbia to California.[86] The forwarding of the letter was delayed, and Montgomery ordered its recall on September first. Actually the vessel was wrecked at the mouth of the Columbia in October 1846.

On August 5 Purser Watmough was ordered to San Jose with a small body of mounted men, to take command there, replacing James Stokes who had acted after Fallon's departure for San Juan. During the month, Watmough received further increments from Sutter's and Yerba Buena, and by local enlistments. However, the Californians at San Jose and Santa Clara were not generally cooperative. Raids by Indians in the vicinity were troublesome. Watmough and Fauntleroy recaptured some stolen horses and inflicted some punishment on the Indians.

During August, Montgomery made several appointments in his district to replace recalcitrant Californian officials. The following alcaldes were named: August 5, Stephen Smith at Bodega; August 12, Lieut. Washington A. Bartlett, acting, at Yerba Buena; and George Hyde, a *Brooklyn* passenger, at San Jose.[87] Also on August 12 Bartlett and Hyde were ordered to try jointly Yerba Buena cases, one of which was that of Elisha Hyatt, from the *Brooklyn* and charged with theft. On August 11 Revere was ordered to appoint an alcalde at Sonoma, and soon Edward McIntosh was acting in that capacity. Sutter was continued as justice of the peace at New Helvetia.[88]

It will be remembered that an emergency signal of a blue light had been prescribed for use between Watson's marines and the *Portsmouth* in the event of an attack on the town. After midnight August 13-14 the watch on the ship saw just such a blue light burning on shore. Downey, Duvall, and Brown, each tell amusing stories of the incident, too long to be repeated here. Responding to the call, a landing party from the ship confusedly poured into the boats and with equal confusion debarked at the beach and waded to shore. The alarm was caused by a sentry who fired his gun when horses were heard. No attack developed. Later, says Downey, the alarm was "explained by Jose Jesus de Noe, who deposed and said that his 'manada,' consisting of some 30 or 40 mares, had been running through and around town all night." Most of the landing party returned to the ship by 2:30 A.M., but an extra guard of twenty-five men under Mdn. Charles S. Bell was left on shore.[89]

A brief examination of the progress of events in the south is desirable. We left Stockton at San Pedro and Frémont at San Diego. General Castro and Governor Pío Pico, finding themselves unable to submit to Stockton's terms, left Los Angeles for Mexico on August 10. The forces of Stockton and Frémont joined at Los Angeles on August 13 and raised the American flag there without resistance. Stockton, on August 17th, proclaimed himself Commander-in-Chief and Governor of California, and announced his policies. The same day Capt. Joseph B. Hull arrived in the *Warren* at San Pedro via Mazatlan and Monterey, carrying news of the declaration of war. On the 22d of August Stockton called for local elections to be held September 15 in Alta California. Frémont was appointed military commandant of California and was ordered to recruit his battalion to a strength of 300, and to meet Stockton at San Francisco October 25. Gillespie was appointed commandant of the Southern Department, headquarters at Los Angeles. He was given an inadequate force of about fifty, from which a small detachment under Merritt was sent to San Diego. Lulled by his easy victories, Stockton left Los Angeles September second and arrived at Monterey on the fifteenth. Captains Ford and Swift, with their depleted companies, had already arrived at Monterey on the second. Frémont moved north, left a small garrison at Santa Barbara, and by the end of September was near Soledad with about thirty men.

At Monterey on August 15 was published the first issue of a weekly, *The Californian*, first newspaper of California. The editors were Chaplain Walter Colton of the Navy, and Robert Semple, who had served with the Bears, Frémont, and Fauntleroy. An extra was published on September 5, which contained Stockton's proclamation of August 17 and his August 22d call for municipal elections.

Stockton had plans for the invasion of the west coast of Mexico, and Montgomery was ordered to be in readiness for a cruise at a moment's notice. The latter in turn ordered Revere, Kern, and Watmough immediately to put their accounts in order. Each was furnished copies of Stockton's proclamation and call for elections, and prompt distribution was enjoined. Watmough's copy was mentioned as a printed one, so it may have been the *Californian* extra of September 5.[90]

Mention of printing brings up the matter of the early imprints of Sam Brannan at Yerba Buena. What appears to be the first of such issues was a broadside containing Montgomery's "Rules and Regulations, for the trade of the Bay of San Francisco," dated September 6, 1846. The next imprint found is a broadside proclamation by Montgomery, prohibiting the enslavement of Indians, issued September 15, 1846. Then came an imprint, dated September 17, 1846, concerning regulations for the detection and punishment of frauds in the tallow trade of the Bay of San Francisco and also dealing with the registration of launches and boats. It did not carry Brannan's name as printer, but certainly may be attributed to his press. Brannan's program for the reception of Stockton will be mentioned later.

September tenth was a busy day for Montgomery. On that day he received from Fort Sacramento (Sutter's Fort) a report that a thousand Walla Walla Indians were approaching the fort; that on the 8th a hundred were already at Feather River; and that their object was to avenge the murder of one of their tribe about a year before by Grove Cook. Kern asked for immediate assistance.

Montgomery took the following action. Orders were at once dispatched to Revere at Sonoma to proceed with all his effective force to Fort Sacramento. Actually, Revere had the news and was already on his way to the fort. Missroon was sent to Sonoma with a marine guard to occupy the post in the absence of the regular garrison. He was ordered to receive any men furnished by General Vallejo; to keep communications open with Fort Sacramento; and to report any advance of the Indians on Sonoma, in order that Montgomery might proceed in person with all the force of the *Portsmouth* if necessary. Watmough, on an Indian expedition with Fauntleroy, was ordered to Fort Sacramento. The person remaining in command at San Jose was ordered to arrest and confine Grove Cook. Mervine was requested to send the recently arrived Frémont troops (the Ford and Swift companies) to the Sacramento. A letter was dispatched to Kern, advising him of the action taken. General Vallejo's offer of personnel assistance was accepted with gratitude. Within a few days Missroon forwarded from Sonoma to the Sacramento nineteen Californians under Moses Carson, and eight Indians from Bodega.[91]

On September 12 Mervine ordered Ford, with his company and Swift's, to the Sacramento. If encountered by Ford, Fauntleroy was to accompany. The men of Ford and Swift refused to march from San Juan Bautista, for they considered their engagements fulfilled. Pay also seems to have been a factor. Fauntleroy returned to San Juan Bautista from the Indian expedition on September 14, and Watmough got back to San Jose about the same time. None of these troops got under way for the Sacramento.[92]

Soon the Walla Walla worries were ended. The Indians, under Chief Yellow Serpent, were found to number only about forty—they came to talk and trade, not fight. Some later rendered good service with Frémont's battalion. Grove Cook represented to Montgomery that he had already been tried for the murder of the Indian, so the order for his arrest was countermanded.[93] By the end of September Revere had returned to Sonoma; the temporary garrison was relieved; and General Vallejo was suitably thanked by Montgomery for his help.

On September 14 Montgomery wrote to Leidesdorff that he had received the petition of a number of non-Californian residents of Yerba Buena requesting that he dispense with the approaching election. This Montgomery refused to do, pointing out that the holding of the election was required by Stockton. The following day these officers were elected: Washington A. Bartlett, alcalde; José de Jesus Noé, second alcalde; John Rose, treasurer; and Peter T. Sherreback, collector. Montgomery considered that the election had failed with respect to the first alcalde, since the naval officer Bartlett, rather than a civilian, had been elected. He so informed Stockton by letter on September 16, but said he would continue Bartlett in office pending Stockton's decision. Actually, Bartlett served as alcalde until relieved in February 1847. William F. Swasey says: "Mr. Bartlett was generally respected and liked by the community, his administration gave general satisfaction, and was, comparatively, without friction. He was a fine Spanish scholar."[94]

Edwin Bryant tells of a visit to Yerba Buena and the *Portsmouth* in September 1846:

"She [the *Portsmouth*] is regarded as the finest vessel of her class belonging to our navy. By invitation of Lieutenant Bartlett, I went on board of her between ten and eleven o'clock. The crew and officers were assembled on deck to attend Divine service. They were all dressed with great neatness, and seemed to listen with deep attention to the Episcopal service and a sermon, which was read by Commander Montgomery, who is a member of that church.

"On the 21st, by invitation of Captain Montgomery, I dined on board of the sloop-of-war Portsmouth. The party, including myself, consisted of Colonel [William H.] Russell, Mr. [Richard K.] Jacob, Lieutenant Bartlett, and a son of Captain Montgomery. There are few if any officers in our navy more highly and universally esteemed, for their moral qualities, than Captain M. He is a sincere Christian, a brave officer, and an accomplished gentleman. We spent the afternoon most agreeably, and the refined hospitality, courteous manners, and intelligent and interesting conversation of our host, made us regret the rapidly fleeting moments."[95]

William Heath Davis, a resident, also had much praise for Montgomery:

"Captain Montgomery was highly regarded by the people, and became a great favorite with all classes, both American and foreign, and also with the Californians. He was about fifty years of age, with a pleasant, intelligent face; a man of considerable ability, officer-like in appearance, and in demeanor polite to all; kind and conciliatory in his intercourse with the people, winning their esteem and affection. He was much liked by his officers, who spoke of him as one of the best commanders in the service. During the six or seven months that he remained at Yerba Buena, he never had the slightest trouble with any one."[96]

A favorite gathering place for the naval officers was the hotel opened by John H. Brown early in August at the southeast corner of Kearny and Clay streets. It was named the Portsmouth House, says Brown, at the request of several non-commissioned officers from the *Portsmouth* who furnished and painted the sign board.[97] The social tempo increased, for on September 8 a grand ball was held at Leidesdorff's, at which upwards of one hundred Californian and American ladies were present. Capt. Bezer Simmons reciprocated with an affair of September 18 on the *Magnolia,* for which one hundred and fifty family invitations were issued.[98]

There are persistent traditions that Montgomery conducted the first Protestant services on shore at Yerba Buena, but a supporting primary source is not found. It is entirely possible that he may have led such a service on shore before the arrival of the *Brooklyn,* but John H. Brown, a contemporary, says: "The first sermon delivered in the English language at Yerba Buena was preached by Sam Brannan."[99]

About 1 P.M., September 26, the station on the hill at Yerba Buena signalled the approach of a ship of the American Navy. The *Savannah* soon came in and anchored near the *Portsmouth.* About 3 P.M. another vessel was signalled. "The Congress under topsails was coming in magnificently—we saluted her, she returned it, passed between us and the Savannah and took her berth."[100]

On the *Congress* was Commodore Stockton, now ready to complete his plans for the invasion of Mexico, but an annoying reverse intervened. A courier, John Brown, arrived at Yerba Buena from Los Angeles, after a ride which was an amazing feat of speed and endurance. The message he carried, delivered to Stockton on October 1, was sent September 24 by Gillespie. It said that Gillespie was attacked the day previous, and was then besieged by a large force of Californians.

The supplies of Stockton's ships had been replenished by the storeship *Erie,* and he had issued orders for their movement from San Francisco Bay. Now he ordered Mervine to proceed in the *Savannah* to San Pedro for the aid of Gillespie. Mervine made a start, but did not leave the Bay until several days later. Montgomery's orders to move were countermanded and he was directed to remain at Yerba Buena.

Since Stockton was not to leave at once, grand plans were made to give him a public reception on October 5. The program for the affair, printed on blue satin by Sam Brannan, is the most interesting of his early imprints at Yerba Buena.

The "Order of the Day" provided for the formation of the procession at 8 A.M. in the Plaza, newly designated as "Portsmouth Square" in honor of Montgomery's ship. Leading was Chief Marshal Frank Ward with aides. Then came the band from the *Congress;* Military Escort under Capt. Jacob Zeilin; Capt. Montgomery with Officers, U. S. Navy; Capt. John Paty, Hawaiian Navy; Lieut. Bonnet, French Navy; Lieut. Rudacoff, Russian Navy; Washington A. Bartlett, Magistrate of Yerba Buena; Col. William H. Russell, Orator of the Day; Consuls Larkin and Leidesdorff; Strangers of Distinction; Committee of Arrangements; Masters of Ships in Port; and Citizens Generally.

The procession moved down Portsmouth Street (probably the later Clay Street) to Water Street (now Montgomery Street) and there formed line. The tide was high, and the Commodore's barge landed at a temporary wharf which had been constructed for the occasion. A salute of seventeen guns was fired, probably by all the warships and by the battery at Montgomery Point. Commodore Stockton was met and conducted in front of the line by Montgomery, Bartlett, and Ward. The red-coated band played "Hail Columbia." Orator Russell delivered a fulsome welcome, and Stockton replied with a bombastic speech. The principals moved to Leidesdorff's, where many ladies passed the Commodore's receiving line. Then he was taken on a horseback tour of the Mission and Presidio. On his return, a dinner was served at Leidesdorff's. The day ended there with a grand ball where, says *The Californian,* "the utmost hilarity and unanimity of spirit prevailed." Hilarity, yes, but not complete unanimity, for there were several discreditable brawls, and Watmough became engaged in a controversy with Leidesdorff. Gen. Vallejo and his brother Salvador were at the dinner, were toasted by Stockton, and became guests of the *Portsmouth's* wardroom.[101]

PUBLIC RECEPTION
OF HIS EXCELLENCY
ROBERT F. STOCKTON,
GOVERNOR, AND COMMANDER-IN-CHIEF
OF CALIFORNIA, &C., &C.

The Citizens of the District of San Francisco and vicinity, having, united for the purpose of giving a public reception to His Excellency, ROBERT F STOCKTON, on the occasion of his landing, on Monday, Oct. 5th, 1846; The following is the

ORDER OF THE DAY.

1st. The citizens will assemble in "Portsmouth Square" at 8, A. M. and form in procession in the following order

CHIEF MARSHALL

AID. AID.

MUSIC

Military Escort, under command of
Capt. J. Zeilin, U. S. M. C.

Capt. John B. Montgomery, U. S. N.,
(Commanding the Northern District of California)
and Suite.

Officers, U. S. N.,

Captain John Paty,
Senior Captain of the Hawaiian Navy.

Lieut. Commanding Bonnet,—French Navy.

Lieut. Commanding Kuracoff,—Russian Navy.

The Magistracy of the District,
and the
Orator of the Day.

FOREIGN CONSULS.

Thos. O. Larkin and Wm. A. Leidesdorff, Esqs.,
(Late U. S. Consuls for California.)

U. S. Navy Agent,
and the
U. S. Collector of the District.

Gentlemen who held Civil or Military Comissions
under the late Government.

STRANGERS OF DISTINCTION.
COMMITTEE OF ARRANGEMENTS.
MASTERS OF SHIPS IN PORT.
CITIZENS GENERALLY.

2d. The procession will move at half past eight o'clock, to take up a position to receive His Excellency at the point of landing.

3d. The Governor and Suite will land at 9 A. M. under a salute of seventeen guns.

4th. The Governor will be received by His Honor Wash'n A. Bartlett, Magistrate of the District, attended by the Corporation.

5th. The Governor will be addressed by Col. Wm H. Russell, Orator of the day.

6th. The procession will then move through the principal streets to the residence of Wm. A. Leidesdorff Esq. where the LADIES will be presented to His Excellency; after which a cavalcade will be formed to escort him on his tour of inspection.

7th. On returning from the tour a collation will be served up at the residence of Wm. A. Leidesdorff Esq.

8th. The following gentlemen will be known as Aids to the Marshall viz. C. E. Pickett, Wm. H. Davis, Frederick Teschmaker, and J. K. Wilson Esqrs; the Aids will appear in uniform.

FRANK WARD, Marshall.

Yerba Buena, October 5th., 1846.

(S. Brannan, Printer.---San Francisco.)

RULES AND REGULATIONS,

FOR THE TRADE OF THE BAY OF SAN FRANCISCO.

REGLAMENTOS

PARA EL COMERCIO Y NAVIGACION DE LA BAHIA DE SAN FRANCISCO.

It having come to the knowledge of the Commander of the District of San Francisco &c &c

That persons are engaged in stealing and killing cattle, and then selling the produce to any purchaser: and it being necessary to put every possible check upon such practices, and to secure all property to the proper owners thereof.

It is ordered that from and after this date, no shipments of the products of the country will be permitted to be made in any boat, launch, or other vessel, except under the following regulations:

1st. The points of shipment where boats or launches will be permitted to take freight on board are at "Sausolito," Corte "Madera," (the wood landing between Sausolito and San Raphael") San Raphael" Petaluma, Sonoma, and only at the usual landing of those places for the north of the bay.

2d. For the Sacramento Valley and River at Suter's Landing.

3d. For the San Joaquin River, Dr. Marsh's landing. Inspectors will be appointed for all the above named points with instructions for their guidance.

4th. For that part of the Bay called the Contra Coast, commencing at the mouth of the San Joaquin River, and extending as far as the landing of the mission San Jose, Hides, Tallow &c., may be shipped under the following regulations: The shipper to give a Bill of Sale in writing, signed by himself, certifying to the marks in said bill to correspond with the marks on the articles, particularly the marks on the Hides and bags of Tallow.

5th An office of inspector of hides and tallow will be established at the Pueblo of San Jose and a sub inspector at the landing of said Pueblo. The Inspector General will be at Yerba Buena

6th. Shipments may be made at any point from the Pueblo to Yerba Buena, under the same regulations contained in art., 4.

7th. The Inspector general at Yerba Buena will inspect all launches or boats on their arrival, and ascertain if the freight corresponds with the Bill of Lading, and particularly as to the marks being the same as expressed on the bills.

8th. An Inspector of tallow will be appointed to ascertain if it is of a merchantable quality, and if it corresponds, that no fraud has been attempted by the introduction of other substances to defraud in weight.

9th. Any person found guilty of selling or disposing of hides that are not legally his own, will be severely punished by fine and labor on the public works, according to the nature of the offence.

10th. Any person found guilty of an attempt to defraud by introducing improper articles in bags of tallow, will forfeit the whole package, and suffer a further penalty, according to the nature of the offence.

11th. In order to meet the expenses of the inspectors which are intended to protect all who are engaged in a just and honorable trade, a tax of 3 cents on each hide, and 25 cents on each bag of tallow will be assessed.

12th All such certificates, and certified bills of lading will be deposited in the office of the superintendant of the port for the benefit of all concerned.

13th. All boats or launches arriving at the anchorage of Yerba Buena must be entered for inspection before they can be permitted to unload.

By order of JOHN B. MONTGOMERY, Esq., Comdg. Northern District of California.

WASH'N. A. BARTLETT

Collector & Superintendant,

Port San Francisco.

Yerba Buena, Sept. 6th., 1846.

Por cuanto que el Senor Gobernador y Commandente Militar del destrito de San Francisco, ha sabido que algunos Ladrones han robado, y estan robando reses, matandolos y vendiendolos a los que pueden, y siendo necesario para dar fin a estos males, y asegurar todo propiedad a sus dueños.

Queda ordenado desde esta fecha, deno embarcar los productos del pais sino en "Sousolito",—"Corte Madera"—San-Rafael—Petaluma—Sonoma—y Nappa, para la costa del Norte de la bahia.

2o En el Rio del Sacramento, y para el valle del Rio, a el embacadero de "Suter".

3 En el Rio de San Joaquin al embacadero del Rancho de Doctor Marsh, y para dichos puntos seran nombrados inspectors, o jueces de campo, con instrucceiones para su gobierno.

4o Para aquella parte de la habia llamada la "Contra Costa"—Comprendido de la embocadura del San Joaquin hasta el embarcadero de la mision de San Jose, Cueros y Sebo puede ser embarcado, bajo los reglamentos siguentes. El embacador se dara una carta, o seguridad de venta, firmada por el; certificando que las marcas, en dichos efectos corresponden con las marcas o senales de la carta de venta—y si no es del hierro de el que vende—que es legalmente su propiedad. Esto es particularmente para las marcas de los cueros y botas de sebo.

5o El Inspector General de cueros y sebo tendra su oficina en Yerba Buena, y sera nombrado un inspector para el Pueblo de San Jose, y un sub-inspector al embacadero de dicho Pueblo.

6o Efectos de toda clase puede ser embacados en toda la costa, entre el embacadero de San Jose hasta Yerba Buena bajo las mismos condiciones y reglamentos de la Centra Costa, espresado en art. 4o.

7o El Inspector General en Yerba Buena registrara todas las lanchas, o embacaiones cuande lleguen al fondeadero o playa—y examinara la carga a ver si el Flete corresponde con las cartas de venta, ó inspeccion de los puntos adonde hai inspectores.

8 El Inspector General tambien tiene ordenes para examinar, y ver, si el sebo esta de la calidad Mercantil; y que no hai engano, ni introducion de alguna cosa espuria para anadir al peso.

9 Cualquiera persona culpable de vender cueros o sebo, u otra propiedad no siendo de su pertenencia, sera castigado severamente con Multa, y a las obras publicas segun el clase de la ofensa.

10 Cualquiera person o personas culpable de enganar algun comprador con la introduccion de cosas espuria en las botas de sebo—aumentando el peso—perdera todo la bota y sufrira castigo segun la ofensa.

11 Para cobrar los gastos de las inspeciones que estan para protejer los derechos de todos que entran en comercio justo y honorable, se pagara por cada cuero 3 centavos, y 2 reales per cada bota de cebo como sueldo del Inspector General en Yerba Buena. A los Jueces de Campo—se pagara como antes—por los cueros que se embarquen con su inspecion.

12o Las cartas de venta cirtificadas por el inspector seran depositadas en la oficina del inspector, para la seguridad de todos los interesados.

13 Todos las lanchas o embacaciones, que lleguen a la Yerba Buena han de ser registradas antes de des-cargar,

Por orden Del Sr. Comdte. y GOBERNADOR del distrito, Don JOHN B MONTGOMERY Capitan de la marina de los Estados Unidos. WASH'N. A. BARTLETT.

Administrador de la Aduana,

Districto de San Francisco.

Yerba Buena 6 de Setr'e. de 1846.

S. BRANNAN, *PRINTER.*

A PROCLAMATION

TO THE INHABITANTS OF THE NORTHERN DISTRICT OF CALIFORNIA.

PROCLAMA

A LOS HABITANTES DEL NORTE, O DISTRITO DE SAN FRANCISCO EN CALIFORNIA.

It having come to the knowledge of the Commander in Chief of this district, that certain persons have been and still are imprisoning and holding to service Indians against their will, and without any legal contract, and without a due regard to their rights as freemen when not under legal contract for service.—It is hereby ordered, that all persons so holding or detaining Indians shall release them, and permit them to return to their own homes, unless they can make a contract with them which shall be acknowledged before the nearest Justice, which contract, shall be binding upon both parties.

The Indian population must not be regarded in the light of slaves, but it is deemed necessary that the Indians within the Settlements shall have employment, with the right of choosing their own master and employer; and after having made such choice, they must abide by it, unless they can obtain permission in writing to leave, or the Justice on their complaint shall consider they have just cause to annul the contract, and permit them to obtain another employer.

All Indians must be required to obtain service, and not be permitted to wander about the country in an idle and dissolute manner; if found doing so, they will be liable to arrest and punishment by labor on the PUBLIC WORKS at the discretion of the Magistrate.

All Officers, civil or military, under my command, are required to execute the terms of the order, and take notice of every violation thereof.

Given at head quarters in Yerba Buena.
Sept. 15th, 1846.

(SIGNED,) - - - - JNO. B. MONTGOMERY,
Commanding District of San Francisco.

Published for the government
of all concerned.
WASH'N. A. BARTLETT,
Magistrate of San Francisco.

Habiendo llegado a la noticia del comandante Militar de este distrito, que algunas personas han tenido, y aun tienen en su servicio, los indegenas de este pais por coercion, y como Esclavos; pues no consideran que los Indios gozan de los derechos de hombres libres, y no se les podran compeler a ningun servicio sino un contrato estipulado.

He venido en mandar, que desde esta fecha en adelante, la persona o personas que tuviesen en su servicio algun INDIO o INDIOS, sin el requisito arriba espresado; los pongan en entera libertad, para que vuelvan a sus hogares, o que elijan a su libre alveldrio el amo a quien quieran servir: en la inteligencia que todo contrato con Indios sirvientes, debe ser autorisado ante su respectivo Juez. No se debe mirar a los Indios como esclavos; pero es indispensable que todo Indio tenga un modo visible de viver honestamente, es decir que han de tener amos, y despues de haber escogido estos, no pueden dejar su servicio sin causa justa y con permiso por escrito, para entrar en el servicio de otro.

A ningun Indio se le permitira andar de holgazan ni tampoco transitar por este distrito, sin pasaporte de su respectivo juez. Y el Indio que se encuentra sin dicho pase, sera aprehendido y puesto a trabajar en obras publicas a la disposicion de los magistrados.

Requiero a todos los oficiales civiles y militares quien estan bajo mi mando, que ejecuten estos ordenes y que toman cuenta del primero violacion.

Cuartel General del distrito en Yerba Buena.
JNO. B. MONTGOMERY,
Commandante en Gefe del Distrio. el
Norte de California.
Set'bre 15 de 1846.

Publicado para la Gobernancia del Dirstrito,
WASH'N A. BARTLETT,
Juez 1o de San Francisco.

(S. Brannan, Printer.----San Francisco.)

REGULATIONS

For the detection and punishment of frauds in the Tallow Trade.

Office of Collector and Superintendent of the Port of San Francisco.
Sept., 15th. 1846.

Gentlemen:—

In consequence of the fraud and imposition heretofore practised in the Bay of San Francisco in the quality of the tallow sold as merchantable, which on being exported to foreign markets has seriously injured the purchasers and is fast destroying the reputation of the California tallow in all markets—it has now become necessary to put some salutary check on the fraud. I deem it necessary therefore that a true standard of merchantable tallow be at once established to protect shippers from this Port.

I therefore request that you will consent to act as a board of examiners in this matter, and from your long experience in the trade and customs of California, decide and declare what shall be the character of tallow, which shall be held to be merchantable in the market—placing in my office samples corresponding to your decision for the government of the buyer and seller—and also of the inspector.

Very Respectfully your ob't., serv't.

Signed - - - - WASH'N. A. BARTLETT
Collector and superintendant,
Port of San Francisco.

MESSRS.
ELIAB GRIMES.
WM. A. LEIDESDORFF.
FRANCISCO GUERRERO.
WM. H. DAVIS.
PETER DAVIDSON.
JOSE DE JESUS NOE.
JOSE JOAQUIN ESTUDILLA.
JOHN C. DAVIS.
NATHAN SPEAR.

Report of Committee.

We the undersigned having been called upon to give our opinion upon certain samples of tallow produced before us, in order to establish a standard which shall hereafter govern both buyer and seller; do pronounce, said samples of good merchantable quality, and as such they be the standard for the inspector.

Yerba Buena Sept. 17. 1846

Signed - - - - ELIAB GRIMES.
W'm. A. LEIDESDORFF
FRANCISCO GUERRERO.
W'm. H. DAVIS
PETER DAVIDSON.
JOSE DE JESUS NOE.
JOSE JOAQUIN ESTUDILLA.
JOHN C. DAVIS.
NATHAN SPEAR

To WASH'N. A. BARTLETT Esq. Collector &c.

Therefore it is ordered, That —

Any Tallow sent into the market which shall fall short of the standard, shall be forfeited to the use of the District, said tallow to be sold at public auction, and after defraying the expenses of transportation, the ballance of the proceeds to be deposited in the public treasury. Any tallow so sold shall not be exported without a re-inspection.

Any bags which upon inspection shall be found to contain substance introduced in order to defraud in the weight, shall be forfeited and the owner subjected to a fine.—

For the first offence $25.00
2d do 50,00
3d do 100,00

and imprisonment at the direction of the court, not to exceed six months.

Every farmer in putting up tallow for sale shall mark each bag distinctly with his brand, in default of which he shall forfeit each and every bag not thus mark d.

Approved by JOHN B. MONTGOMERY Esq., Commanding Northern District of California.

WASH'N. A. BARTLETT.
Collector and Superintendent,
Port San Francisco.

Yerba Buena, Sept. 17th, 1846.

GENERAL ORDER

The owners or agents of Launches or boats belonging to and navigating this bay, are hereby notified, that it is necessary to register them in this office, and take out a patent or license for the bay; said patent to state the name of the owner and master of said launch or boat, and the service in which employed.

WASH'N. A. BARTLETT.
Collector and superintendant
of the Port of San Francisco.

Approved by JOHN B. MONTGOMERY Esq, Comd'g. Northern District of California.

REGLAMENTO

Para la averiguacion y castingo del fraude en el trafico de sebo.—

Oficina del superintendente y colector del Puerto de San Francisco,
Sep'bre. 15 de 1846

Muy Senores mios:—

A consecuencia del fraude e impostura que hasta aqui ha sido tan general en este puerto, en el sebo vendido por de buena calidad, el que siendo exportado, ha perjudicado gravemente a los compradores, y ha desconceptuado mucho al sebo de California en todas partes.

Es necesario ya, reprimir semejantes fraudes. Y para ello, me ha parecido conveniente que se establezca inmediatamente una regla fija, para el resguardo de los comerciantes de este puerto.

Portanto, suplico aVV se sirvan de admitir el nombramiento de una comision de examen de este asunto: y apoyados en su larga esperiencia del comercio y costumbres de este pais, decidan y declaren cual sera la calidad del sebo vendible en esta plaza: poniendo en mi oficina, las muestras correspondientes para el gobierno del comprador, vendedor e inspector.

Soy de VV su Servidor,

WASH'N. A. BARTLETT.
Superintendente y Colector del
Puerto de San Francisco,

A LOS SRES.
ELIAB GRIMES,
WM. A. LEIDESDORFF,
FRANCISCO GUERRERO,
WM. H. DAVIS,
PETER DAVIDSON,
JOSE DE JESUS NOE,
JOSE JOAQUIN ESTUDILLA,
JOHN C. DAVIS,
NATHAN SPEAR.

Resolucion de la Comision.

Puerto de San Francisco,
Setbre 23 de 1846.

Nosotros los abajo suscritos, habiendo sido llamados por Vd para dar nuestro dictamen sobre el establecimiento de una regla fija para el conocimiento del sebo, que en lo futura se venda por bueno, y que sea observada por el vendedor y comprador de este articulo, hemos examinado la muestra que se nos ha presentado, y declaramos que es de la primera calidad, y asi debe ser reputada por el inspector.

Signed - - - - ELIAB GRIMES,
W'M. A. LEIDESDORFF,
FRANCISCO GUERRERO,
W'M. H. DAVIS,
PETER DAVIDSON,
JOSE DE JESUS NOE,
JOSE JOAQUIN ESTUDILLA
JOHN C. DAVIS.
NATHAN SPEAR.

At Sor D. WASH'N. A. BARTLETT,
Superintendante y Colector
del Puerto de S. Francisco.

DECRETO.

Oficina del Superintendente
y Colector del puerto de San
Francisco.
Setbre, de 1846.

Habiendo sido depositadas en esta oficina varias muestras de sebo que en lo futuro debe ser reputado por de buena calidad; he venido en decretar, que en adelante todo sebo vendido sera inspeccionado y lo que no sea igual a estas muestras, sera confiscado y vendido en publica subhasta para el uso del distrito: y despues de pagar los gastos, el sobrante sera depositado en la tesoreria publica.

El sebo asi confiscado, no podra ser exportado sin ser inspeccionado de nuevo.

Cualquiera botana de sebo que al inspeccionarse se le encontrase cualquiera cosa, introducida para defraudar en peso o calidad, sera confiscado y el dueno sufrira una multa.—

Por la primera ofensa 25 pesos
segunda 50, „
tercera 100, „ y prision qui no pasara de 6 meses a la discrecion de las autoridades.

Todo Ranchero estara obligado a poner su marca o fierro en cada una de las botanas de sebo, y en falta de esta marca perdera el dueno el sebo.

Aprobado por el Sr. Don JUAN B. MONTGOMERY Com'dte del Norte de California.

WASH'N. A. BARTLETT
Superintendente y Colector,
De la Aduana.

BANDO.

Los duenos o ajentes de Lanchas o embarcaciones pertenecientes a esta bahia, estan notificados, que es menester registrarlas en esta oficina, y de obtener permiso o patente de navegacion declarando el nombre del piloto o director de dicho embarcacion y el servicio en que estan empleados.

WASH'N A BARTLETT
Administrador de la Aduana,
Distrito de San Francisco,

El 6 de Setbre. de 1846.

Frémont was busy recruiting on the Sacramento. Small boats were sent for him and his party. On arrival, he and about 160 men boarded the chartered merchantman *Sterling* and sailed with the *Congress* and Stockton on October 14. The vessels became separated in a fog. Stockton met the *Barnstable*, which carried a message from Maddox indicating that Monterey, which he commanded, was threatened; so Stockton put in, reinforced Maddox and proceeded south. Frémont spoke the *Vandalia*, learned of the shortage of horses at Santa Barbara, where he had been ordered, and landed at Monterey.

Montgomery was now in a position similar to that of the commander of a zone of the interior, and was responsible for the protection of lines of communication, and the procurement and forwarding of replacements and supplies. His letter book contains many orders in fulfillment of that duty. An intensive search was made for horses and equipment. Charles M. Weber returned from the south, where he had been transported as a prisoner by Castro. Montgomery placed Weber in command at San Jose, ordered him to increase his garrison, then to call in the arms of local Californians. Captain Weber's papers include extensive records of horses and equipment commandeered, together with the names of owners. This dedicated and zealous man knew the country and its people. He used firm and uncompromising methods, and thereby gained the resentment and even the hate of many Californians. His contribution to the American cause has not been overestimated. After the war he moved to the San Joaquin and founded Stockton, which he named for the Commodore.

Montgomery ordered Revere and Kern to push recruiting and to forward the men and available horses to San Jose, which was to become a replacement depot for recruits and remounts. Edwin Bryant and Charles D. Burrass, late emigrants, were sent to the

Sacramento, the former to assist in recruiting, the latter to escort a caballada (a drove of horses) for Frémont. There was hope that Frémont could march south before the rainy season, but he required about 1000 horses. On October 26 Montgomery ordered Lansford W. Hastings to relieve Capt. Weber at San Jose, but not to interfere with him. This was apparently done to facilitate Weber's procurement duties. Arms, percussion caps, lead, powder, and clothing, as well as recruits from Sonoma, were forwarded from Yerba Buena for Frémont.

On November 7 the *Warren,* Capt. Joseph B. Hull, came in and anchored at Sausalito. It was intended that Hull should relieve Montgomery in command of the Northern Department of California, and that the *Warren* should replace the *Portsmouth* as guard ship in the Bay—Montgomery with his ship then to join Stockton. Much remained to be done to effect an orderly transfer. Accounts had to be settled. Both officers were out of funds, so Montgomery borrowed locally at a high rate of interest. Bread was in very short supply; it was ordered from Santa Clara and from Fort Sacramento.

A subordinate should, if practicable, be furnished the means to accomplish his assigned mission. This axiom had been violated by Stockton in the case of Gillespie at Los Angeles. Left there with a force which could expect no prompt reinforcement, Gillespie made a show of firmness, and established regulations obnoxious to the Californians. The attack of September 23 was by a Californian force under Sérbulo Varela, but he was soon joined by José María Flores as Comandante, and the investment was complete. Outnumbered by a force of about 600, Gillespie was allowed to withdraw. He boarded the merchantman *Vandalia* at San Pedro, where he was joined on October 6 by Mervine in the

Savannah. The combined force advanced the next day, but was defeated by the Californians, who had cannon and animals, lacked by the Americans. Mervine then sent some seamen and volunteers in the *Magnolia* to San Diego, there to reinforce Merritt, who had withdrawn to the whaler *Stonington.* Stockton joined at San Pedro October 25 and landed, but on the 30th left with Gillespie in the *Congress* for San Diego and commenced plans for an advance on Los Angeles. Mervine, with the *Savannah,* was sent to Monterey.

The conquest of Southern California was far from complete.

A Father's Sorrow

SOON AFTER THE *Warren* came to San Francisco Bay, her Sailing Master, Passed Midshipman William Henry Montgomery, came on board the *Portsmouth* for a happy reunion with his father and brothers, John and Larry. Doubtless he was pressed for the story of his part in the recent "cutting out" of the prize brig *Malek Adhel* at Mazatlan in September last, and the others told him of the exciting happenings in Alta California.

Since pay to the amount of $846 was due the garrison at Fort Sacramento, it was decided between Montgomery and Hull that the money should be forwarded to Kern in the *Warren's* launch. On November 12, 1846, John Elliott Montgomery, captain's clerk, made his last entry in his father's letter book, a letter to Kern, and prevailed upon his father to allow him to accompany in the launch.

William H. Montgomery was placed in charge; Mdn. Daniel C. Hugunin was pilot; John E. Montgomery was passenger; and the crew, all from the *Warren,* consisted of: Coxswain George Redmond, John Dowd, Gilman Hilton, Milton Ladd, Samuel Lane, Philip L. Lee, Alexander McDonald, Anthony Sylvester, and Samuel Turner.[102] After meridian on November 13, the log of the *Warren* records: "Commences with light breezes and pleasant. Armed the Launch and sent her in charge of the Master to the 'Sacramento.'"

William T. Wheeler, who served on the *Warren* at the time, recalled many years later: "Sam Turner was my chum on the ship—

when he was going over the side into the launch, he gave me his hand, & bid me goodbye which was something unusual. I laughed, & asked him if he was going to run away with some of those squaws up the Sacramento—the reply he made was, 'You'll hear of us.'" Wheeler thought nothing of the answer at the time.[103]

During the next two weeks several boats came down from the Sacramento, but none had seen or heard of the *Warren's* launch. Now thoroughly apprehensive, Hull arranged for an intensive search of the waterways, including the sloughs, inlets, and deceptive false passages. On November 29 the *Warren* "sent 4 men in the Barnstable's boat, provisioned for 10 days to search for the Launch, also a bbl of Pork and a bag of bread for the Launch when found." Other boats joined in the search. Finally, the *Warren's* log for December 21 says: "All the boats that were sent in search of our Launch having returned without having received the least intelligence in regard to her fate; It is, therefore to be conjectured that she is lost. . . ."

Lost indeed—but the circumstances remained for many years a matter for further conjecture, rumors, and investigation. A day or two after the departure, there were violent gales which were believed by some to have foundered the launch, but had it made strait or river, someone should have made shore. Furthermore, no vestige of the launch, its equipment or water cask, were found, unless the following account is to be credited.

Writing June 5, 1848, from San Francisco, to Lieut. Joseph Lanman, commanding the *Warren,* Acting Master Selim E. Woodworth stated as follows:

"A resident of this town, by the name of Stephen Harris, having just returned from the Gold District, has informed me that while on the Spot, that the Mormons have selected (about 35 miles above 'Sutters') at the house of one Daniel Clark, he was informed by this same Clark that the fate of the Crew and Officers of the Warren's Launch was no mystery to him (Clark) and upon further interrogatory, Clark informed him (Harris) that the Officers in charge of the boat were thrown overboard, after having their throats cut, and the Crew then proceeded up the 'Tulerries' [tule swamps] & concealed the boat, after having divided the money and other articles, 5 of the Crew of the Launch returned to the United States last Summer overland, and that three of the remainder of the Crew were at work washing Gold, near at hand.

"Besides many other particulars related by Mr. Harris, we learned from another person who also was at Clark's at the same time, a Mr. [J. D.] Marston (formerly the School Master of this place). He informed me that one morning, while standing on the Bank of the American Fork, he saw a person come up to 'Clark,' and ask for something which Clark said was in the house, & immediately went into the house and brought out a small Mahogany box or case, which from his description, I would suppose was a pistol case, as the man after receiving it from Clark, put it inside his shirt and immediately left the house. 'Marston' then asked Clark, 'Who that man was?' (meaning the man that had taken the case). Clark replied 'Yes I know him well—he is one of the Crew of the Warren's Launch, and there are two more of them about here digging Gold.' Marston then asked 'what case that was he had just given to the Man.' Clark replied, 'It is a case of Instruments that was in the Launch and I have been keeping it for him some time and have just brought it up from below.' His wife, Mrs. Clark, then remarked, 'Yes we have had that box of Nautical Instruments in our house ever since last December, a year, and I always thought there was something wrong about the way in which this man came in possession of it.'

"The above comprise the substance of what I have learned in

the matter, and from my knowledge of the men who have communicated to me these facts, together with the fact of the man, Clark, having been employed on one occasion by Capt. Hull, as Pilot, for this very Launch, leaves but little doubt in my mind of the statements being correct. Clark also observed that he knew all the men, having made their acquaintance during his trip in the Launch as Pilot.

"I am unable to take any steps for the recovery of the Launch, and other property belonging to the 'Warren,' or arresting the three Men, who are undoubtedly at work at the Gold Mine, and could be readily found, if one of the Officers of the Warren were sent up the Sacremento to identify the Men."[104]

As a result of that letter, and in order to identify the mutineers, an officer from the *Warren* was sent to accompany Governor Richard B. Mason on a trip to the gold fields, but nothing further is found regarding that mission. Commodore Thomas ap C. Jones, in his letter of July 27, 1848, to Secretary Mason, stated: "I would most respectfully suggest as a very sure means of apprehending such of the Mutineers as may attempt to reach the sea-board of the Atlantic States overland, that confidential agents be appointed at St. Louis, Independence and New Orleans, to look out for and apprehend *all sailors* making their way from the Pacific Coast, who do not produce certificates or other clear evidence of having been discharged regularly from their engagements on this coast." Mason approved and said, "Measures are taken to apprehend the wretches who were concerned in the horrid crime referred to, if they cross the Continent. If you succeed in apprehending them, be pleased to bring them to trial."[105]

Many years passed. Then came rumors from across the continent. The San Francisco *Evening Bulletin* of June 17, 1869, published a letter to the editor, stating in part:

"Three or four years ago I met an early Californian, who related the circumstance of having met one of the [crew's] number in Broadway, New York, and having known him in California, the conversation that sprung up was of a startling and deeply interesting nature. The sailor said that he himself had no hand in the matter, but related the fact that some of the crew, when the launch had reached the vicinity of Sacramento (I think) seized some instruments, iron bolts, belaying pins, or something of that kind, with which they broke the skulls of the three young men, Montgomerys and Hugennin, cast them overboard, scuttled the launch and with the money $1,500 fled inland and overland."

Those rumors would not be repeated here except for a later confirmation in part. Gen. Theophilus F. Rodenbough, a grandson-in-law of John B. Montgomery, wrote what seems to be the last and definite word on this mystery. Says he: "For some time it was thought that the boat was capsized in a squall, but many years after the grey-haired father was called to the bedside of a dying sailor, who confessed that he had taken part in the murder of the officers, and that the crew, after scuttling the boat, divided their plunder and separated. Although the late admiral would never discuss the subject, yet this theory has been adopted by the other members of his family."[106]

It had been on July 25, 1846, when John Elliott Montgomery, aged sixteen, wrote a postscript to his mother: "If father buys land out here I shall want to stay here it is a lovely climate & country."[107]

Stay he did, with his brother William.

The episode had a legal aftermath. Montgomery sued for the title to a lot, the grant for which John E. Montgomery had petitioned Alcalde Bartlett before leaving on the *Warren's* launch.

The case of John B. Montgomery v. Thomas P. Bevans, *et al,* was heard by the U. S. Ninth Circuit Court. The attorney for the plaintiff offered a certificate of Bartlett that on December 1, 1846, he had granted to John E. Montgomery lot number 113, 50 Spanish varas square, in Yerba Buena. But Bartlett's signature was lined out, and across the record was written, "This title not given out in consequence of the loss of the petitioner before he [Bartlett] could have done so. Feb. 1847. Wash A. Bartlett, Chief Magistrate." Mr. Justice Stephen J. Field opined that the grant was inoperative to pass the title since John E. Montgomery died before the first of December 1846.[108]

In the South

On November 19, 1846, Montgomery had written to Hull a long letter that was a model of briefing by an officer who was about to turn over command. A proper transfer having been effected, *Portsmouth* stood out of the Bay of San Francisco on the afternoon of December 5. The run to San Diego was without incident. At 3 P.M. on the 9th, the ship entered the harbor and found the *Congress* present. *Portsmouth* was at once practically stripped of its complement. A detail of 152 officers and men was sent on shore by order of the Commodore.[109] The reason for this emergency action follows.

Brig. Gen. Stephen W. Kearny, with Companies C and K, First U. S. Dragoons, had come overland to California from Santa Fe. Enduring great hardship, the command reached Warner's Ranch on December 2. Thence Kearny sent a letter telling of his arrival and requesting that Stockton open communication and furnish information of the situation. In response, Stockton detailed Gillespie, who left San Diego on the evening of December 3 with 26 volunteers, a small cannon, and several officers, including Lieut. Edward F. Beale, of the *Congress*. Gillespie met Kearny on December 5, and the combined command halted at the Santa Maria Rancho.

Kearny planned a dawn attack on Californians who were reported in the valley of San Pascual. He sent out a reconnaissance party during the night of December 5-6, but it was detected, and the Californians, numbering about 75 under Andrés Pico, were aroused. The American advanced element made a premature charge. In the swirling melée of that cold dawn it was carbine and saber against lance. The Californians used the latter weapon with deadly effect, and before they left the field about eighteen Americans were killed and an equal number wounded. Among the killed were Captains Benjamin D. Moore and Abraham R. Johnston, and Lieut. Thomas C. Hammond. The wounded included Kearny and Gillespie. The Californian casualties were very few.

The Americans camped in the vicinity and buried their dead. Capt. H. S. Turner, who assumed command after the wounding of Kearny, sent a message to Stockton, telling of the situation and calling for provisions and transport for the wounded. The three messengers included Alexis Godey and Thomas Burgess. On the 7th the Americans moved to Rancho San Bernardo and took position on a low, rocky hill since known as Mule Hill, and located near the present Lake Hodges. Water was lacking, so was food other than mule meat. It was the 8th when it was learned that the Godey party had been captured on its way back from Stockton. Kearny, again in command, dispatched another message to Stockton during the night December 8-9. This time the messengers were Lieut. Beale, Kit Carson, and an Indian, identified as Che-muc-tah by Downey.[110] Suffering much hardship, all of Beale's party reached San Diego; the Indian was first in.

Now thoroughly aroused, Stockton speeded up his preparations to aid Kearny. A relief column of 215 marines and sailors was placed under Lieut. Andrew F. V. Gray of the *Congress*. Lieut. Watson of the *Portsmouth* commanded the marines. Musketeers from the *Congress, Savannah,* and *Portsmouth* were included. The officers from the latter ship were Lieut. Hunter, Purser Watmough, and Boatswain Robert Whittaker. The column departed on the night December 9-10 and reached Kearny early on the morning of December 11. By the 12th all were at San Diego.[111]

There Stockton placed Montgomery in command of the town and proceeded with the organization, training, and supply of a land force of about 600, drawn from his ships, the Dragoons, Gillespie's men, and a few Californians. On December 29 that force, under Stockton as Commander-in-Chief, but with Kearny commanding troops, commenced its march on Los Angeles. Included from the *Portsmouth* were Asst. Surg. Henderson and the musketeers with Lieut. Hunter and Mdn. Edward C. Grafton. A month earlier Frémont had left San Juan Bautista with a reorganized, mounted battalion of about 425, and was now at Santa Barbara, refreshing his men and animals after a passage in bad weather of much difficult terrain.

Stockton entered Los Angeles on January 10, 1847, after fighting and winning two engagements with Flores—the San Gabriel River crossing on the eighth and the Mesa on the ninth. The American casualties were light; the two from the *Portsmouth* were Frederick Strauss, seaman, killed, and Pvt. William Scott, marine, wounded.

By the 11th Frémont reached San Fernando. This pincer action of Frémont and Stockton convinced the Californians that further resistance was useless, and on the 13th the peace commissioners of the Californians and those appointed by Frémont signed articles of capitulation at Cahuenga. Major William H. Russell carried the treaty to Los Angeles, Kearny and Stockton concurred, and the conquest of Alta California was complete. We shall not concern ourselves with the bitter controversy that soon was conducted between Stockton and Frémont, on one side, and Kearny on the other.

At San Diego, hearing of the overland approach of Lieut. Col.

P. St. George Cooke with the Mormon Battalion, Montgomery wrote him on January 14, assuring him of a welcome reception, but warning against sending out small detachments unless well mounted. Montgomery stated that the Californians had been underrated, and that some of their leaders might pass near Cooke on their flight to Sonora.

Soon Montgomery received from Stockton orders to be ready for a cruise on the Mexican coast. His detachments having been returned to him, Montgomery sailed on February 3, and on the 17th ran into the roads at Mazatlan. On the latter date he announced the blockade of Mazatlan and so notified the Governor and Commandant there, the various consular agents, and Capt. John A. Duntze, of the British frigate *Fisgard*.

Immediate complaints came from all quarters, the gist of the protests being that the original blockade of the coast in 1846 was illegal as it had not been enforced by a sufficient force, and that it had been abandoned. Arrayed against Montgomery in this battle of words were not only Duntze but also the resident Minister of Prussia and the Spanish Consul, who represented France as well. To the latter's objection that only a sloop of war was enforcing the blockade, Montgomery replied that he would carry out his assigned mission, and that his superior deemed the force quite sufficient.

The *Fisgard* was relieved by the ship *Constance*, Capt. Sir Baldwin Walker. He continued the British position, and he and Montgomery, orally and in writing, exchanged citations of precedents to support their respective views. The outcome was an agreement that the officers would submit the case to their superiors; that Montgomery would allow the captain or supercargoes of English ships bound for Mazatlan to communicate with their consignees for fresh instructions; and that Walker would avoid interference with Montgomery's duty of examining and warning vessels off from the port of Mazatlan.[112]

Montgomery later reported to the Naval Commander in the Pacific:

"The blockade of Mazatlan was effectually maintained by the Portsmouth for nearly six weeks, although generally opposed and protested against on the ground of illegality, and the service was not relinquished until I had satisfactorily secured the means of communicating Commodore Stockton's orders to Lt Comdr Turner as directed, and the low state of my provisions admonished me of the necessity of immediate attention to duties assigned me on this coast.

"I think it proper, Sir, with the view of averting from others the serious embarrassments through which I deemed it my imperative duty (in obedience to specific orders) to persevere in maintaining the recent blockade of Mazatlan, to apprise you that, unless commencing de novo by proclamation, any attempt to re-establish a blockade of one or more ports, short of all named in Commodore Stockton's proclamation of August last, will be strenuously opposed by the representatives of neutral powers. Nothing but the amicable forebearance and courtesy of Sir Baldwin Walker, of H.B.M. Frigate Constance (such as could only with safety have been exercised by a superior to a very inferior force), prevented a serious difficulty (possibly collision between our ships) growing out of conflicting orders respecting the blockade."[113]

In turn, Montgomery received this citation by the British Government:

"FOREIGN OFFICE
June 30, 1847

"Sir:—Captain Sir Baldwin Walker, commanding Her Majesty's Ship *Constance*, on the west coast of Mexico, has mentioned in his reports in very favorable terms the kind and considerate manner in which Captain Montgomery, of the United States Frigate *Portsmouth,* has conducted himself toward neutral vessels whilst he has been employed in blockading the Port of Mazatlan, and I have to desire that you will take an opportunity of conveying to the United States Secretary of State the acknowledgments of Her Majesty's Government for Captain Montgomery's courteous treatment of British subjects upon this occasion.

I am, etc., etc.,
PALMERSTON"[114]

Before leaving Mazatlan, Montgomery had a windfall which augmented his dwindling supply of provisions. On the 11th of March, Lieut. Revere, stationed with the prize tender *Joven Eliza* off Mazatlan, captured the Mexican schooner *Magdalena,* which carried over 40,000 pounds of flour. Montgomery took on the flour and later turned over the unseaworthy schooner to its former owner. On March 25 Montgomery wrote a farewell letter of appreciation to Walker, and the same day stood out of the Mazatlan roads, to carry out his mission in Lower California.

Arriving at San Jose del Cabo, near the southern tip of Lower California, Montgomery sent Lieut. Missroon on March 29 with a summons for the alcalde to surrender the town. Lieut. Hunter landed with the marines and 100 seamen the following day. No resistance was encountered; the American flag was raised and saluted with twenty-one guns, and a proclamation was issued. A local man was appointed U. S. Collector and Captain of the Port, and arrangements were made for the baking of much-needed bread. The American flag was also raised at near by San Lucas on April 3.[115]

Montgomery found at San Jose the American merchantman *Admittance,* Capt. Peterson. The vessel was from New Orleans, bound for San Blas with a cargo of cotton, although cleared for Honolulu. Montgomery seized the ship, placed Lieut. Revere in command, and later ordered him to take her to Monterey, there to deliver her with cargo and papers to such court as would adjudicate the case.

On April 8 the *Portsmouth* got under way and on the 13th appeared before La Paz, capital of Baja California. Missroon presented to the authorities Montgomery's demand for surrender. Again no resistance was offered, and on the 14th there was the usual landing of seamen and marines, the raising and saluting of the American flag, and the reading of Montgomery's proclamation. Missroon and Henderson represented Montgomery at a meeting, and articles of agreement were signed with a local commission.

The principal articles provided that an inventory of public arms, munitions, and property be delivered up; that local officials continue in office, and that they and their employees pledge neutrality; that authorities at Loretto be notified that they must likewise preserve neutrality; that Mexican military officers give their paroles; that the forces of the United States would respect the property of private individuals and their civil and religious rights; that all citizens of Lower California be assured the same rights and privileges as enjoyed by citizens of the United States; that the articles should "continue in force until the resolution of the commander-in-chief of the naval forces of the United States in the Pacific ocean be known, and, in the meantime, the country will continue to govern itself by its own laws." Certain articles provided for the control of local shipping.

Back in Alta California, Commodore W. Branford Shubrick had arrived at Monterey in the *Independence* January 22, 1847.

He replaced Stockton by reason of seniority, but was in turn outranked by Commodore James Biddle, who arrived from the Orient at Monterey in the *Columbus* on March 21. Biddle revoked Stockton's paper blockade of the entire Mexican coast and declared specific ports blockaded. He placed Shubrick in command of the blockading squadron.

Montgomery was at San Jose, Lower California, when, on April 23, the *Cyane,* Cdr. Samuel F. Dupont, arrived with an order from Biddle for the *Portsmouth* to proceed to Monterey. The *Independence* arrived at San Jose April 26. Montgomery was much disturbed by the situation, and before departing for Monterey on the 27th addressed a letter to Shubrick, stating in part:

"The unexpected withdrawal of the Portsmouth, so immediately after hoisting the flag of the United States at the ports along this coast, appears to have produced in the minds of many of the people here, apprehensions that ill-disposed persons in the interior may take advantage of the absence of all force, and visit them with resentment for their recent quiet submission to the United States authorities; and however strange it may appear that a large community should attach importance to the presence of a handful of armed men, (and those afloat,) it is still true that I am desired by the municipal junta, with whom I had an interview in session this day, to apply to you for a vessel to be placed here, if nothing more than one of the small prize vessels captured by the United States ship Cyane, with ten or twelve men on board, esteeming the very presence of a national authority as sufficient to curb the turbulent spirits among them, and to secure quietude to the community. Should it meet with your approbation, sir, I would respectfully recommend that the request of the Californians be complied with, or otherwise, the occasional visit of one of our vessels in the gulf might prove serviceable to the end desired."

These words proved to be prophetic, but Montgomery's estimate of the force required was totally in error.

The *Portsmouth* reached Monterey May 24, and Montgomery reported to Biddle that the terms of 120 members of his crew would expire by the end of the year. On the 26th the watch officer entered (probably resentfully) in the log that "In taking on 17 bbl of Whiskey 2 men rolled a barrel each off the dock which stove them with a loss of 48 galls." Other necessities were loaded, and on June 11 the ship sailed for the Mexican coast. There, the tour was of nearly constant cruising. The *Portsmouth* was at Monterey again on August 1, and the following day she came to San Francisco Bay.

Yerba Buena had been renamed San Francisco; the town was much enlarged, and the population was mostly American. Two newspapers appeared weekly. Sam Brannan had started the *California Star,* and the *Californian* had moved to the metropolis from Monterey. The return of the crew after nine months' absence was welcomed, for, Downey relates, they paid off to the man their debts to the shop keepers.[116]

On August 18 the ship left San Francisco Bay, on the 21st made Monterey, departed September 3, and on September 19 arrived off San Jose, Lower California. Continued cruising carried the ship as far as San Blas. Montgomery came under the direct command of Capt. E. A. F. Lavallette, who followed to Mexican waters in the *Congress.* The Chilean brig *Argo,* en route from Honolulu to the Mexican coast, was boarded by Montgomery on October 10, but several weeks later the cargo was ransomed by the American owner for $4,000.

The *Congress* and the *Portsmouth* were in the outer harbor of

Guaymas on October 17. Both moved to the inner harbor and soundings were made. By the evening of the 18th the ships had warped to positions within range of the enemy batteries defending the town. Two guns were landed at vantage points during the night; one was a brass seven-pounder commanded by Lieut. Bartlett, who had rejoined the *Portsmouth*. On the 19th Montgomery was sent to Col. Antonio Campuzano, the military commandant, with Lavallette's demand for the delivery of the town, forts, and armament. This was refused. At sunrise the following day a signal gun was fired from the *Congress*, and both ships fired ranging shots. Then followed very effective broadsides. After about three-quarters of an hour a white flag was shown on shore, and the firing ceased.

Portsmouth had fired her first shots in anger.

The military had withdrawn the night before, and the town was practically deserted. Lavallette raised the American flag and issued a proclamation to the inhabitants. Marines from both ships were placed on shore under Lieut. Jacob Zeilin. This shore force made a signal about 7 P.M., because of the reported return of Campuzano. In about a half-hour, a force of five companies organized as infantry, and two of artillery, was landed from the ships and remained on shore over night. No attack occurred. Lavallette departed in the *Congress* on the 23d, leaving Montgomery in command at Guaymas.[117]

On October 29 was captured the brigantine *Carolina*, which sailed under the flag of Ecuador, but was suspected of being of Mexican ownership. Montgomery ordered the transfer from the vessel to the *Portsmouth* of "nine half barrels of liquor now on board the prize—only with a view to the safety of the vessel and the better preservation thereof." Lieut. Bartlett was made prize master of the *Carolina*.

Meanwhile, the situation across the gulf in Lower California was not as stable as the Americans might have wished. Following Montgomery's flag raisings there, many Mexicans at San Jose and La Paz had openly collaborated with him. When the *Portsmouth* then withdrew, all seemed quiet for a while, but the Mexicans in the interior became emboldened and brought pressure on the collaborators, and later in some cases seized their property.

In July, Companies A and B, First New York Volunteers, under Lieut. Col. Henry S. Burton, took station at La Paz. The regiment had arrived at Yerba Buena via Cape Horn in the preceding March. These troops not being mounted, their radius of action was limited. Some supplies and a few Mexican troops came west across the gulf. A force from the *Dale,* Cdr. T. O. Selfridge, had a skirmish at Mulege with Mexicans under Manuel Pineda, who had assumed general command in Lower California.

Commodore Shubrick arrived off San Jose and on November 4, 1847, issued a proclamation to the people of Lower California, designed to allay the fears of those friendly to the American cause. It included this implied promise, which was never fulfilled with respect to Lower California: "The flag of the United States is destined to wave forever over the Californias. No contingency can be forseen in which the United States will ever surrender or relinquish their possession of the Californias."[118] Hostile Mexicans vacated San Jose when Shubrick landed Lieut. Charles Heywood there with four officers and twenty marines on November 8. Shubrick then left for Mazatlan.

On November 19 a Mexican force appeared, and the surrender of Heywood's party was demanded. Upon refusal, the Mexicans deployed and opened a fire which was continued until dark and resumed during the night. There was little action during daylight of the 20th, but that night the Mexican attack recommenced.

On the morning of the 21st, the American whalers *Magnolia,* Capt. B. Simmons, and the *Edwards,* Capt. John S. Barker, hove in sight, and the Mexican force left for La Paz. The Americans had but one man seriously wounded, and none killed, while the Mexican casualties probably totalled at least a score.

On November 9 Montgomery left Guaymas, where he was relieved by Cdr. Selfridge in the *Dale.*[119] Putting in at La Paz November 12, the *Portsmouth* left there the 14th and on the 17th was at Mazatlan. There Montgomery found that on November 11 Shubrick had taken that important port, unopposed, with parties from the *Independence, Congress,* and *Cyane.* When Shubrick received notice of the attack on Heywood at San Jose, he dispatched Montgomery in the *Portsmouth* with instructions to render Heywood all possible aid, then to proceed home to Boston via Valparaiso.

Montgomery left Mazatlan December 2, and the following day was at San Jose. A detachment of fifty, under Revere, was landed to reinforce Heywood in the face of an expected attack which did not materialize. Several weeks were spent in strengthening the American position at San Jose. Montgomery tried to induce some of his own men, scheduled to return to the States, to volunteer to remain with Heywood. In this, he had much success, and on December 29 was able to furnish sixteen volunteers to Heywood. Montgomery called an officers' council at which it was decided that everything practicable had been done to aid Heywood.[120]

New Year's Day found the *Portsmouth* on the first leg of her journey back to the United States.[121]

New Commands and Later Days

Sailing from Valparaiso February 23, 1848, *Portsmouth* reached Boston on May 5, without intermediate stop. A number of administrative details required the attention of Montgomery. He reported his arrival to Secretary Mason, and received approval of his departure from San Jose. He made a report of repairs needed by the *Portsmouth*. He turned over to the Commandant, Boston Navy Yard, four flags; three were the Mexican flags replaced by American flags at Yerba Buena and at San Jose and La Paz, Lower California. The fourth was the original Bear Flag, obtained by John E. Montgomery after the American flag was raised at Sonoma. This flag was later secured from the Navy Department by Senator John B. Weller of California, and was deposited with the Society of California Pioneers. As before related, it became a casualty of the San Francisco fire of 1906. The sum of $15,000 prize money came with the ship, and presumably was soon disbursed. On May 17 Montgomery acknowledged to Mason receipt of orders for a leave of three months.[122]

Montgomery and *Portsmouth* came to a parting of their ways.

His next important assignment was to the Washington Navy Yard as executive officer in April 1849. He was commissioned captain on January 6, 1853, and was placed in command of the new steam-frigate *Roanoke* in April 1857. Sailing from Norfolk to Aspinwall, he returned to New York in August with a reported two hundred and fifty of General Walker's filibusters.

Then came duty on the court of inquiry on retired officers. In

April 1859 he was ordered to the command of the Pacific Squadron, and on May 12, 1859, he reported to the Secretary of the Navy that he had raised his flag on the steam-corvette *Lancaster* off the Philadelphia Navy Yard. Arrival at Norfolk was on June 19. Montgomery named his son, David Edwards, as his official secretary. Arriving at Panama on August 15, Montgomery relieved Flag Officer John C. Long. The *Lancaster* proceeded around the Horn. Other ships which became available to Montgomery were the screw-sloops *Narragansett* and *Wyoming,* the side wheel sloop *Saranac,* and the sailing sloops *St. Mary's* and *Cyane.*[123]

Among the ports visited by Flag Officer Montgomery on this tour were San Francisco and Mazatlan. At each place has was received with unusual respect and honors. When the Civil War broke out, his most important duty became the guarding of the steamer routes from Panama to California.

Rodenbough is responsible for this information of Montgomery's stand: "When the late war opened Captain Montgomery personally assured himself of the status of his officers by assembling them upon the flagship in Panama Bay and causing the prescribed oath of allegiance to be administered with the most impressive solemnity. Only one officer in the entire squadron—then the largest afloat—declined to take it. Many, supposed to be wavering, were confirmed in their fealty, a result largely due to the energy and patriotic action of the flag officer."

Also quoted by Rodenbough was this private letter by Montgomery, which appeared in the correspondence of the New York *Tribune* from Washington:

"I honestly believe, under an all-wise Providence, that great and permanent good to the Union under our present glorious Constitution will result from our present agitation. I glory in the patriotic course pursued by Major Anderson [at Fort Sumter]. For my own part, knowing and having acknowledged no obligation but that which I solemnly swore to the Constitution and Union nearly fifty years ago, it would, indeed be humiliating to be now reduced to the position of being a citizen of a seceding section of our country; and while two stars and stripes of our proud flag shall be found together I shall adhere to it with my whole heart, affection and devotion. I have great hopes in the wisdom, patriotism and strong sense of Mr. Lincoln, who may, by an all-wise Providence, have been reared for the present crisis in our own history. *That the Union shall endure and arise from her present difficulties in greater strength and permanency—I will say, in greater glory than ever—I fully believe.*"[124]

Montgomery was placed on the retired list, by requirement of law, on December 21, 1861. His successor was Flag Officer Charles H. Bell, by whom he was relieved in January 1862. He left the Pacific Squadron with the reported "best wishes of the entire native and foreign population, and of every officer and sailor in the fleet, to all of whom he has endeared himself by his kind and courteous manners, his moderation and good sense."

There was a period of waiting orders, and in May 1862 came assignment to command of the Boston Navy Yard. The rank of commodore came to Montgomery July 16, 1862. At year end, 1863, he assumed command of the Washington Navy Yard.

This last assignment involved some duties which were unexpected and certainly unusual. At the Yard, in April 1865, were the monitors *Saugus* and *Montauk*, wherein were imprisoned most of the conspirators alleged to have been involved in the assassination of President Abraham Lincoln and related plots. Montgomery was required to provide for the placing of bags over the head of each prisoner "with holes for proper breathing and eating but not seeing"; to secure Lewis Paine against his self destruction; and to transport from the *Montauk* to the Arsenal Penitentiary the body of John Wilkes Booth. Montgomery reported the latter duty as having been accomplished at 2:45 P.M., April 27, 1865. On May fourth, half-hour guns sounded from the Yard from noon to sundown, closing with a national salute—all on the occasion of the funeral of the President at Springfield, Illinois.[125]

Commodore Montgomery was relieved as Commandant of the Washington Navy Yard by Commodore William Radford on October 13, 1865, and was then placed on waiting orders. On July 10, 1866, came orders, possibly at his own request, for Montgomery to proceed to Sacket Harbor, his very first station as a midshipman fifty-four years earlier. He was promoted to the rank of Rear Admiral July 25, 1866.

Mrs. Montgomery died January 19, 1869, at a place not stated. The Admiral was relieved from duty at Sacket Harbor on September 1, 1869, and moved to Carlisle, Pennsylvania. There he lived with relatives until his death on March 25, 1873, at the home of his daughter, Julia Maria, who had married David N. Mahon, M.D.

The funeral services were held at the Mahon home. The officiating clergymen were the Reverend Dr. W. C. Leverett, Episcopal Church, and the Reverend Dr. C. P. Wing, of the First Presbyterian Church. Interment was at the family plot in Oak Hill Cemetery in Washington.[126]

The Navy honored Montgomery by naming a destroyer for him. This ship was launched March 23, 1918, at Newport News, Virginia, and was commissioned July 26 of the same year. She was converted to a mine layer and was at Pearl Harbor when the Japanese struck. *Montgomery* received the Navy Unit Commendation for her part in the Palau operation and was awarded four battle stars for participation in operations at Pearl Harbor, Guadalcanal, New Georgia, and Palau Islands. On October 17, 1944, she was severely damaged by an exploding mine, but was repaired and made San Francisco under her own power. The ship was decommissioned April 23, 1945, and sold.[127]

Admiral Montgomery's life was so long devoted to the naval service that it is virtually impossible to separate the man from the officer. He was a fully competent naval officer, who was given important assignments and who performed them well. His loyalty was unquestioned. He evidenced much diplomatic ability. He was a deeply religious man. He gained the respect and often the admiration of those with whom he was associated.

The Ship's Wake

After arrival at Boston May 5, 1848, the *Portsmouth* was repaired at a cost of nearly $28,000.[128] She sailed for the coast of Africa August 29, 1848, under Cdr. William M. Armstrong. On February 1, 1849, Lieut. Cdr. Henry Darcantel relieved Armstrong, who reported at length on the splendid sailing qualities of the *Portsmouth*. In September 1849 she returned to New York, was repaired, and sailed again for the Africa station under Cdr. Elisha Peck. She returned to the States in June 1851, and was repaired for about $35,000. During these tours of African service, *Portsmouth* was the flagship of Commodores Benjamin Cooper and Francis H. Gregory, whose ships cooperated with the British for the suppression of the slave trade.

On December 16, 1851, *Portsmouth* left Boston under Cdr. Thomas A. Dornin, to join the Pacific Squadron of Commodore Charles S. McCauley. Of the dozens of ports of call during this long service under Dornin, but a few shall be mentioned here. Lancey tells of two incidents which caused excitement on the ship.[129] Of the first he relates: "[The *Portsmouth*] arrived at San Francisco August 12, 1853, 22 days from Honolulu and sailed again September 15, 1853, at 1½ P.M. in a race with the Clipper Ship 'Harriett Hoxie,' the Hoxie having 2 hours start and nearly hull down ahead. At sunset the 'Portsmouth' had come up with her & both ships made all sail possible. For three hours the contest was quite exciting; but at midnight the Hoxie began to drift astern showing signs of fatigue and at daylight next morning she was nearly out of sight and by sunrise was not visible."

The second incident was a tragedy which occurred after the arrival of the ship at Honolulu. On October 26, 1853, at a drinking bout at a house called "The National," Quartermaster Addison Soames killed John Stinchfield, who had served long as the *Portsmouth's* captain of the hold. Stinchfield's funeral was held at the Seaman's Chapel and was largely attended. Later, on recommendation of the King's officers and of Cdr. Dornin, a charge of manslaughter against Soames was withdrawn.

About this time the filibustering operations of William Walker became a cause for the concern of the military and naval authorities on the Pacific Coast. In mid-October 1853 Walker sailed from California with a small band in the *Caroline*. He easily took La Paz, on the east coast of Lower California. Later meeting resistance, he determined to increase his force and moved to the Bay of Todas Santos, also called Ensenada, some sixty miles southeast of San Diego.

In 1854 orders for the suppression of filibustering came from the Navy Department, and Dornin was assigned such a mission by Commodore Bladen Dulany. The Pacific Mail Steamship Company's *Columbus* was chartered and, with *Portsmouth* in tow, passed through the Golden Gate for Baja California on February third. Although towing was arranged to expedite the movement, we can almost hear the curses of the old timers when the *Portsmouth* submitted to such an indignity. Adverse, though light winds were encountered, and the vessels arrived at the Ensenada February 10. Walker, already considerably reinforced, soon left to continue his abortive effort. His wounded, about nine in number, were sent by Dornin to San Diego in the *Columbus*. The San Francisco *Alta California* commented: "If the filibusters have left their camp there, one or both vessels will enter the Gulf to watch the proceedings of the latter day Quixottes." Early in

March Dornin sailed to San Diego for supplies, thence to Mazatlan where he obtained the release of some twenty American prisoners, whom he sent to San Francisco on a revenue cutter.

After service at Acapulco in protection of American shipping interests, *Portsmouth* sailed for Callao, thence to Honolulu where Dornin and officers of his ship and those of the *St. Mary's* were given an audience by the King. A continuous salute of twenty-one guns was fired by each of the American, British, and French men-of-war when the King paid them return visits. *Portsmouth* arrived at Tahiti December 23, 1854, and within a few days sailed for home.

Arriving at Norfolk April 5, 1855, after one of the longest of her cruises under a single captain, she was placed in ordinary (out of commission) during extensive repairs. There she "was fitted with a new and most powerful battery of 16 8-inch shell guns each of 63 cwt. . . . and the day she was ready for sea there was not in any Navy in the World a finer looking, more compact, or powerful ship, of her rate and tonnage."[130] On April 22, 1856, her command was assumed by Cdr. Andrew H. Foote, who later would gain great fame as Flag Officer in command of the operations of his gunboats on the Mississippi and tributaries during the Civil War.

Ordered to join the East Indian Squadron of Commodore James Armstrong, Foote sailed from Norfolk May 4, 1856, and reached Batavia in ninety-five days, encountering heavy gales en route. Thence *Portsmouth* went to Hongkong and in October was with the *Levant* at the Whampoa anchorage below Canton.

Because of hostilities between the English and the Chinese, and upon request of the American Consul for a force to protect American interests, Foote sent a strong party to Canton from his ship and the *Levant*. Commodore Armstrong joined from

Shanghai in the steam frigate *San Jacinto*. It was decided to withdraw the American force at Canton. On November 15, while completing arrangements for the withdrawal, Foote was fired upon from the Chinese "barrier forts," located about midway between Whampoa and Canton. Foote's small boat was struck, but the party returned uninjured.[131]

Armstrong sent for the American steamers *Kum Fa* and *Willamette* to tow the *Portsmouth* and the *Levant* off the forts, with his orders "to redress this outrage upon our flag."[132] The next morning *Kum Fa* was first sent to Canton, from which she evacuated most of the American force. Meanwhile Lieut. James G. Williamson was sent in a cutter to sound the channel to the forts. He returned, having sounded within about a half-mile of the forts, and having been fired upon with the loss of one man. The channel was too shallow for the *San Jacinto,* so part of her crew was sent to the *Portsmouth* and part to the *Levant*.

Armstrong hoisted his pennant on the *Portsmouth,* which started up the river in tow of the *Willamette*. The *Levant,* towed by the *Kum Fa,* grounded about a mile below the forts and took no part in the ensuing action. Before the *Portsmouth* could anchor near the forts she was fired upon, returned the fire, and anchored about 500 yards from the nearest fort. In position about 4:20 P.M., she continued to fire for about three hours. Says Armstrong:

"Never before had I seen such precision of firing or more steadiness in battle. . . . The Chinese fired exceedingly well and hulled the *Portsmouth* six times, but doing no material injury to her. . . . The largest of the forts, and the one nearest us, was silenced early in the evening; and the fire of the others became very languid at the close of the action."

On the 17th there was no action; the forts did not fire. *Ports-*

Battering Down the Canton Barrier Forts in 1856

mouth, which became grounded, and the *Levant,* already grounded, got out kedge anchors to free themselves. Armstrong became ill and retired to the *San Jacinto,* leaving Foote in command, "with orders to keep in position on the forts, but not to fire unless assailed by them." The orders were changed on the 19th, for the Chinese were detected improving their defenses. Foote was ordered "to take such measures as his judgment would dictate, if it were even the capture of the forts."

Such latitude was much to the liking of Foote, for at 6:30 A.M. on the 20th *Portsmouth* and *Levant* were firing on the two nearest forts. After an hour of engagement the enemy fire slackened. Foote personally led a storming party of 287 in three columns of small boats. After landing and forming up, the party moved through rice fields, a creek, and a village, pulling along three howitzers. A fort was taken by an attack in its rear, and the American flag was raised on it by a lieutenant from the *Portsmouth.* Fifty-three guns were captured, some of which were turned on another fort, resulting in its silencing. Thousands of Chinese counterattacked twice, but were repulsed.

By 4 A.M. the next day, the last of the landing party had reembarked, and at six both ships engaged the three remaining forts. One was silenced, and the *Kum Fa* towed ashore a party in boats, again commanded by Foote. The fort with 41 guns was taken, and the standard bearer of the Marine company raised his flag on the wall. The boats had been brought up, and were used for a crossing to an island fort. The howitzers and captured enemy guns were used to cover this movement, which was successful. Among the 38 guns captured here was an enormous brass cannon of twenty-two feet five inches in length and eight and one-half inches bore. Again the flag of the Marine company was raised. The one remaining fort was silenced, and the next morning it was captured. This time, says Lancey, a boatswain's mate of the *Portsmouth* planted the American flag on the ramparts. About ten working days were spent in the further demolition of the forts.

During the actions against the barrier forts, Foote's casualties were about thirty; the killed and wounded of the Chinese were about two hundred and fifty. *Portsmouth's* new Dahlgren guns proved their worth against the massive stone walls of the Chinese forts. The ship received some eighteen shots in hull and rigging. Capt. William Curry of the *Willamette* came in for a well-deserved share of Foote's commendation. One result of the capture of the forts was a treaty of amity and commerce with the Chinese.

Foote says: "As the gallant Portsmouth dropped down the river, the ship of the British admiral, Sir Michael Seymour, as well as his commodore's vessel, manned the rigging and gave three rousing cheers for the Portsmouth, while the bands struck up 'Hail Columbia' and 'Yankee Doodle'—a compliment rarely paid to our ships by rival nations."[133] Of course, that compliment was likewise intended as a tribute to the leadership, resourcefulness, and bravery of Foote himself.

Just inside the Sands Street gate at the New York Naval Shipyard stands a marble monument which was erected in 1857 to honor those who took part in the Barrier Forts action. Inscribed on the sides of the monument are the names of the twelve men killed during the engagement.[134]

The remainder of *Portsmouth's* tour in the Orient was rather routine, but many interesting ports were seen. In April of 1857 there was a visit to Singapore to investigate the case of the Dutch bark, *Henrietta Maria,* claimed to have been salvaged by the American ship *Coeur de Lion.* In May 1857, Dr. Bradley, carrying a treaty, was taken to Siam. The *Portsmouth's* officers were presented to both kings, one of whom visited the ship with a retinue of forty. There was drydocking at Shanghai and a trip to Japan. On nearing Shimoda, uncharted breakers were discovered and named "Portsmouth Breakers." In March 1858, orders for home having been received, the ship sailed from Manila by way of Java and St. Helena, and arrived at Portsmouth, N. H., June 13, 1858, having cruised over 49,000 miles since leaving the United States.

After repairs the ship sailed for the African Station, under Cdr. John Colhoun, in May 1859. After the outbreak of the Civil War, she returned home in September 1861, was repaired at Kittery and, under command of Cdr. Samuel Swartwout, took over blockading duties off the Texas coast. Captures made were the *Wave,* the *Pioneer,* and the *Labuan.* In April she joined Flag Officer Farragut's squadron, and took part in the action of April 24 when Farragut effected a passage of Forts Jackson and St. Philip, below New Orleans. The *Portsmouth* brought up the rear of the third division and was towed into position to enfilade Fort Jackson. No sooner was she in position and firing, than she was taken under heavy fire by a well-masked water battery. Her spring (hawser to hold her in firing position) was shot away, and she swung around so that her guns could not bear on fort or battery. By the time the squadron had passed the forts, the *Portsmouth* had accomplished a slight diversionary effect, but she was now helpless and ineffective. So Swartwout reluctantly ordered that her cable be slipped, and she drifted downstream. After the surrender of New Orleans, and during the remainder of the war, she was stationed at that city, for the protection of the Federal garrison.[135]

In 1866 *Portsmouth* was on quarantine duty and had an ordnance assignment; she was on special service under Cdr. Joseph S. Skerrett in 1867-1868; during 1869 to 1871 her duty was largely in the South Atlantic Squadron. In 1872 she was fitted for surveying duty in the Pacific. Her armament was reduced to 14 guns; she was provided with two steam launches and with a steam windlass for deep sea sounding. In this assignment she was again under Cdr. Skerrett. She sailed from New York in September 1872, and corrected many charts of many islands in the Pacific. Then came drydocking at Mare Island, California, in April 1874.

On September 15, 1874, still under Skerrett, *Portsmouth* sailed from San Francisco for Alaska, with a committee of Icelanders who investigated the practicability of the territory for colonization by their countrymen. Returning to San Francisco in November, the ship then cruised to Honolulu and the Mexican coast. In September 1875 she became a school ship under Cdr. Silas Casey, Jr., and was stationed at the foot of 3d Street, San Francisco. She went out of commission in August 1876, but a year later was prepared for a trip around the Horn. Captained by Cdr. Norman H. Farquhar, she left San Francisco and arrived at Chesapeake Bay in February 1878, after a voyage of 15,270 miles without anchoring in 112 days—something of a feat. In March she sailed from New York for Havre, France, with exhibits for the Paris Exposition, and returned to New York in December. In 1879 she became a training ship for naval apprentices, and so served to include 1894.

One of the apprentice trainees was the late Fred J. Buenzle, whose *Blue Jacket* is a fine story of his experiences in the old Navy.[136] He devotes many pages to his service on the *Portsmouth,* which he joined in 1889. His interest in things naval continued after his retirement, and he made the extremely fine, large model of the *Portsmouth,* now on loan to the Maritime Museum of San Francisco. The model is uncommonly detailed; included are many small figures representing members of the crew at their various tasks on deck and aloft. Of course Buenzle depicted the ship as he knew it, when it had a complete spar deck and double topsails. The latter were added to facilitate the handling of canvas by the apprentices, but incidentally brought greater beauty to one of the very finest ships of our sailing Navy. It is to Downey and to Buenzle that one must turn for those intimate details of daily sailor life on the *Portsmouth,* beyond the scope of the present work.

In 1895 *Portsmouth* was transferred to the Naval Militia, State of New Jersey, from which assignment she was returned to the Navy Department on March 4, 1911, and was then loaned to the Marine Hospital Service.

Already, several efforts were under way to bring the *Portsmouth* to the Pacific Coast. A group of Washington men, who had served on her, wanted her for Seattle. California interest intervened. The *San Francisco Chronicle* reported on October 16, 1910, that some months before, the Navy Department had given the *Portsmouth* to San Francisco. The article continued: "Congressman Julius Kahn and other influential citizens eagerly accepted the vessel with a view to establishing her as a floating museum in San Francisco Bay, as a reminder of the romantic beginnings of that great city and greater State. But the Portsmouth still lies on the New Jersey shore."

Zoeth S. Eldredge, the California historian, was a champion of the cause. He wrote to the California Governor that a board of examiners had said that it would cost $25,000 to place the vessel in condition to make the voyage, and only $1,120 to fit her for quarantine duty, so she had been ordered to Norfolk for the latter service. Eldredge called it an indignity to which the gallant ship should not be subjected, and added: "The 'New York Sun' in an editorial yesterday, said that the ship should be fitted out and sent around the Horn to San Francisco . . . and should surely be on hand in San Francisco Bay when the Panama Canal is opened." Many other letters were written by Eldredge to persons and agencies within and without California.[137]

The act of March 4, 1913, making appropriations for the naval service, contained a provision that the *Portsmouth* should be turned over to the State of California under certain conditions. Senator Shanahan's bill (Senate 383), "Providing for the Acceptance of the U. S. Ship Portsmouth . . ." was passed by the California Legislature and on March 22, 1913, sent to the Governor. He vetoed the bill, reciting that the ship repairs would run to something over $25,000, and that the necessary appropriation did not accompany the bill. The Senate postponed consideration of the objections of the Governor, and the matter died in file on May 12, 1913.

So California lost the *Portsmouth*. She had been returned to the Navy by the Marine Hospital Service, and on April 17, 1915, she was stricken from the Navy List. On July 22, 1915, she was sold to John F. Burke, of Brighton, Massachusetts, for $4,689.

On July 27 *Portsmouth* left Norfolk under tow, equipped with steam pumps, and by August 2 was at Constitution Wharf, Boston, ready for stripping by her latest purchaser, the Thomas Butler Company.

It would be a pleasure to learn of the locations of all relics salvaged from the *Portsmouth*. Undoubtedly the finest example is a helm, supposed to be hers, which is now at the San Francisco headquarters of the Bank of America. It was obtained from the Portsmouth (New Hampshire) Yacht Club, and is a handsome, double wheel of mahogany. Staff members of the Bank of America raised a fund for the purchase of the helm and in 1941 presented it to the Bank's founder, A. P. Giannini.

The ship was taken to Governors Island, Boston Harbor, and burned there on the night of September 6-7, 1915. The spectacle was the culmination of a South Boston carnival, and was well attended by politicians and others. The torch was applied, and "as the flames shot out from the empty gun ports, the siren of the fireboat mournfully shrieked a salute."[138]

The ashes of the *Portsmouth* joined the sea.[139]

Appendix A

COMMANDING OFFICERS OF THE *PORTSMOUTH*

Name	*Assumed command*	*Detached*
Montgomery, Cdr. John B.	Nov. 10, 1844	May 6, 1848
Armstrong, Cdr. William M.	Aug. 7, 1848	Jan. 30, 1849
Darcantel, Lt. Cdr. Henry	Feb. 1, 1849	Sept. 5, 1849
Peck, Cdr. Elisha	Sept. 6, 1849	July 3, 1851
Dornin, Cdr. Thomas A.	Nov. 27, 1851	Apr. 9, 1855
Foote, Cdr. Andrew H.	Apr. 22, 1856	June 21, 1858
Colhoun, Cdr. John	May 4, 1859	Oct. 1, 1861
Swartwout, Cdr. Samuel	Dec. 2, 1861	Apr. 13, 1863
Sartori, Capt. Louis C.	Apr. 13, 1863	Aug. 3, 1863
Richmond, Acting Master Gilbert	Aug. 3, 1863	Oct. 2, 1863
Sartori, Capt. Louis C.	Oct. 2, 1863	Apr. 22, 1865
Franklin, Lt. Cdr. Samuel R.	Apr. 22, 1865	July 10, 1865
Gover, Act. Vol. Lt. F. J.	July 10, 1865	July 26, 1865
Smith, Lt. Cdr. Robert B.	July 26, 1865	Sept. 11, 1865
Skerrett, Cdr. Joseph S.	June 3, 1867	Oct. 15, 1868
Semmes, Cdr. Alexander A.	Jan. 1, 1869	Nov. 2, 1871
Robertson, Lt. Cdr. James P.	Nov. 3, 1871	Nov. 21, 1871
Caldwell, Capt. C. H. B.	Apr. 8, 1872	June 27, 1872
Nicholson, Capt. James W. A.	June 27, 1872	Aug. 23, 1872
Skerrett, Cdr. Joseph S.	Nov. 4, 1872	Dec. 22, 1875
Casey, Cdr. Silas, Jr.	Dec. 29, 1875	Aug. 9, 1876
Farquhar, Cdr. Norman H.	Oct. 8, 1877	Mar. 7, 1878
McNair, Cdr. Frederick V.	Mar. 7, 1878	Aug. 21, 1878
Crowinshield, Lt. Cdr. A. S.	Aug. 21, 1878	July 9, 1881
Hoff, Cdr. A. B.	July 9, 1881	Dec. 8, 1882
Wise, Cdr. William C.	Dec. 8, 1882	Oct. 11, 1884
Terry, Cdr. Silas	Oct. 11, 1884	May 12, 1886
Gridley, Cdr. Charles V.	May 12, 1886	Dec. 10, 1886
White, Cdr. Edwin	Dec. 10, 1886	Oct. 8, 1888
Schouler, Cdr. John	July 10, 1889	June 25, 1891
Sigsbee, Cdr. Charles D.	June 25, 1891	May 3, 1893
Barclay, Cdr. Charles J.	May 3, 1893	May 23, 1894
McGowan, Cdr. John	May 23, 1894	Jan. 17, 1895

Appendix B

ASSIGNMENTS OF THE *PORTSMOUTH*

Pacific Squadron	1844–1848
African Squadron	1849–1851
Pacific Squadron	1851–1854
East India Squadron	1856–1858
African Squadron	1859–1861
West Gulf Squadron	1861–1865
Quarantine Ship, New York Harbor	1866
Fitting as a training ship and on special duty	1867–1868
South Atlantic Squadron	1869–1871
Special service to Brazil and Pacific Squadron	1872–1877
Training ship for boys, San Francisco	1877
Special service in connection with Paris Exposition	1878
Training ship for apprentices, Atlantic Coast	1879–1894
Transferred to the Naval Militia, State of New Jersey	1895
Returned to Navy by Naval Militia, New Jersey	1911
Loaned to Marine Hospital Service	1911
Returned to Navy by Naval Militia, New Jersey	1911
Loaned to Marine Hospital Service	1911
Returned to Navy	1912
Stricken from Navy List	1915

NOTES

The oil portrait of Montgomery, reproduced here as the frontispiece, is in possession of his great-grandson, John Montgomery Mahon, and is attributed to Jacob Eicholtz. Mrs. James H. Beal informs me that Eicholtz was born at Lancaster, Pa., Nov. 11, 1776, and died there May 11, 1842; also that he painted in Pennsylvania, in Maryland, and elsewhere in the East. This portrait is presumed to have been done about 1841.

The headpiece of the title page is drawn by Walter Loos from a National Archives photograph of the *Portsmouth,* in her later days. This stern view is symbolic, for here we follow the wake of the ship during her long life.

The Skerrett depiction of the *Portsmouth* in action is a wash drawing heightened with Chinese white, and is in possession of the writer. Other illustrations are mentioned in the main text.

These notes are selective rather than all-inclusive. The general plan is to present many lesser-known authorities. These are sufficiently identified, so a separate bibliography is not essential. Letters from Montgomery for the period 1844-1848 may be assumed to appear in his *Letter Book* for that period unless otherwise indicated.

In using dates recorded in ships' logs, necessary conversion has been made from "sea time" to the time used on land.

1. The principal biographical and genealogical references used in this chapter are: Theodore F. Rodenbough, *Autumn Leaves from Family Trees* (New York, 1892); Thomas H. Montgomery, *A Genealogical History of the Family of Montgomery* (Philadelphia, 1863); and Lewis R. Hamersly, *Records of the Living Officers of the U. S. Navy . . .* (Revised ed., Philadelphia: Lippincott, 1870).

2. Letter, Mr. Mahon to F. B. Rogers, Feb. 25, 1957.

3. Howard I. Chapelle, *History of the American Sailing Navy* (New York: W. W. Norton & Co., 1949), pp. 269-272.

4. U. S. *Statutes at Large,* III, 141.

5. Montgomery to Francis A. Thornton, Nov. 16, 1821 (MS at Yale Library).

6. Rear Adm. George H. Preble traces beginnings on the waters of the Piscataqua from 1603 when Martin Pring, first European visitor, arrived with the small vessels, *Speedwell* and *Discoverer*. *History of the U. S. Navy-Yard, Portsmouth, N. H.* (Wash.: Bur. Yards & Docks, 1892), p. 3. This rare work is the best on its subject for its era.

7. See Chapelle, *op. cit.*, as indexed, for details on most of the ships named in this volume.

8. John B. Montgomery, *Letter Book*, entry Nov. 21, 1844 (MS volumes at National Archives).

9. Letter, John E. Montgomery to his mother, July 25, 1846 (MS at Yale Library).

10. The cat-o'-nine-tails was a whip with nine lashes, and the colt was a knotted rope.

11. In this chapter, and many others following, data from the *Portsmouth's Log*, 1844-1847, at National Archives, will be used in the main text without continual identification by date in these notes.

12. Montgomery, *Letter Book*, Dec. 16, 23, 1844.

13. *Odds and Ends*, I, 102-107. This is a two-volume MS in the Western Americana Collection, Yale Library. Its publication, perhaps under another title, is expected soon.

14. *Ibid.*, I, 113.

15. Extracts from the journal, herein cited as *Montgomery Journal*, were edited by Theophilus F. Rodenbough and appeared in "The Navy on the Pacific Coast, 1845-47," in *Journal of Mil. Serv. Inst. of the U. S.*, XXXI (1902), 709-720, and XXXII (1903), 247-253.

16. Honolulu *Polynesian*, Mar. 14, 1846.

17. Muster rolls and log of *Portsmouth*.

18. Camilla L. Kenyon, "In Mazatlan in the Forties," *Soc. of Calif. Pioneers Quarterly* (May 1957), p. 9.

19. Area 9 file, U. S. Navy (at National Archives).

20. *Montgomery Journal*, April 23, 1846.

21. *Ibid.*, April 28, May 4, 1846.

22. *Ibid.*, May 9, 1846.

23. Joseph T. Downey, *Filings from an Old Saw* (San Francisco: John Howell, 1956), p. 25.

24. Marius Duvall, *A Navy Surgeon in California, 1846-1847* (San Francisco: John Howell, 1957), p. 12. Downey, *Filings*, p. 26.

25. See Boyd F. Huff, *El Puerto de los Balleneros* (Los Angeles: Dawson, 1957), for "Annals of the Sausalito Whaling Anchorage."

26. Duvall, *op. cit.*, p. 12.

27. Montgomery, *Letter Book,* June 3, 1846.

28. Duvall, *op. cit.*, p. 13.

29. *Portsmouth Log,* June 11, 1846.

30. Chapelle, *op. cit.*, p. 508.

31. Duvall, *op. cit.*, pp. 13-14.

32. John C. Frémont, *Memoirs of my Life* (New York, 1887), p. 519.

33. Charles S. Sawyer, *Documents,* pp. 36-37 (MS at Bancroft Library).

34. The best account of the Bear Flag Revolt, by a participant, is that of Ide in *A Biographical Sketch of the Life of William B. Ide* (Claremont, N. H., 1880), written mostly by Ide and here cited as *Ide Biography*. Ide's role as a delegate at the Mormon political convention appears in the *Nauvoo* (Ill.) *Neighbor,* May 22, 1844. Information, courtesy of Dale L. Morgan.

35. Ford's MS, *The Bear Flag Revolt* (at the Bancroft Library) ranks next to the Ide item. See Fred B. Rogers, *Bear Flag Lieutenant* (San Francisco: Calif. Hist. Soc., 1951), for the life of Ford and scores of references on the revolt, too numerous to be repeated here.

36. Duvall, *op. cit.*, p. 22.

37. Todd wrote a short biography for the scrap book of the Territorial Pioneers of California (MS now at Calif. Hist. Soc.). After service in the south with Gillespie, who listed him as a good man, Todd was discharged March 6, 1847, and returned north. He was at Sutter's Fort in 1849, and also lived in Yolo County and various places north and south. He seems to have disappeared from the California scene sometime after his listing in the Eldorado County *Great Register* for

1879. His wife, Mary, writing from Lodi, California, to the Society of California Pioneers, states that he died suddenly in Italy, date not disclosed.

38. Ford, *op. cit.*, pp. 2-3.

39. *Ide Biography*, pp. 124-25.

40. Duvall, *op. cit.*, p. 15; *Montgomery Journal*, June 13-17, 1846.

41. Downey, *Filings*, p. 33; see also Duvall, *op. cit.*, pp. 19-20.

42. *Ibid.*, pp. 21-24.

43. Area 9 file, which also contains a letter, Gillespie to Montgomery, June 16, 1846, briefing the latter on the latest events at the Sacramento.

44. MS at Yale Library.

45. See Rogers, *op. cit.*, pp. 15-17, for details of the Olompali affair.

46. Area 9 file.

47. *Ibid.*

48. Montgomery, *Letter Book*.

49. Area 9 file.

50. Montgomery, *Letter Book*.

51. Both Larkin letters in Area 9 file.

52. *Ide Biography*, p. 181.

53. San Jose (Calif.) *Pioneer*, June 7, 1879.

54. Duvall, *op. cit.*, pp. 53-54.

55. *Ide Biography*, pp. 187-90.

56. Duvall, *op. cit.*, p. 26.

57. Area 9 file.

58. *Ibid.*

59. Ruiz was released July 31. *Portsmouth Log*, July 8 and 31, 1846.

60. John H. Brown, *Reminiscences* ... (San Francisco, 1886); Downey, *Filings*.

61. Testimony of William A. Richardson in land case 421, U. S. Court Northern District, California; William S. Clark, quoted by Ann Clark Hart, *Lone Mountain* (San Francisco, 1937), p. 14; Soulé, *et al*, *Annals of San Francisco* (San Francisco, 1855), p. 158; Edward C.

Kemble, *Yerba Buena—1846* (San Francisco, 1935), p. 13. All these concur on the boat landing situation at the Montgomery Street beach and at Clark's Point. Clark says that Montgomery "brought his instruments ashore and ran the line of Montgomery Street."

62. Ho. Rep. 30th Cong. 2d Sess., *Ex. Doc. 1* (later cited as *Ex. Doc. 1*), p. 1014.

63. *Ibid.*, p. 1015.

64. Wm. Heath Davis, *Seventy-five Years in California* (San Francisco: John Howell, 1929), facsimile opp. p. 298.

65. Downey, *Filings*, pp. 35-36.

66. I am informed by the U. S. Naval Observatory that the moon was on meridian at Yerba Buena at 0:25 A.M., July 9, 1846. The U. S. Coast and Geodetic Survey reports that the times of the tide in the vicinity and near the time of landing were: "low water 6:04 A.M., high water, 1:17 P.M. Local mean time for the meridian of San Francisco is used. The time on ship board was also probably local mean." See also the evidence cited in note 61 above.

67. Downey, *Filings*, pp. 36-37.

68. *Ex. Doc. 1*, pp. 1016-17.

69. *Ibid.*, p. 1015.

70. *Ibid.*, p. 1017.

71. *Ibid.*, p. 1021.

72. *Ibid.*, pp. 1018-19.

73. *Ibid.*, pp. 1017-18.

74. Brown, *op. cit.*, p. 32.

75. *Ex. Doc. 1*, pp. 1022-23.

76. *Ibid.*, pp. 1021-22.

77. Duvall, *op. cit.*, pp. 34-35.

78. *Ex. Doc. 1*, pp. 1026-27.

79. Area 9 file.

80. In *Calif. Hist. Soc. Quarterly*, XV, No. 1 (March 1936), pp. 58-69.

81. Stockton to Montgomery, July 27, 29, 1846, Area 9 file.

82. Montgomery to Watson, July 21, 1846; Duvall, *op. cit.*, p. 36.

83. Montgomery to Mervine, Aug. 3, 1846.

84. *Filings,* pp. 45-46.

85. Montgomery to Revere, Sept. 7, 1846.

86. Montgomery to Kern, July 29, 1846.

87. H. H. Bancroft, *Hist. of Calif.* (San Francisco, 1886), V, 295, states that Bartlett's appointment as alcalde was on August 26, but I prefer to accept the date of August 12, as shown in Montgomery's *Letter Book.*

88. Montgomery to Kern, Aug. 18, 1846.

89. *Filings,* pp. 70-73; Duvall, *op. cit.,* p. 49; Brown, *op. cit.,* pp. 29-30; *Portsmouth Log,* Aug. 14, 1846.

90. Montgomery to Watmough, Sept. 7, 1846. A reproduction of the extra is in Duvall, *op. cit.,* opposite p. 54.

91. Montgomery to Revere, Sept. 14, 1846.

92. See John A. Hussey and George W. Ames, Jr., "California Preparations to meet the Walla Walla Invasion, 1846," *Calif. Hist. Soc. Quarterly,* XXI, No. 1 (March, 1942), pp. 9-21.

93. Montgomery to George Hyde, Sept. 15, 1846.

94. William F. Swasey, *Early Days and Men of California* (Oakland, 1891), p. 182.

95. Edwin Bryant, *What I saw in California* (5th ed.; New York, 1849), pp. 323, 326.

96. Davis, *op. cit.,* pp. 272-73.

97. Brown, *op. cit.,* p. 26.

98. *Californian,* Sept. 26, 1846.

99. Brown, *op. cit.,* pp. 24-25.

100. Duvall, *op. cit.,* p. 58.

101. Principal references in addition to the program are: Duvall, *op. cit.,* p. 60; *Filings,* pp. 61-64; *Californian,* Oct. 24, 1846; Montgomery to Watmough, Oct. 8, 1846.

102. J. B. Hull to W. B. Shubrick, Sept. 30, 1847. Area 9 file.

103. William T. Wheeler, *Loss of Men & Launch of U. S. Ship "Warren" in 1846* (MS at Bancroft Library).

104. Copy in Letters Pacific Squadron, at National Archives.

105. Cover letter by Jones, and Mason's indorsement in *ibid.*

106. Rodenbough, "John Berrien Montgomery," *Magazine of Am. Hist.* (July, 1878), pp. 422-23.

107. MS at Yale Library.

108. L. S. B. Sawyer, *Reports* . . . (San Francisco: Bancroft, 1873), pp. 653-70.

109. *Portsmouth Log,* Dec. 10, 1846.

110. Downey's account of the battle is in *Filings,* pp. 84-90.

111. The best narrative of the battle and related events is that of Arthur Woodward, *Lances at San Pascual* (San Francisco: Calif. Hist. Soc., 1948).

112. Montgomery Journal in *Jour. Mil. Serv. Inst.,* XXXII (1903), 249-252.

113. *Ibid.,* p. 252.

114. *Ibid.,* p. 253.

115. For a detailed description of Lower California see the report of Lieut. H. Wager Halleck, U. S. Engrs., and the accompanying map, in Ho. Rep., 31st Cong., 1st Sess., *Ex. Doc. 17,* "California and New Mexico," pp. 606-612.

116. *Odds and Ends,* II, 41.

117. See *Ex. Doc. 1,* p. 1075 ff., for the Guaymas affair and many other events in the theater.

118. *Ibid.,* pp. 1084-85.

119. After relieving Montgomery, Cdr. Selfridge had been wounded in the foot during a skirmish near Guaymas. Cdr. Dupont later criticized Montgomery for departing before Selfridge could join for transportation to the States. Also, Dupont felt that Montgomery feared that Commodore Jones (en route to supersede Shubrick) would countermand the orders of the latter. Samuel F. Dupont, *Extracts from Private Journal-Letters* (Wilmington, Del., 1885), p. 325. Fortunately, Selfridge recovered from his wound and later became a rear admiral.

120. Lieut. Heywood and his small band at San Jose were invested by a large force of Mexicans in late January, 1848. Attacks continued

until February 15, when the garrison was relieved by a landing party from the *Cyane*. Heywood's losses were one officer and two men killed, four wounded, and two officers and six men taken prisoner, but later recaptured. *Ex. Doc. 1,* pp. 1130-31, 1138-47.

121. Dr. Robert E. Johnson in his unpublished Ph.D. dissertation (Claremont Graduate School, Calif.), "U. S. Naval Forces on Pacific Station," p. 162, says: "Able Commander Montgomery commanded his crew's respect and affection to a degree seldom seen, and on his recommendation Shubrick decided that the fine sloop [*Portsmouth*] should be allowed to return." A passenger on the ship was J. Quinn Thornton, who boarded at San Jose, Lower California, and who was en route to Washington to present to the Congress matters pertaining to the Oregon country.

122. Various letters, Montgomery to Mason, Feb. 18–May 17, 1848. See John A. Hussey, "New Light on the Original Bear Flag," *Calif. Hist. Soc. Quarterly,* XXI, No. 3 (Sept. 1952), pp. 205-217, for much data on the travels of the Bear Flag.

123. Many incidents regarding Montgomery's service in command of the Pacific Squadron are contained in his letters for the period to the Secretary of the Navy, at National Archives.

124. *Magazine of Am. Hist.* (July 1878), p. 425.

125. Condensed from MSS Nos. HM 23885, 23883, 25253, and 3636, permission of the Huntington Library, San Marino.

126. *Magazine of Am. Hist.* (July 1878), pp. 426-427; Carlisle (Pa.) *Herald,* Apr. 3 and 10, 1873; information from John W. Collier, Supt. Oak Hill Cemetery, Washington. It has been noted that Bryant, *op. cit.,* p. 323, named Montgomery as an Episcopalian in 1846. However, the records of the First Presbyterian Church of Brooklyn, N. Y., show that Montgomery and his wife joined that church in 1831. Phillips P. Elliott to Clifford M. Drury, Aug. 18, 1948, held by Dr. Drury. Whether Montgomery continued in the Presbyterian faith during the rest of his life does not appear to be a matter of record.

127. Data from the Div. of Naval History, Department of the Navy.

128. Among the references found useful in the preparation of this chapter are the following. The Div. of Naval History, Department of the Navy, furnished a concise history of the *Portsmouth*. Thomas C. Lancey's MS "History of the Portsmouth," at Special Collections, Univ. of Calif., Los Angeles, contains some data not to be found elsewhere. Representative articles which appeared in the *U. S. Naval Institute Proceedings* are: Charles O. Paullin, "Early Voyages of American Naval Vessels to the Orient," Vol. XXXVII, 392-397; Thomas O. Selfridge, "Origin of the U. S. Ship Portsmouth," Vol. XLII, 913-914; Robert W. Neeser, "Historic Ships of the Navy: Portsmouth," Vol. LII, 1349-1355.

129. His *History of the Portsmouth.*

130. *Ibid.*

131. Reports of Armstrong and Foote are in Paullin, *op. cit.*

132. See Edward K. Haviland, "American Steam Navigation in China, 1845-1878," *American Neptune,* XVI, No. 3 (July 1956), pp. 168-172, for data on the *Willamette,* and *ibid.,* XVII, No. 2 (April 1957), p. 144, regarding the *Cum Fá* (spelled *Kum Fa* by Foote). *Willamette* was an iron propeller which came under sail around the Horn to Oregon in 1851. She came to California in 1852, was renamed the *Thomas Hunt,* and plied inland and coastal waters. At an undetermined time prior to sailing to China in 1855, again under her original name, she was converted to a side-wheeler. Sacramento *Union,* May 7, 1855.

133. James M. Hoppin, *Life of Andrew H. Foote* (New York: Harper, 1874), p. 122.

134. Capt. John H. Levick, Hq. 3d Naval Dist., Aug. 13, 1957, to F. B. Rogers.

135. See *Official Records of Union and Confederate Navies in the War of the Rebellion* (Washington, 1905), Ser. I, Vols. 17-19, as indexed, for the service of the *Portsmouth* during the Civil War.

136. Published by W. W. Norton & Co. (New York, 1939).

137. Eldredge letters at Society of Calif. Pioneers.

138. *Boston Herald,* Aug. 1 and 2, Sept. 19, 1915; *Boston Globe,*

Sept. 7, 1915. The rotogravure section of the last-named issue of the *Herald* contains a picture of the burning hull of the *Portsmouth*.

139. The name *Portsmouth* was continued in the Navy when the third of that name, a light cruiser, was launched at Newport News on Sept. 20, 1944. She was named jointly for the cities of Portsmouth in New Hampshire and in Virginia, and was commissioned June 25, 1945. World War II soon came to an end, and *Portsmouth* (3d) was placed out of commission, in reserve, on June 15, 1949.

INDEX

Streets named are in San Francisco. Unless otherwise indicated here or implied in the text, place names are of California proper, and ships are American.

Muscovite and Mandarin

Muscovite and Mandarin: Russia's Trade with China and Its Setting, 1727-1805

Clifford M. Foust

The University of North Carolina Press   Chapel Hill

Library of Congress Catalog Card Number 72-80923
Manufactured in the United States of America
Printed by the Seeman Printery

For My Parents

Preface

This study was begun as a general investigation of Russian relations with China in the final three-quarters of the eighteenth century. In the beginning I intended to inquire into the entire spectrum of events and episodes in that intercourse, including diplomatic, commercial, and cultural matters. Chinese actions and reactions were to be treated equally with Russian ones; the aim was to construct an historical "synthesis" of these differing societies encountering one another. This original aim was eroded in the very process of historical investigation. Another set of objectives almost completely replaced those I began with.

What came to seem important to me was not so much the encounter itself of these two societies and their governmental and commercial representatives, although that encounter does have a fascinating and at times exciting history, but the historical dynamics of one or the other of these parties to a meeting of East and West. To try to make complete sense of both parties and to describe both meaningfully would likely prove to be unsatisfying at best and unimportant at worst. I determined to focus primarily on Russia, Russian acts and decisions, Russian motivations, and Russian dynamics of expansion.

The primary emphasis on Russian commercial relations with the Chinese also emerged only in the process of research and writing. I am now convinced that, in these early years of Russian interaction with the Chinese, trade was the dominant goal of most Russians, both state and private persons. For most Russians all else was subordinate. Yet the commerce that grew in the eighteenth century was intimately affected by a variety of factors and matters of noneconomic character. Decisions made in St. Petersburg and the accommodations agreed upon by Russian and Chinese diplomats and courts not only affected, but at times dictated, the circumstances, condition, and size of trade. Such things as the location of the borders, the control of runaways and deserters across established frontiers, the residence of Russian priests and students in Peking, and the forms of diplomatic correspondence, all at one time or another disturbed the relations between Russia and China, and as a consequence impinged on trade. Sometimes the impact was so great that trade was cut off for years. Were these noncommercial matters well known and chronicled it could be argued that they should not be dealt with as fully as I have done here. But they are almost completely unknown, especially to the English-reading audience. Russian trade with China is therefore seen, throughout this study, in a setting of noncommercial events, decisions, and factors.

Russians went to China to exchange goods for profit. Both state official and private trader went for that purpose. Until roughly the mid-eighteenth century, the Russian state monopolized a variety of goods marketed in China and reserved for itself all trade in the Chinese capital. Private merchants (after 1727) were limited to border trade. Hence Russian trade with China must be presented as an instance of rivalry between state commercial monopoly (sometimes the state operated the monopoly and sometimes it farmed it out to private entrepreneurs) and private commerce. This does not suggest that this rivalry in the China trade may be taken as a microcosm of Russian experience in economic enterprise in the eighteenth century. Certainly much of what is examined here has applicability to the general economic history of eighteenth-century Russia, but in a variety of ways the China trade was a special case—distant, exotic, chancey, discriminatively administered by the state, and participated in by a breed of traders (both state and private) of unusual cut. After the Treaty of Kiakhta (1727), the Russian state's involvement in the China trade was great and persistent. Hence considerable emphasis is laid here on state policy and state regulation of its own monopolies and of private trade. This emphasis has also required the explanation of changes in the administrative and governmental structure, both in St. Petersburg and in eastern Siberia, that affected trade.

This monograph begins fairly abruptly with the year 1727. In that year a new treaty—the Treaty of Kiakhta—replaced the earlier and better known Treaty of Nerchinsk. The Kiakhta agreements significantly and substantially altered the conditions and terms of trade between Russia and China, among other things clearly establishing the distinction between commerce carried on in the Chinese capital and that conducted at the border. New patterns of trade replaced the older ones, and the "Kiakhta system," as one author puts it to draw comparisons with the "Canton system," developed. That "system" was further defined later in the eighteenth century and thereafter remained much the same until the mid-nineteenth century.

This account is concluded in the early years of the nineteenth century because, by that time, the arrangements for trade and the agreements on noneconomic differences were set. They remained largely unchanged until after the stunning defeats suffered by the Chinese in the Anglo-Chinese Wars. Between 1803 and 1806 the Russians attempted to change those patterns drastically but, with the adamant refusal of the Chinese, they made no further effort until the world situation of China had altered dramatically.

Russian-Chinese relations, including trade, have been comparatively closely studied for the seventeenth century and the Petrine period. By far the finest work yet published is that of M. Gaston Cahen.[1] Although over a half a century old, it stands well the ravages of academic time. His study ends with the Treaty of Kiakhta and the subsequent Chinese embassies to Russia. A recent and most promising study, Professor Mark Mancall's doctoral dissertation on Sino-Russian relations prior to 1728, has, unfortunately, been unavailable to me.[2] The nineteenth century, also, has been treated in considerable detail, although by no means thoroughly dredged.

Hence, the main subject of this monograph is Russian trade in China and with the Chinese. It may be taken as a selective study in Russian economic and entrepreneural history of the eighteenth century, although I have made no particular effort to fit the China trade into the broader picture. It is too early to do that in a systematic way, for eighteenth-century Russia still very badly needs much monographic treatment before even the general patterns of the economy emerge. This is particularly true for the post-Petrine period, as persuasively argued by Professor Arcadius Kahan in his recent articles.[3]

By the same token, I have made no attempt at comparative history. It is left to others to contrast Russian penetration of the East with that of the Portuguese, Spaniards, English, and later the

1. Gaston Cahen, *Histoire des relations de la Russie avec la Chine sous Pierre le Grand, 1689-1730* (Paris: Félix Alcan, 1912).

2. Mark Mancall, "Sino-Russian Relations to 1728: The Search for Stability" (Ph.D. dissertation, Department of History, Harvard University, 1963).

3. Arcadius Kahan, "Continuity in Economic Activity and Policy during the Post-Petrine Period in Russia," *The Journal of Economic History,* XXV (March, 1965), 61-85, and "Entrepreneurship in the Early Development of Iron Manufacturing in Russia," *Economic Development and Cultural Change,* X (July, 1962), 395-422.

Americans. There is a very great deal that can be done in the comparative study of Europeans in East Asia, and it seems obvious on the surface of it that such study will reveal important insights into the nature and flavor of the societies back home.

No exceptional problems arose in the transliteration of Russian and Chinese. The Wade-Giles system, in spite of its archaisms, has been used for Chinese. For Russian, the Library of Congress system was employed, with the usual simplifications, such as the omission of ligatures. In almost all things, the advice of J. Thomas Shaw was found sound and sensible.[4] Manchu and Mongol names and terms proved to be a far greater problem, since transliteration of these languages has not yet stabilized in the academic world. Mongol is here transliterated by the convention adopted for Arthur Hummel's great compilation of the lives of Ch'ing dynasty personages.[5] Where this was not possible, the Chinese form, in the Wade-Giles system, was substituted, a somewhat unhappy device defensible on at least one ground—that the Mongols of that time are usually as well known in Chinese texts as in Mongol. Manchu names and terms are, contrarily, usually given in Wade-Giles transliteration, with the Manchu form following on first occurrence. The only justification for this practice is that Manchus (and even Manchu terms) are best known in the Ch'ing period through Chinese texts.

The Julian calendar, which was in general use in eighteenth-century Russia, has been used throughout. To convert to the Gregorian, add ten days in the seventeenth century, eleven in the eighteenth, and twelve in the nineteenth.

In order to simplify many bibliographic citations, Russia—as author—was assumed throughout. Thus where the issuing authority (e.g. Pravitel'stvuiushchii Senat) appears as author, Russia must be added by the reader, except, of course, when the country is specifically indicated.

It is a pleasant occupation to recall the many people who have contributed to this study, most of whom, I suppose, contributed unknowingly and perchance unwillingly. I am grateful to Professors George B. Carson, Leopold H. Haimson, Charles O. Hucker, and Donald F. Lach. To Professor Earl Hampton Pritchard I owe

4. J. Thomas Shaw, *The Transliteration of Modern Russia for English-Language Publications* (Madison: The University of Wisconsin Press, 1967).

5. Arthur W. Hummel (ed.), *Eminent Chinese of the Ch'ing Period (1644-1912)* (Washington: U.S. Government Printing Office, 1943).

a great debt of gratitude for his unfailing patience and steadfast loyalty to the muse. My colleague, Professor David M. Griffiths, read the later chapters and made valuable suggestions, many of which I have incorporated. Several of my students have written on related matters of eighteenth-century Russia and these have proved helpful: Wallace L. Daniel, Jr., David N. Jones, George E. Munro, and above all Mary E. Wheeler. My wife, Roslyn, and my daughters, Amy, Emily, and Polly, have each and severally suffered too much in a project which at many times seemed quite unworth the pain. And my parents have waited very long very patiently for substantial evidence of their commitment; it is to them this book is dedicated.

Clifford M. Foust

Chapel Hill
July 1968

Contents

Tables

Illustrations

Abbreviations

BSE	*Bol'shaia sovetskaia entsiklopediia*
Chteniia OIDR	*Chteniia v Imperatorskom Obshchestve istorii i drevnostei rossiiskikh pri Moskovskom universitete*
GAIO	Gosudarstvennyi Arkhiv Irkutskoi Oblasti
PSZ	*Polnoe sobranie zakonov rossiiskoi imperii s 1649 goda*
RBS	*Russkii biograficheskii slovar'*
Sbornik RIO	*Sbornik Imperatorskago russkago istoricheskago obshchestva*
SFPC	*Shuo-fang pei-ch'eng*
TsGADA	Tsentral'nyi Gosudarstvennyi Arkhiv Drevnikh Aktov

Muscovite and Mandarin

Chapter I. The Road to Kiakhta

Russians of means knew well of Chinese silk velvets in the fifteenth and sixteenth centuries; they were brought to Muscovy by Central Asian intermediaries long before a Russian tsar or his courtiers dreamed of dispatching their countrymen to make direct contact. The lure of the East quickened Russian hearts in the later sixteenth century; Ivan IV initiated the Russian state involvement in eastern affairs which grew by fits and bounds until, by the early eighteenth century, it was a permanent fixture of Russian history—long before the rightly famed Murav'ev-Amurskii. The first Russian visitors to Chinese dominions in the modern era were probably the cossacks Petrov and Ialychev of Ivan's times, albeit they did not succeed in gaining a reception at court. But the preconditions of regularized contact and commerce between Russia and China began to be fulfilled at the same time: the raising of Russian towns, actually only rude frontiers forts, in Siberia. Tiumen' (1586), Tobol'sk (1587), Tomsk (1604), Eniseisk (1619), and all the other posts later served as way stations on the road to Peking. Even before the mid-point of the seventeenth century, Russians bathed in the cold North Pacific, and in 1654 the key city of eastern Siberia was laid out on the boiling Angara—Irkutsk. In far less than a century, they walked, sailed, portaged, fought, traded, and duped their ways across the expanse of northern Siberia.[1]

Many and varied impulses set loose the Russian trek eastward: Orthodox proselytization and courtly glory mixed, if at times un-

1. For an overview of this process, consult George Vernadsky, "The Expansion of Russia," *Transactions of the Connecticut Academy of Sciences*, XXXI (July, 1933), 393-425; Raymond H. Fisher, *The Russian Fur Trade, 1550-1700* (University of California Publications in History, 31 [Berkeley: University of California Press, 1943]); Robert Joseph Kerner, *The Urge to the Sea; The Course of Russian History. The Role of Rivers, Portages, Ostrogs, Monasteries and Furs* (Berkeley: University of California Press, 1942); John F. Baddeley, *Russia, Mongolia, China. Being Some Record of the Relations Between Them from the Beginning of the XVIIth Century to the Death of the Tsar Alexei Mikhailovich, AD. 1602-1676, Rendered Mainly in the Form of Narratives Dictated or Written by the Envoys Sent by the Russian Tsars, or Their Voevodas in Siberia to the Kalmuk and Mongol Khans & Princes; and to the Emperors of China . . .* (London: Macmillan & Co., Ltd., 1919); and George V. Lantzeff, *Siberia in the Seventeenth Century, A Study of Colonial Administration* (University of California Publications in History, 30 [Berkeley: University of California Press, 1943]).

easily, with the drive for commercial profits, the need for release from the social restraints back home, and the thirst for high adventure and derring-do. Business profit may not have been the prime motive, but it was ubiquitous. Beyond the acquisition of Siberia's magnificent furs, the Muscovite court, for example, gave little evidence of sustained interest in Siberia in the sixteenth and seventeenth centuries; ". . . Siberia was like the remote estate of a very wealthy landowner; its possession was appreciated as the source of an additional income and of a few interesting and pleasant items, but it played only a small role in the general economy of the domain and little attention was paid to it."[2] Income from Siberia and its bordering lands derived mainly from fine furs; Siberian furs were carried from early times back to the capital for ultimate sale both in Russia and in Europe, but, as time went by, it was learned there was yet another market for these pelts, China itself. The China market had a double advantage; Chinese finery and exotica could be obtained in exchange for the easily trapped and processed furs and carried back to Russia (and thence in part shipped to Europe). The first Russian "diplomats" in China, Ivan Petlin (1618-19) and Fedor Isakovich Baikov (1654-58), were charged with investigating the potentialities of trade and the best avenues by which to get there and to India and Persia as well.[3]

Regularized and treaty-sanctioned trade between the two great empires had to await a sharp armed confrontation. Russian trappers reached Dauriia shortly before the middle of the seventeenth century; they discovered to their dismay that the Manchus considered the Amur River basin as their private preserve. Superior Manchu military and naval forces persistently frustrated the Russian trappers' efforts to build ostrogs (forts) and villages on the Amur; the struggle culminated in the now familiar sieges of the

2. Marc Raeff, *Siberia and the Reforms of 1822* (Seattle: University of Washington Press, 1956), p. xv.

3. Consult the carefully edited reports of Petlin and Baikov in Natal'ia Fedorovna Demidova and Vladimir Stepanovich Miasnikov, *Pervye russkie diplomaty v Kitae ("Rospis'," I. Petlina i stateinyi spisok F. I. Baikova)* (Moscow: Izd. "Nauka," 1966). Also Lo-shu Fu (comp. and trans.), *A Documentary Chronicle of Sino-Western Relations (1644-1820)* ("The Association for Asian Studies: Monographs and Papers," 22 [Tucson: The University of Arizona Press, 1966]), I, 15-16, 20; and the colorful account in Hugh Murray, *Historical Account of Discoveries and Travels in Asia, From the Earliest Ages to the Present Time* (Edinburgh: Archibald Constable and Co., Ltd.; and London: Longman, Hurst, Rees, Orme, and Brown, 1820), III, 314-17.

ostrog of Albazin in 1685-86.[4] The Manchus won the day and settled the Russian survivors in Mukden and Peking. The Albazin fighting underscored the increasing necessity for the amicable delimitation of the known territories of Russia and China and for agreement on the fundamentals of relations between the two. In 1685 Moscow selected its first ambassador plenipotentiary to China, Fedor Alekseevich Golovin.

Golovin was instructed to negotiate a definition of the Amur border if at all possible, and in doing so to retain the right of Russians to trade along the river and its tributaries.[5] His initial orders specified as his maximal concession relinquishment of Russian settlements along the Amur, but an amendment of 1687 authorized him to cede the embattled Albazin in exchange for the *summum bonum*, regularized commercial avenues between Muscovy and the Middle Kingdom. He was to avoid violence and bloodshed, which obviously would jeopardize successful trade relations. And the Emperor K'ang-hsi was to be given an invitation to send a mission to Moscow in return for this embassy, which mission it was hoped would come laden with precious stones, silver, velvets, damasks, and spices. The Russian government promised to purchase all of these elegant goods. Were he to fail in all of these tasks, Golovin was to persuade the Manchu court to leave the door open for some future Russian embassy.

The original site of the negotiations was to be the Russian ostrog of Selenginsk, on the River Selenga south of Lake Baikal, but the Peking representatives en route were forced back. The eruption of the Dzhungars led by Galdan blocked the route. Golovin's suite was itself besieged in Selenginsk by Mongols apparently driven north by Galdan's raids. As we shall see, the Dzhungar affair continued to complicate Russian-Chinese inter-

4. See, among other items, Fu, *A Documentary Chronicle*, I, 72-90.

5. On Golovin and the Treaty of Nerchinsk, see Gaston Cahen, *Histoire des relations de la Russie avec la Chine sous Pierre le Grand, 1689-1730* (Paris: Félix Alcan, 1912), pp. 33-50; Fu, *A Documentary Chronicle*, I, 94-103; Gerhard Friedrich Müller (Miller), "O pervykh rossiiskikh puteshestviiakh i posol'stvakh v Kitai," *Ezhemesiachnyia sochineniia, k pol'ze i uveseleniiu sluzhashchie* (St. Petersburg: Imp. Akademiia Nauk, 1755-64), I (July, 1755), 15-57; Dmitrii Nikolaevich Bantysh-Kamenskii, *Slovar' dostopamiatnykh liudei russkoi zemli* . . . (Moscow: Izdan A. Shiriaervym, 1836), I, 1-28.

Golovin returned to Moscow in January of 1691. In reward he was made a boiar. He was a great favorite of the young Peter and an intimate friend of Lefort. He commanded infantry at Azov and accompanied Peter's famed first European junket. In 1700 he became a field marshal. He died in 1731.

course for a large part of the next century. This mighty band, one of the Mongol Eleuth tribes of Central Asia, gradually consolidated its hold over neighboring peoples and augmented its military strength, beginning in the 1630's.[6] It was inevitable that the new and expansive Manchu power would contest the Dzhungars for hegemony over Central Asia. By 1668 Galdan, aided by firearms and armorers obtained from the Russians, launched his bid for supremacy in the region; it might well have proved to be a bid for supremacy in East Asia. Eastern Turkestan fell; Hami and Turfan were invested. K'ang-hsi's effort to pacify the Dzhungars in a conference in 1686 miscarried, and Galdan attacked the Khalkhas. His hordes swept eastward. At the time Golovin and his colleagues arrived at the extremity of Siberia, control of Central Asia was quite in doubt. Only after the Russians and Manchus came to agreement in the Treaty of Nerchinsk (1689) was Galdan bloodied at the critical battle of Ulan-butung (Yu-lan-pu-t'ung); although not decisively defeated he was forced to relinguish his march on the Chinese capital and to accept an oath of peace. Galdan took his own life in 1697, and the first great contest between Dzhungar and Manchu ended; the final one took another sixty years.

Compelled by the Dzhungar fighting to convene the negotiations further east in the Russian frontier ostrog of Nerchinsk on the Shilka River, Golovin, leading the Russians, and Lungoto (Lung-k'e-to), the Chinese, aided by the Jesuits Gerbillon and Pereyra as interpreters, began discussions on 12 August 1689. Two weeks later agreement was reached. It has been a common belief that Golovin acceded to a distinctly unfavorable treaty in part because the ten thousand Manchu fighting men on the scene badly out-

6. On the Dzhungars, see Sir Henry Hoyle Howarth, *History of the Mongols, From the 9th to the 19th Century* (London: Longmans, Green, and Co., 1876–1927), I, *passim*; Maurice Auguste Louis Marie Courant, *L'Asie centrale aux XVIIe et XVIIIe siècles; Empire Kalmouk ou empire Mantchou?* (Lyon: A. Rey, 1912), pp. 45-63; Vasilii Vladimirovich Bartol'd, *Four Studies on the History of Central Asia*, trans. V. & T. Minorsky (Leiden: E. J. Brill, 1956), I, 160-65; Boris Grigor'evich Kurts, "Kolonial'naia politika Rossii i Kitaia v XVII-XVIII v.v.," *Novyi Vostok*, Bk. 19 (1927), 199ff; Arthur W. Hummel (ed.), *Eminent Chinese of the Ch'ing Period (1644-1912)* (Washington: U.S. Government Printing Office, 1943), I, 265-68, 757-59; Il'ia Iakovlevich Zlatkin, *Istoriia dzhungarskogo khanstva (1635-1758)* (Moscow: Izd. "Nauka," 1964), esp. Chapters 3 and 4; and V. S. Batrakov, "K istorii torgovykh sviazei Kazakhstana s Rossiei v XVIII-XIX vv.," *Trudy Sredneasiatskogo Gosudarstvennogo Universiteta im. V. I. Lenina*, New Series, Vypusk 78; Istoricheskie nauki, Bk. 11 (Tashkent, 1956), pp. 3-39.

numbered his soldiers, but it is not a foregone fact that the treaty was disadvantageous to Russia's primary aims. Golovin, as his amended instructions allowed, ceded all Russian right to the Amur valley; but he secured what Moscow most wanted—direct trade in Peking on a treaty basis. The Russians preferred the real and concrete advantages of Peking trade to the uncertain benefits of trapping in the Amur basin and sailing the river's waters to an unknown sea.

The Treaty of Nerchinsk, the first international accord signed by the Middle Kingdom in modern times, was in six very short articles.[7] The frontier between Russia and China was fixed at the Argun and the Gorbitsa (a left bank tributary of the Shilka), and along the watershed of the basins of the Lena and Amur Rivers, as far as the Uda and the sea, which is to say, the Russians lost Albazin. All deserters or captives on either side were to remain as they were, but future fugitives had to be extradited. And finally, for the Russians, commerce was to be maintained, with access to Peking by those merchants identified by letters of authorization from the Russian government; the Treaty allowed the Chinese to visit Russian territories under the same conditions.

The treaty provisions on trade and merchants were vague and incomplete, but the important thing was that they opened the interior of China to regular Russian caravans. The Muscovite bureaucracy moved quickly to assert Russian state control over the potentially lucrative trade route. Fewer than four years after the signing of the Treaty of Nerchinsk, an Imperial ukaz of 30 August 1693 laid down general and specific regulations for Siberian customs and colonial officers, the broad principles of which remained the same until the middle of the eighteenth century.[8] Initially the Muscovite state did not attempt to monopolize fully

7. For texts of the Treaty, consult *Russko-kitaiskie otnosheniia, 1689-1916; Ofitsial'nye dokumenty*, comp. Petr Emel'ianovich Skachkov and Vladimir Stepanovich Miasnikov; Issued by Akademiia Nauk SSSR, Institut Kitaevedeniia (Moscow: Izd. Vostochnoi Literatury, 1958), pp. 9-11; and China, Inspectorate General of Customs at Shanghai, Statistical Department, *Treaties, Conventions, Etc., Between China and Foreign States* (Shanghai, 1908), I, 3-7.

8. Imperatorskaia Kantseliariia, *Polnoe sobranie zakonov rossiiskoi imperii s 1649 goda*, First Series: 1649-1825 (St. Petersburg: Pechatano v Tipografii II Otdeleniia Sobstvennoi Ego Imperatorskago Velichestva Kantseliarii, 1830), III, No. 1474, 160-67, dated 30 August 1693/7201 (hereafter cited as *PSZ*). For an excellent summary, see Cahen, *Histoire*, pp. 56-57.

Some of the following description has been drawn from the author's "Russia's Peking Caravan, 1689-1762," *South Atlantic Quarterly*, LXVII, No. 1 (Winter, 1968), 108-24.

the China trade, i.e. to reserve it exclusively for its own caravans, but rather endeavoured to regulate closely the activities of the private merchants and traders interested in travelling to Peking and to other cities. Since the Treaty of Nerchinsk required official passports for all merchants seeking entry into Chinese territories, the 1693 ukaz notified all Siberian officials that no one was to cross into China without an Imperial ukaz and a "patent" *(gramota)* from the Siberian Prikaz, the governmental department which since 1637 enjoyed general responsibility for the Siberian colony and its borderlands.[9] These documents were to be checked by the customs officials at Verkhotur'e in the Urals, the prescribed city of entry for Siberia, and again at Nerchinsk, the usual exit at this time into Manchuria and China proper, as well as at all stages along the way. Each merchant's passport was required to contain a full list and description of all merchandise carried, in order that the proper amount of state customs duties might be charged. At Verkhotur'e and Nerchinsk the usual Siberian duty of 10 per cent *(desiatina)* was extracted in kind and a receipt issued marked by an imperial seal. This receipt had to be inspected and compared with the goods at every major governmental town in Siberia; all goods carried and not listed as having been taxed were ordered confiscated. Were a merchant twice apprehended in attempting to deceive the customs houses, he was to be knouted and his kin and household tortured to provoke them to reveal any other effort at fraud. No state official nor his near kinsmen, regardless of rank or station, might engage in the China trade, with the sole exception of the soldiers and serving men *(sliuzhilye liudi)* accompanying the caravans to Peking or serving at the border customs station. These latter were granted, because of their low pay, permission to invest in the private caravans up to maximum of fifty rubles.

Tsar Peter, not yet the Great, issued in 1698 an ukaz which eased somewhat the stringent 1693 regulations and rules.[10] The goods of private merchants were no longer to be inspected at every

9. On the Siberian Prikaz, consult Lantzeff, *Siberia*, pp. 4-6, and on its later structure, *Gosudarstvennye uchrezhdeniia Rossii v XVIII veke (zakonodatel'nye materialy), Spravochnoe posobie*, ed. N. P. Eroshkin, prepared for publication by A. V. Chernov (Moscow, 1960). This most useful guide was issued by the Ministerstvo vysshego i srednego spetsialnogo obrazovaniia RSFSR and the Moskovskii gosudarstvennyi istoriko—arkhivnyi institut.

10. *PSZ*, III, No. 1654, 491-517, dated 12 November 1698/7207; and III, No. 1518, 206-7, dated 21 September 1695/7204. For a summary consult Cahen, *Histoire*, pp. 57-58.

town and in every market fair, but only at the seminal and terminal points, Verkhotur'e and Nerchinsk, the customs office of each to send a copy of the inventory of the merchant's goods to the other, the latter simply verifying its accuracy. The customs tithe was collected, but only once; one-twentieth by weight was extracted in kind from all goods purchased in Siberia and goods exported to China did not pay again. Goods brought from China paid the one-twentieth at Nerchinsk and even if they were sold in Siberia, the merchant paid no more. The buyer did however pay another one-twentieth.

As for the caravans themselves, the 1698 decree provided that they were to travel no oftener than once every two years; in the four years prior to the issuance of the decree, caravans had apparently been annual and threatened to satiate the Chinese markets. During these early years many of the goods carried by the caravans were privately owned and accompanied by the merchants who owned them to protect their investments, although state-owned merchandise, especially Siberian furs and pelts, probably constituted half of the total. To direct and administer the caravan, men were selected from among the larger merchants in Siberia who, as often as not, were already in the service of the state. Smaller merchants served as sworn-appraisers or sworn-men (*tselo-val'niki*, literally "those who kissed the cross," i.e. had taken an oath), whose task it was to price the state's commodities and to keep accurate accounts.[11] Foreigners were excluded from participation in this China trade, except with specific permission granted by the Siberian Prikaz. Russian merchants from west of the Urals might take part without a passport, but only with the payment of a nominal fee of one ruble each and after a year's residence in Siberia.[12] Falsification in the declaration of goods or the altering of receipts for customs duties paid resulted in the loss of trading privileges in the China market.

Initially then, the Russian state set out to control and to regulate the trade to Peking by organizing the caravans under the direction of substantial merchants in its service, by insisting on the use of established routes of transport across Siberia and on accurate report of merchandise carried, and by demanding immediate payment of customs duties levied at the "port" cities of Siberia. The

11. See Vladimir Antonovich Ulianitskii, *Russkiia konsul'stva za granitseiu v XVIII veke* (Moscow: Tip. G. Lissnera i A. Geshelia, 1899), I, 159-60.

12. *PSZ*, IV, No. 1800, 59-60, dated 18 June 1700.

simple goal of Moscow was the maximization of customs revenues; the device it adopted to do this was the close regulation of this international trade, taking care to allow room for private merchants to operate profitably.

Supervision of the caravans was only one side of the coin of state control of the China trade; the other was the flat prohibition of enumerated commodities for private trade in Siberia or to China and Chinese domains. Some of these items were denied to private merchants for political-security reasons: firearms, gunpowder, and lead. These were prohibited for sale to Bukharans and other Siberian border peoples in an imperial edict of 1693.[13] The sale or exchange of gold, silver, and foreign coinage (*efimki*, especially Albert talers and Joachim talers) across Siberian borders was also forbidden by the same decree, and remained prohibited or restricted throughout most of the seventeenth and eighteenth centuries.[14] Finally several commodities were reserved to the state (or leased by the state to private monopolists) because they were considered to be especially lucrative items. Ungulate rhubarb, extremely popular in Russia and Europe as an astringent drug, the best varieties of which came from western China, Mongolia, and Tibet, was prohibited to private import as early as 1657.[15] At one time or another the importation and manufacture of fine silks

13. *Ibid.*, III, No. 1474, 164, Article XV, ukaz dated 30 August 1693/7201.

14. The Russian state had long been interested in encouraging the inflow and discouraging the outflow of gold, silver, and foreign silver coinage. See, for example, the New Commercial Regulation of 1667 *(Novotorgovyi ustav)*; A. I. Pashkov (ed.), *Istoriia russkoi ekonomicheskoi mysli*, Vol. I: *Epokha feodalizma*, Chast' 1: *IX-XVIII vv.* (Moscow: Gospolitizdat, 1955), 287.

Efimki or *efimka* (sing. *efimok*) is mentioned repeatedly in eighteenth-century Russian texts, yet remains difficult to define with precision. The *Slovar' sovremennogo russkogo literaturnogo iazyka* describes it as "Foreign, chiefly silver, money (talers, Dutch marks, etc.) formerly in circulation in Muscovite Russia in the 16th and 17th centuries" *(Slovar' sovremennogo russkogo literaturnogo iazyka* [Moscow-Leningrad: Izd. Akademii Nauk SSSR, 1950-65], III, 1286). Apparently *efimki* was European coinage, most commonly Germanic, which was stamped with the tsar's seal or other official mark. Thereafter these coins circulated freely, although how they were evaluated in local markets and transactions is not well known. In eighteenth-century edicts on money and customs duties, the word seems to have been used as synonymous with foreign coinage.

15. In the early years of the eighteenth century, trade in rhubarb was leased to several private merchants, but after Peter the Great established his Medical Chancellery *(Meditsinskaia kantseliariia)* the state reserved the root for itself and except for a brief period in the 1720's maintained the monopoly until the 1780's.

were restricted and granted as a special privilege to favored petitioners, although the state never took upon itself the exclusive right to make or to trade in this fine fabric. Trade in tobacco was one of the earliest Petrine monopolies given to private persons, although in the eighteenth century it was at various times forbidden and permitted to nonmonopolists.[16]

The valuable and expensive Siberian furs, pelts and hides—by a wide margin the most important items in the China trade—were declared by Peter the Great illegal for private trade. Sporadic prohibitions against the sale of certain furs to Asian merchants trading in Muscovy dated as far back as the sixteenth century, but it was the last decade of the seventeenth before any large-scale monopoly was attempted. The declining supply of fine pelts together with the great potential profits combined to induce Peter in 1693 to prohibit the export by private individuals to China or elsewhere of sables valued at more than forty rubles and all black fox pelts.[17] Finally in 1706 in an ukaz to the Eniseisk *voevoda* Glebov, Siberian officialdom was reminded that no one might trade in Chinese domains without an Imperial "charter" and the monopoly on the sale of fine Siberian pelts to the Chinese was *ipso facto* the exclusive right of the state.[18] As in the instance of the caravans to Peking, the monopoly of the prime items of trade began modestly, but it did not take long for the temptation of quick and easy profit to entice the Muscovite court to extend its grasp.

Prior to the issuance of the 1689 rules, apparently four commercial caravans reached Peking, and in the two decades there-

16. After being held briefly by a Russian citizen, it was given over to Sir Thomas Osborne, Marquis of Carmarthen, in 1689. Osborne enjoyed the sole privilege of importing tobacco from the New World through Arkhangel'sk to Siberia, where Siberians in large numbers were addicted to the habit. The state held the monopoly until 1727 when traffic in the leaf was opened to private trade. Not until 1748 was the monopoly reinstated and the privilege of trading in Siberia and European Russia held by several entrepreneurs consecutively. The monopoly fell in 1762, along with most others. Consult Jacob M. Price, *The Tobacco Adventure to Russia; Enterprise, Politics, and Diplomacy in the Quest for a Northern Market for English Colonial Tobacco, 1676-1722* ("*Transactions of the American Philosophical Society*," New Series, LI, Pt. 1 [Philadelphia, 1961]).

17. See especially the fine description in Fisher, *The Russian Fur Trade*, pp. 210-14. Four years later the state extended the monopoly to all sables, stipulating that these furs be taken only by the state treasury by purchase, or as tribute *(iasak)* or tithe levied on the trappers and traders.

18. *PSZ*, IV, No. 2089, 336, dated 28 January 1706.

after an additional ten.[19] Most of them were substantial operations as far as may be gathered from scattered and incomplete records. The first caravan under the new rules was said to have carried thirty-one thousand rubles worth of state goods and twenty-six thousand rubles in goods in private hands. The state treasury reportedly profited to the extent of twenty-four thousand rubles. The next caravan was even larger, primarily because of the many more privately-owned goods carried, and it returned a state profit nearly twice as large. By the time of the third venture (1702-4), under the direction the substantial merchant Ivan Savateev, the "typical" size of the Peking caravan for decades to come was attained: goods both private and state valued at 223,320 rubles (at Nerchinsk prices) and a caravan complement of more than four hundred men. Although no profit figure for the Savateev caravan survives, the fifth caravan, Petr Khudiakov's of 1705-9, was said to have returned a profit of two hundred seventy thousand rubles, an exceptionally large figure for the day.[20]

Of the total of fourteen state caravans to Peking between 1689 and 1722, most were probably financial successes for the state, provided that only immediate costs are calculated and overhead expenses of the Siberian colonial apparatus are excluded. The main commodity of export, Siberian furs and pelts, was after all obtained at minimal cost, except for the expense of maintaining a substantial colonial administration in Siberia. Were it possible accurately to establish these expenses, and it is not, it is highly likely that the state could have maximized its revenues by encouraging private merchants to carry on the entire China trade and then extracting from them the usual customs duties and other imposts for the use of state warehouses, etc. This assumes, of course, that state officials in Siberia could successfully interdict all illicit and illegal carriage into Manchu territories, an assumption that evidently could not and cannot be made.

The evidence is plentiful that—in the Petrine period—at least

19. The finest study of these by far is that of Boris Grigor'evich Kurts, *Gosudarstvennaia monopoliia v torgovle Rossii s Kitaem v pervoi polovine XVIII st.* ("Naukovi zapiski Kiivs'kogo institutu narodn'ogo gosudarstva," 9 [Kiev, 1928]), especially pp. 1-27. See also the same author's *Russko-kitaiskie snosheniia v XVI, XVII i XVIII stoletiiakh* (Khar'kov: Gosudarstvennoe Izdatel'stvo Ukrainy, 1929).

20. Aleksei V. Semenov, *Izuchenie istoricheskikh svedenii o rossiiskoi vneshnei torgovle i promyshlennosti s poloviny XVII-go stoletiia po 1858 god* (St. Petersburg: Tip. I. I. Glazunova i Ko., 1859), III, 197.

as many goods, and probably more, were carried to China proper or to Chinese territories by enterprising but illegal private traders as were carried by the state caravans. Between the signing of the Treaty of Nerchinsk and the Chinese cessation of this trade in 1722, two special embassies of a mixed diplomatic and commercial nature were dispatched (the first led by the long-time European merchant in Russia Evert Ysbrandszoon Ides, in 1692-95, and the second by Lev Vasil'evich Izmailov, 1719-20), in addition to the fourteen Russian state caravans approved by Imperial charter for passage to Peking. Yet when the Muscovite ambassador Sava Lukich Vladislavich-Raguzinskii reached Peking in 1726, he was astonished to discover that the Manchus had received fifty "ambassadors" and "envoys" from Russia, which is simply to say that many private traders found their way to Peking without the required imperial sanction.[21] Some secured passports signed by the governors and local officials in Siberia, others in all likelihood merely forged credentials. It was quite impossible for the Manchus to distinguish successfully between legal passports and cleverly contrived ones.

As time went by, the state caravans found themselves at an increasing disadvantage in competing with these interlopers. Part of the problem was that some caravan officials, in league with Siberian officials and customs officers, were the chief connivers. All of these soon discovered that there was immense personal profit in trafficking in furs illicitly and in accepting bribes to overlook the contraband carried by both the caravans and private merchants who travelled alone. A few of these officials were apprehended; the Siberian governor from 1710 to 1719, Prince Matvei Petrovich Gagarin, was the highest ranked of them, and the full fury of the law fell on him as an example to others. He, his relatives, and his friends had grown rich from illegal participation in the China trade, for which he was eventually recalled; charged with theft, nepotism, and ineptitude; tried, and hanged.[22] But the great distance from St. Petersburg and the lacunae in the Siberian administrative system insured that others would and did continue

21. As early as 1706, an Imperial edict recognized the existence of this "illegal" commerce; instructions to the *voevoda* of Eniseisk insisted on the enforcement of the prohibition against trading in all of China itself by all persons not associated with the state caravans; Cahen, *Histoire*, p. 59.

22. *Russkii biograficheskii slovar'*. Ed. A. Polovtsov (St. Petersburg: Izdanie Imp. Russkago Istoricheskago Obshchestva, 1896-1918), vol. Gaag-Gerbel, 78-80. Hereafter cited as *RBS*.

cutting corners on the law. There were constant complaints at this time and later, for instance, that the sworn-appraisers of the caravans were not always realistic in evaluating the state pelts. The prices they set were often far too high, at least in comparison with those of privately carried pelts.

Even more striking is the realization that many Siberian and Russian merchants never reached Peking itself, but carried goods only as far as the major Manchurian and Mongolian towns, especially Naun and Urga, whence Chinese merchants transshipped them to northern Chinese cities. Private merchants, after all, could purchase their pelts at the most convenient markets and market-fairs of Siberia, journey to Urga in only ten or twelve days, dispose of their furs after two or three days of trading, and return to make several more journeys during the year. Caravans, on the other hand, usually remained in Peking from three to six months because of the slow trading and the time wasted occasionally in long ceremonies of welcome. Lorents Lange, a Scandinavian in Peter's service in the East, estimated in 1721 that the Urga trade alone was four to five times greater annually than the trade carried on by the state caravans.[23] It is also obvious that the expenses of carriage to Peking, particularly of provisions and forage, were several times greater than those sustained in carriage to Urga or Naun. Lange noted that before the Urga trade developed, the Chinese merchants trading with the caravans became rich, but thereafter "traded to their own loss, and many may be deemed at present quite ruined. . . . All these circumstances well considered, it is easy to comprehend that upon closing the accounts of the caravan, the profits cannot, at this time, be much more than the disbursements."[24]

Other considerations of a noncommercial nature complicated the decision-making of the St. Petersburg authorities on the China trade. If the state's involvement in the caravan trade directly to

23. Lorents Lange, "Journal of the Residence of Mr. de Lange, Agent of His Imperial Majesty of All the Russians, Peter the First, at the Court of Peking, During the Years 1721 and 1722," published as part of John Bell of Antermony, "Travels from St. Petersburg in Russia, To Various Parts of Asia, in 1716–1719, 1722, &c." in John Pinkerton, *A General Collection of the Best and Most Interesting Voyages and Travels in All Parts of the World* (London: Longman, Hurst, Rees, Orme, and Brown; and Cadell and Davies, 1811), VII, 456.

24. *Ibid.*, VII, 457. See also Iulii Andreevich Gagemeister, *Statisticheskoe obozrenie Sibiri* (St. Petersburg: V Tipografii II Otdeleniia Sobstvennoi Ego Imperatorskago Velichestva Kantseliarii, 1854), II, 590.

Peking were to be reinvigorated and Russia's private merchants were to be restrained and regulated, there were prerequisites.[25] Siberian administrative and customs personnel had to acquire senses of honesty, duty, and efficiency. The same may be said of the staffs of the caravans. If contraband were to be suppressed, the border between Russian and Chinese dominions would have to be defined in the Baikalia region and effectively enough patrolled to intercept (or to threaten to intercept) contraband carriers. And for that matter it would prove an enormous advantage were private merchants excluded completely from Manchuria and Mongolia; competition between private merchant and state caravan might then be brought nearly to an equality.

Most of these considerations had to be decided by the two powers in concert. Unilateral efforts could only be piecemeal. And most of them inextricably involved the relations of both empires with the third most powerful force in eastern Asia, the resurgent Dzhungars. The death of Galdan in 1697 only temporarily clipped the Dzhungars' wings. Fighting broke out again in 1712, when Tsewang Araptan, Galdan's successor, sacked Hami. Manchu armies retook and retained it; and Tsewang's intrigues shifted in other directions, particularly toward Tibet. Peremptorily K'ang-hsi summoned him to restore all the rights and lands he had wrested from the other Dzhungar princes and to that end to convene a conference, at which a representative from Peking would be in attendance. Accession to these demands meant submission to vassalage. Tsewang spurned them and the struggle continued.

Russia persisted in the facade of neutrality in the Manchu-Dzhungar rivalry, but became deeply involved in Dzhungaria in the first quarter of the eighteenth century. In 1698, for example, she granted favorable commercial privileges to the Bukharans, a Mongol tribe noted for its mercantile skill and activity, which acted, in a sense, as the commercial agent of the Dzhungars.[26]

25. In 1723 merchants returning from Chinese territories were no longer required to pay customs duties in Chinese gold or silver, but still had to sell all gold or silver they imported to the treasury. Several of the most important items of the China trade were shortly released to private trade—rhubarb in 1725, tobacco in 1727. And even sable was freed for trade within Siberia, although its private export to China remained interdicted.

26. Cahen, *Histoire*, p. 140. Like most of the Central Asian peoples, prior to very recent times, the Bukharans are almost impossible to define. No eighteenth-century source provides an adequate and verifiable definition. The main body of Bukharans *(Bukhartsy)* located in the region of Bokhara were, it seems, "Turkic" in linguistic composition. There was and is a Buriat-

Those who came to Siberia to trade were required to pay only one-twentieth in duties instead of the usual tenth, and were exempt altogether if they came in the name of Tsewang Araptan. Still the Russians avoided committing themselves to an open alliance with the Dzhungars, as is evident in the Volga Turgut affair.

Early in the seventeenth century, part of the Turguts migrated to the Volga-Don region. In spite of the great distance, they managed to maintain close connections with their Mongol brothers in Dzhungaria. Intermarriage between the ruling clans of the Turguts and the Dzhungars served as a major link. The link served to keep alive, among both the Russians and the Manchus, the apprehension that the Turguts might remigrate and, in doing so, quicken the tempo of central Asian affairs. Peking thus found in 1712 a pretext to dispatch an embassy to the Turguts, the real purpose of which was to augment its influence with these potential allies (or enemies). The *Li-fan-yuan*[27] requested passage across Siberia for an embassy carrying a letter to Ayuki (A-yu-ch'i), chief of the Turguts, which concerned a nephew of Ayuki's who, because of the state of war in Dzhungaria, was unable to return from a pilgrimage to Tibet and sought refuge in Peking. Prince Gagarin, Siberian governor, cautioned care that an attempt not be made to commit the Turguts to offensive action against the Dzhungars, an exigency likely to engage Russia. The Russian Governing Senate resolved to permit the embassy, but instructed the governor of Kazan' to try to discover its true intent and, if necessary, to dissuade Ayuki from a precipitous act. The narrative of T'u-li-shen, the only record of the discussions between the Manchus and the Turguts, reveals that the conversations were restricted to the disposition of the errant nephew.[28]

Then early in the second decade of the eighteenth century, a

Mongol branch in Transbaikalia also known as *Bukhartsy*; it is this branch with which we are mainly concerned here. An added complication is that the Russians and Siberians commonly referred to many or all of the Mongols who came to trade as Bukharans. For the eighteenth century, the designation can only be used to refer, very loosely, to any Turkic or Mongol Central Asians who traded with the Russians.

27. For explanation of *Li-fan-yuan*, see n. 50 of Chapter 2.

28. Sir George Thomas Staunton (tr.), *Narrative of the Chinese Embassy to the Khan of the Tourgouth Tartars, in the Years 1712, 13, 14, & 15; by the Chinese Ambassador, and Published, by the Emperor's Authority, at Pekin* (London: John Murray, 1821), pp. pp. 148-76; Cahen, *Histoire*, chap. v; Gaston Cahen, "Les cartes de la Siberie au XVIIIe siècle, Essay de bibliographie critique," *Nouvelles Archives des Missions Scientifiques et Litteraires*, Nouvelle Serie, Fascicule 1, pp. 136-37.

wild gold fever in the Tarim Basin further complicated Russian-Manchu-Dzhungar relations. Unsubstantiated rumors of fabulous gold mines provoked Governor Gagarin in 1713 to send a Tobol'sk boiar to Sining and Tapa to locate the riches. The first results were negative, but a larger expedition, more than 1,500 strong, set out shortly thereafter. It was commanded by Lieutenant-Colonel Ivan D. Bukhol'ts, of whose later activities we will speak. The band reached Iarkand in 1717, where engineers prospected for the illusive gold. Tsewang Araptan's warriors were a clear and present danger to the safety of the Russians, and Gagarin promised tangible aid to the Mongol prince if the latter resisted interference with the expedition. But one of Tsewang's subordinates besieged the Russians, forcing them to raze a fort they had built at Iamyshev and to return down the Irtysh. The hapless survivors reached Tobol'sk in December, 1716, and Bukhol'ts returned to St. Petersburg to explain away his failure.

The fever did not abate. The next year another expedition set out, and in 1719 Peter appointed a general to supervise all of the prospecting efforts. Tsewang Araptan, defeated by the Manchus near Hami and elsewhere, and encouraged by his ability to turn back Russian military units, refused a Chinese offer of vassalage and sent off an envoy to St. Petersburg, who in September, 1721, offered passage for the Russian gold seekers in return for a defensive alliance against the Manchus. Peter succumbed to the temptation. He sent Ivan Unkovskii with a proposal that Russia obligate herself to adopt a stern attitude toward China and, if necessary, to make a demonstration of military strength. Tsewang was to submit to formal Russian vassalage and to permit the raising of additional ostrogs within Dzhungaria. In spite of a few years' residence with Tsewang, Unkovskii did not accomplish a binding agreement. The death of K'ang-hsi in 1722 and an offer of peace from his successor, Yung-ch'eng, ended the need for Russian support. For the next thirty years, friendly relations and caravan trade existed between Russia and Dzhungaria.

Complicating the strained relations which resulted from the undisciplined Russian trade in China itself and in Chinese territory, and from the Dzhungarian imbroglio was the matter of deserters fleeing from Central Asia and Mongolia to Siberia. Fugitives from the Manchu and Dzhungar armies crossed into Siberia in large numbers requesting asylum.[29] Local Siberian authorities

29. Fu, *A Documentary Chronicle*, I, 124-25 and *passim*.

were reticent to force their return, not only for humanitarian reasons, but because Siberia was sparsely populated and always needed additional sources of tribute, taxes, and military conscripts. Some of the "deserters" were probably not that, precisely speaking, but no more than pastoral nomads wandering in search of land and fodder. The Manchus nonetheless demanded their return, for to them they were no less a source of tribute, taxes, and military conscripts. As with Russia's merchants, there was no solution to the problem of fugitives and wanderers short of agreement on a marked and patrolled border between Mongolia and Siberia.

By 1719 these several aggravations to Russian-Chinese intercourse approached emergency level, and the Peking court refused entry to the capital to the Russian caravan commanded by Fedor Stepanovich Istopnikov in June of that year.[30] The immediate reason given was that the court no longer wished to bear the heavy expenses of the caravans. Just a month earlier, Tsar Peter appointed as envoy to Peking a young soldier-diplomat, Lev Vasil'evich Izmailov, a captain in the Preobrazhenskii Regiment. Izmailov's mission, like that of Ides in the 1690's, was primarily commercial; his main task was to try to "open" the entire interior of China to Russian trade.[31] He was to press for an increase in the volume of trade and the number of caravans permitted to enter Peking. The highest hope was that the Peking court would be convinced of the value of complete freedom of trade for Russians throughout China—unlimited numbers of merchants purchasing Chinese valuables wholesale, exporting them duty-free, and selling Russian goods without impost. To aid these merchants, a permanent Russian commercial agent or consul would be installed in Peking, with subordinates in the provinces, and a commercial tribunal would be organized to handle the differences arising between merchants of the two countries. In exchange for these concessions, St. Petersburg would grant similar rights of

30. Cahen, *Histoire*, p. 111.

31. Izmailov, born 1686, served in 1710 on a diplomatic mission to Denmark. After returning from Peking, he resumed his military career and rose to the rank of lieutenant-colonel before his death in 1738; *Azbuchnyi ukazatel' imen russkikh deiatelei dlia Russkago biograficheskago slovaria,* published as vols. 60 and 62 (1887-88) of Imperatorskoe Russkoe Istoricheskoe Obshchestvo, *Sbornik Imperatorskago russkago istoricheskago obshchestva* (St. Petersburg, 1867-1916) (hereafter cited as *Sbornik RIO*), I, 300. Also Julius Heinrich von Klaproth, *Mémoires relatifs à l'Asie, contenant des recherches historiques, géographiques et philologiques sur les peuples de l'Orient* (Paris: Librairie Orientale de Dondey-Dupré Père et Fils, 1824-28), I, 4.

trade in Siberia and Russia. To assuage the fears of the Manchus with regard to the Russian role in Dzhungaria, Izmailov was to assure them that the Russian ostrogs along the Irtysh were nothing more than a fulcrum directed against the Dzhungars—not a prelude to offensive action against Manchu armies.[32]

Klaproth asserted that Izmailov and his companions produced "un heureux effet" in Peking, but they failed anyway.[33] Istopnikov's caravan was allowed to enter, but its primary thrust—to open China—was turned aside.[34] Minor accomplishments salvaged something of the day. A system of seals was agreed upon to identify official caravans and to eliminate interlopers. Lorents Lange, who accompanied Izmailov as first secretary, was permitted to remain temporarily in Peking, but not as an officially recognized consul, only to lend the caravans a hand. And Russian merchants of the caravans henceforth had to accept sole responsibility for all expenses incurred and for the recovery of any debts contracted by Chinese merchants. Izmailov departed on 2 March 1721, leaving Lange behind to serve the caravan. It seems that the refusal of the Chinese to entertain widening of the trade was related to the broader outstanding differences symbolized, to them, by the failure of Siberian border authorities to return to Mongolia some seven hundred Mongol runaways who had fled in 1720. No misunderstandings were abated; if anything they intensified.

At first successful in disposing of its wares, Istopnikov's caravan met with increased obstacles to unhampered trade.[35] To make

32. Cahen, *Histoire*, chap, vii, pp. 153-69. For an entertaining, but rather irrelevant, account of Izmailov's journey, see "A Journal from St. Petersburg in Russia, to Pekin in China, with an Embassy from His Imperial Majesty, Peter the First, to Kamhi Emperor of China, in the Year 1719," and "Travels from St. Petersburg in Russia, to Various Parts of Asia, in 1716, 1719, 1722 &c. by John Bell, of Antermony," in Pinkerton, *A General Collection*, VII, 318-434. Also Murray, *Historical Account*, III, 321-23; Kurts, *Gosudarstvennaia monopoliia*, pp. 27-29; Nikolai Nikolaevich Bantysh-Kamenskii, *Diplomaticheskoe sobranie del mezhdu rossiiskim i kitaiskim gosudarstvami s 1619 po 1792-oi god,* Sostavlennoe po dokumentam, khraniashchimsia v Moskovskom arkhive gosudarstvennoi Kollegii inostrannykh del, v 1792-1803 godu (Kazan': Tipografiia Imperatorskago Universiteta, 1882), pp. 91-103; and I. F. Kurdiukov, "Iz istorii russko-kitaiskikh otnoshenii (1695-1720 gg.)," *Istoricheskii arkhiv*, No. 3 (May-June, 1957), 183-84.

33. Klaproth, *Memoires*, I, 4.

34. Vladimir Kalistratovich Andrievich, *Kratkii ocherk istorii Zabaikal'ia ot drevneishikh vremen do 1762 goda* (St. Petersburg: Voennaia Tipografiia, 1887), p. 129.

35. For more on the Istopnikov caravan, see particularly Lange's "Journal" in Pinkerton, *A General Collection*, VII, 459-80; Arkheograficheskaia komissiia,

matters worse, while still on the road to Peking, the caravan director had run short of ready cash with which to purchase "the necessities of the caravan." He requested through Lange, who had gone ahead, the loan of two thousand *liang* (approximately twenty-six hundred rubles) from the Manchu court, promising to repay soon after the bartering began. Only after considerable trouble was Lange able to forward to him at the gate of Kalgan some fifteen hundred *liang*.

The Russians reported that the warehouses provided for Russian merchandise were in a sad state of disrepair, and the overseer *(chien-tu)* of the Russian compound (the *O-lo-ssu kuan* or *Russkii dom*) ignored Russian requests to have the leaking roofs repaired or to permit the Russians themselves to fix them. Many of the Russian goods had to be left in the open courtyard and were badly damaged by seasonal rains. And four Chinese officials arrived insisting on a complete inventory of the Russian goods that they might select the finest for the Emperor's choice; to the Russians this was a transparent excuse for them to acquire the most desirable goods on their own accounts at very depressed prices (three *liang* per pair of sables, for example, some of which had cost twenty to thirty rubles each).

Although the caravan reached Peking on 29 September 1721, it had to wait more than two months before general trading began, and then the Chinese officials detailed to supervise the caravan's activities demanded a small fee from all Chinese merchants who appeared to trade. Korean merchants were simply driven away. The Russians learned, further, that the K'ang-hsi emperor had been persuaded by his ministers to throw on the market sables stored in the imperial treasury, on the pretext that so many had been accumulated that they were likely to deteriorate. Twenty thousand Amur sable pelts were advertised for sale at favorable prices, enticing many Chinese merchants from the Russian compound and further depressing an already slow market.

Finally on 8 May 1722, before the caravan succeeded in disposing of all it brought, Lange received word from the court that no more Russians would be permitted in Peking until some solution were found to the problems which arose from the undefined Siberian-Mongolian border and until all Mongol runaways had

---

Pamiatniki sibirskoi istorii XVIII veka (St. Petersburg: Tip. Ministerstva Vnutrennykh Del, 1882–85), II, 394-96, Document 87; and Kurts, *Gosudarstvennaia monopoliia*, pp. 30-31.

been returned. The "Imperturbable Tranquillity" of K'ang-hsi had been disconcerted by the Russians. Shortly thereafter (17 July), the Istopnikov caravan departed, and Lange accompanied the influential minister T'u-li-shen (Tulisen) to the frontier to investigate the state of the deserter situation. For the first time since the Treaty of Nerchinsk, Peking was closed to Russians. If St. Petersburg wished to continue this trade, the next move was its. And if we may believe the French envoy in the Russian capital at this time, the stoppage of the China trade must quickly have been noticed, since for some years many of the officers of the army and navy, as well as *chinovniki* in various colleges, had been paid wholly in fine Chinese silks.[36]

Late in the 1710's Peter began to sponsor a series of "mercantilist measures" aimed at encouraging private enterprise (within limitation) and easing the restrictions on internal and external commerce, among other things. In April, 1719, for example, ukazy proclaimed freedom of trade in the interior of Siberia for all goods, except pitch, potash, and sables and other furs.[37] These commercial measures (and it need not concern us here as to whether or not they were "mercantilist") reflected the view that foreign trade was extremely important in helping to develop a modest factory system in Russia by stimulating the flow of bullion into the country, the importation of raw materials, and the carriage abroad of Russian fabricated products, although this last was of relatively less importance to Peter. Toward these ends, Petrine policy resulted in the loosening of innumerable and hampering restrictions on private foreign trade.[38] The Peking trade itself benefited only incidentally from these specific edicts, but the generalized issue inherent in them did relate directly to it: state involvement in and control of commerce (as well as industry) vs. encouragement of private trade and merchants. The ultimate criterion for deciding between the two (or for achieving a balance between the two) was the benefit of the state, i.e. the degree to which one or the other contributed to the industrial base required to support Peter's military might, to the stability of the currency, and to the solvency of the treasury. A large measure of the history

36. "M. Magnan au comte de Morville," St. Petersburg, 17 December 1726, *Sbornik RIO*, LXIV (1888), 474-75.

37. For discussion of decrees of 8 April and 11 May 1719, see Cahen, *Histoire*, p. 238.

38. *PSZ*, V, No. 3360, 696, dated 30 April 1719.

of the Peking trade in the second quarter of the century is, as shall be seen, the history of the competition between state and private interests and the debate that emanated from that competition.

Specifically, the Russian court needed badly to make a set of clear decisions with regard to the China trade, although prior to 1727 there was no sign that it was prepared to do so. The choices open to the court may be regarded as a translation into the concrete instance of the issues inherent in Peter's "mercantilist measures." For example, the court had the choice of pressing forward the liberalizing measures, releasing additional monopolized goods to private trade, and, as far as the China trade was concerned, abolishing the state Peking caravan altogether, thereafter promoting the formation of a private company or companies to assume the monopoly. This was not an entirely novel idea; Peter I had proposed as early as 1711 the giving over of the China trade (which at that time meant trade in Peking) to a "good company." The other general choice was to reinvigorate the faltering state caravan. This necessarily meant the elimination in whole or in part of private merchants from at least the Peking trade and at most from all trade with the Chinese both in Peking and in the other cities where barter had recently developed. And some compromise between these two extreme choices was also possible. None of these choices was excluded by the peculiar brand of "mercantilism" represented in the edicts of the later years of Peter's reign, if for no other reason than that "mercantilism" was not a closely defined ideological doctrine. The dubious experience of the Peking caravans, the swiftly increasing private trade both in Peking and other cities, the persistent difficulties with the Chinese in Peking, and now the stoppage of trade by the Chinese required that some effort must be made to put the trade on a new basis or to reinforce the old one.

Yet no decision on the China trade, no matter how well founded in current economic doctrine, could be taken by St. Petersburg authorities unless it came to terms with the noneconomic problems of intercourse with the Chinese. A series of issues plainly had to be negotiated and settled to the mutual satisfaction of both sides, or trade of any consequence had no chance of restoration. The Mongolia-Siberia border had to be demarcated and sealed to unauthorized persons in order to reduce the runaway and migration problem, to localize the Dzhungarian fracas, and to restrain private Russian merchants. Until all of these were accomplished, it seems clear that Peking would not again allow trade within its walls, nor was it likely to allow private Russian merchants to continue to visit Naun and Urga. And none of these abrasive issues could be abated unless agreement with the Chinese led to the creation of a finer and more dependable administrative structure in Siberia. Neither state monopoly nor regulation of private merchants could succeed unless the state's administration were enlarged, its enforcement powers increased, and its officials impressed with the virtues of efficiency. To put it another way, on the level at which trade was actually conducted, the decisions with regard to the organization of commerce were and had to be made on the basis of real and concrete circumstances, circumstances which necessarily included many factors of noneconomic and nonfiscal character and excluded most of what we usually know as economic doctrine or ideology.

By mid-1722, Russian policy toward China and her trade had begun to be clarified. There was a swing toward the avoidance of hostilities over the several issues mentioned above, and increasing anxiousness to negotiate them. Orders came from St. Petersburg that Siberian officials must strictly comply with the Treaty of Nerchinsk, particularly with regard to runaways. Finally in January, 1724, Lorents Lange and his colleague, Ivan Glazunov, assisted by Colonel Bukhol'ts and two thousand troops under his command, were designated to attempt to bargain with the Manchus. Before anything could come of this, another diplomat-merchant of high repute and great skills was appointed to take Lange's place. On 11 August 1725, Sava Lukich Vladislavich-Raguzinskii received a patent as Ambassador Extraordinary and Minister Plenipotentiary to China to undertake to reason with the Manchus on all of the issues in dispute.[39] The initial meetings Lange had held with Chinese representatives gave him hope of eventual solution of the differences in a peaceful way. The Governing Senate seized upon the hope and dispatched to China one of Russia's most experienced, most adroit, and wiliest negotiators.

39. *Ibid.*, VII, No. 4746, 517-20, Senate decree dated 5 July 1725.

Chapter II. The Treaty of Kiakhta

In March of 1726 the Illyrian Count Sava Lukich Vladislavich-Raguzinskii[1] and fifteen men of his ambassadorial suite struggled up the final miles of the swift and treacherous Angara river and reached the city of Irkutsk. The journey from St. Petersburg had taken an arduous five months, a taxing experience for a man in his late fifties. But Irkutsk, the largest and by any measure the most cultured town of Eastern Siberia, might permit him a few days respite to reflect on the fortuitous adventures of his already full life.

Vladislavich was born of noble family in Herzegovina and came to be trusted agent and favored merchant of Peter the Great, selected now to negotiate a new treaty with the sly Manchu rulers of China. Resting quietly in a comfortable wooden house of Irkutsk after an excellent dinner of Baikal sturgeon, he recalled tales of Turkish depredations and tribute demands in his homeland, the "flight" of his family to Venice and to Ragusa, and his early years as a merchant in the eastern Mediterranean and in Constantinople where he first determined to enter Russian service. He arrived in Moscow in April of 1703 with plans for trading operations between that city and Azov on the Black Sea. Brusque Peter quickly recognized his value to Russian aspirations to extend political and commercial influence to the south and particularly to the Balkans, a value recompensed by grant to Vladislavich of a series of special trading privileges over the years, a fine estate in Moscow formerly owned by the Naryshkin family, properties in Ukraine, and a Russian court rank (*nadvornyi sovetnik*, court councillor, the seventh rank in Peter's Table).[2] For this bounty

1. There is no uniformity, even in contemporary eighteenth-century Russian sources, as to the spelling or form of Vladislavich's name. A recent and careless work even makes it Raduzinski (J. V. Davidson-Houston, *Russia and China, From the Huns to Mao Tse-tung* [London: Robert Hale, Ltd., 1960], p. 74). Raguzinskii is, properly, not his surname, but an appelation similar to Murav'ev-*Amurskii* and Potemkin-*Tavricheskii,* derived from the city of Ragusa on the Adriatic where his family lived for a time and to which he returned to receive the title of Count. In Chinese texts he is usually identified by his given name Sava or Savva (Sa-wa).

2. His family background is the subject of some debate and distorted by many errors. He was most probably an Orthodox Greek born in Herzegovina in a family that had cause to fear Turkish reprisals. He certainly lived in

he in part repaid the Russian court by serving with Peter on the Prut campaign as advisor on the anti-Turkish sentiments of Balkan peoples whom Peter's agents were trying to provoke into revolt against the Ottoman Empire. In later years Vladislavich spent several years in Ragusa, Venice, and Rome on delicate and complex missions for Russia. The Roman mission involved, in the first instance, several marble statues by the master Pietro Baratta given by Pope Clement XI to Russia, but not released by local Roman authorities. In the end, he had to negotiate the entire question of the freedom of Roman clerics to preach and teach in Russia, and to travel to the East across her lands.

The good Tsar chose wisely in selecting Vladislavich to represent St. Petersburg in the negotiations with the Middle Kingdom. The Herzegovinian was already an exceptionally successful merchant, and long accustomed to operating within the framework of Russia's state monopolies in trade and industry.[3] He knew that state monopoly of certain trade routes or items of trade could bring great profit to the Tsar's Treasury or to the private entrepreneur or investor granted an imperial monopoly, provided of course that the state's officers made the monopoly effective by preventing or prosecuting interlopers. His advice to the state in future years on the China trade and other commercial matters

---

Venice and Ragusa after leaving Herzegovina, and as an adult appeared in Constantinople in the 1690's. For additional biographical detail, consult *Bol'shaia sovetskaia entsiklopediia* (2d ed.; Moscow: Gosudarstvennoe Nauchnoe Izdatel'stvo "Bol'shaia Sovetskaia Entsiklopediia," 1949-58), XXV, 467 (cited hereafter as *BSE*); Cahen, *Histoire*, pp. 193-95; Nikolai Nikolaevich Bantysh-Kamenskii, *Obzor vneshnikh snoshenii Rossii (po 1800 god)* (Moscow: Tipografiia E. Lissnera i Iu. Romana, 1894-1902), Pt. 2, pp. 215, 239, 242-44; Benedict H. Sumner, *Peter the Great and the Emergence of Russia* (London: The English Universities Press, Ltd., 1951), p. 78; Bertrand Gille, *Histoire économique et sociale de la Russie du moyen-âge au XXe siècle* (Paris: Payot, 1949), pp. 93-94; Andrievich, *Kratkii ocherk*, Prilozhenie, n. 1, p. 214; Kurts, *Russko-kitaiskie snosheniia*, p. 70; *PSZ*, IV, No. 2510, 821; and Aleksandr Sergeevich Pushkin, *Eugene Onegin, A Novel in Verse*, trans. with a commentary by Vladimir Nabokov ("Bollingen Series," 72 [New York: Pantheon Books, 1964]), III, 419-23.

3. *PSZ*, IV, No. 2510, 821, dated 28 March 1712. Vladislavich and a *konsul* Gutfel' were given on farm the right to export potash (usually a state commercial monopoly prior to this) over a three-year period to any lands abroad, except English and British territories. Of 1000 *bochki* of potash warehoused in Arkhangel'sk, 200 were given free to Vladislavich for his service to Peter I the year before, and the rest he was to pay for at the rate of 15 *efimki* per *berkhovets*. See Pavel Alekseevich Khromov, *Ocherki ekonomiki feodalizma v Rossii* (Moscow: Gospolitizdat, 1957), p. 240. A list of contemporary weights and measures may be found in Appendix I.

reflects this understanding. Then too his political and diplomatic experience in Constantinople, Rome, and the Balkans was useful preparation for the difficult and sensitive task of treating with these *kitaitsy* of whom the Russians yet knew little. To compensate for the one serious flaw in his qualifications, a complete lack of experience in Asian affairs, Vladislavich was given as members of his suite several of the best and most knowledgeable men in Chinese matters then available in the Russian Empire. The most useful of these, it turned out, was Lorents Lange.

Lange, of vague Scandinavian antecedents, the adopted son of a Scottish medical doctor long resident in Russia, had been in Peking intermittently for a decade as agent of the Russian state caravans. Unfortunately we know little of the background, the private life, and the thoughts of this talented man.[4] In later years, as we shall

4. Lorents Lange (sometimes Lavrentii Lang) has been identified variously as a Swede, Dane, and German. V. M. Florinskii, for example, reported him born in Stockholm (N. N. Bantysh-Kamenskii, *Diplomaticheskoe sobranie*, "Pribavleniia," p. 532). Consult also Leonhard Hess Stejneger, *Georg Wilhelm Steller, The Pioneer of Alaskan Natural History* (Cambridge: Harvard University Press, 1936), p. 468, n. 14. Lange was the adopted son of a noted medical doctor, Robert Karlovich Areskin who had come to Russia from Scotland and Paris in 1706 and was privy councillor to the Tsar. A. I. Andreev, citing Stejneger (*ibid.*, pp. 444-45), accepts the interpretation that Lange was a coronet in the Swedish cavalry taken captive at Poltava in 1709 and accepted into Russian service three years later. The extant evidence for this conclusion seems inadequate. Consult Aleksandr Ignat'evich Andreev, *Ocherki po istochnikovedeniiu Sibiri*, Vypusk 2: *XVIII vek (pervaia polovina)* (Moscow-Leningrad: Izd. "Nauka," 1965), p. 267. Andreev failed to report Stejneger's refusal to identify Lange as one Johan Lang in the Swedish forces at Poltava because of the clearly circumstantial evidence available. It seems sensible to conclude that Lange began his service in Russia at least by 1706, when he performed a diplomatic mission to Denmark to appeal to generals and engineers to serve the Tsar. He also spent some time in Berlin improving his German and his scientific knowledge.

Lange was in China as early as 1715, and in 1719 accompanied Lev Izmailov as secretary. After the Izmailov embassy left Peking, Lange remained until he joined Vladislavich's suite. He seems to have been in high favor in St. Petersburg: the French envoy de la Vie in a dispatch of 21 January 1718 noted that after Lange returned from conducting a caravan to Peking, Peter the Great conferred with him on several occasions, each lasting six hours, and "l'a pris en grande affection" (*Sbornik RIO*, XXXIV [1881], 303). On Lange consult also N. N. Bantysh-Kamenskii, *Obzor*, Pt. 1, p. 239; *RBS*, vol. Labzina-Liashenko, 59, wherein he is listed as Ivan-Lorents Lang; and [Lorents Lange], *Le livre de comptes de la caravane Russie à Pékin en 1727-1728*, trans. and commentary by Gaston Cahen (Paris: Félix Alcan, 1911), p. viii, n. 5. In Chinese, Lange is usually rendered Lan-ku.

Even Lange's adoptive father, Areskin, a fascinating figure in his own right, presents biographical problems. He was the sixth son of Sir Charles Erskine of Alva, Baronet (hence Robert's Russian patronymic), although on the son's

see, he rose to the vice-governorship of Irkutsk and State Councillor, and according to one report served on a mission to Constantinople. One thing is certain, there was no man at this time in Russian service, either native or of foreign extraction, who knew Peking or the Chinese better than this "Swede." And his long concern for commercial matters especially recommended him as advisor on the fundamental task of the embassy, the reestablishment of trade. In fact nearly eighteen months prior to the appointment of Vladislavich, Peter the Great through his Senate created a commission on the Chinese border to settle the existing disputes; Lange was to head the commission and to negotiate with Chinese representatives to secure passage for the delayed caravan and to discuss boundary delimitation.[5] For the safety of the frontier Lt. Col. Ivan Dimitrievich Bukhol'ts, recently returned to Siberian service, was to take command of one thousand regular garrison cavalry and one thousand infantry. Neither Lange nor Bukhol'ts were in any sense to be plenipotentiaries: all demands of the Chinese had to be remanded to the Collegium of Foreign Affairs *(Inostrannaia kollegiia)* for firm reply. Within a year the decision had been taken to send out a full plenipotentiary, and by 3 March 1725 Lange was sent an ukaz ordering him to announce this to the Chinese court.[6] Apparently it was a report of July 1724 from

medical indenture papers in Scotland the name was already spelled Areskine. He became chief of the Apothecary Office *(Aptekarskii prikaz)* which eventually was known as the Medical Chancellery *(Meditsinskaia kantseliariia)*. On the doctor, consult Robert Paul (ed.), "Letters and Documents Relating to Robert Erskine, Physician to Peter the Great, Czar of Russia, 1677-1720," *Publications of the Scottish History Society*, XLIV; *Miscellany* (Second Volume) (February, 1904), 371-430; J. L. Stevenson, "Introduction," to John Bell of Antermony, *A Journey From St. Petersburg to Pekin, 1719-22*, ed. by J. L. Stevenson (Edinburgh: The University Press, 1965), pp. 8-9; Douglas K. Reading, *The Anglo-Russian Commercial Treaty of 1734* ("Yale Historical Publications, Miscellany," XXXII [New Haven: Yale University Press, 1938]), p. 72, n. 28; and Archibald Francis Steuart, *Scottish Influences in Russian History From the End of the 16th Century to the Beginning of the 19th Century* (Glasgow: James Maclehouse and Sons, 1913), p. 78.

5. *PSZ*, VII, No. 4429, 208-9, dated 20 January 1724. See also Arkheograficheskaia Komissiia, *Pamiatniki sibirskoi istorii XVIII veka*, II, 447-48, Document 190, dated 31 March 1724.

6. Bantysh-Kamenskii, *Diplomaticheskoe sobranie*, p. 124; E. P. Silin, *Kiakhta v XVIII veke, iz istorii russko-kitaiskoi torgovli* (Irkutsk: OGIZ, Irkutskoe Oblastnoe Izdatel'stvo, 1947), pp. 23-24. Lange immediately sent his own secretary, David Grave, to the border to announce the plenipotentiary to the Chinese, but difficulties with the Chinese border officials with regard to passage of the frontier delayed him, and he left for Peking only at the end of February, 1726.

Lange informing St. Petersburg of the arrival on the frontier of two Chinese ministers proclaiming the pacific intent of the new Manchu emperor (Yung-ch'eng) and his desire to better order the frontier that determined the Russian Senate to send a larger delegation and to appoint Vladislavich.[7]

Other than Vladislavich and Lange, we can do little more than name and identify the remaining members of the embassy. Between the original orders of July 1725 and the crossing of the border in August of the next year, many changes were made in personnel. Of the military commander, Colonel Bukhol'ts, it is known only that he had served for some time in Siberia and was not unacquainted with conditions there.[8] And on the embassy itself he commanded a security force of thirteen hundred infantry and one hundred dragoons. Overall responsibility for the important task of mapping the vague frontier between Siberia and Mongolia and general geographical investigation was given to one Stepan Andreevich Kolychev, a *stol'nik* by rank and Master of Petitions *(reketmeister)* of the Senate. Originally there were to be two geodesists but both the original colleague of Kolychev and his successor died, leaving Kolychev alone in his task, one for which he was well prepared by earlier work in delimiting borders with Poland and Turkey.

Of the rest, there were secretaries of whom Ivan Glazunov was the chief, and an interpreter, plus two language students from the Moscow Slavonic-Greek-Latin Academy, who were to study Chinese and Manchu.[9] In addition to Kolychev two geometrists were taken along the surveying purposes. Religious consolation was administered by the Bishop Innokentii Kul'chitskii and two priests.[10] A

7. *PSZ*, VII, No. 4746, 517-20, dated 5 July 1725.

8. *RBS*, vol. Betankur-Biakster, 564-65. Numerous variations of this Teutonic name exist in the literature: Bukhgol'ts, Buchholz, etc. The Chinese rendered it Pu-ch'ih-ho-ssu.

Governor-General of Siberia Gagarin had sent him earlier on an expedition against the Kalmyks, but for some reason he fell into disfavor. By this time he was again in good grace and was promoted. In 1731 he reached the rank of Brigadier (5th of the military ranks) and after 1728 served as Border Commandant at Selenginsk. By ukaz of 3 March 1740 he was pensioned.

9. These were Luka Voeikov and Ivan Khrestopalov Iablontsev. The latter died on his return from China on 24 December 1727. Vladislavich complained that Voeikov was too old to learn new languages, gave him over to Kolychev for service, and replaced him with one Stepan Pisarev.

10. Innokentii Kul'chitskii was born in Ukraine, enrolled in the Kievan Ecclesiastical Academy, and became a monk in the Kievo-Pecherskii monastery. From 1714 to 1718 he served as prefect of the Moscow Slavonic-Greek-Latin

foreign physician took care of more mundane needs. In all about one hundred men were escorted by about fourteen hundred troops.[11]

The Embassy's Instructions

Such a large and expensive (Cahen estimated a total outlay of one hundred thousand r.) operation must have important substantive objectives, and this one did. Vladislavich's original instructions issued on 5 July 1725, as amended and augmented in the months thereafter, reveal the intent of the Russian Senate and the full powers granted Vladislavich to negotiate and decide on the spot.[12] Vladislavich was designated ambassador extraordinary and minister plenipotentiary *(Chrezvychainyi posol i polnomochnyi ministr)* and within the broad and necessarily somewhat vague limitations placed upon him, he wielded full power to negotiate, to commit the Russian government, and to demand of Siberian officials nearly every means of support he needed. The pretext of the mission was to felicitate the new Manchu emperor, the Yung-ch'eng emperor,[13] and to announce the accession to the throne of Peter's widow, Catherine I. The sum of ten thousand rubles was allocated for gifts for the emperor. Three thousand rubles were earmarked for gifts to high-ranking ministers and personages "manifesting good will" toward the embassy.

The central task of Vladislavich, the one by which all others need to be seen and interpreted, was commercial: to restore the caravan trade and to so arrange commercial relations that the Russian state might reassert its monopoly, or at least control, of this most valuable trade. The original instructions called for the drafting of a new commercial agreement with the Manchus or at

---

Academy and took the opportunity to study philosophy. In 1718 he was transferred to the Aleksandro-Nevskii monastery in St. Petersburg, and three years later was appointed bishop *(episkop)* of Pereiaslavl'. He was posted to China in 1721. Consult Bantysh-Kamenskii, *Diplomaticheskoe sobranie*, p. 533.

11. See Cahen, *Histoire*, pp. 198-200; Andrievich, *Kratkii ocherk*, pp. 138-39.

12. *PSZ*, VII, No. 4746, 517-20, Senate ukaz dated 5 July 1725. Reproduced in Bantysh-Kamenskii, *Diplomaticheskoe sobranie*, pp. 434-56, 480-84. See also the excellent summary in Cahen, *Histoire*, pp. 203-5.

13. In Russian eighteenth-century materials, the Manchu emperor is referred to usually as the "Bogdykhan" or Bogdokhan," a term apparently used by the Kalmyks and Bukharans of the time for the Manchu leader; Baddeley, *Russia, Mongolia, China*, II, 442, n. L.

least a renewal of the trade that had been interrupted. The state caravans must travel again to Peking, preferably without the payment of any duties or taxes, and if at all possible permission should be obtained for a permanent commercial resident (consul or agent) in Peking, who would of course be Lange. All means had to be devoted to this end, including if necessary wooing the Jesuit advisers of Yung-ch'eng by promising them the long-sought privileges of free correspondence through Russia and uninhibited travel across Siberia. Chinese permission for Russian merchants to trade freely throughout China should be sought, although certainly the prospects were not bright. Vladislavich was ordered secretly to gather a wide variety of commercial intelligence: the comparative advantages of the several routes and methods of transportation across Siberia, the extent of Chinese trade with Western European merchants at Canton, including the items of exchange and their prices, the cost of transport from Canton to Peking (an extremely important factor in Russian competition with her rivals in Canton), the weights, measures and monies in use in China, and the nature of Chinese trade with Japan.[14] In general Vladislavich was cautioned that, whatever arrangements were negotiated, trade should be as unfettered as possible and, if the Manchus insisted on customs duties, they should not be levied as high as previously.

The delimitation, definition, and marking of the frontier, although invariably stressed by recent writers, were in fact only the second order of priorities in the Russian scheme of things; Vladislavich was to strive to put off to some future time the delimitation of the border. Were the Manchus to insist on delimitation of the unsettled frontier west of the Argun, Vladislavich was to concede it in the interests of the all-important trade. Under no circumstances was he to cede the territories of Transbaikalia, Udinsk, Selenginsk, Nerchinsk, or the Irtysh territory in the west.[15] All valuable lands, especially those with gold or silver mines, or of potential military worth, were not to be ceded. Actual demarcation was to be done by a joint Russo-Chinese commission. To strengthen the Russian hand in this work, a detailed map was to be drawn, which

14. In addition to these commercial matters, the secret instructions asked for data on the military posture and dispositions of China.

15. A rumor was current to the effect that the Chinese intended to build a stronghold on the upper reaches of the Irtysh, although it did not come up in the discussions. The Chinese still did not have effective control of the region; the *Kontaisha* of the Dzhungars held sway. Bantysh-Kamenskii, *Diplomaticheskoe sobranie*, p. 484; Kurts, *Russko-kitaiskie snosheniia*, p. 70.

finally had to be done at the border, since no adequate survey of the region existed.[16] Dissatisfied with the first maps drawn by an Irkutsk surveyor, one Petr Skobel'tsyn, chosen by the Siberian governor-general (only a single river, the Argun, was shown), Vladislavich had a second map prepared by him and three other surveyors, who were sent to the border in the spring of 1726. Skobel'tsyn and his three assistants explored and mapped the almost unknown Mongolian frontier, the upper Enisei, the lower basin of the Selenga, and the upper waters of the Amur, and even the established border all the way to the sea.[17] They were ordered to take particular care to observe any Buddhist markers which might substantiate Chinese claims to lands in Transbaikalia, claims which the Russians intended to resist firmly.

The third major issue was that of deserters, especially the Dzhungars and other Mongols who evaded Chinese armies or authority by fleeing to Siberia and Russian asylum. The Chinese negotiators had to be made to understand Russia's good intentions; the ambassador was to refer to a Petrine ukaz of 22 July 1722 which had ordered that such persons be returned to Chinese dominions, to Fefilov's arrangements for the extradiction of eighty-four deserters, and to Lange's returning them in August of 1724. The Collegium of Foreign Affairs and the Senate seemed aware that this issue was by far the most critical in the minds of the Manchus—assuredly informed to this effect by innumerable reports from Lange and others at the border. The extension of Manchu military and political power over Mongolia and Dzhungaria was not easily possible until the borders were sealed off and deserters promptly extradited. Fugitives already in Russian territory were not to be returned if possible, although this last point Vladislavich might concede if the resumption of trade relations was threatened.

Fourth, to eliminate the perenially sensitive issue of protocol in correspondence with the Chinese, Vladislavich was to work out with them some scheme of equality whereby state offices and officials of comparatively equivalent rank and stature be designated to correspond on all problems. His instructions here were intentionally loose; he was to negotiate whatever modus vivendi was possible.

16. Sergei Mikhailovich Solov'ev, *Istoriia Rossii s drevneishikh vremen* (2d ed.; St. Petersburg: "Obshchestvennaia Pol'za," 1894-95), IV, 1135. See also Silin, *Kiakhta*, p. 26.

17. The details of this map have been preserved in a copy by one Mikhail Zinov'ev; Cahen, *Nouvelles Archives des Missions scientifiques et littéraires*, pp. 164-65.

Finally, the embassy was to attempt the entry into Peking, secretly if necessary, of the Bishop of Pereiaslavl', Innokentii Kul'-chitskii, and to obtain permission for him (or at least for several common priests) to remain in the city to carry on parishional work among the Russians and Russian descendents in Peking, which endeavour had been active since the seventeenth century, and also to make pastoral visits to the provinces; in other words, to evangelize in modest fashion. The Bishop had been waiting in Selenginsk and Irkutsk since mid-1722 with his small suite of two priests, two deacons, and three lay servants, denied entry by Peking officials until all matters in dispute were settled. If this solicitude for the spiritual welfare of Orthodox communicants in Peking proved unconvincing to the Chinese, the Bishop was to be left at the border (in the end he was, and replaced by the lower-ranking archimandrite Antonii Platkovskii on the request of Vladislavich of 31 August 1726[18]) and in the negotiations the minimum to be demanded was the concession of a parcel of land in Peking on which to build a church, the expense to be defrayed by St. Petersburg. In addition two young students were to be permitted to stay in Peking to study Chinese and Manchu.

The embassy's instructions overall contained very little that was new. Many parts of them, particularly the orders from the Commerce Collegium *(Kommerts-kollegiia)*, duplicated the instruc-

18. V. M. Florinskii insists that Jesuit "intrigue" blocked the passage of Kul'chitskii to Peking, but the evidence is slim; Bantysh-Kamenskii, *Diplomaticheskoe sobranie*, "Pribavleniia," p. 533. He remained in Selenginsk through 1725 until an ukaz of the Holy Synod directed him to Irkutsk, where he lived in the Irkutsk Vosnesenskii monastery. There he established a school for youths of all ranks and stations, and evangelized widely among the native Irkuts, Tungus and Buriats. He became known as the Apostle of Siberia. Serge Bolshakoff, *The Foreign Missions of the Russian Orthodox Church* (London: Society for Promoting Christian Knowledge, 1943), p. 64.

Platkovskii, archimandrite of Irkutsk, was skilled in the Mongol language and well acquainted with border affairs. He had accompanied Izmailov to Peking and was likely to prove of more value to the embassy than Kul'chitskii. He had recently (1725) established a school in Irkutsk for the study of Mongol, using native lecturers and informants. Several students of this school later distinguished themselves, particularly Illarion Kalinovich Rossokhin *(infra)* who was subsequently sent to Peking to learn Manchu and Chinese as well. The school survived until 1740 or 1741. Mikhail Nikolaevich Tikhomirov (ed.), *Ocherki istorii istoricheskoi nauki v SSSR* (Moscow: Izdatel'stvo Akademii Nauk SSSR, 1955), I, 514-15; N. P. Shastina, "Istoriia izucheniia Mongol'skoi narodnoi respubliki (Kratkii ocherk)," in *Mongol'skaia narodnaia respublika, sbornik statei*, ed. I. Ia. Zlatkin (Moscow: Izdatel'stvo Akademii Nauk SSSR, 1952), p. 18.

tions given earlier to Izmailov. In two regards only were substantial additions made: the delimitation of the mutual frontier and the arrangements for the extradiction of deserters. These additions, it turned out, were of the utmost importance, and they were the matters of uppermost consideration to the Chinese. As indicated above, Peking authorities were distressed about the lack of order in trading operations in the Chinese capital and elsewhere, but even this was subordinated to their main concern—the control of Central Asia. The Governing Senate and the Collegium of Foreign Affairs had done well to expand Izmailov's powers and instructions; otherwise the cherished trade with the East would not have been restored.

The Preparations and the Negotiations

In the late spring and summer months of 1726, Ambassador Vladislavich soon learned that lengthy orders from St. Petersburg were not always immediately translatable into effective and intelligent action two thousand miles to the east. Not only did he see fit to request the replacement of the Bishop Kul'chitskii and to order completely new geographic surveys and maps, but a multitude of other problems, some trifling but many critical, faced him swiftly one after another. Two months after his arrival in March, he was informed of the death of Stepan Mikhailovich Tret'iakov, merchant and director of the state caravan halted since 1724 at Strelka on the Chikoi river.[19] He selected the chief sworn-appraiser of the caravan, Dmitrii Molokov, in his place.[20] Then word arrived from the Chinese that no caravans, state or private, would be permitted to travel all the way to Peking (prior to the negotiation of outstanding differences), but to go only to Urga to trade, and then no more than three hundred carts per year. This was a severe disappointment to Vladislavich, who had hoped to arrange the immediate departure of the caravan, and put him on notice that the Chinese were not prepared to conclude an agreement at any price. Already in May, Vladislavich reported from Irkutsk that as

19. Tret'iakov died on 2 May 1726.

20. Molokov was of a lower rank of serving men *(boiarskie deti)* of Tobol'sk. He was apparently one of only six sworn-appraisers at the time, although normally about ten were employed; Kurts, *Gosudarstvennaia monopoliia*, p. 34; Lange, *Le livre de comptes*, p. x; and Cahen, *Histoire*, p. 229. The initial appointment was only temporary, but was confirmed in an Imperial ukaz to the Senate of 30 December 1726; *PSZ*, VII, No. 4994, 722-24.

far as he could judge at that time the Chinese court was "little inclined toward a reestablishment of commerce and pleasant correspondence with the Russian empire," at least until the problems of deserters and theft of cattle across the border were settled to their satisfaction.[21] And he was given to understand by Lange and other Russian officers at the border that any mutually acceptable solution of the deserter matter "will not be without difficulty," and he so reported to the Collegium of Foreign Affairs.

As if these presentiments of strenuous times ahead were not enough, the Siberian Governor-General Dolgorukii reported to St. Petersburg that Chinese armies were gathering for another major strike against the Dzhungar *Kontaisha.* The meaning of this for the weak and deteriorated Russian forts near the border was obvious: Vladislavich reported that the forts of Nerchinsk, Udinsk, and Selenginsk were in extremely bad shape, and artillery and ammunition supplies were in a state of complete disorder. Not only were these rude forts vulnerable to the attack of Mongol or Chinese regular or irregular troops, but they could hardly be expected effectively to suppress thievery and other deceptions practiced by the merchants who traded in the vicinity. The border had to be strengthened and, within the broad discretionary powers granted him, Vladislavich ordered the local governor to refurbish the forts.[22] If funds available from local poll taxes were insufficient, soldiers, serving men, convicts, and any other local dwellers were impressed or induced to do the work. When he finally ascended the Selenga to the frontier in August of 1726, Vladislavich observed the poor physical location of the important Selenginsk fort, and requested that it be built anew at a spot on that river chosen by him. He picked a place on the "high road" where water was more plentiful. An imperial ukaz of 30 December 1726 confirmed the request and ordered soldiers under the command of Colonel Bukhol'ts to do the work and the Military Collegium *(Voennaia kollegiia)* to dispatch immediately an engineer and an artillery

21. Protocol of the Supreme Privy Council of 28 September 1726; *Sbornik RIO*, LVI (1887), 146. Report of Vladislavich from Irkutsk dated 26 May 1726.

22. *Ibid.*, 149. The authority to demand material support from the governor-general of Siberia was given in a Senate decree of 19 August 1725. It was followed up on 15 September 1726, evidently on recommendation of Vladislavich, by a Supreme Privy Council decree that Vladislavich and Governor Dolgorukii provide adequately for the safety of Siberia by building border palisades and strongpoints, and transferring artillery to the frontier; *ibid.*, LXXXIV (1893), 57, 129.

officer to aid.[23] This time the fort was to be permanent, of stone and earth; time was short and could not be wasted on crude and depressing little frontier *ostrogi*.

Vladislavich passed quickly through Selenginsk, continued up the river to the small settlement called Strelka ("Spit" or "Cape") on the Chikoi stream, where the Molokov caravan had long waited. (He found that town also to be in poor shape.) One more effort to secure permission for the caravan to accompany him had to be made; from Selenginsk he sent an aide, Captain Miklashevskii, to the border to meet with the Chinese officials who were to escort the Russian to Peking. The Captain was to announce his imminent arrival. Vladislavich hurried on to the rendezvous and to another disappointment. The first meeting was on the banks of the small river Bur on 25 August. The Chinese repeated the proscription against commercial caravan travel to Peking, at least without a pass from Peking, and there was no choice now but for the embassy to push on by itself. In just over a week, Vladislavich and his embassy of 120, guarded and escorted by fourteen hundred troops under Bukhol'ts, crossed over into Mongol territory, and the great adventure was finally underway.

Actually Vladislavich obviously assumed, even before meeting the Chinese, that the Molokov caravan would temporarily remain, for at Strelka he ordered it back to a better waiting spot (Selenginsk). Also he was completely aware that until private merchants were effectively prevented from carrying Siberian furs to Peking, directly or indirectly, little or no profitable state trade was feasible. In his last long report to his superiors in St. Petersburg, written on 31 August, Vladislavich requested renewed prohibition against private trade in peltry across the frontier while the caravan was in Peking.[24] The Tsar responded with an ukaz to the Senate on 30 December 1726, which prohibited private traffic in peltry to Urga, Naun, and other markets under Chinese hegemony "in order that Our crown caravan will not suffer loss in sales of peltry in China."[25] Other than peltry, private merchants might continue to export whatever legal goods they wished, on payment of the existing customs duties. At this moment at least, the Ambassador

23. *PSZ*, VII, No. 4994, 724-25, dated 30 December 1726. Also "Zhurnal Verkhovnago tainago soveta," No. 264, 21 December 1726, in *Sbornik RIO*, LVI (1887), 567.

24. Kurts, *Russko-kitaiskie otnosheniia*, p. 71. Protocol of the Supreme Privy Council, No. 274, 23 December 1726, in *Sbornik RIO*, LVI (1887), 583-85.

25. *PSZ*, VII, No. 4994, 722-24.

seems to have had little faith in the profitability of state caravans to Peking. As early as May he had doubts that the Chinese would in the end permit renewal of trade directly to Peking and suggested that in such case state peltry be shipped to Urga, fifty thousand rubles worth each year, and new stocks not dispatched until the earlier shipments were completely sold.[26] His August report bemoaned the fact that private Russian merchants now carried such a great amount of peltry to Urga and elsewhere that more was exported privately each year than was carried in two state caravans! In customs duties on these goods alone, the state had lost twenty thousand rubles since the Chinese suspended trade. The lack of cooperation from the Chinese in sealing off the frontier, the weaknesses of Russian frontier organization, the unlimited inventiveness of private merchants in avoiding state officials and customs payments, and the surfeit of privately transported furs in Peking, all these left the future of state caravan trade very dim at best. But then one must wait and see what arrangements might be made with the Chinese.

The journey from the banks of the Bur, across the Mongol steppes and the sparse Gobi desert, to the gates at Kalgan and Peking was as uneventful and comfortable as could be expected in those days in those lands, and the first echelons of the caravan arrived in Peking on 21 October 1726. After a relatively brief wait of two weeks, the Ambassador of Her Imperial Majesty, Empress of All the Russias, was received in the court of the Heavenly Emperor and all proprieties were maintained. It was not long, however, before the Russians complained loudly of mistreatment. Vladislavich and Lange objected that their movements were carefully circumscribed, that their quarters were guarded constantly by soldiers, that all the Russians housed in the Russian House were sealed in every night, that the Chinese provided them with insufficient food ("starved"), that they were given only debilitating salt water to drink, that they were all threatened with prison were they not more tractable in negotiations. During the discussions, Vladislavich himself did in fact fall ill, together with half of the suite (some writers then attributed the malady to the salt water), but a story with the ring of authenticity describes Yung-ch'eng hurriedly dispatching his own physician to minister to the chief Russian.[27]

26. *Sbornik RIO*, LVI (1887), 150.

27. Petr B. Shumakher, "Nashi snosheniia s Kitaem (s 1657 po 1805)," *Rus-*

If the Chinese resorted cunningly and deviously "to obstinacy, to subterfuge, and even to intimidation," Russian tactics in balance seem no more genteel. Cahen reports that prior to leaving St. Petersburg, Vladislavich leased his house to the French Ambassador Campredon and received from him a letter of introduction to the Jesuit missionary Father Dominique Parrenin.[28] In Peking Vladislavich had a pleasant and fruitful interview with the skilled Jesuit and secured a letter to the Grand Secretary *(Ta-hsueh-shih)* Ma-ch'i (Maci), a member of the Manchu Bordered Yellow Banner and long involved in relations with the Russians in Peking and on the border. Father Parrenin then served as something of an intermediary and also helped with the interpreting.[29] Ma-ch'i on the other hand seems to have been even more useful; he apparently kept the Russians accurately and well informed of discussions and affairs within the Chinese court and among the Chinese negotiators, and this in spite of a great reputation for incorruptibility. At least Vladislavich thought highly enough of his aid to enrich him to the extent of one thousand rubles worth of peltry, and Father Parrenin for his intercession was awarded one hundred rubles.[30] All this is slightly euphemistic; Vladislavich successfully utilized ill-disguised bribery to secure his ends.

The actual negotiations, in spite of these questionable tactics on both sides, were terribly long and difficult, and at time stormy. Some thirty separate conferences were held over a six-month period. The main Chinese negotiators were highly placed, competent, and well informed: Ch'a-pi-na or Ch'ia-pi-na (Chabina in Russian,

---

skii arkhiv, XVII, Bk. 2 (1879), 176; Kurts, *Russko-kitaiskie snosheniia,* p. 72; Cahen, *Histoire,* p. 214 (quoting from Vladislavich's long report of 10 May 1727). The French ambassador reported to Paris on 27 January 1729 that Vladislavich was in Peking "comme aux arrêts sans avoir la liberté d'aller voir les manufactures; son hôtel était fermé en dehors pendant la nuit et entouré de troupes" and during the day all members of the embassy were accompanied on their rounds by Chinese soldiers; *Sbornik RIO,* LXXV (1891), 302. Late in the negotiations the Chinese even threatened to hold the crown caravan in Peking as hostage, if Vladislavich did not cede on the territorial issue. He is reputed to have replied that the Swedes lost five provinces and more than 100 towns in trying to seize one province, and that the Persians, despoiling one Russian caravan, paid with the loss of five provinces and more than ten cities; Bantysh-Kamenskii, *Diplomaticheskoe sobranie,* pp. 148-49.

28. Cahen, *Histoire,* p. 212.

29. Parrenin is said to have used a special code for his correspondence with the Russians, although it may simply have been Latin.

30. Hummel, *Eminent Chinese,* I, 560-61; Cahen, *Histoire,* pp. 215, 219, lxiv-lxv. Also Kurts, *Russko-kitaiskie snosheniia,* p. 72, and Solov'ev, *Istoriia,* IV, 1139.

often Tschabina in western languages) was a Grand Secretary *(Ta-hsueh-shih)* and member of the Chinese "foreign ministry," the *Li-fan-yuan*; T'e-ku-t'e (Tegout) also a Grand Secretary and President *(Shang-shu)* of the *Li-fan-yuan*; and as a perfect colleague in these meetings, T'u-li-shen, likely the most knowledgeable man in the Manchu court on matters Russian.[31] In the end agreement was reached, agreement, as shall be seen, incorporating the main wishes and needs of both sides. By 21 March this accord was substantially complete, and the decision was made to move the final meetings to the frontier to deal with the specific problems of delimitation of the Siberian-Mongol border and to set out markers on that border. There is a romantic little story, probably apocryphal, that Vladislavich in audience with the Emperor asked for the move from Peking and received it as a consequence of the Emperor's magnanimity and his solicitude for the Russian's health: "Your Majesty, you cured me of illness, cure [me] of grief: permit that the affair, much presented and incompleted in Peking, be finished on the border."[32] More practical considerations undoubtedly led to the move: not only was the border little known to the Russians, save for the hurried surveying done in the summer, the Chinese had charted it no more fully. Also the border was the logical place to draft the final version of the delimitation agreements. And for the Russians it would be easier there to balance the obviously strong hand of the Chinese in Peking.

Shortly after a final audience with the Emperor on 2 April 1727, the Russians left Peking (on the twenty-third). The secretary Glazunov was sent ahead to prepare the meeting place on the border fixed on the stream Bur, roughly one hundred versts south of Selenginsk. Vladislavich shrewdly assembled there a substantial military force calculated to impress the comparatively powerless Manchu negotiators. In all nearly eight hundred military or para-military men—a company of dragoons, four hundred Buriat irregulars and many Russian serving men—faced the Manchus.[33] Conferences began on 23 June and ended on 16 August, after eight major and hectic sessions. So tempestuous were they at times that suspension was threatened, but the distinguished Prince Lung-k'e-to (Lungkoto), President of the *Li-fan-yuan* intermittently

31. *Shuo-fang pei-ch'eng,* ed. Ho Ch'iu-t'ao (1881), ch. 37.16b-17a. Cited hereafter as *SFPC*.

32. Shumakher, *Russkii arkhiv,* XVII, Bk. 2 (1879), 176.

33. Andrievich, *Kratkii ocherk,* p. 140.

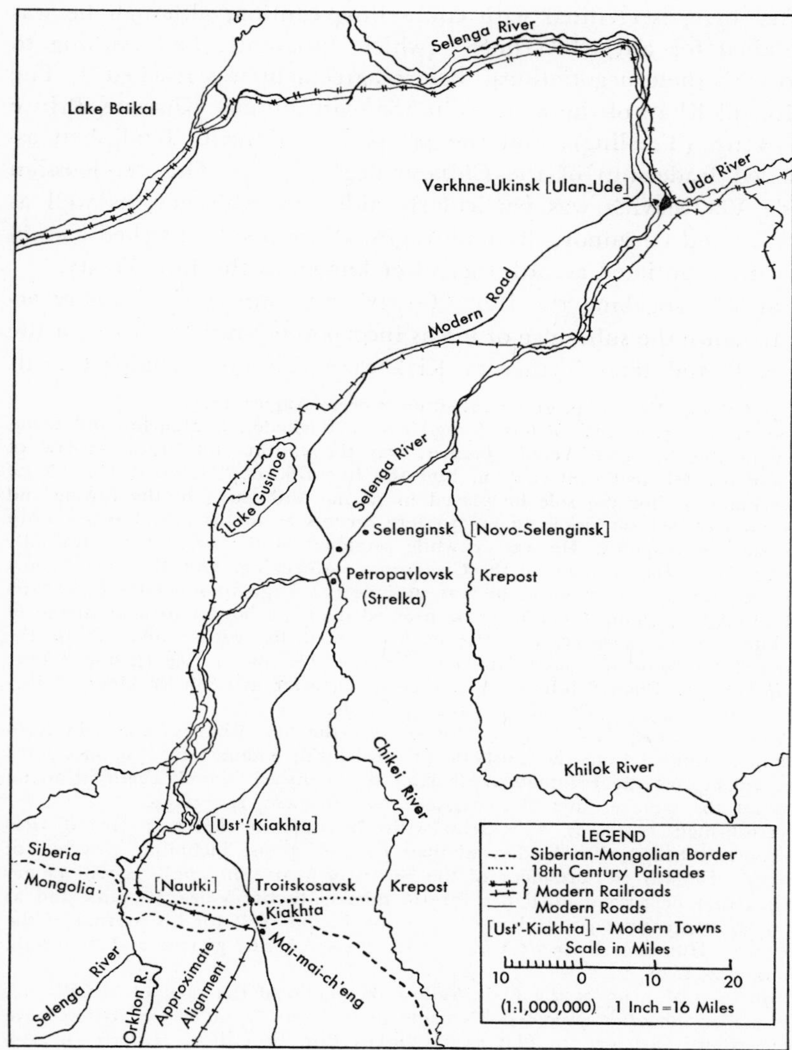

Figure 1. Map of the Kiakhta Region.

after 1720, is credited with counselling caution, although he was recalled for alleged "crimes" (which apparently had nothing to do with these negotiations) before agreement was reached.[34] The Mongol Khan of the Sain Noin (San-yin no-yen) Khanate, Prince Tsereng (Ts'e-ling), and the peripatetic Manchu T'u-li-shen assumed leadership of the Chinese negotiators.[35] On the Russian side Vladislavich was particularly aided by Kolychev, as well as Lange and Glazunov. By mid-August the two sides reached a stubbornly negotiated accord, thereafter known as the Bur Treaty.

Strictly speaking the Bur "Treaty" was only a preliminary accord, since the substance of it was incorporated into Article 3 of the overall and later Treaty of Kiakhta.[36] The Bur compact dealt

34. Cahen, *Histoire,* p. 218; recalled on 8 or 10 August 1727.

35. *SFPC,* 37.16b-17a. Prince Lung-k'e-to (Lungkodo), a Manchu and member of the Bordered Yellow Banner, was the cousin and brother-in-law of K'ang-hsi. He had conferred on him the honorific of "Maternal Uncle" (of the Emperor) for the role he played in raising Shih-tsung to the throne and this has caused confusion among western writers as to his actual relationship to the new emperor. He was erstwhile president of the *Li-fan-yuan* (initially in 1720) and commandant of the Gendarmerie of Peking. Out of favor at court in 1725 for obscure reasons, he was stationed at Urga to supervise the affairs of the Altai region. From Urga he proceeded to the border to take charge of Peking's negotiators, i.e. he was "again allowed to redeem himself" in the eyes of the Manchu court; Hummel, *Eminent Chinese,* I, 552-54, and *Ch'ing shih-kao,* ed. Chao Erh-hsun *et al.* (cited hereafter as *CSK*) (Peking: Ch'ing-shih-kuan, 1927-28), Chuan 301, Biography 82.

Prince Tsereng (Ts'e-ling), a Mongol, was the first Khan of the Sain Noin Khanate formed from the Tushetu (T'u-hsieh-t'u) Khanate in 1725 in reward for aid against the Dzhungars. He later distinguished himself again in action against the same enemy; Hummel, *Eminent Chinese,* II, 756-57.

T'u-li-shen (Tulisen), a Manchu with the rank of *shih-lang* (board vice-president), had earlier held a number of high posts, including governor of Shansi. He was vice-president of the Board of War *(Ping pu).* It will be recalled that he accompanied the 1712-15 mission to the Volga Turguts, and as a consequence gained considerable attention in the West for his journal of the journey; Hummel, *Eminent Chinese,* II, 784-87; *SFPC,* 37.17a; and Klaproth, *Mémoires,* I, 28, n. 4.

Ssu-ke, a Manchu of the Plain Yellow Banner, held the rank of "Earl" *(po).* Since his rank often preceded his name in the sources, numerous writers have inadvertently referred to him as Po-ssu-ke. Consult Cahen, *Histoire,* p. 219, n. 3.

36. A thoroughly scholarly discussion of the several extant texts of the treaties negotiated in 1727-28 (the Treaty of the Bur, the two supplementary protocols, and the overall Treaty of Kiakhta) is to be found in Agnes Fang-chih Ch'en, "Chinese Frontier Diplomacy: Kiakhta Boundary Treaties and Agreements," *Yenching Journal of Social Sciences,* IV (February, 1949), 151-205. Miss Ch'en's discussion is concerned in the first instance with the authenticity of the Chinese texts printed in several treaty collections, all of which she deems to be later translations (some full and useful, others abbreviated and interesting mainly

largely with the sketchy delimitation of the border, and provision was made for the actual marking of the long frontier and the determination of the allegiance of certain border peoples, particularly those in the Uriankhai (Wu-liang-hai) region. Joint border commissions immediately set out to the east and the west of the Bur to erect stone markers or cairns (*obo* in Russian, *o-po* in Chinese). Eastward went Ivan Glazunov and Semen Kireev for the Russians, and Hu-pi-t'u (Khubitu) and Na-yen-t'ai (Nagitai); westward, Stepan A. Kolychev, Ssu-ke, Pao-fu, and Araptan (E-erh-pu-tan).[37] Upon return of these commissions two protocols supplementary to the Bur accord were concluded and signed, stipulating the precise locations of the sixty-three markers to the east and the twenty-four to the west.[38]

---

as curiosities) and therefore of generally dubious value. The Bur or Burinskii Treaty *(Pu-lien-ssu ch'i yueh)* was signed by Vladislavich for Russia and by Ts'e-ling, Ssu-ke, and T'u-li-shen for China on 20 August 1727. Copies in Russian, Latin, Mongol, and Manchu are preserved in Moscow archives. The first Chinese translation was not made until 1907; Miss Ch'en considers the list of stone markers appended to the Treaty to be a separate document signed two days after the general agreement (known as the Kiakhta Obo Treaty of 22 August 1727); *ibid.*, 183. No separate Russian version of this document was made, however. For easily accessible Russian and Latin versions of the various treaties and documents, see Inspectorate General of Customs at Shanghai, Statistical Department, *Treaties, Conventions, Etc. Between China and Foreign States* (2d ed.; Shanghai: Inspectorate General of Customs, 1917), I, 14-17; Ministerstvo Inostrannykh Del, *Sbornik dogovorov Rossii s Kitaem, 1689-1881 gg.* (St. Petersburg: Tip. I. Akademii Nauk, 1889), pp. 11-26 (which includes Russian, Latin, and Mongol texts, plus a Chinese translation from the Mongol); and *PSZ*, VII, No. 5143, 840-41.

37. Bantysh-Kamenskii, *Diplomaticheskoe sobranie*, p. 242; Andrievich, *Kratkii ocherk*, p. 141; and *Sbornik RIO*, LXIX (1889), 299-300.

38. Sychevskii, "Istoricheskaia zapiska o kitaiskoi granitse, Sostavlennaia sovetnikom Troitsko-Savskogo pogranichnogo pravleniia Sychevskim v 1846 g.," V. N. Basnin (ed.), *Chteniia v Imperatorskom Obshchestve istorii i drevnostei rossiiskikh pri Moskovskom universitete* (Moscow: Obshchestvo Istorii i Drevnostei Rossiiskikh pri Moskovskom Universitete, 1846-1918), Bk. 2 (April-June, 1875), 19-20 cited hereafter as *Chteniia OIDR*. The boundary markers *east* of the meeting place (the Selenga river, near modern Kiakhta) were listed in the agreement known usually as the "Treaty of Abagaitu" *(A-pa-chia-i-t'u yueh)*, exchanged at Abagaitu Hill, the easternmost *obo* on the source of the Argun 12 October 1727). Sixty-three markers were provided for, rather than the forty-eight stipulated in August. Russian guardposts (*karauly* in Russian, *ch'ia-lun* or *k'a-lun* in Chinese, often *karun* in western language materials) were to be built opposite the *obo*, with guards selected from the Russian frontier subjects. Originally Buriats usually served as guards; later Cossacks were also settled along the border for this purpose. Russian buildings south of the *obo* were to be destroyed and Russian subjects transferred northward. The protocol was signed and exchanged in Russian and Mongol; *Treaties, Con-*

The Treaty in its final form fixed approximately twenty-six hundred miles of the Mongolia-Siberia frontier. From a marker placed near the small rivulet Kiakhta the line ran east to the source of the Argun, i.e. to the westernmost demarcated point of the Treaty of Nerchinsk, and west to the Shabina Dabeg range (Sha-pi-na-i ling), north of the Altai mountains and beyond which neither Russians nor Chinese knew or really controlled. The long frontier between the greater empires of the Middle Kingdom and the Tsardom was now fixed, with small exceptions, from the Sea of Okhotsk to the regions still under Dzhungarian sway and so it was to remain, with small changes, until after the middle of the nineteenth century. But a thin line on a map and small piles of stone hardly sealed the frontier and solved the fundamental problems of settling the nomadic herders of the region and identifying their loyalties and tax obligations.[39] The protocols additionally provided that Russian guardposts be placed opposite the stone cairns and that Russian dwellings and hamlets in the immediate vicinity of the cairns be destroyed and the inhabitants relocated farther north.[40] Save for the border guards, all trespassers could be taken *ipso facto* as illegal. By no means did these arrangements

ventions, Etc., I, 18-24; *PSZ*, VII, No. 5180, 876-82; Ch'en, *Yenching Journal of Social Studies*, IV (February, 1949), 183-85.

The boundary markers *west* of the meeting place were listed in the agreement known as the "Treaty of Selenginsk" *(Se-leng-e yueh)*, exchanged on the Selenga or the Bur on 27 October 1727. Forty-eight *obo* were placed on twenty-four sites, one Chinese and one Russian marker for each. Border guard-posts were also provided for; Russian guards were to be chosen from among the local Siberian tribes, as in the Treaty of Abagaitu. This Treaty was signed by Vladislavich and Ts'e-ling, and was exchanged in Russian, Mongol, and Manchu; *Treaties, Conventions, Etc.*, I, 25-27; *PSZ*, VII, No. 5189, 887-90; Ch'en, *Yenching Journal of Social Studies*, IV (February, 1949), 190-91. For a detailed specification of the responsibilities of the selected tribes for each guard-post, consult Sychevskii, *Chteniia OIDR*, Bk. 2 (April-June, 1875), 20-25.

For lists of the surviving border posts in the later eighteenth and nineteenth centuries, consult the following: Grigorii Efimovich Grumm-Grzhimailo, *Zapadnaia Mongoliia i uriankhaiskii krai* (Leningrad: Izdanie Uchebnogo Komiteta Mongol'skoi Narodnoi Respubliki, 1926), II, 825-28; Korsak, *Istoriko-statisticheskoe obozrenie*, p. 53; Ministerstvo Torgovli i Promyshlennosti, *Sbornik torgovykh dogovorov zakliuchennykh Rossieiu s inostrannymi gosudarstvami*, Nikolai Vladimirovich Verkhovskii (ed.) (St. Petersburg: Izd. Otdela Torgovli, 1912), p. 315. For description of the posts, see Klaproth, *Mémoires*, I, 8-27.

39. Some native tribes were split by the division and suffered from dual obligations for a time; Klaproth, *Mémoires*, I, 10.

40. Silin, *Kiakhta*, pp. 34-35. In reality only fifteen posts, served by the men of five to ten iurts each, were maintained in the first half of the eighteenth century.

end the vexing problem of deserters, runaways, defectors, and smugglers, but they were a beginning, and none of the other very real accomplishments of the negotiations were possible without this beginning.

After the Bur negotiations were finished, Vladislavich retired northward to Petropavlovsk, where Molokov had long waited with the caravan. Vladislavich ordered the caravan to Peking, as the Chinese had earlier agreed, and instructed it to hurry on its way, to remain no more than forty days in the Urga market. He also issued more orders with regard to fortification of the frontier and the building of a new border trading post, which took its name from the stream Kiakhta. Shortly, too, word came from St. Petersburg that the likeable Catherine had died, and young Peter II had risen to the throne of the double eagle. This was certain to delay final ratification and exchange of the treaty.

Vladislavich returned to the border to await final exchange ceremonies. But when in early November 1727 a Latin draft of the overall treaty which had been in Chinese hands since March arrived it did not conform with Russian understandings of the Peking accord in several small but sensitive points.[41] Vladislavich flatly refused to accept it. After trying some intimidation which seemed not to get results, he went over the heads of the Chinese negotiators and sent a strong complaint to Peking with Lange who accompanied the caravan. Still another long Siberian winter was endured before the Treaty of Kiakhta was formally completed; the final ratified copies in Manchu, Russian, and Latin were not exchanged until 14 June 1728, even though they carried the date of Yung-ch'eng's ratification, 21 October 1727. The mission which began nearly three years earlier was now discharged.

The final treaty, its several parts and versions collectively known as the Treaty of Kiakhta, contains eleven articles, or rather six major subjects.[42]

41. Cahen, *Histoire*, pp. 219-20. The border delimitation did not agree with the Bur Treaty and the use of the title of the Manchu Emperor unnecessarily inferred the subordinate status of the Tsaritsa. Noting that the Chinese negotiators did not seem in a hurry to contact Peking on these disputes, Vladislavich bypassed them by sending a complaint to the Chinese court through Lange who was en route with the Molokov caravan; Kurts, *Russko-kitaiskie snosheniia*, p. 73.

42. The Treaty of Kiakhta *(Ch'ia-k'e-t'u chih yueh)* is available now in numerous copies, versions, and translations. Since Chinese was not an official language of the Treaty, all Chinese versions are of comparatively late translation. The original copies in Russian and Latin signed by the negotiators

The Treaty

Eternal Peace

Article 1 proclaimed eternal or perpetual peace *(vechnyi mir)* between the two greatest empires of the world; the subjects of both should be so governed and disposed that no occasion for dispute should arise. The Treaty made *no* specific reference to the Dzhungarian wars of China, nor to Russian neutrality in them, in spite of the obvious influence of this factor on the Chinese decision to suspend trade in 1722. However the weight of not only this article but those mentioned below dealing with the return of border violators is that Russia would in fact withhold aid or succor from the Dzhungarians.

Delimitation of the Frontier

As we had mentioned, the border delimitation accords of the Bur treaty were included in the general Treaty of Kiakhta as Article 3, and excellently accurate maps and topographical descriptions of the frontier were exchanged.[43] There was some question at the time and there has been some debate since then as to whether or not the Russians secured strips of territory which in fact they had not held or had no claim to earlier.[44] The argument is largely senseless;

---

were preserved in the Moscow archives, and have been published several times since: *PSZ,* VIII, No. 5286, 49-53; Bantysh-Kamenskii, *Diplomaticheskoe sobranie,* pp. 365-73; Kurts, *Russko-kitaiskie snosheniia,* pp. 78-82, n. 22; *Treaties, Conventions, Etc.,* I, 50-60. For French and English translations see *Archives diplomatiques; recueil mensuel de diplomatie, d'histoire et de droit international,* I, 276; John M. Maki (comp.), *Selected Documents, Far Eastern International Relations (1689-1951)* (Seattle: University of Washington Press, 1951), pp. 2-6.

There is no uniformity in the literature on the precise terminology to apply to the various agreements concluded in 1727-28. All writers agree that the Treaty of Kiakhta, dated 21 October 1728, is properly termed a "treaty." The provisions of the "Treaty of the Bur," included in substance in Article 3 of the Treaty of Kiakhta, have been designated a treaty, a convention, a preliminary agreement, and a protocol; the "Treaties" of Abagaitu and Selenginsk have been similarly treated.

43. Cahen, *Nouvelles Archives,* pp. 164-65, 173-74.

44. See, e.g., "Russo-Chinese Relations (112-1912)," *Edinburgh Review,* CCXV (January, 1912), 201. Hsü is typical of a number of recent works: "For Russia acquisition of land had always been a cardinal principle of her policy toward China. By the Treaty of Nerchinsk in 1689 she gained 93,000 square miles of territory from China, and by the Treaty of Kiakhta in 1727 she secured nearly 40,000 square miles. . . . The occupation of some 1,224 square miles of

neither the Russians nor the Chinese knew the territory well, only in time when travellers and scholars observed and described the border peoples did it become clear that the demarcation only poorly took into account demographic considerations. Some tribes and peoples were divided between the two empires, but little better could have been done at this time. The demarcation was largely on the basis of *uti possidetis,* at least to the degree that the negotiators' geographical and demographic knowledge permitted.[45]

Vladislavich carried out his instructions admirably with regard to border delimitation. The regions of Dauriia (Transbaikalia), Selenginsk, and the Angara were retained by Russia, and Russian sovereignty was extended to regions south of Selenginsk practically unknown to the Russians. The Chinese court, on the other hand, had greater cause for unhappiness with the specific line delimiting the frontier. Yet in actuality it was as favorable as could have been expected: all of Mongolia reverted to the Middle Kingdom, much of which was only tenuously controlled. Her pretensions to the Angara region remained unsatisfied, but it is likely that this claim was more of a bargaining gambit than a serious intent. Above all else the Manchus desired and needed delimitation, and this certainly outweighed any possible dissatisfaction with the specific demarcated line. Notably China made no great effort at any time in the eighteenth century to alter the line, only to tighten control over it to prevent unauthorized crossing.

Violation of the Border

Of course the major reason for fixing the border was to make possible the control of the native populations in the vicinity and, especially for the Russians, the merchant trading across the border. Articles 3 and 10 deal directly with this matter. It was first stated

territory in the Ili Valley in 1871 was but another step in the fulfilment of Russia's age-old policy of land acquisition from China" (Immanuel C. Y. Hsü, *The Ili Crisis, A Study of Sino-Russian Diplomacy* [Oxford: The Clarendon Press, 1965], pp. 2-4).

45. The question of redefining or more precisely defining the boundary east of the Argun arose in the discussions, i.e. in terms of the Uda River valley, the line set by the Treaty of Nerchinsk (1689), but Vladislavich insisted he had no authority from his Empress to deal with it. The Chinese permitted the question to be dropped, with the admonition that Russia exercise sufficient discipline over her subjects to prevent them from violating the old border (Article 7). See D. I. Uspenskii, "Iz istorii russkikh snoshenii s narodami Vostoka (Russko-kitaiskiia nedorazumeniia)," *Russkaia mysl',* XXV (November, 1904), 79-80.

that all disputes and transgressions of the past be forgotten, whether disposed of or not, that is, deserters would be left where they were, a victory for Vladislavich. Fairly exact regulations then governed the handling of future illegal trespassers in either direction. Common people crossing the border without the required passports had to be extradited and punished; cattle or camels stolen across the border had to be returned, and the thief or thieves required to make ten-fold restitution for the first offense, twenty-fold for the second, etc. Fugitives from either side would be punished where seized—deserting soldiers would be beheaded, if Chinese, and strangled, if Russian. All stolen merchandise, other than animals, had to be returned to rightful owners. All in all these were stringent measures, even for the day, but the problem had long and seriously disturbed peaceful border relations. And even more to the point, the Chinese imperial war against the Dzhungars simply demanded an end to the privileged sanctuary that Russian Siberia had been for many of the Chinese enemies and the source of supplies and animals for others.[46] Although the Russians had given no real evidence of warlike activities in the region, nor indeed did they have the military power there to do so, the Treaty did serve to isolate the Dzhungars and make possible, in time, their total conquest. It still took Chinese armies another quarter of a century.

Commerce

Delimitation of the frontier and regulation of border crossing were not clearly to the disadvantage of Russia, but her most intense concern was trade. Article 4 dealt with both Russian trade directly to Peking and trading posts on the border. One Russian caravan (the treaty itself made no distinction between state or private enterprise) could journey to Peking each three years; it could have no more than two hundred merchants (i.e. members). No taxes or imposts might be levied on either buyer or seller in this capital trade. Any draft animals or provisions required on crossing Chinese lands might be purchased, but at the merchants' own expense, rather than, as was the Chinese tradition, assumed in part or whole by the Chinese court. Any goods might be bought and exchanged except for those specifically forbidden in the future by either country. There was little change here from the provisions of the

46. Cahen, *Histoire,* 190-91.

Treaty of Nerchinsk; as we shall note later the real difference was that the mutual eagerness to demarcate the border and to limit much of the total trade to the posts established there made feasible the *effective* operation of monopolistic caravan trade for the first time.

For that trade not conducted in Peking, two locations were provided for continuous barter; one near Selenginsk to replace Urga and the other near Nerchinsk to replace Naun (these became Kiakhta with its neighbor across the border Mai-mai-ch'eng, and Tsurukhaitu). Each of these trading centers was to be surrounded by fences and palisades, if necessary for protection. Merchants arriving to trade had to follow direct routes to the towns, at risk of confiscation of their merchandise on the assumption that they were, prima facie, intent on illicit and illegal trade. An equal number of officials must be appointed on both sides to administer border affairs and to assume responsibility for protection of merchants. The Treaty provided only the skeletal structure for what became at Kiakhta a very thriving commerce.

Vladislavich achieved the practical expectations of his masters in St. Petersburg, but not their most sanguine hopes. The persistent Russian effort renewed here to obtain permission for Russian merchants (state or private) to travel in the interior of China did not bear fruit. Nor was he able to induce the Chinese to allow a permanent consul or commercial agent to remain in Peking when the caravans were not trading; not until the latter half of the nineteenth century was Russia to obtain these privileges, along with all other western powers.[47]

By deflecting the Russian desire to penetrate the provinces, China in her own official eyes profited by the treaty. Her reply to the request of Vladislavich was reputed to have been a single line: "Really . . . it will be your China, your agents and free merchants will breed throughout all of China."[48] The transfer of continuous private trade from Urga and Naun, both deep in Chinese dominions, to Kiakhta and Tsurukhaitu, on the very edges of the

47. Ministerstvo Inostrannykh Del, *Svod mezhdunarodnykh postanovlenii, opredeliaiushchikh vzaimnyia otnosheniia mezhdu Rossieiu i Kitaem, 1689-1897* (St. Petersburg: Tip. V. F. Kirshbauma, 1900), pp. 11-12, 14-15, 71. Consuls and diplomatic agents were not permitted until the Treaty of Tientsin (1858). Internal trade, i.e. access to the Yangtse, was not accepted by Peking until the agreement of 1862.

48. Quoted from the Moscow archives in Kurts, *Russko-kitaiskie snosheniia*, p. 78, n. 21.

empire, removed the divisive influence of rowdy Russian merchants and permitted close scrutiny and regulation of them, particularly as concerned traffic in prohibited items of exchange. It has been suggested that Chinese merchants were not as pleased with this new arrangement for it meant a longer and more expensive trek from Peking, and at Urga they had been able to trade readily with both Russians and Bukharans, but for the court it was pure gain.[49]

Both sides then profited by the commercial arrangements. That Vladislavich did not obtain complete access to all of China must have been no more than a minor disappointment; while Russian private merchants were restricted to the border trading emporia, Russian state trade, especially the caravans, was given a new lease on life, and was exempt from Chinese taxation. Now undisciplined and uncontrollable private merchants could not depress Chinese markets for furs and other lesser items, and ruin the profitability of state ventures. At the border private merchants might now be closely regulated, especially valuable items of trade successfully prohibited to private trade, and customs duties more fully collected. The courts of both empires had little cause to be dissatisfied with this vigorous control of trade, although the private merchants of both might well complain; even they in time used the new arrangement to their advantage—after a bit, trade prospered as it had not before.

Diplomacy and Correspondence

Especially to the Chinese court, but of only somewhat less interest to the Russians, was the question of the forms of correspondence and diplomatic intercourse between the empires. The ticklish matter was the designation of the particular offices that should carry on the correspondence; the Chinese haughtily declined to recognize direct correspondence with any office or official higher in rank or importance than their own *Li-fan-yuan*,[50] and the Rus-

49. *Ibid.*, p. 75.

50. The *Li-fan-yuan* has been known in western writings by a wide variety of names; the Mongolian Superintendency, the Colonial Office, the Court of Colonial Affairs, etc. It was originally established to superintend the affairs of the border Mongols. Since the Russians penetrated to China through Mongol lands, it was natural that relations with them should be handled by the same office, at least in the beginning. The *Li-fan-yuan*, although similar in organization to the Six Boards, with the exception that it had only one president instead of two, was not on an organizational level with them. It is of course impossible to equate Russian and Chinese governmental organization, but it is apparent that a closer equivalent to the Russian Governing

sians, as is so typical in affairs such as this, refused to have their Governing Senate (*Pravitel'stvuiushchii senat,* or *Sa-na-t'e* in Chinese) degraded in such a manner that Russia became, in form at least, a tributary nation to China. All diplomatic notes were required to carry proper seals. Any delay in forwarding of correspondence would be cause for the rupture of commercial and diplomatic relations. Finally all diplomatic agents or officials, regardless of rank, had to present themselves at the border and announce their business and rank. They also were not to suffer unnecessary delays or be caused senseless waiting.

These issues of the forms of and terminological exactitude for state correspondence bothered the Chinese to the extent that they made innumerable efforts to fashion a form that would subtly emphasize the superior stature of the Manchu emperor and his administration. The Chinese negotiators probably gained a slight diplomatic advantage in the end, although the principle of equal correspondence prevailed (as it did not in repeated eighteenth-century negotiations with other western powers). The Russian Senate was after all the highest administrative-judicial body of the realm; the *Li-fan-yuan* was not one of the Six Boards *(liu-pu),* but a *yuan* or office the function of which at that time was to regulate and superintend the affairs of tributary states and peoples, among whom the Russians were obviously included. If anything, the *Li-fan-yuan* was equivalent to the Siberian Prikaz, rather than the Senate, but St. Petersburg officialdom seemed not disturbed by the slight. In fact by avoiding correspondence directly from the Chinese throne it delicately avoided an issue that terribly perturbed the English.[51]

Senate in the Manchu scheme was the Grand Council *(Chun-chi-ch'u),* a kind of privy council to the emperor. See Hippolit S. Brunnert and V. V. Hagelstrom, *Present Day Political Organization of China,* rev. by N. Th. Kolessoff; trans. A. Beltchenko and E. E. Moran (Shanghai: Kelly and Walsh, Ltd., 1912), p. 160; William Frederick Mayers, *The Chinese Government. A Manual of Chinese Titles, Categorically Arranged and Explained, With an Appendix* (3rd ed.; Shanghai: Kelly & Walsh, Ltd., 1897), p. 23; Valentin A. Riazanovskii, *Customary Law of the Mongol Tribes (Mongols, Buriats, Kalmucks)* (Harbin: "Artistic Printing House," 1929), pp. 54-56; and Michel N. Pavlovsky, *Chinese-Russian Relations* (New York: Philosophical Library, 1949), pp. 39-40, 169.

51. On the other hand, the Chinese objected to the Senate being termed a Tribunal, i.e. equating it to the *Li-fan-yuan.* However, in the Russian text of the Treaty the Senate was referred to as the "Senat ili Tribunal Rossiiskii" (Senate or Russian Tribunal). In the Manchu copy it was simply the Senate. How this variant came to be is not clear.

Ecclesiastical Matters

Article 5 permitted the erection in Peking of a Greek Orthodox (Russian) church to minister to the Russian community there. Four ecclesiastics would staff the church, led by Archimandrite Platkovskii. (The Treaty itself made no distinction in rank among the four, although Bishop Kul'chitskii was rejected and the ranking cleric thereafter was no higher than an archimandrite.)[52] The Manchu Emperor supported the mission, as was in the Chinese tradition, in both money and provisions and promised not to interfere in the exercise of the faith. Further the Chinese accepted not two but six Russian students in Peking, three of whom reached the city in June 1729 with Platkovskii and three of whom travelled with the Molokov-Tret'iakov caravan in the autumn of 1727. Awaiting the completion of the new Orthodox church, these stu-

---

The crux of the problem was of course the difficulty of finding a means for the Chinese-Manchus to communicate "down" to the Russians, short of an overt offense to St. Petersburg. Vladislavich accepted the ambiguous solution to avoid the necessity of receiving communications from the Manchu emperor, which by established custom were transmitted down to subordinates. The problem did not end here, as shall be seen below. For a discussion of the matter, see Kurts, *Russko-kitaiskie snosheniia,* p. 74.

52. *PSZ,* VIII, No. 5286,51. On orders of Vladislavich, Platkovskii arrived in Selenginsk on 12 August 1728, but waited until 20 February of the next year to proceed from there to Kiakhta. The delay was caused by the procrastinating contractor engaged to prepare the carriages and carts of the small religious suite. On 17 March he finally left Kiakhta for Peking, arriving on 16 June. He took with him one cleric, Ivan Filimopov (or Filipov) and a deacon, the *ierodiak* Ioasaf. Three of the six young students sent to Peking under the provisions of the Treaty also travelled with Platkovskii: Gerasim Shul'gin, Mikhail Ponomarev, and Illarion Rossokhin. The other three (Luka Voeikov, Ivan Pukhort who replaced the deceased Ivan Iablontsev, and Fedot Tret'iakov) had set out earlier with Lange and the Molokov caravan. Archimandrite Platkovskii was assigned a salary of 550 r. annually; all other members of the ecclesiastical-academic group, including the students, received 130 r.

Platkovskii stayed in Peking until 1737, when he was replaced because of his advanced age and, we gather, his devotion to spiritous beverages. He had, seven years before, been involved in an altercation with Filimopov in which the archimandrite's hand was injured. After a second such disturbance, Filimopov was put in irons by the Chinese and, with the archimandrite's approval, was expelled from China.

The students probably deported themselves in more acceptable fashion, although only Rossokhin returned to Russia to make use of his acquired linguistic skills. The latter part of his life was spent in scholarly effort in the Academy of Sciences. Shul'gin and Ponomarev both died natural deaths in Peking. See *inter alia* Petr E. Skachkov, "Istoriia izucheniia Kitaia v Rossii v XVII i XVIII vv. (Kratkii ocherk)," in *Mezhdunarodnye sviazi Rossii v XVII-XVIII vv. (Ekonomika, politika i kul'tura), Sbornik statei,* ed. L. G. Beskrovnyi, M. M. Shtrange, and P. T. Iakovleva (Moscow: Izd. "Nauka," 1966), pp. 122-51.

dents would reside at the Russian House (*Russkii dom* or *O-lo-ssu kuan*), a kind of consulate compound sans consul, which the caravans used when in Peking, and they would be provided stipends and provisions by the Chinese. Both the church and the Russian compound were to be built or refurbished at the Chinese court's expense.

In a manner of speaking both sides gained from these provisions. A rumor persists that Yung-ch'eng was strongly anti-Catholic and anti-Jesuit, because of Jesuitical intrigue which attempted to replace him on the throne by someone favorable to Romanism.[53] Were the Russian clerics as skilled technically as the Jesuits had been since the days of Ricci, the Chinese might well have been able to supplant the latter with Russian court advisers. And the Russians might also have served as translators and interpreters, as well as a source of knowledge of the western world. St. Petersburg on the other hand obtained indispensible translators from Manchu and Chinese, again relieving the Russians in Peking of overdependence on Jesuit interceders, such as had been necessary during the negotiations for both the Nerchinsk and Kiakhta treaties. Some of these students and clerics did in fact become reputable scholars in later years: Illarion Rossokhin, Aleksei Leont'ev, and the justly famed monk Iakinf (Hyacinth) Bichurin, among others. In spite of strong charges to the contrary, not all of the Russians in Peking were dissolute, licentious, lazy, rude, perverted, dishonest, or deceitful, only most of them.[54]

53. Consult, e.g., John Dudgeon, "Sketch of Russian Ecclesiastical Intercourse with, and the Greek Church in, China," *The Chinese Recorder and Missionary Journal*, IV (June, 1871), 36-37. Dudgeon attributed the principal motivation of the Manchus in admitting Russian ecclesiastics and students to their intent to expel Roman Catholic missionaries from China. The Yung-ch'eng Emperor was considered to be anti-Catholic because of the missionary desire to place on the throne "a prince converted by them to Catholicism." Yung-ch'eng is reputed to have said to the Jesuit Father Moyriac de Mailla in 1724, "You desire, that all Chinese become Christians, I know, your teaching demands this; but what will come of this? They will become subjects of your king. The people who listen to you will know only you; during insurrections they will listen only to your voice. . . . Now there is nothing to fear, but when ships begin to arrive from thousands of miles, then there will be more disorders." Vysheslavtsev, *Ocherki perom i karandashom, iz krugosvetnago plavaniia* (St. Petersburg, 1862), p. 232, quoted in Uspenskii, *Russkaia mysl'*, XXXV (November, 1904), 76.

54. As argued with verve by Albert Parry in his "Russian (Greek Orthodox) Missionaries in China, 1689-1917: Their Cultural, Political and Economic Role" (Ph.D. dissertation, University of Chicago, 1938), and his article bearing the same title in the *Pacific Historical Review*, IX (December, 1940), 401-24.

Above and beyond the specific provisions of the Treaties themselves, the embassy served still another valuable purpose for the Russian state: the collection of extremely valuable information and impressions on China, Chinese trade and military preparations, and Siberia. Vladislavich's intelligence exceeded in detail and accuracy any available to Russian policy makers prior to that time; he passed on data on the cities of China, China's population, the imperial court, the administrative system, etc.[55]

In contrast the Chinese had no first-hand knowledge of European Russia since the mission to the Turguts in 1712-15, although it was not to be long before this was rectified. Between 1730 and 1732, as we shall describe below, two embassies travelled to European Russia on several pretexts, the formal one of which was to felicitate the Tsar Peter II and his successor Tsaritsa Anna. But not incidentally, much knowledge of Russia and more particularly of the Volga Turguts was gathered. This was only the second embassy dispatched abroad by the Chinese in modern times, and both went to Russia.

Immediate Aftermath and Reception

It is tempting to pass judgment on the gains and losses, the advantages and disadvantages, the satisfactions and dissatisfactions on both sides with the treaty arrangements; most who have done so have erred in making assessments in the light of nineteenth-century events. The effort to exclude later consideration results in a somewhat different picture. The ruling bodies of neither country commented directly on the merits or demerits of the treaty, although both in effect commented through their actions. The reception of the negotiators on returning home and their subsequent careers provide some evidence.

On the Chinese side, it will be recalled that Lung-k'e-to was ordered back to Peking before the Bur Treaty was concluded. Apparently (although the materials are not precise) his adamancy on certain questions threatened the breakdown of negotiations, and the Peking court *did* desire a favorable treaty settlement. In

55. "Graf Vladislavich o Kitae v XVIII veke," *Russkii arkhiv,* XXXVIII, Pt. 2 (1900), 572-80. Originally published in *Russkii vestnik* in 1842. These notes were composed in 1730 on the order of Count Gavriil Ivanovich Golovkin. The manuscript is preserved in Moscow.

Peking Lung-k'e-to was tried and imprisoned for various crimes; he died the following year while still under house arrest.[56]

His colleagues fared little better. Ts'e-ling on his return was tried for ordering a cannon salute fired to thank Heaven upon completion of the Bur Treaty and was fined three years' stipend and demoted a rank. Several years later he regained imperial favor by virtue of valorous conduct in the Dzhungarian wars, and he eventually became a prince of the first order *(Ho-shih ch'in-wang)* and the first governor of Uliassutai (1732). T'u-li-shen similarly was accused of "unlawful" acts in the erection of wooden tablet markers at the frontier on his own initiative, instead of first obtaining imperial consent. Even beyond that he was charged with divulging military secrets while governor of Shansi, and was sentenced to death. An imperial pardon commuted the sentence, but he appears never to have regained favor. He lived on until 1741.[57]

Extreme caution is in order in attempting to draw broad conclusions from this evidence. Radically differing concepts of administrative responsibility, punishment, accolade, and personal conduct are involved; notably none of the Manchu officials were brought to trial directly for having acceded to an unfavorable treaty, but rather were judged for other matters only tangentially related to the treaties. Still the treatment meted out to the negotiators strongly suggests some displeasure with aspects of the treaty or perhaps the tactics used in negotiating it.

In contrast to the singularly shabby treatment of the Chinese, the Russians were by and large granted the accolade. Vladislavich, at the time past sixty, reached Moscow late in 1728. He was honored as a privy councillor (*tainyi sovetnik,* the third rank in the table of civil ranks and four above that he had held earlier), and made cavalier of the Order of Aleksandr Nevskii.[58] He was then quickly set to work at a task for which his lifelong experiences admirably suited him, to advise on the rewriting of the customs tariff of 1724 and on the impending trade agreement with England. Reportedly Vladislavich recommended that England be granted no special privileges.[59]

56. Hummel, *Eminent Chinese,* I, 552-54; *CSK,* ch. 301, Biography 82.

57. Hummel, *Eminent Chinese,* II, 784-87.

58. *PSZ,* VI, No. 3890, 486-93; Solov'ev, *Istoriia,* IV, 1139; Kurts, *Russko-kitaiskie snosheniia,* p. 83, n. 23. In the words of the French ambassador in St. Petersburg (dispatch dated 27 January 1729), Vladislavich "a rempli sa mission à l'entière satisfaction du Czar," *Sbornik RIO,* LXXV (1891), 300.

59. By order of the Supreme Privy Council (16 May 1729), Vladislavich was

In March of 1729 Vladislavich petitioned Peter II for a twenty-year renewal of a Ukrainian tax farm granted three years earlier to his nephew Gavriil.[60] The privilege was renewed within five days, in recompense for the service of the new privy councillor at the Chinese border, and this time the farm ran for twenty years rather than the original four! On another occasion (1734), Tsaritsa Anna at the request of Vladislavich forwarded a remittance of two hundred rubles to another of his nephews, one Ivan Stanislavich, a senior non-commissioned officer *(Vakhmistr)* in the Perm' dragoon regiment.[61] Finally near the end of his life, Vladislavich requested of Anna through the Court Office *(Pridvornaia kontora,* that office which was responsible for court ranks, some court titling, etc.) that his townhouse and court on Admiralty Island in St. Petersburg be taken back by the court for ten thousand rubles and "in recompense" that he be given another such house and court on Nalichnaia Street "along the canal [and] opposite the meadow where your sister Tsarevna Ekaterina Ioannovna is permitted to reside."[62] The request was granted of course; such beneficence is evidence alone of the regard with which he was received in St. Petersburg. In terms of the post-treaty treatment of and honors enjoyed by Count Vladislavich it may be inferred that the Russian court was more than content with the Treaty.

The others prospered, if not as affluently. Colonel Bukhol'ts, in command of the troops present during the frontier negotiations, was appointed Commandant of Selenginsk by Vladislavich and given general oversight over border affairs, perhaps the most critical task in Siberia. In 1731 he was promoted to Brigadier in spite of his earlier besmirched service record and was finally pensioned

attached to the Commission on Commerce for this work; *Sbornik RIO,* XCIV (1894), 619. The French Foreign Ministry regarded the work and the new schedules sufficiently important to request that M. Magnon in Moscow obtain a copy if possible; *ibid.,* LXXV (1891), 354. See also *ibid.,* LXXV (1891), 349-51, 374-75, and 382-86.

60. These lands originally belong to the Ukrainian Hetman Skoropadskii and then to Prince Aleksandr D. Menshikov, Peter's favorite; *Sbornik RIO,* LXXIX (1891), 1, 5-7. Also consult *ibid.,* XCIV (1894), 423-24; XIV (1898), 25-26; and CVI (1899), 295-96, 301, 336.

61. *Sbornik RIO,* CVIII (1900), 326-27.

62. *Ibid.,* 422-23. Regarding his death, testament, his designated heir Gavriil, etc., see *ibid.,* CXX (1905), 490, 511; CXXIV (1906), 14, 78-79. Vladislavich died on 17 June 1738.

nine years later.[63] Lange continued to serve with the state caravan to Peking and travelled with the caravans of 1727-28, 1731-32, and 1736-37. From 1735 he held the post of councillor of the Selenginsk Chancellery and from 1739 vice-governor of Irkutsk—other than the governor-generalship of Siberia, certainly the most important post east of the Urals.[64] And in 1737-38 he was entrusted with a diplomatic mission to Constantinople. Of the rest of the embassy members we know little: Glazunov apparently continued to serve in important posts, for his talents were utilized during the Chinese embassies to Russia between 1730 and 1732.

This evidence supports the contention that the Russian government obtained about what it wished from the Treaty, or so it seems. The fact that Vladislavich was regally treated may indicate little more than the respect accorded an elderly diplomat who had worked diligently at an extraordinarily difficult task. And the improved status of the others may simply represent normal promotion within civil or military bureaucracy of those whose service records were clean or at least who were not associated in a decision-making capacity with an unsuccessful operation. But I think not.

M. N. Pavlovsky considered the Treaty of Kiakhta to be unfavorable to Russia on the grounds that she lost "all the advantages in Outer Mongolia which she had created by her efforts during more than a century. . . ."[65] The argument is weak. Not only did Russia have no real advantages in Mongolia nor any real power in the region, but *at that time* control south of Selenginsk promised little profit. No gold or silver mines had yet been discovered there and the supply of fur-bearing animals was paltry. Trade with the Bukharans, especially in rhubarb, was the only other attraction for the Russians, but the Bukharans could and did trade after 1728 at Kiakhta on the border, saving Russian merchants the long and expensive journey to Urga.

63. *RBS*, vol. Betankur-Biakster, 564-65; Fedor Fedorovich Martens, "Le conflict entre la Russie et la Chine, ses origines, son développement, et sa portée universelle," *Revue de droit international et de législation comparée*, XII (1880), 535. In the journal of Anna's Cabinet is an Imperial resolution of 18 November 1731 signed by the Tsaritsa which makes reference to the fact that she granted Bukhol'ts a salary from the Siberian *guberniia* above that permitted by the 1720 table; *Sbornik RIO*, CIV (1898), 12, 21, 25, 28-29.

64. *RBS*, vol. Labzina-Liashenko, 59; Bantysh-Kamenskii, *Diplomaticheskoe sobranie*, 194, 198-99, 218-19, 273; Sychevskii, *Chteniia OIDR*, Bk. 2 (April-June, 1875), 228; Pravitel'stvuiushchii Senat, *Senatskii arkhiv* (St. Petersburg: Senatskaia Tip., 1888-1913), II, 18.

65. Pavlovsky, *Chinese-Russian Relations*, p. 23.

Pavlovsky pursued his argument by insisting that a document signed by Vladislavich and several Siberian chiefs on 23 August 1727, and forwarded then to St. Petersburg, testifies to Vladislavich's fear that the treaty would be critically received back home. He needed this testimony to assure his superiors that he had not bargained away territory that Russia might well have retained, by force if necessary.[66] As shown above however, Vladislavich more than fulfilled his orders in the matter of border demarcation; he had retained those regions deemed essential in his instructions. If anything, the Manchus rather than the Russians had cause for discontent over the demarcation line. The documents sent back shortly after the conclusion of the Bur Treaty may well be taken as nothing more than a description of the earlier unmapped border region, together with assurances from those who knew it best, local native chieftains, that in fact Russian hegemony had been extended "a distance of several days' march and in certain sections of even several weeks," rather than diminished.[67]

Later in 1729 when he petitioned for Gavriil's tax farm and in 1731 in a special report, "Secret Information on the Strength and Condition of the Chinese State," Vladislavich gave us something of his own interpretation of his mission and of the several alternatives then open to acceptance of the treaty.[68] He deemed the treaty not only the best possible, but one that gave the Russians precisely their first needs: a restoration of commerce, and an arrangement of the frontier and its several problems that both state and private trade might in the future prosper. In fact as we shall see, it was the Treaty and only it that made possible the reinvigoration of the system of the state monopoly of trade. He declared that the only alternative was to war against China (there was another which he did not mention for it obviously was no solution in terms of Russian aims in the east: stalemate and no trade), "but we must take into consideration the fact that this would not be an easy undertaking." Vladislavich concluded that at least ten regiments of the line and an equal number of irregulars would be necessary to face the enemy. "The cost of such an undertaking, even assuming that it would be successful, will never be recovered

66. *Ibid.*, p. 29.

67. Bantysh-Kamenskii, *Diplomaticheskoe sobranie*, pp. 344-46.

68. Sava Vladislavich, "Sila advantazha rossiiskago imperiia vo vruchennoi mne komissii pri dvore kitaiskom," *Sbornik RIO*, XCIV (1894), 424-25, and "Sekretnaia informatssiia o sile i sostoianii kitaiskogo gosudarstva," in Bantysh-Kamenskii, *Diplomaticheskoe sobranie*, pp. 373-75.

even in a hundred years," an overstatement but a well-taken point. Were the insufficiency of troops in Siberia and the monetary cost of a remote war not reason enough, Russia would still lose that which she most desired, regular trade. Consequently Vladislavich recommended that "minor vexations be disregarded," and in fact they were, throughout most of the eighteenth century. Safety of the Siberian possessions was best obtained by improving the frontier fortifications in the Selenginsk and Nerchinsk regions, supplying them with artillery, and even manufacturing it on the spot. Distances were too great, the population too thin, and communications too difficult for any other alternatives. Later eighteenth-century observers confirmed the Ambassador's counsel.

The Chinese Embassies

Gaston Cahen has insisted that China obtained from the Treaty of Kiakhta "the assurance that Russia would not conclude an offiensive alliance against her, the neutralization of Russia, that is to say, the complete freedom of action against the Eleuths [Dzhungarians]."[69] This meticulous scholar has overstated the point. No specific mention of the Dzhungarian conflict and of Russian neutrality appears in the Treaty, although it is possible to read into the "eternal peace" proviso an implicit Russian agreement to refrain from becoming embroiled in Central Asian affairs. Were Chinese armies to renew the campaign against the Dzhungars however, presumed implications of Article 1 of the Treaty were certainly no insurance of Russian noninvolvement. The lack of definitiveness in the extradition provisions further complicated the question of Russian role in Central Asia. And finally there was the question of the Volga Turguts, the Russian vassals in the Volga River valley who had been the target of Chinese pressure more than a decade earlier. The Turguts could greatly strengthen the Chinese hand against the Dzhungars by putting an army in the field in the Dzhungarian rear, or threatening to do so. Although the Peking court probably realized that there was little chance for an active military alliance with the Russians, the value of Turgut aid must have occurred to them. The best that might be expected from the Russians was neutrality, the best from the Tur-

69. Gaston Cahen, "Deux ambassades chinoises en Russie au commencement du XVIIIe siècle," *Revue historique*, CXXXIII (January-February, 1920), 84.

guts was military aid. These several considerations suggest that the Treaty of Kiakhta did not entirely satisfy Peking officials and that they had good reason to try to carry it one step further.

The Dzhungarian situation had worsened. The *kontaisha* Tsewang Araptan died in 1727, succeeded by his able son Galdan Tseren. The son continued applying pressure on the western Mongols under Manchu suzerainty, and appeared to have achieved a major victory over Chinese armies in August 1731.[70] This renewed strife caused hundreds more Mongol iurts to cross the border into Russian territory, from Tsurukhaitu in the east westward, especially in 1730.[71] Even more dangerous to Chinese desires in Central Asia, at least potentially, Galdan Tseren at this time dispatched an embassy to Russia, a development not unnoticed in Peking.[72] Were this mission to ripen into open or covert Russia support of the Dzhungar armies, Chinese hopes of subduing the distant region would be seriously jeopardized. There was no choice but for the Chinese to assemble an army, reputedly three thousand-strong by 1730.[73] Or perhaps in light of the recent successful negotiations with the Russians, to extort from them or from their Turgut vassals direct military support.

On 3 June 1729 the *Li-fan-yuan* directed to the Governing Senate a letter indicating the desire of the emperor to send a mission to congratulate Peter II on his recent accession to the throne of the Russias, in return for the Vladislavich embassy of felicitations to China.[74] The Senate replied on 23 October that the mission would be most welcome and would be escorted to Moscow with full honors, provided only that Peking authorities inform Moscow of the numbers and ranks of the embassy members. Titular Councillor Ivan Glazunov, formerly with Vladislavich, was ordered to the border almost immediately (31 October) to prepare to meet and greet the ambassadors with cannonades in Selenginsk, Irkutsk, and Tobol'sk.[75]

70. *Ibid.*, 88-89. See also Hummel, *Eminent Chinese,* I, 264.

71. Bantysh-Kamenskii, *Diplomaticheskoe sobranie,* p. 167.

72. Kurts, *Novyi Vostok,* XIX (1927), 172; Bantysh-Kamenskii, *Diplomaticheskoe sobranie,* p. 191.

73. *Sbornik RIO,* LXVI (1889), 172.

74. Bantysh-Kamenskii, *Diplomaticheskoe sobranie,* p. 159, received in Moscow 29 September 1729. Rondeau also reported from Moscow on 25 March 1730 that the task of the embassy was "to sollicit this court and Ayook-khan, to attack the great Contaysha. . . ." (*Sbornik RIO,* LXVI [1889], 172). This knowledge came from "a gentleman lately come from China."

75. Bantysh-Kamenskii, *Diplomaticheskoe sobranie,* p. 165.

But congratuations to Peter II were only one ostensible purpose of the mission: Yung-ch'eng's message of June also made reference to greetings to be carried to Ayuki Khan of the Turguts. When Glazunov reached the border post of Kiakhta on 3 March 1730, he found that the Chinese had been there since mid-August of the preceeding year.[76] Not only were they chafing at the long delay awaiting the escort from Moscow and even threatening Bukhol'ts and Lange to return to China, but they seemed at first ill prepared for and rather vague about their appointed tasks. Although they were to carry gifts to Peter II, they carried no correspondence directly to the Tsar, but only from the *Li-fan-yuan* to the Senate and from the Ch'ing emperor to the Turgut chieftain. Glazunov reported back that he was informed by members of the suite that an active alliance "by the aid of troops" was sought.[77] Other than this reference only scattered and partly circumstantial information reveals Chinese aims beyond all doubt. That real concessions were sought is an inescapable conclusion: a specific stipulation that the Dzhungar *kontaisha* or other Dzhungar leaders who defected in the heat of battle would be returned to Chinese authorities; a more explicit statement on Russian neutrality in the form of a renewed promise to respect Chinese borders; and permission for an active alliance with the Volga Turguts. Since Peking already had general extradition agreements with the Russians in the Treaty of Kiakhta (and presumably through the Russians with their vassals the Turguts), the most important of these aims must have been positive alliance, perhaps an active military alliance, with the Russians and/or the Turguts.[78] To the Chinese, then, the mission was a sequel to the negotiation of the Treaty of Kiakhta, an effort to make more precise and, if possible, to extend the cooperation between the two empires on Central Asian matters.

And for the Russians this new confrontation presented an opportunity to press again for the conditions for amicable and profitable commerce. The state caravan commanded by Molokov spent the winter and spring of 1727-28 in Peking, but reported failure to dispose of its goods.[79] Chinese bureaucratic interference in the actual exchange of goods was one of the major reasons for this failure in the caravan officers' minds. As early as 14 August

76. Glazunov left Moscow on 6 December.
77. *Ibid.*, p. 169.
78. Cf. Cahen, *Revue historique*, CXXXIII (January-February, 1920), 87.
79. See Chapter 3 for full discussion.

1730 the Russian court drafted two notes to Peking, *inter alia*, complaining of the failure of the caravan to sell its goods because it had been ordered to leave too early and requesting the Ch'ing emperor to guarantee complete freedom of purchase and sale of goods without any time limit nor any duty or tax on the sales.[80] With another caravan now readying at the border and Chinese worry over the Dzhungars so intense, the timing and appropriateness of the Russian request is obvious. The Chinese reply denied categorically that restraints were placed on trade: if Russian goods had not been sold, the reasons were that prices were too high and some goods damaged, and as for the complaint of Lorents Lange that the Molokov caravan had been compelled to leave Peking too early, the Treaty of Kiakhta after all said nothing of the time period caravans might be permitted to remain in Peking.[81] Nonetheless the Senate, meeting with the embassy on 1 March 1731, reiterated the Russian desire for "the free dispatch of merchants without any hindrance."[82] The Russians were intent on using the mission as an unsolicited but welcome chance to press for distinct commercial advantages, while at the same time exercising great caution to avoid commitment in the Dzhungarian area where Russian power was weak and dispersed.

The suite of thirty-five led by an official of the *Li-fan-yuan* reached Moscow in early January of 1731, and was housed in the small suburban village of Alekseevskoe.[83] In three days the visitors were conducted to the suburban house of Acting Privy Councillor Vasilii Fedorovich Saltykov where they were treated to huge tables of food, confections, and potables, and serenaded with music.[84] The 26th of January finally was set for the first imperial audience; nine coaches preceded the ambassadors carrying gifts of porcelains, lacquer ware, fine steel sabres in golden settings, and other valuable items. The audience itself was more oriental than Muscovite; the Chinese performed one of their several versions of *k'ou-t'ou*, approached the throne on the order of the Chancellor Golovkin, and

80. Bantysh-Kamenskii, *Diplomaticheskoe sobranie*, pp. 170, 181; *Sbornik RIO*, LXVI (1889), 172.

81. Bantysh-Kamenskii, *Diplomaticheskoe sobranie*, p. 172; Kurts, *Russko-kitaiskie snosheniia*, p. 84.

82. Bantysh-Kamenskii, *Diplomaticheskoe sobranie*, p. 177.

83. Arrived in Alekseevskoe on 9 January to prepare for formal entry into Moscow.

84. *Ibid.*, p. 182, n. 1, and p. 175. Cf. *Sbornik RIO*, LXVI (1889), 283.

read a brief greeting to the "All-illuminating, Most Powerful, Great Sovereign Empress, Autocratrix of All the Russias. . . ."

In the time between the embassy's arrival and the imperial audience, Privy Councillor Stepanov met with the Chinese several times in a vain effort to elicit from them the "real" reasons of the mission. But two formal sessions later did reveal, as much as can be gathered, the substantive interests of the embassy; one of the sessions was at court (on Her Majesty's birthday, 28 January) and the other in the Senate on 1 March.[85] The ambassadors formally petitioned for permission to detach a group to visit the Turguts and to greet their new leader, the successor of Ayuki Khan. The Russian reply was affirmative, although with the caveat that in the future no contact to be made with the Turguts, except with Her Majesty's approval, for these Mongols were after all Russian subjects.[86]

With regard to the Dzhungarian wars directly, the Chinese requested Russian recognition of lands wrested by Chinese armies, to which the Tsaritsa grandiloquently replied that great Russia coveted no more lands and desired only peace. The Chinese again alluded to the expectation that Siberian authorities would deliver the leaders of any fugitive tribes to Chinese border officials and would contain the remainder of the fugitives in fortified areas of Siberia to forestall any hostile activities in the vicinity of the border. The Russians responded only that the Manchu emperor should inform Russia of any border transgressions.[87] Finally the

85. The English minister Claudius Rondeau described the 28th in detail in a despatch of 1 February 1731, since as he noted, this was the "first embassy from that court [Peking] to any prince in Europe" (*Sbornik RIO*, LXVI [1889], 281-83). The Chinese were in attendance at this birthday celebration and had the honor to dine in the same room with the Empress and other especially distinguished guests. At night there was a huge ball and a striking fireworks display. Rondeau noted that there was some surprise that the Empress did not, as was customary, announce the promotion of any officers, but she did take the occasion to give over to General Saltykov some 800 serf families and to permit Naryshkin to return from the exile earlier imposed on him for supporting the claim to the throne of the Duchess of Holstein rather than Peter II. This Naryshkin had been in England in earlier years and had served as President of the Collegium of Finance in the reign of Catherine I.

86. Wang Chih-hsiang (trans.) and Liu-Tse-jung (comp.) *Ku-kung O-wen shih-liao Ch'ing-K'ang ch'ien-chien E-kuo lai-wen yuan-tang* (Peiping: National Palace Museum, 1936), pp. 107-20, 177-88, 304-12.

87. Western Mongols, as well as Eastern, crossed the Siberian border in substantial numbers at this time, as a result of incessant Manchu requisitions and army levies for the Dzhungarian wars; Cahen, *Revue historique*, CXXXIII (January-February, 1920), 88-89.

Chinese expressed the hope that Russia would not take umbrage if Manchu armies found it necessary to violate the border in pursuit and apprehension of fleeing Dzhungars. Tsaritsa Anna was hardly pleased with the idea of foreign soldiers on Russian soil, but promised that Chinese requests with regard to fugitives would in general be honored.

All of the Russian replies were properly circumspect and evasive. The Chinese did not propose an explicit alliance, but their requests certainly presumed honest Russian neutrality or passive alliance.[88] Was the mission then a total failure? By no means. Although the Russian court refused open alliance in the Central Asian wars and even categorical assurances that fleeing Dzhungar troops would be immediately returned, entry of Chinese troops on Siberian soil was not flatly forbidden and vague promises were made to negotiate locally the disposition of future fugitives. For Peking these were substantial diplomatic successes, and they did augment and clarify the Treaty of Kiakhta, even if not formally. The Russians used the opportunity to complain—as they did many times in the future—of restrictions laid upon the crown caravans travelling to Peking. Each side learned considerably of the other's main concerns and interests, and in passing it should be mentioned that the officials and courts of both received handsomely valuable presents. The Chinese returned with select Siberian furs and some brocades for themselves and their Emperor.

The embassy departed the Russian capital on 8 March, after a final audience at court on the second, half of the suite descending the Volga to confer with the new chieftain of the Turguts, Tseren (Cheren)-donduk, and the remainder travelling directly to the border. As far as is known, little transpired on the Volga that had not already been basically decided in Moscow. Conversations between the ambassadors and the very new Turgut chieftain were held in the presence of the Russian Lieutenant-Colonel Beklemishev; the sessions were brief and largely sterile, although a note from Yung-ch'eng was read to the Turguts. It was mainly a review of past relations of the Turguts and China, hence justifying

88. B. G. Kurts wrote that the Manchu envoys in the conferences announced the new campaign against the Dzhungars, and indicated that after the conquest of Dzhungaria the Manchu emperor wished to effect its division with Russia. The Russian court reportedly replied to this enticement that Russia had no need of new lands, but that if Dzhungaria was to be partitioned, Russia would certainly be an interested party (*Novyi Vostok*, XIX [1927], 200). There is no corroboration of this exchange in other materials.

the present journey. Verbally the Chinese described Dzhungarian depradations on Mongols, and substantively the Turguts were asked to detain any Dzhungarian runaways and to consider sending their leaders on a pilgrimage to Peking. The ambassadors left on 15 June, carrying a note from the Khan to Yung-ch'eng, thanking him for the mission and for gifts, and asking that they be remembered in the future. The Khan was said to have given his verbal promise that any Dzhungar fugitives would be detained, but for a pilgrimage to Peking the will of the Russian Tsaritsa was decisive. Apparently the Turguts gave no evidence of proclivities to take the field against the Dzhungars, although there is a report that Tsaritsa Anna specifically ordered the Turguts not to concern themselves in the Dzhungarian wars.[89]

To effect a rendezvous with the remainder of the embassy, the suite returned to Tobol'sk. Thence via Baraba the entire embassy moved on to Tomsk, where in a series of conferences (early January 1732), particularly with State Secretary Vasilii Bakunin, who accompanied the group to the Turgut villages, several other matters were discussed, although evidently not decided: the allegiance of the Tatars of the steppes of Baraba who paid tribute *(iasak)* to both Russia and the Dzhungarian hegemons (the Chinese questioned whether they should not be removed to the territories of Irkutsk or Saratov that they might be more closely supervised), the need for a Russian embassy to Peking in response to the Chinese embassies (otherwise the Ch'ing court would suffer chagrin), evidence that St. Petersburg had received a Dzhungarian embassy and that a Russian army major, one Ugrimov, had been sent to confer with Galdan Tseren (hardly demonstration of Russian neutrality), and the possibility of a Chinese mission through Russia to Turkey (the Chinese inquired of its size and the name of its capital). Apparently Bakunin offered explanations, although we do not know their substance. The fact alone that such reasonably delicate matters were discussed is ample evidence of the great measure of amicability achieved in the long negotiations since 1726. The Chinese embassy reached the border in mid-February 1732.

At the time the embassy first arrived in Siberia, word was given it that Tsar Peter II, to whom they were accredited, had died on

89. Report of the English minister in Moscow, Claudius Rondeau to London (15 March 1731); *Sbornik RIO*, LXVI (1889), 300-301.

18 January 1730.[90] Yung-ch'eng on learning this quickly sent off a *second* embassy while the first was still in Russia, under the pretext of carrying greetings to the new Tsaritsa Anna.[91] This suite of more than twenty men arrived in Kiakhta on 21 April 1731, and beyond its curiosity value would hardly have been worth mention, save that a week later, there arrived at the border a second embassy accredited to the Turguts and dispatched by the Kalmyk khan (Namki Retsuli), then residing in Peking. This was a larger suite of fifty-three men and three distinguished leaders, the appointed task of which was to induce the Turguts to war against the Dzhungars—the tempo of the Chinese-Dzhungar was quickening, to arm them for this conflict, and to urge them to hand over Galdan Tseren, the runaway brother of the Dzhungarian *Kontaisha* who lived in a Turgut *ulus.* Four notes regarding this embassy were sent to the Governing Senate on 18 July and 11 August, but were not received in St. Petersburg until 4 January 1732.[92] The substance of them was a request for permission for the embassy to travel through Russia and be accredited to the Turguts.

The Collegium of Foreign Affairs responded to the Chinese in memoranda of 12 January and 31 May 1732 to Vice-Governor of Irkutsk Zholobov and to Colonel Bukhol'ts instructing these Siberian officials to deny access to the embassy intending to visit the Turguts, and to inform Peking officials to that effect, but to welcome and bid godspeed to the new embassy to St. Petersburg. Zholobov passed on these orders to the Chinese in a note of 30 March, a reply to which did not arrive in St. Petersburg until nearly seven months later (23 November 1732).[93] Even then the Chinese still pursued the vain hope that the Tsaritsa would permit her subjects to fight against the Dzhungars, or at least would

90. Formal announcement of the death and replacement went to Peking in a note of 14 August 1730, carried overland by the soldier Afonasei Solov'ev and the translator Semen Kriazhev. They reached Peking on 24 December 1730, and returned to Moscow with the *Li-fan-yuan*'s reply on 17 June 1731; Bantysh-Kamenskii, *Diplomaticheskoe sobranie,* pp. 170, 186, and Andrievich, *Kratkii ocherk,* p. 150.

91. For the best sources on this embassy, consult Bantysh-Kamenskii, *Diplomaticheskoe sobranie,* pp. 170-203.

92. *Ibid.,* p. 187.

93. Zholobov replied to the *Li-fan-yuan* on 30 March 1732 stating that the Collegium of Foreign Affairs had refused permission to travel to the Turguts. Peking responded on the 10th day, 3rd month, 10th year of Yung-ch'eng (the document arriving in St. Petersburg on 23 November 1732) in a long letter requesting Russia's permission for correspondence with the Kalmyks and for the visit of the Kalmyk leader Lobzan-Shuna to Peking. *Ibid.,* p. 193.

open the way for greater Chinese influence by permitting a Turgut leader to visit Peking.

The mission to the Turguts having been turned back, the suite directed to St. Petersburg went on its way. It reached Tobol'sk on 13 February 1732 and was quartered in the Moscow suburb Aleksandrovskoe by the end of April. A splendid welcome greeted it, with three infantry regiments lining the road, drum rolls and music, and thirty-one salutes from the Admiralty cannon. On the day after its arrival in St. Petersburg, the anniversary of Anna's coronation (28 April 1732), the Empress received the Chinese in a gorgeous display befitting the day. Vice-Chancellor Osterman officially greeted them only because the Chancellor Count Golovkin was indisposed with the gout, and he accepted two notes from the *Li-fan-yuan*, one congratulating Anna and the other expressing the satisfaction of the Ch'ing emperor with a letter from Bukhol'ts to the Tushetu Khan to the effect that fugitive Mongols would be henceforth deported, together with their cattle and possessions. As with the first embassy, gifts were ceremoniously exchanged and after a stay of less than three months the embassy left St. Petersburg on 15 July, reaching Selenginsk a bit more than six months later. Few concrete accomplishments came from this second embassy, except that together with the first it contributed significantly to the beginning of a long period of cordial relations between the two empires, a prerequisite to sizeable and successful commerce.[94]

The two embassies in retrospect constitute the final chapter in the long and difficult negotiations that began in 1725. Although Russian authorities were patently unwilling to commit themselves or to permit the Turguts to be committed to an active alliance against the Dzhungars, it seems apparent that St. Petersburg accepted a kind of passive neutrality somewhat beyond that reflected in the Treaty of Kiakhta. Realistically that was probably all that the Manchu court desired. These embassies helped to attain the free hand the Manchus needed and desired against the Dzhungars; the only mar on otherwise pleasant proceedings was the renewed dispute over the title of the Russian Senate used in correspondence, and this was not very serious. If the Peking court were not convinced that the Treaty of Kiakhta provided the assurances she

94. *Ibid.*, p. 191. In Gaston Cahen's words, the second embassy, save for the richness of the gifts, was "un simple prolongement" of the first; Cahen, *Revue historique,* CXXXIII (January-February, 1920), 88.

needed for the free hand, she certainly was assured by the experiences of the missions.[95]

To be sure the embassies themselves had little direct influence on the course of war in Dzhungaria. The struggle repeatedly ravaged local Mongols, whether they were combatants or not, and caused large-scale treks into Siberia. In 1733-34, the imperial armies of China took the field in force, and after reoccupying some territory, struck a peace with Galdan Tseren in 1735.[96] That the

95. The pleasure of Peking is obvious in the astonishingly valuable gifts sent to Russia following the first embassy. Cottons, silks, precious stones, etc., all in all some 468 chests of goods valued at 100,000 *liang* (circa 130,000 r.) were received by Colonel Bukhol'ts. He forwarded this munificence to Moscow, a portion of which was divided among five high Russian officials, and the remainder reverted to the Collegium of Foreign Affairs. To what extent the Manchus intended this generosity to influence or "bribe" the Russians to remain neutral in the Central Asian conflicts remains a matter of speculation. The traditional Chinese tributary system involved often exceptionally dear gifts to tributary nations or peoples, often far exceeding the market value of tribute brought to Peking. Nonetheless it would be naive to consider these gifts to Russia as no more than demonstration of gratitude for the pleasant reception of the first embassy. Although the embassy was not ostensibly a commercial venture, it is relevant to note that the value of these gifts roughly equalled the value of the average Russian caravan to Peking of this period. The net profit to the favored Russian officials and to the Collegium must have been substantially larger than that produced by any one of the caravans! The cost of transport to Moscow was only 3,800 r., and there was apparently no reciprocal gift of commensurate value. Although it is not possible to determine precisely the value of the gifts exchanged personally by Anna and the envoys, items of approximately equal value seem to have changed hands—6,000-8,000 r. worth. Consult Bantysh-Kamenskii, *Diplomaticheskoe sobranie,* p. 182, n. 1; p. 201, n. 3.

Although wholly irrelevant to our concerns here, it is of passing curiosity value to report that the members of the embassy, with the Tsaritsa's happy permission, visited the St. Petersburg Academy of Sciences on 6 June 1732. The Academy must not have been too impressive to the Chinese; it was authorized only eight years before and still in its infancy. Nonetheless the tour lasted six hours and the visitors expressed particular interest in the printing press of the Academy, which had begun operations in 1727; M. I. Radovskii, "Pervaia vekha v istorii russko-kitaiskikh nauchnykh sviazei," *Vestnik Akademii nauk SSSR,* No. 9 (September, 1959), 95-97.

96. Kurts attributes the maintenance of Dzhungarian independence at this time to the peace agreement, which he views as a direct result of general Russian colonial policy, i.e. the refusal to permit the Volga Turguts to war against the Dzhungars and the aloofness of St. Petersburg from the conflict (*Novyi Vostok,* XIX [1927], 200-201). It is dubious whether any such direct influence of Russian policy on Dzhungarian autonomy can be documented. To be sure Turgut aid in the Dzhungarian rear would have helped the Manchu armies, but whether decisively or not is moot. Russian "aloofness" was after all what China wished, although there never was imminent prospect of Russian entry into the fray against the Dzhungars.

Treaty of Kiakhta and the subsequent emendations did not result in the final triumph of Manchu arms in Central Asia cannot casually be attributed to the reticence of Russia to participate actively in the fray, nor did Peking so believe. For China as for Russia, the settlements ushered in a period of good will and permitted each to concentrate primarily on things at hand—trade for one, empire for the other—in spite of some minor bickering over Mongol deserters not returned expeditiously by Russia and the proper forms and styles of diplomatic correspondence.[97]

The Treaty of Kiakhta and the subsequent Chinese embassies settled for the moment the major differences between Russia and China. All of these differences relate to trade, at the very least in the sense that compromises and accommodations agreed upon allayed them, making possible the resumption of commercial intercourse. It goes further than that. The solutions found to the Dzhungarian problem—delimitation of the Siberian-Mongolian frontier, agreement in principle on the return of fugitives, and the mechanism for the regular consultation of border officials on disputed issues—intimately affected and perhaps dictated the future structure of trade between the two countries. Hence private trade could be and was strictly limited to two frontier locations, and any trade in Peking would be carried on only as specified by the Treaty, a single caravan of limited size every three years. Nothing in the Treaty required that the caravans had to be operated as Russian state monopolies, and by the same token nothing prohibited the Russian state from monopolizing for itself or leasing out to selected private merchants portions of the border trade or particularly valuable items of trade. The details of the organization of Russian trade still had to be worked out. The Treaty made possible the restoration and continued growth of the China trade, and, as shall be seen in the next three chapters, contributed directly to the particular ordering of that trade that in time came to be. The Russian state came to reserve for itself all Peking trade and a portion of the border trade, at the same time permitting and even encouraging the expansion of private commercial operations at Kiakhta and Tsurukhaitu.

97. See, for example, Fedor Fedorovich Martens, "Le conflict entre la Russie et la Chine, ses origines, son développement, et sa portée universelle," *Revue de droit international et de législation comparée* (Ghent), XII, Bks. 5-6 (1880), 536.

Chapter III. The New Milieu of Trade

Peter the Great employed no fixed, consistent, or persistent economic philosophy or policy throughout his long reign. All historians of the period agree, to a greater or lesser degree, on the ad hoc character of his individual economic measures, which has resulted naturally in widely varying interpretations and labels.[1] It is not, nor can it be, our task here to reproduce, to order, and to analyze those measures. Nor shall any effort be made to distinguish between native measures and policies, and those imported from Western Europe. The primary concern here is to describe one set of economic and commercial experiences, both state and private, to see what sense can be made of the decisions with regard to those experiences if general economic philosophy and doctrine are eschewed.

Particularly after Peter's journey to Paris in 1717, his administration promulgated measures intended to encourage private enterprise (within limitation), to facilitate the production of raw materials at home, to solve the factory labor shortage, and to ease the restrictions on trade and commerce, both internal and external. Peter's commercial ukazes at this time reflected the view that foreign trade was extremely important in helping to develop a modest factory system in Russia by stimulating the flow of bullion into the country, importing needed raw materials, and carrying abroad Russian fabricated products, although this last was of lesser importance to Peter. Toward these ends, Petrine policy loosened the innumerable and severe restrictions on private trade. State monopolies were not abandoned out of hand, nor did any of these measures imply they would be. Rather private merchants were encouraged to trade abroad, to bring more gold and silver into the country, and to deal in hitherto restricted goods (such as sable,

1. Consult, among other things, E. V. Spiridonova, *Ekonomicheskaia politika i ekonomicheskie vzgliady Petra I* (Moscow: Gospolitizdat, 1952); Vladimir Vladimirovich Sviatlovskii, *Istoriia ekonomicheskikh idei v Rossii*, Vol. I: *Merkantilizm, fiziokratizm, klassicheskaia shkola i ee razvetvleniia* (Petrograd: "Nachatki Znanii," 1923); B. I. Syromiatnikov, *"Reguliarnoe" gosudarstvo Petra Pervogo i ego ideologiia*, Chast' 1 (Moscow-Leningrad: Izd. Akademii Nauk SSSR, 1943); Konstantin Nikolaevich Lodyzhenskii, *Istoriia russkago tamozhennago tarifa* (St. Petersburg: Tip. V. S. Balasheva, 1886), especially pp. 49-56; Pashkov, *Istoriia russkoi ekonomicheskoi mysli*, Vol. I: *Epokha feodalizma*, Chast' 1: *IX-XVIII vv.*, especially pp. 266-317.

rhubarb, and tobacco in Siberia), although these merchants might expect to compete in many cases with state and state-farmed monopolies, which continued to bring profit to the state treasury. Siberia and the China trade were affected by these measures to varying degrees.

With regard to the China trade, the Russian court needed to make a clear decision by the mid-twenties, although prior to 1727 there was no sign that it was prepared to do so. On the one hand, it had the choice of pressing forward with these liberalizing measures, releasing monopolized goods to private trade, and perhaps abolishing the state Peking caravan and promoting the formation of a private company to assume the monopoly or at least to enjoy privileges not granted to competing private merchants. From early years of the century Peter favored the formation of private companies for commercial endeavour; indeed as early as 1711 Peter ordered the Governing Senate, "having organized a good company," to give over the China trade to it.[2] Apparently nothing came of the order. The Prut defeat and military concerns dominated the day, at least until 1719, when a temporary truce was arranged with Sweden. But the notion of a private company to assume the choice Peking trade reappeared in later years, as we shall see in Chapter 4. Were the Russian court to accept a full measure of private entrepreneurship in the China trade, either through promoting a single monopolistic private company or attempting to regulate individual merchants competing for Chinese goods, it could expect to earn considerable state revenue from the taxation of these merchants and from customs revenues. It would no longer be saddled with the heavy costs of operating its own caravans. To achieve this alternative however, the state would have to improve its administrative and legal structure in Siberia in general and on the Mongolian border in particular. Contraband trade and all other sharp and deceptive practices would have to be minimized, and past experience in Siberia did not hold very great promise that this could be achieved.

The other distinct possibility was to reinstitute state monopoly of the most valuable commodities which had been permitted private merchants in the years since 1717 and to reinvigorate the faltering state caravan to Peking. This choice also required that the state strengthen its administrative apparatus in Eastern Siberia,

2. *PSZ*, IV, No. 2330, 643, Ukaz dated 2 March 1711; consult Pt. 8 of the Ukaz.

no less than if it removed its hand from the China trade. In any case, the necessity of a finer and more dependable administrative structure was imperative and long overdue.

In the end the choice between these two broad approaches was made as much in Peking as in St. Petersburg. Simply enough, the treaty arrangements negotiated by Vladislavich made feasible the renewal of state monopolies in the China trade or laid the foundations for the extension of private operations closely regulated by officers of the state, whichever the St. Petersburg officialdom chose. The founding of border trading posts at Kiakhta and Tsurukhaitu, the delimitation and fortification of the Siberian-Mongolian border, and the explicit provisions covering caravans to Peking all worked to encourage the state to exercise a stronger hand in ending the disarray in this valuable commerce. Vladislavich and Lange, however, contributed to the immediate decision—to persist in direct state caravan trade with Peking and to limit private traders to border trade in legal goods under the close scrutiny of an augmented corps of government officials.

Vladislavich and the Reaffirmation of Monopoly

The Treaty provisions provided the possibility of reinvigorated state monopoly, but new ukazes enforced by capable administrators had to make that monopoly viable. Vladislavich and Lange both used their considerable influence in St. Petersburg to persuade the court to reassert the monopoly system and to give it a reasonable chance of success by tightening up the controls all along the line. There was nothing especially new about this; as early as 1722 Lange, for example, had deplored the excessive number of private caravans to Peking and Urga.

Vladislavich left no doubt that he was convinced that Siberian and Chinese trade had immense potential for the court and the country. Shortly after his arrival in Selenginsk he dispatched a report, dated 31 August 1726, to the Collegium of Foreign Affairs which rhapsodized on the expansiveness of Siberia and contrasted its natural magificence with the mean and minute Russian settlements:

> The Siberian province, as much as I have been able to see and hear, is not a province, but an empire, with many in-

habited places and prolific embellishments. . . . However . . . in all of Siberia there is not a single flourishing town nor a stronghold, particularly on the border on this side of the Baikal sea. Selenginsk is not a town, nor a village—but a hamlet *(derevushka)* with 250 houses and two wooden churches, built on a spot worthless for anything and exposed to attack; a square wooden stronghold such that in the event of unfortunate attack in two hours [it] will all be consumed; and Nerchinsk, so they say, is still worse.[3]

In addition China was a vast potential market, a source of treasure, well-populated, and rich. To Russia's good fortune China was poorly defended, rent by divisions between Manchus, Mongols and Chinese, and capped by a shaky "foreign" sovereign. Vladislavich interpreted these debilities as offering an alert Russian administration great opportunity for commercial and possibly political expansion. Still he noted in 1726, private merchants seemed to be the only ones successful in tapping this potential, even though they were compelled to operate illicitly for the most part:

Russian trading people carry from Siberia to Urga a large quantity of peltry; in a year more than in two [state] caravans . . . is delivered, and of customs duties *(poshlini)*, not only on peltry but also on other goods carried to Urga and to the Chinese state, more than 20,000 rubles to the treasury . . . . are not gathered, and such great and disorganized trade in peltry, by and large, the Chinese still do not investigate.[4]

To inhibit the incursions of private merchants on the state's prerogative, Vladislavich suggested that before the next caravan set out an imperial ukaz be issued which strictly prohibited all private trading in China, under threat of loss of goods and possibly life. The conduct of the caravans should be carefully cir-

3. Solov'ev, *Istoriia,* IV, 1135; paraphrased in *PSZ,* VII, No. 4994, 724-25, Ukaz dated 30 December 1726.

4. *PSZ,* VII, No. 4992, 723-25, which extracts Vladislavich's report of 31 August 1726. Quoted also in Silin, *Kiakhta,* p. 29; see also Cahen, *Histoire,* p. 242. Vladislavich submitted three major pieces on the potential of the China trade: his report of 31 August 1726 on his departure for Peking, another report of 28 September 1727 on his return, and his secret memorandum of 1730. See Cahen, *Histoire,* pp. lxxiii-lxxx, for partial text and French translation of the second report.

cumscribed, the caravan officials paid fixed salaries instead of being permitted to trade on their own accounts, and exact and detailed account books kept.[5]

The Supreme Privy Council *(Verkhovnyi tainyi sovet)* accepted part of Vladislavich's advice. On 30 December 1726 it issued an ukaz forbidding private commerce in furs to China or Chinese controlled territories while the Tret'iakov-Molokov caravan traded in Peking.[6] At this juncture, the treaty arrangements with China not yet known, the Council decided to end the state caravans: this caravan was to be the last, after which private merchants would be permitted to carry all goods directly to the China markets.[7] The decision was never carried out, for on 26 June 1727, even before the details of the treaty settlement were known in St. Petersburg, the usual prohibition against private trading in Chinese dominions was repeated. Finally three and one-half years later, on 3 January 1731, came the definitive decision. Trade in peltry to China was for the third time interdicted and the precise organization of all future caravans was laid down.[8] Caravans were henceforth to be purely state operations, all officials of them to be paid salaries and forbidden to trade on their own. The choice had at last been made. Until the reign of Peter III, the Russian state was destined to attempt by a variety of means to enforce the reinstituted caravan monopoly. Except for several abortive efforts in later years, which we shall comment on in the next chapter, private merchants were prohibited from crossing the frontier to trade directly in Chinese territories and from trafficking in rhubarb, fine pelts and several other reserved goods. Vladislavich by deed and word helped to swing St. Petersburg policy makers, flirting with the complete freeing of private merchants, back to deep state involvement in this distant trade. Private merchants labored under severe restriction for over three decades more.

5. When Tret'iakov asked appointment as commissar of the caravan early in 1722 he petitioned to trade on his own account. The Senate granted the petition on 9 March 1722, and subsequently issued an ukaz to the Collegium of Foreign Affairs informing them of the appointment and of the fact that Tret'iakov would be permitted to carry 3000 r. worth of merchandise of his own. Ten sworn appraisers also were permitted to trade another 3000 r. worth or a total of 6000 r. of private goods on which would be charged the usual customs duties; see Cahen, *Histoire*, pp. 227-28.

6. *PSZ*, VII, No. 4992, 723-25.

7. Consult Silin, *Kiakhta*, p. 29.

8. Cahen, *Histoire*, p. 243, and Silin, *Kiakhta*, p. 46.

The Organization of the Border

On the Russian Side

The deeds of Vladislavich did not end there. He left his mark on the frontier as well, by helping to create the conditions indispensible to the successful renewal of the state's monopolies.

On 20 August 1727, shortly after signing the Treaty of the Bur, Vladislavich returned to Selenginsk to send off the caravan of Tret'iakov-Molokov and to indicate the construction of frontier trading posts and fortifications. The final duties of the ambassador were discharged the following spring (1728), after the ratification of the Treaty of Kiakhta. He issued a series of highly detailed instructions to the several officials appointed to regulate border affairs, instructions dealing with border organization, the division of administrative responsibilities, lines of reporting and responsibility, and the construction of posts and facilities.[9]

General responsibility for the conduct of border matters was entrusted by Vladislavich to Colonel Ivan D. Bukhol'ts, appointed Border Commandant *(Pogranichnyi komandant)* and chief of the General Border Administration *(General'noe pogranichnoe upravlenie)* located in Selenginsk, some fifty to sixty miles north of Kiakhta and by water 265 miles from Irkutsk.[10] The Border Commandant was charged with carrying out the new treaty and agreements, supervision of two new border trading posts to be built (Kiakhta and Tsurukhaitu), and maintenance of pacific relations with the Manchu officials in Urga and at the border. To accomplish the latter, he was empowered to communicate directly with his counterpart on the Mongolian side, the Tushetu Khan, utilizing a newly minted seal for this purpose. When travelling to Urga to consult with the Khan or Manchu officials, Bukhol'ts was to order in advance that post horses be provided him by the Manchus and to demand an immediate reply as provided for in the treaty. He had to take special care with envoys from either Moscow or Peking who bore instructions to proceed through to the other capital. For delegations which came from Peking with papers from the

9. The *Instruktsiia* dated 30 June 1728 in Selenginsk; Sychevskii, *Chteniia OIDR*, Bk. 2 (April-June 1875), 56-77; Bantysh-Kamenskii, *Diplomaticheskoe sobranie*, pp. 156-59; summary in Cahen, *Histoire*, pp. 221-24.

10. Sychevskii, *Chteniia OIDR*, Bk. 2 (April-June 1875), 56-77. Selenginsk was founded as an *ostrog* in 1666; some twenty years later it became a *krepost'*.

Figure 2. Selenginsk. From James Gilmour, *Among the Mongols* (New York: American Tract Society, n.d.), p. 39. Probably made in the 1860's.

Li-fan-yuan and with passport, Bukhol'ts was to allow two or three individuals to travel on and to give to them whatever supplies they needed. If a Russian courier arrived from either Moscow or Tobol'sk, Urga had to be informed immediately and reminded that under the Treaty the courier was to be permitted to travel unimpeded to Peking.

As Border Commandant, Bukhol'ts commanded all military units in the vicinity and was to keep one battalion in readiness on the Chikoi and in outposts elsewhere, in addition to the regiment to be stationed at the new border fort of Troitskosavsk. He had no discretionary powers to declare war or take the offensive, however, but rather was to avoid involvement in the old Chinese feud with the Dzhungars. Specifically Vladislavich ordered him to prevent the export of cattle to Mongolia which might be used to revictual the Chinese armies in the field. He was to keep in close touch with Lorents Lange on matters of treating the Chinese and to communicate with him only in cipher on confidential subjects. Vladislavich counseled the colonel against direct interference in the day-to-day conduct of border affairs and the trading towns, since other officials were designated for these duties with their own specific directives. He was ordered to report on all matters directly to the *voevoda* of Irkutsk (Izmailov) and the governor-general of Siberia in Tobol'sk (Dolgorukii). This gave him fairly quick access to higher authorities although still within the colonial chain of command in Siberia.

Rebuilding of the Selenginsk *krepost'*—Bukhol'ts headquarters—in the new location did not progress with dispatch. On 15 January 1728 there arrived in Selenginsk a Bombardier Lieutenant of the Preobrazhenskii Guards Regiment, Abram Petrovich Gannibal, none other than the Blackamoor of Peter the Great *(arap Petra Velikago)*, father of Lt.-General Ivan Abramovich Gannibal noted for his command and rebuilding of the Kherson fort in 1778-81, and maternal great-grandfather of Pushkin.[11] Gannibal reputedly was the son of an Abyssinian prince, a Turkish vassal, given over to the Sultan's seraglio in Constantinople at an early age, whence he was brought to Russia in or about 1705 on order of Peter I by the envoy Vladislavich-Raguzinskii![12] Peter sent Gannibal to France in 1717 for military engineering training and, as it turned out, for great adventures as a volunteer in the French army in Spain where he was wounded and captured. After his return to Russia five years later, he performed engineering tasks at Kronshtadt and Kazan' before being posted to Selenginsk. Gannibal was completely disheartened when he saw the task facing him. By late spring he complained sharply to Vladislavich in a letter and petitioned that he be released from the assignment.[13] He insisted, all too modestly, that he had no experience in fortress building; he lamented that necessary manuals and instruments were unavailable and that his pay and expense money had not reached him. Abruptly and without orders, he left for Tobol'sk. Another ukaz of 17

11. *PSZ*, VIII, No. 5254, 22-23. Also consult Andrievich, *Kratkii ocherk*, p. 144, and Bantysh-Kamenskii, *Diplomaticheskoe sobranie*, p. 145. The name Gannibal (Hannibal) was used as early as 1723, although the blackamoor's baptismal name was Petr Petrovich Petrov. He preferred Abram or Avraam, Russian equivalent of Ibrahim, as he was known in Constantinople. Apparently the Gannibal was formalized after his Selenginsk adventure, in the 1730's. He retired from government service of old age in 1762, and died in 1781. A superb investigation of Gannibal, a little gem of historical research, is the account of Vladimir Nabokov in Pushkin, *Eugene Onegin*, III, 387-447.

12. *RBS*, vol. Gaag-Gerbel, 217-18; *Sbornik RIO*, LXXXIV (1893), 129.

13. *Sbornik RIO*, LXXXIV (1893), 129; CI (1898), 542.

July 1728 ordered him to return to Selenginsk, but he remained obstinate and was eventually taken under guard to Tomsk.[14] He was replaced by an Engineer-ensign *(Inzhener-praporshchik)* Semen Babarykin (Bobarykin) who for various infractions was also in 1731 disciplined. Vladislavich's plans for a new and powerful fortress remained unfulfilled.[15]

Although it never became a powerful military installation, Selenginsk grew rather impressively, at least contrasted with other Siberian towns of those days. J. G. Gmelin, a German naturalist who accompanied G. F. Müller on the Second Kamchatka Expedition, visited there in 1735 and described it as a substantial frontier town.[16] It had then five warehouses for grain, two powder magazines, two churches, some shops, two taverns, and a cellar for brandy. By the end of the eighteenth century, it claimed 2,597 male inhabitants, or a total population of probably at least 6,000.[17]

Vladislavich devoted his closest attention to the two trading posts to be raised at the border, Kiakhta on the border and Tsurukhaitu far to the east on a site on the Argun River.[18] The two mercantile towns were to be built and administered by serving men under the command of officers appointed by Vladislavich in his Instructions: a Captain Fedor Kniaginkin of the Tobol'sk Guards Regiment for Kiakhta and a Captain Mikhail Shkader (or Chkader) of the same regiment for Tsurukhaitu. They bore the title *osteregatel'*, probably derived from the verb *osteregat'*, "to caution" or "to warn." Kniaginkin was aided by the Selenginsk gentryman *(dvorianin)* Aleksei Tret'iakov (probably kin of the deceased caravan commander) for minor judicial matters and a corporal in

14. *Ibid.*, LXXXIV (1893), 128, Ukaz of the Supreme Privy Council signed by General-Admiral Count Apraksin and Chancellor Golovkin: *PSZ*, VIII, No. 5309, 66, and Andrievich, *Kratkii ocherk*, p. 144.

15. Bantysh-Kamenskii, *Diplomaticheskoe sobranie*, p. 162.

16. Johann Georg Gmelin, *"Voyage au Kamtschatka par la Siberie,"* in Antoine François Prevost (ed.), *Histoire générale des voyages* (Paris: Rozet, 1746-91), XVIII, 194.

17. Heinrich Friedrich von Storch, *Statistische Übersicht der Statthalterschaften des Russischen Reichs nach ihren Merkwürdigsten Kulturverhältnissen* (Riga: Johann Friedrich Hartknoch, 1795), p. 86.

18. The town Kiakhta took its name from the stream on which it was located, a small branch of the Selenga. Bodnarskii claims the name originally derived from the Mongol *Kiet-tu* meaning "covered with rushes"; Mitrofan Stefanovich Bodnarskii, *Slovar' geograficheskikh nazvanii* (2d ed., Moscow: Gos. Uchebno-Pedagogicheskoe Izd., Ministerstva Prosveshcheniia RSFSR, 1958), pp. 182-83. Tsurukhaitu, sometimes rendered Tsuru-Khaitu, is obviously of Manchu or Mongol origin.

charge of a small body of troops. Tret'iakov evidently was especially well skilled for the task. He was said to understand the Mongol and Chinese languages because he was a member of earlier caravans to Peking. Shkader was also to share his authority with a gentryman and a corporal. Both captains received extraordinarily minute instructions from Vladislavich, which defined their administrative responsibilities and provided them with precise plans for the trading posts to be constructed, although leaving exact locations to their discretion.[19] They exercised specific jurisdiction over the collection of customs charges and the regulation of public liquor vendors, and were in general to maintain law and order through the use of the troops stationed at the posts.

Three hundred and fifty men of the Tobol'sk Guards Regiment, paid from the state treasury, were assigned to Kiakhta throughout the summer and early fall of 1728 to carry on the construction. These were the same troops that accompanied the embassy to Peking. Some thirty serving men—Cossacks—from Udinsk were instructed to come with twenty-five carts and horses to work for three months, although they had to bring their own provisions. The main market place at Kiakhta was designed in a square, approximately 215 yards on each side, with watchtowers at each corner. Within this square the merchants were to live in thirty-two huts *(izby)*, each with a Russian stove *(pech')*, and in the middle of the town was a bazaar *(gostinnyi dvor)* of twenty-four stalls *(lavki)*, twelve on a side, on the first level and storerooms *(ambary)* on the second.[20] These small stalls, constructed as was usual in

19. Sychevskii, *Chteniia OIDR*, Bk. 2 (April-May 1875), 37-47; summarized in Cahen, *Histoire*, p. 222, n. 2.

20. The number of shops or stalls was increased in later years; Falk reports some sixty "boutiques": Nicholas Gabriel Clerc, *Histoire physique, morale, civile et politique de la Russie Moderne par MM. Le Clerc pere* [*and*] . . . *Le Clerc fils* (Paris: Froulle, 1783-94), III, 387. The *gostinnyi dvor* is a peculiarly Russian market place, described by Strahlenberg about this time in these words: "*Gostinoy-dwor*, are a kind of large Squares walled in, within which are built, on every Side, convenient Ware-Houses and Shops, for all Sorts of Commodities; And in the Middle, Room enough is left for Carriages to go in and unload. These Square Places are erected at the Charge of the Government, in all Capital trading Cities, as *Muscow, Petersburg, Archangel, Kiow, Novgorod*, &c. The Word signifies a Store-house for Strangers." Philip Johan Tabbert von Strahlenberg, *An Historico-Geographical Description of the North and Eastern Parts of Europe and Asia; but more Particularly of Russia, Siberia, and Great Tartary; Both in their Ancient and Modern State: Together with an Entire New Polyglot-Table of the Dialects of 32 Tartarian Nations . . .* trans. from the German (London: W. Innys and R. Manby, 1738), p. 364. Strahlenberg was a Swedish officer taken by the Russians after the defeat of

Old Russia at state expense, were let to merchants for the profit of the treasury. Each merchant's cart passing through Kiakhta was also required to pay a toll of one ruble and twenty kopecks, to be devoted to help maintain the post (5 per cent of which would revert to Captain Kniaginkin for "pocket expenses").[21] The instructions for Tsurukhaitu were no less detailed; the town and all its dimensions were simply smaller.

In spite of the great care taken by Vladislavich, later eighteenth-century and early nineteenth-century travellers agreed unanimously that the location of Kiakhta was most unfortunate.[22] One Russian marvelled "that two powers like Russia and China had not treated themselves to something grander,"[23] another that "everything, in short, denotes a frontier situation."[24] Kiakhta was situated in a broad, shallow, but elevated basin, with topographically the most impressive thing being the rising hills on all sides. The valley it-

---

Charles XII; together with the well-known Prussian naturalist Messerschmidt he explored the lower basins of the Ob' and the Enisei. His description is excellent, except for his etymological explanation. By the eighteenth century *gost'* had long since taken on the special meaning of "large merchant" in addition to "stranger" or "guest," and *dvor* retained its use as "court" or "court-yard," although here signifying "storehouse." The *gostinnyi dvor* of Kiakhta was to be 112 ft. long and 21 ft. wide; the *izby* of two sizes, five meters square and six meters by three. Nineteenth-century photographs of Kiakhta show a *dvor* very similar to the plans of Vladislavich, although of course the original ones were rebuilt in later years. A stone court was built in 1842 on the site of the wooden structure, although it also was replaced. Messerschmidt's account of his Siberian travels is being reprinted in East Berlin: Daniel Gottlieb Messerschmidt, *Forschungsreise durch Sibirien, 1720-1727*, ed. E. Winter, G. Uschmann and G. Jarosch (Berlin: Akademie-Verlag, 1962—), see especially Bd. VIII, Teil 2, pp. 226-39.

Today the outline of the original structure of the Kiakhta *dvor* can still be seen, although it is now used as a general factory: S. P. Kostarev, *Istoricheskie pamiatniki Buriatii (Kratkii spravochnik)* (Ulan-Ude: Buriatskoe Knizhnoe Izd., 1959), p. 84. Still today in the great *GUM (Gosudarstvennyi Universal'nyi Magazin)* on Moscow's Red Square and the *Gostinnyi Dvor* on *Nevskii Prospekt* in Leningrad can be seen the same basic arrangement.

21. Sychevskii, *Chteniia OIDR*, Bk. 2 (April-June 1875), 227; Cahen *Histoire*, p. 222, n. 2; *Baikal*, No. 10 (3 August 1897), p. 3.

22. See, for example, Gmelin, *Voyage*, XVII, 190-91 (1735), Peter Simon Pallas, *Voyages de M.P.S. Pallas, en différentes provinces de l'empire de Russie, et dans l'Asie septentrionale*, trans. M. Gauthier de la Peyronie (Paris: Maradan, 1788-93), IV, 150 (1772); John Dundas Cochrane, *Narrative of a Pedestrian Journey through Russia and Siberian Tartary, From the Frontiers of China to the Frozen Sea and Kamchatka; Performed During the Years 1820, 1821, 1822, and 1823* (London: J. Murray, 1824), II, 167-68 (1823).

23. Pavel Iakovlevich Piasetskii, *Russian Travellers in Mongolia and China*, trans. J. Gordon-Cumming (London: Chapman & Hall, 1884), I, 6-7.

24. Cochrane, *Pedestrian Journey*, II, 166.

Figure 3. A general view of Kiakhta, showing the "Neutral Ground." A steel engraving from a sketch by G. A. Frost. From George Kennan, *Siberia and the Exile System* (New York: The Century Co., 1891), II, 103.

self was largely treeless and denuded, and the soil so poor and the precipitation so scant that ordinary vegetables were raised only with great care.[25] Firewood had to be carted from distant forests; cattle and horses had no adequate grazing land. Worst of all there was no adequate supply of safe drinking water nearby (much of it had to be carried from the Mongol side of the border, or animals driven there for watering). In later years the stream Kiakhta was dammed, and a small but rank pond partly alleviated this shortage. In brief, this was no rural paradise, although after an inauspicious beginning, the town grew slowly over the years and achieved certain hallmarks of culture—a manner of living that was "polite and sociable, which one does not encounter in another town of Siberia, except Irkutsk,"[26] merchant houses with stairs and balconies which in some cases "are painted and embellished with architectual ornaments,"[27] a stone church to replace the original wooden one, and eventually, in the later eighteenth century, the rise of Ust'-Kiakhta, some miles away on the Selenga and about six hundred feet lower in elevation, described as "an agreeable summer residence for the merchants of Kiakhta."[28] When the town was still only seven years old, Gmelin described ordinary baths, a cellar for beer, another for brandy, a brewery, and a tavern.[29] In time the original merchants' *dvor* proved too small and other larger shops were built of stone "as have been built in St. Petersburg," while the cost of construction was to be paid out of the proceeds of Kiakhta customs duties and private merchants were to continue to pay for their use.[30] There rose outside of the ramparts of Kiakhta proper a dwelling suburb, which housed most of the permanent inhabitants. Pallas reported 120 houses in 1772, but Gagemeister's later account lists only 32 in 1829 and 31 in 1852 (a population in 1829 of 326 including 119 merchants, and of 594 in 1852 with 214 merchants).[31] These figures likely apply only to "Old Kiakhta," i.e. the original

25. Gmelin described it as "plus aride, puis que d'est une miserable steppe qui ne produit rien"; *Voyage*, p. 190.

26. Pallas, *Voyages*, IV, 150.

27. Adolph Erman, *Travels in Siberia: Including Excursions Northwards, Down the Obi, to the Polar Circle, and, Southwards, to the Chinese Frontier*, trans. William Desborough Cooley (Philadelphia: Lea & Blanchard, 1850), II, 162. Observation made in 1850.

28. *Ibid.*, II, 161.

29. Gmelin, *Voyage*, p. 191.

30. Senate report to Catherine II on 5 June 1763: *Senatskii arkhiv*, XII, 459.

31. Gagemeister, *Statisticheskoe obozrenie Sibiri*, II, 188-89. Today the town has a population of about 10,000: Bodnarskii, *Slovar'*, pp. 182-83.

Figure 4. Kiakhta. From George Frederick Wright, *Asiatic Russia* (New York: McClure, Phillips & Co., 1902), II, facing p. 474.

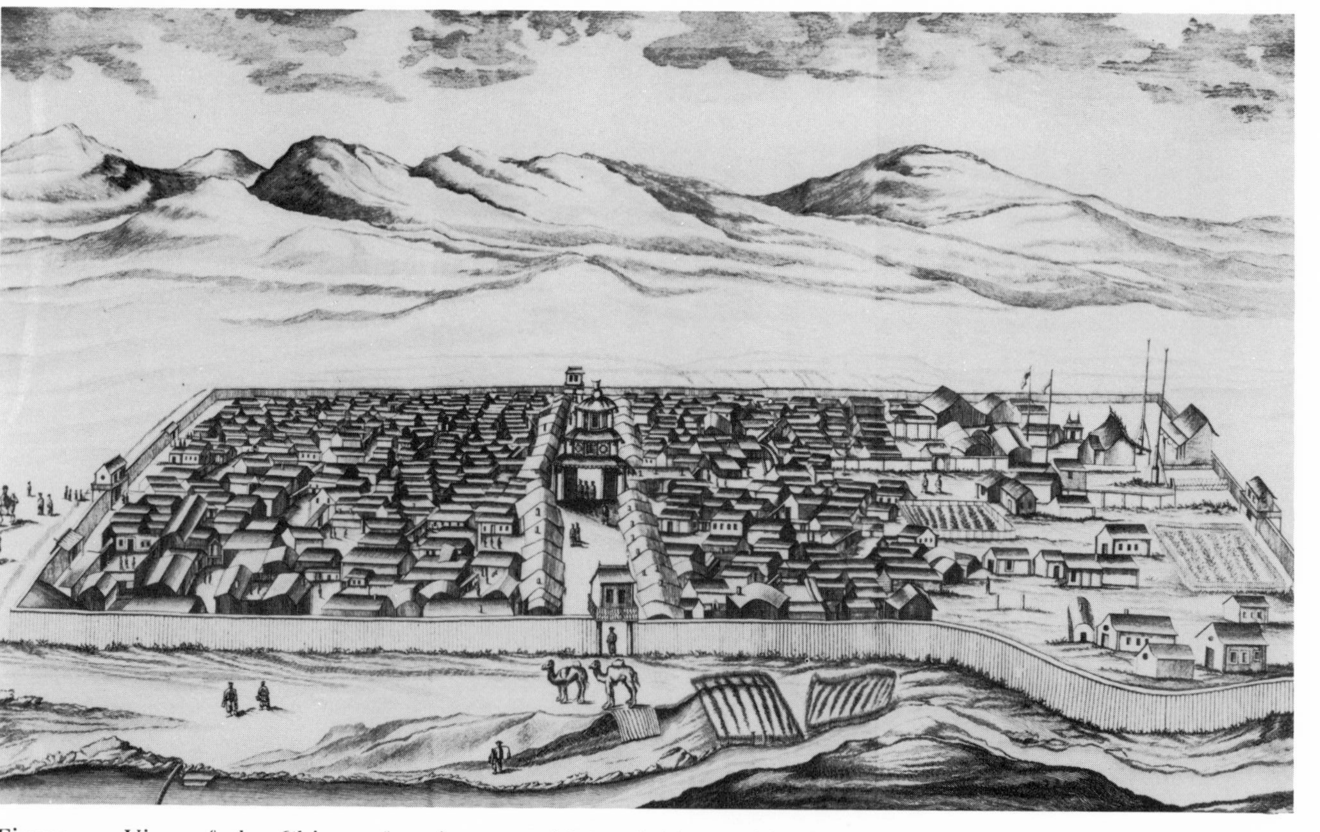

Figure 5. View of the Chinese frontier town Mai-mai-ch'eng with the Brook Kiakhta, taken from the west. From William Coxe, *Account of Russian Discoveries Between Asia and America* (London: T. Cadell, 1780), between pp. 210-11. This engraving is "represented with the greatest exactness" as Coxe was "informed by a gentle man who has been on the spot" (p. 221, n.).

site surrounded by *chevaux-de-frise* and reserved for merchantry, for Cochrane reported in the year 1823 some 45 houses there, with greater Kiakhta having 450 houses and a population of 4000.[32]

In later years Kiakhta developed something of a town administration, headed by a *zemskaia izba* or "local town hall."[33] Prior to 1774 the Kiakhta *izba* was subordinate to the Selenginsk *gorodovaia ratusha* ("town hall"), then to the Verkhneudinsk *gorodovoi* ("mayor"), and finally to the Irkutsk governor's office. It properly reflected the exclusive mercantile character of the town: it had at its head an elder *(starosta)* selected from among the merchants residing in Kiakhta. The elder was chosen from among the substantial and "first-rank" *(pervostateinye)* merchants in meetings held of all those registered as merchants. Beneath the elder served aldermen *(al'dermany)* who had to be guild artisans *(tsekhovye)* representing "various masters" and who were literate. The merchants and artisans *(tsekhovye, remeslenniki)* together selected several literate men of good character to serve in the Selenginsk chancellery as valuers *(otsenshchiki)* and sworn-appraisers *(tseloval'niki)* of the merchandise presented for customs inspection and taxation. And in addition Kiakhta was represented in the Irkutsk provincial chancellery by two "petitioners" *(chelobitchiki)* who took part in tax, commercial and judicial matters that affected Kiakhta residents.[34]

Vladislavich instructed that another fort be built—Troitskosavsk (Troitskaia fort or Novotroitsk) nearly three miles downstream on the Brook Kiakhta and north toward Selenginsk, on the site of an earlier wintering spot, Barsukovskoe *zimov'e*. The fort was to be 1680 feet in diameter, to have a wooden church named *Presviataia*

32. Cochrane, *Pedestrian Journey*, II, 167. Silin (*Kiakhta*, p. 91, quoting a document in the *Gosudarstvennyi arkhiv Irkutskoi oblasti*) gives 380 merchants (males) for 1768 and 874 guildmen *(tsekhovye)*, and for 1774, 488 merchants and 908 guildmen. In 1761 Selenginsk commandant Iakobi supported by Siberian governor Soimonov did request permission to remove the town and its fortifications some distance back from the border to a spot between Troitskosavsk and Kiakhta. The main reason seems not to have been the poor location, but the desire to get further from the prying eyes of Chinese whom it was considered gained something of a commercial advantage by spying on the Russians. In any event the Senate refused the request. *PSZ*, XV, No. 11322, 777-79, Senate ukaz of 4 September 1761, and Andrievich, *Kratkii ocherk*, p. 188.

33. Silin, *Kiakhta*, pp. 91-92.

34. The Kiakhta *zemskaia izba* also employed some ten messengers *(khodoki)*, put to good use maintaining communications with Selenginsk, Irkutsk, and the other Russian towns and with the Mongol capital of Urga, four collectors *(sborshchiki)*, and one watchman *(storozh)*.

Troitsa (Most Holy Trinity),[35] a large wooden customs house of six rooms, a prison, stables, warehouses, and all other accoutrements of the town which was to be the administrative, customs, and military headquarters of the immediate border region. To bar the roads and prevent smuggling, palisades and *chevaux-de-frise* were raised, eventually reaching all the way to Kiakhta in one direction and to the Chikoi River in the other. The soldiers who guarded the frontier in this area were normally quartered in the casernes of Troitskosavsk. Kiakhta was the main commercial settlement; Troitskosavsk was the administrative and military center. Merchants were required to take the route directly there, where their goods were to be inspected and state customs duties levied.

A little less than fifty miles further north and within five to eight miles of Selenginsk was still another fort, Strelka or Petropavlovsk, also part of the only legal route of travel for merchants. Located on a spit of land at the confluence of the Chikoi and Selenga Rivers, palisades which stretched from the river to the mountains were eventually raised here as well, and were intended to effectively bar the road. At times Strelka served as the main customs collection point. In the years after the treaty was signed, it was used as a staging place for the Peking caravan and a military garrison as well, although Gmelin reported that the regiment assigned there had been reduced to 220 men, the remainder being detached elsewhere.[36]

The actual patrolling and arming of the long frontier from the Shabina Dabeg in the west to the Argun silver mines in the east were placed in the hands of two newly appointed Border Inspectors *(Pogranichnye dozorshchiki),* Grigorii Firsov (to inspect east of Kiakhta) and Onasim Mikhalev (to inspect west of Kiakhta).[37] Firsov was a Selenginsk gentryman, appointed by Vladislavich to the customs house in his hometown. In later years he commanded one of the state caravans to Peking, as we shall see. Mikhalev was of a lower rank of serving men *(boiarskie deti)* from Irkutsk, who had helped delimit the border west of Kiakhta in

35. Bantysh-Kamenskii, *Diplomaticheskoe sobranie,* pp. 156-57. When Vladislavich reached Moscow he sent back on 29 January 1729 five bells weighing over 700 lbs.

36. Gmelin, *Voyage,* pp. 193-94.

37. Sychevskii, *Chteniia OIDR,* Bk. 2 (April-June, 1875), 25-37; Bantysh-Kamenskii (*Diplomaticheskoe sobranie,* p. 157) gives Mikhalev as Mikhnev and his class as *syn boiarskii.*

1727. Each summer the two were to tour the border, maintain the boundary markers, inspect the native border guards, and as much as possible prevent passage of contraband and deserters in either direction. Sixty-four guardposts, manned by local Siberians (Buriats and Tungus) and settled Cossacks, were to be erected along the frontier. Eventually eight small forts guarded the border from Tomsk *oblast'* to the sea.[38] Local Siberians of Nerchinsk and Selenginsk *uezdy* were permitted to sell horses, cattle, and sheep in and near Kiakhta and Tsurukhaitu with the payment of high customs duties of fifty kopeks per horse and five per sheep. The reason for this special privilege was the general poverty of these people and their inability to pay the annual *iasak* tax laid upon them. Even for this privilege they had to pay however, for each family *(rod)* was to provide five workers to aid in building the forts and to provide twenty sheep every three years to feed the forts and those having business at the frontier.[39]

The second of the new border trading towns, Tsurukhaitu on the Argun, intended to replace the Manchurian city of Naun as a place of Russian travel, earns only brief mention. The site on the river known locally up to that time as Tsurukhaitu was picked early in 1728 in a meeting between a *komissar* of the Argun silver mines, one Timofei Burtsov, and a Chinese officer.[40] Although as carefully provided for in Vladislavich's instructions as was Kiakhta, the town made little headway in the next seven years because of the predilection of Vice-Governor Zholobov for another location well within Russian territory.[41] Not until 1736 was his successor, Bibikov, ordered to commence the job. Tsurukhaitu's physical setting was unhappy; according to Gmelin who visited there in 1735, "it would have been difficult to choose a location more inhospitable. . . ."[42] Firewood was over twenty-five miles distant, grazing was poor, and the town repeatedly flooded by the uncontrolled Argun. In 1756 St. Petersburg authorized Siberian Gov-

38. Gorbitsa, Tsurukhaitu, Chananturukussk, Kudarinsk, Troitskosavsk, Kharaitseisk, Tunkinsk, and Akchinsk; Aleksandr Kazimirovich Korsak, *Istoriko-statisticheskoe obozrenie torgovykh snoshenii Rossii s Kitaem* (Kazan'; I. Dubrovin, 1857), p. 53. See Pallas (*Voyages*, IV, 151-54) for a list of fortified places along the border in the 1770's.

39. Bantysh-Kamenskii, *Diplomaticheskoe sobranie*, p. 158.

40. *PSZ*, VIII, No. 5268, 36. Letters exchanged confirming the selection.

41. Zholobov preferred the side of the village of Olonchinskaia, more than sixty miles within Russian territory; Bantysh-Kamenskii, *Diplomaticheskoe sobranie*, pp. 223-25.

42. Gmelin, *Voyage*, p. 217.

ernor Miatlev to move the post some distance downstream to a spot less susceptible to chronic inundation, and although this was done it seems to have had very little impact on the commercial value of the town.[43]

From the founding of the town, the bulk of the trade carried on there was performed by the Chinese border inspectors who passed through at least once annually. They usually camped across the river from the post for a period of ten days to one month in early summer; unlike at Kiakhta the Chinese never erected a permanent suburb of their own in Manchu territory. Initially the trade was so modest that no customs duties were collected on it, which permitted some of the small band of Cossacks stationed there to accumulate tidy sums. Eventually Tsurukhaitu formally became a market town *(iarmarka)*, and held a fair in June and July,[44] but even then it seems to have been largely a local operation. The larger merchants who had traded at Naun earlier all moved their operations to Kiakhta or to the city of Irkutsk itself.[45]

There were several obvious reasons for this stagnation. The overall journey from Irkutsk to Peking via Tsurukhaitu, Naun, and Shanhaikuan was many hundreds of miles farther than by way of Kiakhta and Kalgan. The terrain of the trek, although not desert, was as difficult, especially the highlands between Lake Baikal and the Argun; the danger from marauding bandits was every bit as great. Merchandise from Russia could be brought nearly to Kiakhta by boat or raft, utilizing the Selenga River, but the Tsurukhaitu route required expensive and time-consuming overland travel. Perhaps more important than these physical difficulties was the fact that Kiakhta was adjacent to the Central Asian peoples who supplied several major items of commercial value, particularly rhubarb and some cottons. Manchurians apparently could offer no distinctive and valuable product that was not equally available at Kiakhta. Finally, Manchu military activity and colonization in Central Asia in spite of the great danger to peace and

43. Bantysh-Kamenskii, *Diplomaticheskoe sobranie*, p. 263.

44. Mikhail Dimitrievich Chulkov, *Slovar' uchrezhdennykh v Rossii iarmarok, izdannyi dlia obrashchaiushchikhsia v torgovle* (Moscow: V Tip. Ponamareva, 1778), p. 212.

45. See Chapter 9 for statistics of Tsurukhaitu trade; Lange reported in 1736 that the Tsurukhaitu trade was very small, "less than 10,000 r. per year" and in some years "even only as little as 1000 r." Lorents Lange, "Drevnyia zapiski karavannomu puti chrez naunskuiu dorogu ot Tsurukhaitu do Pekina, 1736 godu." *Akademicheskiia izvestiia na 1781 god*, Chast' 7 (April, 1781), 467.

order with which they were regarded by local Russian officials and the court back in St. Petersburg, helped to stimulate the Kiakhta trade. Although in times of threatened danger the export of cattle, horses, and provisions to the Mongolians was prohibited by the state, this commerce was always lucrative, so much so that it gave rise to a substantial portion of the illicit trade.

The administration of the border trade, both at Kiakhta and Tsurukhaitu, of the Peking caravan, and of the border region itself was as complicated and authorities were as overlapping and non-rationalized as the central administration of the Russian Empire itself. At the highest level, policy decisions (and on many occasions decisions on seemingly minor interpretations and applications of general policy) were made by the Governing Senate or, while it lasted from 1726 to 1730, the Supreme Privy Council, which was charged with making decisions swiftly and easily, as the Senate was not always able to do.[46] During the reign of Tsaritsa Anna Ioannovna (1730-40), her Cabinet *(Kabinet)* often supplanted the Senate, as had the Supreme Privy Council earlier, in dealing with Siberian considerations or China matters. In the case of all three of these organs, action might be taken with or without formal imperial approval, which was usually noted, when it was given, by the traditional phrase of approbation of the throne, *byt' po semu.* In judicial matters, the Senate acted as the highest appellate court and the final court of adjudication. With regard to the China trade, the usual kind of issue it dealt with was peculation and malfeasance on the part of officials of eastern Siberia, or the misuse of state commercial monopolies granted to private merchants. The cases were few, but those that were decided by the Senate were of overriding concern to the state, often apparently because they might serve as examples to dissuade others from playing free and easy with the state and its prerogatives. Of course, these highest bodies usually did not act except on report or request from subordinate offices. Here the administration of Siberia and the China trade becomes quickly very complex. Siberia itself was administered by the reconstituted Siberian Prikaz between 1730 and its abolition in 1763.[47] The Siberian Prikaz was subordinate to the

46. *Gosudarstvennye uchrezhdeniia,* pp. 53-55.

47. *Ibid.,* pp. 229-30. The Siberian Prikaz was originally established in the seventeenth century primarily "for the development of the trade of Russia with this region," and it always retained much of the flavor of a state commercial operation. It was located in Moscow and presided over a large merchants' court *(gostinnyi dvor)* "for the storage and sale of peltry, rhubarb, and

Senate according to the ukaz which established it, and it enjoyed from 1732 authority over all Siberian affairs, including designation of the governor-general.[48] In 1719 the great expanses of Siberia *beyond* the Urals were divided into two provinces *(provintsii),* Tobol'sk and Irkutsk; in both cases the provinces were known by the names of the leading towns of the region. Perm', most of which lay west of the Urals, was also included within Siberia. The Selenginsk area earlier administered by the Eniseisk *voevoda* was transferred to the dominion of Irkutsk. Vice-governors *(vitse-gubernatory)* were to rule in the provinces, but it proved impossible to find good and suitably ranking men, and to Irkutsk was appointed a lower-ranked *voevoda,* in Vladislavich's time, Izmailov. An ukaz of 8 November 1729 from the Collegium of Foreign Affairs to the Siberian Vice-Governor Boltin requested that he specifically sanction *voevoda* Izmailov to preserve and maintain the treaties newly signed with the Chinese and guard the border trading posts.[49]

The Siberian Prikaz was only one of many departments and colleges with some measure of responsibility or concern for eastern Siberia and the China trade. The Collegium of Foreign Affairs throughout the last three quarters of the eighteenth century exercised dominion over relations with the Chinese empire, and at times extended this dominion to essentially domestic matters, such as the military posture of Russia in eastern Siberia, when those matters bore on foreign relations. Although it was of course primarily commercial in aim and organization, the Peking caravan was in large part directed by the Collegium of Foreign Affairs, particularly in all matters of protocol and diplomatic intercourse.

The Commerce Collegium, established in 1717 and given its basic Instruction two years later, was charged with general direction of all sea and land trade, and with the organization and

---

other products of Siberia and China." After a very bad fire in its quarters, it was reestablished in 1731 under the supervision of the Governing Senate and headed by General Iaguzhinskii. Its prerogatives were broad; it governed all Siberian towns, gathered all customs duties and other treasury imposts, preserved for itself the China trade as a state monopoly, and directed the commercial aspects of the Peking caravans. Consult Nikolai Ivanovich Kaidanov, *Sistematicheskii katalog delam Sibirskago prikaza, Moskovskago kommisarstva i drugikh, byvshikh, uchrezhdenii po chasti promyshlennosti i torgovli, khraniashchimsia v Arkhive departamenta tamozhennykh sborov* (St. Petersburg: Tip. V. Kirshbauma, 1888), p. 3.

48. *PSZ,* VIII, No. 5659, 351; No. 6165, 911.

49. *PSZ,* VIII, No. 5479, 235.

direction of Russian merchantry within the realm. Specifically this Collegium established and maintained the customs houses, levied the customs duties, and appointed customs house officers. Also the special Commission on Commerce *(Komissiia o kommertsii)* was given exceptional powers to investigate trade and to make recommendations to the court and to the various governors and *voevody*. It was originally organized in 1727, disbanded two years later, reestablished briefly in 1760, and then permanently in 1763. The first of these commissions compiled the first Regulation on Promissory Notes *(Ustav veksel'nyi)* which encouraged Russian merchants to engage in long-distance trade by permitting them to defer payment of customs duties and other fees for varying numbers of months, in order that they might turn over their goods prior to payment.[50] More shall be said later of this important measure. The Commission established by Catherine in 1763 was also given the task of investigating means to strengthen merchants' sources of credit. It finally passed from existence on 21 December 1796, declared by Paul to be "unnecessary."

These major administrative bodies, and others less highly placed and more irregular in their impact, all had a hand in the organization and conduct of the China trade, both private trade at the border and the state caravans to Peking. Coordination between them was not always perfect; in fact at times they seemed to operate at cross purposes, each attempting to influence the higher organs of decision toward their favorite policies. Sometimes decisions that should have been taken were left wanting because, it seems, they fell in the interstices between the colleges and offices, or involved several state offices unable or unwilling to arrive at a consensus.

In eastern Siberia itself, this situation was no happier, partly as a result of too many incompetent or demonstrably dishonest officials and too few of the calibre and evident rectitude of Lorents Lange. In the light of the past growth and importance of the China trade, accentuated by the new treaty arrangements which held such great promise for a restoration of trade at ever more profitable levels both for private merchant and state treasury, the *voevoda*-ship in Irkutsk quickly appeared anachronistic and anomolous. The Senate with the Tsaritsa's approval appointed a vice-governor in Irkutsk: "since Irkutsk province is a border province

50. *PSZ*, VIII, No. 5410, 147-97, dated 16 May 1729, printed 5 July 1729.

and both for the administration of customs affairs and collection and for the maintenance of the border treaty made with the Chinese and the ordering of correspondence [with them], a vice-governor is necessary," i.e. a man of gentry background and sufficient rank to make his weight felt in the complicated apparatus of state.[51] Notably the two reasons given recognize the predominant roles of Chinese relations and trade. The State Councillor *(Statskii sovetnik)* Aleksei Zholobov was appointed in place of the "old and ill" Boltin, who was retiring.[52] But he was replaced within the year and subsequently caught up in a legal net for peculation, influence peddling, and other gross but common iniquities.[53] There began a parade of holders of the office throughout the next decade. Brigadier Afanasii Arsen'ev received the office on 14 December 1731, but since he was "old and decrepit" and his doctor advised he could not stand the journey, he declined, and three months later on 30 March 1732 the State Councillor Kirilla Sytin was given the place.[54] Sytin actually did travel to Irkutsk, arriving on 5 January 1733, but he soon fell ill and died, leaving for the moment only Colonel Bukhol'ts to administer all affairs at the frontier. The journal of Anna's Cabinet contains on 7 May 1733 an entry that takes note of the death of Sytin and requests of the Senate to compile a list of candidates for the oft-vacated office.[55] In an Imperial Rescript dated 5 July 1733, Anna selected Colonel and Privy Councillor Andrei Pleshcheev who remained at the post only three years. But in this time the next major step was made in recognition of the importance of the Irkutsk area.

Already implied in the order five years earlier which authorized the appointment of a vice-governor in Irkutsk, an Imperial ukaz of 30 January 1736 given by the Cabinet to the Senate announced the division of the entire Siberian *guberniia* into two administratively equal parts, Tobol'sk and Irkutsk, each with a vice-gov-

51. Bantysh-Kamenskii, *Diplomaticheskoe sobranie*, pp. 171-72; Fedor Aleksandrovich Kudriavtsev and German Aleksandrovich Vendrikh, *Irkutsk, ocherki po istorii goroda* (Irkutsk: Irkutskoe Knizhnoe Izdatel'stvo, 1958), p. 58.

52. Zholobov was appointed on 5 January 1731, his instructions from the Siberian Prikaz dated 4 February 1731; Bantysh-Kamenskii, *Diplomaticheskoe sobranie*, pp. 173-74; Andrievich, *Kratkii ocherk*, p. 158.

53. *PSZ*, IX, No. 7009, 876-79; Silin, *Kiakhta*, p. 55. Zholobov was hailed into court on 9 July 1736 for accepting large bribes to permit private merchants to carry contraband merchandise into Chinese territory and using the state seal to mark these goods.

54. *Sbornik RIO*, CIV (1898), 223-24, 245.

55. *Ibid.*, CVI, 201.

ernor.[56] The formal reason given for this was the size of Siberia and the extreme distance between major cities and towns, but of course the reason for singling out Irkutsk was the steadily growing importance of the region in Russian foreign trade. The new vice-governor of Irkutsk province, State councillor Aleksei Iur'evich Bibikov, replaced Pleshcheev, who was convicted of theft.[57] The new office was no longer to be under the direct command of the Tobol'sk governor, but rather of the Siberian Prikaz itself, although Bibikov was ordered to report to both. Any need he had for prompt decision was to be directed to the Siberian Prikaz, and the ukaz stressed the reception and dispatch of reports and accounts "without unnecessary delay."

Bibikov's instructions were issued from the Collegium of Foreign Affairs and cautioned him on four matters.[58] (1) Since, it was noted, the Chinese *Li-fan-yuan* was chary about carrying on correspondence with other than the Governing Senate or the Siberian governor in Tobol'sk, the Vice-governor should avoid entering into correspondence, "except in dire necessity." (2) During the seven years that had elapsed since Vladislavich ordered the building of Tsurukhaitu, very little had been done. Hence Bibikov was to gather men and supplies where he could and erect the post. (3) The *Li-fan-yuan* had complained that the territory to the east between the Amur and Uda Rivers, which was Chinese territory according to the Treaty of Nerchinsk, was still undemarcated. The Collegium felt that the territory was too little known to mark the border accurately, and ordered Bibikov to obtain further data on these lands and to have a good map made, for which he should consult with the governor at Tobol'sk and Commander Vitus Bering, then engaged on his great expedition of exploration. (4) Finally, and as had been ordered many times earlier and was to be many times in the future, especial effort had to be made to forestall or capture runaways trying to cross into Siberian territory from Mongolia. Although the Chinese-Dzhungarian fighting was for the moment dormant, the problem was a sensitive one, at all times threatening to thoroughly disrupt the China trade.

56. *PSZ*, IX, No. 6876, 733, Imperial ukaz dated 3 January 1736; Bantysh-Kamenskii, *Diplomaticheskoe sobranie*, p. 223; *Sbornik RIO*, CXIV (1902), 48, 111; CXX (1905), 344-45; Andrievich, *Kratkii ocherk*, p. 159.

57. Bibikov had earlier been Master of Petitions of the Senate *(Reketmeister)*; *RBS*, vol. Betankur-Biakster, 20-22.

58. Bantysh-Kamenskii, *Diplomaticheskoe sobranie*, pp. 223-25, Ukaz dated 9 June 1736.

In spite of all these efforts to strengthen the administrative structure of eastern Siberia, to appoint good men and true to public office, and to remove those who fell prey to the temptation to misuse their offices for personal gain, the extant evidence strongly suggests that little immediate change was made in these regards. For over a century Siberia had been for many a rare opportunity to wax wealthy, distant from the prying eyes of the central administration and from the restraints of moral and social standards.[59] Indeed, two of the vice-governors of Irkutsk in the 1730's alone were charged with thievery and tried in court. How many other officials went uncharged for failure of detection or lack of good evidence is problematic, but assuredly there were many. Siberia was in these years for the Muscovite what India was to the Londoner later, save that Russians did not have a populous and old culture to plunder and enjoy. Repeatedly state edicts and ukazes commented on the sad state of governance in Siberia, and as often were directed at doing something about it, but only time, improved communications, and an enlarged population seem in the end to have turned the trick, and then only in the nineteenth century after the famed reform of Mikhail Speranskii.[60] An ukaz of 12 January 1739 points up the problem of staffing this huge empire, particularly with regard to the casual way in which town *voevody* were appointed:

> It has been known to us that in many towns *(goroda)* of the Siberian *guberniia, voevody* have been designated from amongst the local inhabitants, namely: from the merchantry, Cossacks, and others similar to that, who were taken in [state service] as recruits, but obtained official rank through service and not by holding patents *(gramoty),* and now actually Cossacks who have not served [in state ranks] have been added to gentry ranks and to [service as] *voevody*; also there are several persons formerly in slave bondage *(kholopstvo),* etc., who have been under [criminal] investigation and punishment.[61]

59. See C. M. Foust, "Russian Expansion to the East through the Eighteenth Century," *Journal of Economic History,* XXI (December, 1961), 469-82.

60. Raeff, *Siberia and the Reforms of 1822,* passim.

61. Andrievich, *Kratkii ocherk,* p. 161. Partly of course the complaint here is that untitled and unranked persons of rude antecedents were rising to high office and achieving acceptance in Siberian "society." There is no doubt that this was often true. Much later (1786) Martin Sauer remarks on Irkutsk

The ukaz concluded by ordering search for new candidates for the *voevoda* offices.

In 1739 Irkutsk, at long last, achieved a vice-governor distinguished both for his great skills, his peerless knowledge of the East, and his unblemished record—Lorents Lange. Within the year he requested that when the Tsaritsa select men for the office of *voevoda* she designate the best for Iakutsk and Nerchinsk *uezdy*; "for the best advantage it is necessary that in Iakutsk and in Nerchinsk such *voevody* be designated who will be of good conscience . . . particularly because in these two *uezdy* [there is] the best peltry."[62] Next to the China trade there was no temptation greater than that of fine pelts.

On the Mongolian Side

The Manchus, on their part, were somewhat slower in establishing the border trading post permitted by the Treaty of Kiakhta on the Mongol-Siberian border. Once begun however, they erected a town no smaller than Kiakhta and by all indications no less favorable for substantial border trade. In 1730, perhaps five hundred to eight hundred feet up the stream Kiakhta from the post Kiakhta, construction began of the trading town eventually known as Mai-mai-ch'eng, literally the "buy-sell city," a Chinese name rare for Mongolia.[63] By the time Gmelin visited the little outpost

(*An Account of a Geographical and Astronomical Expedition to the North Parts of Russia* . . . [London: T. Cadell, jun. (etc.), 1800], p. 17): "Number of mechanics, artists, and artificers of great ability, whose exertions were selfish in Russia, here exert themselves for the benefit of the community; and, as merit is the chief introduction to independent society, so all who possess it meet with liberal encouragement; and, unless their characters are sullied by acts of criminality, they are countenanced and supported. The unfortunate are generously distinguished from the villainous.

"The officers here, both military and civil, are very numerous; the former, in consequence of this being the seat of government in the vicinity of the Chinese and Mongol territories; the latter, on account of the numerous courts of justice, and the necessary distributions to be made for the vast extent of its jurisdiction. I shall rate these in two classes; for rank is only a secondary recommendation here: the gentleman, who behaves himself with propriety, though poor, is completely independent, and every house is open to him; while the worthless are only attended to in the execution of their duty, and then with great reserve."

62. Andrievich, *Kratkii ocherk*, p. 161.

63. The *Sibirskaia sovetskaia entsiklopediia* (Novosibirsk: Sibirskoe Kraevoe Izdatel'stvo, 1929-32), II, 1149, says it was not established until 1740, but this is evidently in error. George Kennan (*Siberia and the Exile System* [New York: The Century Co., 1891], II, 101) judges the two towns to be 450-

of Chinese civilization in 1735, it was probably about as large as it was to remain throughout the eighteenth century. Mai-mai-ch'eng was carefully laid out, adhering to the necromancy rules of *feng-shui*, "wind and water." The town was square, surrounded by wooden walls and protected after 1756 by a ditch some three feet in breadth. Each wall had a gate in the center, and these gates led to the two major streets, which intersected in the middle of the town, and divided it into four quadrants. Over each of these four main gates was a small wooden "corps de garde" which was manned by members of the Mongol garrison of the town. These troops were usually armed only with heavy sticks. Outside the four gates were erected wooden watchtowers about twenty-five feet in height to permit surveillance of the approaches to Mai-mai-ch'eng.

In spite of the modest size of the trading suburb, westerners, including Russians, were alternately startled and revolted by what they saw. One nineteenth-century Russian traveller remarked, "On entering the street I was struck by the singularity of the scene, for I seemed as if transported to another world. Nothing I saw had the slightest resemblance to anything I have beheld in Europe."[64] European civilization was abruptly shucked off in the five hundred feet or so between Kiakhta and Mai-mai-ch'eng, and the sight and smell and touch of oriental quaintness and "decadence" seized the uninitiated. Within the town the streets and houses were mostly carefully aligned. The main avenues were about twenty to twenty-five feet in width, adequate for most commercial purposes, but all other streets and alleys were so narrow that travellers consistently commented on the difficulty of moving about the town, with a Russian *drozhki* at least. Still the houses themselves were quite large and were in the genre of the Chinese courtyard, with living quarters, kitchen, storerooms, etc. grouped around a central

---

600 ft. apart; the Brokgauz and Efron encyclopedia (*Entsiklopedicheskii slovar'* [St. Petersburg: Semenovskaia Tipo-Litografiia (I. A. Efrona), 1890-1904], XVII, 170) says 560 ft. (80 *sazhen*); Kurts (*Russko-kitaiskie snoshenna*, p. 75) says 840 ft.

Properly speaking, Mai-mai-ch'eng is not a name, but a description: lit. the "buy-sell city" or "city of commerce." Often referred to by the Russians as the Chinese suburb *(Kitaiskaia sloboda)*, or by others as a *fauburg*. The town was badly burned in 1869 and the modern city is not on precisely the original site. Today it is known as Altan-bulak. Pallas, *Voyages*, IV, 154; E. M. Murzaev, *Mongol'skaia narodnaia respublika, Fiziko-geograficheskoe opisanie* (Moscow: OGIZ, Gosudarstvennoe Izdatel'stvo Geograficheskoi Literatury, 1948), pp. 11, 21.

64. Piasetskii, *Russian Travellers*, I, 7.

Figure 6. A street in Mai-mai-ch'eng. Steel engraving by H. Sandham. From George Kennan, *Siberia and the Exile System* (New York: The Century Co., 1891), II, 109.

court. On the exterior gate of the court could usually be read the name of the proprietor, the title of his establishment and the characters for Good Fortune and Long Life. Within the courtyard dogs were often kept for protection and small gardens were tended to provide the vegetables indispensible to good Chinese cuisine. Although most western visitors thought the town unkempt, crowded, noisy, and unappealing in general, individual courtyards and houses were scrupulously clean, neat, and comfortable. The actual bartering was usually done within the merchant's courtyard where he kept his goods in accessible display rooms. As expected the haggling and bargaining was slightly civilized by the consumption of much Chinese tea and pastries.

The most notable public edifices were the pagoda-style temples, one in the precise center of the town, the sumptuous quarters of the Manchu commandant of Mai-mai-ch'eng and the border region, and the theater. When permitted Russian visitors delighted in the presentation of classical Chinese opera, with its colors if undecipherable language. One corner of the town, the southwestern, was occupied by Bukharans, an almost generic name for all Mongols, who traded with both Russians and Chinese. Apparently, save for their lack of personal cleanliness, they were to the casual observer indistinguishable from Chinese and Manchus, since they affected Chinese dress.[65]

One aspect of the town struck nearly all western observers as extraordinary and unnatural—the absence of the fairer sex because of a government prohibition, strictly enforced throughout the eighteenth century (and for that matter into the twentieth).[66] The rationale for this appears to have been the desire of the *Li-fan-yuan* to prevent the Chinese merchants from becoming permanent fixtures in this non-Chinese region and absorbing dangerous Western ideas and practices. Nevertheless, the merchants clearly did not go unconsoled. Not only did the woman of Kiakhta "enrich themselves with them at the expense of their [the women's]

65. This description of Mai-mai-ch'eng is taken mainly from three contemporary accounts: Gmelin, *Voyage,* 191 ff.; Pallas, *Voyages,* IV, 154-68; Klaproth, *Mémoires,* I, 63-66.

66. Lindon Bates noted that the prohibition was "in full force" in the early twentieth century, although at an earlier time the subterfuge of keeping wives across the border in Kiakhta was used; Lindon W. Bates, *The Russian Road to China* (Boston: Houghton Mifflin Co., 1910), pp. 178-79. See also Cochrane, *Pedestrian Journey,* II, 169-70; Piasetskii, *Russian Travellers,* I, 32.

67. Pallas, *Voyages,* IV, 168; Klaproth, *Mémoires,* I, 66.

honor," but rich merchants reportedly kept Mongol mistresses. The charge of pederasty was several times directed against the Chinese, as Cochrane put it in the early nineteenth century, "that dreadful degeneracy which is said to pervade all ranks of society among them."[68]

As trade shifted from Urga to Kiakhta-Mai-mai-ch'eng there evolved a fairly elaborate administrative structure on the Mongol side. Immediate police and administrative functions at the border were in the hands of a Manchu official known as the "dzarguchei" *(Cha-erh-ku-chi)*.[69] He was responsible to and reported to the Urga officialdom and ultimately to the *Li-fan-yuan*; he was chosen from among *Li-fan-yuan* officials and replaced every two years. He was expected to supervise commerce and the merchants, carrying out the general regulations of the realm but making minor ordinances on the spot. Usually men of rank and education were chosen for the post, although frequently, as was Chinese habit, an official who was deemed to have misbehaved was "exiled" here. A fixed salary at the rate of one *liang* per day was paid. However "gifts" and bribes from merchants could be expected to augment this modest stipend, probably several times over. All minor altercations and

68. Cochrane, *Pedestrian Journey*, II, 169-70. At least one nineteenth-century observer spied also some of the magnificent pornography of the Chinese. Erman (*Travels in Siberia*, II, 188) remarked on the scrolls and paintings depicting "their favorite subjects"—"licentious adventures" and "indecent themes." "The same indecency prevailed in the painting on all the porcelain tea-cups in Maimachen, without exception; but here, also, licentious reminiscence seemed intended wholly for the wealthy, for the obscenest paintings always bore the highest price."

69. This is a very strange title. It was originally a Mongol term used by the Manchus in the early Ch'ing dynasty, but by the eighteenth century it had been dropped everywhere but in Mongolia. The Chinese equate it to *tuan-shih-jen*, i.e. an administrator with aspects of a legal judge. Hoo Chi-tsai (*Les bases conventionnelles des relations modernes entre la Chine et la Russie* [Paris: Jouve & Cie., 1918], p. 80) says the Chinese equivalent is *pou-yuan*. The dzarguchei of Mai-mai-ch'eng carried the honorary appelation of "Imperial Agent" (*amban*, see n. 76). The Russians considered the title equivalent to *nachal'nik*, a "lieutenant-governor," who normally mixed administrative and judicial powers. Brunnert and Hagelstrom (*Present Day Political Organization of China*, pp. 454-55) translated it as "Judicial Commissioner for Chinese Affairs," which suggests, but does not entirely capture, the dual judicial and administrative nature of the dzarguchei, nor does it indicate that he conducted relations with the Russians as well as governed native Chinese and Mongols. There were four such officials in Mongolia, one each at Urga, Mai-mai-ch'eng, Uliassutai, and Kobdo. See especially Nieh Ch'ung-ch'i, "Man-kuan han-shih," *Yen-ching hsueh-pao*, No. 32 (June, 1947), 107; P. G., "Ukazatel' neposredstvennoi torgovli chrez Moskvu s Kitaem," *Zhurnal manufaktur i torgovli*, ch. 4, no. 11 (1836), 124; Klaproth, *Mémoires*, I, 67; and *SFPC*, 37.17a-17b.

disputes were handled first by the dzarguchei, and only if he was unable to settle them at the local level were they passed on to Urga or Peking. He had the power to judge and ship off any officials beneath him in rank.[70]

The most important task of the dzarguchei was to regulate trade and the merchants. He functioned as something of a factor, keeping the individual Chinese merchants in line, preventing cutthroat competition between them, enforcing a certain standardization of price and offer, and when necessary consulting with the Russian commandant of Kiakhta. As early as 1720 the *Li-fan-yuan* began to set down strict and rigid regulations for the conduct of Chinese and other merchants in Mongolia.[71] The ranking tribal leader in central Mongolia, the Khan of the Tushetu tribe of Khalkha Mongols exercised close surveillance over the Russians trading in the main Mongolian city, Urga, and regularly reported to the *Yuan* on the total amount of merchandise that changed hands in the city and the number of merchants involved. The *Yuan* required licenses of every Chinese merchant arriving from China proper and strictly prohibited munitions, military goods in general, and several other things, under very heavy penalty. To insure respect for these measures, the *Yuan* sent one of its people as assistant *(chien-shih kuan)* to the Tushetu Khan, and carefully rotated him every two years. As time went by this Peking official seems to have aggrandized more and more authority of the Khan although formally the Tushetu Khan exercised overall jurisdiction in eastern and northern Mongolia even after the Treaty of Kiakhta.[72]

Gradually additional regulations led to tightened control over trade with the Russians, and the sealing off of the border as much as possible. In 1727 Peking ordered that especial efforts be made

70. The dzarguchei continued in much the same role well into the nineteenth century. Erman (*Travels in Siberia*, II, 170) reported in 1850 as follows: "With respect to tolls and duties, and other similar matters liable to dispute, they are either arranged between the Russian customs' director and the sarguchei, or chief officer in Maimachen; or, when they are of a more general and important nature, between the governor-general of Irkutsk and the van or Manchoo lord-lieutenant in Urga. The rank and functions of the sarguchei are compared in Kiakhta with those of a Russian officer of the seventh class; but, in the exercise of his local authority, he is not careful to confine himself within the narrowest limits. He sits to administer justice, orders very severe punishments, and reports only in criminal cases to the van in Urga; who, on the other hand, cannot inflict the punishment of death until he receives confirmation of the sentence from Peking."

71. *SFPC*, 37.15a-16a, the fifty-ninth year of K'ang-hsi.

72. *Ibid.*, 37.19a, citing a 1747 Imperial decree to that effect.

to prevent neighboring Siberian natives ("Russian Khalkhas") from stealing acrosss the frontier.[73] If horses were stolen (presumably across the border), an investigation was to be opened quickly and every effort made to follow the horse thieves, to apprehend them and regain the horses. If not returned, the owners had to be indemnified by the border guardpost in whose territory the theft occurred. If deserters from Mongol territory were involved and they returned, they were to be dealt with harshly—they should not receive food and maintenance from the state. The chief Manchu border official, i.e. the dzarguchei, was specifically instructed not to levy any toll duties on goods exchanged with the Russians, since Peking interpreted the Treaty of Kiakhta to prohibit any surtaxing. Finally he was to send off directly to the *Li-fan-yuan* any correspondence that arrived from the Russian Senate. In order that all Khalkha Mongols in the border regions understood and complied with these new regulations, they were printed and widely disseminated.

As on the Russian side, the Manchus tried to seal off the frontier to all deserters and runaways, and to merchants evading the prescribed routes of travel. A chain of small military posts known as *k'a-lun* faced the Russian *karauli*. A minor officer (a *chang ching*), with a few soldiers, manned each of them.[74] Piles of stones *(o-po)*, marked the line of the frontier again as the Russians had done.

In later years the *Li-fan-yuan* sanctioned stationing in Urga an imperial agent, who was replaced every three years to avoid his becoming entrenched, nepotistic, and susceptible to bribe.[75] The Military Board *(Ping Pu)* requested that this agent prohibit items of actual or potential military value for trade with the Russians (saltpeter, ox horns, high quality iron). Chinese merchants "pilferingly" entering Mongolia were to be apprehended and remanded to the Board of Punishments *(Hsing Pu)* for judgment. Officials entrusted with guarding passes who neglected their duties were to be removed from office, and their superiors degraded five ranks and transferred to other posts. This new imperial official seems to have been the one who in later years evolved into a full-blown

73. *Ibid.*, 37.17b-18a; 46.4b.

74. *Chang-ching* is usually translated as "secretary," but signifies an assistant or subordinate in either civil or military employ: Mayers, *The Chinese Government*, p. 13.

75. *SFPC*, 37.19a.

Imperial Agent in Urga *(K'u-lun pang-shih ta-ch'en)*.[76] A Mongol subordinate bearing the title *K'u-lun pang-pan ta-ch'en* assisted him[77].

Both sides, then, reorganized the border in the light of and to take advantage of the Treaty of Kiakhta. Both Russians and Chinese government officials saw it as to their advantage to seal off the frontier as much as possible and to supervise, more or less, the comings and goings of their own merchants. Except for the Russian state caravan to Peking, both sides almost eagerly welcomed the opportunity to restrict private trade to only two border towns, and for that matter only one with any real possibility of growth. Both established, as best they could, the means to guard and patrol the border, a border in frontier country almost equally unknown to both. Both attempted to extend down to the lowest levels an intimate and direct control over commerce which stretched really over five thousand miles from Moscow to Peking, so as to utilize it to their own best advantages.

Trade Routes

Moscow to Peking

To say nothing of the nearly five-thousand mile routes over which Chinese silks were carried to Moscow (and for many of them thence to Europe) and Russian leather goods taken to Peking would not only ignore much of the dramatic character of this longest of overland trading routes, but more importantly would neglect one of the serious considerations in the competition between Russian state caravan and private carriage in the years after the Treaty of Kiakhta. Certainly the sheer distance of the trade routes and even the great physical difficulties were not by themselves decisive factors in the overall profitability of the trade, nor did they alone account for the solvency or insolvency of state caravans. Nor did all private merchants personally escort their merchandise the entire arduous way. In fact, most of them seem not to have done so,

76. More simply known as the *Amban*. *Amban* is a Manchu title equivalent to the Chinese *Ta-chen, Ta-kung,* or *Ta-jen,* rendered *An-pan* in Chinese. Mayers, *The Chinese Government,* pp. 100-101; Nieh Ch'ung-ch'i, "Man-kuan han-shih," *Yen-ching hsueh-pao,* No. 32 (June, 1947), 99.

77. Brunnert and Hagelstrom, *Present Day Political Organization,* p. 453; Mayers, *The Chinese Government,* pp. 100-101; and Louis Richard, *Comprehensive Geography of the Chinese Empire and Dependencies,* trans., rev. and enl. by M. Kennelly, S. J. (Shanghai: T'usewei Press, 1908), pp. 517-18.

but to have depended on agents or local merchants in Siberia to conduct the transactions and arrange for transport. Nor were all goods exchanged at Kiakhta-Mai-mai-ch'eng carried the full distance east to Peking or west to Moscow-St. Petersburg. The single largest item of Russian exchange—furs and pelts—came mainly from Siberia and eventually North America, not European Russia. Several particularly important Chinese items—rhubarb above all—came from Mongolia or the foothills of Tibet, not Peking or Nanking. In terms of items imported, some on both sides were consumed on or near the border and never shipped on: Mongolian tobacco balls, for instance, preferred by Siberian natives; and Siberian horses and cattle, which remained in Mongolia itself. Nevertheless the trade routes that were used, the extreme distances, the physical deprivations and dangers, all had relevance to the success or failure of the trade as a whole, and as far as the Russians were concerned were factors in the contest between state and private entrepreneur, as we shall see later.

No single route adequately served as an all-purpose, all-weather way across Siberia. Many factors helped determine the routes used by private merchants and state caravans: the direction of river flows, the strength of rapids, the distance of portages between river systems, the condition of roads, and not the least the location of customs collection points and state regulations on the legal routes to be followed to pass through these points. Surprisingly, the usual route across that great land mass was mainly a water route, used especially in the summer months but also in the deep winter when slow and swift rivers alike were covered with thick ice. This was a very indirect route. It began really in Iaroslavl', northeast of Moscow, from which merchants carried their goods, partly by land and partly by water, through Vologda, past the old fair town of Velikii Ustiug to Verkhotur'e, the main Siberian customs center just across the Urals on the River Tura. Some merchants preferred an alternate journey from Moscow to Nizhni-Novgorod, Kazan', Kungar, Ekaterinburg, and Tiumen', since it was shorter by about 260 miles and included several important commercial and fair cities. The government did not always permit the use of this route. Between 1754 and 1763, for example, private merchants were ordered through Verkhotur'e; in the latter year Verkhotur'e customs was abolished.[78]

78. Departament Tamozhennykh Sborov, Statisticheskoe Otdelenie, *Statisticheskiia svedeniia o torgovle Rossii s Kitaem* (St. Petersburg: Tipo-litografiia

The long water passage began from Verkhotur'e: the Tura River down to Tiumen', then the Tobol to Tobol'sk, long the capital and leading city of Siberia. From Tobol'sk goods were moved down the Irtysh to its junction with the mighty Ob', the first of the great Siberian rivers met by travellers going eastward. Then began the tedious task of partly sailing and partly towing merchandise barges up the Ob' as far as Narym. At Narym the River Ket' was entered and ascended as far as Makarskoi Fort (or Makovskaia *pristan'*, landing). At this point there had to be performed the first major portage *(volok)* in Siberia, a carriage of some sixty miles to the important central Siberian city of Eniseisk, a portage known as the Makarskoi portage. Goods transferred from the river barges to carts *(telegi)*, or sledges *(sani)* in winter months, were laboriously dragged over to Eniseisk and the Enisei River system, the next east of the Siberian systems. Up to this portage the carriage might be entirely by water save for a short Ural portage, and once the Enisei system had been entered the remainder of the journey nearly up to Selenginsk, except for portages necessary around some rapids, might also avoid cartage by land. However from Eniseisk the river route was very tortuous and at times endangered life and goods. The route went up the Enisei to the Angara River (at this time the river was usually divided into two rivers at Olekminsko-Vitimskaia Mountain, the Lower Angara or Upper Tunguska, and the Upper Angara). The Angara was most dangerous, its rapids were swift and the currents tricky, violent, and at one point at least—at a rapid known as Padun (now the Bratsk Electrical Power Station)—goods had to be taken ashore and the rapids bypassed. In the middle of winter even the Angara froze sufficiently to permit the goods to be hauled up by sledge to Irkutsk. To avoid these difficulties meant continuing up the Enisei beyond Makarskoi to Krasnoiarsk, and then striking overland by cart to Nizhneudinsk and Irkutsk. This alternate route was used primarily in the mid-summer, when the roads dried hard, because the passage of the Ob', the Ket' and the Angara was so difficult, even during summer months, that it usually required more than a single summer season. From Irkutsk locally-built flatboats *(doshchaniki)* carried the goods up the Angara to Lake

M. P. Frolovoi, 1909), p. 3. Compare William Tooke, *View of the Russian Empire, During the Reign of Catharine the Second, and to the Close of the Eighteenth Century* (2d ed.; London: Printed by G. Woodfall, for T. N. Longman and O. Rees, 1800), III, 469-70.

Baikal, and across Baikal to Verkhneudinsk. When the winds were favorable, the Baikal was sailed; when they were not or when the water was too rough, particularly in early winter and early spring, the boats had to be rowed hugging the southern shore all the way. After mid-January the Baikal normally iced up thick enough to use sledges. From Verkhneudinsk the flatboats were pulled or poled up the Selenga beyond Selenginsk to Strelka (Petropavlovsk), where the goods were usually placed on carts and taken finally to Kiakhta.[79]

The whole passage from European Russia to Kiakhta was much more difficult a trip than the reverse, because it necessitated much sailing against the current. Often animals and men, the latter on the boats, simply pulled the loads up the rivers. Not only a slow process but possibly a dangerous one. The return trip was otherwise much the same as the journey out. Sometimes a variant route from Eniseisk took goods by land to Tomsk to the south, and from there on boats on the Tom' and Ob' Rivers, and up the Irtysh to Tobol'sk. Beyond Tobol'sk, the Tobol and Tura Rivers were most popular up to Turinsk, and then to Irbit fair, which in the eighteenth century lasted from two or three weeks in the middle of January. Irbit was one of the major market fairs in Russia, with a huge-cornered *gostinnyi dvor* of two rows of fifty-eight *lavki*, according to Chulkov.[80] Here many of the merchants ended the journey and disposed of their goods. Others carried beyond to Makar'skaia *iarmarka* and to Moscow, typically by land until the place was reached where the River Chusovaia was deep enough for floating, they drifted down the Chusovaia, transhipped about thirty miles by land up to the Utkinskaia landing. The Kama River took them to the Volga, thence to Markar'evo or the great fair of Nizhni-Novgorod. Like Irbit, Nizhni-Novgorod served as a major entrepôt for goods from the East, although it rivaled Irbit only toward the end of the century.

In the 1760's, a second over-all route began to take shape, the land road eventually known as the Great *(Bol'shaia)* Road, but then known as the Moscow Tract. It proceeded from Ekaterinburg

79. Not until 1763 did the Russian government make an effort to provide Lake Baikal with larger boats with higher freeboard worthy of the world's deepest freshwater lake. Up to that time merchants used their own river flatboats and barges, which were potentially dangerous, and in the storms that rose swiftly they often lost many of their goods and at times the boats themselves. Silin, *Kiakhta*, p. 86; *PSZ*, XVI, No. 11840, 268.

80. Chulkov, *Slovar'*, p. 72.

through Tobol'sk or Ishim nearby, across the Baraba steppe through Kainsk, Tomsk, Krasnoiarsk to Nizhneudinsk and on to Irkutsk. It was a long and hard road of over three thousand miles. Travel during much of the spring and autumn and part of the summer was vexing; many of the stretches were mired and impassable for other than mounted travellers.[81] Once the ground froze solid, the journey might be made in seventy to eighty days with good luck, an average of fifty to fifty-five miles per day. Travellers not burdened with goods carts could make eighty or more miles per day.[82]

In the final three decades of the century this Great Road came to be heavily used. Aleksandr Radishchev reported in the 1790's that during the winter season there gathered in Irkutsk up to ten thousand carts, three thousand drivers, and two thousand other workers—amazingly large numbers for Siberia of the day.[83] Radishchev also reported that the men of the Baraba steppe across which the Road ran drew large profits from this carriage, contrasting sharply with the meager earnings of other Siberian peasants. Convoys of fifty to one hundred carts or sledges were common. Post-stations dotted the Road providing both horse and vehicle so that the "caravans" could push on from Irkutsk to Moscow at nearly maximum rate of speed. The consequence of this was extremely low cost of transportation per weight carried. One mid-nineteenth-century traveller reported that even then a packet of one pound could be sent from St. Petersburg to Kamchatka for one ruble![84]

The best and most common route for private merchants' travel eastward was via the southern land route after the frosts had hardened the roads, with stops at the various markets, fairs, and the many small settlements in order to barter and to purchase pelts and other goods. The Mongolian border was usually reached in January or February, and throughout the winter the merchant traded with the Chinese and Bukharans at Kiakhta-Mai-mai-ch'eng.

81. Kh. Trusevich, *Posol'skiia i torgovliia snosheniia Rossii s Kitaem (do XIX veka)* (Moscow: T. Malinskago Moroseika, Chelovekoliubivago Obshchestva, 1882) p. 78.

82. Major-General Sarychev of the Billings' expedition made eighty miles per day: Gavrila A. Sarychev, *Account of a Voyage of Discovery to the North-East of Siberia, the Frozen Ocean, & the North-East Sea,* trans. from the Russian (London: Printed for Richard Phillips by J. G. Barnard, 1806-7), p. 6, note f.

83. Aleksandr N. Radishchev, "Pis'mo o kitaiskom torge," *Polnoe sobranie sochinenii* (Moscow: Izd. Akademii Nauk SSSR, 1938-52), II, 15.

84. Erman, *Travels in Siberia,* II, 155.

In the spring after the river ice had broken up, the Chinese and Mongol goods acquired in the long winter of trading were embarked on rafts or flatboats and carried to Tobol'sk via the water route. From Tobol'sk to Moscow or Perm' or the other destinations, overland routes were normally used in the winter, and the Kama and Volga river routes in the summer. This schedule not only utilized the best features of each route, but allowed the bulkier Chinese goods (cottons, silks, teas, and enameled and porcelain wares) to be carried by water. Still the total elapsed time in either direction was anywhere from one to three years, depending of course on how much time was spent bargaining and bartering in the fairs. Were goods carried directly through without barter or changing hands, five to six months was sufficient between St. Petersburg and Kiakhta, and even as little as three months if the Great Road were used in ideal season. By the end of the century an individual could travel "by post" between Moscow and Irkutsk in no more than one month.[85]

Kiakhta was the end of the road for private merchants after the Treaty of Kiakhta, except for a few who risked illegal entry into Mongolia. For the crown caravans to Peking the worst ordeal in many ways still lay ahead. Two general routes to Peking predominated after 1727. The northerly route started from Selenginsk or Verkhneudinsk and crossed into Manchuria via Nerchinsk and Tsurukhaitu. This stage alone likely consumed seven weeks.[86] Beyond the Argun, the route threaded southward by way of Naun (now Tsitsihar), and usually penetrated the Great Wall at the Shanhaikuan pass near the sea. This was the longer of the two routes by approximately 550 miles, but avoided the extreme priva-

85. This description of the Siberian trade routes derived largely from the following: Kudriavtsev and Vendrikh, *Irkutsk*, pp. 40-41; M. I. Sladkovskii, *Ocherki ekonomicheskikh otnoshenii SSSR s Kitaem* (Moscow: Vneshtorgizdat, 1957), p. 72; Coxe, *Account*, pp. 246-48; Erman, *Travels in Siberia*, II, 155 ff.; Radishchev, *Polnoe sobranie sochinenii*, II, 14-15; Departament Tamozhennykh Sborov, Statisticheskoe Otdelenie, *Statisticheskiia svedeniia o torgovle Rossii s Kitaem*, pp. 3-4; Jacques Savary des Bruslons, *Dictionnaire Universal de Commerce* . . . (Paris: J. Estienne, 1723-30), II, 643; Gagemeister, *Statisticheskoe obozrenie*, II, 649-67; Ministerstvo Vnutrennykh Del, *Statisticheskoe obozrenie Sibiri, sostavlennoe na osnovanii svedenii pocherpnutnykh iz aktov pravitel'stva i drugikh dostovernykh istochnikov* (St. Petersburg: Tipografiia Shnora, 1810), p. 32; Strahlenberg, *An Historico-Geographical Description*, p. 385; Pallas, *Voyages*, IV 373-74; and *Sbornik RIO*, CXXXVIII (1912), 78-80.

86. G. I. Constantin, "The Transbaikalian Routes to China as Known to or Explored by Nicolaie Milescu (Spathary)—1675," *Studia et Acta Orientalia*, I (1957), 98.

tions of the Gobi desert with which the Russians yet had little experience. The Russians preferred to take this course during those times when the Dzhungarian wars disrupted western and central Mongolia.

The southern route followed one of two paths: either straight through the Gobi Desert by way of Urga, or skirting the desert by way of the Kerulen River. By either route the caravan entered China proper at the Kalgan gate. Once the Russians learned to cope with the problems peculiar to desert travel—the lack of animal forage, firewood, inhabitants, and especially water; the heat by day and the cold by night; and the vicious winds strong enough to carry away any poorly secured tent—they preferred to take advantage of this shorter route. The Gobi could be crossed by caravan in thirty to forty days, although it often took twice that long. A Chinese postman on foot was expected to reach Urga from Peking in forty-eight days—a distance of nearly one thousand miles.[87]

While private merchants often did set out from European Russia and return within a year, the members of the state caravans usually could expect three years to pass before they again saw the spires of the Moscow Kremlin. They travelled all the way to Peking and remained there a number of months. In addition caravans usually waited a minimum of several months at the border awaiting approval of Peking before they were allowed to enter Mongolia. The China trade was not a business for the weak in spirit or body.

Without the peaceful settlement of differences incorporated into the Treaty of Kiakhta, there would have been no substantial licit trade between Russia and China in the eighteenth century. But the Treaty itself was only the possibility, not the actuality. The acts taken on both sides in the years after 1728 were what set the milieu of both state and private trade as it was to develop throughout the century. Both sides built border trading posts in which private merchants (and government officials) might gather to barter their wares; both tried to seal off the border to compel merchants to use only the prescribed trading towns; both made relatively minor but essential changes in their administrative structure in the border region. The results for trade are the substance of the next three chapters.

87. John King Fairbank and Teng Ssu-yu, "On the Transmission of Ch'ing Documents," *Harvard Journal of Asiatic Studies*, IV (1939), 28; and U.S. War Department, *Siberia and Eastern Russia* (Washington: Government Printing Office, 1918), II, 114-21.

Chapter IV. The Caravan to Peking

Before the Treaty of Kiakhta was signed, ratified, and the copies exchanged, Ambassador Vladislavich, with Chinese permission, ordered the crown caravan to proceed to Peking with all possible speed. The heat of the summer had passed and the skies were clear and bright on the two September mornings in 1727 when the two divisions of the caravan set out for Mongolia and Urga.[1] In spite of the enormous relief all felt in getting on the road after such a long delay both the caravan commissar, Dmitrii Molokov, and his well-versed aide, confidant, and trouble shooter, Lorents Lange, harbored mixed feelings. The prospects for this, and for any caravans that might follow it, were not at all great. The caravan had after all been waiting at the border for over three years, and for that matter many of the goods it carried had been accumulated at least seven years earlier. Some furs had already begun to deteriorate, and moths threatened the textiles. Furthermore, favorable exchanges in Peking and in Urga on the way were not going to be easy to make. The state always insisted on unrealistically high prices for its merchandise, especially for that which was no longer in first-class condition. To make matters worse, Siberian merchants had been permitted to trade freely in sable, other Siberian furs, and rhubarb in order to encourage the bringing of Chinese gold and silver duty free into the country, provided only that they turn it in to the Mint *(Denezhnyi dvor)* as they had been permitted to do since 1723. The sole item of great significance to Chinese and Mongol trade still strictly prohibited to private trade was Chinese tobacco balls, and even that was freed by the Supreme Privy Council on 26 September 1727. An imperial ukaz only a little over two months earlier granted all these liberties.[2] Private merchants were, to be sure, prohibited from carrying sable and other fine furs into Chinese territories while the caravan travelled and traded in China, and the Chinese had closed even Urga since late 1724.[3] Nonetheless the markets of Peking were likely to be saturated with Russian furs legally or illegally there, and the prevailing market prices were much below those demanded by the Siberian Prikaz. Lange's fears

1. 5 and 13 September 1727.
2. *PSZ*, VII, No. 5110, 819-21, dated 26 June 1727.
3. Edict of 14 December 1726.

in this regard were well founded, as he was to find out shortly. The caravan directors nourished sufficient pessimism that they petitioned Vladislavich for fixed salaries in silver, in lieu of permission to trade on their own accounts as was usual earlier. The Ambassador agreed, and Molokov received 600 rubles per year; the sergeant of the bodyguard, Ivan Nognev (Nozhnev), 100 rubles; and each of the two interpreters, 50 rubles.[4] Only the sworn-appraisers did not receive salaries, but were accorded claims on the caravan merchandise to the extent of 200 rubles each, with payment of the usual customs duties, upon bringing goods back into the country.[5] Since the state's goods must be sold before privately owned merchandise, the prospect of doing well in private trade in Peking was not at all good.[6]

The passage to Peking was comparatively uneventful, although no crossing of the Gobi at any time was unforgettable. The caravan set out at full strength: 205 men in all, 1,650 horses (of which 400 were cavalry mounts), 475 carts with goods, 162 with provisions and stores, and 562 head of horned cattle and three calves to feed the men on the way in.[7] It carried a total of 285,404 rubles worth of pelts, manufactured goods, and money with which to purchase gold and silver. Siberian peltry comprised the bulk of the merchandise—nearly a million and a half squirrel pelts, plus smaller quantities of ermine, sable, fox, lynx, otter, etc.[8]

4. Cahen, *Histoire*, p. 230.

5. Eight sworn-appraisers were assigned to the caravan: Filat Liangusov, Ivan Ikonnikov, Maksim Bobrov, Iudas Khmelev, Pantelei Nepein, Ivan Pivovarov, Ivan Sukhanov, and Nechaevskii. Whether all eight travelled to Peking is unlikely; perhaps only five did. Apparently two died before 1726 (Bobrov and Nepein) and Nechaevskii may not have made the journey. Kurts, *Gosudarstvennaia monopoliia*, p. 34, 43, n.; Lange, *Le livre de comptes*, p. x; Cahen, *Histoire*, p. 231, n. 6.

6. Kurts, *Gosudarstvennaia monopoliia*, p. 32.

7. Bantysh-Kamenskii, *Diplomaticheskoe sobranie*, p. 142; Kurts, *Gosudarstvennaia monopoliia*, pp. 35, 42-43, n. This was over twice as many carts as the Chinese earlier seemed willing to permit to travel to Urga and no further. In addition to the goods themselves, some carts carried tools necessary for the journey—yokes, axes, adzes, augers, chisels, rope, etc. Of the 205 men who made up the roster, Lange and his suite constituted nine; Molokov and his suite, six; the sworn-appraisers, eight (?); the soldiers, eighteen; the laborers *(rabotniki)*, 140; and twenty-four others, including three students assigned to the Orthodox mission in Peking to learn eastern languages. Of the provisions taken the main item was hardtack *(sukhar')* of which 600 *pud* was carried, plus 100 *pud* of barley groats *(iashnaia krupa)*, 200 *pud* of oats to feed the cattle, and 400 *pud* of rice.

8. See Appendix II for Lange's daily account of goods sold and purchased. Kurts notes that there are small errors in Cahen's calculations, but none large

Emperor Yung-ch'eng directed the *Li-fan-yuan* to aid the Russians while the caravan was on the road.[9] A *Yuan* official joined the caravan especially to protect its horses and animals against theft. With Chinese approval, the Russians corralled their extra horses and cattle in enclosures outside of the Great Wall, as they had requested. If any cattle or horses were stolen, compensation had to be paid to the caravan, since "Russia was a small foreign land," according to the Emperor's message to the Russians. Still the weight of the message was not quite so felicitous. The Emperor held the caravan commander responsible for keeping his men in line, preventing fighting and brawling, and suppressing thievery and brigandage. All in all the harbingers were not particularly auspicious.

After a fast but costly trip of fewer than four months, the caravan reached Peking on 26 December 1727. Between Selenginsk and Kalgan it lost 489 horses and 258 head of cattle. The cost of maintenance of animals in Peking was prohibitive, and Molokov was ordered to graze them on the Kalgan grasslands and pick them up on return. The Chinese received the travellers cordially, perhaps accounted for by the fact that the Treaty of Kiakhta was still not ratified and exchanged. On the very day after arrival, the Peking court approved trade to begin at the Russian quarters, the so-called "Russian House" located slightly south and east of the Forbidden City. This was a surprisingly gracious turn of events, for typically the caravans sat for weeks waiting for an imperial reception at which the "tribute-bearing barbarians" would present themselves, their quaint gifts, and receive in return Chinese curiosities and permission to trade. However the honeymoon was brief; there soon appeared before the Russian House some 750 men, reportedly 500 to "guard" the caravan and its goods, and another 250 to keep close watch on the gates of the Russian court.[10]

---

enough to be significant in the final accounting; Kurts, *Gosudarstvennaia monopoliia*, p. 43, n. 1.

9. Issued 5 November 1727 (o.s.) (the 4th day of the 10 month of the 5th year of Yung-ch'eng); *SFPC*, Chuan Shou 2.1a-1b.

10. This is of course a Russian estimate, but exaggerated as it may seem, it may well be, on balance, roughly accurate; Bantysh-Kamenskii, *Diplomaticheskoe sobranie*, p. 160. Cf. Meng Ssu-ming, "The E-lo-ssu Kuan (Russian Hostel) in Peking," *Harvard Journal of Asiatic Studies*, XXIII (1961), 26-27, for a brief recitation of extant Chinese regulations on the Russians' quarters. Meng says that there was normally a *chien-tu* (inspector) appointed by the *Li-fan-yuan* to oversee the Russian operations and to serve as intermediary between

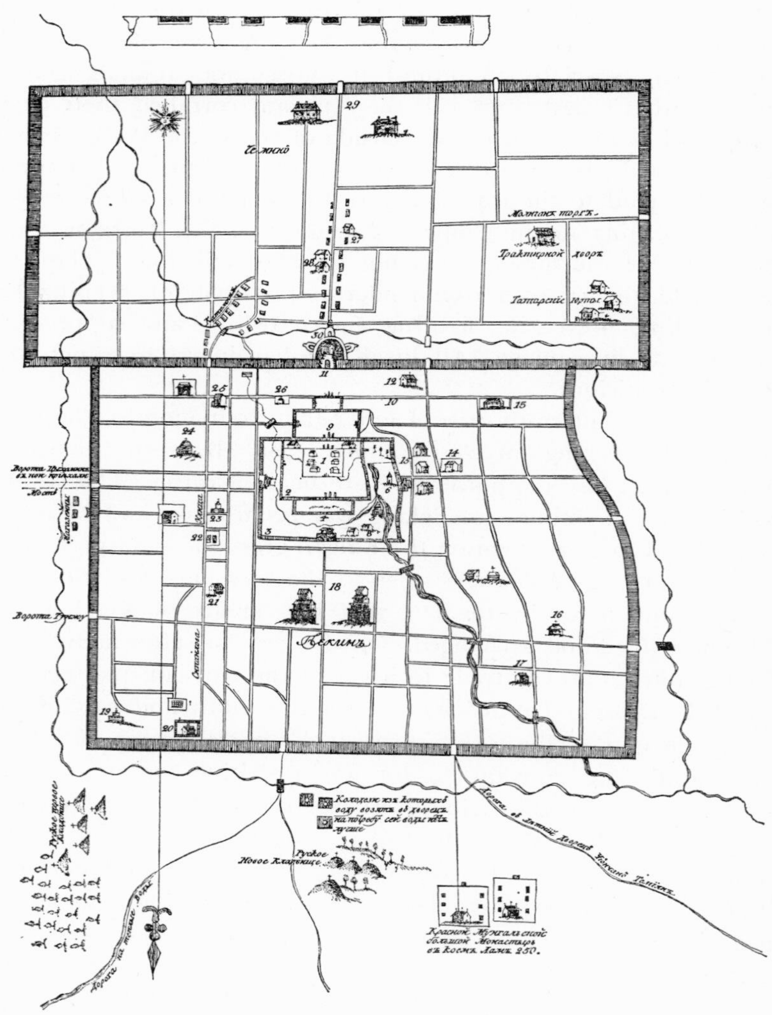

Figure. 7. Peking in the eighteenth century. From *Akademicheskiia izvestiia na 1781 god* (St. Petersburg: Pri S. Peterburgskoi Imp. Akademii Nauk, 1779-81), VIII, following p. 677. Reproduced from the collections of the Library of Congress. No. 1 is the Imperial Palace; No. 19 is the Russian Church of St. Nikolai Chudotvorets; No. 26 is the Russian compound *(Russkii dom)*, located on what seems now to be Ch'ang-an Avenue.

According to Russian claims, Yung-ch'eng and his bureaucracy tried in nearly every way to hinder trade. They tried to turn away wealthier and more prosperous Chinese, Japanese, and Korean merchants, intercepting everyone who came to trade and subjecting them to thorough investigation—what they wished to sell, how much cash they brought, and how they came into possession of these goods and money. Once passed by the investigators stationed near the Russian House, each merchant received a pass to enter the Russian compound and to commence barter. Agent Lange complained repeatedly to the Chinese court that this procedure dissuaded wealthy merchants from revealing themselves to the interrogating bureaucrats, and as a result only poorer merchants came with highly inferior goods. As the weeks went by, Russian goods deteriorated, and the *Li-fan-yuan* admonished the Russians to sell at the offering prices of the Peking merchants rather than hold out for higher prices. To increase the pressure, the *Yuan* put on the market some of its own store of Siberian furs, acquired no doubt from private Russian merchants, further depressing an already poor market. The Chinese merchants who appeared at the Russian House brought only small quantities of silks, at least at first, wholly insufficient for the Russians to dispose of their pelts.[11] Before many weeks went by, Lange turned, as he had earlier, to "middlemen" (*baryshniki*, "profiteers" or "jobbers"; more politely *maklery*, "brokers"). At least six of these go-betweens aided the caravan at one time or another, of which three or four were Peking-born, recently-baptized Russians. They either brought Chinese merchants to the Russians (on 17 January 1728 Efim Gusov brought a wealthy Chinese who had earlier had dealings with Vladislavich and now bartered silver and damasks for sea otter

the Russians and the court. Porters guarded the *kuan* gate and a censor *(yu-shih)* kept the Russians from learning things they had no need to know.

When a caravan arrived it was met by a temporarily-assigned officer *(tsung-li E-lo-ssu shih wu)*, a superintendent of Russian affairs, who assumed general responsibility for the entire caravan business. And a force of some 260 officers and men was mounted as a guard for the *kuan* and to accompany each Russian as he went about town.

11. Lange wrote to Vladislavich on 11 March 1728: "Unfortunately, we see every day a great quantity of Chinese merchandise that they bring to us to sell for silver, but so far we have only been able to get for our own merchandise silver enough for the provisioning of our men and our horses, and none of the larger merchants has shown himself willing to exchange goods for goods"; Cahen, *Histoire*, p. 233, n. 3.

and Arctic fox) or arranged for exchanges as merchants' agents.[12] Each earned from 1.5 to 3 per cent of the value of the goods sold, although they asked 5; in all these services cost the caravan 2,203 *liang* (3084 rubles) and accounted in all probability for a very large portion of the total sales, perhaps as much as three-quarters.

In spite of this device business continued poor for the Russians. Even after six months of trading many of the pelts remained unsold, especially the rarer and more expensive varieties. The Russians quickly blamed the Chinese court for restricting them and their customers and for contributing to the surfeit of furs already on the Peking market. The Chinese for their part accounted for the difficulty by the absence of interested purchasers for the Russian wares, because of "the poor quality *(plokhost')* of the goods and the hot weather."[13]

At length Lange, so he claimed, was hailed to the court and asked, "Did he think to die in Peking, that he lived here so long?" The Chinese officials requested him to fix a departure date, and failing to do so he would be "dispatched with dishonor."[14] Molokov and Lange held counsel and determined to wait, if at all possible, until 1 August, but when Lange so informed the *Li-fan-yuan* the President of the *Yuan* insisted the date be moved back to 13 July (the fifteenth day of the sixth month). Six days before the deadline Yung-ch'eng granted Lange an audience. The Emperor began by reminding Lange of the good relations that his

12. Efim Gusov, described as born in Peking of Russian parentage and as with many of the Russians there descended from Cossacks taken at Albazin or from runaways. Other Peking Russians mentioned are Iakov Savin, Aleksandr Il'in, Semen Sakhaltui, Sange Liugin, Danzhilai, and Syge. See *ibid.*, p. 233; and Kurts, *Gosudarstvennaia monopoliia*, p. 44.

On 19 January 1728 Lange contacted Père Parrenin whom Vladislavich had earlier as a source of information, but apparently Lange did not use his good offices to aid in the trade. On the twenty-first the two visited and Parrenin described to Lange the persecution of Jesuits of the Portuguese embassy who were charged with trying to buy religious toleration with gold.

Lange also learned of the disgrace of Lung-k'e-to after the signing of the Treaty of Kiakhta; Cahen, *Histoire*, pp. 234-35.

13. The Chinese statement was made to Lange in his final interview at the court on 7 July 1728, when it may well have been warm in the Chinese capital, although it could hardly have been said of the months previous; Bantysh-Kamenskii, *Diplomaticheskoe sobranie*, p. 161; Kurts, *Russko-kitaiskie snosheniia*, p. 76; and Silin, *Kiakhta*, p. 45.

14. Bantysh-Kamenskii, *Diplomaticheskoe sobranie*, p. 161. In 1730 the Senate reproved the *Li-fan-yuan* sharply for so summarily dispatching the caravan before its sales were completed, to which the latter responded that the Treaty of Kiakhta specified no length of time for a caravan's stay; *ibid.*, pp. 170, 181.

father, the K'ang-hsi Emperor, had enjoyed with him, implying that there was no reason for them not to continue. Seeing several important ministers present, Lange inquired of the Chinese commitment in the Treaty of Kiakhta to build an Orthodox church in Peking and to provide for the teaching of Russian students. Two of those who had negotiated with Vladislavich, Ch'a-pi-na and T'e-ku-t'e, assured Lange of the good will of the court toward the church and the students. The church building begun in January would be finished, they said, and the students' teachers were already selected.[15] The good will seems to have been genuine. The Chinese, it must be remembered, had already determined to send an embassy to Russia. The audience ended with the Chinese reminding Lange of something he knew too well, that there seemed to be no demand for Russian wares in Peking, and the caravan was formally bid farewell.

The caravan remained in Peking more than six and one-half months, an unusually long sojourn for Russian caravans or for those of any "tribute-bearing" peoples. Lange and his superiors in St. Petersburg later charged that the long stay accounted for the failure of the caravan to dispose of all of its goods.[16] Not only was this sharply denied in correspondence from the *Li-fan-yuan* two years hence,[17] but it is hardly persuasive on the face of it. Trading started unprecedentedly soon after the Russians' arrival and as far as may be gathered continued until they left. Other caravans required far less time to achieve far greater success.

The late departure forced travel across the Gobi during the wretchedly hot summer, and it took two and one-half months to reach Kiakhta.[18] The luck of the caravan remained poor to the end. It carried back to the border over one-half of its goods in value, i.e. one-fifth of its pelts (404,000 pieces of a total of over 2,100,000). The best and most expensive furs did the poorest over-

15. Lange reported to St. Petersburg from Selenginsk on 31 December 1728 that five days earlier there arrived a messenger from Peking to escort Archimandrite Platkovskii to Peking. Lange sent him off with about 2,000 r. for maintenance of the ecclesiastical establishment in Peking, the pupils, and the priests, for two years. The money came from the treasury of the caravan. Construction of a church in Peking began on 12 January 1728 and, according to Lange, was going well; Cahen, *Histoire*, p. 235.

16. Bantysh-Kamenskii, *Diplomaticheskoe sobranie*, pp. 170-72; Kurts, *Russko-kitaiskie snosheniia*, p. 84.

17. Bantysh-Kamenskii, *Diplomaticheskoe sobranie*, p. 181.

18. They reached Kiakhta on 30 September 1728 and Selenginsk on 4 October; Cahen, *Histoire*, p. 234.

all.[19] The inexpensive squirrel, well over one-half of the total pelts shipped to Peking, nearly sold out, but the rare and choice ermine, fox, sable, and lynx, which sold at anywhere from twice the price of squirrel to nearly 100 times, all were returned to the border in large quantities. Only the most expensive sea otter, of which somewhat fewer than 600 were brought, held its market. Of the small quantities of other goods brought, few did well. Most of the Dutch cloth found no buyers; all the seal skins and all but one of the mirrors were left unsold.

Curiously one finds a similar pattern in the Chinese goods imported.[20] Although at other times and places in the eighteenth century silks were purchased in large quantities, they were far overshadowed here by the less dear cottons, approximately 125,000 yards of various kinds of silk fabrics compared with 570,000 yards of cottons. Over 30,000 pounds of both green and black teas were carried, but this is a small amount compared to the great tea trade of the latter decades of the eighteenth century, plus small quantities of anise, tobacco, untanned ox-skins, certain medicants, and pearls. Finally Lange acquired substantial amounts of both gold and silver, 31,600 rubles worth of gold and 33,800 rubles of silver, in both cases mostly in bullion. Since the acquisition of Chinese gold and to a lesser extent silver was throughout these years a major goal of the Russian treasury, Lange's greatest success may be considered to have been here. Since he took with him only a very small amount of cash (9,596 rubles), Lange succeeded in bartering furs for bullion.

What caused the relatively poor business showing of this caravan? It is impossible to say conclusively. Of the many factors mentioned earlier, any one alone could have accounted for it. Perhaps most persuasive is the Chinese allegation that the merchandise was inferior in part and the sworn-appraisers were reluctant or forbidden to cut prices, at least beyond a certain minimum. It is not unlikely that many of the pelts carried back to Selenginsk (including even 40,000 of the low-priced squirrel) were already in second-class condition, having been gathered ten years or more earlier and, in spite of continued effort of the government to compel careful pack-

19. See Appendix II for a complete listing. Cahen reported inaccurately that all of the caravan goods were sold (*Histoire*, p. 235).

20. Gaston Cahen distinguishes between two types of goods, "les produits de luxe" and "les objets de première nécessité," and remarks that although the caravans always seemed to be in search of the former, the bulk of the trade was in the latter (Lange, *Le livre du comptes*, p. 139).

ing and handling, had lain in dampness or been exposed to worms and bugs. We do know that even before the caravan left Kiakhta, caravan officials declared a large number of furs damaged by moths, including 100,000 ermine pelts, 32,500 squirrel, etc.[21] Whether these were removed from the caravan or simply left in the distant hope that some dull-witted Chinese merchant might be hoodwinked in dim light, we do not know.[22] That other pelts were inferior by the time trading opened is highly likely.

A full account of the caravan's goods is impossible. Apparently after a lapse of six months, Vladislavich sent an order on 24 May 1729 to Lange authorizing him to sell all surplus goods on the border, and any not disposed of there (presumably at prices set by the appraisers) should be transshipped to Moscow where, Vladislavich noted, prices were higher than obtained in China.[23] Two of the caravan's sworn-appraisers, Liangusov and Nechaevskii, seem to have had a hand in bartering unsold pelts at the border. Molokov turned over to Liangusov 102,995 rubles worth of Russian goods (of which 22,506 rubles were in the possession of Nechaevskii), 5,979 rubles in goods and money of Madame Tret'iakova (representing a deficit in the accounts of the caravan while her husband was commissar and of which 2,400 rubles were diamonds and pearls), 4,157 rubles in cash (presumed to be expense money for Liangusov), and 695 *liang* of silver (whether part of the silver taken to China or whether purchased there is not evident). Excluding the diamonds and pearls, which evidently came from China, and the silver, the remainder represents at least 106,000 rubles worth of the goods unsold in Peking.[24] The sworn-appraisers disposed of most of these goods in 1731 and 1733, 88,016 rubles worth, for which they received Chinese goods worth 91,623 rubles at the border prices or 125,333 rubles evaluating the goods at Moscow prices, a "profit" of 37,317 rubles over original assigned value.[25] This meant, it would seem, that in the end some 36,000 rubles worth of furs and other goods remained unsold, and may be counted as sheer loss for the caravan. We know also that in the

21. Kurts, *Gosudarstvennaia monopoliia*, p. 41; compare Trusevich, *Posol'skiia i torgovliia snosheniia*, p. 132.

22. The surviving account figures suggest, but suggest only, that these pelts were not taken to Peking; see Kurts, *Gosudarstvennaia monopoliia*, p. 41.

23. *Ibid.*, p. 48, citing the Moskovskii Glavnyi Arkhiv, Ministerstvo Inostrannykh Del, Snosheniia Rossii s Kitaem, *karton* 26, *delo* 1729 g., *Nr.* 4, p. 3.

24. *Ibid.*, p. 49.

25. *Ibid.*, pp. 48-49.

final accounts of four of the sworn-appraisers "discrepancies" of nearly 4,000 rubles appeared, although this is probably only faulty accounting revealed by auditors *(vyborshchiki)*, rather than theft of state property.[26]

Of the Chinese goods imported, some 335,301 rubles worth were brought to Moscow for sale, including the 91,623 rubles acquired at the border by Liangusov and Nechaevskii, according to the final verification *(proverka)* made on 20 December 1733 of the accounts of Tret'iakov and Molokov.[27] Sales began in 1730 in the Moscow Siberian Office *(kontora)*, although not all of the goods reached that city until the following year. The important merchant Ivan Lakomkin supervised the transactions, but even a skilled trader such as he fell short of complete success. Many of the goods were purchased by private merchants for resale in Russia or for shipment to western Europe, but civil and military servants, generals, state councillors, colonels, even sergeants and artillery serving men made purchases. Most of the sales were small, forty or fifty rubles, or even one and two. Only the tea went in large consignments, several thousands of rubles.[28] By 1733 nearly one-third of the goods remained unsold (77,287 rubles), and even by 1735, when the acquisitions of the next caravan began to arrive in Moscow, there remained some, although probably few, which were turned over to the account of the new caravan.

One matter for consideration is left, the question of the financial success or failure of the entire venture, one which finally stretched over more than fifteen years from the initial gathering of furs and goods to the giving over of unsold goods to the account of the next caravan. Surviving records and accounts are most incomplete, and except for the months in China itself, detailed accounting was apparently never made. Within these limitations we can surmise that the caravan was a relative failure, i.e., had the same trade been conducted by private entrepreneurs and taxed by the state, far greater returns to the state would probably have been realized. It may have been an absolute failure and suffered "very great losses," as insisted by B. G. Kurts.[29] Counting together the basic

26. *Ibid.*, p. 50: Liangusov, 2,811 r. 36 k.; Nechaevskii, 995 r. 52 k.; Bobrov, 48 r. 25 k.; Sukhanov, 82 r. 57 k.

27. *Ibid.*

28. A first-guild merchant bought 1,550 r. worth at 12½ r. per *pud* in February 1732, and in July the merchants Andrei and Vasilii Evreinov bought 8,045 r. at 14 r. per *pud* of plain green; *ibid.*, p. 51.

29. *Ibid.*, p. 53.

monetary expenses of the caravan reported by Molokov in 1733, 63,687 rubles, and the total of goods and monies carried to China, 285,404 rubles, we get an initial outlay of 349,091 rubles. Against this investment must be balanced some 335,301 rubles worth of Chinese goods brought to Moscow for sale. Had all of the Chinese wares been sold and sold dearly, which as far as may be gathered was not the case, the caravan might be said to have been financially successful. Notably this does not assign *any* value to the overhead expenses involved in such a complicated operation, such as the costs of maintaining an enlarged Siberian Office operation in Moscow, the expenses of the Collegium of Foreign Affairs in conducting its business with the *Li-fan-yuan*, etc.

If trade of these same proportions had been conducted by a single private company or by individual merchants investing in a caravan, all of the goods, both Russian and Chinese, would have been taxed, as was usual at the time, 10 per cent ad valorem. This would have produced, say, 28,000 rubles on the Russian goods actually carried to Peking, and 16,000 rubles on the Chinese goods brought directly from Peking, or about 44,000 rubles total. The government assuredly did valuate its pelts at prices higher than those that usually obtained in the open market place, but then we have not included in our calculations any but the *actual* expenses of the caravan.

Or to look at it another way, if the state had invested 350,000 rubles elsewhere, a modest 6 per cent return would have yielded over 20,000 rubles with a great deal less risk and likely much less headache. Direct costs of the caravan, here 13 per cent on the Chinese goods brought back, were considerably higher than the 5 per cent reported by Vockerodt in 1737, and if Strahlenberg was told at this time that the operation "frequently made *Cent. per Cent.*" his informant was ignorant or perverse.[30] Vockerodt's observation may have more than a grain of truth to it: "Only the poor and strange ordering of business and supervision of the Siberian Prikaz during the storage and sale of these goods, and the swindling by officials [charged with] looking after them, cause a great part of the profit to be lost or transferred to their pockets."[31]

30. Strahlenberg, *An Historico-Geographical Description*, p. 341.

31. Johann G. Vockerodt, "Rossiia pri Petre Velikom, po rukopisnomu izvestiiu Ioanna Gottgil'fa Fokkerodta," trans. from the German by A. N. Shemiakin, *Chteniia OIDR*, Bk. 2 (April-June, 1874), Pt. IV (Materialy inostrannye), p. 62.

Perhaps another set of *chinovniki,* with more liberal standards of pricing the state's goods and altering prices according to the will of the market, might have turned business failure into a model of business acumen; it is always pleasant to speculate. We cannot say how well lined were the pockets of officials from *iasak* collector to supervisor of sales in Moscow. Charges of peculation and malfeasance abounded, the indebtedness incurred by caravan commissar Tret'iakov being a case in point. The discharge of this debt fell to the caravan treasury and ultimately to the widow Tret'iakova.[32] Trusevich alleges that the caravan was often bilked by having to pay excessively high prices for animals and other things necessary for their maintenance, which suggests under-the-counter payments to caravan personnel, although he could offer no more evidence than that several prices seemed to him to be out of line.[33]

Long before the final accounts of the caravan were closed and the financial failure thoroughly evident, the Supreme Privy Council sought out and solicited the opinions of those most knowledgeable about the caravan operations and most concerned with the future involvement of the state. There were sharp and valid differences of opinion. Vladislavich strongly supported the continuation of state caravans to Peking, and went so far as to propose that trade in Siberian peltry be denied to private merchants *both* in Chinese territories *and* on the border, making the border towns local marts for Siberians and Mongols.[34] Under no circumstances should private merchants be permitted to carry goods into Chinese territory, under penalty of death. The caravans must be closely regulated, their members strictly denied the privilege of private trading and instead paid in fixed salaries; private trading throughout Siberia to be closely watched by government officials stationed at a series of new forts and barriers. This extreme view was guaranteed to provoke resistance, especially among the merchantry, but no less among those government officials who were chary about

32. Trusevich, *Posol'skiia i torgovliia snosheniia,* p. 126.

33. *Ibid.,* p. 128.

34. Kurts, *Gosudarstvennaia monopoliia,* p. 54. For Vladislavich's three pieces of 31 August 1726, 28 September 1727, and 1730, see Cahen, *Histoire,* pp. 241-42, lxxiii-lxxx. For Dolgorukii's memorandum of 1727 ("Na mneniia Grafa Savy Vladislavicha my nizhaishee nashe mnenie o rossiiskom torgu s kitaiskim gosud. ob"iavliaem") in abridged form see Cahen, *Histoire,* pp. lxxx-lxxxiv. Consult also Silin, *Kiakhta,* p. 45.

restricting private operations lest state customs revenues be severely jeopardized.

The Siberian Governor-General since early 1724, Prince Mikhail Vladimirovich Dolgorukii, was one of those who took issue with Vladislavich. Arguing on the basis of the potential loss of customs revenues if private border trade in peltry were prohibited, he resisted turning over to state functionaries the lion's share of trade in the finest Siberian furs. Dolgorukii did not favor dispensing with the state monopoly of trade in Peking, but insisted that private trade in pelts be permitted on the frontier, and the members of the caravans be paid not in money, as recommended by Vladislavich and requested by the members of the Tret'iakov-Molokov caravan, but in the prerogative to sell furs privately in the Chinese capital, as had been the common practice prior to 1727. No caravan members should be permitted, however, to offer their furs for sale until all of the crown pelts had been disposed of. To make even more attractive their positions, the caravan commissar and his sworn-appraisers should even be permitted to purchase Chinese merchandise on their own accounts and carry them to Moscow for private sale.

In substance what the Governor-General proposed was that the caravans should in every way compete with private enterprise in providing Chinese markets with furs, although with private trade limited to the border (except for the caravan leaders' business), the state operation would continue to enjoy the advantage of carrying directly to the main Chinese markets and the not inconsiderable disadvantage of a costly journey. Under no circumstances may the proposals of Dolgorukii be passed off lightly as ill-conceived or a reflection of a strong mercantile lobby. His reasoning was good, if his conclusions somewhat impractical. As governor the economic welfare of border Siberians necessarily concerned him, and he recognized the importance of the China trade to them. He certainly desired to encourage trade, to promote the prosperity of the region, and at the same time to reap good benefit to the state through increased customs revenues. As for caravan personnel's trading in apparent competition with the state's goods, therein lay a good check on these merchants-*cum*-state officials. If the sworn-appraisers and commissar purchased the state goods they carried to Peking at excessively high prices, they ran the risk of failing to dispose of their own pelts. If the prices they paid for Chinese goods were too high, the Muscovite treasury assessors *(tsenovniki)*, as was their wont, would appraise them low, the caravan would be a financial failure, and these men risked punishment for malfeasance and perhaps misuse of state funds.

At least one other acknowledged expert was sought for advice. On 4 June 1729 the Supreme Privy Council ordered Lorents Lange in Selenginsk to report as quickly as possible to Moscow.[35] He brought with him, as ordered, the account books of the Tret'iakov-Molokov caravan, such as they were. Lange presented his report to the Senate on 30 June 1730, although the substance of it must have been available to the Privy Council long before that.[36] Lange was somewhat more imaginative, innovating, and sweeping in his memorandum than Vladislavich and Dolgorukii. It began by proposing that all Siberian furs be acquired by the State Treasury, rather than allow them to be acquired directly by merchants and traders. The treasury would then sell them to any Russian merchants who desired to buy, but they might be sold to Chinese only on the Siberian-Mongolian border, not in Peking. With these profits, together with customs duties revenues, the treasury could purchase from Russian merchants additional quantities of European silver coin *(efimki)*, carry it to Peking in smallish caravans (some thirty to fifty thousand rubles in total value) and exchange it for precious metals and stones, and other portable but valuable commodities.[37] He insisted this would be a profitable *modus operandi*, because costs of transportation of such a small caravan would be comparatively low and the business in Peking could be done much more quickly that could that of disposing of several million pieces of fur. Lange's scheme was logical and took into account all of the dreadful disadvantages and hardships, which he knew so well, entailed in the journey to Peking. He had no intention of discouraging private trade, quite the contrary. Private merchants would enjoy the privilege of exchanging Siberian furs with the Chinese unhindered by competition with the state. Lange was primarily concerned, though, that the state obtain what

35. Bantysh-Kamenskii, *Diplomaticheskoe sobranie*, pp. 164-65. For unknown reasons Lange did not leave the border until 23 October 1729, assigning his personal assistant and secretary, David Grave, to act in his stead. He reached Moscow on 23 February 1730.

36. Kurts, *Gosudarstvennaia monopoliia*, p. 55; also see Cahen, *Histoire*, pp. lxxxv–xcvi.

37. Consult Chapter 5 for a discussion of the Russian state's policy and practice in the import and export of precious metals.

he judged then to be among the most valuable items of Chinese origin: gold and silver, and other non-bulky goods. Furthermore most of the risks of the caravan would be obviated or reduced: loss of furs through damage, water or moths; danger of limb and life; the irascibility of the Manchu court, and so forth.

Vladislavich, Dolgorukii, and Lange all proposed retention of at least some kind of state caravan and some limitation of the private sphere of operation. There was one other possibility, short of simply turning loose all Russian and Siberian merchants to travel, trade, and barter where and as they saw fit, and that was to create a private company or companies to trade with the Chinese, within, or course, the treaty limitations. Not since 1711 had this even been suggested, but in December of 1728 a Jewish merchant of Riga, one Solomon Sampson, memorialized His Imperial Majesty on the creation of companies "to trade freely with China," in return for which advice Sampson petitioned for a gratuity of ten thousand rubles and permission for him to trade freely throughout the Russian state.[38] As was usual in Russia in those days, Sampson invoked the image of Dutch and English companies trading in China and India, and insisted that the Russian state might similarly make "great profit" from such a commercial organization. Russian and foreign private persons willing to invest four hundred or five hundred rubles each must be sought out so that the new company would have an initial capital of four to five million rubles. The specific individual investment should be at the discretion of the company head *(komandir).* Several men from among the "eminent and learned" of the nation should be designated as directors, one of them serving as factor *(konsul)* in the company office at the border. The factor was to send back detailed lists of the company's goods passed through customs, lists that would always be available to the tsar, to insure that no attempt be made to deceive the state and the investors. The company should have a monopoly on all goods it brought from China and should be permitted to re-export them freely abroad if necessary to obtain good prices. Finally, to allay any false expectations that returns to the state would be immediate and enormous, Sampson warned that at first customs returns were likely to be modest, although in time as trade grew, profit would redound to the benefit of His Imperial Majesty.

38. Chulkov, *Istoricheskoe opisanie,* III, bk. 2, 180-81; also Silin, *Kiakhta,* p. 48.

Sampson's project appears to have lain dormant for a year and a half, until on 27 July 1730 the newly established Commission on Commerce, formed to review the whole situation of Russia's internal and external trade and to make recommendations for its improvement and amelioration, ordered the Commerce Collegium to forward to it all proposals it had for reconstituting the Siberian trade "on the basis of the East India Company."[39] Still nothing came of the notion of a Russian East Indian Company at this time, although in less than a decade Lange revived the idea. At this point the notion of a great trading company seems not to have gone beyond the stage of discussion in the Commission; later a diligent search actually was made for potential investors.[40]

On 17 July 1730, the Senate at long last issued its decision on the caravan business.[41] The counsel of Vladislavich and Lange seems to have been most persuasive, that of Dolgorukii less so, and for the time being the Sampson proposal was ignored. At least for the moment the state monopoly of Peking trade received the Senate's *imprimatur,* although the next caravan was to be smaller by nearly two-thirds than the Tret'iakov-Molokov one, and it was, as Lange proposed, to make a greater effort to secure Chinese gold. The next caravan was to carry goods and silver worth 100,000 rubles (in comparison with the 285,000 rubles worth in the earlier caravan), included within which was to be fifty *pud* (approx. 1800 pounds) of *efimki* or of silver utensils, plates, etc. (no more than five *pud* of the latter as a trial venture) for the precise purpose of purchasing Chinese gold. The recently created Money Office *(Monetnaia kontora)*[42] in Moscow provided the silver and worked closely with the Commerce Office *(Kommerts-kontora),*[43] also in Moscow and a branch of the Commerce Collegium. Since the new caravan was to carry a much smaller amount of Siberian peltry, all surplus furs already gathered were to be shipped to Moscow for quick sale by the Siberian Office. The

39. Chulkov, *Istoricheskoe opisanie,* III, bk. 2, 184. An imperial ukaz was issued on 13 August 1730 which requested of the Commerce Collegium that all the information it had with regard to "the representation and project in the Collegium to increase Siberian trade on the model of the East India Company be sent to the Commission."

40. See pp. 146-47 of this chapter.

41. *PSZ,* VIII, No. 5589, 298-99; Chulkov, *Istoricheskoe opisanie,* III, bk. 2, 183-84. Directed to be announced to Vladislavich, Lange, and Molokov.

42. *Gosudarstvennye uchrezhdeniia,* pp. 221-23.

43. *Ibid.,* pp. 190-91.

Senate's labors had only begun, for within six months it issued the fullest set of regulations for the operation of the Peking caravan the Russian administration ever elaborated.

On 3 January 1731, after hearing the thoughts of all the concerned state offices, the Governing Senate published a long, eighteen-point ukaz which in a sense completed its earlier statement of December 1726.[44] Now for the first time in a decade the State made clear its role in the China trade: no private persons might sell the varieties of peltry reserved for the state caravan, either in Peking, in Chinese territories elsewhere, or across the border, on pain of loss of all illegal goods apprehended. To insure that ignorance of the law was no excuse, this ukaz was ordered published in all Siberian towns. The caravans themselves (as stipulated in the Treaty of Kiakhta) were to travel to Peking once every three years, and to barter their goods there, as well as in Urga or other Mongol cities where trade was possible. The ukaz explicitly defined the personnel of the caravans. Lorents Lange was to serve in the capacity of consul, although this meant simply chief commercial adviser, not resident in Peking. He was given an associate *(tovarishch)* to be sent out from the Siberian Prikaz. As earlier, general command of the personnel of the caravans fell to the commissar, although now two were to be designated, one to accompany a caravan to Peking and the other, together with half of the personnel mentioned below, to remain in Siberia preparing the succeeding caravan. There were to be four sworn-appraisers (fewer than before), two chancery clerks *(kantseliaristy)* to maintain all of the account books of the caravan and handle all necessary paper work, two copyists, and two interpreters. None of these people might trade on his own account, contrary to the recommendation of Dolgorukii and as permitted Tret'iakov in 1722, each to be paid a fixed salary: Lange, 2000 rubles; Lange's associate, 1500 rubles; the commissar, 1000 rubles; the sworn-appraisers, 300 rubles each; the clerks, 200 rubles each; the copyists, 50 rubles each; and the translators, 100 rubles each. None of these people could carry any Russian or Chinese goods so as to eliminate any opportunity

44. *PSZ,* VIII, No. 5666, 354-58. See also Chulkov, *Istoricheskoe opisanie,* III, bk. 2, 186-90; Cahen, *Histoire,* p. 243; and *Sbornik ukazov po monetnomu i medal'nomu delu v Rossii pomeshchennykh v Polnom sobranii zakonov s 1649 po 1881 g.,* M. Demmeni (comp.) (St. Petersburg: Published by Grand Duke Georgii Mikhailovich, 1887), vyp. 1, 145-47.

for private trade and damage to the caravan's trade.[45] In future caravans, this scheme of remuneration might be used, or as was the customary arrangement between private merchant and his agent in the field, a percentage of the caravan profits might be paid in lieu of fixed salary, as calculated by the Siberian Prikaz. One hundred Cossacks, selected from among "the very best" and captained by a *piatidesiatnik* (commander of fifty men) of Irkutsk, were detailed to protect the caravan from thieves and highwaymen, each Cossack to receive twelve rubles per year, plus provisions: three *chetvert'* of wheat or rye grain, one and one-half *chetvert'* of groats *(krupa)*, twenty-four Russian pounds of salt per year, and double these figures for the chief.[46] These provisions were in fact pay, since the men were to be fed out of caravan provisions en route.

Lange and his associates were to enjoy overall commercial command *(vysshaia komanda)* of each caravan and to travel with it to Peking. Earlier this command responsibility seems to have been vague and shared with the commissars. In the absence of Lange, the commissar was to assume captainship, although at all times he was specifically charged with protecting and preserving the caravan, and settling arguments or altercations between Russians or between the Russians and the Chinese. Were a commissar to die in China, the first sworn-appraiser should succeed him, until such time as the second commissar could assume leadership. Each commissar was to function as an active participant in all preparations and conduct of his caravan. The one remaining behind in Siberia was to personally travel with his sworn-appraisers through-

45. There was some difficulty over this in the next caravan. Several of the officers of the Molokov caravan, including the commissar himself, returned from Peking with Chinese goods (especially furniture) of their own: according to a report of 2 December 1736, Molokov had 32 r. 21 k. worth; sworn-appraiser Ivan Oskolkov, 702 r. 41 k.; sworn-appraiser Andrei Pushkarev, 545 r. 85 k.; and chancery clerk David Grave, 85 r. 59 k., or a total of 1,376 r. 6 k. worth. Lange testified, and the offenders protested, that these goods were not obtained in barter, but purchased with salaries paid them before leaving Peking, and were not intended for resale but for personal home use. In spite of this testimony, the Siberian Prikaz decided that the rule of 1731 was violated and requested an ukaz confiscating all of these goods. Although some of the furniture was destroyed in the Siberian Prikaz fire of 1737, the remainder the Senate ordered taken and lumped with crown goods. The officers were then paid in cash for their losses: Molokov, 500 r.; the sworn-appraisers, 150 r. each; etc. *Sbornik RIO*, CXIV (1902), 477; CXXIV (1906), 164.

46. A *chetvert'* was a grain measure of about eight bushels; a *funt* (lb.) was 0.90 lbs. avoirdupois.

out Siberia helping to select and acquire the finest peltry and other goods to be carried.

The Senate laid great emphasis on the means whereby the state controlled and checked on the caravan operations. All furs and other commodities acquired by purchase, *iasak,* or tithe (customs or turnover tax) for carriage to Peking and left behind in Siberian collection points had to be carefully packaged, marked as to how obtained—purchase, *iasak,* or tithe—and stamped with the seal of the local town or city, then dispatched to the Siberian Office in Moscow, together with lists identifying each item as to package in which it was contained. These goods had to be shipped directly through, and not repacked or broken up in Tobol'sk or Verkhotur'e. In Moscow they were to be priced according to their customs values and sold publicly. Those goods accepted for carriage to Peking, and Chinese goods brought back, all had to be carefully packed, sealed, and full lists kept of the exact location of each item. A copy of this inventory (*opis'* or *rospis'*) must always be with the caravan goods, and upon returning from Peking one copy was to be given over to the Irkutsk vice-governor or *voevoda* and the other sent to the governor-general in Tobol'sk and eventually to the Siberian Prikaz. The vice-governor or *voevoda,* together with the customs officials, was ordered to examine the goods and the inventories carefully and to certify that the latter were wholly accurate. To make certain that a full and meticulous inspection took place, the caravan officials were instructed to inform the customs officials "in good time," prior to arrival, on what day the caravan might be expected to reach the customs point. Not only did the caravan goods themselves have to be inspected, but every worker and soldier as well, to insure that none secretively carried goods to or from Peking. If any were found, they were subject to confiscation, and one-third were to be distributed among those who ferreted out the deception. A new caravan seal was authorized, entrusted to the vice-governor or *voevoda,* and a sketch of it kept available in Tobol'sk, Verkhotur'e, and Moscow customs houses.

Chancery clerks were to keep full account books (*prikhodnie i raskhodnie knigi,* literally receipt and expenditure books), which listed every sale, purchase, exchange, or expenditure, including duties paid on entering or leaving Peking, with details such as where the transaction took place. The books themselves were to be directed to the Siberian Prikaz, a long extract to the Examining Collegium *(Revizion-kollegiia)*,[47] and a short one to the Governing Senate. Such an account had been maintained by the earlier Tret'iakov-Molokov caravan.[48]

These were the general regulations and directives set down in 1731 for all future caravans. Although seventeen of the eighteen sections of the ukaz dealt with the state caravans and the mechanism by which the state's monopoly would be preserved and strengthened, one brief section, the last, at least recognized the value to the state of private trade, so persuasively argued by Dolgorukii. The Siberian Prikaz, in addition to dispatching the next and future caravans, was to observe closely the effect of the monopoly on private trade with the Chinese and Mongols, that it be not "overburdened" by the reinvigoration of the monopoly. The Senate further promised that future measures would be taken, presumably with the aim of improving the conditions of trade for Russia's private merchants.

In two regards this ukaz altered or augmented the decree of 1730 which had ordered the preparation of a new caravan. The original decree called for the carriage of goods and silver to the extent of 100,000 rubles total; now the figure was substantially raised, although, if adhered to, would still be smaller than the Tret'iakov-Molokov caravan. The Senate now permitted merchandise, mostly Siberian peltry, up to a limit of 100,00 rubles but sanctioned in addition the carriage of *efimki* and silver up to another 100,000 rubles, or as much as the Siberian Prikaz deemed practicable. The Siberian Prikaz was strictly cautioned to keep secret the actual amount of silver eventually sent. The Money Office provided the actual *efimki* and silver, the Siberian Prikaz paying for as much as possible in Russian currency and the rest put on the account of the caravan in the Prikaz. As it turned out, the Monetary Office released 100,000 in *efimki,* by weight 168 *pud,* 36 *funt,* 14 *zolotnik,* (nearly 7000 pounds), and according to its value in contemporary Russian paper money, 114,893 rubles, i.e. over thrice the amount originally projected.[49]

47. The *Revizion-kollegiia* (Inspection Collegium) was founded in 1717 to examine and inspect all state accounts; *Gosudarstvennye uchrezhdeniia,* pp. 150-55.

48. Lange, *Le livre du comptes.*

49. In the papers of Anna's Cabinet; *Sbornik RIO,* CIV (1898), 409, *Prilozhenie* to the journal of 17 September 1732.

Second, the Senate now ordered the caravan commissar to escort four young students to China. Four students from the Academy of Sciences, of gentry rank and studied in geometry and trigonometry, were assigned to the caravan, to learn all they might of the caravan operation while with it. If the students left earlier in Peking had completed their studies of the Chinese language, these were to replace them. If their studies were not finished, then one or two of these new boys might be left to study closely the patterns of trade in Peking.

With only slight change, the structure for the Peking trade laid down here, early in 1731, remained essentially the same for the next twenty-five years and for the five caravans that reached Peking during that time. The Senate and the Supreme Privy Council determinedly held tight their grasp on this important commercial route and on one of Russia's finest sources of bullion and markets for its Siberian furs. Short of trying to manipulate the entire Siberian fur store, which probably would have been in vain, in view of the thinly scattered state officials, troops, and customs houses across the great stretches of Siberia, the St. Petersburg administration did about all it could to preserve its nearly antiquated venture. Even for eighteenth-century Russia, the whole structure of the caravan was obsolete and irrational. One animus—the acquisition of bullion—was itself somewhat archaic; the returns to the state in customs revenues from enhanced and stimulated private trade would unquestionably have been far greater at far less monetary cost, although the bullion was usually used to coin money. Probably none of the succeeding caravans was a financial success, if all of the costs, including the overhead required in the Siberian Prikaz and other state offices in Moscow, St. Petersburg, Tobol'sk, and Irkutsk are calculated. As for the caravans themselves, the organization of each, like a convoy of ships, under the sole command of a single responsible officer, from acquisition of merchandise to delivery and sale in Moscow or St. Petersburg, was awkward and cumbersome.

Still, within the limitations of the Treaty of Kiakhta which permitted only a single caravan of limited size every three years, the only other choice was to commission a private company or partnership to assume all the risks and to submit itself to close state scrutiny, and hopefully to thorough and honest taxation. As we shall see later that was not a real alternative, simply because of the lack of investors with ready capital.[50] The caravans, so reminiscent of the Manila galleons, continued to struggle to Peking and back.

The Molokov Caravan

There was great bustle and hurry in the organization and outfitting of this caravan, the officers of which were appointed only eighteen days after the Governing Senate issued its great ukaz. Vladislavich later charged that there was carelessness as well, which accounted for the failure of it to show great profit.[51] Lange naturally served as "director" and Molokov as commissar. In all 113 men comprised the suite, much smaller than its predecessor. There were four sworn-appraisers (Ivan Oskolkov, Andrei Pushkarev, Glazunov, and Marem'ianinov), two chancery clerks (David Grave and Nikifor Syreishchikov), and four young students (Mikhail Pozniakov, Ivan Bykov, Gerasim Barshchikov or Baryshnikov, and Aleksei Vladykin) to replace several of those left in Peking four years before. To effectuate its renewed conviction, the Senate sent strict orders to Eastern Siberia which prohibited the private carriage of peltry to Chinese territories by "persons of all ranks and stations either secretly or openly."[52]

Prospects for the success of this caravan were much greater than for the Tret'iakov-Molokov one. The Chinese amicably responded to Lange's complaints with regard to the restrictions imposed on the last caravan. They blamed its commercial failure on the Russians, but nonetheless promised an absence of all impediments to trade in the future.[53] Behind these written pleasantries was the significant fact that the first Chinese embassy had arrived in Russia in early 1731. It served as a kind of hostage for the good reception of the caravan in Peking. Never before or after was every Russian request or demand so promptly fulfilled.

After receiving his patent *(gramota)* as agent of the caravan on 21 January 1731, Lange set out quickly from Moscow and arrived in Irkutsk on 13 May and in Selenginsk on 19 July. Since the

50. See pp. 146-47 of this chapter.

51. Bantysh-Kamenskii, *Diplomaticheskoe sobranie*, p. 377, from his *Informatsiia (Iz"iaznenie)* of 19 July 1734 given to Vice-Chancellor Osterman.

52. Gosudarstvennyi Arkhiv Irkutskoe Oblasti, Fond Ilimskoi Voevodskoi Kantseliarii, *delo* 335, *list* 20, as cited in Silin, *Kiakhta*, p. 46.

53. See Chapter 2; Bantysh-Kamenskii, *Diplomaticheskoe sobranie*, pp. 170-72, 181.

initial authorization for this caravan had come from the Senate almost precisely a year before, it is presumed that it was in readiness by Lange's arrival, but because of the dilatoriness of the Chinese border officials in reporting the caravan's presence to Peking, it was November before it left Kiakhta. However on 12 October Lange received a most cordial piece of correspondence from the *Li-fan-yuan*.[54] In recognition of the long wait on the border and of the fact that the harsh winter season had set in, the *Yuan*, in the name of the Emperor, granted Lange ten thousand *liang* (roughly fourteen thousand rubles) for the higher costs of maintaining horses and cattle in the winter, and the replacement of those that had died. A grand gift indeed, considering that it was probably one-fifth or one-fourth of the total expenses of the caravan. On their part, the Chinese promulgated a new set of rules for the treatment of the Russian caravans, rules designed to regularize the means and improve the speed with which the Russians were dealt. On memorial of the *Li-fan-yuan*, the Emperor ordered that upon the arrival of the Russian caravans at the border the Tushetu Khan should immediately report to the *Li-fan-yuan*, requesting dispatch of an official from Peking to Kiakhta to ride post for the caravan. As stipulated in the Treaty of Kiakhta, the caravan would sustain all costs of maintenance and provisioning on the road, and should supply its own horses and cattle. Once Kalgan, the Great Wall gate, was reached, Chinese troops would escort and protect the Russians, and would continue to do so in Peking. The Board of War *(Ping pu)* would depute a brigadier general *(Fu-tu-t'ung)* to command the troops guarding the Russian House. Several high officials were entrusted with the general supervision of the Russians in the capital, and two others, appointed from the ranks of the Readers of the Han-lin Academy *(Shih-tu-hsueh-shih)* and the Censors *(yu-shih)* of the Six *Pu* and Fifteen *Tao (k'o-tao)*, were given immediate direction of the Russian House and the trading.[55]

On 6 November 1731 Lange and his compatriots crossed the Mongolian border and proceeded on the northerly Mongolian

54. There is an unresolved discrepancy here in dating. Russian sources record that Lange received the note on 12 October 1731 (o.s.) (e.g. *ibid.*, p. 173), but Chinese sources record the Imperial Edict to the *Li-fan-yuan* ordering the note as 10 October (the tenth day of the ninth month of the ninth year of Yung-ch'eng) (*SFPC*, Chuan Shou 2.1b-2a).

55. *Ibid.*, 37.6b-7b, 18b; cf. Meng Ssu-ming, *Harvard Journal of Asiatic Studies*, XXIII (1961), 26-27.

route, that route that followed the Kerulen River part of the way, in order to avoid the rigors of the Gobi route to the south. It proved to be a bad choice. The journey took four months and marauders robbed the caravan in the Chechen Khanate of eastern Mongolia.[56] Once Peking was sighted however, affairs improved. The Russians soon discovered that they were allowed to roam rather freely about the town and to arrange meetings with the Jesuit missionaries. The sole hindrance mentioned was the insistence of Chinese officials that Russian merchandise and Chinese merchants "even as far as their shirts" be inspected by them to prevent the sale of prohibited items, such as gunpower—a chronic Chinese demand and after all not an unreasonable one, in spite of Lange's protestations.[57] Lange also had difficulty in corresponding with the *Li-fan-yuan* and the Court, and was informed that in the future no direct correspondence from him would be received since the Treaty specified only the Governing Senate and the governor-general of Siberia as legitimate initiators of direct correspondence.[58]

Trade commenced quickly and Russian goods sold well. Even though a small quantity remained unsold after about five months trading, business was much improved over that of two years earlier. No daily account of transactions, such as that kept by Lange for the preceding caravan, is extant, nor beyond partial accounts compiled in 1736[59] and in 1743 do we have any real notion of the accounting of the caravan. The Siberian Prikaz suffered a serious fire in 1737, in which some of the caravan's goods were destroyed,

56. *SFPC*, 37.6a-6b. The caravan left St. Petersburg on 23 August 1731, arriving in Peking 14 February 1732; Bantysh-Kamenskii, *Diplomaticheskoe sobranie*, pp. 194-95. On the road a courier, Sergeant Solov'ev, passed the caravan and reached Peking a month before it. He carried a Senate note formally announcing the caravan and, among other things, requesting of the *Li-fan-yuan* total freedom of trade in Peking and permission for the caravan to return to Siberia via Manchuria, because of the disturbances in Mongolia threatened by the resurgent Dzhungars. After a two-month wait Solov'ev was summoned to the *Yuan*, given three notes in return and urged to hasten to St. Petersburg. Yung-ch'eng granted permission to leave via Naun.

57. Bantysh-Kamenskii, *Diplomaticheskoe sobranie*, pp. 196-97; Kurts, *Russko-kitaiskie snosheniia*, p. 84. Sufficiently embarrassing was this to well-to-do Chinese merchants that they sent "worthless" persons to receive their goods from the Russians.

58. Bantysh-Kamenskii, *Diplomaticheskoe sobranie*, p. 197.

59. The caravan's account was closed in 1736, as was the case of the last caravan long before the Chinese goods were disposed of; *Sbornik RIO*, CXIV (1902), 398, 507.

along with many of its records. Even in 1743 it was impossible for the state to completely account for its investment, for the surviving records were kept only in Moscow prices. Presumably Molokov carried about 100,000 rubles in furs and other commodities;[60] whether the 114,000 rubles worth of *efimki* and silver was taken is not entirely clear, although considering the amount of Chinese goods returned it seems impossible that it was not. Before the end of trading in 1736, the account already showed (in Moscow prices) Chinese goods of 214,699 rubles, plus 1,144 *liang* 48 *fen* of silver and 11,102 rubles of Russian money, or a total of 216,300 rubles, excluding the Russian money.[61] Even discounting the Moscow prices by at least 10 per cent and possibly 20 or 25 per cent, the total Chinese imports seem much too large to have been obtained from bartering 100,000 rubles worth of furs.[62]

Of the 100,000 rubles of furs carried (in all 72,000 pelts) the largest item in ruble value was fox, including the more valuable red and plain *(prostoi)* worth 12,000 rubles and the brown, grey, and crossed at 6,000 rubles.[63] Grey and black squirrel held second place (15,000 rubles worth) which indicates there were certainly many more squirrel pelts than any other variety, as in 1727-28. Then came medium and low priced sable at 14,000 rubles (including 2,000 in bellies), Arctic fox at 13,000 rubles, lynx and *korsak* (a small grey fox) at 10,000 rubles each, glutton from the Ob' basin at 8,000 rubles, sea otter at 6,000 rubles, otter at 3,000 rubles, and the remaining at 1,000 rubles or less.

After five and one-half months of trading, the caravan departed Peking on 8 September 1732, but not until the Court honored it with a fine reception. The officers of the suite enjoyed a "magnificent" table, were entertained with a puppet show and other *diver-*

60. Two accounts give the precise figure of 104,390 r., but indicate no source; Aleksandr Kazimirovich Korsak, *Istoriko-statisticheskoe obozrenie torgovykh snoshenii Rossii s Kitaem* (Kazan': I. Dubrovin, 1857), p. 56, and Trusevich, *Posol'skiia i torgovliia snosheniia*, p. 96.

61. Kurts, *Gosudarstvennaia monopoliia*, p. 61, again calculating one *liang* as 1 r. 40 k.

62. See also *Sbornik RIO*, CXI (1901), 515-16, wherein it is reported that in December 1735 the Siberian Prikaz had on hand 7 *funt* 73¼ *zolotnik* of gold, 13 *funt* 32 *zolotnik* of Khanish silver and commercial silver, and diamond items.

63. Petrogradskii Arkhiv Departamenta Tamozhennykh Sborov, *Katalog* 1888 g., *Dela Sibirskogo Prikaza No.* 30, *Sviaska* 13, *d.* 131, *l.* 4, *l.* 5. cited in Kurts, *Gosudarstvennaia monopoliia*, p. 56. Trusevich (*Posol'skiia i torgovliia snosheniia*, pp. 131-32) lists more precise figures, but since his work is often undependable, they must be ignored. See also *Sbornik RIO*, CXI (1901), 140.

tissements, the whole affair lasting over three hours.[64] Lange accompanied only by his translator, Stefan Savinov, was ushered into audience with the Emperor, permitted to sit, and receive tea. Evidently Lange impressed the Manchu Emperor every bit as much as he had his own; the Emperor asked his age, gave him six pieces of *kamka* as a personal gift, promised that he would be held in high esteem, and wished him Godspeed on the road. Before he left, Lange arranged to replace the Russian students in Peking: two of the four he brought with him (Ivan Bykov and Aleksei Vladykin, of whom much will be said later) replaced Ivan Pukhort and Fedot Tret'iakov, both judged to have finished their studies.[65]

With the permission of Peking to use the northern route, the caravan set out in three parts for Tsurukhaitu by way of Naun. Although the rigors of the Gobi were avoided, highwaymen were not. The caravan suffered two attacks by armed Mongols, three Russians were wounded (one died on arrival in Selenginsk), and in all ninety horses and twenty-three oxen were lost. The *Li-fan-yuan* quickly restored the losses, fined the Mongol tribes in the region 1,263 horses, cattle, and camels, captured the "offenders" or their surrogates, of which nine were executed and their heads sent to Kiakhta as token of the good will of the Peacock Throne. The distance and the depredations caused the caravan to spend nearly as long on the road as it had in Peking. And when Tsurukhaitu was finally reached on 23 April 1733, it was little improvement. For lack of closed storage space there, the Chinese goods lay in the open field, sustaining considerable damage, and in two months, when the caravan was ready to push on, Lange had great difficulty finding Russian or native laborers to help repack and move the goods.

Lange took the time to submit a lengthy report to the Collegium of Foreign Affairs in which he complained bitterly of the miserable location and circumstance of Tsurukhaitu.[66] His most valuable comments were, however, on the strength of the Chinese and their

64. Bantysh-Kamenskii, *Diplomaticheskoe sobranie,* p. 198.

65. The Archimandrite Antonii Platkovskii also sent back a report dated 30 June 1731 requesting a communion cloth (for consecration of the newly built Orthodox church), an ikonostatis, priestly raiment, Church books, an altar, a bell, 500 silver crosses, and several small images of the Savior as gifts to newly baptized Chinese. He wished funds for maintenance of the Church and to pay small sums to Chinese converts; he claimed to have baptized twenty-five; *ibid.,* p. 198.

66. *Ibid.,* pp. 199-200.

involvement in Dzhungarian affairs. He felt the situation faced by the Manchus in their struggle with the Dzhungars was critical, and he recommended that the time was ripe for Russia to intervene with demands for removal of the surveillance imposed on caravans, a favorable settlement of the recurring controversy over deserters at the frontier, and the extension of the Russian frontier once again to the Amur. He warned of Chinese construction of a fort on the Kailiar River, an east bank affluent of the Argun, and counselled that Russia should counter with a new fort at the Turgia River, north of Tsurukhaitu. This intelligence and counsel apparently went unheeded, for it was over twenty years before St. Petersburg showed renewed interest in the Amur River valley.

It took the entire summer for the caravan to reach Irkutsk, arriving in September 1733, hence it was the following year before the selling of goods began in Moscow and 1735 before all the goods arrived in the Siberian Prikaz.

By early 1736 the Siberian Prikaz reported to the Senate that sales of the Chinese goods were not going well.[67] Many were spotted, discolored, and mildewed, and the few merchants who did come offered less than the set price or expressed no interest in purchasing at any price, even though the prices then were judged to be lower than usual. The Prikaz revealed a sharp gap between the prices fixed by the sworn-appraisers and those offered by the merchants; on some goods the appraisers were high and on others low. Hence the Governing Senate ordered that new appraisers be selected from amongst Moscow's first-guild merchants, and in the presence of officials from the Siberian Office *(Kontora)*, the Siberian Prikaz, and the Procuror's Office that all goods—item by item—be re-appraised and sold at prices so fixed that they would move. A complete report had to be submitted to the Senate, with former and new prices, and comparisons with Siberian and Chinese prices. Although business improved after that, the account still showed 73,724 rubles worth undisposed of after the fire of 1737. By 1738 only 7,404 rubles worth remained.

The difficulties encountered by the Siberian Prikaz in disposing of these caravan goods (as well as Chinese merchandise extracted

67. *PSZ*, IX No. 6916, 779-82, dated 15 March 1736. In May, 1734, the silk entrepreneur Aleksei Miliutin requested permission to buy some 200 *pud* of raw Chinese silk which had arrived at the rate of seventy rubles per *pud*, twenty above the appraised value, for use in his mill. The Empress approved sale of 100 *pud* at the price he offered, to be paid for over the next two and one-half years; *Sbornik RIO*, CVIII (1900), 184-85.

from private merchants trading at the border) is well revealed in a Senate ukaz of 30 June 1737.[68] Two first-guild merchants—Grigorii Osipov and Vasilii Shaposhnikov, both representing a number of associates—appeared in that year with offers for the goods before revaluation. They had bid on specific goods after obviously close inspection of quality and condition, and Osipov at least sought large quantities, in all 96,254 rubles worth of Chinese fabrics, of which 30,818 rubles were on the account of the caravan. After revaluation Osipov's offer would return a profit of 2,475 rubles to the caravan. The Siberian Prikaz refused the offer, however, on the ground that the profit was too small. The Court Broker *(Gof-makler)* reported that, in spite of considerable efforts to attract other merchants, both large and small, none appeared, and the offers of the two merchants were finally accepted. The broker cautioned the Siberian Prikaz to take care that sound and spoiled goods were sold together in large lots of 500 to 5000 rubles, to avoid the latter being left over. The goods that arrived in the Prikaz in the years 1734 and 1735 must be sold out before those of 1736 were offered to the public. In all likelihood the worst hindrance to successful trade was the bureaucratic outlook that insisted that all inventory be accounted for and disposed of, regardless of the fact that this would deter merchants from offering high bids. Willingness to take loss on defective and spoiled goods for the sake of overall profit seems to have been beyond the understanding of St. Petersburg officialdom.

Kurts attempted to assess the profitability of this second caravan under the Kiakhta Treaty, but found it nearly impossible on the basis of extant data.[69] Calculating only *goods* imported and exported, the total turnover may be said to have been at least 312,000 rubles. Customs duties on this, had it been in private trade, would have been 31,000 rubles. Since the valuations of the Chinese goods are available only in Moscow prices, this customs duties "loss" may perhaps be reduced to 25,000 rubles. No expense account has survived for the caravan, but judging from former and subsequent caravans it must have cost at least 60,000 rubles.[70] If gross profits

68. *PSZ*, X, No. 7305, 196-99.

69. Kurts, *Gosudarstvennaia monopoliia*, pp. 62-63.

70. On order from the Siberian Prikaz, Vice-Governor of Irkutsk Zholobov gave over to Lange 28,000 r. in customs house and public house revenues prior to the departure of the caravan. On its return Lange demanded and received another 10,000 r. to transport the caravan from the Manchurian border and 2,000 r. for boats and barges for use on the rivers around Selenginsk, plus

are taken at 114,000 rubles (214,000 rubles worth of Chinese goods minus 100,000 rubles worth of furs), the net profits could have been no more than 29,000-30,000 rubles, i.e., gross profits less expenses and estimated loss of customs revenues. And this does not take into account the merchandise lost in the fire of 1737, a loss Kurts is willing to fix at the hypothetical figure of 15,000 rubles. An accounting profit of 15,000 rubles remains, spread out of course over the eight years from 1731 through 1738. If the entire investment were 200,000 rubles (100,000 rubles in peltry, 60,000 rubles for direct expenses of the caravan, and an additional 40,000 rubles for cost of transportation, etc. within Russia), the investment returned approximately 2,000 rubles per year, a profit of 1 per cent annually.

If the caravan as a whole was a financial failure, as it would appear from these figures and as Vladislavich charged, some people benefited. Early in 1733 several specially marked bales arrived in the Siberian Office with valuable gifts and curiosities sent by Lange and Platkovskii: Vladislavich got a tea service, Ober-secretary of the Holy Synod Mikhail Dudin a bold of *kanfa,* and General Count Iaguzhinskii also received some fineries.[71] Late in the year and early in 1734, ten more chests appeared and were ordered shipped to Count and Ober-Gofmeister S. A. Saltykov in St. Petersburg, presumably for distribution to the worthy.[72]

The reasons for the failure of this caravan to do better than the Tret'iakov-Molokov one are several. Lange still alluded, as we have seen, to what he considered to be decisive restrictions on free trade in Peking. So persistent is this charge we are compelled to lend it some credence, although it is impossible to say how much. Vladislavich, as we have also seen, insisted in his 1734 report to Osterman that hastiness in organization of the caravan, done in only a few months, was the critical factor in the poor showing of the caravan, not private competition.[73] Of course this is the judgment of a man thousands of miles distant from the scene. As so many times earlier, state sworn-appraisers and others of the Siberian Prikaz officialdom exhibited a bureaucratic unawareness

---

3,000 r. for undetermined purposes; in all 43,000 r. for only a part of the journey; *Sbornik RIO,* CXI (1901), 141.

71. *Ibid.,* CVI (1899), 28, 53.

72. *Ibid.,* CVI (1899), 589, 591; CVIII (1900), 19; CXI (1901), 515-16.

73. The 19 July 1734 *Informatsiia;* Bantysh-Kamenskii, *Diplomaticheskoe sobranie,* 375-78.

of the private marketplace in Moscow and its current prices. But the most telling cause—at least the only one the government acted positively to eradicate—was the old bugaboo of private competition. Lange in a report of 1734, submitted no doubt on his arrival in Moscow on 25 June 1734,[74] stressed that Russian merchants who purchase *kamka* and *kitaika* on the frontier caused "not a little disarray in the sale of crown goods," and he proposed that such Chinese goods be forbidden for shipment to Moscow.[75]

The Siberian Prikaz chose to allow carriage of Chinese goods from Kiakhta and Tsurukhaitu to Moscow and to Siberian market fairs, but instructed Lange to investigate and to determine which crown goods sold poorly in Moscow, and in the future to sell them in Siberia or in other European Russian market fairs in the course of the caravan's journey from Kiakhta. As for the other side of the coin, the illicit sale of forbidden peltry, in April of 1735 a special ukaz was sent to Selenginsk elder *(starosta)* Ivan Mostovskii, which ordered him to announce once again to all Russian merchants and their agents that certain valuable furs were prohibited to private trade: sea otter, lynx, Nerchinsk and Iakutsk squirrel, brown, grey, crossed and red fox, and Kamchatka and Iakutsk sable and young Arctic fox.[76]

The Firsov Caravan

Dmitrii Molokov was in the last years of his life and his place as caravan commissar was taken by Erofei Firsov, a long time Siberian merchant. Lange for the final time in his long career of service in the East served as director, but now his services had brought him the rank of chancellery councillor *(Kantseliarskii sovetnik)*.[77] The

74. *Sbornik RIO*, CVI (1899), 553, 555; CVIII (1900), 252.

75. Gosudarstvennyi Arkhiv Irkutskoi Oblasti, *fond* Ilimskoi Voevodskoi Kantseliarii, *delo* 270, *l.* 216, cited in Silin, *Kiakhta*, p. 44.

76. Tsentral'nyi Gosudarstvennyi Arkhiv Drevnikh Aktov (cited hereafter as TsGADA), Selenginskaia gorodovaia ratusha, *fond* 1801, *ed. khr.* 8, *ll.* 229-229a, Ukaz Irkutskoi ratushi Selenginskoi zemskoi izbe o zapreshchenii vyvoza russkikh mekhov v Kitai pomimo kazennykh torgovykh karavanov, 29 April 1735. See also Silin, *Kiakhta*, p. 47.

77. Lange received his orders from the Collegium of Foreign Affairs on his way back to the border (dated 5 May 1735). The caravan took two translators Frolov and Stefan Savinov, who had accompanied Lange earlier, and at least two sworn-appraisers, including a Ponomarev. Lange also took along a young chap, son of a director of the Nerchinsk mines, Stepan Domes (or Damesov), whose task it was to discover what he could about Chinese mineralogy and alchemy, especially how "to separate silver from gold." But Lange reported

grumbling of Vladislavich bore some fruit: on 16 December 1734 the Senate ordered the Siberian Prikaz to prepare another caravan, but a year and a half passed before it crossed into China.[78] Lange's orders cautioned him to maintain friendly relations at all times with the *Li-fan-yuan* and the Court, but to hew strictly to the Treaty of Kiakhta and to insist persistently on unfettered trade.[79] To help him in his duty, he carried over 3,000 rubles worth of fine furs and other goods as gifts to the Emperor.

The new caravan represented about the same capital investment as the last one: Russian goods valued at 100,315 rubles, plus cash including 276 rubles which remained at Strelka from the preceding caravan.[80] Expenses totaled 23,008 rubles for all horses, camels, cattle, carts, and other material, in addition to which the caravan

---

in July, 1738, that the boy was not of the cloth or skill of his father, and he proved to be useless in Peking. The Cabinet ordered him returned to his parent, tutored, and then at Lange's discretion, taken again to Peking with the same mission. Lange did not return empty handed however; he forwarded to the Cabinet a fine map of all of China drawn by the student Rossokhin, for which the latter was honored with the rank of ensign *(praporshchik)* and given 150 r. per year as a special incentive bonus; *Sbornik RIO*, CXIV (1902), 156, CXXIV (1906), 96-97; and *PSZ*, X, No. 7650, 602. See also Fu, *A Documentary Chronicle*, I, 169-70.

78. Actually the caravan was authorized early in 1735 and scheduled to leave in the early summer of that year, but the death of Yung-ch'eng caused it to wait at the border until December, when a courier arrived from the *Li-fan-yuan* with permission for it to proceed. With the winter jouney so difficult, Lange chose to defer departure until spring. TsGADA, Selenginskaia gorodovaia ratusha, *fond* 1801, *ed. khr.* 8, *ll.* 1-1a, Ukaz Selenginskoi voevodskoi kantseliarii o vydache deneg tseloval'niku torgovogo karavana, otpravliaiushchegosia v Kitai, E. Firsovu, 8 January 1735; and Selenginskaia gorodovaia ratusha, *fond* 1801, *ed. khr.* 8, *ll.* 7-7a, Donoshenie Selenginskogo distrikta v Selenginskuiu zemskuiu izbu o vydache deneg E. Firsovu soglasno ukazu Selenginskoi voevodskoi kantseliarii, 7 February 1735. See also Bantysh-Kamenskii, *Diplomaticheskoe sobranie*, p. 222.

79. Bantysh-Kamenskii, *Diplomaticheskoe sobranie*, p. 219.

80. Kurts, *Gosudarstvennaia monopoliia*, pp. 64-65. TsGADA, Selenginskaia gorodovaia ratusha, *fond* 1801, *ed. khr.* 8, *ll.* 210-210a, Ukaz Selenginskoi voevodskoi kantseliarii Selenginskoi ratushe o predostavlenii deneg na zakupku loshadei i verbliudov dlia torgovogo karavana, otpravliaiushchegosia v Kitai, 3 June 1735; *l.* 211, Prigovor Selenginskoi zemskoi izby o predostavlenii deneg v rasporiazhenie Selenginskoi voevodskoi kantseliarii na zakupku loshadei i verbliudov dlia torgovogo karavana, otpravliaiushchegosia v Kitai, 3 June 1735; *ll.* 212-212a, Donoshenie Selenginskoi ratushi v Selenginskuiu voevodskuiu kantseliariiu o predostavlenii deneg na zakupku loshadei i verbliudov dlia torgovogo karavana, otpravliaiushchegosia v Kitai, Prilozhena kopiia kvitantsii o vydache deneg, 9 June 1736; *ll.* 290-end of book, Perepiska mazhdu Selenginskoi voevodskoi kantseliariei i Selenginskoi zemskoi izboi o zakupke loshadei i verbliudov dlia torgovogo karavana, otpravliaiushchegosia v Kitai, 25 July 1735.

took on account another 41,875 rubles for other expenses, such as salaries, which if otherwise unused could be spent for Chinese goods. Thus the total value of the caravan was some 165,198 rubles, not including the 3,582 rubles in fineries for the Emperor.

Peltry was of course the main item carried: 19,571 sables valued at 25,604 rubles, 33,874 red white-necked fox at 38,030 rubles, 116,943 Ob' ermine at 10,442 rubles, 1,006 grey-necked fox at 1,523 rubles, 40,584 squirrel at 854 rubles, and others in smaller amounts. There were other commodities, but none in large quantities: Russian textiles, German and Russian mirrors, etc.

The caravan spent four months on the road track from Irkutsk to Peking via Manchuria, arriving 10 November 1736. This time it experienced an unavoidable delay.[81] The Yung-ch'eng Emperor had died, the new Emperor—whose reign is known as Ch'ien-lung, one of the truly extraordinary Manchu dynasts—and his family and most of the court were absent attending to the cremation. Lange orally and in writing inquired of the *Li-fan-yuan* when he might expect the audience that traditionally preceded the opening of trade, and there began an overly long colloquy between the two on the protocol of the audience. It seemed as though the Peking officialdom took the opportunity of a new and inexperienced monarch to test the limits of its independent authority. When a courier from the Governing Senate arrived in town (18 November 1736), the *Yuan* tried to induce him to hand over the notes he brought before Lange was officially received. Probably aware of their content, Lange objected and on the twenty-third both the courier, a Major Sharygin, and Lange presented the notes to the *Yuan*. But then the *Yuan* brought up the matter of the audience and the presentation of the Russian gifts, insisting that Lange perform a full *k'ou-t'ou*, which he refused to do since it had never before been necessary. Pledging his faith in the honor of both monarchs, he threatened to leave Peking immediately and promised never in the future even to reply to such a demand. The *Yuan* relented and on 6 December 1736 Lange and Sharygin had their audience, both bowing deeply from the waist three times. Lange presented his Tsaritsa's gifts, and he and the Emperor exchanged the usual pleasantries and concern for each other's health. They sat, had tea, and retired to an anteroom with the usual heavy table. On leaving Lange requested of the ministers that merchants be per-

81. Bantysh-Kamenskii, *Diplomaticheskoe sobranie*, pp. 226-28; Dudgeon, *The Chinese Recorder*, IV (August, 1871), 70-71.

mitted to come freely to trade, and probably much to his surprise the very next day news was spread throughout Peking of the opening of trade. Beginning on 11 December, Chinese merchants came in good numbers so that "in a short time" almost 50,000 rubles of the Russian goods were sold.[82]

The honeymoon was brief, and before long the Russians complained of more impediments to trade than had earlier caravans.[83] Lange sharply objected to the practice of issuing "passports" to Chinese merchants coming to trade, which he insisted kept wealthy merchants warily at home. But the only reply he could elicit from the *Yuan* was that Peking was so full of thieves there was no other way to insure that they did not harm the Russians, and as for larger merchants not appearing, the *Yuan* could hardly be expected to compel them by force to trade. A month after this, on 14 February 1737, the *Yuan* did distribute a proclamation inviting Chinese merchants to trade with the Russians, but warned them that they must incur no indebtedness, nor extend loans to the Russians, nor traffic in prohibited items (saltpeter, sulphur, powder, shot). Soon thereafter trade quickened, and Lange determined to sell the remainder of his pelts at any possible price and to prepare to leave. By mid-February all crown sables were sold and by 9 April all of the peltry was gone. Preparations began for departure a month hence.

In the Chinese bureaucracy dissatisfaction with the conduct of Russian trade in Peking mounted, until one of the overseers of the Russian compound, the Censor He-ch'ing, memorialized the Emperor that consideration should be given to limiting Russian trade to the border.[84] Russian purchase of Chinese gold and

82. In the midst of these mundane concerns, the Russians neglected not the higher matters. According to Lange's daily journal, on 12 December 1736, a religious image brought from Siberia was carried in a ceremony to the newly completed Church in the Russian compound, and eight days later the Church was consecrated in a fine celebration attended by all of the Russian people; *Akademicheskiia izvestiia, Soderzhashchiia v sebe istoriiu nauk i noveishiia otkrytiia onykh* . . . (St. Petersburg: Pri S. Peterburgskoi Imp. Akademii Nauk, 1779-81), VIII, 604-31; also *PSZ*, VIII, No. 6057, 816-17; IX, No. 6666, 458-59. Meng Ssu-ming (*Harvard Journal of Asiatic Studies*, XXIII [1961], 28), following Cahen (*Histoire*, p. 262), says, inaccurately, that the consecration took place four years later.

83. Bantysh-Kamenskii, *Diplomaticheskoe sobranie*, pp. 229-35; Kurts, *Gosudarstvennaia monopoliia*, p. 67. Lange referred to it as "captivity in trade," "which formerly has not been"; caravan goods obtained prices "only half of what they might bring."

84. *SFPC*, 37.7b-8a.

silver galled He-ch'ing and doubtless disturbed others, for he proposed that other foreigners trading in Peking should be permitted only to barter goods for goods and that they be prohibited from exchanging gold and silver. As for those ill-disguised commercial spies, the Russian students in Peking, they should not be allowed to travel freely in the hinterlands of China, nor to acquire maps or other prohibited articles. There is no evidence that this memorial was implemented by Ch'ien-lung, although numerous writers erroneously have assumed that Russian trade in Peking ended at this time.[85] Three more caravans came and went before the journeys ceased, and then on the initiative of the Russians, not the Chinese.

Three years later (1740) the Dzhungars received commercial privileges in Peking and were admonished to "follow the Russian example," by which is meant that the arrangements for trade were to be similar to those of the Russians.[86] The Dzhungars might not exceed two hundred men in a suite, nor remain over eighty days. In order to avoid direct competition and possibly collusion with the Russians, they must trade in years other than those in which the Russian caravans were expected: the third, seventh, and eleventh years of the twelve year cycle, since the Russians were expected in the second, sixth, and tenth years. And they must cultivate the virtuous principles of conduct in *li* and must reverence study *(tu)*. This Dzhungar trade may well have done serious damage to the already flagging Russian caravan, for these Mongol people regularly traded with private Russian merchants at the border. They may well have carried Russian goods to Peking.

The Russians left Peking in two echelons on 8 and 10 May 1737; twenty-five men were sent ahead to round up the Russian animals beyond the Wall.[87] Nearly a month before, on 13 April, a final audience with the Emperor was held, during which the usual felicities were exchanged. In spite of differences of opinion between Lange and the Chinese ministers, the Emperor gave over to Lange

85. He Ch'iu-t'ao, chief editor of the *Shuo-fang pei-ch'eng*, appears to have considered this memorial as the end of Russian capital trade; *SFPC*, 37.18a-19a. See also Ch'eng Po-wen, *Chung-O wai-chiao shih* (Shanghai: Commercial Press, 1929–32), p. 18; A. K. Wu, *China and the Soviet Union, A Study of Sino-Soviet Relations* (New York: John Day, 1950), p. 25; Davidson-Houston, *Russia and China*, p. 76; and Ken Shen Weigh, *Russo-Chinese Diplomacy* (Shanghai: Commercial Press, 1928), p. 26.

86. *SFPC*, 37.8a-8b. Also Fu, *A Documentary Chronicle*, I, 171.

87. Bantysh-Kamenskii, *Diplomaticheskoe sobranie*, pp. 232-34.

expensive gifts for his Tsaritsa—110 postavs of silk brocade, *kanfa* and other fabrics.[88] Only one thing was left to do before departure, the securing of permission of the *Li-fan-yuan* to leave the priest Illarion Trusov, who had formerly travelled as priest with the caravan and was then in the Tobol'sk bishopric, in place of the aging Platkovskii (reportedly given to strong drink) and the student Ivan Shikhirev in place of two young Russians—Luka Voeikov and Gerasim Shul'gin—who had died in Peking in early 1734 and early 1735 respectively. The *Yuan* approved these, and the caravan set out across the Gobi and reached Kiakhta on 23 August and Selenginsk on 1 September. Lange remained at Strelka while Firsov accompanied the goods on to Moscow.[89] Because of the 1737 fire in Moscow, Firsov moved his goods on to St. Petersburg, arriving in the spring of 1738, and for the first time an open auction was held for the sale of Chinese goods.[90]

The Chinese goods were disposed of in three ways.[91] The smallest third sold at public auction, arranged by the Commerce Col-

88. When the president of the *Li-fan-yuan* presented Lange with gifts, he—the president—took a valuable cup and handing it to Lange requested that he face the entrance to the emperor's inner chambers and prostrate himself. Lange inquired of the significance of this low bow, but when told it was customary after receiving gifts from the emperor to give one cup in return, Lange declined, arguing that it had not been done when his tsaritsa's presents were given and would not be now. The ministers did not press the point; *ibid.*, p. 232.

89. From Selenginsk Lange forwarded on 21 October 1737 to St. Petersburg three notes from the Chinese (written Ch'ien-lung, 2nd year, 4th month, 21st day), along with his own report. The first of these notes granted permission for the caravan to take the Gobi route, the second accepted the replacement of Platkovskii by Trusov, and the third dealt with the student exchange; *ibid.*, p. 234. Lange sent along also his daily notes of the journey and the stay in Peking; *Akademicheskiia izvestiia*, VIII, 604-31. With regard to the road back to Moscow and St. Petersburg, see *Sbornik RIO*, CXX (1905), 10, 29, 88, 391, 397-98.

90. A list of tea prices in the auction is given in Kurts, *Gosudarstvennaia monopoliia*, p. 71, n., taken from the Petrogradskii Arkhiv Departamenta Tamozhennykh Sborov, *Sv.* 2, *d. no.* 23. Although half of the tea went unsold, the profits on that turned over was from 100 to 200 per cent, depending on whether contrasted with Siberian or St. Petersburg prices. The remaining stores went to the Court Office.

91. Except for silver, all of which was turned over to the Money Chancellery for conversion into coin; *Sbornik RIO*, CXX (1905), 504-5; Kurts, *Gosudarstvennaia monopoliia*, pp. 70-72. Eventually some 46 *pud* 10 *funt* 36 *zolotnik* in Chinese silver was sent to the Chancellery and coined into Russian money, which amounted to—after deduction of the expense of conversion—35,063 r. 14½k. It was split between the Bodyguards of the Izmailovskii Regiment and the Horse Guards, both Anna's favorites; *Sbornik RIO*, CXXIV (1906), 108.

legium in the "Italian House" on the Fontanka.[92] Sales began, on order of the Tsaritsa, on 8 September and continued on Mondays, Wednesdays, and Fridays until all the goods were gone. Newspapers carried announcements in both Russian and German. Generally the poorest and least expensive goods were offered for auction to avoid their being left over. In all some 38,386 rubles worth (at assessed valuation with expenses included) sold for 53,319 rubles, a profit of 14,933 rubles.

The second third was given over to the Tsaritsa's court, specifically to the Court Paymaster's Office *(Kamer-tsal'meisterskaia kontora)* and the Court Office *(Pridvornaia kontora)*.[93] Since the former office, established sometime in the 1730's, had the task, among other things, of paying court servitors, it is likely many of these goods were used for that purpose. The latter office had general charge of the budgeting of the Imperial court. Some 69,931 rubles worth was given over by the Commerce Collegium to these court offices, for which the caravan account received 86,721 rubles, or a paper profit of 16,760 rubles.

The goods which remained after auction and selection by the court (some 52,078 rubles in value) were transferred to the Commerce Collegium. Presumably the Collegium attempted to sell these goods within Russia or abroad, but their disposition is not clear. In total then the caravan disposed of 160,988 rubles worth of goods, for a profit of at least 32,137 rubles.[94] From this profit, Lange, Firsov, the sworn-appraisers, and other serving men of the caravan received salaries *(zhalovaniia)* of 2,667 rubles, leaving a net profit of 29,470 rubles.

Although substantially complete, these figures were not the last accounting for the caravan. In 1757 on order of the Governing Senate, then considering the dissolution of the crown caravan, there was compiled an account *(Vedomost')* for this and other caravans beginning with that of Molokov, the purpose of which

92. In addition to the auctioned goods, small amounts were sold on the way across Siberia (as Lange had been ordered earlier to try to do): 604 r. 17 k. worth was sold for 1,048 r. 8 k. Silks worth 30,000 r. sold at auction, plus silver ware, precious stones, copper and other utensils, and tea. Some 2,672 r. 40 k. worth of tea sold (mostly *Dzhulan*), although less than half of that offered—146 *pud* of a total of 272 *pud*.

93. Those goods that went to Her Majesty or to the Paymaster's Office were counted in the accounts of the caravan; *Sbornik RIO*, CXXIV (1906), 110.

94. Kurts notes that one *vedomost'* in the archives give the alternate total figure of 200,816 r. 16 k., the value of the goods at St. Petersburg and Moscow prices (*Gosudarstvennaia monopoliia*, p. 72).

was to reveal the profits, if any, of the caravans.[95] This tabulation differs somewhat from others. The total value of the caravan as it proceeded to Peking was listed as 159,719 rubles, of which 100,000 rubles was in furs and 59,719 rubles represented the expenses of salaries, supplies, animals, materials, etc. Of the Chinese goods brought back, silks and similar goods constituted only 59,190 rubles (given at St. Petersburg prices) of the total, an unusually small figure for these caravans. Precious stones, gold, silver, diamonds, and other especially valuable curiosities amounted to 105,441 rubles, or total imports of 164,631 rubles (compared with 160,998 rubles worth of Chinese goods disposed of in one way or another in St. Petersburg). These imported wares realized, when sold, 200,816 rubles according to this account. Therefore, profit of 41,096 rubles was realized, when the total sale value is compared with the value of goods exported to Peking, or 36,184 rubles when compared with the book value of goods (again at St. Petersburg prices) imported.

Since customs duties of 10 per cent would normally be extracted from the silks and other goods (not from bullion, precious stones, etc.), a figure of 5,919 rubles must be deducted from the profits to represent the state's "loss." This leaves a clear (net) profit of 35,177 rubles, when compared with exports and 30,265 rubles when compared with value of imports. Considering that the caravan account stretched over seven years (1734-41) and taking the basic investment to be 160,000 rubles in round figures, we have an annual profit of a little over 3 per cent at best; Kurts prefers 2 to 2.5 per cent.[96] Like the Molokov caravan, the Firsov one was in the black, but not by a wide margin.

Lange's Company

The first three state caravans in the dozen years after the signing of the Treaty of Kiakhta proved to be no great successes. The first was probably a financial failure, the other two turned modest

95. Petrogradskii Arkhiv Departamenta Tamozhennykh Sborov, *Katalog* 1884 g., *Dela Kommerts-Kollegii, No.* 476, *Sv.* 9, *d.* 224, cited in *ibid.*, p. 73. Cabinet member A. P. Volynskii ordered on 26 June 1738 that all Chinese goods be reassessed by two appraisers *(tsenovniki)* and lists *(tsenovye rospisi)* be kept recording Siberian value, Moscow and St. Petersburg values of each item; *Sbornik RIO*, CXX (1905), 504-5; CXXIV (1906), 173.

96. Kurts, *Gosudarstvennaia monopoliia*, p. 74.

profits, but the time was propitious for another of what had become periodic reappraisals of the monopoly. This time it came from the man most knowledgeable of and skilled in this trade over its long history—the State Councillor and new Irkutsk Vice-Governor Lorents Lange.

Lange resurrected the idea of the creation of a private company to assume the state monopoly in capital trade in China. He submitted a long project dated 13 September 1739, the most thorough such proposal to reach the higher levels of Russian administration.[97] The first step was to create a bank with an initial capital of two million rubles, negotiable shares in which would be sold at three hundred rubles each to any and all interested purchasers whether men of substance or base born, Russian or foreign. Careful account books were to be kept, and payments for the shares made quickly so that the bank might begin operations as quickly as possible. Subscription books should be distributed throughout the realm, to each *guberniia* and *provintsiia* and to each town hall *(ratusha)*. Since apprehension lest the state sequester such exposed funds in the face of military or other state "necessity" had always been one of the greatest deterrents in Russia to the formation of private companies or banks, Lange took special efforts to assure investors that capital would be safe. He recommended that Her Imperial Majesty purchase shares in the bank and announce widely that the state's loss, were the venture to fail, would far exceed that of any single investor, since it would lose not only its investment but also the great customs duties it stood to gain from taxation of the trade. The crown should guarantee that the investments would not be confiscated, even if the investor committed a crime "or a major sin" which subjected the remainder of his property to seizure by the state. The company, not the state, should inherit all shares of investors who died without heirs and intestate, and a stockholder without close kin should be allowed to designate business associates to inherit his stock. If an initial stockholder wished to divest himself of his stock, he should be able to do so, but only two years after the company was actually established, so

97. Chulkov, *Istoricheskoe opisanie,* III, bk. 2, 242-50. There is a report that two Englishmen appeared in Russia in 1735 with a proposal for expansion of Russia's East India and China trade, but they do not seem to have inspired Lange's proposal; N. N. Bantysh-Kamenskii, *Obzor vneshnikh snoshenii Rossii (po 1800 god)* pt. 1, 141.

as not to jeopardize its resources. These same guarantees should extend to foreign investors as well.

Once the bank was viable, a company was to be formed, with all those who owned ten or more shares to act temporarily as directors, for the purposes of fixing the organization and bylaws, electing a director-general *(General-direktor),* and establishing a company office. Those large investors geographically distant from St. Petersburg should appoint agents *(korrespondenty)* with full powers of surrogate. These directors must have full and sole control of the company; no government office or official should be permitted to meddle under any pretext. The officers of the company who actually took part in trade and served in the company office were to enjoy immunity from arrest, except in the most aggravated cases, when the arrest had to be ordered by a *gubernator* or other official of similar authority.

Lange highly recommended that the crown endow the company with complete monopoly of all trade to Peking and with all nations and peoples bordering Siberia, in return for which the company would be obligated to purchase—at a "deserving price" —all Siberian peltry! All goods carried into China and all Chinese merchandise brought back would be taxed at a rate of twenty rubles per one hundred rubles ad valorem, excluding only those goods stipulated by the state to be free of duty. Goods of the company not exported abroad or shipped to non-Chinese lands should pay only the usual customs duties, internal and external. The company, Lange insisted, should be permitted to import from China and elsewhere goods that had no market within Russia, but were useful for transshipment abroad. In such case these goods should not be charged customs duties twice, unless they were a second time carried from abroad and then should pay a second duty of 10 per cent ad valorem.

The director-general and the people employed in the company offices should be designated only after the share money was paid and the bank functioning. The permanent directors should be selected only from among those with commercial knowledge and of good station *(dobroe sostoianie)* and who owned not less than eight shares; the director-general should have at least twelve shares. Company offices should be set up in St. Petersburg, Moscow, Tobol'sk, and Irkutsk, each headed by a director. The director-general, the individual directors, and all the company employees were to take oaths of fidelity to the company and the crown. Complete account books were to be kept of all company transactions, available at any time to public scrutiny. And to expose "rascals" in company ranks the director-general should employ a number of "deputies" *(deputaty)* to inspect the books of all offices and factories. Any miscreant found should be divested of his rank and his offense publicized, that he remain a pariah and no other contemplate such deceit.

To facilitate the activities of the company throughout Siberia, Lange asked that the state establish "a regular post" to all corners of the empire. Beyond that he expected the state simply to keep hands off and positively to give the throne's assurance to protect the company against any disturbance or danger within or without the country.

Profits of the company should be distributed annually among all of the shareholders, either paying them personally or providing their agents with promissory notes *(veksely)*.

Such was the original proposal, but as soon as the Governing Senate raised some questions, Lange responded with further arguments dated 21 September 1739. He insisted that the Imperial Treasury stood to gain greatly from turning over to the company the exclusive right to purchase from the state all *iasak* peltry, for no longer would it suffer the losses from furs lying around for long periods of time and possibly deteriorating. Further, customs revenues, he predicted, would far exceed those collected previously, simply because it would be in the interest of the company to secure the greatest expansion of trade, and to aid in suppressing all illicit trade across the border on which losses in customs revenues were notoriously great. Her Imperial Majesty might purchase as many shares as she liked, even to the extent of that normally invested in a crown caravan, and from these shares she would enjoy an annual profit, not just an unsure return every third or fourth year (or more) as with the caravans. Lange predicted that the company could sell at least two hundred thousand rubles worth of Siberian peltry annually to the Chinese at the border, and the periodic Peking caravans would carry more than they had in the past. Since the company would purchase all Siberian peltry, the state would know at all times precisely how much was exported from Russia. If any private merchant wished to trade peltry at locations where the company did not choose to operate, he would have to purchase his furs from the company, hence the deception of the customs offices would be minimized. Such peltry as the company did not export would be put up for auction every year at a convenient location, for example Tobol'sk in February. Finally, if the level of capital investment Lange recommended for the bank (two million rubles) seemed unrealistic, he commented that the Senate might wish to investigate the annual intake of *iasak* furs and to fund the bank at that level. The advantage would be that the initial bank resources would match the loss to the state of *iasak* pelts, which now of course would by collected by the company. The Treasury could still purchase annually and freely all of the non-*iasak* pelts it needed for its own purposes.

Lange completely convinced the Senate and the Tsaritsa, even though they would be creating an unprecedented private business operation in the Russian Empire, were the full project of Lange realized. It would be the first "chartered" company of any consequence with shares issued from a bank "guaranteed" and protected by the state. To it would be given one of the most lucrative sources of state income for several centuries past, Siberia's furs, not to speak of the Peking caravan itself. There would be created the largest and probably the most powerful quasi-governmental economic enterprise Russia would have seen until at least the mid-nineteenth century. But in spite of all this, an imperial order was issued on 21 September 1739 authorizing the dispatch to Peking of the caravan in preparation, after which the Commerce Collegium would encourage all "substantial merchants and other persons who wish to invest capital in this Chinese company" to write to the Collegium.[98]

About this time Lange forwarded two other suggestions to the Cabinet, which if accepted would have extended and tightened the monopoly of his proposed company, although neither was directly connected with it.[99] He hoped that the Siberian Prikaz would strictly forbid both Siberian and Russian merchants from purchasing peltry directly from Tatars and other Siberian natives in the villages and tribal settlements; only the Treasury should ob-

98. *PSZ*, X, No. 7906, 908. On 17 October the Senate ordered the Commerce Collegium and the Siberian Prikaz to investigate thoroughly the entire proposal and to report back their findings. Chulkov gave the date of the Imperial ukaz authorizing the company as 11 September, rather than the twenty-first as in *PSZ; Istoricheskoe opisanie*, III, bk. 2, 251-52.

99. *PSZ*, XI, No. 8017, 20-31, dated 1 February 1740.

tain peltry, as *iasak,* at the local level. Merchants should acquire peltry in the towns (where of course closer surveillance was possible), upon which sales customs duties of 5 per cent should be levied, and the merchants in addition should pay 10 per cent of fur purchases in cash or in kind when it was more advantageous for the Treasury to acquire the best pelts of the merchants. The Senate pointed out that under Siberian Prikaz regulations of 1721 and 1727, the 10 per cent tax on merchant-purchased furs was extracted in kind, excepting only incomplete tenths which were taxed by value in money. Also the order of 1727 taxed Russian goods arriving in Siberia at 5 per cent in the Tobol'sk merchants' court through which they had to pass, and no goods were to be traded to Siberians for peltry until the state *iasak* was collected. In the light of these practices, the Senate rejected Lange's proposal to take 5 per cent customs duties *after* the collection of *iasak.* As for taxation of purchased furs in money rather than in kind, this was no improvement.

Lange also proposed that correspondence with the Chinese be directed in the future from Irkutsk rather than Tobol'sk, simply because Irkutsk was closer to the scene and privy to better intelligence. For this purpose the state seal recognized by the Chinese should be transferred to Irkutsk. Not only the Peking caravan, but growing Chinese interest in undelimited portions of the Siberian-Monolian border, concerned Lange. Nonetheless the Senate disagreed, pointing to the Treaty of Kiakhta, which specifically identified the governor in Tobol'sk as the proper initiator of correspondence. Although the Senate was properly circumspect in view of the abrasiveness of the issue, Lange's suggestion was promising; the pressure of disputes at the border tended to mount while authorities on both sides waited long weeks for judgments from Tobol'sk or St. Petersburg, Urga or Peking. The Senate did accede to Lange's request that the results of the surveying and mapping done by the great expedition under Professor G. F. Müller in the watersheds of the Amur and Uda Rivers (the demarcation line of the Treaty of Nerchinsk) be forwarded to him. Although the Chinese-occupied territory north of the Amur was not to be seriously contested for some time to come, Lange was well advised to keep informed, as shall be seen below.

Soon after the decision was reached to form a Russian company of merchant adventurers to the east, notices were widely circulated requesting all those interested to make themselves known.[100] There was *no* response to this first announcement, and in September 1740 the Senate instructed that a second be made and published widely.[101] Another year went by with no merchants or other investors coming forth. On 31 August 1741 the Senate took cognizance of the fact that "still no one interested in a China company has appeared" and commanded republication of the ukaz of two years earlier.[102] Finally in March of 1742 the Senate requested of the Commerce Collegium that it send "by the next post" the bylaws *(ustav)* of this company to be established "on the example of the Dutch East India Company," but the effort was in vain.[103] As far as may be ascertained, neither Russia's merchants nor foreigners found enticing the prospect of investing in such a company. Until Tsar Paul chartered the Russian-American Company in the last year of the century, there was to be no other serious effort to turn over the state's monopoly to private hands. The Russian business and mercantile community had no experience with joint-stock operations; it is not surprising that the first such in Russian history was created by imperial decree.

The Last Three

There was no choice now but to persevere with the state caravan system. So long as it turned even a modest profit and did not enmesh Russia in dangerous commitments far from Russian military and strategic strength, it served useful purposes. Besides, delicate Chinese furnishings were fine conversation pieces in St. Petersburg's best houses.

Actual organization of the next caravan began shortly after its

100. Silin unearthed an ukaz in the State Archives of Irkutsk Oblast' dated 7 August 1740 and sent from the Irkutsk *ratusha* to the Selenginsk *zemskaia izba* which ordered the chief *(starosta)* there to gather all the merchant people in the town offices to announce the formation of a China company, and, for those interested, to inquire how much they wished to invest. The news *did* reach the hinterlands; Silin, *Kiakhta*, p. 48. TsGADA, Selenginskaia gorodovaia ratusha, *fond* 1801, *ed. khr.* 8, *ll.* 229-300a, 318-318a, Ukazy Irkutskoi ratushi i Selenginskoi voevodskoi kantseliarii ob organizatsii kompanii russkikh kuptsov dlia torgovli s Kitaem, 9 August 1740.

101. *PSZ*, XI, No. 8234, 247; XI, No. 8237, 256; Chulkov, *Istoricheskoe opisanie*, III, bk. 2, 254-55.

102. *PSZ*, XI, No. 8436, 480, dated 21 August 1741; Chulkov, *Istoricheskoe opsanie*, III, bk. 2, 255; *Senatskii arkhiv*, IV, 364, an item of 4 September 1741.

103. Chulkov, *Istoricheskoe opisanie*, III, bk. 2, 256.

authorization in September 1739. A Senate ukaz of 26 February 1740 once again prohibited "secretly or openly" the carriage of peltry by private persons into Chinese dominions,[104] although by September the deleterious effect of such blanket proscriptions on private trade at the border was recognized. The Senate then, on the advice of Lange in consultation with the dzarguchei in Mai-mai-ch'eng, gave to the Irkutsk Vice-Governor almost complete discretionary powers as to what items be permitted to free trade and when, since he "knows more than others" from his long association with the caravans and St. Petersburg was too distant from the border for accurate information.[105]

The history of this fourth caravan after the Treaty of Kiakhta began innocuously enough. Erofei Firsov received his patent as caravan director and his passports at the end of October 1739, and a little over a week later learned of his promotion to the distinguished rank of Collegiate Assessor *(Kollezhskii asessor,* eighth rank in the civil list).[106] A courier of the Cabinet, Major Mikhail L'vovich Shokurov, left St. Petersburg for Peking on 25 January 1740 to announce the caravan, to request passage for it, and to secure permission for two long-time Russian students in Peking Illarion Rossokhin and Mikhail Ponomarev, to return with the caravan. Only the news that Ponomarev had unfortunately died in the meantime may have been taken as something of a harbinger of the difficult times ahead for the caravan.[107]

An old and sensitive issue in relations between Russians and Chinese reappeared at this time and brought considerable grief to the caravan. Seven years earlier in 1733 the Kalmyks of the Volga sent a small embassy to pay homage to the Dalai Lama, but since then it had sat waiting in Peking for permission to return. Now the Kalmyk Khan Donduk-Ombo petitioned the Tsaritsa to permit another envoy and some seventy-three companions to make the journey to the Lama. She not only gave her leave for them to travel across Siberia, but sent along the interpreter Ivan Savinov with several serving men to accompany them and a note from the Senate (of 29 May 1740) which asked the *Li-fan-yuan* to provide safe passage for the Kalmyks to Tibet and return. Savinov left

104. *Ibid.*, III, bk. 2, 252.

105. *Ibid.*, III, bk. 2, 253-54; *PSZ*, XI, No. 8234, 247, dated 9 September 1740.

106. Bantysh-Kamenskii, *Diplomaticheskoe sobranie*, p. 238.

107. Shokhurov arrived in Peking on 16 April 1740, received the Chinese reply on 6 July, left the following day, and reached Kiakhta on 6 August, and St. Petersburg on 2 January 1741.

the border on 16 November on his fruitless mission. With unassailable logic Emperor Ch'ien-lung refused to allow the Kalmyks to proceed: since the second Chinese embassy nearly a decade earlier had been refused the right to visit the Kalmyks on the grounds that these Volga natives were Russian subjects, they could hardly be permitted passage of Chinese territories, since the Treaty of Kiakhta made no provision for Russian citizens except those properly certified as members of the tribute-bearing caravans.[108] Savinov reached the border 6 March 1741 and reported to his superiors in the Collegium of Foreign Affairs that the Emperor seemed favorable toward the Kalmyk pilgrimage, but his ministers were not and they carried the day.

Another of those trivial, but often annoying, and at times crucial circumstances disturbed the Chinese: the conduct or unseemly misconduct of some of the ecclesiastics in Peking. In January 1741 Rossokhin brought back a report from his student colleague, Aleksei Vladykin, detailing extravagances of Archimandrite Illarion Trusov. He exercised no solicitude for the students there, succumbed to drunkenness and sacrilege, and diverted himself by donning Chinese women's dress which he even wore in church. Mercifully for this religious endeavour, Illarion died in April, but the Chinese again were given cause to compare the Russians with the astute and disciplined Jesuits who had served so long and so well in Peking.[109]

All these aggravations contributed to the delay of the *Li-fan-yuan* in authorizing the entry of the caravan; it waited over a year in Irkutsk, and not until 9 June 1741 crossed the border and arrived in Peking 24 September. A month later the *Yuan* allowed trading to begin but it went slowly, and the caravan remained over the whole winter before Firsov concluded that all had been done that could be done, and the caravan left on 20 April 1742. On his return to Moscow in February of the next year, Firsov lamented that he and his men received the same unfavorable treatment accorded to Lange earlier, and both in Peking and on the road the

108. Bantysh-Kamenskii, *Diplomaticheskoe sobranie*, pp. 241-42.

109. *Ibid.*, pp. 242-43. The Holy Synod gave the Collegium of Foreign Affairs authority to permit the priest Lavrentii Uvarov, already in Peking, to serve temporarily as head of the mission. Trusov was replaced by Gervasii Lintsevskii of the Kievo-Mikhailovskii monastery and with the latter were to travel two other priests, both of the Kievo-Sofiiskii monastery—Ioil Rublevskii and Feodosii Smorzhevskii. These replacements tried at first to travel alone, but were refused by the Chinese and awaited the next caravan; *ibid.*, pp. 248-49.

Chinese gave him far less in maintenance money and gifts. He confirmed that a "majority" of the mission in Peking had grown to enjoy Chinese wines too well and were often raucous and belligerent.

As for the business history of the caravan, little can be said from available sources. Apparently the caravan carried furs and goods worth about one hundred thousand rubles, perhaps somewhat less than earlier caravans.[110] Exchanged for the Russian goods were all of the typical Chinese fabrics, teas, furniture, lacquerware, porcelains, copper work, and a wide variety of bric-a-brac and objets d'art. Sale of them began at auction on 1 June 1743 in the house of Lieutenant-General and Acting Chamberlain Balkpolev on Great Nemetskaia Street of Admiralty Island. The goods were open for inspection and bid every Monday, Wednesday, and Friday both in the forenoon and after.[111]

Of curiosity value is one sworn-appraiser of this caravan, the Siberian merchant and silversmith Osip Semenov Miasnikov. Earlier (in 1736-37) he had served as part of Lange's suite in Peking, charged with investigating the wonders of Chinese porcelain artisanry.[112] Because of his complaint that he had been paid only four rubles per month subsistence and 150 rubles per year remuneration, he came to the attention of the Senate and the Cabinet, which decided to return him to Peking to do a thorough job of discovering all of the Chinese tricks and habits of skilled craftsmanship. He was to learn how they gave red copper its hardness and the appearance of gold, how lanterns were made from ram's horns, how jade was fashioned into such magnificent figurines and dishes, whence came white copper, etc., in return for which the caravan treasury would grant him a gratuity of three hundred rubles and a salary of the same amount per year. The caravan director was instructed not to burden him with gross business duties that his research be unimpeded and to give over to him any caravan goods he might need to barter for Chinese curios. While the caravan readied he could scour the frontier about Kiakhta for information (his wife and children were even moved from Tobol'sk to Strelka to encourage him) and to select three

110. Semenov, *Izuchenie* III, 199.

111. Chulkov, *Istoricheskoe opisanie,* III, bk. 2, 256. Lieut.-Gen. Pavel F. Balk-Polev.

112. *PSZ,* X, No. 7898, 897-98, dated 27 September 1739; Upravlenie Imperatorskimi Zavodami, *Imperatorskii farforovyi zavod, 1744-1904* (St. Petersburg: Izdanie Upravleniia Imperatorskimi Zavodami, ca. 1906), p. 4.

apprentices in Tobol'sk, Irkutsk, and Selenginsk to take to China at one hundred rubles per year to learn his secrets.

On his return in 1743 Miasnikov reported to the Cabinet that all had not gone well, that he had learned little of the techniques he was to investigate. The malevolence of Firsov, he charged, provoked him to refuse to hand over sufficient money to line the pockets of Chinese who had promised to provide him with porcelain secrets. Russian appetites for fine porcelains had long been whetted, and the Empress Elizabeth the very next year approved the establishment of the Imperial Porcelain Works in St. Petersburg. The next caravan under Lebratovskii also indulged in this industrial espionage, apparently with little more success.

The coolness increased between Russian and Chinese in the years after the Firsov caravan. Major Shokurov returned to Peking in November 1742 with the primary task of announcing the accession to the throne of the daughter of Peter the Great, Elizabeth.[113] He took with him three students of the Moscow Ecclesiastical Academy to replace those in Peking, one more of whom had died, Ivan Shikharev, there only since 1741.[114] He met resistance long before he reached Peking; in Urga the Tushetu Khan recalled that the Treaty said nothing of students travelling with a courier, rather they were expected to go with a caravan, and he refused them entry. Shokurov left them in Urga and went on alone to Peking, which he reached on 12 May 1743. In three days he had an audience, and the Emperor did permit the students to come on, although they did not reach Peking until 16 October.

No sooner had this small matter been disposed of than another equally minor arose: the Emperor chose to send gifts to the new Tsaritsa. Shokurov uncharitably refused to accept them after he was advised by the Russian clerics that they were sent "not in honor, but in disdain." Why they told the courier this is a mystery. Ch'ien-lung then determined to send an embassy to felicitate Elizabeth, but Shokurov learned later from a local official

113. Bantysh-Kamenskii, *Diplomaticheskoe sobranie*, pp. 245-47; Andrievich, *Kratkii ocherk*, pp. 180-81. He left Moscow on 29 December 1742, arrived at Irkutsk on 19 March 1743, left Kiakhta on 10 April 1743, arriving in Urga a week later.

114. Aleksei Leont'ev, Andrei Kanaev, and Nikita Chepanov (or Chekanov). Only two students were still in Peking—Aleksei Vladykin and Ivan Bykov. The Senate ordered the Irkutsk treasury to provide them with 200 r. per year maintenance and fifty rubles in pay. These new students were instructed to learn Japanese, as well as Chinese and Manchu, but as it turned out Japanese teachers were in short supply in Peking.

that the Emperor's advisers opposed it and prevailed. They apprised the Emperor that Peking had sent two embassies to Moscow to greet new arrivals to the Russian throne, but save for Izmailov many years before, none had come from Moscow to Peking. Shokurov reported that he tried to mollify the ministers by pointing out that Russia had not known of the death of Yung-ch'eng because the Chinese court had not seen fit to send the news. Nonetheless the damage was done. When he reached Moscow again in early January 1744, he passed on two notes from the *Li-fan-yuan.* The first greeted Elizabeth in proper fashion but stressed the refusal of the courier to carry the gifts of *kamka* and porcelains, and the second insisted that students in the future must travel with caravans. Furthermore the young Russians would no longer be given monetary support by the Chinese. Only the infinite grace of His Majesty permitted these three to enter with such impropriety.[115]

Despite all of this, the Senate voted to mount another caravan, and in fact took several new measures to strengthen its prospects. The Commerce Collegium informed the Senate in 1743 that foreign merchants in St. Petersburg regularly imported from abroad, by sea and by land, large amounts of Chinese (and Indian) silks, rhubarb, anise, copperware, sealing wax, porcelain, and others, which cause "great damage" to the caravan trade.[116] The Collegium requested a Senate ukaz prohibiting all such trade on pain of confiscation. The Senate was at first more temperate; on 23 September 1743 it ordered that all Chinese damasks and *svistun* (a silk fabric also) already imported be taxed in the usual manner in the Collegium and carried to the Court, after which no more of these fabrics were to be permitted in any Russian ports. A month and a half later the Senate added all processed Chinese silk, twisted and nontwisted, to the proscribed list, along with lacquerware. These orders were published and distributed in French and German, as well as Russian. On 5 December came the last and most inclusive edict.[117] All Chinese silks stuffs, many listed by name

115. Shokhurov was quite shocked by the demeanor of the Chinese ministers when he arrived at court. He reported it was the hottest July Peking had experienced for 900 years (!), and in the *Yuan* during his visit the ministers sat "stark naked."

116. Chulkov, *Istoricheskoe opisanie,* III, bk. 2, 257-59.

117. *PSZ,* XI, No. 8828, 955; Chulkov, *Istoricheskoe opisanie,* III, bk. 2, 259-60.

and others included generically, and all those items listed in September, were prohibited. Any imported would be confiscated, and offenders would be fined "without receiving any mercy." Customs officials of the frontier regions (Ukraine, Lifland, Estland, and Finland) were particularly admonished to be alert for these items.

In the East renewed steps were undertaken to seal off the Mongolian border. On 11 January 1744 at the insistence of the Siberian Prikaz and the Collegium of Foreign Affairs, the Senate provided for the building of breastworks and trenches, and in the forests, abatis and palisades, between the Chikoi and Selenga Rivers, the only legal route from the border.[118] Although the immediate provocation of this measure was illegal trade in rhubarb (the merchant Svin'in, recently granted a monopoly of rhubarb trade, made the initial request), the effect was to inhibit the passage of any contraband from China or Mongolia.

In August of the same year, the Senate authorized new stamps to be used, not on paper but sealing wax, to mark all goods coming and going through Siberia in the customs offices of Kiakhta, Verkhotur'e, Nerchinsk, and Iamyshev.[119]

Against the background of deteriorating relations with the Chinese and strong evidence of both legal and illegal competition for the goods caravans brought to St. Petersburg, the Assessor Gerasim Kirillovich Lebratovskii was selected in March 1744 to take charge of the caravan. Nearly a year later he informed border officials of the readiness of his train to cross the border, but correspondence was slow and not until 25 August 1745 did he quit Kiakhta.[120] While he waited, the *Li-fan-yuan* reproved Russian authorities for failure to punish two Russians who had, two years before, killed two Chinese in a drunken fray, couching the notes in language that suggested border trade might be suspended unless Chinese merchants were assured that their lives were not in danger in mingling with Russians.[121] Actually the Military Collegium *(Voennaia kollegiia)* arranged for the culprits to be taken secretly some distance from the border and from any public thoroughfare, lashed, and then let go. The Border Commandant at that time, Iakobi, afterward informed his counterpart across the frontier that the mur-

118. PSZ, XII, No. 8852, 3.
119. *Senatskii arkhiv*, VII, 34.
120. Bantysh-Kamenskii, *Diplomaticheskoe sobranie*, pp. 249-50.
121. The Senate received two notes on this on 14 July 1744.

derers had escaped from detention and were still at large.[122] At least for the moment the Chinese seemed content with the explanation.

Lebratovskii reached Peking by early December and with his entire suite was summoned to the *Li-fan-yuan* on the fifteenth. Trade began shortly, but as the director detailed in his report the hindrances to barter were if anything greater than ever. The Russian House was held "under scrutiny as if for security" by four men who sat at the gates and observed all who entered, what they bought and at what price—"small as it was already."[123] One thousand soldiers, changed every morning, surrounded the Russian House and accompanied every Russian who left and all Chinese who came. These were old tales, but Lebratovskii's description of the "company" organization of the Chinese merchants was quite new and probably not by accident dovetailed with what is known of Chinese monopolistic practices after the 1720's in Canton.[124] Some fifteen to twenty Chinese merchants were allowed to take part in the "company" trading with the Russians, were not allowed to trade independently on their own nor to form other companies. Other merchants had to attach themselves to this select inner circle to participate in the trade. Naturally the favored merchants exercised considerable discipline themselves to insure that only those they approved reached the Russian compound. The caravan chief reported that this device led to Russian goods going cheaply and Chinese goods, many unfit and inferior, coming dear. He was not merely rhetorical when he asked "What can be expected of caravans in view of this?" Many Russian goods had to be sold "for

122. The sources reveal that justice did triumph. One culprit, the soldier Selivan Ufimtsev, drowned in 1750 while fishing in the Barguzinsk region, and the other, the *d'iachok* Sazhin, was lost at sea four years later; Bantysh-Kamenskii, *Diplomaticheskoe sobranie*, p. 250, n. 1.

123. *Ibid.*, pp. 251-52; see also *Senatskii arkhiv*, VII, 86.

124. The "Co-hong" *(kung-hang)* merchant guild first appeared in Canton in 1720, although it did not acquire a fully monopolistic position until the 1760's. It originally consisted of sixteen prominent *hang* merchants, i.e. traders of "Substance or Credit" who, upon presenting proper security, were granted the privilege of opening a hang or "company"; Earl H. Pritchard, *Anglo-Chinese Relations during the Seventeenth and Eighteenth Centuries* ("University of Illinois Studies in the Social Sciences," XVII, nos. 1-2 [Urbana: University of Illinois Press, 1929]), p. 109, and Sybille Van der Sprenkel, *Legal Institutions in Manchu China, A Sociological Analysis* ("London School of Economics, Monographs on Social Anthropology," 24 [London: University of London, the Athlone Press, 1962]), pp. 89-96.

half the usual price." Repeated complaints to the *Li-fan-yuan* went unheeded.[125]

If one may believe the allegations of Archimandrite Gervasii, Lebratovskii suffered from another disability—his own taste for the good life.[126] The cleric charged that the director occupied himself "for the most part" "with various kinds of diversions, music, drink and various banquets" all charged to the expense account of the caravan, and distracted the sworn-appraisers from their appointed tasks and the Russian students in Peking from obedience to the archimandrite.

His caravan apparently a business failure, Lebratovskii requested permission to leave on 6 June 1746. He took with him the two students who had survived a long novitiate in Peking since 1731—Aleksei Vladykin and Ivan Bykov—leaving in their places only one, Efim Sakhnovskii. Both of these returned students proved useful; Vladykin became the next and last caravan director, and Bykov was posted to the Academy of Sciences as a translator.

At Irkutsk the caravan was divided into two sections, one under the director which reached St. Petersburg in March of 1747, and the other under Grigorii Kartashev which did not arrive until August. Precisely how much merchandise was taken to China, how much returned, how it was sold or given away, and how much profit if any this caravan made—none of these questions can be answered.

Some small gain, at least, came from the caravan; Lebratovskii took up the investigation of Chinese handicraft secrets, especially of porcelains. Although he had no special instructions in this regard, he took it upon himself to spend some 3,286 rubles of the caravan's funds to secure from the Chinese knowledge of their skills in porcelain casting and firing.[127] Although Miasnikov still served as sworn-appraiser on this caravan, the director hired the services of another silversmith, the Kiakhta resident and native of the town of Iaransk, Andrei Kursin, who had for some years experimented with porcelains with some success. With the aid of

125. Lebratovskii got along no better with the often useful Jesuits. He reported he gave one, a Bishop Polikarp, 1400 r. which the latter obviously took as a contribution to the spiritual endeavour, for he did not return it, much to Lebratovskii's chagrin. The Bishop later wrote a colleague passing through Russia that in the future such an "ungrateful man" must not be recommended to him; Bantysh-Kamenskii, *Diplomaticheskoe sobranie*, p. 253.

126. *Ibid.*, p. 254.

127. *Imperatorskii farforovyi zavod*, pp. 5-6.

the students Vladykin and Bykov, Kursin successfully bribed a Chinese porcelain master, with one thousand *liang* of silver, to show him the process of casting hollow porcelain idols in a workshop some twenty miles from Peking. Even more fortunate, Kursin received various recipes, a plan of the workshop, and forms necessary to the art. Wary lest he waste the money, Lebratovskii had Kursin sign a written deposition to the effect that the raw materials required for porcelains were actually available in Russia; Kursin assured him that near Kiakhta and Irkutsk were all that was necessary.

On the caravan's return Lebratovskii sent Kursin and Gerasim Barshchikov, formerly with the Molokov caravan, on to Irkutsk to launch an experiment in reproducing Chinese porcelains with Russian raw materials. The caravan director passed all this information on to St. Petersburg, and in 1747 went to the capital with Kursin, Kursin's brother Aleksei, Vladykin, and Barshchikov. Under Imperial ukaz, the group retired to Tsarskoe Selo to carry on the porcelain experiments, with Lebratovskii serving as director of the enterprise. Clays were brought from Siberia, quartz from European Russia. But the effort was stillborn. Whether the Chinese informer sold incomplete or intentionally altered recipes, whether the Russian technicians were too unskilled, or whether Russian clays and stones were not of the same composition as those the Chinese used are not clear. During the late 1740's Russian porcelain craft came to pattern itself after Swedish and European techniques.

After a very long interval, Aleksei Matveevich Vladykin assumed command of what was to be the last Russian caravan to Peking, not ordered formed until 20 February 1753. Vladykin, now raised from ninth to eight civil rank (Collegiate Assessor), was unquestionably the best prepared caravan director since Lange. If this long-time resident of Peking could not persuade the Chinese to ease the restrictions there, no one could. No one did.

A courier left Moscow for Peking at the end of March 1753, with a note more specific and blunt than usual. It requested that Chinese merchants bring to the Russian House only those goods in which the Russians expressed an interest and that all of the guards around the Russian residence be removed, so that all Chinese merchants might come without fear. The son of the Selenginsk Commandant, Lieutenant Ivan Varfolomeevich Iakobi, hurried with this message to Peking and as quickly hurried back. He rode into Kiakhta on 24 September 1753. But his news was disheartening: the *Li-fan-yuan* blandly denied that there had ever been any oppression; the treatment of the Russians was always according to the letter of the Treaty of Kiakhta.[128] The *Yuan* promised that all goods would be traded freely and only prohibited items inspected. The Chinese officials did not reveal how they planned to detect prohibited items without inspecting all. Iakobi also brought back a letter from Archimandrite Gervasii Lintsevskii, chief of the Russian church in Peking at this time, with the news of the death of still another student, Nikita Chepanov, although praising the study of Chinese and Manchu by three others, Aleksei Leont'ev, Andrei Kanaev, and Efim Sakhnovskii. The good cleric recommended that in the future language students be sent there for a specified period of time only.

The caravan set out with nearly a complete replacement for the personnel of the church mission in Peking, including Gervasii's successor, Archimandrite Amvrosii Iumatov, although he was to be called only cleric *(sviashchenik)*.[129] Amvrosii survived in Peking until July 1771. With him went two priests, Sil'vestr, who died in Kazan', in 1773 on his return, and Sofronii, who passed away in Peking, the deacon Sergei, who also died in Peking, and three Church serving men, Stepan Zimin, Il'ia Ivanov, and Aleksei Danilov. The Holy Synod had recommended all of these churchmen, and the Senate had duly approved them. Students Vladykin and Bykov were also to be replaced by four others—Vasilii Ermolaev, Stepan Sokolov, Stepan Iakimov, and Ivan Ozerov—each given one hundred rubles for journey expenses and subsistence of two hundred rubles annually.[130] And finally a Greek, skilled in the assay of gold and silver and knowledgeable of precious stones, accompanied the Russians.

The group entered Peking on 23 December and remained for six and one-half months, longer than any Russian caravan since that led by Tret'iakov and Molokov. No sooner had trade com-

128. Bantysh-Kamenskii, *Diplomaticheskoe sobranie*, p. 259.

129. Father Gervasii became bishop of Pereiaslavl' in Ukraine, where he died 2 December 1769.

130. A geodetist, Lt. Eremei (Ermil) Vladykin, was also part of the suite and compiled a land map of the territory covered by the caravan, a plan of Peking, and a journal, all preserved by the Senate. He also acquired a sixteen-volume descriptive work on China given to the Academy of Sciences for translation; *Senatskii arkhiv*, IX, 196-97, 488-89, 511.

menced (only a little over a month after arrival) than the *Li-fan-yuan* demanded a list of all goods imported and a detailed price list. This in spite of their recent guarantees that trade would be unimpeded and free. Vladykin flatly refused, and the *Li-fan-yuan* thereafter represented him to the Governing Senate as "an unprecedented and stupid" man who had the extraordinary gall to demand that ten horses secretly be given to him personally, and whose persistence and impertinance had various untoward consequences. The Chinese asked that in the future none as unskilled in trade as he be sent.[131] Still the sale of Russian goods was fairly good, although Vladykin reported he was disconcerted because the Chinese insisted on paying in money, rather than in goods.

If the trade was not a great success, and it was not, the replacement of priests and students was even less so. *Yuan* mandarins called to Vladykin's attention that the Treaty of Kiakhta specified only that six young men would study in Peking and said nothing of their replacement. Hence the four he brought had to be returned to Russia. A specious argument at very best, for *thirteen* young Russians had already spent greater or lesser periods in Peking. Although the director was shocked at this treatment after nearly three decades of Russian students in Peking, he had no choice but to transport them back to their homeland. He brought back also Aleksei Leont'ev, who proved later to be a valuable member of the Collegium of Foreign Affairs and an aide to Rossokhin in the Academy of Sciences, translating many books from the Chinese and attaining the rank of Chancellery Councillor, and Efim Sakhnovskii, who was left as an assistant in the Kiakhta customs house at a salary of two hundred rubles.[132] Andrei Kanaev died on the journey. The clerics and their serving men remained in Peking, as we have said, but three assistants brought with them were also returned to Russia.

So ended, without ceremony, the passage of these great caravan

131. One of three Chinese notes to the Senate carried by Vladykin, all dated Ch'ien-lung, 29th year, 5th month, 6th day; Bantysh-Kamenskii, *Diplomaticheskoe sobranie*, pp. 262-63. See also Silin, *Kiakhta*, p. 51, and Kurts, *Russko-kitaiskie snosheniia*, pp. 87-88.

132. Vladykin had been ordered in a Senate ukaz of 15 August 1754 to bring back from Peking two of the students of whom one, skilled in Chinese and Mongol, was to be left at Kiakhta. The Senate noted, on the basis of a report of the Collegium of Foreign Affairs report, that there was "not a single man" from among the former Peking students available for service in the Kiakhta customs house as a translator; Chulkov, *Istoricheskoe opisanie*, III, bk. 2, 283.

fleets to the East. The Russians, neither in St. Petersburg nor in Siberia, had made a conscious and formal decision to abandon the long and dangerous trip from the border to the Northern Capital. In 1760 the Senate requested a report of the Collegium of Foreign Affairs on the advisability and propitiousness of sending still another caravan, to which the Collegium merely said that the Dzhungarian campaign of the Chinese had inflamed the area and a caravan was at that time out of the question.[133] The Senate instructed the Collegium to wait until circumstances bettered. Two years later, in the first year of the reign of Catherine the Great, the Peking caravan was formally given over to free private trade, by which time there was little prospect that private merchants would take advantage of the opportunity.[134] Any private merchants who desired might trade in Peking in conformity with the Treaty of Kiakhta, in the manner of the former crown caravans, and naturally with the payment of full customs duties. When merchants gathered, the bodyguard, Captain Kropotov, recently returned from Peking, would accompany the caravan back. As for a director, the merchants should select one of their own number. All earlier prohibitions on select Siberian peltry were now lifted; all wares not specifically prohibited to export abroad were free to private carriage. Thereafter no private caravans reached Peking, but the crown did not turn its back completely. It continued to send small lots of pelts to the Russian church for sale.[135]

In retrospect the state monopoly of trade in Peking was no great and glorious success. The surviving statistics suggest strongly that if the monopoly over the years operated in the black, it was not by much, and several of the caravans undoubtedly lost money. Still a just assessment of the operation must mention the disadvantages under which caravan directors had to operate, as well as certain obvious advantages it enjoyed.

When state caravans began at the end of the seventeenth century, the country through which they travelled had, at best, ill defined boundaries, an extremely light population, and above all the flimsiest governmental apparatus to enforce the restraints placed upon the competition, the private merchants. Until the

133. *Senatskii arkhiv,* XI, 399, reported at a Senate session of 18 July 1760.

134. *Ibid.,* XII, 158; *PSZ,* XVI, No. 11630, 34; Chulkov, *Istoricheskoe opisanie,* III, bk. 2, 328-29. Senate edict dated 31 July 1762.

135. P. Golovachev, *Irkutskoe likholet'e 1758-1760 gg.* (Moscow: Izd. A. V. Kas'ianova, 1904), p. 25, as quoted in Silin, *Kiakhta,* p. 51.

Treaty of Kiakhta there was no effective way to restrain private merchants from poaching on the government's assumed prerogative, nor to discipline them when they did. And Russia's Siberian merchants were no gentle lot anxious to exercise self-discipline and responsibility; were they not a lusty and avaricious lot, they would not have been in eastern Siberia in those days. Prior to 1727 there were no effective barriers to illicit private trade and only a handful of soldiers to enforce the state's prohibitions.

After 1727 the situation changed somewhat. Vladislavich and others strove to shore up the administrative apparatus of the border, or rather to create one *de novo*. Unfortunately for their objectives, capable government servants with a sense of obligation to their offices and duties were rare on the frontier. Even at the highest level in Siberia, the drive for quick fortune overcame easily, it would seem, any lingering sense of fiscal responsibility. Zholobov, for example, vice-governor of Irkutsk in the early 1730's, was later tried and executed for a variety of malpractices, among which were permitting illegal goods (primarily expensive peltry) to be carried secretly across the border, and even allowing the imperial seal in his charge to be used to stamp these goods.[136] The damage these acts did state trade in Peking is impossible to measure, but the persistent complaints of Lange and other caravan directors of the surfeited peltry market in Peking suggests strongly that Zholobov, and most certainly others, played a major role in the financial failure of Russian state barter in Peking. If even the redoubtable Lange could have his integrity questioned at one point, how much the more so for the sworn-appraisers, customs officials, and all others who in small ways undoubtedly stole from the caravan, but escaped detection and cashiering. Korsak estimated that in 1739 the amount of illegal peltry that crossed the border was three times that usually carried in a caravan.[137]

Had St. Petersburg officials acted on the repeated suggestion that it end the caravans, and draw even larger revenues from customs duties on private trade, then enormously heavy costs would have been avoided. The transportation of pelts, or for that matter any goods, probably doubled, or nearly so, the caravan's cost of carriage

136. See *PSZ*, IX, No. 7009, 876-79; *Sbornik RIO*, CXI (1901), 41-42, 45, 46, 58–59, 69, 75, 76, 105-6, 138-42, 190, 415; CXXIV (1906), 58-60, for a complete account of Zholobov's investigation, trial, and condemnation. He was decapitated on 1 July 1736.

137. Korsak, *Istoriko-statisticheskoe obozrenie*, p. 38.

from Moscow to the border.[138] Draft animals and carts accounted for this. The crown tried to establish its own stables at Arguzinsk ostrog, but even there private persons carried on trade using "crown carts, workmen, horses, cattle, and other prerogatives."[139] The bulk of goods carried to China were Siberian, but carriage to Peking still probably raised the asking prices at least 50 per cent on an average. In addition to transportation costs, the state of course would have completely avoided fifty or sixty thousand rubles in necessary overhead expenses associated with every caravan.

Finally the sheer cumbersomeness of the caravans contributed a large measure of their disadvantage. Slow accumulation of furs over a period of several years prior to a caravan's departure resulted in a high percentage of badly deteriorated and nearly valueless pelts. The archaic system of caravan directors and commissars bearing responsibility for each caravan from acquisition of furs to sale of them in Moscow or St. Petersburg is a measure of the badly outmoded administrative machinery of Siberia, not brought up to date until the nineteenth century. The inflexibility of the pricing mechanism, both of Russian goods and Chinese, slowed sales on both ends, and contributed to the Chinese distaste for the entire arrangement. The failure to realize soon enough that Siberia itself might be a valuable market for many Chinese goods, tobacco, rhubarb, and others in addition to fabrics, cut the caravan off from the flourishing market fairs of Siberia and of Russia between Moscow and the Urals. In short the insistence of St. Petersburg authorities that all decisions and operations be centralized in the Russian capital, compounded by the inefficiences and losses of time in communicating with Siberian governmental authorities and caravan personnel, laid a dampening influence on what might have been a sparkling enterprise.

Probably the greatest disadvantage of the caravan system was,

138. Departament Tamozhennykh Sborov, Statisticheskoe Otdelenie, *Statisticheskiia svedeniia o torgovle Rossii s Kitaem*, p. 4. See also, e.g., TsGADA, Selenginskaia gorodovaia ratusha, *fond* 1801, *ed. khr.* 8, *l.* 102, Postanovlenie Selenginskoi zemskoi izby o predostavlenii podvod dlia perevozki kitaiskikh tovarov, 27 March 1736; *l.* 103a, Vedenie A. Parshevnikova v Selenginskuiu zemskuiu izbu ob otpravke 30 podvod dlia perevozki kitaiskikh tovarov iz Kiakhty do Sinopskoi strelki, 28 March 1735; and *l.* 104, Donoshenie iz Selenginskoi zemskoi izby v Selenginskuiu voevodskuiu kantseliariiu ob otpravke 30 podvod dia perevozki kitaiskikh tovarov, 29 March 1735.

139. Trusevich, *Posol'skiia i torgovliia snosheniia*, p. 127.

all in all, the restrictions and limitations it laid upon the growth of private trade in Siberia. Except in small ways between 1727 and Catherinian times, Russian and Siberian merchants were cut off from legal traffic in many of the most lucrative commodities of the area—the finest pelts, Chinese gold and silver, tobacco, rhubarb, horses, cattle, etc. The next several chapters treat in greater detail the other government monopolies and private trade at the border, but enough has already been said to conclude that the heavy hand of the faraway government guaranteed that merchants would indulge in illicit trade, bribe, and negotiate their ways around all barriers and prohibitions, and would adopt an attitude of thorough mistrust of any open or government-sponsored venture. It is not at all surprising that the real effort to bring into being the bank and company proposed by Lange elicited absolutely no response from Russia's mercantile or business communities; they had for too long properly feared exposing themselves and their monies to government seizure or taxation.

The other side of the coin is the one truly extraordinary advantage the state caravan enjoyed over all private merchants—its great store of the finest Siberian peltry obtained through *iasak,* purchase, customs tithe, or "gift," in any event obtained at very low cost. Peking was potentially, and actually as it turned out, a fine market for these furs, which otherwise were shipped back to European Russian cities or transshipped to western European markets. Only for accounting purposes may these furs be taken as worth one hundred thousand rubles or more per caravan. Actually they were almost free to the state. Why in view of the poor (at best) profits of the succeeding caravans were they carried on so long and formally ended only by Catherine's administration which was theoretically at least devoted to the economic principle of "free trade?" Simply because they did not lose money so far as the state apparatus as a whole is concerned. The only question was, could much more gain have flowed into the imperial treasury had the state disposed of its pelts elsewhere, say to a company such as Lange proposed, and in addition taxed all private trade in peltry across the boundaries of the empire? And the answer in all likelihood is in the affirmative; at least Lange was convinced of it.

This argument is not to be taken as a twentieth-century brief for free and private commercial enterprise in eighteenth-century Russia. The Treaty of Kiakhta was—in one sense—the result of the inability of Russia's private trade to exercise a modicum of discipline upon itself. The unruliness of merchants and Peking's inability to cope with them led the Chinese to cast out all Russian traders in 1722. The Treaty and the bureaucratic structure to control and organize this commerce were, in part, the responses of the Russian state to the excesses of her Siberian colonists.

Chapter V. Rhubarb and Other Things

Fine furs and their carriage to Peking were not the only commercial monopolies of the Russian state in the last three quarters of the eighteenth century. Chinese tobacco, gold and silver, and most important of all, ungulate rhubarb, were all at various times and in various ways denied to private merchants. Rhubarb was popular throughout Europe as a drug, and though Dutch and other ships brought it from the East Indies, it was commonly accepted that the finest came from the mountains and highlands of Tibet, Chinese Central Asia, and Kansu. The Russians, to their delight, stood between the source and the upset stomachs of western Europe.

Rhubarb was then, as it still is today, regarded as a particularly useful drug because it "possesses the double virtue of a cathartic and astringent."[1]

> ". . . it readily evacuates particularly the bilious humors, and strengthens the stomach walls. It is given with great success in all obstructions of the liver, in the jaundice, in diarrhoeas, and in the fluor albus and gonorrhoeas; it is also an excellent remedy against worms. It is sometimes given as a purgative, sometimes as only an alterant; and which way ever it is taken it is an excellent medicine, agreeing with almost all ages and constitutions. The only cases in which it's use is to be avoided, are those in which the blood and viscera are too hot. Fallopius says it is never to be given to people who have disorders of the kidneys or bladder, as it is apt to occasion an extraordinary heat in those parts; and Simon Pauli tells us of vertigoes brought on by a too free and continued use of it."

1. Savary des Bruslons, *The Universal Dictionary of Trade and Commerce . . .* II, 611-12. A recent medical text affords an interesting comment on the modernity of eighteenth-century pharmacology: "The laxative quality of rhubarb is due to its anthraquinone content and differs from the other drugs of this group in that it has a high tannic acid content, thereby preventing free movement of the bowels after complete evacuation has been obtained. This tannic content was believed to be advantageous because it possesses a constipating effect following its laxative action. . . . Rhubarb is a valuable remedy in simple constipation;" *The Cyclopedia of Medicine, Surgery and Specialties*, ed. by George Morris Piersol and others (Philadelphia: F. A. Davis Co., 1948), XIII, 585-86.

Such a universal remedy could hardly be expected to escape the sharp eyes of the directors of the Russian court and the Commerce Collegium. As early as the mid-seventeenth century, imperial edict prohibited its trade by private merchants, both Russian and Siberian, under penalty of death with no expectation of mercy.[2] By the end of the century the rhubarb trade was given to a large merchant, I. Isaev, as an exclusive farm for a five-year period. Isaev could import duty free up to 2100 pounds (fifty *pud*) of the dried root of rhubarb, but no more, so as to maintain a high price on it. When his lease expired, the monopoly was renewed for five years to the Hamburg merchant Mathias Poppe, after which the state itself tried to assume the monopoly.[3] In 1704 it permitted a courtier, the *stol'nik* Siniavin, to import into Siberia over 10,000 pounds (300 *pud*) per year.[4]

The Russian court's great interest in the rhubarb trade came only with the establishment in Peter's reign of a Chief Apothecary Office (*Glavnaia apteka*, 1706), and sometime thereafter of a Medical Chancellery *(Meditsinskaia kantseliariia)*, inspired by the Scottish doctor whom Peter met in Holland, Robert Erskine, or Areskin as he preferred in Russia.[5] The Chancellery was early given general control of the collection, distribution, and sale of all medical drugs to all apothecaries in Russia, including the relatively small number of private druggists. The Chancellery in later years repeatedly insisted that all rhubarb for medical use in Russia pass through its hands, that none be imported from Europe through Riga or Revel', and this not so much for fiscal profit as to insure that the fairly potent drug be prescribed properly and only when in good condition. At irregular intervals the Chancellery purchased small lots of rhubarb, usually fifty *pud* or less, from the Commerce Col-

2. *PSZ*, I, No. 215, 442-44, edict dated 21 November 1657/7166.

3. Cahen, *Histoire*, p. 62.

4. *PSZ*, IV, No. 1967, 245-46.

5. *Gosudarstvennye uchrezhdeniia*, pp. 179-82. On Areskin see Chapter 2, n. 4; also John Cook, *Voyages and Travels Through the Russian Empire, Tartary, and Part of the Kingdom of Persia* (Edinburgh: Printed for the Author, 1770), I, 26-28. The *Glavnaia apteka* became, apparently, the *Aptekarskii prikaz* which moved from Moscow to St. Petersburg in 1712 and two years later was designated a Medical Chancellery. Its head was termed an *Archiator*, "reviving an old Roman title first given by Nero to his Imperial body physician;" Paul, *Publications of the Scottish History Society*, XLIV; *Miscellany* (Second Volume) of the Society (February, 1904), 380. Areskin was the first archiator with an annual salary of 1500 ducats (£700 sterling). The Chancellery became the main supplier of drugs for both military and naval forces as well as the civilian sector of the realm.

legium for distribution to state apothecaries, and private doctors and chemists. In 1738, for example, the Cabinet permitted sale of rhubarb by the Chancellery to private pharmacies of no more than ten *funt* at not less than six rubles per *funt*. Private persons with no medical credentials were not to be sold any, except in those areas of Russia where there were no druggists or doctors, and then only one-half to one *funt* was permitted per person.[6]

In spite of this close control, rhubarb shared in the loosening of restrictions on Siberian and Chinese trade of the 1720's. It was declared free to private trade on 26 June 1727, although the State Treasury Office in Tobol'sk was instructed still to acquire annually 200-300 *pud*, either by purchase at local Tobol'sk prices from private merchants who brought it from the frontier, or by giving over the acquisition to a private farmer.[7] Only that amount requested by Moscow should be sent from Tobol'sk, part of which would be transferred to the Medical Chancellery and part for sale in Moscow or shipment abroad at prices established by the Commerce Collegium. For that exported to the West through St. Petersburg or Arkhangel'sk, the edict requested that any Russian or foreign merchants interested in participating in this trade present themselves to the Commerce Collegium. Even during this period of free trade, the state did not relinquish completely its involvement in the rhubarb trade, and private trade in the drug did not last long in any event.

In the four years of free trade in rhubarb, it was badly mishandled by private traders, according to depositions of the newly created Stores Accounting Commission *(Shchetnaia proviantskaia komissiia)*.[8] The quality of the root declined, and it often arrived in great batches, which caused prices to fluctuate widely and do harm to that offered for sale by the Commerce Collegium. The state's offices traded only 200-300 *pud* per year, but private merchants often brough quantities many times larger than that.

As a result of this situation, the Governing Senate, with the advice of the Commerce Collegium, determined in 1731 to reassert the role of the state; rhubarb once again was interdicted to private merchants, and the Imperial Treasury, the Commerce Collegium and the Siberian Prikaz were enjoined to cooperate in contracting

6. *PSZ*, X, No. 7555, 454-55.
7. *Ibid.*, VII, No. 5110, 820, especially Point 9 of the long ukaz.
8. *Gosudarstvennye uchrezhdeniia*, pp. 236-37.

for rhubarb on the Mongolian border in quantities sufficiently limited so as to maintain "a high price and state profit."[9] The Senate requested that the Collegium undertake a thorough study of the acquisition and especially the marketing of rhubarb, and that it provide the Siberian Prikaz with full information on the market demand and the offering prices. The Prikaz, in its turn, would then contract with a specially designated merchant to obtain supplies at the border, taking great care that supply and demand be so balanced that European prices remain high, yet no great stores of the drug be permitted to spoil from long storage in Moscow warehouses.

All private merchants possessing rhubarb or having already contracted for it on the border were required to deliver it to the Imperial Treasury or its branch offices in Moscow or Tobol'sk, in exchange for the current purchase price, plus whatever transportation costs were incurred. For several years the Treasury depended on the large quantities purchased or contracted for by Russian merchants prior to 1731. The Muscovite merchant Semen Kalinin and his associates imported over 900 *pud,* contracted before 1731 and delivered to the Commerce Collegium four years later. Another merchant, Filipp Kriukov, delivered to the Treasury Office in Tobol'sk 136 *pud* 28 *funt* of ungulate rhubarb that he had obtained at Kiakhta in exchange for Russian tanned hides *(iuft').* And the textile manufacturer Ivan Dmitriev claimed in his petition of 1733 that he had contracted three years earlier for 300 *pud* which he intended to export to Spain for raw linen to process in his textile mill.[10]

This acquisition by the state *after* importation proved unfair to private merchants and made it almost impossible for the state to regulate the flow of rhubarb to its advantage. Dmitriev, for example, prevaricated in his petition to export rhubarb to Spain, and so the Commerce Collegium decided upon investigation. The 300 *pud,* valued at the "foreign price" of 38,640 rubles was far greater in value than the modest amount of linen he imported, and were he to be permitted to export all of the rhubarb, he could do so only over a long number of years doing irreparable damage to the state monopoly and sharply lowering the foreign price. The

9. *PSZ,* VIII, No. 5741, 450, Senate ukaz dated 8 April 1731.

10. For all of these cases, see *Sbornik RIO,* CXVII (1900), 223, 641-45; CXXXVIII (1912), 357, 419-22; Chulkov, *Istoricheskoe opisanie,* III, bk. 2, 191-96.

Senate concluded that he must turn over to the Treasury all of the rhubarb he had on hand and expected to carry to Moscow, in return for which he would receive a 12 per cent profit above the cost of the rhubarb and expenses. Kriukov initially received only twelve rubles per *pud* for his rhubarb in Tobol'sk, i.e., the price the Treasury determined to be the current purchase price in Kiakhta. He and his brother after his death were forced to badger government officers for years to obtain what they pleaded was their actual investment, over twenty-seven rubles per *pud* (3,487 rubles 50 kopeks of *iuft'* given to a Bukharan trader, plus 232 rubles 99 kopeks in transportation expenses to Tobol'sk). Not until 1740 did Kriukov's heirs receive a settlement from the government—eight years after the merchant had borrowed the money to buy *iuft'*.

Supplementing another strong prohibition on private trade of 7 October 1734, the Senate instructed the Siberian Prikaz to purchase and to brack, i.e., to inspect and to grade, up to 1,000 *pud* annually, both for export and use in Russian apothecaries.[11] If more was offered for sale by the Mongol and Bukharan merchants it should be purchased so as not to discourage a steady and large supply.[12] In future years the amount acquired would vary depending on market price and supply. Any above 1,000 *pud* must be stored in the dry climate of the border, rather than shipped to Moscow or St. Petersburg where good storage was very difficult.

In spite of these strict prohibitions against private carriage and great plans for expanded state trade, illicit trade persisted. In the spring of 1735 the Senate noted that in that year alone fifty *pud* was exported illegally from Russia, and much more than that must have escaped the attention of customs officials and border guards. New and stricter prohibitions were quickly ordered, violation of which earned large fines for foreigners, and fines and death for Russians. This time the orders were published throughout Russia as was not uncommon, but Russian merchants were to be inspected not only at home, but "in England, Holland and other [European]

11. The brack system *(brakovanie)* developed in Russia's European ports to guard against fraud and deception in the timber and naval stores sold to England, Holland, and France in the Petrine years; Reading, *The Anglo-Russian Commercial Treaty*, pp. 20, 201ff.

12. *PSZ*, IX, No. 6634, 412-13. In years immediately thereafter the Senate usually requested 1000 *pud; ibid.*, IX, No. 7058, 931-32, dated 16 September 1736; IX, No. 7093, 966-67, dated 5 November 1736.

places" as well.[13] Illicit trade was never successfully suppressed, and these same decrees appear repeatedly in the succeeding decades.

There were really two general problems that the state had to solve were it to enjoy the fruits of great profit from its monopoly: acquisition of good rhubarb at a reasonable price, and sale of most of it in western European markets at prices high enough to cover all costs and still yield a good return. As for the former, the first step was to post to the border someone medically knowledgeable to inspect, grade and evaluate the rhubarb as it came from the border, i.e., to brack it. Prior to the 1730's, St. Petersburg itself did not seem to have had the trained and skilled personnel to do this.[14] The large amounts of inferior or spoiled rhubarb arriving in St. Petersburg led to the dispatch to the border of one Petr Rozing, probably Dutch. Since his tasks were critical to the success of the monopoly, the Cabinet sanctioned the high salary of 500 rubles per year, or 400 if the person selected were Siberian.[15] Of the good root brought by private merchants from the border, Rozing was to ship 800 to 1000 *pud* as specified by the Commerce Collegium to St. Petersburg for shipment abroad, and any rhubarb unfit to bring a good price was to be burned there in Irkutsk.[16] Beyond this general directive, Rozing received finely drawn instructions.[17] Genuine ungulate rhubarb *(kopytchatnyi reven')* must be segregated from the inferior root, pendunculated (*cherekovyi reven'* or *rapontik*) and "stone" rhubarb *(kamennyi)*, and then inspected piece by piece to eliminate any rotted pieces or fresh ones susceptible to rot. Pendunculated root was described as oblong

13. *Ibid.*, IX, No. 6749, 531, dated 15 June 1735; IX, No. 6750, 531, dated 22 July 1735.

14. In May, 1736 the Commerce Collegium was ordered by the Senate to acquire a bracker *(brakovshchik)* in England or Holland expressly for this purpose; Chulkov, *Istoricheskoe opisanie*, III, bk. 2, 205.

15. *PSZ*, IX, No. 7098, 970-71, dated 11 November 1736.

16. *Ibid.*, IX, No. 7058, 931-32, dated 16 September 1736. Of the normal 1000 *pud* for shipment abroad, 50 *pud* of ungulate and 20 *pud* of pendunculated were to be shipped to the Medical Chancellery for use in St. Petersburg, for which the Chancellery paid the Collegium at the going market price; *ibid.*, IX, No. 7076, 953.

17. *Ibid.*, IX, No. 7112, 992-93, dated 28 November 1736; *Sbornik RIO*, CXIV (1898), 592; Chulkov, *Istoricheskoe opisanie*, III, bk. 2, 223-24. Rozing served well for an exceptionally long time and was retired in 1748 because of ill health. He was replaced the next year by the senior apothecary's assistant *(starshii gezel')* Pavel Rung, who lasted for fourteen years. Andrei Brant, also an apothecary's assistant, took his place in 1764 at 300 r. per year; *Senatskii arkhiv*, XIII, 40-41.

and wooden in appearance with a taste more bitter and astrigent than genuine ungulate and with an odor like Russian leather. The finest rhubarb could be distinguished as generally round, with coloring ranging from dark gold through deep yellow to whitish, from the best to the poorest. Each of the grades had to be packed separately in tight, waterproof bales, stored in newly built and guarded warehouses, and then shipped only in the dry summer. To aid Rozing were one or two merchants thoroughly experienced in rhubarb trade and several of the best available laborers.

When it assumed monopoly of the rhubarb trade in 1731, the state apparatus began looking about for a merchant or merchants capable of acting as agent of the treasury for the actual bartering and contracting with Bukharan Mongols for large and regular shipments. As with most of the directors of the Peking caravans, the state put its trust in the skill of the accomplished merchant, rather than the long-time civil servant. Simon Svin'in was selected at the end of 1736. He was a merchant of Velikii Ustiug of Norse background, who had, for several years at least, traded in rhubarb.[18] He was permitted to select one other merchant to aid him (he chose the Muscovite Manuil Skerletov as his associate), and he was assigned a chancellery servingman from his home town, Ivan Petrovich Shurkov (Oshurkov), two copyists, and later an interpreter. This small band came to be known as the Kiakhta Rhubarb Commission *(Kiakhtinskaia revenskaia komissiia)*. Svin'in's original orders from the Commerce Collegium were exceedingly long and later amended at his request.[19] They charged him to inquire all along the way from Moscow to Kiakhta of any privately, although legally transported rhubarb not yet turned over to the Treasury or the Siberian Prikaz, to note the prices on it, to make complete lists of the goods, and to take from the owners signed letters that they would not sell any rhubarb before reaching Moscow—an extraordinarily haphazard way to enforce a monopoly the violation of which ostensibly merited death. Similarly he was to inspect the rhubarb in the Tobol'sk and other Siberian chancelleries, in order to separate the ungulate suitable for export from

18. *Sbornik RIO*, CXIV (1898), 491, 495, 592, 645.

19. Chulkov, *Istoricheskoe opisanie*, III, bk. 2, 210-23, 232-35. The original instructions were dated 24 November 1736, his addenda December, 1737. The formal Senate decree approving him came on 19 February 1737; *PSZ*, X, No. 7181, 53-54.

the penduncculated and other inferior roots, to burn the useless, and to fix his own seal on the bales of the good. He was to request the Siberian governor to send off the selected rhubarb immediately to the Siberian Office in Moscow brooking no delay on the road. The Collegium authorized Svin'in to purchase privately carried rhubarb both on the road and in Kiakhta, at the price the state favored, twelve rubles per *pud*, or less whenever he was able. For any rhubarb trade on the Argun, a dependable man selected by the Irkutsk vice-governor was to be sent to Nerchinsk to perform these same inspecting functions and to purchase any private rhubarb. In short Svin'in was to serve as the eyes and ears of the Tsaritsa while journeying to the border.

Once on the border his main task began, and one that was to occupy him for well over a decade—the acquisition of exportable rhubarb. He was advised to buy the rhubarb already on the market there, both useable and worthless, so as not to offend the Bukharan and Mongol traders. Thereafter he must inform them to bring only good quality ungulate rhubarb. To reinforce his point, he should brack on the spot any rhubarb he purchased, and burn before the suppliers' eyes the penduncculated and valueless pieces. Furthermore all rhubarb must be bracked thrice, the best third dispatched back to European Russia first, and if that did not amount to the 1000 *pud* needed for export then, the second and third selections should be sent. To assure that the best quality was brought for sale to Russians, Svin'in could pay two or three rubles above the usual price, i.e. fourteen or fifteen rubles per *pud*.

Svin'in's instructions show that St. Petersburg commercial authorities were well aware that rhubarb from the Dzhungarian regions of Chinese Turkestan often found its way to Turkish Mediterranean ports through Bokhara, Khiva, Astrakhan, and Persia. He was ordered to make a special effort to investigate that source and those routes. In general he was to track down the source of any rhubarb that arrived at the Russian border, either in the Kiakhta area or on the Irtysh line, to record the asking price of that rhubarb, and to inquire as to the amount and kind of goods necessary for exchange. From Tobol'sk a special emissary should be sent to the Dzhungarian Kontaisha and provided with Russian goods up to 1000 rubles in value which seemed suitable for barter.[20] The

20. According to a 1739 Senate decree, Svin'in's assistant, Skerletov, was eventually sent to the Kokonor region, not with 1000 r. worth of pelts and goods, but with only enough for gifts for local leaders, and not necessarily to

Commerce Collegium made it patently clear that it wished all the rhubarb possible to end up in Russian hands, and to that end Svin'in should make whatever arrangements he could with any local tribal leaders, so that they would send to him all they produced each year, at a single established price. The Commerce Collegium lectured Svin'in that this was exactly what the Dutch did, with such great success, in the East Indies with cinnamon, nutmeg, and cloves. Of all of these transactions Svin'in was warned to keep thorough and accurate accounts.

Finally he had one secret bit of intelligence to perform, a successful one according to later documents—to acquire "even if for great price" 300-400 *funt* of rhubarb seed and to learn all he could of the soil conditions necessary for good growth, whether the seedlings needed transplanting, how they were tended, etc. All the information he gathered he was to forward to Moscow with dispatch and discretion.

Svin'in submitted to the Collegium a supplement to his instructions in six points. Since the Russian state had for long objected to the export of bullion, the problem of which goods to exchange for rhubarb was a major problem. Svin'in petitioned that he be granted permission to purchase Chinese tobacco balls, highly prized by the Siberian natives and normally prohibited to private trade, to carry to Siberian markets to exchange for pelts, including the best usually reserved for the caravans—sea otter, Arctic fox, glutton, fox, squirrel, etc. He should not have to depend on using the furs and others goods returned unsold from Peking by the state's caravans. In spite of the obvious infringement this represented on the state caravan, he was granted such permission. His commission was in this regard potentially as lucrative to the state or more so than the caravans themselves. He asked that orders be sent from Moscow to the distant *voevody* in Siberia ordering that the furs he purchased be sent without delay or prevarication to the border.

Svin'in stated that he had no faith in the ability of local officers already at the border to brack rhubarb for apothecary purposes. They were far too accustomed to the cruder standards of commercial brack, and he asked that only capable apothecaries do the selecting and grading. Because of the distance of Irkutsk from the

make a contract, but mainly to secure accurate and full information on the rhubarb trade of the region; *Senatskii arkhiv*, II, 17; Chulkov, *Istoricheskoe opisanie*, III, bk. 2, 240.

border, purchased rhubarb should be bracked and stored at Kiakhta, rather than at Irkutsk as earlier and the actual work done by twenty-five men provided by Irkutsk Provincial Chancellery. When it was ready for shipment to St. Petersburg, he would hire the carts and the Irkutsk vice-governor should provide the horses. In that way he might exercise closer surveillance over the entire operation, control better the import of good rhubarb, and reject those goods he judged of no use. At the very end of his petition Svin'in asked, and was given, greater return for his efforts. Normally he would have gotten 4 per cent of value of goods he handled. The Collegium allowed him to claim an additional 2 per cent, because of the great distance from home at which he served. He, his father, his brothers, and a nephew were granted release from the service obligation *(sluzhba)* and any surtaxes *(podat')*, and his own household was relieved from the post system obligation, all of which left him only the poll tax *(podushnye den'gi)* and the recruit duty.

At the end of January 1738, an imperial ukaz given from the Cabinet to the Siberian Prikaz specifically approved of the purchase by Svin'in of Siberian pelts, rigidly prohibited to private trade, but "in order that both the rhubarb and caravan trades show profit in the future," only those that the caravan commissars deemed of no value to them.[21] A year later another imperial ukaz put it this way: Svin'in should "in payment for the rhubarb, select goods and peltry of medium quality, but not the very best. . . ."[22] Svin'in was eventually permitted to use pelts gathered for the caravans, but only if the caravan commissars, with Lange's approval, released them because of their limited value in the Peking market. And on all rhubarb imported customs duties of 10 per cent must be paid in Irkutsk but none elsewhere.

St. Petersburg attempted to defray the initial expenses of the rhubarb trade as much as possible from the Siberian colony, rather than the Imperial Treasury. In 1738 from the large public funds collected in the Kiakhta and Selenginsk city halls, Svin'in was given 11,778 rubles, and in the next year, from the Irkutsk chancellery 13,824 rubles, although the latter only for purchase of gold apparently.[23] If sufficient funds to carry on the trade were not

21. *PSZ*, X, No. 7498, 398-99.

22. Chulkov, *Istoricheskoe opisanie*, III, bk. 2, 240, Imperial ukaz of 14 March 1739. See also *Senatskii arkhiv*, II, 17.

23. Silin, *Kiakhta*, p. 53; *Sbornik RIO*, CXXXVIII (1912), 123-24; and Kaidanov, *Sistematicheskii katalog delam Sibirskago prikaza*, p. 10.

available in eastern Siberia (especially because of the heavy obligations already of the caravan expenses, and the salaries of serving people in the large Kamchatka expedition), then the receipts of the Siberian *guberniia* in the Money Chancellery were to be used and if these were still not enough, the Chancellery would forward other funds from Moscow. These monies were used for the purchase of gold and furs and other goods to exchange for rhubarb.

Svin'in at first purchased rhubarb from the several Bukharan merchants who regularly traded at Mai-mai-ch'eng, and evidently he did so quite successfully. A report of the Siberian Prikaz of 30 June 1737 stated that he had already purchased 1091 *pud* 20 *funt*, although shortly thereafter an imperial ukaz given to the Prikaz instructed the rhubarb commissar to make contracts with those suppliers who wished to barter rhubarb for goods, in order that stocks of Russian commodities might be built up in Kiakhta.[24] In the ensuing year Svin'in purchased even larger amounts.[25]

At this point Svin'in succeeded in negotiating a contract with a single supplier, the Bukharan of Selim, Murat Bachim, who agreed to supply 2000 *pud* of "good, clean, large and dry ungulate rhubarb" annually over a four-year period. Svin'in agreed to brack the "very best" at 9 rubles 80 kopeks per *pud*, which meant that the contract could amount to 78,400 rubles in rhubarb root if all of it were the "very best." Actually things did not go quite so well. In early 1741 Svin'in reported to the Senate that of 4216 *pud* brought in the preceding three years, less than half (1976 *pud*) was judged by the apothecary to be satisfactory for acceptance by the Treasury, and the remainder was all publicly burned (as Svin'in was repeatedly ordered to do). The poor root was destroyed at the expense of the Bukharan, whose loss was obviously very great.[26] Of the sound rhubarb 1002 *pud* had already reached St. Petersburg, and another 50 *pud* 9 *funt* was retained in Moscow

24. *PSZ*, X, No. 7324, 217.

25. *Sbornik RIO*, CXXIV (1906), 275. A total of 4584 *pud* although it is not clear whether this included the amount he bought earlier.

26. *PSZ*, XI, No. 8633, 683-87; *Senatskii arkhiv*, V, 396-411; *Sbornik RIO*, CXXIV (1906), 453. In the *Sbornik RIO* may be found the 7 December 1738 Cabinet order that all unusable purchased rhubarb be burned. A Senate ukaz of 15 November 1740 demanded that Murat bring only suitable rhubarb, all other would be refused. Three days later another ukaz insisted that during brack in Siberia the rhubarb must be cleaned and only the clean sent to St. Petersburg; Chulkov, *Istoricheskoe opisanie*, III, bk. 2, 255. In 1741 again, Svin'in and the apothecary were ordered to put into effect all instructions and orders previously issued; *Senatksii arkhiv*, V, 396-411.

for use by the Medical Chancellery.[27] Much of what was received at the border was also thoroughly handled and bad spots pared out with knives, which was, Svin'in insisted strictly, not in the contract.

In spite of the unsatisfactory fulfillment of the contract, Svin'in recommended at the end of the four years that Murat Bachim not be disavowed, for he was the only trustworthy and honest contracter to be found at the border.[28] Other suppliers demanded 10 rubles per *pud* (the going price at Kiakhta-Mai-mai-ch'eng) and something less than half of what the rhubarb brought bracked clean, he argued. Hence, for 2000 *pud* of clean root per year, it would be necessary to buy 4000 for 40,000 rubles. Murat on the other hand, now apparently asking 16 rubles per *pud*, would supply 2000 *pud* clean, for a total of 32,000 rubles, or a saving of 8,000 rubles per year (80,000 over a ten-year contract period). Murat himself would, of course, sustain any losses that resulted from deteriorated root under this arrangement. Since the losses to Murat over the past year amounted to 58,800 rubles, even if this were repaid over the ten-year period, there would still be a "saving" of 21,000 rubles. The effect would be to raise Murat's price per *pud* to 18 rubles 90 kopeks, but Svin'in insisted that contracts with other Bukharans at 10 rubles promised no more "safety" than did renewing the Murat contract under these new conditions. The Commerce Collegium from its empyrean heights in St. Petersburg was unpersuaded by Svin'in's calculations, and simply ordered him to purchase 700 *pud* per year of good and unrotted rhubarb at a price not above 9 rubles 80 kopeks, the original contract price, although he might exceed that by one, two, or three rubles, if he could no longer find rhubarb at that price level. Apparently Svin'in failed to obtain such a favorable contract with Murat, for on 18 June 1743, he concluded a ten-year pact with him for 500 *pud* annually at 16 rubles per *pud*.[29] To conduct this trade Svin'in was permitted to draw 18,000 rubles from the Treasury, which as shall be noted below he was not able to fully account for later.[30]

These first dozen years of the reinstituted monopoly (1731-42)

27. *Sbornik RIO*, CXXXVIII (1912), 52. It was shipped clandestinely from Moscow to St. Petersburg in packages marked "confiscated Siberian items."

28. *PSZ*, XI, No. 8633, 683-87, an Imperially approved report of the Senate dated October 13, 1742. Also *Senatskii arkhiv*, V, 420-22, 429-31.

29. *Senatskii archiv*, VII, 364.

30. *Ibid.*, VIII, 464.

were evidently extremely prosperous. One source has it that from 1735 through 1740 alone, the state received profits of 384,309 rubles from the shipment of rhubarb abroad.[31] This represented the export of 2434 *pud* 36 *funt* valued at 121,600 rubles in St. Petersburg, including all expenses there. The increment in value between Kiakhta and western European markets, we know to have been great. For the root usually purchased freely in Kiakhta at twenty rubles or a bit more (or less than ten on contract from Murat prior to 1743), the St. Petersburg value was still only thirty-seven rubles seven kopeks for the period of the initial Murat contract or about 50 rubles per *pud* if all expenses were included. This sold abroad for 169 to 289 rubles per *pud* (an average of 208 rubles per *pud*) depending on the condition of the markets![32] Comparison of these representative prices with those of pre-Murat days suggests that most of this profit came during the Svin'in direction of the monopoly, for the usual St. Petersburg value was no more than seventy to eighty rubles then.

Part of the credit for such successful business undoubtedly must belong to those back in St. Petersburg who performed the final brack before shipment abroad and arranged for the consignments to major European commercial cities and their sale. Prior to the resumption of the state monopoly, England seems to have dominated rhubarb imports into western Europe, and it is not at all surprising that the English firm of Shiffner and Wolff, long trading in St. Petersburg, received a commission in 1735 to ship crown rhubarb at eighteen guilders per *funt*.[33] These two had been

31. *Ibid.*, VII, 365. Troitskii gives a figure of 382,636 r. 21 k. for the years 1735-41, which he extracted from a December, 1745 report of Commerce Collegium President B. G. Iusupov to Elizabeth entitled, "Proekt o privedenii revennogo torgu v lutchii poriadok"; Sergei Martinovich Troitskii, *Finansovaia politika russkogo absoliutizma v XVIII veke* (Moscow: Izd. "Nauka," 1966), p. 173.

32. *PSZ*, XI, No. 8633, 683-87.

33. Wolff later served as English consul general in St. Petersburg; Reading, *The Anglo-Russian Commercial Treaty*, pp. 44-45, 287. On the English domination of the trade see the statement of the French consul Villardeau in 1731, in Walther Kirchner, "Relations économiques entre la France et la Russie au XVIIIe siècle," *Revue d'histoire économique et sociale*, XXXIX, no. 2 (1961), 161.

A Scottish physician who ministered to Elizabeth I, Dr. James Mounsey, is credited with having introduced the root into England. Throughout much of the eighteenth century, it brought a very good price. Claudius Rondeau (in a letter of Lord Harrington of 31 December 1737) reported that he had tried diligently but failed to acquire rhubarb seeds, or even a plant, "even for a

trading in Russian rhubarb since at least 1732, and the year before their commission the Russian minister in England, Prince Kantemir, received instructions to propose to English merchants the purchase of rhubarb at a price not less than 100 or 150 rubles per *pud*.[34] These agents operated through correspondents *(korrespondenty)* in leading European cities, especially Amsterdam and London, of whom the most important at this time was probably Andrew (Andrei) Pel's (?) in Holland, who in the forties and fifties became the leading contractor for Russian rhubarb sales on the continent and the best source of information on market conditions for the Commerce Collegium, and Samuel Golden in London.

However by the first years of the 1740's, faults began to show in the system and the lean years set in. In 1741 Amsterdam merchants through Pel's ordered 700 *pud* to meet the pent-up demand created by the Swedish war. Only 488 *pud* 17 *funt* were shipped, and even that was not completely sold after five years.[35] Stockpiles began to mount in St. Petersburg and Siberia, enough to gross nearly a million and a half rubles, if it sold favorably in western Europe.[36] Or to look at it another way, the backlog represented ten to fifteen years of good sales.

The Commerce Collegium sent repeated notices to the Senate of deteriorating and rotted rhubarb, all of which was secretly burned "in a favorable place and under dependable scrutiny," but such prudent secrecy seems not to have improved sales.[37] In 1742-44 Pel's apparently disposed of none, in 1745 only 100 *pud*, and in the following year 150 *pud*; in 1746 and 1747 Wolff arranged for 100 *pud* to be shipped to England.[38] Small amounts were also transferred to the Medical Chancellery for use in Russia, and likely some was dispersed in eastern Europe, but by mid-1748 the Commerce Collegium reported of both ungulate and "stone" rhubarb,

---

bribe of 200 ducats." As late as 1777, the eminent Edinburgh physician Sir Alexander Dick (an acknowledged expert on rhubarb) sold his year's crop of nine and one-half pounds for one guinea the pound; John Bell of Antermony, *A Journey from St. Petersburg to Pekin, 1719-22*, p. 108, n.

34. Chulkov, *Istoricheskoe opisanie*, III, bk. 2, 201.

35. *Senatskii arkhiv*, VII, 365. Compare Troitskii, *Finansovaia politika*, p. 173.

36. *Senatskii arkhiv*, VII, 366; also VII, 131-32. By mid-1744 there were 2973 *pud* in St. Petersburg and 4229 in Kiakhta; *ibid.*, VI, 216-18, 281.

37. *Ibid.*, VII, 221, 359.

38. *Ibid.*, VII, 131-32, 221, 370. The prices were somewhat depressed; the 1747 lot of 100 *pud* to London brought only 196 r. per *pud*, somewhat off the usual price.

2113 *pud* stockpiled in St. Petersburg and 4229 *pud* in Siberia—in all 6342 *pud*. And this still left six years of the second Murat contract to run, according to which there was another 3000 *pud* yet to come.[39]

Official Russian sources blame this decline in fortunes heavily on a single cause: new and damaging competition from European suppliers. The French, English, Dutch, Swedish, and Danish all carried greater or lesser amounts of rhubarb from the East, mainly from Canton, although also from Dzhungaria through Smyrna and Aleppo, and invariably sold for prices far below those demanded by the Russians.[40] Compared with the enormous quantities in Russian warehouses, the individual cargoes brought by western ships do not seem exceptionally large. The Commerce Collegium learned that 60 *pud* arrived in Copenhagen on 2 September 1744, to be sold at auction on the twenty-first, from which "disruption" in Russian trade was expected. The next year Dutch and Danish ships brought 234 *pud*; in 1748 Commerce Collegium President, Prince Iusupov, informed the Senate that an Amsterdam newspaper recorded the arrival of a Dutch ship from Canton with 58 *pud*.[41] The low price of the competitive root came from purchase in Canton at figures considerably below those paid by the Russians at the border (a decade earlier Lange reported rhubarb selling in Peking for seven rubles sixty kopeks per *pud* compared with the ten to twenty at the border), together with the extremely inexpensive cost of ship transport, and no doubt quick turnover in the European markets.

But all this suggests something more—malfeasance or misfeasance on the part of the rhubarb bureaucracy in Russia, or at least an intolerably inefficient system of expediting transport and sale. We do know that Svin'in, like so many of his fellow adventurers in Siberia, was caught in a legal web for his failure to account fully for the funds at his disposal. He was arrested in 1745, and over the next several years his accounts were thoroughly investigated, until it was concluded that he misused state funds and forwarded to St. Petersburg an unnecessarily small amount of rhubarb at an unnecessarily high price. It was claimed he connived to do this

39. *Ibid.*, VII, 370.

40. In 1760 a report even had it that European-carried rhubarb from Copenhagen, Amsterdam, and Hamburg could be imported to Riga at a price below that of the Russian-carried; Chulkov, *Istoricheskoe opisanie*, III, bk. 2, 314.

41. *Senatskii arkhiv*, VI, 216-18, VII, 287.

with his agents and assistants *(prikazchiki)*, "among whom for the most part were his relatives."[42] It is impossible to say just what effect this malfeasance by Svin'in had upon the solvency of the rhubarb trade. Suffice it to recall that the opportunities were legion for personal aggrandizement at the expense of the state, and in view of the European competition any needless addition to the cost and hence sale price of the rhubarb obviously placed the Russians at a distinct disadvantage. In the absence of more precise information however, the simpler explanation of bureaucratic mismanagement is probably a truer explanation.

The technical work of selection and bracking seems to have been done well. Prior to the time of Catherine the Great, Kiakhta had only three brackers, Rozing, Rung, and Andrei Brant, and each seems to have done exceptional service. In St. Petersburg on the other end, one man—the apothecary's assistant *(gezel')* Fridrikh Adol'f Meingart—distinguished himself over a period of at least twenty years. Appointed in 1746 to the Commerce Collegium by the Medical Chancellery, he proved so successful that in the next year the Collegium asked that he be posted permanently to the Collegium, which he eventually was, at the rather good salary of 300 rubles per year.[43]

On the higher policy level, however, suspicion of ineptitude is legitimate. The Vice-President of the Collegium (later President) Iakov Evreinov was responsible for the rhubarb trade during the 1740's, and in at least one major way he erred. Permitting such very large stores of rhubarb to accumulate without any reasonable guarantees of sale was a grave miscalculation, both because of certain deterioration after years of storage, and the high costs of warehousing. The notion accepted by the Commerce Collegium and the Senate that contracts for large amounts had to be made with a single Bukharan merchant to assure an adequate supply of clean and dry rhubarb seems, on balance, to have been inaccurate. The Russian state in these years seemingly understood and preferred these kinds of limited monopolistic arrangements, but bargaining on the open market in Mai-mai-ch'eng may well have proved more advantageous, even if a higher price were paid for smaller amounts carefully inspected prior to purchase by the bracker stationed at Kiakhta. Evreinov's record was blemished

42. Silin, *Kiakhta*, p. 53; Chulkov, *Istoricheskoe opisanie*, III, bk. 2, 268-69.
43. *Senatskii arkhiv*, VIII, 200-202.

from this rhubarb business, although there is no evidence that he was reprimanded or disciplined.

A third, although probably minor cause of the disruption of the trade and damage from the saturation of European markets with low-priced root was the persistence of contraband. Throughout the 1740's and 1750's state officials apprehended private persons illicitly carrying rhubarb, but the quantities were always small. In 1745 the Siberian *guberniia* chancellery sent to the Siberian Prikaz ten *pud* twenty-nine *funt* eighty-four *zolotnik* of ungulate and pendunculated rhubarb confiscated in various places in Siberia.[44] Two years earlier the soldier Kostygin was apprehended in Verkhotur'e customs for possessing twenty-two and one-half *funt*, which it turned out he had bought in Iakutsk *uezd*. Instead of death, as stipulated in the edict of 1735, he was knouted and sent to convict labor *(katorga)* in a state factory.[45] Most of the other cases also involved small amounts, the most noteworthy being that of the registered peasant Osenev, who purchased in 1744 and 1747 seventy-five *pud* at the Irbit market fair from Dzhungarians who came there to trade.[46] This enterprising man carried the rhubarb to a village near Moscow and returned to Siberia with Russian goods purchased in Moscow and Kazan'. The rhubarb he secretly sold to a Moscow merchant and to a Smolensk Jewish retailer at sixty rubles per *pud*, certainly a fine profit. The Smolensk merchant was apprended carrying his thirty-seven *pud* out of the country. Even if one multiplies these instances of contraband many times over, it is difficult to believe that serious damage was done to state sales in western European markets.

Still not untypically, the Senate placed great emphasis on the suppression of contraband rhubarb and accepted the proposition that failure to do so had cost the state monopoly dearly. In 1748 the Senate ordered the prohibitions of 1735 republished and specifically directed instructions to all border *gubernii* and provinces to take strong measures to prevent carriage by private persons of any rank or station. The Military Collegium similarly instructed

44. *Ibid.*, VII, 62-63.

45. *Ibid.*, VII, 385-86.

46. *Ibid.*, VIII, 427-29, 435-36. For other cases see *ibid.*, VIII, 90-91, 183-89, 231-33, 266-67, 268-71, 282-83, 386-87, 427, 496, 575, 576-78; *PSZ*, XII, No. 9531, 891-94; XV, No. 11201, 645-46; Chulkov, *Istoricheskoe opisanie*, III, bk. 2, 309-10.

its officers.[47] Three years later the Senate again ordered republication in Russian and German in Riga, Revel', Vyborg, Narva, and on all borders and shores.[48]

The response of the Senate and Commerce Collegium was not limited to these restated prohibitions. As early as 1744 the Governing Senate ordered Count Golovkin, returning to the Hague as the Russian ambassador, to quietly investigate the rhubarb market in Holland, to report on all rhubarb offered for sale, both Russian and foreign, whence it came, whether by land or sea, and at what prices good rhubarb sold.[49] Early that same year the Commerce Collegium, at the Senate's request, temporarily suspended the export abroad of rhubarb, so that an excessive amount would not cause the price of the Russian product to decline.[50] Nonetheless the situation steadily deteriorated in the following three to four years, in spite of the hope spurred by small ladings to Amsterdam and London.

The Senate in 1747 turned to the problem of distribution, and concluded that the Russian rhubarb must be sold directly in other major European cities as well as Amsterdam. It hoped for sale of at least 500 *pud* annually, if not 700 or 800.[51] Pel's reported that sales were doing poorly, but predicted increases in Italy, the German lands, France, and other places, even though of the last lot of thirty-nine boxes, twenty-four were still unsold and four of them were in poor shape. By July 1748 the Senate, on representation of the Commerce Collegium President Boris Grigor'evich Iusupov decided that "utmost need" demanded the preparation by the next spring of 500 *pud* of the "very best rhubarb" for loading on the first ships departing for all those places where there were *komissionary*, with the price fixed in the Amsterdam market at ten gulden per *funt* and in other places (excepting the Baltic littoral) above that only to the extent of added expenses.[52] Even that price might be reduced by two gulden if it helped the rhubarb to move

47. *PSZ*, XII, No. 9493, 853-54.

48. *Ibid.*, XIII, No. 9873, 464-66, dated 12 August 1751, published 2 September; Chulkov, *Istoricheskoe opisanie*, III, bk. 2, 270-73; *Senatskii arkhiv*, VIII, 335-38.

49. *Senatskii arkhiv*, VI, 216-18. It was decided also to send Commerce Collegium councillor Evreinov to Holland in the following year, but it was not done, probably because shipments to Pel's picked up in 1745-46; *ibid.*, VII, 364.

50. Chulkov, *Istoricheskoe opisanie*, III, bk. 2, 261.

51. *Senatskii arkhiv*, VII, 164-65.

52. *Ibid.*, VII, 367-68; VIII, 202; XI, 436.

quickly. All conditions in contracts with local correspondents had to be laid down exactly to avoid future disputes, although they were to have a free hand in sales. The Commerce Collegium of course maintained contact with these agents to keep abreast of changes in the markets. A memorial was sent to the Medical Chancellery to remind them that only Russian rhubarb might be used and no foreign root imported. Foreign competition was severe—". . . in Europe the Canton rhubarb trade increases hour by hour . . . ." Yet the efforts helped little; in 1749 and 1750 only 710 *pud* was shipped to the distributor in Amsterdam, and in 1751 only 200 *pud* and that to England.

The Russians turned elsewhere. In 1747 the Senate experimented with transshipment through the Arab world. Thirty *pud* was sent secretly to Persia through the Russian consul Ivan Danilov so that it would be identified as of Chinese origin rather than Russian.[53] The hope was that it would find its way through Smyrna and Aleppo to Europe at a price not less than forty-five rubles. But even this exotic device proved faulty. In 1751 the consul died and the six boxes of rhubarb were held up in Astrakhan for new orders. A new consul was sent out, a secretary of the Collegium of Foreign Affairs, Petr Chekalevskii, but nothing came of the scheme.[54]

One more little expedient attracted Russian bureaucrats—the cultivation of Tibetan rhubarb in suitable places in Russia. Svin'in had been instructed years earlier to obtain rhubarb seeds if possible, and it seems he did. Then in 1749 his associate and successor Skerletov, now director of the Kiakhta Rhubarb Commission, induced a Bukharan merchant to bring him three *pud* twenty *funt*, which he forwarded quickly to St. Petersburg. The Medical Chancellery tried sowing the seeds in dry regions around Astrakhan, Orenburg, and elsewhere in Siberia. All this was carefully kept most secret, but there is no evidence of observable impact on the markets of Western Europe.[55]

By the early 1750's there was talk of ending the monopoly and turning over the purchase, carriage, and sale of rhubarb to pri-

53. *Ibid.*, VII, 343-46; VIII, 317-21, 389; IX, 184.

54. A report of 1760 noted that the rhubarb in the Astrakhan *guberniia* chancellery "remaining from sale in Persia" was given to the Astrakhan state apothecary at his request; *ibid.*, XI, 421.

55. *Ibid.*, VIII, 398-400; IX, 68. The scheme did succeed in growing medically usable penduncIulate rhubarb in Siberia, however; *PSZ,* XVIII, No. 13081, 484-86.

vate merchants of Russia. Disappointment appeared in nearly every aspect of the monopoly: sales in Western Europe continued to lag, Svin'in and Skerletov had been adjudged to have damaged the purchase of rhubarb and both were gone from the scene; competent and trustworthy men to carry on the operation were not to be found in St. Petersburg or Kiakhta, and in 1753 the contract with Murat was due to expire.[56] In several pronouncements of the Senate in 1751, 1752, and 1753, mention was made of the return of the trade to private hands.[57] Nothing was done for another five years, possibly because hope sprang anew with the order by Pel's in 1753 of twenty to twenty-five boxes of not less than 100 *pud* each, and the Medical Chancellery every now and then requested fifty *pud* for use in the army, navy, and in local apothecary shops. The Senate made it clear that it had no wish to relinquish the monopoly until all of the warehouses of the Commerce Collegium were clear of the disappointing drug.

By the spring of 1758 the Senate came to an overdue decision; it commanded that no more rhubarb be dispatched through the correspondents in St. Petersburg and Amsterdam, but that all remaining in St. Petersburg and Kiakhta be placed on sale for use within Russia, as well as exported abroad at a price not less than 100 rubles per *pud* (plus internal and port duties), much below the price that earlier was gained in western Europe but high enough to cover costs.[58] Eight per cent of the proceeds would be retained by Treasury for insurance and commission fees, and after all stores were disposed free trade would again prevail, with the payment of all customs duties and charges. If this did not solve the problem of surpluses the Senate would at its discretion reduce the price. In Kiakhta alone at this time there were 8,339 *pud*, of which only 3402 were still judged to be in good condition and of good quality, and in St. Petersburg about 900 *pud* and of that only 318 *pud* was bracked first-class root.

In October of 1760 the Senate ordered the public announcement of sale of this crown rhubarb in large quantities or as small as half a *funt* at the rate of 100 rubles per *pud*.[59] A year and a half later,

56. Skerletov died in 1751 and Iakobi requested that another from among the local gentry be appointed in his place. Also since Irkutsk was distant from Kiakhta Iakobi was ordered to appoint a Captain Ostiakov to exercise surveillance over the trade; *Senatskii arkhiv*, VIII, 464-65.

57. *Ibid.*, VIII, 351-54, 468; IX, 129.

58. *Ibid.*, XI, 434-37.

59. *PSZ*, XV, No. 11118, 528-29; *Senatskii arkhiv*, XI, 455.

the Treasury listed still available 3,127 *pud* of good rhubarb and 4,937 of inferior, and the Senate had already lowered the price to sixty rubles, plus duties of sixteen rubles, thirty-two and one-half kopeks.[60] The great liberal commercial ukaz of 31 July 1762, widely accepted as clear evidence of Catherinian economic progressivism, merely promised in its Point Six the release of rhubarb to private trade when the government's rhubarb was disposed of at sixty rubles.[61] Sales of Treasury rhubarb continued slowly thereafter, and the liberal free-trade philosophy of Catherine II to the contrary, the prohibition against private trade continued. In 1763 an English merchant offered to buy thirty to forty boxes, but at only forty-five rubles including customs duties. The Collegium bargained and agreement was struck at fifty-one plus customs duties. Catherine approved the transaction, but cautioned "in the future to attempt to sell more dearly."[62]

Then in 1764 the merchant David Lev Bamberger and his associates of Novorossiisk *guberniia* proposed to purchase all of the crown rhubarb then in St. Petersburg and Moscow and all that would arrive in the next two years.[63] This would amount to 2000 *pud* at sixty rubles, plus customs and port duties, paid for in copper money. The proposition was enticing, and Catherine secretly ordered Selenginsk Commandant Iakobi to continue to purchase rhubarb at sixteen rubles, although not more than 500 *pud* per year. The skilled apothecaries Meingart in St. Petersburg and Brant in Kiakhta were both kept on the job through the 1760's, and on the recommendation of Iakobi a crown apothecary shop *(kazennaia apteka)* was erected in Selenginsk to better serve this trade imminently to be free.[64] The Kiakhta Rhubarb Commission under the direction of Irkutsk merchant Artem Pakholkov continued to inspect all contracts of Russian merchants with Bukharans and to stamp all arriving rhubarb with the crown seal, although in at least one case in these years a private merchant was permitted to carry his contracted rhubarb up to St. Petersburg for

60. *Senatskii arkhiv*, XII, 155-56; XIII, 25-28.

61. *PSZ*, XVI, No. 11630, 33, Ukaz of 28 March, i.e. compiled during the brief reign of Peter III and issued as an Imperial Ukaz on 31 July.

62. *Senatskii arkhiv*, XIII, 280-82. English, German, and Dutch merchants purchased small amounts in 1764, at the negotiated prices of 52 and 53 rubles; *PSZ*, XVI, No. 12144, 729-30.

63. *Senatskii arkhiv*, XIII, 13-14, 70-71; XIV, 246-48.

64. *PSZ*, XVII, No. 12477, 340-341, decree of 21 September 1765; *Senatskii arkhiv*, XIII, 39-40, 47-48.

crown inspection.[65] The Commerce Collegium through the Rhubarb Commission purchased the root at the border at sixteen rubles and offered it for sale in St. Petersburg at sixty as late as 1770.[66] And the Commerce Collegium with imperial permission sold rhubarb within Russia to help cover the running expenses of the Collegium Chancellery.[67] Finally in 1782 private merchants received the right to trade freely in rhubarb.[68] This wondrous drug which strengthened the stomach, diminished the colic, and completely cleared up the flux was one of the last of the state commercial monopolies of the eighteenth century to be abandoned.

Gold and Silver

Simon Svin'in was employed by the Russian state to import rhubarb, but it may well be that his arrangement with Murat Bachim to provide "the very best pure gold" (and later silver as well) was of equal or greater value to the state treasury. By 1738 when Svin'in began procuring bullion from his Asian providers, the state caravans, as we have seen, were already actively seeking Chinese gold and silver in Peking. The explanation for the very great Russian intrest in gold and silver from China lies in Russian monetary policy for the first three decades of the eighteenth century.

As early as 1698, Peter's administration succumbed to the temptation to solve its heavy financial needs by manipulating the monetary system.[69] Partly this was done by debasing coinage, especially silver, the basic or accounting ruble of Russia. The silver ruble before 1698 represented nine and eleven-twelfths *zolotnik* of pure silver, after only six and two-thirds *zolotnik*. In other words, the *stopa* or quantity of money coined from one *funt* of silver was raised. At that time the fineness or *proba* of silver coin was not fixed

65. *Ibid.*, XIII, 35-39.

66. *PSZ*, XIX, No. 13526, 163-64.

67. *Ibid.*, XXI, No. 15533, 694.

68. *Ibid.*, XXI, No. 15169, 133; also see the comment of the Siberian traveller Samuel Bentham (brother of Jeremy) in 1781, in Walther Kirchner, "Samuel Bentham and Siberia," *The Slavonic and East European Review*, XXXVI (June, 1958), 479: the furs exchanged for rhubarb were undervalued by the crown causing the real price for rhubarb to rise and the monopoly to prove unprofitable. Cf. Senate ukazes of 8 March and 31 October 1772, in Chulkov, *Istoricheskoe opisanie*, III, bk. 2, 338.

69. Much of the following historical description of Russia's monetary practice is taken from Troitskii, *Finansovaia politika*, pp. 197-212.

precisely, although it remained about eighty-four fine for some years. In 1718 silver coin was established at seventy fine and thereafter was usually seventy or seventy-seven, a sharp reduction in the actual value of the coin.

In addition to altering the fineness of silver (and other) coins, the Money Court (*Monetnyi* or *Denezhnyi dvor*) also failed to refrain from the issuance of large amounts of coin, especially copper and silver, from which it earned the State Treasury very large profits. Copper began to appear in 1700 in small denominations, and especially during the 1720's it was issued in large amounts. In 1723, for example, copper five-kopek pieces were coined with a value of 500,000 rubles.[70] And the *stopa* of this issue was set at forty rubles from a *pud* of copper, far above the 1704-17 rate of twenty. Later in 1727 Catherine I approved the coinage of even more copper money, still at forty rubles from a *pud*, at which time the value of a *pud* of copper on the open market varied between six and eight rubles. Between 1723 and 1731, copper five-kopek pieces with face value of 3,491,000 rubles were coined, in addition to a largish amount of copper kopeks and polushkas (one-quarter of a kopek). Silver coins were minted in these years with the same disregard for future consequences. In 1725-29, the mint issued silver coinage valued at 3,985,000 rubles. Only gold was coined in small amounts.

On the books the Treasury profited enormously from these monetary practices. In the year 1724 alone, the Treasury's income was recorded as 216,808 rubles, of which 137,210 rubles represented profits from silver coinage. In the following two years, silver coin accounted for state income of 215,974 rubles and 144,915 rubles. In these three years, silver coinage returned nearly half a million rubles to the Treasury! Copper was no less profitable, even though minted almost entirely in small coins. It brought in upwards of 2,000,000 rubles between 1723 and 1731. It seems apparent that without these very great profits the administrations of Peter I and his successors could not have afforded the expanded state activities undertaken in the first quarter of the century: long and costly wars, investment in industry and mines, lavish court functions, etc.

Of course these monetary profits were not without some unhappy and unforeseen consequences. One of these was a tendency

70. *PSZ*, VII, No. 4393, 188, dated 20 December 1723.

for coin of higher fineness, which remained in circulation when debased coinage was issued, to flee the country. In the 1710's it was observed that private merchants carried abroad seventy-seven fine silver coins, rather than the newly minted seventy fine ones. The general shortage of raw metals, the large profits realized in the issuance of debased coins, and the prevailing notion of state wealth as bullion combined to confirm the standing Russian policy prohibiting the private carriage abroad of precious metals in any form, except for small amounts used for personal expenses of merchants. As early as 1693 an ukaz forbade the payment of customs duties in gold, silver, or Albert talers.[71] By edict of 1721, reinforced in 1744, 1751, and during Catherine's reign in 1769, 1782, and 1791, private persons were strictly forbidden to carry abroad any bullion.[72] Close control over the export of Russian bullion and coin remained the steadfast policy of the state, although the reiteration of export prohibitions suggests that the state was not always successful in enforcing the policy.

The other side of the state monopoly of precious metals was the regulation of their import. The Russian state insisted on the monopolization of all imported gold and silver long before the large issues of coin in the 1710's. In 1697, for example, a Petrine ukaz demanded that all of these metals brought into the country by merchants be delivered to the state offices for purchase or be used by the merchants in payment of their customs duties.[73] Also silver *efimki*, especially the Joachim taler, was encouraged for import that it might be stamped for circulation within Russia, melted down and reminted at lower fineness or, as shall be seen below,

71. Cahen, *Histoire*, p. 60.

72. *PSZ*, XII, No. 8940, 105-12, dated 11 May 1744; *ibid.*, XII, No. 8942, 113, dated 17 May 1744; *ibid.*, XII, No. 8985, 173-74, dated 17 July 1744; *ibid.*, XII, No. 9063, 259, dated 9 November 1744; *ibid.*, XIII, No. 9833, 400-403, dated 8 February 1751; *ibid.*, XVIII, No. 13308, 905-6, dated 3 June 1769; *ibid.*, XXIII, No. 17007, 287, dated 23 December 1791; *ibid.*, XXI, No. 15520, 678-81, dated 27 September 1782 (the tariff of 1782).

73. *Ibid.*, III, No. 1606, 410-11, dated 5 December 1697/7206. In 1711 the Merchants' Chamber *(Kupetskaia palata)* was established to purchase gold, silver, copper, and other coin for conversion into newly minted Russian money. The Money Court or Mint (*Monetnyi* or *Denezhnyi dvor*) accomplished the actual smelting and minting. It was composed originally of three elected merchants and was subordinate to the Chancellery of the Governing Senate. It lasted until 1728 when its functions were taken over by the newly created Money Office *(Monetnaia kontora)* in Moscow. In 1734 the Money Office became the Money Chancellery with its director in St. Petersburg.

exported to China to purchase pure Chinese silver or gold.[74] And Chinese gold and silver were sought after from the earliest days of Russian penetration in Asia. Both Spafarii and Golovin on their missions to China carried invitations to Chinese representatives to visit Moscow with gold and silver, which the Imperial Treasury guaranteed to buy from them. It will be recalled that the state caravans to Peking after 1727 persisted in carrying some Russian coin for the purchase of Chinese pure gold and silver and, in addition, attempted to exchange goods or *efimki* for bullion. The Tret'iakov-Molokov caravan brought back 65,400 rubles in bullion, most of which was obtained from exchanging Russian goods, and the next—the Molokov—caravan took with it over 168 *pud* of *efimki,* worth 114,893 rubles, but from what is known had far less success than its predecessor. Later caravans probably also acquired some Chinese bullion, although in all likelihood in smaller quantities, for the Chinese grew cautious about permitting its export.

The Treasury experienced a severe shortage of precious metals by the 1720's as a result of the heavy issue of new coin, which contributed to the easing of restrictions on the private importation of gold and silver. It will be recalled that this coincided with the loosening of a wide variety of restraints on private trade and the release to private merchants of many goods in foreign trade earlier reserved to the state. The problem simply was that the "gold fever" of the 1710's had failed to lead to the discovery of new mines of gold and silver adequate for the enlarged monetary demands of Russia. Consequently foreign bullion and coin became increasingly important to the Treasury and the Money Court. State missions and commercial ventures such as the Peking caravans apparently were unable, as we have noted, to supply enough of the metals; the only remaining solution was to encourage the private importation of gold and silver, from both East and West, although at the same time making every effort to insure that it passed into the hands of the Treasury. In 1723 gold and silver were declared free for import without customs duties.[75] The sole requirement was that the merchants must turn over all of the metals to the Money Court in exchange for Russian coin, failure to do so carrying the death penalty. Even this requirement was lifted four years later as a

74. Pashkov, *Istoriia russkoi ekonomicheskoi mysli,* Vol. I: *Epokha feodalizma;* Chast' 1: *IX-XVII vv.,* p. 287.

75. *PSZ,* VII, No. 4397, 189, dated 20 December 1723.

further and reasonably drastic enticement to induce merchants to return to Russia with more foreign coin and bullion and fewer goods; after June 1727 private merchants could legally sell imported gold and silver to private persons within Russia.[76]

No one of these contrivances nor all of them together provided a solution to the deepening monetary problems of the Russian state in the 1730's. The Treasury reached the point at which it could no longer issue metal coin in the large amounts it had in the previous decade. Nor could it have the Money Court recall substantial amounts of the debased coin in circulation, for it did not have the precious metal on hand to purchase it. The Treasury was impoverished and the monetary system badly needed reorganization. A special commission was created in 1730, partly state official in composition (Musin-Pushkin, Tatishchev, etc.) and partly private merchant (Solov'ev, the Evreinovs, etc.), charged with finding the means by which to withdraw from circulation especially the nearly worthless copper coin.[77] It was soon obvious that no clear solution upon which all could agree was available, but in 1731 the commission did propose the issue of a new copper coin minted at the rate of ten rubles from a *pud* which was to be exchanged for the copper already in circulation minted forty rubles from a *pud*. The losses to the Treasury of this operation were major, some 2,500,000 rubles, and it was soon abandoned.

Silver received equal attention. At this time all silver coin was fixed at seventy-seven fine and by decrees of 1731 and 1734 the Treasury began withdrawing from circulation all silver money issued in the first two decades of the century in order to remint it at the standardized fineness.[78] The recalling and reminting of silver coin went on for several decades, from which, it appears, the Treasury profited, although, according to Troitskii, it is not possible now to determine with any exactitude how great these profits were.[79] It is certain, however, that the Treasury was persistently in difficulty, that there was continued pressure to withdraw copper entirely from circulation (although it was never done and in fact more copper was issued), and that pure silver was always in short supply. It is in the context of these monetary difficulties that Rus-

76. *Ibid.*, VII, No. 5110, 819-21, dated 26 June 1727. Also to be found in *Sbornik ukazov po monetnomu i medal'nomu delu*, I, 112.

77. *PSZ*, VIII, No. 5578, 294, dated 19 June 1730.

78. *Ibid.*, VIII, No. 5677, 366-67, dated 22 January 1731.

79. Troitskii, *Finansovaia politika*, p. 203.

sian state efforts to acquire silver (and also at times gold) from Chinese lands must be seen.

Svin'in's contract with Murat in 1738 was by no means the first attempt of the Russian administration to acquire both gold and silver at the border. For example, Irkutsk Vice-Governor Pleshcheev reported, late in 1735, the purchase of 15,000 *liang* worth of commercial or "khanish" silver, of which he sent 116 *liang* five *chin* (ten *funt* fifty-four *zolotnik* in Russian weight) to the Cabinet in St. Petersburg.[80] Pleshcheev remarked that the price was very favorable, one ruble per *liang*, and he announced that he hoped to purchase an additional 50,000 *liang* in the future. The Cabinet heartily concurred in the project, although cautioned Pleshcheev not to pay over that price. All Chinese silver already acquired at the border and any obtained thereafter, the Cabinet stressed, had to be sent immediately to Moscow for conversion into Russian coin at the Money Chancellery. There is no record of further purchases of silver by Pleshcheev, but again in 1744 the Senate decided to try to buy silver abroad, in Persia and on the Chinese border.[81] Vice-Governor Lange was instructed to purchase Chinese commercial silver in Kiakhta-Mai-mai-ch'eng, or in any other places he could, exchanging for it Russian goods whenever possible.

From 1738 on, it was through Simon Svin'in, rather than the Peking caravans or the state's officers in Transbaikalia, that the Treasury attempted to acquire large amounts of both gold and silver. Initially gold was the main commodity, not because silver was unneeded, but only because the Bukharan Murat Bachin first proposed the sale of gold. It will be recalled that some gold coin continued to circulate in Russia in these years. Svin'in proposed to Murat that the latter supply him with pure gold in quantities as large as his superiors wanted at the rate of two rubles per *zolotnik*. He recommended to St. Petersburg that the operation be kept informal and secret, that no contract as such be drawn up. His reason was that private merchants trading at Kiakhta already had a difficult time carrying on profitable trade, and the knowledge that they now faced state competition at the border as well as in Peking was not likely to be received with great joy. This solicitude for the Kiakhta merchants is now wholly persuasive; it is probable

80. *PSZ*, IX, No. 6843, 654, dated 16 December 1735; also in *Sbornik ukazov po monetnomu i medal'nomu delu*, I, 230-31.

81. *PSZ*, XII, No. 8898, 48-50, dated 15 March 1744; see also Silin, *Kiakhta*, p. 56.

that Svin'in felt far more comfortable in far off Siberia unhindered by contracts precisely drawn. He argued that it was better for the state to openly barter goods and Russian coin for any gold that was brought to the frontier by any supplier.

The Tsaritsa's Cabinet, after assay of two small gold pieces forwarded by Svin'in and as thorough as possible an investigation of the merits of buying from Murat, rejected Svin'in's request for a free hand, and ordered him at the end of 1738 to contract with the Mongol for an initial delivery of not less than ten and not more than twenty *pud* of gold at the price proposed.[82] If Murat Bachin wished Russian goods in return, the Vice-Governor of Irkutsk was to provide any not needed for carriage in the Peking caravan; if he insisted on money, the Siberian *guberniia* office was to provide coin. To test the purity of the gold, a learned assay master was ordered sent to aid Svin'in. All gold acquired was to be dispatched without delay to the Money Chancellery for conversion into Russian coin. In all of these operations, the Cabinet stressed the need for "utmost secrecy."

The Mongol's price was very favorable, according to the Money Chancellery's calculations. After deduction of the cost of transportation, smelting, and minting, a profit of 1356 rubles from each *pud* of pure gold could be expected, or thirty-three and five-twelfths kopeks profit for each ten-ruble gold piece *(chervonets)* coined. Hence Svin'in and his assistant Skerletov contracted with Murat in October 1739 for twelve *pud* of gold of purity equal to the samples he had given them earlier to be imported during the next three years at the price of one ruble eighty kopeks per *zolotnik.* The Senators were delighted: even more, if Russian goods were to be exchanged for the Bukharan gold, no Russian silver coin would be lost abroad, and on the goods exported, the Treasury could charge the usual customs duties and bring even more gain to the state.

This bright beginning of the importation of precious metal from Chinese dominions did not last long. It soon became obvious that much silver coin (presumably the less fine issues) was necessary to obtain the amount of gold desired by the Treasury. The Cabinet arranged for Svin'in to secure as much silver as he needed, but the contract with Murat did not produce the results so fondly hoped.

82. *Sbornik RIO,* CXXIV (1906), 487-89, also 247, a Cabinet decree signed by Andrei Osterman and Artemii Volynskii. See also *Senatskii arkhiv,* II, 2, 19-20.

In 1739 the Irkutsk Chancellery provided Svin'in with 13,824 rubles in silver with which to purchase two *pud* of gold, and gave him to understand that were that sum insufficient he had permission to use some unneeded pelts gathered for the Peking caravan.[83] The Chancellery was in no position to undertake this kind of subvention long however, a fact that was brought to the attention of the Senate. The Senate admitted that the Irkutsk Chancellery, usually short of funds, already contributed to the expenses of the Peking caravan and helped pay the salaries of many of the members of the Kamchatka Expedition, but found no better source of funds than the receipts of the Siberian *guberniia* which came to the Siberian Prikaz. So important did the Senate consider the acquisition of this gold, that it ordered the Money Chancellery to forward whatever funds it could put its hands on, when and if Siberian *guberniia* funds were exhausted.

Yet it does not seem to have been a shortage of cash and goods that proved to be the main impediment to the financial success of this state business. For reasons not entirely certain, Svin'in apparently was unable to carry out his end of the transactions. At the end of the contract period, 15 October 1743, he had forwarded to Moscow only a small amount of gold, and reported that he had on hand at the border an additional eleven *funt* sixty-one and three-quarters *zolotnik*, i.e. gold of a total value of 2011 rubles 5 kopeks.[84] But he had been given 39,174 rubles from the funds of the Siberian *guberniia* and 3552 rubles in expense money. Svin'in was not able to account for all of these funds, and shortly he was arrested.

It was at this point that St. Petersburg authorities turned to Lange. The Money Chancellery, the Treasury, and the Senate had for some years considered a variety of projects for ridding the country of the debased copper coinage and of small silver money as well. Most of these required increased use of silver coin. The need for pure silver was greater than ever by this time (March 1744), for the Money Chancellery reported that in its St. Petersburg and Moscow coffers was over 712 *pud* (about 25,700 pounds!) of silver alloy which it considered could not economically be brought up to the prescribed commercial fineness by smelting. Hence *efimki* or other high-test silver was needed to mix with it. The Com-

83. *Sbornik RIO*, CXXXVIII (1912), 123-24.
84. *Senatskii arkhiv*, V, 321; VI, 142-45, 265-66.

merce Collegium attempted to acquire as much silver as possible in return for Russian goods marketed in Amsterdam, but Acting State Councillor Golitsyn estimated that it would take five years to accumulate the 5,432 *pud* of *efimki* required for the conversion. The only immediate solution was to buy as much Persian and Chinese silver as possible; Lange was instructed to purchase all he could at the border.[85]

We do not know what success Lange had in securing silver from Chinese lands, but it can be noted that in later years the Russian state repeatedly ordered that both gold and silver be purchased whenever and wherever they were available in the East. In 1751, for example, Bukharan merchants brought small quantities of both to the Orenburg Line, and the Senate instructed that it be purchased by the Treasury with *guberniia* funds and that an assay master be sent to test its purity.[86] The price per *zolotnik* was one ruble for the gold and nine kopeks for the silver. Trusevich cites, without acceptable documentation, many other instances in the 1750's and 1760's of small quantities of gold and silver in various forms—ingots, bars, coin, and gold dust—purchased from Bukharan merchants, mostly it would seem on the Orenburg Line and in its vicinity.[87]

All in all the state's attempt to regulate the circulation of precious metals in the China trade appears to have met with little greater success than did the rhubarb monopoly. It is virtually impossible to detail the fiscal impact of gold and silver purchases at the Mongol border and by the caravans in Peking on the monetary situation of Russia in the middle half of the eighteenth century. The evidence strongly suggests that the total amounts of precious metals actually imported from Chinese dominions were far less than desired, needed, and anticipated by the Treasury. The cashiering of Svin'in further suggests that his most important and promising effort to secure Chinese gold and silver was ineptly and perhaps dishonestly managed, although it is now not possible to judge conclusively whether or not another official of the rectitude and ingenuity of a Lange could have succeeded in importing the very large quantities necessary to have had a significant effect

85. *PSZ*, XII, No. 8898, 48-50, dated 15 March 1744.

86. *Senatskii arkhiv*, VIII, 309-10.

87. Trusevich, *Posol'skiia i torgovliia snosheniia*, p. 103; see also Grigorii Nikolaevich Potanin, "O karavannoi torgovle s dzhungarskoi Bukhariei v XVIII stoletii," *Chteniia OIDR*, Bk. 2 (1868), 68.

on the Treasury's staggering problem. It seems difficult to imagine that the Chinese court would have permitted the leakage of very large amounts of gold or silver; in fact it does seem that later Peking caravans had far less success in obtaining the metals than did the first two or three after the Treaty of Kiakhta. In any event, it is reasonable to conclude that the attempt of the Russian state to reserve for itself what appeared to be a most productive source of gold and silver failed to develop a trade sufficiently large to have a significant effect on the continuing monetary distress of the country, a distress which led in the 1760's to the issuance of large amounts of paper currency. Some gold and silver was imported by private merchants through Kiakhta throughout the century, most of which the Treasury was able to acquire. And there must have been some illicit importation as well, but it cannot be established how much.

Silk

At one time or another, silk—its importation and manufacture—was granted as a special privilege to favored private petitioners, but the state itself never assumed the exclusive right to make or to trade in this fine fabric. As early as 1717 Peter the Great gave the monopoly of the processing of silk and silk brocades in Russia to the Muscovite merchant Ivan Evreinov and his colleagues.[88] Twenty years later, when the privilege was up for renewal, Evreinov, on his petition, was granted a very great commercial advantage over all other merchants trading at the frontier; he was permitted to ship Russian merchandise up to 10,000 rubles in value with the Peking caravans.[89] These goods were to be exchanged for silks only, and even then under the close scrutiny of the caravan chief so that these private exchanges did no harm to the state's trade. Evreinov's petition argued that his newly founded Moscow silk

88. Evreinov was a member of the Moscow "merchants' hundred."

Other than China, Persia was the great supplier of raw silk to Russian mills. In 1724 Peter gave to Armenian merchants the monopoly of Persian silk trade on reasonable terms of 3 per cent transit duty. These Armenians also had the sole right to carry European goods to Persia, and doing so were exempt from the usual heavy customs duties (25-75 per cent) placed on all goods to Persia. Most of their imported silks were transshipped to Holland, at least at this time.

89. Chulkov, *Istoricheskoe opisanie,* III, bk. 2, 228; *PSZ,* X, No. 7217, 97, Imperial resolution dated 1 April 1737.

mill had not been able to acquire sufficient quantities of fine silk for processing, not even by trading at Kiakhta-Mai-mai-ch'eng, where, he claimed, the finest raw and semi-processed silks did not appear. Evreinov asked also that his silk imports be charged no duties, but Anna did not see fit to give up customs income. There were, after 1737, only three caravans to Peking, and the absence of account books for them leaves it uncertain as to whether Evreinov used his privilege. If he did, border trade probably suffered little. Then too, Evreinov's prerogatives were primarily manufacturing rather than mercantile in function; they were intended to spur silk processing in Russia.

Sixteen years later (1753) the situation in silk seems to have been about the same. Fine silks suitable for processing were in short supply, according to the testimony of the Manufacturing Collegium *(Manufaktur-kollegiia)*, and were high priced. Consequently on petition of an Armenian merchant from Astrakhan, Artemii Nazaretov, no customs duties were collected on the silks he imported, probably from Persia, for sale to Russian silk mills.[90] Again in 1756 the Senate lifted customs duties from Italian and Persian silks intended for processing.[91]

Not until 1759 did silk become the exclusive commercial monopoly of the Chief Inspector *(Ober-inspektor)* Nikita Shemiakin.[92] Earlier he held on farm the right to import finished silks and silk products from Europe, but now he prevailed upon the Senate to grant him a thirty-year monopoly to bring into the country all sorts of silks and to export all those that proved unsuitable for milling. Both imports and exports were without customs duties. Furthermore, he could export prohibited Siberian pelts: sea otter, all

90. *Ibid.*, XIII, No. 10090, 820-22, dated 2 April 1753.

91. *Ibid.*, XIV, No. 10532, 536-37, dated 2 April 1756.

92. *Ibid.*, XV, No. 10803, 166-71, dated 3 March 1758; XV, No. 11028, 417-20, dated 28 January 1760; XVI, No. 11630, 31-38, dated 31 July 1762; Chulkov, *Istoricheskoe opisanie*, III, bk. 2, 307-8. Exceptions were made in Shemiakin's monopoly. Those silk mills and factories already in existence could continue to import on their own, but only enough for their use. Merchant associations which had been importing Persian silks in the Caspian area were, until further notice, permitted to continue to do so, also. Mainly Shemiakin's prerogative concerned the import of Chinese silks and Italian silks through Turkey and Poland. Shemiakin was the merchant who, as head of the Temernikov Company, obtained in 1755 a monopoly of all Black Sea trade, and two years later petitioned for and obtained for six years a farm for the collection of all customs duties in the Black Sea area in return for a payment of 170,000 rubles annually (150,000 rubles to Her Imperial Majesty and 20,000 rubles to the newly established University of Moscow); Lodyzhenskii, *Istoriia* pp. 93-94.

varieties of squirrel, and Ukrainian and other sheepskins. Shemiakin persuaded the Senate that the small silk mills which had existed for long in Russia had never fulfilled their promise. In part the reason was that each mill entrepreneur was required to be simultaneously his own merchant, dyer, weaver, and distributor, which was patently impossible in view of the heavy capital outlay required for any one of these operations. Hence the mills never enjoyed a regular and reasonably priced supply of silks. He intended, he professed, to rectify this "idiocy" in the business.

The Chief Inspector had little time to profit from his special privileges. In 1762 Catherine approved the return of silk imports to private trade open to all interested, with of course the payment of the normal high customs duties.[93]

Tobacco

Trade in tobacco was one of the earliest of the Petrine monopolies farmed out to private persons. The farm was held briefly by the Russian Bogdanov, and then in 1698 given over in London by Golovin and Lefort to Sir Thomas Osborne, Marquis de Carmarthen, whom Peter had met and liked.[94] Osborne enjoyed the exclusive privilege of importing tobacco from the New World through Arkhangel'sk to Siberia, eventually six thousand barrels per year, five hundred pounds to each barrel. Upon the importation to Russia of the first three thousand barrels he was to pay the Treasury £12,000 sterling, and thereafter to supply the Russian court annually with a thousand leaves of the finest tobacco he could acquire. Infringement on this monopoly carried harsh penalties, including confiscation of one's property, half of which went to the state and half to the monopolist. Not long thereafter the Russian state resumed the tobacco farm for itself, until it was declared in free trade in 1727.

Tobacco was potentially an extremely lucrative monopoly. From the early seventeenth century, addiction to the weed spread rapidly from China to her neighbors and into Siberia. By the end of the century its use was firmly established among Siberians, and regarded, as in China, of multiple value: a good snake bite remedy,

93. *PSZ*, XVI, No. 11630, 31-38, point 11.

94. *Ibid.*, III, No. 1637, 457, dated 11 July 1698/7206. Also see Cahen, *Histoire*, pp. 63-64; and Reading, *The Anglo-Russian Commercial Treaty*, pp. 35-36.

an antidote for certain afflictions, a destroyer of insects, a stupifier of fish. Siberian smoking habits were similar to those of the Chinese. Laufer describes the technique of the Ostiaks of the Ob' region:

> They first filled their mouth with water, and lighting a pipe, swallowed the smoke together with the water. An observer of that time [the seventeenth century] relates that, when they had their first pipe in the morning, they fell to the ground as though attacked by an epileptic fit, as the smoke they had swallowed took their breath away. They were in the habit of smoking only when seated. . . .[95]

Many accounts agree that the Siberians preferred Chinese tobacco to western varieties. Hence the importation there of American leaf, either through England and Russia or the Philippines and China, had to face competition with Chinese and Mongol forms, and so the Russian state in 1701 prohibited the latter under penalty of fine and confiscation. The most popular was Chinese tobacco in balled or rolled form *(shar)*, which throughout these years remained interdicted, although it continued to be carried clandestinely. Chinese tobacco did not share fully in the broad emancipation of interdicted items in 1727, although the state gave up its exclusive monopoly over the importation to Siberia of Circassian and other tobacco leaves.[96] Circassian tobacco from the Ukraine could now be traded freely throughout all of Russia and Siberia, with the payment of customs duties.[97]

Tobacco remained in free trade from 1727 to 1748. In the latter year, the Senate said that the state made "little profit" during these two decades, and gave out tobacco on farm to the Moscow merchant Kozma Matveev and his associates.[98] These farmers carried

95. Berthold Laufer, *Tobacco and Its Use in Asia* ("Anthropology Leaflet," 18 [Chicago: Field Museum of Natural History, 1924]), p. 16. Trusevich (*Posol'skiia i torgovliia snosheniia*, p. 104) quotes this homely description without citing its source: "They [Siberians] began to smoke as young boys, as well as young girls, from ten to twelve years of age; adults smoked at least twenty *ganz* (a Chinese pipe) in a day, [and] since [they were] unaccustomed [to it] or smoked too much, [after] puffing two or three times fell in convulsions on the floor and lay in such a state for half an hour, and when from [dousing with] cold water returned finally to themselves—again fell to smoking."

96. *PSZ*, VII, No. 5110, 821, Point 10, dated 26 June 1727.

97. *Ibid.*, VII, No. 5164, 865-68, dated 26 September 1727.

98. *Ibid.*, XII, No. 9543, 904-11, dated 24 October 1748.

rolled and packaged Circassian smoking tobacco to all cities and towns of Siberia and Great Russia for which they paid 42,891 rubles 6¼ kopeks annually to the Treasury and the existing customs duties as well. Chinese tobacco balls were still forbidden.

The St. Petersburg merchant L. A. Gorbylev petitioned the Senate in 1752 that he be granted the farm for the sale of all tobaccos in Russia. He noted that in 1748 when Matveev was given the monopoly the latter had passed on to him the privilege of tobacco sales in the St. Petersburg *guberniia* and in the Baltic region. Since he owned his own tobacco factories, he would sustain great loss if the monopoly were given over to anyone else. Minimally he requested that he be permitted sole rights to trade in tobacco in the territories given him by Matveev, plus Novgorod *guberniia,* unless Matveev's prerogative were dropped, in which case Gorbylev desired to assume the entire monopoly for a ten-year period. He promised to return to the Treasury 27,608 rubles 93 kopeks annually, considerably less than others paid for the monopoly but probably far more than the state had been earning from duties assessed on private trade before 1748. Gorbylev received his farm, but for only four years.

The General-Field Marshall Count Shuvalov then induced Elizabeth in 1758 to give him and his heirs the right for twenty years to import Chinese and other tobacco.[99] He paid 70,000 rubles annually for the privilege, a measure of the tenacity of Siberian predilection for the Chinese style of smoking and the contemporary assessment of the Siberian market. Shuvalov's privilege fell with so many others in 1762. Point 20 of that famed ukaz ended the monopoly and permitted all who wished to trade in tobacco. In order that the state's income would not drop below 70,000 rubles, customs duties four times higher than usual were charged (twenty kopeks per ruble instead of the usual five), to be paid in Russian specie, not *efimki.*[100] The following year, on recommendation of Selenginsk Commandant Iakobi, very heavy duties were laid on Chinese tobacco, ten kopeks per *funt* (a *funt* at this time was usually imported for twenty-five to fifty kopeks), to assure a good profit to the state.[101] For the remainder of the century, tobacco was a

99. *Senatskii arkhiv,* XIII, 373-74.

100. *PSZ,* XVI, No. 11630, 38.

101. *Ibid.,* XVI, No. 11968, 421, imperially approved report of the Senate dated 17 November 1763; Chulkov, *Istoricheskoe opisanie,* III, bk. 2, 330-31; *Senatskii arkhiv,* XIII, 373-74.

free commodity in trade; Chinese balls were usually imported in amounts of 1000 to 2000 *pud* annually, bringing the Treasury a substantial revenue but nothing close to 70,000 rubles per year.

Siberian Furs and Other Hides

State monopoly of the finest Siberian pelts was intimately, although not exclusively, connected with the Peking caravan, as we have indicated earlier. With the decision in 1731 to continue the caravans, the furs that sold best in Peking were forbidden to private carriage, as it had to be in view of the extreme difficulty throughout all the eighteenth century of the caravans to compete with Siberian furs carried to the Chinese by private traders. The various reiterations of the monopoly were usually made just before the departure of a new caravan and included, at one time or another, sea otter, lynx, Nerchinsk and Iakutsk squirrel, fox of many varieties, and Kamchatka and Iakutsk sable. Since these furs were the staple commodity, in fact the *raison d'être* of the journey to Peking, their monopoly by the state was crucial to its enterprise and constricting, to say the least, on the growth of licit private trade in Siberia and with Chinese lands. Even as late as 1760 the Irkutsk Magistracy refused to permit an Irkutsk merchant Bechevin traffic in sea otter. All peltry was included within the 1762 edict on free trade.

In addition to pelts, raw and unfinished hides (sheepskins, etc.) were at various times prohibited. Peter in 1721 first included untanned hides among the items interdicted for export abroad, although shortly after his death, on 24 May 1725, carriage was permitted, and continued to be free for a dozen years. The purpose of Peter's decree (and all subsequent prohibitions) was not to reserve a valuable commodity to the state, but to protect one of Russia's struggling industries, the tanning and preparation of hides. Processed and finished Russian hides *(iuft')* were popular both in Europe and China, as well as elsewhere. In 1737 an imperial ukaz forbade export of unfinished hides, instructing those who wished to trade in them to deliver them to tanneries for purchase.[102] In another seven years the prohibition was repeated, with the argument that Russia had only one (!) hide factory, and Rus-

102. *PSZ*, X, No. 7183, 55, dated 22 February 1737. Chamois *(losina)* had already the year before been limited to military use for making jackets and breeches. Also, *ibid.*, X, No. 7666, 628-30, dated 7 October 1738.

sian merchants trading *iuft'* abroad were suffering great loss from the competition.[103] However the edict was primarily directed not to the East, but to merchants in Riga, Revel', etc. In 1749 the Senate forbade the carriage abroad of sheepskin *(ovchina),* sheep's wool, and the live animals themselves, but again this seems to have been concerned with the European markets, not the Chinese and reason for it was given as the shortage of sheep products for use by Her Majesty's armies.[104]

The importance of pelts and hides to both the state and the Siberian merchant is beyond question. In Catherinian times the two together almost always comprised upwards of 85 per cent of all Russian barter with the Chinese. More shall be said later of the suppressive effect laid upon private trade between Russia and China by these state prohibitions.

Sundry

There were other items that the state refused to let be exchanged with Chinese or Mongol merchants, but in no cases were they of major commercial value, and in all cases the limitations were not of a commercial nature. Several times during the eighteenth century, for example, cattle and horses could not be driven across the border for sale, but the reasons were the shortage of stock in Siberia, and, at times, the danger of Russia being drawn into the recurrent Chinese-Dzhungarian conflict by seeming to favor one side or the other through the sale of desperately needed draft and food animals. Peter the Great first declared cattle nonexportable, and later in 1736 and in 1758-59 it came up again; between these years local border officials often resurrected the previous decrees.[105] The enforcement of these prohibitions seems not to have been very rigid, for local Siberian officials and St. Petersburg offices recognized that raising and sale of cattle, horses, and sheep constituted one of the most important, in truth, almost the only source of income for the primitive Siberian natives living in the vicinity of the border.

Finally saltpeter and other military paraphernalia were ordinarily

103. *Ibid.*, XII, No. 8850, 2, dated 7 January 1744.

104. *Ibid.*, XII, No. 9657, 119-20, dated 14 August 1749.

105. *Ibid.*, IX, No. 7002, 872-73, dated 3 July 1736; *Senatskii arkhiv,* VIII, 116; X, 595; XI, 36-38.

interdicted (as did the Chinese on their side). Grains occasionally were included on the forbidden list, but evidently only in those years following failure in the harvests. At least once in the 1740's, the Tobol'sk merchant Iakov Nikitich Maslov was reprimanded for selling a Christian cross to a Tatar; his error was in allowing this holy thing to fall into idolatrous hands. A general Senate ukaz issued on the advice of the Holy Governing Synod, strongly rejected the practice of sale or giving of any holy relics to Tatars or any other infidels.[106]

The state's handling of those items prohibited to private trade for economic or fiscal reasons was varied and inconsistent, and it is of limited value to generate patterns or generalizations which seem to incorporate them all. Some, such as rhubarb and precious metals, were closely guarded by the state's offices and administered wholly or nearly so by its officers. They did not enjoy great prosperity, taken all in all. The acquisition of rhubarb was well handled, the activities of Svin'in excepted, but by the 1740's it became evident that the problems of distribution and sale, particularly in Western Europe, was by no means solved. The monopoly must be considered to have been profitable for the first twelve years after 1731, but then it became a millstone the state could not bring itself to cast off until long after it proved to be uneconomic. In spite of endless difficulties in getting rid of warehoused rhubarb, the state persisted in the hope that the highly profitable days of the 1730's would return. They never did. Whether the entire monopoly might have proved more successful after the 1740's if turned over on farm to one or more private monopolists is problematical. Private merchants would likely have had little more success in developing the sales contacts and mechanism in Western Europe at least. And like the Russian state, they may well have had to come to depend heavily upon European agents, a practice the state found to be highly unsatisfactory. Were the rhubarb monopoly abolished by the mid-1740's when it had begun to founder, it is quite possible the state could have realized greater profits by effective collection of customs duties on trade carried on by competing private traders. But even that can now be considered only a possibility.

Tobacco, on the other hand, when prohibited to private trade was granted on farm to private persons, Russian and foreign. The

106. Chulkov, *Istoricheskoe opisanie,* III, bk. 2, 261-62.

incomplete data assembled by S. M. Troitskii suggest that the State Treasury profited far more during those years when tobacco trade was farmed that when it was free to all private merchants (1728-48).[107] An incomplete survey by the Senate recorded state revenues from the taxation of tobacco trade between 1728 and 1736 as being 54,116 rubles 96 kopeks.[108] Yet in those same years the arrears in customs duties collection amounted to more than five times the sum actually collected, 285,994 rubles 48 kopeks, i.e. for reasons that are not revealed the state proved unable to collect the largest part of the duties assessed on the private trade in tobacco. What is suggested here is that the state apparatus more easily and effectively could collect the dues owed it by a single trade farmer than it could the customs duties levied against a large number of private traders. The state could have earned far more by improving and tightening its customs administration than by farming out trade in tobacco, but it chose the latter. Several times during the 1730's and 1740's it attempted to find another farmer, but to no avail until the end of the latter decade. By the time the merchant Matveev came forth to undertake the monopoly customs duties on tobacco were in arrears to the extent of 631,401 rubles! It seems safe to conclude that the State Treasury profited substantially from the farming of tobacco, but at the same time the state missed the opportunity to secure far larger profits.

Finally, there is the case of precious metals. The state's monopolization of much of the trade in gold and silver with the Chinese was not, of course, a usual sort of commercial monopoly, since it was a function of the state's exclusive right to mint and issue currency for the country. As far as we can judge, the officials of the state, including Svin'in and Lange, failed to secure sufficient quantities of gold and silver to have a noticeable impact on the state's monetary debacle. It seems doubtful that it would have made any difference whether or not the state positively encouraged the private import of those metals and guaranteed private merchants a good return on all gold and silver sold to the State Treasury. The Manchu court was not likely to permit its metals to escape the country in the quantities necessary to bring large profits to the Russian Treasury or to help to place Russian currency on a strong metal base.

107. Troitskii, *Finansovaia politika*, pp. 174-75.
108. *Sbornik RIO*, CXLVI (1916), 351.

Chapter VI. Private Border Trade to 1762

In spite of his intimate association with the state caravan and his strong support for its vigorous resumption, Vladislavich was no less concerned with the health and vitality of private trade at Kiakhta, and for that matter at Tsurukhaitu as well. He commented on the loss of state revenues occasioned by Russian merchants trading within Chinese dominions in Urga and Naun, and on the failure of the state to route them through customs barriers. For the merchants themselves, he predicted that removal of their trade to the two new border towns would reduce their transportation costs and induce many more to take part in profitable trade with the Chinese and Mongols. To be sure he advised that only Siberians—no European Russians or foreigners—be permitted to trade with the Chinese at the border; this would improve the depressed economic condition of the natives and likely induce the carriage of more Siberian peltry to European Russia, Poland, Persia, Turkey, and Western Europe. Save for this last, Vladislavich's fondest hopes were fulfilled, but not for several decades.

At the end of August, 1728, the new Selenginsk Chancellery published an announcement to all Russian merchant people inviting them to bring their goods for barter at Kiakhta:

> Those who desire . . . to go for trade in the newly-built trading suburb of Kiakhta, [after] declaring their goods in the Selenginsk customs house and taking an extract [a copy of the merchandise inventory], go by the highway from Selenginsk to the border marker through the Kiakhta gate without delay, where Chinese and Mongol merchants will arrive for the exchange of merchandise. . .[1]

Russian merchants were invited to trade in all goods except foodstuffs *(provianty)* and peltry. The day before this announcement, Selenginsk received a letter from the dzarguchei at Urga asking when the Russian merchants might be expected to gather at the border, at which time Chinese would bring their goods, some of

1. Published on 20 August 1728 by the Chancellery of the General Border Administration *(Kantseliariia general'nago pogranichnago pravleniia)*; Sychevskii, *Chteniia OIDR*, Bk. 2 (April-June, 1875), 223-24.

them having already arrived at Urga.[2] Proprieties notwithstanding, few merchants on either side came to the rude frontier posts for trade. By 11 September 1728 ten Russians had appeared in ones and twos, but on the other side only four iurts of Mongols came, with some goods and some animals to sell. The first active trade was Russian purchase of several Mongol ponies, horned cattle, and sheep, upon which were paid five kopeks duties. There was no rush of either Russians or Chinese to take part in this great meeting of commercial civilizations.

Before the end of the year, the Urga dzarguchei informed the Russians that the transfer of trade from Urga to Kiakhta-Mai-mai-ch'eng displeased many of the Chinese merchants with whom they had bartered earlier. To Urga regularly came people from throughout Dzhungaria bringing a wide variety of exotica popular in China, but at Kiakhta there would be only Russians.[3] The dignitary lamented that the Russian customs commissar Dement'ev had refused to permit sale to the Chinese of Buriat cattle, horses, and sheep, on the hoof or slaughtered, and the Russians brought no *iuft'* or sealskins, which to his understanding, were not forbidden to private trade. Bukhol'ts from Selenginsk directed the customs official to allow the sale of everything not specifically prohibited in ukazes, even a small number of horned cattle.

For its part, the Russian administration had its complaints: the apparent gathering of a Chinese army in Mongolia to pursue the Dzhungarian wars, the demand for large purchases of cattle and provisions, which it was felt were in no plentiful supply on the Siberian side, and the illicit sale across the border of cattle. Before the turn of the year confiscations of contraband began, and they were to continue throughout the history of Russian-Chinese trade at Kiakhta.

The slow start in border trade can be seen in the customs duties collected on the Russian side: in 1729, 113 rubles; and in 1730, 232 rubles, plus 89 rubles for the building of an Orthodox church in Kiakhta.[4] This probably represented a total trade of between 1000 and 2500 rubles, certainly no more than 5000 rubles, astonishingly small by earlier or later standards. Then in the spring of

2. *Ibid.*; and P. Mushkin, "Osnovanie goroda Kiakhty i nachalo torgovli s Kitaem," *Severnaia pchela*, No. 120 (31 May 1851), 480.

3. Kurts, *Russko-kitaiskie snosheniia*, p. 75; and Sychevskii, *Chteniia OIDR*, Bk. 2 (April-June, 1875), 225.

4. Mushkin, *Severnaia Pchela*, No. 120 (31 May 1851), 480.

1731, the Selenginsk resident Parfen Semenov was sent by Bukhol'ts quietly and unobtrusively to scrutinize the status of trade, to determine who the Russian and Chinese merchants were, how they normally conducted their affairs and their trade, etc.[5] He reported the commercial negotiations as orderly, although by no means satisfactory to all. Too few Chinese merchants had come thus far, and the goods they brought were inadequate to satisfy Russian demand. He saw no attempts at secret barter and at deception of Russian customs officials. Above all the facilities for the Russians in the "merchants' court" were so cramped that often ten or more men had to store their goods in one warehouse, and several in fact kept theirs in casernes separately, which was strictly against standing customs policy.[6]

The next years saw trade still struggling to gain a solid footing. On his return from Peking in 1737, Lange composed a strong report to the Siberian Prikaz on the poverty of the Kiakhta trade.[7] There were enough Russian merchants, but so few Chinese, with an inadequate amount of goods for sale, that the Russian merchandise lay for long periods in the Kiakhta "merchants' court," and when it did sell, it brought extremely low prices. Lange reported he had intended to press the case for the improvement of border trade at the Chinese court, but he had his hands full with the caravan's difficulties and made no mention of Kiakhta. Russian merchants themselves aired their grievances; they charged Chinese merchants with collusion to maintain high prices on their commodities and to exclude Mongol and other merchants as much as possible.[8] Some Russians waited with their goods for two or three years without sales, and then were forced to exchange them very unfavorably against high-priced Chinese goods.

Provoked by news from Irkutsk of the paucity of Chinese merchants coming to trade, the Siberian Prikaz ordered Irkutsk Vice-Governor Aleksei Bibikov, in the spring of 1738, to investigate, and on 29 July Bibikov instructed Bukhol'ts to seek a meeting with the dzarguchei to demand more Chinese merchants and freer

5. Sychevskii, *Chteniia OIDR*, Bk. 2 (April-June, 1875), 226. These figures do not include the 23,829 rubles worth of furs sold by the returned Tret'iakov-Molokov caravan in 1729-30; Kurts, *Gosudarstvennaia monopoliia*, pp. 45, 48.

6. See for example *PSZ*, X, No. 7207, 87.

7. Bantysh-Kamenskii, *Diplomaticheskoe sobranie*, p. 235; Sladkovskii, *Ocherki ekonomicheskikh otnoshenii*, p. 58.

8. Kurts, *Russko-kitaiskie snosheniia*, p. 86.

trade.[9] The dzarguchei ingenuously replied that the shortage of animal forage in northern Mongolia persuaded Chinese merchants not to attempt the trip, but that hardly explained sharp business practices in Mai-mai-ch'eng.

In the next year the Governing Senate entered the scene; it sent the Collegiate Councillor and long-time soldier in the Armenian garrison regiment, Semen Liubucheninov, with a copyist, a corporal, and two soldiers, to investigate thoroughly the state of trade, as well as Svin'in's Rhubarb Commission.[10] He was to ferret out any transgressions of state commercial regulations and especially to discover any contraband. He should interrogate Russian merchants individually as to the items of trade they carried to the border, the prices they asked and received, and then to report on all this to the Senate. Svin'in told him that he "did not know" of any illegal transactions across the border, but he had seen Chinese merchants in Mai-mai-ch'eng with various prohibited goods and pelts. There does not seem to have been any immediate repercussion of this investigation on private trade; the Senate only recently had made its attitude toward contraband known once again, by demanding that all merchants returning from Siberia pass through the Verkhotur'e customs barrier, and by promising that all who evaded the barrier by sneaking through Ekaterinburg or other places would find themselves in penal servitude *(katorga)* in Siberia.[11] Other than this preoccupation with suppressing contraband, the St. Petersburg authorities were concerned at this time with the poor sale in the Siberian Prikaz of Chinese goods, silks and others, taken in customs tithe. In June of 1739 and again in 1740, the Cabinet ordered the Siberian Prikaz to provide, prior to their sale, a complete inventory of all Chinese goods in open sale in Siberia, so as to better equip the sworn-appraisers in Moscow in setting prices as favorably as possible for the state.[12]

In positive ways, little seems to have been done from St. Petersburg to improve the conditions of trade for merchants travelling to Kiakhta, except for a series of orders directed at creating a postal system in Siberia.[13] Since the early seventeenth century, letters

9. Sychevskii, *Chteniia OIDR*, Bk. 2 (April-June, 1875), 228; Silin, *Kiakhta*, p. 42; Mushkin, *Severnaia Pchela*, No. 120 (31 May 1851), 480.

10. *Senatskii arkhiv*, II, 16, 21, 22-25, 30-31, 154-55, 205-7.

11. *PSZ*, X, No. 7741, 717-18; Chulkov, *Istoricheskoe opisanie*, III, Bk. 2, 238.

12. *PSZ*, X, No. 7838, 807-8; XI, No. 8223, 234; see especially the sample *vedomost'* attached to the latter.

13. *PSZ*, VIII, No. 5805, 516, dated 16 June 1731; IX, No. 6351, 63-69, dated

could be posted up to Tobol'sk, but beyond that there was no regular system. Now from Moscow to Tobol'sk, post was to be established twice a month utilizing post stations and horses; from Tobol'sk to Eniseisk and Iakutsk, once a month; and from Iakutsk to Okhotsk on the Pacific, once every two months. The Irkutsk vice-governor was responsible for setting up the route between Eniseisk and the border trading posts, once a month normally, and while trading was in progress twice. From the state-owned herds of horses in Siberia, five mounts were assigned to each post station and a "good and responsible family" to operate it; each post family was given the right to brew beer without special lease "for the sake of [those] passing through." The entire system was intended to be self-liquidating; the post taxes, paid by merchants on letters or other items sent were to be returned to the Siberian Prikaz from all places in Siberia, even from Kamchatka and the Chinese border. The primary urge for the creation of the Siberian postal system was the need of the great Bering expedition for quick and dependable communications, but the Kiakhta trade was also specifically mentioned and serviced.

On the recommendation of Vladislavich, two or three boats were built for Lake Baikal but a decade later only one unseaworthy craft was still there, and the merchants as earlier were forced to cross the dangerous lake on their river boats.[14] Not until the 1740's and 1750's did the state, increasingly aware of the shortcomings and failings of the state monopolies, take a more active role in the promotion of private trade in Kiakhta and in the welfare of the merchants.

All in all then, the private trade at Kiakhta-Mai-mai-ch'eng began only slowly and inauspiciously, giving no hint of its great future growth and importance. And the Russian state, preoccupied elsewhere, devoted precious little attention to the needs and prospects of the few hardy traders who found their ways there.

Merchants Russian and Chinese

Who were these merchants and traders who came so far for an uncertain bargain? What were their origins, financial resources, prof-

16 March 1733; IX, No. 6376, 91-92, dated 21 April 1733; and Andrievich, *Kratkii ocherk*, pp. 162-64.

14. *PSZ*, VII, No. 5254, 22-23, dated 29 March 1728.

its, and social fates? How did they actually carry on business? The answers to most of these questions we simply cannot hope for; Russian sources prior at least to the nineteenth century do not permit close descriptions of mercantile or industrial operations because of the absence (except for a few striking examples such as the Demidovs) of private family or business accounts and records. The Chinese situation is, if anything, worse. From suggestions here and there, a sketchy picture can be put together.

During the greater part of the second quarter of the eighteenth century, most of the merchants who frequented Kiakhta were small scale and usually local, i.e. resided in Selenginsk or Irkutsk. Russian immigrants and native Siberians both participated, and commonly sold Siberian goods—pelts, *iuft'*, some small iron goods, animals, foodstuffs, etc. Goods received in return would not be carried far by them, only to Irkutsk or to one of the great Siberian fairs at Irbit, Makar'evsk, or Tobol'sk, although a few did travel to Moscow.[15] Formally Irkutsk did not hold a market fair until the second half of the century, but trading was done in the warehouses and storage bins. Not all of these small merchants were civilly free. At least during the first half of the century a few bound peasants (serfdom was always comparatively lax in Siberia) traded and not always in the smallest quantities. Small trade was in the vicinity of one hundred to four hundred rubles per year. Two merchants, Trapeznikov and Iugov, were fairly large merchants for the day.

From the beginning there were also Great Russians from the northern commercial cities—Moscow, Kostroma, Nizhni-Novgorod, Suzdal', Viatka, Kazan', Tula, Vologda, and others. Typically the investors did not themselves go to Kiakhta but hired agents or assistants (*prikazchiki*, originally a land steward, or *izvozchiki*) to conduct their business for them, or commissioned local merchants to buy in their names. In Moscow alone, the customs books for 1740 list sixty-six merchants acquiring large lots of Siberian and Chinese goods.[16] Among those who sold the Chinese items were ten Muscovites, including the big merchant's son Vasilii Evreinov, Danila Zemskii, and Gavrila Zhuravlev, whose business during the

15. For the Siberian fairs, see Ronald F. Drew, "The Siberian Fair: 1600-1750," *The Slavonic and East European Review*, XXXIX, no. 93 (June, 1961), 423-29.

16. Akademiia Nauk SSSR, Institut Istorii, *Istoriia Moskvy*, Vol. II: *Period feodalizma XVIII v., Moskva v kontse XVII v. i v pervoi chetverti XVIII v. (Chast' pervaia)* (Moscow: Izd. Akademii Nauk SSSR, 1953–64), II, 284.

1730's and 1740's was the largest of the men from Moscow. At that time there were nine Siberians from Tobol'sk and Eniseisk who brought Chinese goods, and the rest were all from Great Russian cities.

None of the Kiakhta merchants were organized into formal joint-stock companys; many operated simply as families. Some cooperated in partnerships, but these seem to have been relatively temporary arrangements. One finds references to "companies" in Kiakhta, but it is quite clear that these were no more than temporary associations of several merchants from the same locale who pooled their resources and ingenuities while at the border, and who, upon leaving, went their own commercial ways.[17] It was only natural that old friends, dealing often in the same items, should appear to some of the casual observers of the time to have organized companies. There is no evidence that any formal companies were organized for the Kiakhta trade per se.

In the 1740's several of the well-to-do merchants connected with the Kiakhta trade formed the Kamchatka Company to exploit the new source of pelts to the east. The Selenginsk merchant Andreian Tolstykh and the Kiakhta merchant Grigorii Volk had large shares in the expedition of the Company, although they sent their own agents to Okhotsk to buy the best pelts as well.[18] The China market was of course the finest outlet by far for these furs, and most were brought to Kiakhta. There is no suggestion that in bartering with the Chinese the participants in the Kamchatka Company expeditions acted together in company fashion to control the market and regulate prices.

Indeed, the most striking thing to most contemporary observers about the Russians at Kiakhta was their almost total lack of organization, mutuality, and appreciation of common cause, giving, from the beginning, the better organized and disciplined Chinese a distinct advantage in the market place. So guileless were the Russians (or so they are often described), that had they not enjoyed the advantage of trading in fine furs obtained at low cost,

17. Moscow merchants acted as a "company" to trade beaver, otter, wools, etc.; Tula merchants to trade cat pelts, sheepskin, etc.; Arkhangel'sk and Vologda to trade *iuft'*, fox paws and pelts, Arctic fox, and otter; Kazan' to trade *iuft'* and hides; Tobol'sk and Irkutsk merchants to trade Siberian furs and *iuft'*; Silin, *Kiakhta*, p. 8.

18. *Ibid.*, p. 85; and Semen Bentsionovich Okun', *Rossiisko-amerikanskaia kompaniia*, ed. Boris D. Grekov (Moscow: Sotsekgiz, 1939), p. 139.

they would hardly have been able to carry on trade profitably.[19] The point is made perhaps a bit strongly by most observers, but there can be no doubt of the inability of the Russians to act in concert with self-discipline. We have already seen their complete unwillingness to take part in the organization of a company for the China trade, at least in a company sponsored by the state and, in their view, open to domination by it. In fact some merchants bore resentment against others and carried it to the point of complaint to state officials, especially the larger traders vis-à-vis the small retailers and the peasants, and doubtless the feeling was reciprocated. In 1747, for example, an Irkutsk official complained to the Siberian Prikaz that the strictly retail merchants, who traded from one hundred to four hundred rubles per year, did great injury to the Kiakhta trade, and by implication to the substantial merchants there.[20] These *petite bourgeoisie* charged lower prices for their goods and thus damaged larger traders with dearer goods and higher prices, and deprived the state as well by reducing the customs duties extracted. Selenginsk Commandant Iakobi investigated, and in September 1748 Kondratov, commissar of the customs house at Kiakhta, reported to him that although these small merchants traded individually in insignificant amounts, together the amount of duties they returned to the state should hardly be overlooked, even though the larger merchants (those above four hundred rubles per year) returned nearly eight times as much. Kondratov also argued that the numbers of Russian merchants arriving to trade in any given year varied widely; since the total turnover of trade (and of course the duties collected) depended upon steady trade (otherwise the Chinese would be provoked to quit bringing their goods), the small merchants served the very useful function of taking up the slack between the arrivals of big merchants with trains of goods. Iakobi recommended that all merchants continue to be permitted in the Kiakhta "merchants' court."

During the latter half of the century, larger merchants, and an increasing number of Great Russians and even foreigners (particularly Prussians and Balts), came to predominate at Kiakhta; men like the three Liventsov brothers, the largest of whom (Vasilii Artem'evich Men'shoi) had a typical gross business of 50,000 rubles

19. As argued by Peter Simon Pallas in his *Voyages*, IV, 183.
20. Sychevskii, *Chteniia OIDR*, Bk. 2 (April-June, 1875), 232-33.

per year during the 1760's and 1770's.[21] At Kiakhta this Liventsov had two stalls, and sold, in one year, 24,000 rubles in furs, hides, and skins to the Chinese. At the same time he traded beeswax and honey out of St. Petersburg for 6,000 rubles and metallurgical goods out of Riga for 17,000 rubles. Kudriavtsev says that Irkutsk merchants who were "poor men" *(skudnye liudi)* during the first half of the century became "eminent citizens" *(imenitye grazhdane)* during the second.[22] Trapeznikov and Iugov were two of these. Trapeznikov for example in 1775 brought from Kamchatka and the Pacific islands 54,929 sea otter, 29,108 fur seal, 17,154 fox, 31,658 Arctic fox, 150 ermine among others, all of which at Kamchatka prices were valued at 3,204,134 rubles, and at Kiakhta prices more than twice that much.[23] And of course those Siberians who took part in the early expeditions to the Aleutians and Alaska, at least those who survived, were "substantial"—Grigorii Shelekhov, Lebedev-Lastochkin, *et alia.*

In 1758 the Senate passed one of the many decrees during the Elizabethan period aimed at defining more precisely the civil status of Russian's bound serfs and peasants and reducing their civil liberties. This one prohibited peasants from trading abroad, either in their own names or others'.[24] Peasants throughout the realm could trade in villages and towns along the major roads and highways, but not in the market fairs of the big cities or across state boundaries, on pain of confiscation of their goods. Customs farmer Nikita Shemiakin was instructed to take special precautions to intercept any peasants exchanging goods illegally. As with many ukazes of the old regime, this one was not flawlessly applied in Siberia; Silin found that in 1778 a rich peasant from Poshekhonsk *uezd* traded at Kiakhta and the assumption is that many others continued to do so.[25] And when Radishchev visited Kiakhta in 1792, he observed many small traders including peasants and Buriats, as well as foreigners and great capitalists.[26] Catherine's famed edicts of 1775 and 1794, which divided Russia's merchants into three guilds according to the amount of capital of each, were

21. Nikolai Ivanovich Pavlenko, *Istoriia metallurgii v Rossii XVIII veka, Zavody i zavodovladel'tsy* (Moscow: Izd. Akademii Nauk SSSR, 1962), pp. 298-99.
22. Kudriavtsev and Vendrikh, *Irkutsk,* p. 49.
23. Silin, *Kiakhta,* pp. 85-86.
24. *PSZ,* XV, No. 10862, 243-44.
25. Silin, *Kiakhta,* p. 93.
26. Radishchev, *Polnoe sobranie sochinenii,* II, 20-21.

likewise never successfully applied in Kiakhta.[27] Irkutsk first-guild merchants tried, in the late 1780's, to limit the Kiakhta trade to themselves, but Radishchev reported that so many third-guild merchants crowded into the first guild, both in their own names and using the names of first-guild merchants, sometimes five, ten, or fifteen to a name, that the effort was a practical failure. Although by the end of the century a few very substantial merchants dominated the trade, small retailers were not wholly forced out.

The Chinese merchants are obscure. North Chinese merchants who had earlier met the Russians at Urga came now to Mai-mai-ch'eng, along with Bukharans, other Mongols, and perhaps Tibetans. The latter people traded both with the Chinese and the Russians. The Chinese themselves seem to have come largely from north China (Shansi, Shensi, Jehol, etc.).[28] We know little of their finances, although, from what we have said of the cost of crown caravans across Mongolia, it is evident that the investment, not only in goods, but in animals, forage, and provisions, prevented any small scale merchants from participating in this trade. The small traders were obviously the Mongol natives; the Chinese had to carry the Russian goods back to north China for the great fur market was there. The Mongols did have the advantage of being the important carriers of rhubarb, silver, and gold, all of which the Russian state in particular was extremely interested in obtaining.

Both Russian and foreign travellers alike commented, sometimes with approbation, sometimes with grudging admiration, on the commercial skill and adeptness of the Chinese. Compared with the disorganized Russians, the Chinese were repeatedly described as secretive, cunning, crafty, and sharp; how much of this judgment reflects the occidental faith in oriental inscrutibility we cannot say.[29] That they seemed to be better organized and more highly disciplined there is little doubt, and that they bargained for high

27. *PSZ*, XX, No. 14327, 145-47; XXIV, No. 17223, 531-32.

28. *SFPC*, 37.18b; William Coxe, *Account of Russian Discoveries Between Asia and America, To Which Are Added, The Conquest of Siberia, and The History of the Transactions and Commerce Between Russia and China* (London: T. Cadell, 1780), p. 231.

29. Klaproth (*Mémoires*, I, 66) puts it this way: "L'amour de l'ordre et un esprit soigneux distinguent le Chinois de toutes les autres nations avec lesquelles il fait le commerce à Kiakhta; il est en même temps plus rusé et plus adroit que le Juif en Europe et l'Arménien dans l'Asie mahométane." Compare P. G., *Zhurnal manufaktur i torgovli*, Chast' 4, No. 11 (1836), 123.

prices for their goods and low for the Russians was a standard charge brought by Russians. As early as 1739, coinciding with a similar development in Peking and Canton, the Chinese reportedly organized themselves into eight "companies," with non-Chinese left out.[30] Each selected an "excellent and substantial" merchant to be *hang* chief *(hang-shou)*, and, under his leadership, were set prices that were mutually adhered to by all members. If these companies were in fact similar to the *hang* at home, they do not seem to have survived the century, and it is likely they were not the well organized, imperially-sanctioned mercantile companies observed elsewhere. Later in the century they are not mentioned, although Peter Simon Pallas described a situation no less disciplined. He noted that Chinese merchants operated in pairs, one traded in Kiakhta with Russians, the other received the goods and carried them to the market in China.[31] But this after all is not very different from the agent-system of the larger Great Russian merchants.

One major difference between Russian and Chinese was the direct control over merchants and trade by the respective border officials. The Russians never willingly submitted to the dictates or even admonitions of the Selenginsk commandant or the Kiakhta customs director. The dzarguchei in Mai-mai-ch'eng from the beginning supervised Chinese merchants with all of the powers of an autocrat.[32] With his judicial and police powers, this official could and did demand absolute commercial secrecy, avoidance of the use of the Chinese language with the Russians so that they would not learn it and be privy to their conversations, unanimity in prices on Chinese goods, common knowledge of Russian offers and deals, limitation of amounts of Chinese goods brought for trade so as to maintain high and fixed prices, etc. The difference is not so much in the merchants, as in the ability of the respective courts to extend to the limits of their empires the power and majesty of state exercised by competent subalterns. As we have repeatedly made allusion to, the eighteenth-century Siberian empire was in this respect notably delinquent.

Between these two merchant groups the actual barter and

30. Sychevskii, *Chteniia OIDR*, Bk. 2 (April-June, 1875), 229; *SFPC*, 37.21a.

31. Pallas, *Voyages*, IV, 168.

32. See for example P. G., *Zhurnal manufaktur i torgovli*, Chast' 4, No. 11 (1836), 124; Murray, *Historical Account* III, 326; Gagemeister, *Statisticheskoe obozrenie Sibiri*, II, 593-94.

exchange of goods was carried on in rather quaint fashion.[33] Ostensibly the trade was barter, that is no coin or bullion could legally be carried from the Russian side, and the Chinese at times strongly discouraged its outflow also. Both sides agreed that credit granted in either direction was potentially dangerous. Hence a much more complicated system of bartering was required, often using other commodities as standards of value—brick tea or baled cottons, for example.

The usual procedure employed—for more than a hundred years —was for the Chinese and Bukharan merchants or their representatives to visit the "merchants' court" in Kiakhta in daylight hours, carefully inspecting goods brought out of the storage bins into the bright light of the courtyard to avoid deception. Over tea, usually taken in the Russian merchants' quarters, items, prices, and quantities were discussed and agreed upon, and the Chinese listed the goods. Mongol was more often than not used in these sessions, for by and large the Russians never mastered Chinese, and it was said that the Chinese use of Russian was grating to the Slavic ear. There were never more than a few interpreters from Chinese to Russian in Kiakhta, and there were many Russian Buriats and other Mongol peoples in the vicinity. Agreement reached, the merchandise was then sealed in the presence of the purchasers. At this point, the whole party repaired to Mai-mai-ch'eng, where in the Chinese warehouses the procedure was repeated with Chinese goods. The goods from both sides were then moved to the other by the day laborers found in substantial numbers in both communities. All this took place during daylight hours, for the gates of both suburbs were closed when darkness fell. This neat pattern presumes of course relatively equal stores of merchandise on each side, in value and in quantity, and of kind wanted by the other. Especially in the early years of trade this was probably true only rarely, and credit came to be fairly commonly extended. Collection was not always easy, particularly if the debtor left the border, and merchant indebtedness came to be a common sore in the relations between the two powers.

33. See descriptions in Petr Andreevich Slovtsov, *Istoricheskoe obozrenie Sibiri* (St. Petersburg: Izd. I. M. Skorokhodova, 1886), II, 221; Pallas, *Voyages*, IV, 181-84; Erman, *Travels in Siberia*, II, 183-84; and Karl Marx and Friedrich Engels, *Sochineniia* (2d ed.; Moscow: Gospolitizdat, 1955-66), XII, 157-60, and article published in the New York *Daily Tribune*, 7 April 1857.

The Russian State and the Kiakhta Trade

Beginning really in the 1740's, i.e., coinciding with flagging efforts to invigorate state monopolies in the Peking trade and in rhubarb, and with the reign of Elizabeth, the several Russian high state offices began to take greater interest in improving conditions of trade for the China merchants. Slowly emerging was the realization of the financial value to the state of increasingly profitable trade at Kiakhta. One of the first steps taken was the recommendation of the Siberian Prikaz, approved by the Senate, to encourage the settlement in Kiakhta of merchants and their families.[34] Prior to this time, no merchants were considered permanent residents of the Kiakhta suburb, but continued to be listed in the tax rolls of their native and adopted cities, and would return to those cities when their trading was completed. Now, under the supervision of Selenginsk Commandant Iakobi, up to one hundred families from elsewhere in the Siberian *guberniia* or Irkutsk province were permitted to move there and be listed in the tax rolls in Kiakhta, "for the expansion of the merchantry." To accommodate them, courts, workshops *(zavody)*, kitchen gardens, and cattle runs had to be provided on land adjacent to the outpost, and a special new suburb erected. These new settlers were to be allowed to cut trees within three to six miles of Kiakhta, although not closer, so that nearby lands not be denuded of a handy source of firewood and lumber. Palisades had to be raised around the houses, with two gates for ingress and egress to prevent goods passing without payment of customs duties. Capitation tax, recruit obligations, and other imposts were lifted for five years, but after that these immigrants were required to pay the same as others. All interested were encouraged to apply, even those not on capitation tax lists elsewhere, provided only they were not runaway serfs, soldiers, dragoons, etc.

Two years later (1745) the Senate issued a supplement to the edict, extending to inhabitants of European Russian cities—Moscow, Kazan', Arkhangel'sk—the right to settle and be registered in Kiakhta.[35] Those who wished to resettle were instructed to report to their own town magistrates, who would in turn report to the

34. *PSZ*, XI, No. 8833, 961-62, Senate decree dated 13 December 1743; Andrievich, *Kratkii ocherk*, p. 187.

35. *PSZ*, XII, No. 9206, 445-46, dated 16 September 1745; Chulkov, *Istoricheskoe opisanie*, III, Bk. 2, 266-68.

Senate the names of applicants and the amount of ready capital they had. Iakobi was instructed to let stay at Kiakhta any townsmen *(posadskie)* and state peasants who had their own dwellings, but to quickly inform the officials of their previous residences, that their names would be dropped in the current revision (census). Great care was to be taken, though, to insure that none was a runaway from a private serf owner, or from church or monastery lands. Nontrading artisans and skilled workers were declared legal to settle; merchants with unsold goods, their agents, and their laborers, need not be dispatched if their passports expired. Svin'in, as head of the Kiakhta Commission, was to renew the passports as long as was necessary, carefully informing these persons' town halls that in their absence they not be overlooked in the revision.

This recruitment of merchants for Kiakhta reveals one of the major problems in the expansion of the China trade, the shortage of Russian populace in eastern Siberia. Merchants alone, after all, were of little consequence, without sufficient population to provide the laborers, artisans, carters, boatsmen, innkeepers, farmers, and herders, all of whom were equally necessary to support a commercial establishment of any great size. Yet at the end of the reign of Peter the Great, Transbaikalia, including the Nerchinsk mining region, could count a total Russian population (including women) of probably no more than 10,000.[36] Sensing the importance of migration to the development of the Nerchinsk mines, Peter ordered the dispatch of hard labor convicts *(katorzhnye)* and 300 households of non-convict labor from western Siberia to settle on arable land in Dauriia.[37] The Selenginsk region, not yet clearly the center of the China trade, was neglected for the moment by the St. Petersburg officialdom.

In the years after Peter's death, the population grew slowly but steadily. By the end of the reign of Elizabeth, the Russian community in Transbaikalia had more than doubled, although it took more than forty years, whereas the native population probably remained about the same. The Selenginsk region as contrasted with the Nerchinsk, however, registered the greatest gains, and although still smaller, the figures reflect the obvious importance and value of the China trade. By 1761 the total population of

36. Andrievich, *Kratkii ocherk*, pp. 120-21. For the 1719 revision see *PSZ*, V, No. 3380, 701-10.

37. Andrievich, *Kratkii ocherk*, pp. 135-36; *PSZ*, VI, No. 3955, 648.

Transbaikalia was probably over 30,000, including about 12,000 natives, most of whom were in the Nerchinsk area.[38] By the end of the century (the Fifth Revision, 1794-96), Irkutsk *guberniia*, now separate from Nerchinsk, listed 53,724 male souls, of which nearly 23,000 were Russian and the rest *iasak*-paying Buriats, Tungus and other natives.[39] The Nerchinsk region came to be overshadowed.

The cities and towns of the Irkutsk territory benefited most from the trade, led by Irkutsk itself, the key city. Irkutsk was founded in 1661 as an ostrog, shortly received a *voevoda*, and by 1721 was designated a provincial town. By the mid-eighteenth century, it was the most impressive and civilized place east of Tobol'sk.[40] In 1769 it had 1153 houses, nearly half occupied by merchants, townsmen *(posadskie)*, and guildsmen *(tsekhovye)* and a male population of about 5,000.[41] The year before it opened its first formal market fair, which gathered twice a year, from 15 November to 1 January and from 15 March to 1 May. The fair was open to all. It attracted Siberians, natives, Great Russians, and foreigners, and displayed a wide variety of European, Russian, and Chinese goods: Siberian furs, skins, wax, copper, cotton fabrics, iron, Spanish, Dutch and German textiles, and the usual Chinese imports.[42] Industry on the other hand was poorly developed; Irkutsk was almost exclusively an administrative and commercial center. There were small silkworks and glassworks, and nearby an ironworks (founded in 1730 by the Irkutsk merchant Lanin, but it failed in 1812), a saltworks, and a copper smelting plant. Some thirty-six miles distant, five merchants of Moscow and Velikii Ustiug opened the Tel'minskaia textile plant in 1731, but it did poorly, and in 1773 passed to the ownership of two Irkutsk merchants, Aleksei and Mikhail Sibiriakov. Twenty years later it was taken over by the Military Commissariat and became the Irkutsk Crown Textile Works. The products of these small factories in part found their

38. Andrievich, *Kratkii ocherk*, pp. 192-94.

39. Ministerstvo Vnytrennykh Del, *Statisticheskoe obozrenie Sibiri*, p. 323. See also Murray, *Historical Account*, III, 484–86.

40. For description of Irkutsk see also Vladimir P. Sukachev (ed.), *Irkutsk. Ego mesto i znachenie v istorii i kul'turnom razvitii vostochnoi Sibiri. Ocherk* (Moscow: Tipolitografiia I. N. Kushnerev i Ko., 1891), passim; Sauer, *An Account*, pp. 14–18; Storch, *Statistische Übersicht*, p. 86.

41. Kudriavtsev, *Irkutsk*, p. 43; also Chulkov, *Slovar'*, p. 73.

42. Kudriavtsev, *Irkutsk*, p. 39.

way into the China trade, but they never became a major portion of the exports.

According to a survey in 1779, a total of 1809 guildsmen *(tsekhovye)*, not counting many artisans and craftsmen unlisted in the guilds, were in Irkutsk *guberniia*, 742 in Irkutsk city, but 953 in Kiakhta and 101 in Selenginsk.[43] As early as 1740, the Cabinet of Anna on the initiative of Lange took measures, including subsidies, to transport to Irkutsk foreign artisans, silversmiths, goldsmiths, bootiers, saddlers, etc.[44] With the exception of the mines of Dauriia, the Irkutsk region boasted far more skilled craftsmen than any other territory east of the Urals. The impact of the China trade is again apparent.

Besides Irkutsk, the towns of the region all grew, although more modestly. Verkhne-Udinsk on the Uda River, built originally in 1649 as an ostrog, became especially important as a permanent residence for rich China merchants and for the boatmen who carried goods between Kiakhta and Irkutsk.[45] Selenginsk and Kiakhta we have described earlier.

In the matter of external customs duties and their collection, state policy was notably favorable toward the China trade (and trade in general in all of Siberia). The basic Siberian tariff, which included Chinese goods, was that promulgated in 1698 and not substantively changed until 1761, which laid down a general tariff of 10 per cent *(desiatina)* extracted in kind on all goods legally carried.[46] In addition all merchants in Kiakhta paid small monthly imposts devoted to local use: to maintain the establishment of the Troitskosavsk commander, to repair a bridge in Troitskosavsk, to help erect and maintain the church in Kiakhta. All merchants also paid the internal customs duties, prior to their abolition in 1753, collected usually as goods passed through the Verkhotur'e barrier.[47] This latter duty varied somewhat from time to time,

43. *Ibid.*, p. 52.

44. *Sbornik RIO*, CXXXVIII (1912), 78-80, 175, 224-26.

45. Ministerstvo Vnutrennykh Del, *Statisticheskoe obozrenie Sibiri*, pp. 327-30; Clerc, *Histoire*, III, 385. The 1956 population of this town now known as Ulan-Ude was 158,000.

46. *PSZ*, III, No. 1654, 491-517, dated 12 November 1698/7207. See also Lodyzhenskii, *Istoriia* (this is the finest work yet done on the Russian customs and tariffs); Pashkov, *Istoriia*, I, Chast' 1, 274-75; Gille, *Histoire*, p. 128; Irina Mikhailovna Bobovicha, *Lektsii po istorii narodnogo khoziaistva SSSR (epokha feodalizma)* (Leningrad: Izd. Leningradskogo Universiteta, 1959), pp. 126-27.

47. Mushkin, *Severnaia pchela*, No. 120 (31 May 1851), 480. Strahlenberg (*An Historico-Geographical Description*, pp. 319-42) reported that goods passing

but was usually more than 10 per cent. What amounted to a turnover tax was commonly charged in market fairs or towns where goods were bought and sold; Strahlenberg reported that this amounted to five kopeks per ruble.[48]

All of these duties were, of course, based on value of goods assigned by the customs house inspectors, and there was no standardization of procedure in calculating that value. Sometimes the actual purchase price of commodities was used, or the expected sale value. In other cases, an arbitrary set value was imposed which bore no necessary relationship to the market values involved. In all cases duties charged tended to be inelastic and fixed, and time and again a little money wisely used to gain favor with collector or official could and did reduce duties, or eliminate them altogether. This was, it will be recalled, one of the charges made against Zholobov in the 1730's.

The great tariff debates of the later years of Peter the Great and his successors had little impact on Siberia and Kiakhta. The first important Petrine measure on tariffs was his 1724 edicts, which were, for the first time in Russian history, forthrightly protectionist.[49] Initially they were established for St. Petersburg, Narva,

---

from west to east paid one *grivennik* (a *grivennik* is one-tenth of a ruble; in Strahlenberg, *griffwen*) in Verkhotur'e, one in Tobol'sk, and four in Selenginsk, or a total of 60 per cent, which is evidently a misunderstanding.

48. Strahlenberg, *An Historico-Geographical Description*, p. 341.

49. *PSZ*, V, No. 3176, 548-49; VI, No. 4006, 676-77; VII, No. 4345, 150-51. See also Lodyzhenskii, *Istoriia*, pp. 56-64, and Arcadius Kahan, "Continuity in Economic Activity and Policy during the Post-Petrine Period in Russia," *The Journal of Economic History*, XXV (March, 1965), 77-78. In his highly contributive article, Kahan takes issue with Soviet historians for their condemnation of the 1731 tariff as a betrayal of Russian industrial interests in favor of those of foreign countries and as a major deviation from normal Petrine tariff policy (1724). He insists that close scrutiny of the 1731 tariff fails to substantiate the charge that it represented a major liberalization of tariff one as "much more selective in its discriminatory features." "It [the latter] was protective with respect to products manufactured within Russia, both by the new manufactories and by the craft or domestic industries. It was protective with regard to the export of manufactured goods and set high duties upon the export of raw materials used by domestic manufacturers. . . . True, it deviated from the 1724 tariff with regard to the level of duties in a number of cases but was much more effective in enforcing them, whereas previous widespread smuggling had rendered many prohibitive duties of the Petrine tariff ineffective. Built upon the reported market prices of Russian commodities, the new tariff resulted in continuous protection of the commodities produced for mass consumption and liberalized the import duties for so-called luxuries, the domestic production of which was clearly inadequate. . . . Therefore, it seems safe to conclude that the tariff policy of Peter's successors was not less

Vyborg, Arkhangel'sk, and Kon'skii, and then applied to all of the Polish border. They did not apply to Siberia. If they had, they would still have had limited impact, in spite of the very steep tariffs, from 25 to 75 per cent, on protected items manufactured in Russia. Some processed silk fabrics (brocades, taffetas, among others) were placed in the highest tax category, along with tobacco pipes (Chinese tobacco pipes were popular with Siberians). Other manufactured imports were in lower tax categories (Chinese silk velvets would have been included here, for example). Raw silk for use in Russia's new silk mills remained at the minimal rate, 4 to 6 per cent. Except for items monopolized by the state or farmed out to private entrepreneurs, the tariff did not exclude foreign manufactured goods, even for the most sorely pressed industries. Peter's attitude was one of granting a modicum of protection when an industry proved it could supply Russia's needs and demands.

Except for certain entrepreneurs, Peter's tariff quickly aroused many opponents, who brought to bear sound arguments for its abrogation. Senators questioned whether it served or hindered the growth of external trade and the prosperity of the merchantry; whether in fact it aided the healthy and prudent growth of industry within Russia; whether it did not reduce state customs revenues by discouraging the carriage of some luxury items, whether it did not foster contraband trade, in spite of new customs houses, barriers, and customs officials, and whether it did not provoke customs officials to accept bribes. And not surprisingly among the first to complain were English, Dutch, and Hamburg merchants trading at St. Petersburg. The Commerce Collegium noted that few goods were as cheap as fifteen years earlier, before there were high duties. Illicit trade conducted by rogues had expanded. And Russian merchants visiting Breslau, Hamburg, Silesia, and other places several times a year carried back nearly all European goods through Riga and other places that were exempt from application of the 1724 tariff.[50] Beginning in 1726 Peter's tariff was lowered on selected articles, culminating in the major revision of 1731. In general this seems to have been a return to preprotection-

effective in its features protective of Russian industry. In fact, it introduced corrections into some of Peter's typical short-run measures which were designed to achieve high rates of growth in some chosen areas to the detriment of others."

50. Lodyzhenskii, *Istoriia*, p. 76; Chulkov, *Istoricheskoe opisanie*, IV, Bk. 2, 114.

ist days, with precious little done for the aid and succor of Russian merchants travelling abroad for trade. Except for diplomatic personnel acting in that capacity, Russia provided no consuls, nor consular apparatus, even though foreigners trading in Russia from major European countries depended heavily on their consuls for advice and even monetary aid.

The Commission on Commerce *(Komissiia o kommertsii)*, established in March 1727, was instructed to inquire into means to ameliorate and strengthen the condition of Russia's merchantry, and one major act it took did have some effect on China merchants.[51] On 16 May 1729 was promulgated that ukaz entitled "Regulation on Promissory Notes" *(Ustav veksel'nyi)* drafted in the Commission.[52] This *Ustav* permitted Russian merchants *(not* Siberian merchants until 1781) to defer payment of customs duties for the period of time it was expected it would take them to carry their goods east to Kiakhta or west to the European cities (especially St. Petersburg) and to sell them. The normal period of *veksel'* was six months, and those who did not pay in this period were charged a penalty of 8 per cent per ruble. Merchants could deposit their pledges to pay either in St. Petersburg or Kiakhta, or put up some of their goods or cash as collateral. It would seem that this was not heavily used by the relatively small number of European Russian merchants who carried their goods the entire way, probably because the time period alloted for payment was simply too short. And all those merchants registered as inhabitants of Siberian cities and towns were excluded in any event.[53] An Elizabethan ukaz of 1754 repeated the conditions of *veksel'* and publicized them throughout Russia.[54]

Beyond these small measures, nothing of great consequence was done by the state to foster private trade with the Chinese until the reign of Elizabeth. As in so many other ways, Elizabeth seemed to

51. *Gosudarstvennye uchrezhdeniia*, pp. 216-17; *PSZ*, VII, No. 5057, 778.

52. *PSZ*, VIII, No. 5410, 147-97, dated 16 May 1729, printed 5 July 1729. Bills of exchange, or perhaps better promissory notes, were used earlier in Peter's reign to transfer monies for the use of the army and crown funds; Aleksandr Fedorovich Fedorov, *Istoriia vekselia, istoriko-iuridicheskoe izsledovanie* ("Zapiski Imp. Novorossiiskogo Universiteta," 66 [Odessa: Tip. Shtaba Okruga, 1895]).

53. *PSZ*, XXII, No, 16402, 607-11. See also the case of Erofei Firsov in *Sbornik RIO*, CXXIV (1906), 508-10.

54. *PSZ*, XIV, No. 10212, 53-55; Chulkov, *Istoricheskoe opisanie*, III, Bk. 2, 278–81.

hark back to the spirit and even to the policies of her father in her attitude toward commerce and the economy. Until late in her reign, exclusive monopolies were again in vogue, although, as we know, they had never been relinquished in the China trade. The Manufacturing Collegium was reestablished, and a variety of decrees substantially changed the picture of trade and tariff. Imported raw materials necessary for Russian factories were permitted duty free, or with reduced duties, including raw silk from China. To cheapen raw materials produced within Russia, export of them abroad was hindered. But the general tariff of 1731 was never thoroughly revised or rewritten.[55] In 1752 and 1753 a new tariff schedule was enacted for the Siberian Line, i.e., for the customs houses at Orenburg and Troitskii fort, through which passed a small number of Chinese goods.[56] The tariff was however very low, 5 per cent, on a list of approved items issued. This schedule, although referred to as the "Asiatic tariff," did not apply to Kiakhta. Elizabeth's closest and most effective adviser in economic and trade matters was Count Petr Ivanovich Shuvalov, Senator and General. One of the last of a series of measures he conceived and engineered was the 1757 tariff, which for the first time in over a quarter of a century altered greatly the tariff structure of Russia.[57] Many of the characteristics of Peter's 1724 protectionist tariff are found in this legislation. On raw and processed materials utilized in manufacturing, duties were low, and on fabricated and manufactured goods relatively high. The main difference was the overall higher duty for all nonprotected imports. The earlier tariff had a lower level of around 6 per cent (three kopeks per ruble *efimki*); this tariff set 12.5 per cent (five kopeks per ruble *efimki*), and the majority of enumerated goods were in the 15 to 20 per cent bracket.[58]

Certainly Elizabeth's tariff had a fiscal aim more than did Peter's. Semiprocessed and raw silks, for example, fell in the lower bracket, and better silks such as Gros-de-Tour, not produced in Russia, were also low. On simple silk fabrics, iron goods, and saltpetre, all found in the China trade at one time or another, duties were higher than they had ever been. This tariff also changed the sur-

55. For the best survey of Elizabethan times, see Lodyzhenskii, *Istoriia*, Chapter VI, pp. 81-97.

56. *PSZ*, XIII, No. 9984, 649; XIII, No. 10156, 934-39.

57. Lodyzhenskii, *Istoriia*, pp. 90-92.

58. *Efimki* at this time was calculated at 2 r. 25 k. in Russian silver money.

charge of 13 per cent (in lieu of internal customs) to a varying charge from 6 to 16 per cent ad valorem, with the lower percentages charged on those items on which customs duties were required in *efimki*. Although the 1757 tariff did not apply to the Asian and Chinese trade, it served as the model for the "Siberian tariff" of 31 May 1761, which lasted fundamentally unchanged until the first years of the nineteenth century.[59]

The "Siberian tariff" of 1761 introduced little that was new. The prohibited items had all been forbidden, at one time or another, to private trade; rhubarb, tobacco balls, copper coin, grain wine, turpentine, arsenic, etc. were nonexportable; and sable, black and brown fox, beaver, precious metals, lead, powder, all firearms, chamois hides, potash, and flax yarn were nonimportable. On the other side, among the goods imported duty free were diamonds, raw cotton, granulated sugar, raw silk, drugs and other materia medica imported for the Crown Apothecary Shop, paints and lacquers, and printed books. These were all items of curiosity value not produced in Russia or raw materials needed for Russian mills. Russian cottons, and paintings or prints of all kinds, were exported with customs duties. Other than these specific items, the 1761 tariff schedule followed closely that compiled for Shuvalov's general tariff of 1757.

The most far-reaching change in Elizabethan times was taken in 1753, and it led to a major alteration of the customs structure and culminated in the tariffs of 1757 and 1761. On the basis of a proposal put forth the year before by Shuvalov, the Senate abolished all internal customs duties and similar retail imposts.[60] The reasoning was simple. Costs of collection were high (ten and one-half kopeks per ruble gathered), and returns were not great enough to warrant that form of taxation. Also as Shuvalov charged, the sworn-appraisers were not above gouging merchants for their own profit. The state had no intention of giving up a long established revenue however, for on Shuvalov's suggestions external customs duties were raised by 13 per cent ad valorem, in effect making up for the loss and relieving the state of a difficult, yea impossible,

59. *PSZ*, XV, No. 11260, 722.

60. Chulkov, *Istoricheskoe opisanie*, III, Bk. 2, 274-76; Lodyzhenskii, *Istoriia*, pp. 87-88; *PSZ*, XIII, No. 10164, 947-53, Imperial manifesto dated 20 December 1753, effective 1 April 1754; also *PSZ*, XIV, No. 10179, 18-22; XIV, No. 10335, 274; XIV, No. 10486, 462-84, dated 1 December 1755, the actual customs regulation *(tamozhennyi ustav)*.

task of collection. The merchant class greeted the measure with enthusiasm.

For Siberia, Verkhotur'e continued to serve as the important customs inspection point. Most Russian goods could pass back and forth through it without duty, but when any of those goods were exported abroad from European Russia or Siberia they were charged the 13 per cent, plus a surcharge of five per cent for maintenance of the border customs house. There were several minor variations: from Siberian peltry exported abroad the traditional tithe was taken in kind, *plus* thirteen kopeks per ruble. From Chinese and other foreign goods imported through Siberia, now was gathered ten kopeks per ruble ad valorem, instead of the previous tithe in kind, *plus* the 13 per cent. Peltry brought from Siberia to European Russia for the personal use of the merchants was still taxed a tithe in kind. Lodyzhenskii, the finest student of Russian tariff structure, points out that the collection of duties became more complicated and difficult in the border posts and in the ports, mainly because the new surcharge was calculated in Russian currency, while (according to the tariff of 1731) the standard customs duties were calculated in gold or in *efimki*. The entire customs structure needed reevaluation, the existing one was already over two decades old, and many common imports and exports were not mentioned in the schedules. Elizabeth was more protectionist in her outlook than Count A. I. Osterman, who had sponsored the earlier tariff.

In the meantime the customs house at the border witnessed some strengthening and improvement. At the recommendation of Siberian Governor Soimonov, the customs house was moved back from the border in 1766 to escape the watchful eyes of the dzarguchei, and in order to satisfy his earlier complaints on the exaction of duties illegitimate under the Treaty of Kiakhta.[61] The collection of duties on Chinese goods rankled the Chinese through the years; they repeatedly insisted that the Treaty of Kiakhta had flatly prohibited any imposts. In the end customs collection was settled in Troitskosavsk, only two to three miles from Kiakhta,

61. *PSZ*, XV, No. 11322, 777-79; XX, No. 14277, 89-97; Silin, *Kiakhta*, p. 57; Nikolai Vasil'evich Semivskii, *Noveishiia, liubopytnyia i dostovernyia povestvovaniia o vostochnoi Sibiri, iz chego mnogoe donyne ne bylo izvestno* (St. Petersburg: Voennaia Tipografiia Glavnago Shtaba Ego Imperatorskago Velichestva, 1817), pp. 10-11.

but far enough away to avoid argument. After 1775 it was moved permanently to Irkutsk.

When the new civil lists of customs personnel were issued on 23 August 1754, Kiakhta received the largest complement in Transbaikalia and one of the largest in Siberia: a director, a paymaster chosen from among the Muscovite merchants, a bookkeeper *(bukhgal'ter)*, two chancery clerks, four copyists, one interpreter, and two guards.[62] Two years later a second director was added to insure that business was not neglected in the event of illness of the director, and although it was unsaid, it was hoped that each would check on the judgment and veracity of the other.[63] In addition to this main cadre, the paymaster had an assistant, four storekeepers *(larets)*, and eight sworn-appraisers, all usually chosen from among the local merchants. Both annual and monthly reports were expected from the customs houses at Kiakhta, Verkhotur'e, Iamyshev, and Semipalatinsk on the Siberian Line, which listed fully all goods that passed through in either direction and all duties collected on them.

As mentioned earlier the Senate reminded Great Russian merchants trading at Kiakhta of their prerogative to give firm pledges of duties payment, rather than to pay immediately in cash, as detailed in the *veksel'* regulations of 1729. Siberian inhabitants were still excluded from the privilege. Even Great Russian merchants trading at Verkhotur'e, Tsurukhaitu, Iamyshev, and Semipalatinsk could not take advantage of *veksel'* pledges, because of the small size of the external trade conducted at these cities and their proximity to Tobol'sk, Irkutsk, or other Siberian *gubernskie* towns. The *veksel'* pledge was sent by ordinary mail from Kiakhta to the Siberian Prikaz which added two kopeks per ruble as charge for the service. Any merchant could avoid the two-kopeks charge by depositing cash in advance of his journey to the border. Still, as earlier, the *veksel'* period was short, and most merchants were unable to dispose of their goods quickly enough and so turned to the money-lender (*baryshnik*, or less kindly, *rostovshchik*) for cash to pay, affording the latter a profit of 200-300 per cent on his loan.

The instructions issued to the newly appointed Kiakhta customs house director, Roman Piatov, give some impression of his wide

62. *PSZ*, XIV, No. 10281, 199-201; Chulkov, *Istoricheskoe opisanie*, III, Bk. 2, 282–85.

63. *PSZ*, XIV, No. 10520, 522-23, dated 8 March 1756.

powers and, by extension, of the nature of this purely commercial town.[64] Beyond the usual sort of admonitions and directives on the procedures to operate an efficient bureaucratic office, this long document (thirty-seven articles) instructed Piatov to insure that no unauthorized persons be permitted in the Kiakhta "merchants' court," i.e., no one except merchants and their designated agents who had goods stored in the warehouses, and any peasants and artisans who directly served trade. Merchants acting on commission for absentee associates *(komissionery)*, merchants' agents, and retail merchants, on the strength of a Senate ukaz of 1744, had to present letters of credit *(kreditnye pis'ma)* or of certification *(veruiushchye pis'ma)* from their masters or associates. Under no circumstances could goods brought for sale be stored in private houses or apartments; they were always to be available for inspection. The inspection for contraband of arriving and departing merchants was the responsibility of the director; his instructions specifically enjoined him to search for lead, silver rubles and other money, precious metals in any form, rhubarb, and tobacco balls, all mentioned in decrees of 1734, 1735, 1744, and 1753. Any culprits were to be reported to the Irkutsk *guberniia* chancellery and the Siberian Prikaz. For maintenance of the border guardhouses Piatov was authorized to appoint officers and detail soldiers, but he was continually to exercise close scrutiny over them to guarantee that they observed and enforced all orders and directives. Even though there existed a "town hall" and a small town administration largely run by the merchants, the customhouse director, at least up to this time, was responsible for local judicial bodies: the local oral court and the tribunal (*slovesnyi sud* and *osprava*). Prior to the establishment in 1774 of a town hall in Kiakhta, the customs house director functioned more in the nature of a frontier *voevoda* with broad administrative, executive, and judicial powers, greater than those of a mayor of a settled city. Together with the leading merchants in the suburb he administered a commercial outpost, not an urban center.

One of the most persistent handicaps for nearly all merchants in eighteenth-century Russia was the almost total lack of credit at nonusurious rates of interest.[65] Prior to the middle of the century

64. Chulkov, *Istoricheskoe opisanie*, III, Bk. 2, 286-304.

65. For a truly excellent recent survey of this see Saul Iakovlevich Borovoi, "Voprosy kreditovaniia torgovli i promyshlennosti v ekonomicheskoi politike Rossii XVIII veka," *Istoricheskie zapiski*, XXXIII (1950), 92-122. Consult

there was no form of organized credit, although for a hundred years merchant and state officials bemoaned the absence and proposed various solutions. The first official credit institution was the Money Office *(Monetnaia kontora)*, founded in 1729 and in operation at least until 1736. Because "many of our Russian subjects, in need of money" had to borrow at usurious rates of 12, 15, or 20 per cent, the Office began small loan operations, but apparently had little impact upon foreign trade and merchants.

The real beginning of loan banking in Russia was the Elizabethan measure of 1754 establishing the State Loan Bank *(Gosudarstvennyi zaemnyi bank)*, sponsored by Shuvalov, the energetic minister responsible for nearly all of the liberal economic measures of the time.[66] The bank had two main sorts of clients: the gentrymen of Moscow and St. Petersburg, notoriously in need of cash, and the Russian merchants trading in the port of St. Petersburg. The latter borrowed from the State Commercial Bank *(Gosudarstvennyi kommercheskii bank)*, as the mercantile branch was known, capital for trade for not less than one month and not more than one year at the marvelously favorable rate of 6 per cent per annum. This bank was subordinate to the Commerce Collegium, and under the direction of its president (Iakov Evreinov) until 1764, when his ineptitude led to general management by the Collegium. It was abolished in 1782, and its remaining capital was transferred to the Petersburg Gentry Bank *(Peterburgskii dvorianskii bank)*.

No loan from the State Commercial Bank could exceed 75 per cent of the value of the goods offered as collateral. The Bank had a capital of 500,000 rubles initially (compared with 750,000 rubles for the Gentry Bank), but was strictly a loan bank; it had no accounts or deposit operations. According to Borovoi, in the six sessions of the Senate that debated the formation of the bank there was some discussion of expanding its role, especially so as to include merchants other than those in St. Petersburg, but in the end only those in the capital were favored. Perhaps this was because—Shuvalov insisted—the Commercial Bank had the major function of strengthening Russian mercantile credit in the Amster-

Dmitrii Andreevich Tolstoi, *Istoriia finansovykh uchrezhdenii Rossii so vremeni osnovaniia gosudarstva do konchiny Imperatritsy Ekateriny II* (St. Petersburg: V Tipografii Konstantina Zhernakova, 1848), pp. 232-33.

66. *PSZ*, XIV, No. 10235, 87-94; XIV, No. 10280, 199; XVI, No. 12127, 707-8; XXI, No. 15534, 695; *Gosudarstvennye uchrezhdeniia*, pp. 142, 262-63; Tolstoi, *Istoriia*, 234.

dam Bourse.[67] Under the aegis of Evreinov the Bank loaned its capital, but its affairs were mismanaged. By 1764 the total capital which then amounted to over 800,000 rubles was lent, but overdue loans reached 382,000 rubles. Borovoi has no doubt but that Evreinov profited personally from the operations, and in light of his nefarious although unpunished handling of Svin'in's rhubarb monopoly, that is not unlikely. After the 1760's, the Bank seems not to have been very active.

In 1760 the newly reformed Commission on Commerce created a local bank in Astrakhan for use by the Armenian merchants trading there. Little is known of its history, and it certainly did not affect the China merchants. Three years later a bank in Madrid was proposed, but nothing came of it. The Assignation Bank *(Gosudarstvennyi assignatsionnyi bank)* was founded in 1769, but it was of the emission type and was not concerned with credit for landowning or trade.

With the possible exception of the St. Petersburg Commercial Bank, none of these new banks or credit institutions had any impact on the China trade. It is possible that one or two of the large merchants, who operated through agents in Kiakhta, did secure loans from the Bank, but the limited loan period was a particular disadvantage to merchants carrying goods from the Mongolian border to the markets of Amsterdam, London, or Hamburg. In 1764 a group of merchants petitioned for an extension of the loan period to four years and were granted permission to defer payment, but by that time the Bank had its own difficulties and soon lapsed into relative inactivity.[68] Shuvalov's efforts at promoting trade were laudable, but so limited in scope and directly focused on the improvement of St. Petersburg and other European outlets, that they had no visible ameliorative effect in Siberia.

The Volume and the Goods

The size of private trade through Kiakhta in ruble value or volume of merchandise is impossible to establish with any certainty. Data is scattered and fragmentary prior to the year 1755. After that, as argued in Chapter 9, there is good cause to accept the ruble figures

67. Borovoi, *Istoricheskie zapiski*, XXXIII (1959), 103; *PSZ*, XVI, No. 12127. 707-8, Imperial decree dated 6 April 1764.

68. Chulkov, *Istoricheskie opisanie*, III, Bk. 2, 305.

available with tentativeness and reservation. None of the data we shall cite take contraband into consideration, which, it must be assumed, continued almost unabated from the Treaty of Kiakhta on and constituted a significant proportion of the total actual trade. In 1758 Kiakhta customs house director Piatov reported that the secretive carriage of goods was impossible to prevent because of the great distances between the customs barriers and guardhouses, and because the Buriats assigned to man the guardhouses took little care to intercept contraband. They even traded in such manner themselves.[69] Since the wooden palisades and breast-high parapets erected many years earlier were, in the majority, rotten, broken, or consumed by fire, Piatov recommended the building of a major barrier near Lake Baikal in the vicinity of the Ambassadorial monastery (*Posol'skii*, in honor of Vladislavich). But the resourcefulness of a dedicated barrier-runner could hardly be so easily nullified. Finally, all of the data extant are derived from customs house figures, which as we have said, are imprecise at best.

Semenov calculates that in 1744 there were acquired by Russian merchants, through purchase or barter, some 287,000 rubles of Chinese goods, and two years later in an eight-month period 177,106 rubles worth, which figures out to be about the same as in 1744.[70] Many consignments ran as high as 10,000 rubles, and those of the first-guild Moscow merchant Zhuravlev several tens of thousands. These figures do not seem out of line and probably represent with reasonable accuracy the high level of exchange obtained in the 1740's, after such a slow start. For 1751 Semenov has Chinese goods fixed at 433,133 silver rubles, slightly over a 50 per cent increase since the mid-1740's, including 103,050 rubles in silk fabrics, 527,940 rubles in cotton goods, 10,810 rubles in raw or unprocessed silk, and a small 46,375 rubles in teas. No figures for the value of Russian exports prior to 1755 are available, but it may be assumed that they are of roughly the same magnitudes as these import figures, which would mean a total turnover of between 500,000 and 600,000 rubles for the mid-1740's, and between 800,000 and 900,000 for the early years of the next decade.

For the last seven years of Elizabeth's reign, the total ruble value of trade ranged from a low of 692,021 rubles in 1756 to a high

69. *Ibid.*, III, Bk. 2.
70. Semenov, *Izuchenie*, III, 199-200.

of 1,417,130 rubles in 1759.[71] From this turnover were extracted duties of 157,000 to 230,000 rubles annually, many times the profits of the most successful of the Peking caravans, and at much smaller investment. Six out of the seven years, the value of Russian exports exceeded the value of Chinese imports, which some contemporary observers attribute to the fact that Russian merchants often set values (in money terms or whatever standard of value was used at the time in actual bartering) far below those of the Chinese goods, causing them to barter "unfavorably." Because of the comparatively low cost of Siberian furs and the high prices Chinese fineries obtained in the Russian markets, they still did well on the entire operation, some Great Russian merchants getting back 200-300 per cent on their investments.

In the early years of Catherine's reign, the Chinese suspended trade at Kiakhta for at least four years as a result of serious disputes between the two powers, which shall be discussed in the next chapter, and the total turnover of trade declined to probably nil in 1767, and not until 1769 did it recover and then exceed all previous highs.

The state monopoly on the carriage and sale of the finest of Siberian furs did not prevent less dear and more plentiful pelts from being the major export of Russian merchants through Kiakhta. During the second half of the century furs were ad valorem well above half of the exports in every year. In 1755, for example, of the 606,000 rubles of exports, furs constituted 69.8 per cent (423,000 rubles).[72] And there is every reason to believe that this predominant place was held in the second quarter of the century. Toward the end of the century the absolute volume of pelts continued to increase, but their relative position seems to have declined, as other goods, particularly European manufactured items, took a more active role. Although the most choice pelts could not be legally traded while the caravans lasted, except as sanctioned by Lange and his successors when they judged their private sale would not do damage to the crown trade, many of the less choice furs were in almost as great demand by the Chinese. The reason seems to have been the skills the Chinese furriers developed in dying and working inferior furs to produce attractive goods.

71. See Chapter 9.

72. M. Andreev, "Iz istorii snoshenii Rossii s Kitaem (XVII-XX v.v.)," *Severnaia Aziia, obshchestvenno-nauchnyi zhurnal*, Bks. 5-6 (1925), 66.

The leading pelt by volume, although not always by value, was squirrel of various qualities and conditions, followed (not in order of precedence) by ermine, fox, cat, beaver, ferret, rabbit, lynx, otter, marten, sea otter, wolf, bear, glutton, mink, marmot, dog, and musk deer. All these were mainly from Siberia. In the second half of the century and increasing as years went by, a significant number of North American furs were sold at Kiakhta, brought either from the Aleutians and Alaska by *promyshlenniki* who braved the dangers of North Pacific crossings, or from Canada and the United States via European carriers. The Dutch in particular carried New World furs to Russia through the Baltic ports and Arkhangel'sk.[73] In the earlier eighteenth century, sixty to eighty Dutch ships annually visited Russia carrying in part staple furs of New Netherlands (especially beaver), in return for which they received old Rijksdallers, gold ducats, spices, textiles, wines, *iuft'*, and Russian beaver! The Russians had a trade secret, reports E. E. Rich, by which they combed beaver pelts leaving only the long guard hairs, a fur widely prized in European haberdasheries. Some of the North American beaver were carried across Siberia and sold to the Chinese, and in spite of the distance they still brought profit to the Russian merchant. From the 1740's on, Aleutian and Alaskan pelts, gathered by merchants or merchants' agents from Irkutsk as often as not, counted for an increasingly large share of the Kiakhta market especially as depletion of the fur-bearing animals in Siberia caused prices to rise.

Russian hides, *iuft'*, lambskins, sheepskins, goatskins, and calfskins, usually were the second general item of trade, along with the popular but expensive Kazan' Morocco *(saf'ian)*. Russian cloth and fabrics were significant—not fine textiles, but coarse heavy fabrics in large part, mainly linens and woolens. European fabrics traded in ever increasing amounts, until by the end of the century, they were greater in volume than the Russian; then too a wide variety of manufactured products sold in small amounts, although together they composed typically, let us say, 15 per cent of the trade ad valorem, especially Russian iron goods—axes, knives, shears, scythes, Tula locks, mirrors, isinglass, etc. Finally animals were one of the most important items of local trade: horses, horned cattle, sheep, and hunting dogs, among others.

73. See for example E. E. Rich, "Russia and the Colonial Fur Trade," *Economic History Review*, 2d Series, VII (1955), 311-16.

Three items comprised the bulk of Chinese exports: cottons, silks, and teas. By far the most important in bulk and value were the cottons. In 1751 for example 257,940 rubles worth of cottons were imported, representing 59.5 per cent of the total value of Russian imports. In later years the percentage increased. Quality ranged from extremely fine dyed and printed fabrics to coarse and inexpensive ones. Silks in all forms—raw, twisted, skeined, and finished dyed and printed goods—were in great demand in Russia, and were also re-exported to Europe. In 1751 silk fabrics comprised 23.8 per cent of the total ruble value of Chinese exports (103,050 rubles), but declined thereafter both absolutely and relatively, in part because of the continuing efforts in Russia to produce silks (and the consequent tariff barriers raised on all but raw silk) and partly because of the competition from Italian silks. Teas were imported from the earliest days of Sino-Russian contact, but not until the eighteenth century, as the Russians became addicted to the brew, did they become a major item of private carriage. Until Catherinian times, brick tea *(kirpichnyi chai)*, used almost exclusively by Mongolian peoples of Siberia, overshadowed dried leaves, both green and black. By the end of the century the situation was reversed, and several varieties of green tea predominated.

The other commodities were of less commercial consequence. When they were not monopolized, tobacco sales were important, but the import of Chinese tobacco, preferred mainly by the static Siberian populace, did not increase much in quantity. A long list of exotica finishes the picture: porcelains, enamels, cosmetics, medicants, etc. All arrived in small quantities, although many had great value in terms of weight and bulk.

Looking back over these items of exchange, it is immediately obvious that the vast bulk of Russian exports were natural or at best semiprocessed goods: furs and hides. Many times in the eighteenth century state offices provoked inquiries, especially in connection with the Peking caravans, as to Chinese material needs and desires and the potential markets within Chinese or Mongolian lands for other Russian goods, but except in small quantities the Chinese neither needed nor wanted Russia's manufactures. By contrast the Chinese provided these Europeans with textiles and other products of sophisticated and unduplicated (at least in Russia) industry. Only tea was "natural," and the handling and preparation in turning a leaf into a potable make it questionable whether it cannot properly be described as a semiprocessed or finished product. This was not a matter of a "colonial" east supplying raw materials and resources to an industrially progressive and energetic western economy.

A Note on Tsurukhaitu and the Siberian Line

The other border trading post we have said nothing of. Tsurukhaitu was intended to draw the trading formerly done at Naun, at Nerchinsk, and in Nerchinsk *uezd*, but it never did. Some small trading began as early as 1729, but because of the great distance lumber had to be carried, building of the town had barely been begun, Bukhol'ts reported.[74] Its location was unblest, but the main reason for the stagnation of trade there was its distance from the centers of Siberian and Mongolian population and commerce. The overall journey from Irkutsk to Peking via Tsurukhaitu, Naun, and Shanhaikuan was over 650 miles farther than by way of Kiakhta and Kalgan, a factor equally important to Russian and Chinese merchants. The terrain was difficult, and as several crown caravans testified, the danger from marauding highwaymen was no less great than across Mongolia. The Russian merchant brought his merchandise nearly to Kiakhta by raft or flatboat, whereas the Tsurukhaitu passage required expensive overland carriage. And Kiakhta was adjacent to the Central Asian peoples, who supplied several major items of commercial value, particularly Bukharan rhubarb and cottons. There was apparently nothing the Manchurians could offer that was not available at Kiakhta. Also, intermittent Manchu military activity and colonization in Mongolia and Central Asia stimulated border trade at Kiakhta in cattle, horses, and provisions, when permitted by the Russian state.

From the beginning, substantially the only trade carried on at Tsurukhaitu was performed by the annual Chinese border inspection team which escorted a few merchants from Naun. The little expedition usually camped across the river from the post for ten days to a month in the early summer, and bartered small amounts with local tradesmen from Nerchinsk, before moving on

74. Andrievich, *Kratkii ocherk*, p. 148.

in small boats to their duties of border control.[75] At first the trade was so light and the post so distant from administrative centers, that no customs duties were collected, which permitted some of the Cossacks stationed there to accumulate tidy sums. The goods exchanged were not out of the ordinary: animals, pelts, skins, and *iuft'* on the Russian side; cottons, silks and tobacco on the Chinese.

Most of the imported goods sold in Nerchinsk and Siberian territory to the northeast, but if the price were particularly favorable some of the cottons might be carried to Irkutsk and thence west. And the best of the Nerchinsk region sable and squirrel funnelled to the Chinese through Kiakhta not Tsurukhaitu. Even the Chinese tobacco and brick tea came in quantities too small to satisfy the needs of Transbaikalian natives, and local merchants carried more back from Kiakhta and Selenginsk.

A Soviet writer gives figures for the total turnover of trade at Tsurukhaitu for the years 1732-35, without citing the source of his data. They work out to an average of 4701 rubles per year.[76] Later data suggest that this is of the proper magnitude. A high of 10,217 rubles volume of trade was reached in 1768, but the usual size in the 1760's and 1770's was 1000 to 3000 rubles per year.[77]

Far to the west on the Siberian Line, trade between Russians and Kazakhs on one side, and Dzhungars and other Mongol peoples on the other, was not significant before the 1740's.[78] The center of the trade was Orenburg on the Irtysh, where in 1745 a customhouse was established and a merchants' court *(menovoi dvor)* built. Thereafter a brisk trade developed there and in the neighboring forts of Semipalatinsk, Iamyshev, Ust'-kamenogorsk, and Zhelenzinsk. After the suppression of Dzhungar power by the Manchu armies of China in the late 1750's, the Kazakhs of the Middle and Great Hordes migrated back to their native region and regular trade with them was carried on by the Russians. Chinese rarely traded directly with the Russians on the Siberian Line, but many goods of Chinese origin were brought by these Asian peoples: silk fabrics, cottons, teas of various sorts, and silver, as well as goods of Tashkent origin, such as cottons, linens, rice meal, and Kirgiz horses, horned cattle, sheep, etc. Throughout the second half of

75. Pallas, *Voyages,* IV, 621; Trusevich, *Posol'skiia i torgovliia snosheniia,* p. 157; Coxe, *Account,* p. 244; Ministerstvo Vnutrennykh Del, *Statisticheskoe obozrenie Sibiri,* p. 335.

76. Sladkovskii, *Ocherki ekonomicheskikh otnoshenii,* p. 62.

77. See Chapter 9.

78. See especially Batrakov, *Istoricheskie nauki,* Bk. 11, 5-18.

the eighteenth and early nineteenth centuries, the Russian government prohibited private merchant caravans in Central Asia and Eastern Turkestan, preferring—mainly for fiscal reasons—all trade to be conducted on the Line under the scrutiny of customs officials.[79] By the same token the Asians were not allowed to penetrate Siberia for trade, as they had long done at Tobol'sk and other Siberian cities.[80] Chinese authorities on their part, prohibited Russians coming to Turkestan to trade after 1758, and the latter simply began to use native Tatar agents as intermediaries. Also the Chinese attempted to monopolize all this trade, requiring all Russian merchants or their agents to turn over to them all of the sheep and other animals they brought in exchange for locally made cottons. These efforts by the officials on both sides to the contrary, private trade persisted, and although mostly barter, the Russians secured gold and silver bullion in substantial amounts.[81]

It is a great misfortune that we do not have the account books and family archives of these private merchants who traded with the Chinese in Kiakhta, and Tsurukhaitu, and on the Siberian Line. We cannot give any direct evidence of the profits or losses of the trade to private merchants, either Russian, Siberian, or foreign. All the indirect information strongly suggests that, at least for many of the larger and more skillful of them, the Kiakhta trade was one of the most lucrative and successful of Russia's eighteenth-century avenues of commerce. The several state monopolies and restrictions unquestionably hindered the growth of a healthy commerce, for it took the state officialdom decades to realize the virtue of promoting private endeavour and of taxing it heavily enough to bring good return, but lightly enough to encourage its growth. Bribable officials in the East partly offset this disability however, and there cannot be the slightest doubt but that contraband continued on a large scale throughout the pre-Catherinian years. What little was done, even during the reign of Elizabeth, to encourage and support private trade had very little impact on the China trade. And persistent disputes between the Russian and Chinese courts, by the middle of the century revolving around the Chinese campaign to subdue the Dzhungars, damaged the course of commerce, and at times cut it off completely.

79. *Istoricheskie nauki*, Bk. 11, p. 16.

80. Chulkov, *Istoricheskoe opisanie*, III, Bk. 2, 263-65; *PSZ*, XVI, No. 11931, 379-83, Point 7.

81. Tooke, *View of the Russian Empire*, III, 459. Through Semipalatinsk in 1777 was imported 72,015 rubles in silver bars.

Chapter VII. Trade or War, Continuing Problems of Intercourse

All commerce between Russia and China, both state and private, was threatened with destruction in the last years of Elizabeth and in the early years of Catherine. No sudden event caused the threat of war between the two empires; rather a series of minor vexations, misunderstandings, and cross-purposes, persisting throughout the years, led to the complete breakdown of diplomatic relations between St. Petersburg and Peking, and the severing of trade, between 1764 and 1768. Most of the matters of dispute had little to do directly with trade; they were matters of state policy, involving territorial acquisition and control, regulation of the natives on both sides of the frontier, and the extension of colonial empire by both powers. Yet they often led to temporary suspensions of private trade at Kiakhta-Mai-mai-ch'eng, and hampered the state caravans, causing them long delays in entering China. These delays and suspensions hindered the growth of trade and caused great damage both to private merchants and the Russian state, particularly as a result of deterioration of goods during the long periods while waiting to be sold.

The critical disputes stemmed largely from the confrontation of the imperial thrusts of China and Russia. During the eighteenth century both powers were concerned to a greater or lesser degree with expanding their Asian empires and consolidating control over those lands and peoples acquired. Except for the Siberian Line and recurrent interest in the Amur Valley, most of the Russian thrust slid tangentially past Chinese domains, as Russian *promyshlenniki,* and then state officials and the church, moved east and north to the Pacific and across it to Alaska. The Manchu court, on the other hand, spent a century slowly pressing its domination westward in Central Asia, into that region where the strong Dzhungars were not willing to submit easily to the foreign hegemony. The Manchu-Dzhungar wars were the backdrop for Russian-Chinese controversies, for it was the fighting that sharply increased the tempo of defection and desertion across the border from Mongolia to Siberia. The return of runaways was one of the most persistent and abrasive problems between the two powers.

The Dzhungar Wars, Runaways, and Rustling

After several years of quiescence, the Dzhungar wars broke out again in 1729. Two years earlier the Dzhungar chieftain Tsewang Araptan was killed in the Ili region, and his son Galdan Tseren, assumed the title of *Kontaisha*.[1] The Ch'ing court dispatched two armies to the west, one to the Altai region and the other to the Barkul. Although he sent a representative to the Yung-ch'eng Emperor, Galdan in 1731 launched a surprise attack on the northern Manchu army and defeated it soundly. Sporadic fighting continued for four years, until Galdan weakened, sued for peace, and was granted it. For a decade after 1735, an uneasy peace prevailed in Chinese Turkestan, marred by Dzhungar pressure on the Kazakhs to the west who had earlier accepted fielty to Tsaritsa Anna in 1734 and in 1740.[2] Upon Galdan's death in 1745, his son and successor Tsewang Dorji quickly displayed truculence toward the Manchus, but he was killed by a brother. From then until 1758, Central Asia was subjected to fighting and disturbance almost without respite.

These continually disturbed conditions, the outbursts of fighting not only between Manchu and Dzhungar, but also between Dzhungar and other neighboring Mongol peoples, tested the Treaty of Kiakhta almost as soon as it was signed. For both sides a major function of the Treaty was to delimit the known border between Russian and Manchu territories, to patrol it, to intercept any natives who crossed it for any reason, and to deport them immediately. As we explained with reference to contraband running, this was no simple task. The natives of the border region, both Siberian and Mongolian, were traditionally nomadic. With no

1. For discussions of the Dzhungarian wars, consult, *inter alia*, Howarth, *History of the Mongols*, especially Pt. 1: *The Mongols Proper and the Kalmuks*, pp. 649-680; Hummel, *Eminent Chinese*, I, 9-11; Kurts, *Novyi Vostok*, Bk. 19 (1927), 199-201; Wu Ch'i-yu, *"China, Russia and Central Asia; a Study of the Political and Diplomatic Relations Between (I) China and Central Asia; (II) Russia and Central Aisa; (III) Russia and China in Regard to Their Respective Interests in Central Asia Beginning Roughly from the Commencement (1644) of the Ching Dynasty to the Year 1895"* (Ph.D. dissertation, Princeton University, 1933), pp. 31-33; Vasilii Vladimirovich Bartol'd, *Four Studies on the History of Central Asia*, 1, 164 ff.; and Andrievich, *Kratkii ocherk*, pp. 152 ff.

2. In a 1735 interview at Orenburg between Governor Tatishchev of Russia and Abulkhair Khan of the Little Horde of the Kazakhs. In 1740 the Middle Horde Khan Abul Makhmet presented letters of submission to the Russian at Orenburg.

censuses and other population checks to go by, it was at times nearly impossible for Russian and Manchu-Chinese administrator and soldier to distinguish between a Siberian Buriat and a Mongol of the Tushetu Khanate, except when large numbers were involved, and large numbers were not easily persuaded to return when they were armed and feared reprisal if they did.

Hardly had Vladislavich left the frontier than Colonel Bukhol'ts reported that Mongol predators crossed the border and fell upon Russian settlers.[3] This was the first of probably hundreds of similar instances over the next several decades. This kind of depradation exacerbated Russian-Chinese relations, but only occasionally resulted in drastic action on either side, and then only when one party believed that the other had not properly punished the apprehended culprits. The major problem was rather the defection to the Russian side of antagonists of the Manchu armies, or simply of those fleeing to escape being caught in the fighting or being ravaged by the ill-disciplined troops.

Still the Collegium of Foreign Affairs carefully instructed Bukhol'ts, in ukazes of August and November 1730, that all runaways and defectors must be returned, by force of arms if they could not be persuaded.[4] These orders were provoked by the passage across the border of a Mongol leader with seven iurts, wives, children, cattle, and provisions, seeking refuge and Russian suzerainty. Border inspectors Firsov and Mikhalev received full and explicit orders to refuse entry to any fugitives from the Chinese, to send back immediately any thievish people to the officials on the Chinese side, to prevent Russian subjects from stealing across the border without proper credentials, to prohibit the sale of provisions, horses, cattle, and camels across the border. If large groups of fugitives caught them unawares, they must immediately inform the Customs House Officer at Kiakhta and refrain from taking open military action against them. At least for the time being, it would seem that Russian officials both in St. Petersburg and on the border had every intention of fulfilling the Treaty to the letter. Later, as we shall see, they were not above a bit of prevarication.

By the autumn of 1731 Vice-Governor Zholobov reported that already ten thousand (!) iurts had found their way to Siberia, of

3. Bantysh-Kamenskii, *Diplomaticheskoe sobranie*, pp. 163-64.

4. *Ibid.*, p. 169; Sychevskii, *Chteniia OIDR*, Bk. 2 (April-June, 1875), 98-102.

which 2142 had been deported.[5] He warned that if hostilities continued in Mongolia, it would be absolutely impossible to seal off the border; it was too broad and too populous, and there were ready for duty only one infantry regiment and one dragoon company of regulars, supported by five thousand armed Tungus and Buriats, loyal but uncertain in an ambiguous situation. His warning was well advised. In the next several years matters worsened.

In April 1732, more than five hundred iurts crossed into the Nerchinsk region, settled in the river valleys, and announced their desire to stay.[6] Bukhol'ts failed to cajole them into returning, and Zholobov reported the next month of the grave danger inherent in the situation. He asked that he be relieved of primary responsibility by the Tobol'sk governor. Later he recommended that the *Li-fan-yuan* be informed that they must take greater precautions to intercept their own people, and that defectors who successfully crossed the border be permitted to stay in Russian villages as long as the fighting went on, under the watchful eye of Tungus and Buriats. By the end of the year, the *Li-fan-yuan* and the Senate exchanged notes, the Chinese accusing the Russians, as they were to do many times in the future, of a lack of haste in returning the runaways, to which the Russians replied "nonsense," citing the difficulties involved in returning large numbers. The Senate wished the Emperor great good fortune in his military operations.

The Russians also had grievances. Tobol'sk Governor Pleshcheev complained, in the late spring of 1734, that border officials had received no satisfaction from repeated requests to Mongol border officials to investigate instances of horse rustling across the border.[7] He charged that the officials themselves connived in the depradations. As for the defectors 2886 iurts had been sent back across the border between 1730 and 1733, but there seemed no end to the problem. And for the moment there was none. Nine hundred thirty-five iurts, with 2150 men of fighting age, entered Nerchinsk *uezd* in the summer, and Firsov's request that they leave was rejected. Bukhol'ts then ordered him to gather 3000 men along the border for a show of military strength, which Firsov did arrange with princes of the Tungus tribes. The Chinese re-

5. Bantysh-Kamenskii, *Diplomaticheskoe sobranie*, p. 203, a report of 16 October 1731.

6. *Ibid.*, pp. 204-5.

7. *Ibid.*, p. 215.

tired, but by October crossed back again when the Russian troops were disbanded.

The year 1735 finally saw relief. In the spring peremptory orders were sent from the Collegium of Foreign Affairs to the Tobol'sk governor that all runaways be returned "with utmost speed," i.e., before the state caravan readying at the border crossed into Mongolia.[8] Displaying a little more assiduousness, Pleshcheev sent off a Captain Petr Porietskii to the border on 10 June 1735, with full powers to ship off the runaways and to settle any Chinese complaints of depradations across the border. The *Li-fan-yuan* was impressed with the Russian efforts in those months and sent a note of thanks to the Senate, together with one hundred bolts of *kamka* and one thousand *tiun'* of *kitaika* which Iakobi distributed among the Tungus and Buriats who took part in the roundups.[9] None too soon word that Galdan had struck a peace with the Chinese came. It took some time to return all the refugees, but the first crisis was passed.[10] With these conditions along the border, it is no wonder that merchants from both sides arrived slowly at Kiakhta and Mai-mai-ch'eng.

These difficult experiences did little to provoke either side to strengthen significantly their border defences and inspection facilities. The Russian Tsaritsa did authorize the formation of one new dragoon regiment and one battalion of infantry formed from among the Siberian gentry, Cossacks, and boiars' sons.[11] The Siberian Office was also detailed to compile complete inventories of all arms available, all ammunition, horses and uniforms. During the fighting with Galdan the Chinese informed the Russians they had raised several new forts in Mongolia, but none of these measures had any visible effect on the porosity of the border.

As the problem of runaways receded for the moment, disputes over rustling and other thievery across the border increased. The

8. *Ibid.*, pp. 220-21.

9. Sychevskii, *Chteniia OIDR*, Bk. 2 (April-June, 1875), 130.

10. Bantysh-Kamenskii, *Diplomaticheskoe sobranie*, pp. 225, 235-37. The Collegium of Foreign Affairs at least was hopeful that the whole business could be forgotten. It instructed the Siberian Governor Buturlin that without doubt all of the runaways were not returned, but he should have his Captain Porietskii investigate only those cases detailed by the Chinese, and then see to it that the claims not be over fulfilled. Porietskii died in Irkutsk on 27 April 1739 and Bukhol'ts replaced him with Major *(Sekund-maior)* Kalina Nalabardin of the Iakutsk Regiment on 2 March 1740 to whom he passed on the same instructions.

11. *PSZ*, X, No. 7261, 155-56; IX, No. 7051, 924-25.

Treaty of Kiakhta stipulated that stolen animals were to be returned ten-fold, a remarkable provision and one almost impossible to enforce on a pastoral economy dependent on animals for livelihood.[12] Such a harsh penalty was probably expected to serve as a deterrent, but the reverse seems to have been the case—thefts, demands for ten-fold restitution, more thefts, more demands, until the situation was thoroughly and preposterously out of hand. One of the first instances of cattle rustling after the Treaty occurred in 1732; a Mongol highwayman killed three Russians and made off with 113 animals.[13] Chinese authorities returned the stolen animals and paid a fine of 203 head of "large" cattle.

The Russians were not as assiduous in making restitution. In the same year, the Chinese demanded 2,087 head stolen since 1729 near Tsurukhaitu in the east. While the Russians vacillated, the demands escalated, until an incident involving the demolition of the house of a Chinese merchant and the theft of his goods provoked the dzarguchei to suspend trade at Kiakhta for several days in 1737.[14] During the two years preceding, Captain Porietskii received from the Chechen and Tushetu Khans itemized lists of 190 separate instances of theft, on the basis of which the Mongol leaders demanded 23,873 camels, horses, and horned cattle from the Russians.[15] He reported early in 1737 to the Tobol'sk governor, and in turn to the Collegium of Foreign Affairs, that he had investigated only forty cases and had turned over to the Chinese 2927 head of cattle. The other 150 cases he left uninvestigated. On the other hand, he inquired into and substantiated thirty-seven instances (of a total of 186 reported) of Russian animals carried off to Mongolia, and secured the return to Siberia of 3665 head of a total of 25,784 claimed. As in the matter of runaways, local Russian officials, backed by the Collegium of Foreign Affairs, regarded the whole business of rustling as best handled by means of a kind of swapping of animals. The Collegium wrote the governor on 15 September 1737 that the Chinese seemed undisturbed by the

12. Owen Lattimore, *Inner Asian Frontiers of China* ("American Geographical Society Research Series," No. 21 [New York: American Geographical Society, 1940]), especially pp. 53-102.

13. Kurts, *Russko-kitaiskie snosheniia*, n. 7, pp. 97-98. Russian sources do not always distinguish between the kinds of animals involved. Horned cattle, horses, camels, sheep, and even deer were mentioned, although the first three obviously were the most important.

14. Silin, *Kiakhta*, p. 58; Trusevich, *Posol'skiia i torgovliia snosheniia*, p. 48.

15. Bantysh-Kamenskii, *Diplomaticheskoe sobranie*, pp. 235-37.

cases not investigated, and there were many small claims still extant on the Russian side, so all should be left "in silence" and not considered. If the Chinese pressed their claims, Porietskii was required to investigate, but as many as he satisfied, he must demand that similar Russian claims be satisfied.

This and other issues led to a series of border conferences (1739-43) between the special investigator Porietskii (and his successors after his death in 1739, Major Kalina Nalabardin and Captain Andrei Grecheninov, both of the Iakutsk Regiment) and several councillors appointed by the Tushetu Khan.[16] Fifteen of fifty-seven cases of runaways, theft, rustling, and murder brought up by the Russians were settled, but no definitive solutions or procedural rules for handling cases in the future were accomplished, although the meeting concluded amicably in November 1743.

The very next year the amicability evaporated in wrangling over the case of the inebriated Russians who killed two Chinese merchants in a scuffle over vodka.[17] This is the incident that threatened the well-being of the Lebratovskii caravan in 1744. The dzarguchei, tired of waiting for assurances from the Russians that the accused had been tried for their felonious attack, finally shut down trade in Mai-mai-ch'eng for seventeen days, until the trial date was set. Even then the legal proceedings made little headway, and it was 1746 before the Chinese were informed that the death penalty had been imposed. It was never carried out, as we know, but the Chinese had no choice but to continue to demand exposure of the corpses at the frontier as proof.

This dispute over the death penalty for frontier miscreants was not an isolated incident. From 1742 on, the two sides continued to quarrel over the punishment, usually the supreme penalty, of apprehended offenders. The Treaty of Kiakhta specified the death penalty for military personnel on either side who deserted, presumably to be carried out on the side of the border on which they were apprehended, but no precise mention was made as to the punishment to be meted out to civilians. This was complicated by the Elizabethan measures that lightened punishments and abrogated the death sentence for some classes and groups in

16. *Ibid.*, pp. 247-48.

17. Kurts, *Russko-kitaiskie snosheniia*, p. 87; Trusevich, *Posol'skiia i torgovliia snosheniia*, p. 49; Bantysh-Kamenskii, *Diplomaticheskoe sobranie*, pp. 249-50; and Sychevskii, *Chteniia OIDR*, Bk. 2 (April-June, 1875), 233.

Russia.[18] In Siberia, however, the death penalty was practiced for some time after it was out of favor in European Russia. The issue rose again in Russian-Chinese relations in 1750 when Iakobi reported that he had unilaterally granted clemency to a Tungus who had been thrice charged with horse theft by the Chinese.[19] His reasoning was ingenuous; the Chinese declined to put to death their own offenders, and as *quid pro quo* until they did, the Russians should not kill their own. Out of sight of the Chinese, Tungus and other Russian natives were to be knouted and fined at the time of *iasak* collection. The Collegium of Foreign Affairs agreed, on 31 July 1750, that Iakobi's reasoning was good, and even if the Chinese began to put to death their own offenders, he should await confirmation of the death sentence from the Senate before inflicting it on any Russian subjects. When informed, the border dzarguchei cut off trade for two days in 1751. Two years later when several Chinese carrying prohibited goods (Chinese wine and ninety kopeks in copper money) were apprehended by the Russians, and they were turned over to their countrymen, but the wine and money was held back at first. A running dispute triggered by this trivial incident provoked the dzarguchei to state that he had never received proof of the punishment of the murderers of a decade before, and on three separate occasions, he suspended trade at Mai-mai-ch'eng for a total of more than five months during the summer season—the longest interruption of trade up to that time. Correspondence between the Senate and the *Li-fan-yuan* continued to debate this matter of punishments for years to come.

In the meantime, another source of friction more directly related to commerce led to brief suspension of trade in 1747. The previous year Russian merchants Mikhail Mushnikov, Andrei Evreinov, and several others informed Iakobi they had extended credit to Chinese and Bukharan merchants of 20,330 rubles 50 kopeks, for which payment was not forthcoming.[20] The dzarguchei

18. *PSZ,* XI, No. 8572, 618; XI, No. 8601, 641-44; XII, No. 8944, 114; XII, No. 8996, 174; XIII, No. 10086, 817-19; XIII, No. 10087, 819-20. Under these decrees many who would have been executed earlier were sent as convict labor to the Nerchinsk mines branded plainly with one letter on the right cheek, two on the forehead and one on the left, spelling out "thief" (*vor"*); see esp. *ibid.*, XII, No. 9293, 558, Imperial edict dated 9 June 1746.

19. Bantysh-Kamenskii, *Diplomaticheskoe sobranie,* pp. 254-55; Andrievich, *Kratkii ocherk,* p. 178; *PSZ,* XIII, No. 9875, 468-69, dated 22 April 1751.

20. Sychevskii, *Chteniia OIDR,* Bk. 2 (April-June, 1875), 230.

initially refused to consider the matter, on the ground that he was absent from Mai-mai-ch'eng when the debts were supposedly contracted. By 1747 the Russian demands mounted to 24,766 rubles, and correspondence with the Urga officialdom only irritated the matter. The Urga amban replied that an earlier dispute, negotiated by Porietskii and a councillor from Urga, resulted in the payment of 150 untanned hides to the merchant Grigorii Shelekhov, after which the debts claimed on both sides were cancelled. An agreement was then made, he argued, that no debts were collectable which were not made in the sight of the responsible border officials, and that not being the case here, the Russians would not be paid. He requested that he hear no more of the case in the future. Still merchants on both sides contracted debts. The absence of convertible currency or bullion almost guaranteed that they would. And the claims and counterclaims continued to be negotiated by a Captain Ostiakov, who replaced Grecheninov, dismissed for mishandling affairs with Siberian natives. By 1752 the Senate directed complaints to the *Li-fan-yuan* which requested that responsible Chinese officials supplement the Mongols at the frontier for settlement of the debts of several Russian merchants, as well as other matters.

During the suspensions of trade in 1753, the dzarguchei took the occasion to fault the Russians on two other matters, neither of which was new.[21] He suggested that Russian prohibitions on the private trade of several valuable commodities—Kamchatka beaver, fine fox, provisions and foodstuffs, and coin—hampered the abilities of Chinese and Mongolian merchants to trade profitably. He complained too that customs duties were extracted at Kiakhta in contravention of the explicit provisions of the Treaty of Kiakhta. The good official was somewhat disingenuous in bringing up both of these issues in apparent good faith. For many decades, the monopolized items he mentioned had been forbidden on and off to private trade. That the monopolies restricted the full growth of private trade is certain; that they were more operative at this time than was usual, is certainly doubtful. The same argument may be made with regard to the custom house at Kiakhta, except that the abolition of internal customs duties and their replacement by

21. *Ibid.*, 235-45; except that in 1737 the courier Sharygin carried back to St. Petersburg a note reminding the Russians that the Uda region was indeed closed to Russian travel; Bantysh-Kamenskii, *Diplomaticheskoe sobranie*, p. 228.

a surcharge on external duties, did substantially raise duties collected on the border. It did not, as we have seen, significantly change the eventual sale value of Chinese goods imported nor of the Russian goods bartered to the Chinese, except perhaps as individual Russian merchants used it as an excuse to demand higher prices. The main problem was that the internal duties were hidden from Chinese view, while this new surcharge was not.

After several interviews with the dzarguchei by subordinate Russian officers, Iakobi met with him on 19 November 1753 in Selenginsk. A variety of issues, most of long duration, were discussed: punishment of border offenders, collection of duties at Kiakhta, Russian prohibitions on certain items of trade, a surfeit (according to the dzarguchei) of Russian soldiers and Cossacks in Kiakhta, delays caused Chinese merchants by the difficulty of locating Russian officials to grant approval for merchandise arranged for barter, and nocturnal visits of Chinese merchants to the Rusian dwellings for "obscene, indecent, and infamous affairs." On most of these matters Iakobi pled that he simply followed orders, and the dzarguchei must inform the *Li-fan-yuan* that it could, after all, correspond directly with the Senate if it wished. Satisfied for the moment with the explanation, the dzarguchei ordered the restoration of trade the next day, although none of the long standing and still potent issues of disagreement between the two nations were settled. Of the minor local grievances, the Kiakhta customhouse was moved shortly, as we have seen, and that was all the dzarguchei wanted. In the course of time Russian state monopolies were abandoned, but certainly not because of official protest by Peking or Mai-mai-ch'eng officials. For all we know, Kiakhta officials may well have become more attentive to their duties when Chinese merchants needed permission to remove purchases from Kiakhta, rather than repeatedly being "at dinner" or "on a visit." Chinese nocturnal appetites remained about the same.

Navigation of the Amur

All of the controversies mentioned up to this point concerned, in one manner or another, local border problems. They were of the kind to be expected from the meeting of two empires with such varying outlooks on trade and diplomacy. Although far from placid, the surprising thing about Russian-Chinese border trade was its general amicability; the prevailing disposition at the border was to find solutions that permitted trade to continue. Prior to the 1760's, there was a total of no more than six years in which trade was suspended at the border, typically not for more than a few day in each case. The five-months suspension of 1753 appeared to have caused as much hindrance to trade as any of the disputes or suspensions, and even it did not completely interrupt trade. It occurred during the "off season," the summer months. In the May-third of the year (May-August) 4010 rubles in duties were collected in Kiakhta, compared with 7480 rubles in the January-third, a respectable sum for the summer season. To this local friction, however, were added in the 1750's two critical conflicts of interest, in the Amur River valley and in Dzhungaria. Rivalry in these areas, at first of only incidental relevance to the Kiakhta trade, honed the edge of the long-standing controversies at the border and threatened eventually to damage or even perhaps to destroy the now established border trade.

Official Russian interest in the Amur River valley lay nearly dormant in the seventy years between the signing of the Treaty of Nerchinsk in 1689, when Golovkin relinquished Russian claims to the region, and the early 1750's.[22] The river remained closed to Russian navigation and settlement. The situation slowly changed in the first half of the eighteenth century as Russian adventurers pushed on to Kamchatka and the Aleutians, and uncovered vast new sources for furs, firing the enthusiasm and acquisitiveness of trappers, merchants, and the state. The Siberian river highways did not extend all the way to the Pacific, and the overland trek from the vicinity of Iakutsk to the Sea of Okhotsk was rugged and expensive. A direct water route from Nerchinsk to Okhotsk, via the Shilka and Amur Rivers, would have greatly facilitated the Russian settlers on the Pacific coast and in Kamchatka, and no less important would have permitted the Kamchatka and Aleutian furs to reach the Kiakhta market more easily or to enter the usual routes to European Russia.

With this in mind the Siberian governor Vasilii Alekseevich Miatlev (Miat'lev) submitted a report to Elizabeth in 1752 empha-

22. Except for the well-known remark attributed to Peter I that the mouths of the Don, the Neva, and the Amur were of immense importance to the future of Russia; Hoo Chi-tsai, *Les bases conventionnelles*, p. 104. The *Li-fan-yuan* received a report in 1742 of the encroachment of Russians on the Amur "to cut brushwood"; *SFPC*, Chuan Shou 2.4b.

sizing the value of the Amur route. The next year the seventy-one year old state employee Fedor Ivanovich Soimonov was commissioned to investigate on-the-spot the channels and currents of the Shilka, Argun, and Amur rivers.[23] It took three years to organize those members of the Second Kamchatka Expedition remaining in Tobol'sk, plus two pilots *(shturmany)* from St. Petersburg, and to build several substantial river boats. In 1757 Soimonov together with his crews and his son Mikhail set out from Nerchinsk in three large boats. They sailed down the Shilka to its confluence with the Argun and there met Chinese resistance, and on order the expedition retraced its path, carefully surveying and measuring the river and the shores. On the basis of this fine geographic work, Soimonov compiled a full description of the region, carried by his son to the Senate.

Russian state interest in the Amur was again whetted. In the spring of 1755 the Senate received Soimonov's preliminary report and also the thoughts of Irkutsk Vice-Governor Vul'f on the value of the Amur. By July it debated the dispatch of a special emissary to Peking to inquire into the possible Russian use of the great

23. Fedor Ivanovich Soimonov (Soimanov, 1682-1780) was born in Moscow of a poorer but old gentry family. After schooling in the Moscow Navigation School, he was assigned by Peter to the navy in 1713 and sailed to Holland and Portugal. By 1719 he took part in a Caspian expedition under K. Verden and helped map the region, and four years later participated in the capture of Baku. In 1740, after much distinguished service, he was swept up in the destruction of Biron's rule, knouted and exiled to Siberia. Elizabeth quickly pardoned him and allowed him to remain in Siberian residence. After completing the work on surveying and charting the Shilka-Argun, Elizabeth in an ukaz of 14 March 1757 promoted Soimonov to the rank of Privy Councillor and appointed him Siberian governor, replacing Miatlev, at a stipend of 2,000 rubles per annum. His six-year term was generally considered to have been preeminently successful and he has gone down as a talented and humane administrator. He caused the building of several boats on Lake Baikal, strengthened the naval school, etc. And in these years his geographic investigations were published (in 1761 and 1764) in the *Monthly Works (Ezhemesiachnye sochineniia)* of the Academy of Sciences. In 1763 at the age of eighty-one Soimonov became a Senator and was transferred to the Moscow *Senatskaia kontora.* There he continued his scholarly career and corresponded on Siberian matters with G. F. Müller. He died on 22 July 1780 at ninety-eight. Consult the following: *RBS,* vol. Smelovskii-Suvorina, 46-47; Nikolai Abramov (ed.), "Neskol'ko svedenii o Fedore Ivanoviche Soimonove, byvshem Siberiskim gubernatore," *Chteniia OIDR,* Bk. 3 (1865), 194; and *Liudi russkoi nauki, Ocherki o vydaiushchikhsia deiateliakh estestvoznaniia i tekhniki: Geologii, geografiia* (Moscow: Gosudarstvennoe Izdatel'stvo Fiziko-Matematicheskoi Literatury, 1962), pp. 298-305. For the Senate discussion of Miatlev's thought on the Amur, see *Senatskii arkhiv,* IX, 188.

river system.[24] In May of 1756 Elizabeth selected Vasilii Fedorovich Bratishchev, a man in the tradition of Vladislavich and Lange, with thirteen years' experience in Persia as a language student and head of the Russian mission there.[25] With a promotion to the rank of chancellery councillor and a salary of 1500 rubles given him in advance, Bratishchev set out for Peking early in 1757. His party consisted of an able assistant and translator in the person of I. V. Iakobi, son of the Selenginsk commandant and recently returned from a Peking mission, two other translators (Sakhnovskii and Sharin), and an escort of three grenadiers and five serving men.[26]

Officially, Bratishchev was only a courier, entrusted with a Senate note to the *Li-fan-yuan,* with no powers to negotiate a change of status of the Amur valley, and there is no evidence that he was granted an imperial reception or performed the *k'ou-t'ou.* But his fifteen-article instructions, issued on 21 December 1756, authorized him to attempt negotiation and conciliation on a variety of issues, particularly the Amur, as well as to secure Chinese replies to his notes. He was to solicit the dispatch of an embassy to Russia to carry felicitations to Empress Elizabeth for her ascent to the throne (over a decade and a half earlier), and to attempt to settle the continuing border disputes over transgressions, thefts, and runaways. Since notes had passed repeatedly between the courts and many meetings had been held on these matters, especially the latter, it is unlikely that he was expected to accomplish much, with only

24. *Senatskii arkhiv,* IX, 365-71, 395. The Collegium of Foreign Affairs considered Court Councillor Andrei Ivanov because of his linguistic talents, but eventually selected Bratishchev.

25. Bratishchev was born in 1714 and studied Latin at the Moscow Academy. In 1732 he was ordered with several others to study Asiatic languages with a Professor Ker in the Collegium of Foreign Affairs. Two years later he was sent to Persia for further language learning, but when the Russian resident in Derbent died in 1742 he came to direct all of the Russian affairs with consuls, Persian ministers, and Russian border commandants. On his return from China, he served in the State Office *(Shtats-kontora)* and the Legal Office *(Iustits-kontora)* in Moscow in the rank of Chancellery Councillor. He left state service in 1765 because of ill health. Consult among other things *Senatskii arkhiv,* XIV, 427-29; XV, 576-78.

26. Bantysh-Kamenskii, *Diplomaticheskoe sobranie,* pp. 264-66; *Senatskii arkhiv,* IX, 618-19; X, 1; Andrievich, *Kratkii ocherk,* pp. 182-83; Slovtsov *Istoricheskoe obozrenie,* II, 276; and Kurts, *Russko-kitaiskie snosheniia,* pp. 88–89. He was allotted 2656 rubles 201½ kopeks for expenses from the Siberian Prikaz and 500 rubles to purchase peltry for gifts. He left Moscow on 27 January 1757, arriving in Irkutsk on 15 March 1758, and in Selenginsk on 28 May.

five hundred rubles worth of fur gifts. He was also to try to persuade the Chinese to accept and maintain several new Russian students in Peking (Vladykin had just failed to accomplish this), and above all to undertake to secure Chinese permission for unimpeded navigation of the Amur by boats carrying grain and other supplies to provision the Russian forts and settlements in easternmost Siberia. Formally he was to hand over three notes, the first repeating the Amur request, the second a reply to two Chinese notes which had protested Russian murders in the Argun region (the Senate assured the *Li-fan-yuan* that both of the murderers had drowned in Bauntovskoe Lake), and the third officially requesting permission for six language students in Peking. The *raison d'être* of the mission was Amur navigation.

Bratishchev's small party left the border in July of 1757 and arrived in Peking on 26 September. It stayed only eight days, reaching Selenginsk on 13 December, whence Bratishchev reported to the Senate. He was graciously received in Peking and provided with foodstuffs, money for expenses, and occasionally even fruit, but he found the ministers adamant, in spite of the intercession of Archimandrite Iumatov. The Ch'ien-lung emperor was deeply perturbed by the Russian failure to return quickly Dzhungars who had escaped to Siberia, and, Bratishchev reported, when he learned of the small Russian military establishment in Siberia he ordered a large force to the border to take the runaways, by force of arms if necessary.[27] As for an embassy to Moscow, the Chinese were wholly uninterested. If the Russians sent to the border a man of distinction with powers to negotiate, Peking would assuredly have met him by an official to deliberate border disputes. Beyond that little could be done. The request for passage of the Amur was not even negotiable; the Chinese attitude was best expressed in the words of the imperial edict to the Councillor of War *(Chun-chi ta-ch'en)* and others:

> A Russian courier arrived at the *Li-fan-yuan* carrying a document from the Senate *ya-men* which stated that on the northeastern border of their country people are in distress and hungry, and that boats are now being built to transport provisions via the eastern route: the Nerchinsk region, the

27. Sychevskii, *Chteniia OIDR*, Bk. 2 (April-June, 1875), 180-81, Iakobi asked that the frontier guards be strengthened to withstand any sudden attack.

> Ingoda River (*Yin-ko-ta ho,* a tributary of the Shilka), the Argun and the Amur. [Permission for] unobstructed passage is requested. Within the eleven articles previously deliberated and agreed upon with the Russians [the Treaty of Kiakhta], [no mention was made of] crossing the boundaries and dispatching men to transport things. [Hence] an order was sent to the *Yuan* to refuse and refute! But the foreign barbarians do not understand [Chinese] affairs, and perhaps consider that presentation of a document to the *Li-fan-yuan* completes the matter, and will not wait for a document in reply before entreating the frontier sentries to let them pass. Therefore this must be done: General *(chiang-ch'e)* Ch'o-le-to will immediately order the frontier patrol-station officials to explain to them [the Russians] saying, "Even though your eminent Senate *ya-men* has sent a document to the *Li-fan-yuan,* we have not yet received from the *Yuan* a document granting permission [for you to pass]. How can we presume to let you enter our territory having received only your one-sided story? Suppose that we said to you we had already sent a document to your eminent Senate *ya-men* requesting to enter your territory, would you believe us?" Guarded houses must devote special attention not to permit them to pass through. In the event they will not listen, stop them. If they use force to proceed, the frontier border patrol officers will report it. Ch'o-le-to will immediately send troops to arrest them and treat them as deserters.[28]

This rebuff stifled Russian efforts to secure rights in the Amur valley for the remainder of the century; not until the Treaty of Aigun (1858) did they achieve permission to navigate the river. When the issue arose in the Senate in 1764, the Collegium of Foreign Affairs advised that, in spite of the obvious value of access to the Amur, the matter should not be pursued because of the "stubbornness of the Manchu court." The only real result of the effort was to deepen latent Chinese suspicions of the aggrandizing aims of the Russians; especially when the encroachment threatened the homeland of the Manchus.

28. *SFPC,* Chuan Shou 2.6a-7b; cf. Solov'ev, *Istoriia,* VI, 42; and Sychevskii, *Chteniia OIDR,* Bk. 2 (April-June, 1875), 147. See also Fu, *A Documentary Chronicle,* I, 206.

The Amursana Affair

The ill will and anger toward Russia that Bratishchev found in Peking did not spring from his Amur mission, but rather from an intensification of the runaway problem as Manchu armies moved to crush for all time the resistance of the Dzhungar nation. After the defeats of the 1730's, Dzhungar cohesiveness and power waned.[29] The flamboyant kontaisha Galdan was succeeded in 1745 by his son, Tsewang Dorji Namjar. Five years later, a series of internecine struggles was touched off when a group of high-ranking Dzhungar leaders rebelled. They captured Tsewang and blinded him, and in his place as kontaisha they raised up the eldest, but illegitimate son of Galdan, Lama Darja. He was opposed only by Davatsi, grandson of the famed Cheren Dondub, erstwhile conqueror of Tibet. Lama Darja defeated Davatsi in 1751, but the latter escaped westward with a few followers. Among these followers was one Amursana (A-mu-erh-san-a), leader of the Khoits *(Hui-t'e)*, a Mongol tribe occupying the Tarbagatai region. Gathering a thousand men, Davatsi and Amursana marched to the Ili region, and killed Lama Darja early the following year. Davatsi succeeded to the title of kontaisha and richly rewarded Amursana for his aid. Within two years, however, Amursana and several other Dzhungar leaders, wearied of the continuous feuding, and smarting under what they thought to be Davatsi's persecution, migrated to Mongolia and surrendered to the Manchus. Amursana brought with him more than twenty-five thousand Khoits. That began the complex chronicle of Amursana.

Recognizing the weakness of the remaining Dzhungars, Ch'ien-lung decided to attempt to put an end to the long but equal contest. An army of two columns set out in 1755 under Bandi (Pan-ti), with Amursana and his retinue as the Northern Route Army (Uliassutai) in the vanguard. The Ili region was easily subdued and Davatsi captured (he was taken to Peking and made a prince of the first degree). The Dzhungar basin now appeared

29. For an excellent summary, see Hummel, *Eminent Chinese*, I, 9-11; cf. "Perevod s dvykh kitaiskikh listov, prislannyi pri donesheniiakh v Kollegiiu inostrannykh del ot Sibirskogo gubernatora ot 1758 g.," trans. and ed. by Nikolai Abramov, *Chtennia OIDR*, Bk. 4, Pt. 5 (1868), 6-8; Courant, *L'Asie centrale*, pp. 97-114; Bartol'd, *Four Studies*, I, 164 ff.; and Agnes F. C. Ch'en, "China's Northern Frontiers: Historical Background," *Yenching Journal of Social Studies*, IV (August, 1948), 72-75.

to be securely in the hands of the Manchus for the first time since the beginning of the Ch'ing dynasty, and the last of the great nomad empires seemed thrust down.

The fickleness of Amursana's allegiance was not taken into account, however. Intoxicated with his successes, he was dissatisfied with the settlement proposed by the Manchus, by the terms of which he would have been recognized as khan of the Khoits (he obviously aspired to khanship of all the Dzhungars). He rejected the proposal and was consequently ordered to Peking. He chose to flee instead. In September, 1755, he evaded his Manchu escort, and set out to organize a revolt. Initially his success was immense, since the bulk of the Manchu armies had already been withdrawn. The helpless Bandi committed suicide. Faced with a full-blown rebellion, Peking authorities reacted with celerity. Another army was sent and Amursana's forces routed; he fled to the Kirgiz Kazakhs. Again Manchu forces retired, again Amursana raised the standard of insurrection, and again the Manchus took to the field, and two armies under Chao-hui and Ch'en-kung-cha-pu pressed Dzhungaria in a great pincers, and the rebel chiefs not killed were taken by an epidemic of smallpox. This time Amursana ran to Siberia, where in Tobol'sk in 1757, he died of smallpox.[30] His death marked the end of the intermittent strife that had plagued Central Asia for nearly a century. The next year Manchu armies despoiled the lands of the Kalmyks, and Dzhungaria disappeared from history, the name Dzhungar itself prohibited—Eleuth or Oirat took its place.

The Amursana affair did not end so abruptly. Four thousand Mongol iurts had crossed into Siberia with the renegade, and fearing that the Russians, in spite of the Governing Senate's denial, would use them as a means of insinuating Russian power into Dzhungaria, Emperor Ch'ien-lung demanded the extradition of Amursana and his followers. When informed of his death, the Manchus were understandably dubious, and insisted on viewing his corpse as proof. The embalmed cadaver was sent to Selenginsk and there witnessed by the border officials in March and April 1758;

30. Siberian governor Miatlev first heard from a native of Uriankhai in the autumn of 1756 in Ust'-Kamenogorsk the rumor that Amursana desired to enter Siberia with all of his armies and possessions; *Senatskii arkhiv,* X, 6. Amursana's wife and son were sent to the Volga Kalmyks after his death. She requested permission to visit St. Petersburg subsequently, and died there on 7 September 1761.

but, still not satisfied, Peking then demanded the return of the corpse.[31] The Russians, assuming that the Manchus wished to expose Amursana's head on a pole at the border as an example to other potential rebels, righteously stalled. The issue of Amursana's corpse irritated Sino-Russian relations for some time to come. Were this not enough, another affair of high international intrigue simultaneously helped destroy the reasonably friendly intercourse achieved by border trade. In the midst of the fighting (1756-57) and directly a consequence of it, many Dzhungar leaders and other Mongols attempted or requested asylum in Russia. In reports of July and September 1756 Siberian Governor Miatlev informed the Collegium of Foreign Affairs of large numbers of Dzhungars who had requested asylum at several Russian border posts (Kolyvan', Biisk, etc.). The first reaction of the Collegium was merely to order Iakobi to remonstrate with the Chinese border officials, pointing out to them that these runaways should not have been permitted to reach Russian territory.[32] At this point the most serious threat to Manchu tutelage in Mongolia emerged.

The Khoshote prince and general, Ch'en-kung-cha-pu, commander of an army guarding Manchu communications in Mongolia and active in the campaign against Amursana, revolted.[33] Peking quickly informed St. Petersburg and requested that he and his compatriots be returned to Chinese authority if they appeared at the Russian border. Given confidence by this bold act of defiance, several top Mongol leaders including the Tushetu and Chechen Khans and even the Hutukhtu, the spiritual leader in Urga, approached Commandant Iakobi, verbally requesting him to forward to St. Petersburg their request to enter into vassalage to Russia.[34] In his report to the Collegium of Foreign Affairs, Miatlev recommended accepting them in the hope that other Mongol chieftains would follow their example. With Manchu armies in Dzhungaria

31. Two of the notes demanding the return of Amursana sent from the *Li-fan-yuan* to the Senate, dated 18 February 1758 and 28 March 1758, have been translated into Russian by Nikolai Abramov; *Chteniia OIDR*, Bk. 4, Pt. 5 (1868), 9-14. See also Fu, *A Documentary Chronicle*, I, 207-12.

32. Bantysh-Kamenskii, *Diplomaticheskoe sobranie*, p. 266, Collegium orders of 16 and 18 November 1756.

33. Announced to the Senate in a *Li-fan-yuan* note of the 21st year, 8th month, 12th day of Ch'ien-lung, received in St. Petersburg 28 November 1756; *ibid.*, p. 268; see also Pavlovsky, *Chinese-Russian Relations*, pp. 32-38.

34. Sychevskii, *Chteniia OIDR*, Bk. 2 (April-June, 1875), 140-43; Bantysh-Kamenskii, *Diplomaticheskoe sobranie*, p. 269.

cut off from their bases in western China, Russia would be in an unprecedentedly powerful bargaining position.

The Russian state was handed a golden opportunity—the only one prior to the middle of the nineteenth century—to extend Russian influence and possibly hegemony into Mongolia and Central Asia. The Senate was not slow to take advantage of it, but neither was it daring. Miatlev was given a free hand to accept the Mongol defectors and to promise the protection of Russian arms.[35] Because of the logistical impossibility of settling ten thousand iurts, more or less, in the frontier regions of Siberia (foodstuffs were chronically in short supply) and as a gesture of compliance with the Treaty of Kiakhta, no attempt was to be made to receive them across the border, and the Mongol chieftains were to be so informed. The Mongols, on their part, desired only Russian protection and support, preferring to remain in their native habitat.[36] St. Petersburg officials nursed high hopes for this intrigue; the Senate considered it a fine lever for obtaining the right of navigation of the Amur—Bratishchev almost simultaneously left Moscow for the East. If the Peking court refused the request, the possible defection of Mongols in the vicinity of the Amur might render Manchu permission practicably unnecessary.[37] If and when Peking raised objections, they were to be told that the Mongols submitted to Russian tutelage of their own free will *(svoevol'no).*

The intrigue simmered throughout 1757, with St. Petersburg preserving a stiffly proper stance. In a note of 17 April, the Senate replied to the *Li-fan-yuan's* announcement of Ch'en-kung-cha-pu's rebellion that Siberian authorities, devoted to the Treaty of Kiakhta, would certainly not offer refuge or succor to the rebel, but in another of 20 May the Senate, harking back to proposals purportedly made by the Chinese embassy at the Russian court in 1731, pointedly drew the attention of the *Li-fan-yuan* to the fact that the Dzhungar nation was, after all, an independent empire contiguous to both the Chinese and Russian dominions. In the midst of this fighting, if Dzhungars or other Mongols (such as Amursana) crossed over into Siberia, it was proper for Russia to keep them, taking care only that they did not use Siberia as a

35. Senate ukaz of 29 October 1756; Sychevskii, *Chteniia OIDR*, Bk. 2 (April-June, 1875), 146-51; and Imperial ukaz from the Collegium of Foreign Affairs to Miatlev of 22 January 1757; *ibid.*, 151-154.

36. Kurts, *Novyi Vostok*, XIX (1929), 201-2.

37. Sychevskii, *Chteniia OIDR*, Bk. 2 (April-June, 1875), 147-48.

privileged sanctuary from which to strike back at Manchu armies and that the Mongol leaders were returned to Chinese authority. Then the note implied that territorial concessions might be made in return for deportation of Mongol chieftains who defected.[38] It was these notes that infuriated the Chinese court at the time of Bratishchev's visit.

While maintaining propriety and adhering formally to the Treaty of Kiakhta, the Russians continued to play the double game. Through the interpreter Grenadier Fedor Sharin, border officials kept in contact with incipient defectors in Mongolia, but for reasons beyond the control of the Russians the whole affair backfired. Early in 1758, the Urga Hutukhtu died, and without his spiritual leadership and blessing there was little prospect of persuading many of the Mongols' princes *(saisan)* to accept Russian suzerainty.[39] Furthermore, the very real threat to Manchu supremacy in Central Asia galvanized Peking into action. Manchu armies moved into Mongolia, and Russia, with a pitifully weak military force available, was in no position to challenge the armies to combat. Peking installed a new governor in Urga, and he swiftly clapped the lid on Mongol movements. Not only were the Mongols forbidden passage to Siberia, they were prohibited from travelling among their own tribes.[40] The incipient insurrection of all of eastern Mongolia was shattered.

Mounting Tension

The five years, 1758-62, were years of degeneration in the relations between Russia and China; there were efforts to settle the border differences, so the deterioration was not even and steady, but seemingly it was irreversible and irrevocable. Both sides made efforts to augment their forces, military or administrative, in the border region, and at least on the Russian side talk of war was taken seriously, even though Russia was then mired in the Seven Years'

38. *Ku-kung O-wen shih-liao Ch'ing-K'ang ch'ien-chien E-kuo lai-wen yuan-tang*, trans. by Wang Chih-hsiang and comp. by Liu Tse-jung, added titles in Russian and in English (Peiping: National Palace Museum, 1936), Document 22 (17 April 1757), pp. 103, 175-76, 303-4; Document 23 (20 May 1757), pp. 107-20, 177-88, 304-12; also Bantysh-Kamenskii, *Diplomaticheskoe sobranie*, pp. 270–71.

39. Sychevskii, *Chteniia OIDR*, Bk. 2 (April-June, 1875), 166-72; Iakobi report to the Senate of 27 March 1758.

40. Kurts, *Novyi Vostok*, XIX (1927), 203.

War. And all this had a delayed effect on trade. In 1759 trade at Kiakhta-Mai-mai-ch'eng reached probably the highest levels yet, in part perhaps due to the fact that it had been several years since a crown caravan travelled to Peking; a turnover of nearly 1,500,000 rubles produced well over 200,000 rubles in customs duties. By 1761 the total turnover had declined to just over 1,000,000 rubles and Russian exports in ruble value were only a little over one-half what they had been in the earlier year.

By early 1758 the threat of war was taken seriously in St. Petersburg. Bratishchev's remarks on the contemplated dispatch of a formidable army to the border to retake Amursana and the other errant Dzhungars seemed to be confirmed in the unmistakably harsh tone of Chinese notes throughout the year.[41] Iakobi stressed the military weakness of Russia in Siberia and requested immediate military reinforcements.[42] Almost simultaneously (November 1757) Brigadier Karl L. Frauendorf reported from the Ust'-Kamenogorsk Line in the Irtysh valley that a Mongol army estimated at six thousand was within about 130 miles of that border fort, ostensibly searching for Amursana.[43] Other Manchu forces reportedly demanded tribute from some of the tribes in the Kuznetsk-Kolyvan' sector who lived in a kind of dual citizenship paying tribute both to Siberian officials and Mongol officials.

Even before these danger signals, the Military Collegium and the Senate had given some consideration to the unpreparedness of the Siberian forces for serious military operations. As early as 1755 Iakobi reminded the Collegium that there was—in full complement—only one regular regiment of three battalions and a grenadier cavalry company on the border in the territory of Selenginsk; Suvorov reported this to the Senate on 15 September.[44] By March 1757 the Senate came to a decision: to augment the Iakutsk regiment by forming new battalions and companies with officers from units then at Tobol'sk and along the Irtysh and Kuznetsk lines and men from the salt mines of Solikamsk, and from among the criminal elements in the army and the garrison regiments (excepted were only those soldiers under death sentences). If these reinforcements were not enough, the first new army recruits would

41. See for example *Senatskii arkhiv*, X, 406.
42. Sychevskii, *Chteniia OIDR*, Bk. 2 (April-June, 1875), 181.
43. *Ibid.*, 187.
44. *Senatskii arkhiv*, IX, 429-34.

be shipped there.[45] This concern was justified. The small regular units in the Selenginsk and Orenburg sectors were wholly inadequate to turn back a determined and well-equipped army, and the Selenga and Irtysh valleys offered relatively easy access to the more developed and important areas of the Siberian colony.

The increased tempo of Mongol defection and the Amursana affair caused an upward revision of defense needs late in 1757 and early in 1758. In September 1757 the Collegium of Foreign Affairs, basing its figures on a 1756 report of Iakobi and citing as reason for increasing the number of regulars on the Selenginsk border, the defection of large numbers of Dzhungars, and the imminent defection of the Hutukhtu, recommended to the Senate the expansion of the military forces in the area to four regiments, two at Selenginsk and two at Nerchinsk.[46] If the Chinese were to fall on the frontier, Selenginsk would need 20,000 regular infantry and 3,000 irregulars, and Nerchinsk 10,000 regulars and 2,000 irregulars. By the end of the year Iakobi, for the second time, bemoaned the weakness of military forces and the great danger involved in Mongol defections. By early January 1758, when all of these recommendations had been advanced to the Senate and the inflammatory words of the Chinese reported by Bratishchev, the Senate ordered that two regiments and one detached battalion with full complements—arms, ammunition, provisions, etc.—be sent immediately from Tobol'sk to the border.[47]

Finally on 9 April 1758, Her Imperial Majesty entertained a major military conference at her court; the Amursana affair was at its height. The assembled military dignitaries gave greatest attention to the Siberian Line to the west, guarded as it was by several small detachments of regulars in distant Orenburg. It was noted that in 1757 four commands of Bashkirs and Meshcheviaks were stationed on the Siberian Line with their families and without provisioning by the government. The conference agreed to ship 1,000 Don and 1,000 Iaik (Ural) Cossacks to Orenburg, plus the dragoon regiment at Ufa, or some similar unit.[48] These were intended to strengthen the long unguarded march from Orenburg to the Kuz-

45. *Ibid.*, X, 22, 52-53.

46. *Ibid.*, XI, 437-38; Sychevskii, *Chteniia OIDR*, Bk. 2 (April-June, 1875), 202–3.

47. *Senatskii arkhiv*, X, 413.

48. *Ibid.*, X, 446; XI, 438; Sychevskii, *Chteniia OIDR*, Bk. 2 (April-June, 1875), 203.

netsk region, and between Kuznetsk and Irkutsk, where not even watchtowers existed. As it was, any penetration of this region would hardly be known, much less turned back, because of the extreme difficulty of moving troops from either Tobol'sk or the Irtysh forts.

During the next three years, until 1761, the Russian court continued—in a variety of small ways—to bolster border military forces and to increase the border population. In March 1759 Governor Soimonov repeated to the Senate Iakobi's estimate of at least 35,000 regulars and irregulars needed between Selenginsk and Nerchinsk, and stressed again the unpreparedness of Siberia for attack.[49] The Kuznetsk-Kolyvansk Line (between the Irtysh and Enisei Rivers) was still also too weak for safety. Rather than import regulars as recommended earlier by Iakobi, Soimonov favored the recruiting of Cossacks in four regional militia regiments, regulars and mounted, with staffing by field and company grade army officers and supplied with arms, ammunition, and provisions. These were to be settled in the Nerchinsk and Selenginsk regions with their families. Two and a half months later, the Collegium of Foreign Affairs reported plans to gather 10,145 officers and men, most of the Cossacks from Tomsk and Kuznetsk *uezdy* assigned to the Kolyvanovoskresensk factory, to be formed up into the four militia regiments, and to scatter them in twenty-two guardposts of fifteen to twenty-five men from Balchikhansk (Bal'dzhikanskaia) east of Kiakhta to Argunsk.[50] They were to be paid out of local Siberian assessed or unassessed revenue, according to army salary and grain specifications, and "in the Ukrainian manner" their horses to be leased for one ruble per year for ten years. Since the regiments would be strung out over a long line, they must be supplemented by conscripts from among townsmen and artisans who had no regular trades or arts.

There was many a delay between the decision and the deed, however, and early in 1760 Iakobi reported his plan to settle along the Kiakhta border, not over 10,000 men, but 1,000 Don and Iaik Cossacks authorized nearly two years earlier for the border from Irkutsk west, 200 of which he proposed to use near Kiakhta and 800 on the Nerchinsk side.[51] Of the 800, 440 would be assigned to twenty-two guardposts dotting the frontier, and 360 held in reserve in

49. Sychevskii, *Chteniia OIDR*, Bk. 2 (April-June, 1875), 189-99; Kurts, *Russko-kitaiskie snosheniia*, p. 92; report dated 9 March 1759.

50. *Senatskii arkhiv*, XI, 439-45.

51. Sychevskii, *Chteniia OIDR*, Bk. 2 (April-June, 1875), 199-200.

two locations, the Akchinsk village and an encampment at the source of the Borza River (which flows into the Onon), so that they might be moved quickly to either the Selenginsk or the Nerchinsk area as the need developed. By the end of the year Iakobi and Soimonov reported that there was no activity on the Mongol side indicating the build-up of a Chinese army for offensive purposes. The armies in Mongolia were reportedly in weakened condition and the one Bukharan amban who came to Kiakhta with 80,000 *liang* of silver, bought 250 mounts at twelve *liang* five *chin* and thirteen *liang* each, but these were for the use of his own people near the town of Selim, and not for military purposes.[52] In 1761 the Senate continued to receive reports from Governor Soimonov on his continued effort to form four land militia regiments for the Selenginsk-Nerchinsk Line, but apparently actual distribution of Cossacks on the border was not completed until the 1770's, provoked then by a new circumstance, the great fear that the famed trek of the Volga Kalmyks back to Mongolia would involve Russia in hostilities with Chinese armies.[53] A 1763 ukaz mentions two regular and four irregular Cossack companies.

Two other concrete and very modest steps were taken to improve the military posture of Russia in the area. Iakobi did form five hundred-man military commands of the Tungus who lived in the border territory to help patrol the frontier under the direction of non-commissioned officers of the Iakutsk Guards Regiment, and under Senate order the Director of Kiakhta Customs House, Artillery Captain Fedor Strekalov, had the frontier surveyed and mapped.[54]

In the west on the Siberian Line rumors and reports seemed to suggest greater danger of invasion. In July of 1760, commanders in the region, Major General Veimarn and Brigadier Frauendorf, observed "several dangers" on the Chinese side and reported the occupation of locations near Ust'-Kamenogorsk fort suitable for settlement and agriculture, and the building of additional fortified points.[55] Shuvalov ordered Governor Soimonov in November to

52. *Senatskii arkhiv,* XI, 462-63, 479-80. He bought another 1000 in Urga.

53. *Ibid.,* XII, 19, 46; Sychevskii, *Chteniia OIDR,* Bk. 2 (April-June, 1875), 221.

54. *Senatskii arkhiv,* XII, 42-53; XIV, 540-42.

55. *Ibid.,* XI, 398-99, 423-28. The Senate heard in July 1759 reports from Iakobi of large purchases of horses on the Chinese side which indicated to Iakobi the gathering of an army. Some of Iakobi's informants reported that this army was prepared to march on the Kirgiz and others believed it would

undertake the building of forts in suitable and advised locations from Ust'-Kamenogorsk further up the Irtysh valley to the Bukhtarma River and Lake Teletsk.[56] Engineers were dispatched to direct the construction, but two years later, when a new commander arrived on the Siberian Line (Major-General Shpringer), his instructions included orders on the building of the same fortifications. In the summer of the following year (1761), the Azov dragoon regiment, which had earlier moved up from the Orenburg Line to the Siberian Line "because of the danger from Chinese armies," was now returned to its regular station.[57] Soimonov advised this because provisioning regular troops was extremely difficult in the Irtysh region. To the east and north in the Kolyvan' sector, deemed extremely important for its mining operations and vulnerable to military penetration from Mongolia, the Senate ordered on 12 January 1761 four infantry and one dragoon companies with their full staffs.[58] The companies were detailed to have good officers always in attendance, and any of them who failed in his duties should immediately be replaced. The officers and staffs must cooperate closely with the Kolyvanovoskresensk Mining Authority *(Nachal'stvo)*, and this authority was to pay the troops on army standards from its funds.

By the end of 1761, and as it happened, at the end of the reign of Elizabeth and nearly at the end of Russian involvement in the Seven Years' War, much had been said of Siberia's military unpreparedness and much planned. Little of a concrete nature had been accomplished in augmenting in any significant way the regular army forces there and in building a defensible line of border forts. But during these years, there was always Prussia and the Seven Years' War, leaving no choice but simply to shift Siberian and Ural regulars and to conscript irregulars on the spot, as danger points seemed to appear.[59]

---

fall on "Great Bukharia." Iakobi judged that there was no indication that the army would descend on Russian territory; *ibid.*, XI, 119-20.

56. Sychevskii, *Chteniia OIDR*, Bk. 2 (April-June, 1875), 216 ff.

57. *Senatskii arkhiv*, XII, 89.

58. *PSZ*, XVI, No. 11943, 391-92.

59. In fact not only were no large number of troops available for transfer from European Russia, but Siberia provided Russian armies with perhaps 40,000 soldiers to fight in Europe. "Undoubtedly, in the ranks of the Russian army, Siberians participated in the victory march on Prussia and they fell on Berlin"; Fedor Aleksandrovich Kudriavtsev and V. I. Dulov, *Boevye traditsii sibiriakov* (Irkutsk: OGIZ, Irkutskoe Oblastnoe Izd., 1942), p. 6.

On the other side of the border, the Chinese were far from inactive, although they also seem to have done little to build up an offensive military force. By early 1758 Dzhungaria was subdued and the potential revolt among the Khalkha Mongols had blown over. The military strength the Manchus could muster along the border, including regular Manchu banners, and irregulars from among the indigenous Mongols, was vastly superior, at least in numbers, to that available to the Russians; certainly many tens of thousands could have been quickly put in the field against the Russians. Thereafter these armies seemed to have declined in military readiness. As we have noted, Russian intelligence fairly consistently reported an absence of warlike preparations or activities.

In the civil and commercial administration of the vast Mongol colony, on the other hand, Chinese colonial authorities tightened the rather haphazard and inadequate controls exercised earlier over Mongolia, and especially over the border trade. In 1758 a new official was posted to Urga—Sansai Dorji (Sang-tsai To-erh-ch'i), an hereditary prince of the Tushetu Khanate—to solidify Chinese suzerainty over Mongolia. He enjoyed full powers to arrest and imprison those responsible for the defections, and above all he was charged to devote attention to the reconstruction and protection of border guardhouses.[60]

A year later new regulations asserted the control of Peking over Chinese merchants trading with the Russians.[61] All merchants must carry *Li-fan-yuan* passports or licences *(ling-p'iao)*, those coming from Chihli and passing through the Kalgan gate of the Great Wall must have theirs checked by the military governor *(tu-t'ung)* of Chahar or the magistrate of Dolon-nor, and those from Shansi by the office of the general *(chiang-chun)* of Suiyuan. Each passport carried the merchant's surname and "style," his residence, the goods he transported, his destination, and the date his journey began. Urga and Kiakhta officials were instructed to examine closely these passports upon arrival of the merchants, and the latter were required to display for inspection all goods and silver. The passports retained validity for one year only, after which the merchants were expected to return to China. Failure to obtain a passport was punishable by confiscation of one-half of the offender's goods, in addition to whatever other punishment the

60. *SFPC*, 46.5b.
61. *Ibid.*, 37.19b-20b.

investigating official felt was commensurate with the degree of his guilt. While at the border no merchant might contract indebtedness with Russian merchants under an assumed name, nor take a Mongol name for any purpose, legal or not, nor marry a native woman. In Mai-mai-ch'eng itself, the merchants were to be organized into eight "companies" *(hang)*, each headed by a substantial and reputable merchant, and all merchants were to mutually evaluate their goods to offer a solid front to the Russians. Judging from Russian references, this organization was successfully accomplished. Many of these restrictions were simply restatements of past policy inconsistently applied earlier. The differences lay in the transfer of new officials charged with enforcing them.

In 1762 direct imperial representatives *(ch'in-ch'iu)* were for the first time appointed in Urga, one a Manchu or Mongol officer from the capital, and the other a Mongol chosen from the Khalkha banners.[62] The term of office was three years. To facilitate defense of the Siberian frontier, these imperial agents maintained close liaison with the left vice-general *(tso-fu chiang-chun)* and councillor *(ts'an-tsan ta-ch'en)* of Kobdo, the administrative center of westernmost Mongolia closest to the Siberian Line, and to the east the general of the Amur region (Hei-lung-chiang) and the vice marshall *(fu-tu-t'ung)* of Hu-lun-pei-erh. Together these were the responsible officials in matters Russian. Hence, from 1762 at least, there was a broad general structure for surveillance of the entire border from the Amur to the Siberian Line.

The First Kropotov Mission and the Curtailment of Trade

By early 1762 none of the chronic disagreements between Russia and China were settled to the satisfaction of both sides.[63] The Chinese continued to press for closure of the Amursana affair; if his corpse had in fact disintegrated, his bones could not have and they should be given over. Claims over cattle thievery continued to mount in numbers until neither side could possibly believe nor satisfy the other completely. Even though the Senate in September 1761 sanctioned the transfer of the customs collection point from

62. *Ibid.*, 37.21a-22a; 46.5b.

63. See especially the summary in Kurts, *Russko-kitaiskie snosheniia*, pp. 92-98.

Kiakhta to some place back from the border, on Soimonov's recommendation, in order that a source of danger to trade would thus be removed, the Chinese throughout the next year persisted in their demand that no duties be charged on any goods involved in the Kiakhta-Mai-mai-ch'eng trade.[64] The Senate instructed that if the Chinese were not satisfied with the shifting of the customhouse and the tavern to Troitskosavsk, they be informed that no duties were being laid on the sale and barter of Russian and Chinese goods themselves, but only upon the Russian merchants—a deceptive and implausible argument at best, but one inclined to carry conviction if the Chinese could not observe the actual extraction of duties directly in the border suburbs. And of course Chinese merchants paid no customs duties on the goods they brought or took away. The Chinese dzarguchei also continued to express his concern over the persistence of small scale rustling and robbery indulged in by people from both sides of the border, and over the failure of negotiations to settle satisfactorily any of these cases. The Chinese also began at this time to object to palisades raised near the border by the Russians to contain cattle and horses and prevent them from wandering across the frontier.

Most of these vexations were discussed in a meeting between Iakobi and the dzarguchei in May and June of 1762.[65] The two failed to come to a meeting of minds on any of the issues, and Iakobi advised St. Petersburg to that effect. The *Li-fan-yuan* quickly sent off a note to the Senate which complained in sharp terms of the lack of agreement and insisted that the Senate take action on the Chinese complaints.[66]

Finally in an effort to stem the deterioration of relations with the Chinese, to preserve open commerce at the border, and to avoid the step over the brink into armed hostilities, Russia's new tsaritsa Catherine II announced to the Collegium of Foreign Affairs on 28 August 1762 her intention to direct an embassy to China. Her Court Chamberlain, Count Ivan Grigor'evich Chernyshev, would be the ambassador, and would formally carry to the throne of the Middle Kingdom the good news of her accession. To prepare the way she appointed Captain Ivan Ivanovich Kropotov, already selected by her late husband to announce in China his ascension to

64. *PSZ*, XV, No. 11322, 777-79, Senate decree of 4 September 1761.

65. 14 May–10 June 1762; Bantysh-Kamenskii, *Diplomaticheskoe sobranie*, pp. 311-12.

66. *Ibid.*, p. 312, n. 1.

the Russian throne.[67] Mainly Kropotov was to express the Russian desire for correspondence from the *Li-fan-yuan* and to couch the desire in words and allusions less harsh in tone than had recently passed between the courts. Specifically he was to request permission for a Russian private commercial caravan to travel to Peking, and to investigate, as best he could without making any formal demands or requests, the Chinese disposition for a mutual exchange of ambassadors.[68] He was given his instructions in Moscow at the end of August 1762, but did not reach Selenginsk until 22 February of the following year. He took time on the way to deliver the Order of St. Aleksandr to Governor Soimonov in Tobol'sk, and the Order of St. Anne to Irkutsk Vice-Governor Vul'f and to Commandant Iakobi in Selenginsk. At the border he added to his small retinue the surgeon Elachich and the Moscow University student Petr Iakimov. He carried a small store of crown peltry with him, not for sale, but rather to contribute to the subsistence of the Russian ecclesiastical mission in Peking.

The mission was entirely without success. The *Li-fan-yuan* censured the Senate for the rude diplomatic correspondence in the past and threatened, if the rudeness continued, to stop all trade at Kiakhta and to refuse entry to Chinese territory of any Russian couriers. The *Yuan* raised again the issue of customs-taking at Kiakhta, and on this issue as well, promised to end border trade if the collection of duties persisted. Kropotov's excursion had no ameliorative effect on Sino-Russian relations.

By the last half of 1762, trade at Kiakhta-Mai-mai-ch'eng was sharply curtailed by the Chinese. Commandant Iakobi sent his

67. Kropotov (1724-69) spent most of his adult life in the army. He was wounded at the Battle of Gross-Jägernsdorf in East Prussia in August, 1757, and was discharged the following year with the rank of captain-lieutenant of the Body-Guards. He gained considerable repute during his life as a dramatic writer and translator, particularly of Molière; *RBS*, vol. Knappe-Kiukhel'beker, 448-49. For his mission, see Kurts, *Russko-kitaiskie snosheniia*, pp. 98-99; *Sbornik RIO*, XLVIII (1885), 10; *SFPC*, 46.6a; Martens, *Revue de droit international et de législation comparée* (Ghent), XII, Bks. 5-6 (1880), 537-38. The great Siberian historian G. F. Müller, who travelled widely in Siberia (and visited Kiakhta) over three decades earlier, was considered for the ambassadorship; Kurts, *Russko-kitaiskie snosheniia*, p. 98, n. 12.

68. This caravan was not to be a state venture per se, as befitted the liberal economic doctrine of Catherine and her liberation of the Peking trade to private merchants on 1 July 1762, but rather a state-sanctioned one in which private merchants might invest their goods as they wished. Kropotov suggested it carry "a small amount of crown peltry," but the suggestion was not taken up; Kurts, *Russko-kitaiskie snosheniia*, p. 98, n. 13.

son to report to the Collegium of Foreign Affairs that Russian goods were piling up in the Kiakhta merchants' court and that the Imperial Treasury had already suffered in reduced customs revenues up to 250,000 rubles in the preceding year.[69] In 1762 the total value of the turnover at Kiakhta was a bit more than 1,000,000 rubles; the following year it declined to 704,000 rubles, and by 1764 was down by 60 per cent (to 296,000 rubles), the largest proportional and absolute decline of the preceding five years. Although some sources suggest that trade was suspended in 1762 and remained suspended for the next six years, Iakobi did not report the complete closure of trade until April 1764.[70] By mid-April Kiakhta officials informed Iakobi that there were no merchants in Mai-mai-ch'eng and except for the dzarguchei's all quarters seemed emptied. Russian carried goods piled up in the Kiakhta stalls by the tens of thousands of rubles worth, and finally on 15 May Kopylov, the Director of Customs, permitted the merchants to begin to return their goods to Irkutsk and other markets. Legal trade at Kiakhta came to a halt. There may have been some permitted in the several years thereafter, but it is not clear. Whatever did take place was a fraction of the usual level.

What caused this sharp curtailment or severance of trade at this time? Neither Russian nor Chinese sources provide a conclusive answer. Between 1762 and the spring of 1764, several new factors troubled Sino-Russian relations, no one of which seems to have been decisive. Correspondence from the *Li-fan-yuan* grew steadily more insolent and vituperous, at least from the point of view of the Senate and Catherine the Great, until during 1765 Catherine declined to respond further. Peking and St. Petersburg remained aloof, one from the other, for most of the next four years.

The wariness with which each judged the other's intentions and motivations can be seen in an incident of 1763, which some sources take to be one of the proximate causes of the curtailment of trade the following year. A certain Ma-mu-te of Uriankhai (Wu-liang-hai, present day Tannu-Tuva) produced a letter which purportedly revealed Russian territorial ambitions in that desolate and little

69. *Sbornik RIO*, XLVIII (1885), 10, 199.

70. Bantysh-Kamenskii, *Diplomaticheskoe sobranie*, p. 317; see also Slovtsov, *Istoricheskoe obozrenie*, II, 310, n. 17; Semivskii, *Noveishiia*, Primechanie, p. 173; Korsak, *Istoriko-statisticheskoe obozrenie*, p. 70; *SFPC*, 37.22a-23a; and Sychevskii, *Chteniia OIDR*, Bk. 2 (April-June, 1875), 258-59.

known region.[71] His tale was given sufficient credence that he was ordered to Peking for interrogation. At the same time Sansai Dorji, in reporting Russian claims for animals rustled across the border, charged Russian officials with lack of good faith in demanding the return of many more than had actually been stolen. An imperial edict castigated the officials for their perfidy. Similar suspicions were rife on the other side of the border.

Catherine and her Collegium of Foreign Affairs increasingly fretted over Chinese pressure on the Siberian Line. In three ukazes of October 1763 the Tsaritsa warned Major-General Frauendorf of Omsk, Orenburg Governor Volk, and Lieutenant-General Shpringer of Ust'-Kamenogorsk, of persistent Chinese attempts to draw the Kirgiz-Kazakhs into tributary relationships with Peking, of the maintenance of Manchu armies in Dzhungaria, of the raising of forts for trade in Central Asia, including even Tashkent and Bokhara, and of the "ruin and captivity" of *iasak*-paying Mongols in the Kuznetsk region.[72] In dispatches to his government in February, March, and April 1764 the British minister in St. Petersburg, the Earl of Buckinghamshire, noted that "the Chinese continue to be troublesome upon the borders," and "it is strongly reported that the Chinese have actually taken possession of three of the silver mines [presumably of the Kuznetsk-Kolyvansk region], but these are facts which it is difficult to ascertain, as the greatest pains are taken to keep secret all the intelligence which comes from that part of the Empire."[73] His longest dispatch is as follows:

> I have taken pains for some days past to get authentick information of the situation of the present disputes with China, as the greatest secrecy is observed in relation to everything that passes on that side. The following, though by no means so satisfactory as I could wish, is the best account I can obtain. In the year 1762 the Chinese seized upon a district of about 20 miles in depth in which, though there are at present

71. *SFPC*, Chuan Shou 2.18a-19a; 37.23a.

72. *Sbornik RIO*, LI (1886), 35-37. All three signed by Catherine on 16 October 1763.

73. John Hobart, Second Earl of Buckinghamshire, *The Despatches and Correspondence of John Hobart, Second Earl of Buckinghamshire, Ambassador to the Court of Catherine II. of Russia, 1762-1765*, ed. for the Royal Historical Society by Adelaide D'Arcy Collyer ("Royal Historical Society, Camden Series," 3d Series, Nos. 2 and 3 [London: Offices of the Society, 1900-1902]), II, 141, 161, 168.

> no mines, it is imagined that the soil is of such nature that mines might be worked to advantage. On this they still keep possession, but no hostilities have been committed since, and both sides continue upon the defensive. Whether this is the truth, or those reports which make it an affair of a more serious nature, in either case it must employ some part of the Russian forces. . . .

It is scarcely easier for us today that it was for Buckinghamshire to assess the seriousness and intensity of the business, either in Siberia or in St. Petersburg. The concern of St. Petersburg over the defence capabilities of the Siberian Line and east is apparent.

In the spring of 1763 the Senate, acting on the reports of Soimonov and Frauendorf, commanded the reconstruction of the road running from Tobol'sk to the Siberian Line.[74] Since the road would be toll the fiscal argument was predominant in the decree, but the obvious strategic advantages, indeed necessity, of the highroad were hardly overlooked. In September Lieutenant-General Shpringer assumed command of the entire Siberian Line with orders to proceed there with all speed.[75] His instructions began by informing him of the recent "seizure of Zengorian [Dzhungarian] localities by the Chinese" and the danger this represented to Russian lands and subjects. Specifically he must undertake the building of a fort in a location of his selection in the fifty-odd miles between the mouth of the Bukhtarma River and the Irtysh above Ust'-Kamenogorsk, and once this was done (he might winter in Omsk and investigate the mouth of the Bukhtarma the next spring), a redoubt and sentry posts must be built "as precaution against a hostile invasion." Dzhungarian crossing of the Line must be interdicted, although to be sure there had been none recently. Of the three major-generals under his command, Shpringer should locate one near Teletsk Lake, another in the Bukhtarma fort when built, and the third in Iamyshev or Omsk, so that sufficient powers of command decision were distributed throughout the Irtysh region. A full regiment of regulars, or at least a battalion, were to be held in reserve in the Kolyvanovoskre-

74. *PSZ*, XVI, No. 11822, 254-56, dated 20 May 1763.

75. *Ibid.*, XVI, No. 11931, 379-83, instructions dated 19 September 1763. See also *Sbornik RIO*, CXL (1912), 247, where Laurent Bérenger, secretary of the French legation and chargé d'affaires, reported on the despatch of Shpringer to take command "contre les Chinois." Also *PSZ*, XVI, No. 11947, 395-96.

sensk sector, to be moved as needed to the Line. The instructions expressed the hope that Shpringer could prevent the usurpation of all lands up to Lake Zaisan itself, since they held special promise for rich mines.[76] These lands had belonged, in one fashion or another, to local powers and tribes, but the Chinese, pridefully victorious over the Dzhungars, gave signs of coveting them. Thus Shpringer's superiors ordered him to send a dependable engineer officer as far as possible toward Lake Zaisan, although cautioning him to avoid arousing the suspicions of any people who might have wandered into the region. He should not take surveying equipment with him, but measure distances with his eyes, feet and a compass. Any information that could be collected on Chinese settlements, trade, and fortifications in the area must be sent to St. Petersburg, exercising always great care to give no cause for umbrage on the part of the Chinese.

Shortly thereafter, Shpringer assumed command of all troops, regular and irregular, in the Siberian Line.[77] Orders were issued in 1762 and 1763 to bolster his and other Siberian units with five infantry and two cavalry regiments formed of Polish deserters to Russia; those deserters unfit for military service were to be settled on lands in the Nerchinsk and Selenginsk regions to help increase desperately needed grain production in eastern Siberia.[78]

It seems impossible now to say which of all of the sources of the contumely and mistrust bestowed by the Chinese on the Russians (and returned more cautiously in kind but returned nonetheless) was the proximate cause of the curtailment of the Kiakhta trade. The whole history of Sino-Russian rivalry along the border

76. See also *Senatskii arkhiv,* XII, 58-59, for evidence of the Senate's interest in the metals of the Altai region.

77. *PSZ,* XVI, No. 11948, 396.

78. *Senatskii arkhiv,* XII, 183; *PSZ,* XVI, No. 11979, 436. Of the *regulars* in Transbaikalia already, nothing was done to increase their numbers. On complaints with regard to arrears in pay and on difficulties in provisioning and clothing the two companies transferred to the Nerchinsk region, the Senate declined to approve increases in pay, but it did order these troops provided with the same uniforms authorized for regulars—shirts, trousers, and neckties—so that the soldiers "seeing themselves with such satisfaction, they will perform service to your Imperial Majesty with pleasure, and they will be able to be restrained from the indecent behavior of desertion and impudence, and they will be clean in their uniforms," a solution to the high cost of Siberian living and the piercing winter cold of the frontier (without the protection of fur garments and blankets) which would have delighted and disheartened Radisshchev as an apt illustration of the horny veil over Catherine's eyes; *PSZ,* XVI, No. 11943, 391-92.

led quite inexorably to this denouement. Minor border altercations and chronic disputes exacerbated the rivalry and exaggerated the mutual lack of faith in territorial and power pretensions. Chinese fears of Russian designs, at least commercial designs, on Dzhungaria, Mongolia, and the Amur valley were not entirely unfounded, although, as we know, it would take another century for the Russians to accumulate sufficient material strength to press claims against a weakened Manchu state. Russian apprehensions that the real goal of the Manchus was the control of the upper Irtysh, and the subjugation of the adjacent Kirgiz and Mongol tribes which had been in tributary relationship to St. Petersburg, were based on less evidence, but it is true that Manchu troops penetrated very close to Russian fortified positions.

Catherine's Conference

Russian military preparations were pushed swiftly ahead in 1764 for what began to look like eventual war with the Chinese. In late spring the Senate listened to reports, once again, of the inadequacy of the forces on the Mongolian border; Iakobi had in his command about twenty-five hundred men in two regiments, one cavalry and one infantry, both understaffed and undersupplied, and an insufficient number of Cossacks.[79] The Senate gave him permission to enroll twenty-four hundred of the local Buriats into paramilitary units.[80] These irregulars were expected to provide their own maintenance in lieu of paying *iasak*, and Iakobi was instructed to keep close watch on them so that they did not defect to the Mongol side, since after all they were close kin to the Khalkas. To compensate for the loss of customs revenues which had formerly been used, in part, to pay the salaries of the Iakutsk infantry and cavalry regiments, the Senate also ordered funds to be released from the Kolyvanovoskresensk mines funds. Already ordered in an imperial ukaz of 29 November 1763, the prohibition against the bulk sale and purchase of grain in Irkutsk and Eniseisk was repeated at this time. Artillery and shells were reported in especially short supply in Selenginsk; the new Siberian Governor Chicherin asked for nineteen three-pounders and a bomb mortar.

79. *Senatskii arkhiv*, XIII, 18-35.

80. He reported in May 1765 that three full regiments of 600 men each had been formed and a fourth with 427; *ibid.*, XIII, 65.

In October of 1764 Catherine summoned a full conference of seven leading civil and military officials to review the deterioration of trade relations with China and to suggest military measures appropriate to the aggravated situation.[81] The conference provided the Empress with a full description of affairs as best they were known and offered recommendations for the defense of the realm in the event of war and for the improvement of the administration of commerce should conflict be avoided. Neither eventuality was slighted.

Reinforcements should be added along most of the frontier, bringing the total strength of Siberian military forces to eleven regiments.[82] Units should be augmented at Petropavlovsk on the Ishim; Omsk, Iamyshev, and Ust'-Kamenogorsk on the Irtysh; Zhelenzensk; Biisk on the Ob'; Kuznetsk on the Tom'; and at Irkutsk and Selenginsk, i.e., across the whole sweep of southern Siberia at all the critical towns. Two dragoon regiments should be transferred from Kazan' to key reserve locations, the Azov regiment to Petropavlovsk and the Revel' to Omsk. Additional artillery must be dispatched to Omsk and Selenginsk, but the majority of regiments must be held in reserve rather than committing them to inaccessible outposts. Since much of the border was mountainous or otherwise impassable, the rapid transfer of units from one point to another was impossible; this was a sensible defensive posture.

In Transbaikalia minor efforts were to be made. Kudarinsk suburb on the Chikoi River was scheduled for strengthening with ditches, palisades, and earthen redoubts, and one thousand rubles were allocated for an arsenal at Kiakhta to provide all inhabitants with weapons. Two companies of the Selenginsk garrison were detached to improve the fortifications of the Cossack-manned Akchinsk fort between Kiakhta and Nerchinsk on the Onon

81. *Sbornik RIO*, LVII (1887), 37-47. See also Solov'ev, *Istoriia*, VII, 98-99; Kurts, *Russko-kitaiskie snosheniia*, n. 27, pp. 99-100. In attendance and signing the rescript were Field Marshall A. Vilboa (Villebois), Nikita Ivanovich Panin, Count Zakhar Chernyshev, Count Johann-Ernst Minikh (von Münnich, son of the great Field Marshall), Vice Chancellor and Prince Aleksandr Golitsyn, Ivan Ivanovich Veimarn (Hans Weimarn), and Adam Vasil'evich Olsuf'ev.

82. The report listed nine regiments already in Siberia: the Dragoon Troitskii in Iamyshev, the Vologda in Ust'-Kamenogorsk, the Sibir' in Zhelenzensk, the Luts in Biisk, the Olonets in Kuznetsk, the Kolyvansk in Irkutsk, the Iakutsk Rifle *(karabineri)* in Selenginsk, the Selenginsk Infantry, and the Tomsk Infantry in Ust'-Kamenogorsk. This is a more impressive list than it should be; most of these units were understrength.

River.[83] Nerchinsk, although unprepared to defend itself, was protected by a mountain buffer and no plans were made to add to its defense.

The mounting crisis provoked the conference to recommend several long overdue administrative alterations. Siberia should be split into two administratively equal provinces *(gubernii)*, Tobol'sk and Irkutsk. The purpose was to transfer decision-making powers farther east, so as to expedite communications between responsible officialdom and the far-flung military and customs outposts in eastern Siberia. Irkutsk for the first time in its history was to have a governor; Major-General Frauendorf who earlier served on the Siberian Line was the first to fill the office. This became law on 19 October in an imperial ukaz creating Irkutsk province.[84]

Cognizant of long-standing criticism of the bargaining weakness of Russian merchants at Kiakhta, the conference strongly recommended the creation of a single private "company" of all merchants trading at the border. The company would be expected to exercise discipline over all private merchants and to end the costly bidding, one against another, for sales to the Chinese. When trade began again and a goodly number of merchants gathered in Selenginsk, three or four merchants should be chosen as directors, or rather brokers, whose duty it would be to secure from all who traded a complete inventory of their goods and the prices expected on them. These brokers would then perform all of the actual sales, purchases, and exchanges of goods in the general interest of all. To prevent a few large merchants from dominating the rest, all merchants had to be stopped with their goods in Selenginsk, and wealthy merchants compelled to leave part of their merchandise, say half, in Selenginsk. Only when their first consignments were sold could they bring up the rest. No individual merchant should be allowed to enter into bargaining or agreements with the Chinese, and any who did could expect to be fined by the brokers, up to 50 per cent of their goods, and permanently to be excluded from participation in the China trade.

83. See Sychevskii, *Chteniia OIDR*, Bk. 2 (April-June, 1875), 222, for reference to the improvement of Kudarinsk and Akchinsk outpost to accommodate the Cossacks already committed at those locations.

84. *PSZ*, XVI, No. 12269, 944; see also Chulkov, *Istoricheskoe opisanie*, III, Bk. 2, 344; and B. Modzalevskii (ed.), "K istorii Sibiri v kontse XVIII veke, Vospominanie T. P. Kalashnikova," *Russkii arkhiv*, XLII, Pt. 3 (1904), 183.

Three years later, with trade at Kiakhta still suspended, the Catherinian Commission on Commerce inquired of the Irkutsk merchant and deputy, Sibiriakov, his attitude toward the organization of the Kiakhta trade and his suggestions for its amelioration. His reply was circulated among Moscow and Tula merchants trading there, but none seemed interested in anything beyond permission to move their goods from the border and Irkutsk to other market towns without the payment of customs duties. Nothing directly came of the suggestions of Catherine's conference for disciplining the China merchants.

All of these military and administrative measures proposed in the conference report of 4 October were approved by Catherine a fortnight later. Plainly they were exclusively "defensive" in character. No offensive military build-up on the border was undertaken, and, as may be gathered, none was seriously considered by St. Petersburg officialdom. Some sentiment for a preventive war, or rather a war of aggrandizement, did exist in the Russian capital. The year before the academician Gerhard F. Müller submitted a long memorandum on the advantages that could accrue from a successful war in the east.[85] The Amur Valley could be regained and the Altai sector of Mongolia secured, among other things. But these enticements failed to impress the court, not because the extension of Russian dominion was not earnestly desired by many, but because the price was too high.

A glorious little war in Siberia's border lands with bountiful returns was obviously daydreaming or wishful thinking. Siberian authorities, as we have seen, were long aware that available military forces were inadequate for defense against a prepared enemy, much less for a campaign deep into the barely known and inaccessible Amur and Altai regions. Far fewer than ten thousand men could have been put in the field, including all irregulars.[86] Use of large numbers of the standing armies in European Russia would critically weaken Russia's ability to defend herself against her western neighbors, and might endanger Catherine's crown, which she felt still lay uneasily on her head. Probably more persuasive than these considerations was the probability that conflict with the Chinese would guarantee for some time to come an end

85. Bantysh-Kamenskii, *Diplomaticheskoe sobranie*, pp. 378-93.

86. In 1763 there were enrolled in Siberia 4640 irregulars (of which 2513 were in Irkutsk province) and in 1765, 4891; *Senatskii arkhiv*, XV, 673; *PSZ*, XVII, No. 12472, 322-28, dated 15 September 1765.

to commerce with them. Through all of the troubles of the 1750's and 1760's, neither Siberian nor capital officials were disposed to directly threaten the course of commerce. Intrigue and meddling in Dzhungarian and Mongol affairs, intransigence in border bargaining, yes, but notably at no time in the eighteenth century did Russia suspend or curtail trade at the border, or fail to dispatch a trading caravan to Peking until it itself proved financially inadvisable, and then Bratishchev attempted to secure permission for a privately organized caravan. The paramount importance of trade with the Chinese was long since granted. Even during its curtailment, effort continued to be made to promote trade, and in the end it was a Russian mission to Peking that restored it.

In the next two years very little was done to increase Siberian military forces beyond that suggested by Catherine's conference. General Shpringer received several orders for the improvement of the forts on the Siberian Line—Omsk, Zhelenzinsk, Iamyshev, Semipalatinsk, Ust'-Kamenogorsk, Biisk—but these simply followed up his original instructions.[87] Iakobi and the other border commander kept close watch on the frontier so as to detect any warlike activities, but they usually reported only that no significant military preparations were observed.[88]

The State of Commerce

What little could be done to encourage Chinese and Mongol merchants to come to Mai-mai-ch'eng was done after 1763. Commandant Iakobi was specifically ordered in 1764 to persist in welcoming trade, exercising caution of course to insure that the proper customs duties were extracted. Part of the reason for his request of that year to transfer the customhouse to Troitskosavsk

87. *Ibid.*, XVII, No. 12410, 150-51, dated 7 June 1765; XVII, No. 12428, 178-79, dated 1 July 1765 (this edict had to do with the prohibition to private use of the forests in the upper Irtysh region so that the timber might be preserved for building and repairing the forts); XVII, No. 12686, 834-35, dated 1 July 1766 (this had to do with the dispatch of skilled artisans from Tobol'sk and other places to help build the forts and the granting them five years' exemption from dues and taxes); and *Senatskii arkhiv*, XV, 985-87, ukaz dated 16 December 1765.

88. *Senatskii arkhiv*, XIII, 74-75, 128, 140-42; TsGADA, Selenginskaia gorodovaia ratusha, *fond* 1801, *ed. khr.* 84, *ll.* 146-148a, Vypiska iz postanovleniia Selenginskoi ratushi ob uchastii zhitelei goroda v ukreplenii kitaiskoi granitsy, 14 October 1768.

was to conceal at least some of the barter from the watchful eyes of the dzarguchei.[89] Much of this trade was carried on with Mongol intermediaries, rather than directly with Chinese merchants, who were not always welcome in Mai-mai-ch'eng. Chinese merchants could and did carry their goods to Urga for exchange with Mongols, and although the Mongol chieftains were instructed to prevent the Chinese from secretively crossing the border to trade with the Russians, it is probable that some did. Rhubarb and other Mongolian goods continued to arrive at the border in dwindling quantities, at least until 1767 when all trade collapsed, at least all legal trade which was observed and taxed by Russian customs officials collapsed.[90]

Some of this trade may have taken place because of the connivance of high Urga officials in contravention of their explicit orders. It is recorded that in December 1765 the three ranking officials in Mongolia—Chouda (Chiu-ta, the Manchu imperial representative from Peking), Sansai Dorji (his Mongol colleague), and Erging (O-erh-ch'ing-e, an assistant of Chouda and formerly secretary of the Six Boards [*ssu-yuan*])—were tried and found guilty of accepting bribes to the extent of several thousand *liang* of silver to look the other way when trading caravans headed north to the Russian suburb.[91] Chouda as the specially deputed capital official received the death sentence, Sansai Dorji was deprived of his title, although it was later restored, and Erging because he only followed orders was shown leniency. Whether these officials by design allowed trade to go on which they knew to be disapproved in Peking, or whether they were scapegoats for a porous structure of border surveillance and were used as examples to deter others from malfeasance in dealing with the Russians is moot. Russian trade statistics, never completely dependable, show a sharp drop in reported trade after 1765, which suggests at least, the authenticity of the charges brought against these high-ranking officials. Also it should go without saying that contraband trade especially with the Mongols existed in spite of the scrutiny of officials on both sides.

89. Kurts, *Russko-kitaiskie snosheniia*, p. 94.

90. Gosudarstvennyi Arkhiv Irkutskoi Oblasti, *fond* 67, *op.* 1, *ed. khr.* 5. l. 131, Ukaz sibirskogo gubernatora general-maiora Iakobi ob ob"iavlenii kupechestvu i drugim liudiam o postavke 600 pudov revenia ot kiakhtinskogo forposta do Tobol'ska, 1766; *Senatskii arkhiv*, XIII, 65.

91. *SFPC*, Chuan shou 2.20a-20b; 37.24a-25b.

The Second Kropotov Mission

Early in 1765 Empress Catherine's court informed the Commission on Commerce that it undertake the discussion of the Chinese complaint of the high duties charged by the tariff of 1761,[92] but before any firm steps could be taken to use a new formulation of tariff policy as a wedge to persuade the Chinese to reopen trade, diplomatic correspondence between Peking and St. Petersburg ceased. Without formal recognition of the fact, diplomatic relations were severed. The offended sensibilities of the Senate and the Imperial Court were soon balanced against the treasury forfeit of up to two hundred thousand rubles annually in customs revenues, a very powerful incentive for Catherine to bid once more for the restoration of normal commercial operations. On 22 December 1766 she signed the documents clothing Captain Kropotov with full powers to negotiate all outstanding border questions with Chinese representatives, either at the border or at any other spot recommended by Peking.[93]

The instructions given both Kropotov and Iakobi stressed the financial losses to private merchants and to the state by the suspension of trade. Kropotov was expected to observe all he could in his stay at the border—and in Peking were he to travel there—about the state of commerce. Iakobi briefed Kropotov as thoroughly as he could on all of the past negotiations with Chinese officials and all of the issues in dispute, and gave him whatever aid and support the mission required. He had Kropotov's letter of introduction translated into Mongol and Manchu and forwarded to the amban in Urga. The letter referred to Russia's primary adherence to the Treaty of Kiakhta and her wish to dwell in peace and tranquility on the border. It informed Peking that the plenipotentiary had been sanctioned to announce to the *Li-fan-yuan* Catherine's accession to the throne. A secretary of the Collegium of Foreign Affairs, Aleksei Leont'ev, and a student accompanied him for purposes of translating and interpreting.

Kropotov was to assure the Manchus that customs duties would no longer be collected at the border, but at Petropavlovsk or at Selenginsk. Border palisades, if erected, would only be in Russian

92. *Senatskii arkhiv*, XIII, 56.

93. *Sbornik RIO*, LXVII (1889), 237-43; LXXXVII (1893), 353-56; CXLI (1913), 311; and Sychevskii, *Chteniia OIDR*, Bk. 2 (April-June, 1875), 260-71.

territory; any inadvertently extending into Mongolia would be immediately removed. It was the Empress' desire that all arguments in the past over border thievery and claims for cattle and horses, should be ended to the mutual satisfaction of all parties. And Kropotov was to request that Peking allow a small merchant caravan to travel to Peking with crown peltry but also to which private Russian merchants could attach themselves if they so desired.

Not until the middle of July, 1768, were the negotiators convened at Kiakhta.[94] Representing China were Kingui (Ch'ing-kuei, the imperial agent at Urga who replaced Chouda), Khutu Ringa (Hu-t'u-ling-a, son of a Mongol prince[95] and the replacement of Sansai Dorji), and Tcheden Dorji (Ch'e-teng To-erh-chi, the Tushetu Khan). The most sensitive topic of negotiation—on the surface of it the most insignificant—was the palisades put up by the Russians near Kiakhta. The Manchus insisted on their destruction, and the Russians adamantly refused. A compromise after weeks of debate settled the matter by more closely defining the border in the vicinity of Kiakhta.

By the end of August agreement was reached on the several major issues, and a protocol was signed on 16 October 1768 which became in effect a supplementary article to the Treaty of Kiakhta.[96] Copies were exchanged in Russian, Manchu, and Mongol. There were three main subjects. First, Kropotov consented to definition of the border delimited in the Treaty of Kiakhta as passing along the mountain ridges in such manner that a portion of the Russian palisades would lie south of the line and hence would be removed. Second, he promised categorically that the collection of customs duties at the frontier would end, although, as we have seen, the customhouse had been moved from Kiakhta already. Third and most important, a new settlement was made with regard to fugitives, defectors, and border depradations. Article 10 of the Treaty of Kiakhta was thoroughly revised. Stringent punishments for thievery were now specified in considerable detail. Thieves caught

94. *Ibid.*, 271; Klaproth, *Mémoires*, I, 45-53.

95. *Beise (Pei-tzu)* of K'e-la-ch'in. *Beise* was a Manchu title bestowed on the sons of Imperial princes (*Beileh* or *Pei-le*).

96. The Russian text may be found in Sychevskii, *Chteniia OIDR*, Bk. 2 (April-June, 1875), 282-85; a French translation from the Manchu is in *Treaties, Conventions, Etc.*, I, 61-66. For the best discussion of the various texts, see Ch'en, *Yenching Journal of Social Studies*, IV (February, 1949), 189-90. See also Klaproth, *Mémoires*, I, p. 53, n. 2, and Kurts, *Russko-kitaiskie snosheniia*, p. 95.

red-handed would receive one hundred blows, the Chinese punishing with the lash and the Russians with the cane. Recovered goods would be returned to the proper owner, a fine paid, and the property of the offender given to the apprehender "for encouragement." A thrice-convicted culprit would merit the death penalty. If the border chiefs on either side failed to apprehend a thief within one month of the offense, they must be fined. All fugitives of the past demanded and not returned were now wiped from the slate, and no requests for their return should be entertained. Thus ended the affair of Amursana and his colleagues. However all future fugitives and defectors must be sought out with all possible effort and returned to the properly designated border officials. Any person, that is particularly any merchant or trader, crossing the border without proper credentials and passport would forfeit his property to his apprehender.

Thus ended the most difficult period in Sino-Russian relations in the eighteenth century. The suspension of trade preceding the Treaty of Kiakhta was longer, but there was then no clear and present danger of border war. During Catherine's reign the Chinese were to shut off trade at Kiakhta at least three more times, the longest for a period of over six years, but again there were to be no serious threats of armed conflict.[97] Trade won out over war for many reasons. Neither side stood to gain much and risked considerable from a resort to arms, whereas both sides profited from spirited commerce, although the Russian court recognized this more openly. Siberia was far too weak militarily to risk becoming mired deep and long in the slippery politics of allegiance and campaigning in Central Asia, especially when these are balanced against the unknown advantages of hegemony in Mongolia and the Amur region. The Manchus for their part had already achieved their long-sought goal—hegemony in Mongolia and Dzhungaria, but only at the cost of a long and bitter conflict. And there was no precedent for Peking to be confident of the allegiance of any of the Mongols in the event of Russian invasion and bold offers of friendship and support. To the Mongol after all the Manchu and the Chinese were equally as foreign and unwanted as the Russian. In one sense the negotiations and settlements at Kiakhta were anticlimactic, for the real issues were decided by the subjugation of

97. Indeed in the thirty-four years of Catherine's reign legal trade was sharply curtailed or suspended for seventeen of them!

Dzhungaria and Mongolia to Manchu vassalage and the reticence of St. Petersburg to press her desires for access to the Amur and part of Dzhungaria after the rebuff of Bratishchev.

In an imperial edict of 27 September 1768, Ch'ien-lung accepted the solutions found at Kiakhta and sanctioned the resumption of trade at the border.[98] The unvirtuous foreigners having displayed "submissiveness, respectfulness and sincerity" should be again extended the privilege to trade with merchants of the Middle Kingdom.

A Peking Caravan?

It will be recalled that Catherine, in her August 1762 orders proclaiming the end of the state monopoly on trade with Peking, proposed the organization of a private caravan to the Chinese capital, directed on his return from there by Captain Kropotov with the choice of a commercial director left up to the discretion of the assembled merchants.[99] Kropotov's utter failure in Peking made the proposal academic for the moment, but Catherine did not give up hope. Among Kropotov's 1767 Instructions was authorization to discuss such a caravan with the Chinese, although the formal protocol signed in Kiakhta made no mention one way or the other. When in February 1769 the Collegium of Foreign Affairs reported Kropotov's success to Her Majesty, it included the emissary's recommendation that a caravan now be directed and that with his passport he would escort it to Peking.[100]

Kropotov reasoned that although Mongol merchants quickly began to arrive in Mai-mai-ch'eng it would take Chinese merchants considerable time to assemble their goods and travel to the border, and in the meantime a caravan with both state peltry and private goods could turn a good profit. But the Collegium unhappily reported that there were no stores of crown peltry at that time in Irkutsk or any of the towns of Irkutsk *guberniia,* although small quantities of sea otter and other pelts were in Tobol'sk and Moscow and could be shipped to the border in time. Catherine agreed this should be done.

Kropotov proposed that the caravan be directed by Major

98. *SFPC,* Chuan Shou 2.21a; 37.25a-25b.
99. Chulkov, *Istoricheskoe opisanie,* III, Bk. 2, 328-29.
100. *Sbornik RIO,* LXXXVII (1893), 353-56.

Vlasov of the Iakutsk Regiment and servitors be drawn from the local region; they must be paid and their expenses on the road defrayed from Chinese silver worth 5,777 rubles then in the custody of the border customhouse, or if this were not enough, crown monies should be used and Iakobi so authorized. As for the private merchants anxious to carry goods, Kropotov suggested that the journey would for them prove difficult and expensive and thought should be given to remitting the usual duties in whole or in part. All of this Catherine approved on 18 March 1769, with one exception, the release of private merchants from customs duties. This she added might be studied in the Commission on Commerce.

It seems that the premature death of Kropotov on 18 May 1769 (at the age of forty-five) ended these plans for a state-private caravan to Peking. Only he bore proper credentials and accreditation to the Manchu court, and in the time it would have taken to report his death to St. Petersburg and to send out another man with new papers, border trade at Kiakhta was not only restored but set a new high in ruble value, over two million in turnover. There was no need to go to Peking, and there was no more talk of it.

Chapter VIII. Catherine and the China Trade

Catherine II and her advisers were variously and in differing degrees smitten by the doctrine of physiocratism and the image of the morally unblemished Rousseauian peasant, as well as by interest in free trade and the inhibitory effect of state monopolies and farmed economic privileges on the economic growth and health of the land. But at all times she was convinced also of the virtue and justice of autocracy, never doubting the right of the state to dispose and arrange the economy (and commerce) to its own advantage—"The Sovereign is absolute" (*Nakaz,* Ch. 2, No. 9).[1]

In her great *Nakaz,* the Empress remarked on the necessity of trade both internal and external, linked trade in a very special way with liberty or freedom *(vol'nost'),* and encouraged the promotion of the total trade of the realm:

> Trade is driven from where it experiences oppression, and settles where its tranquillity is not disturbed. [Ch. 13, No. 317] The liberty of trade is not when merchants [*torguiushchye*] are permitted to do as they wish; that would rather be slavery [*rabstvo*]. What hinders the merchant, does not hinder trade. In free lands the merchant [*kupets*] finds countless obstacles; but where slavery exists, he is never so much constricted by laws. England prohibits the export freely of its own wool; she has decreed the import of coal to the Capital by sea; she has prohibited the export of horses fit for breeding

1. Catherine II, *Nakaz Eia Imperatorskago Velichestva Ekateriny Vtoryia, Samoderzhitsy Vserossiiskiia, dannyi Kommissii o sochinenii proekta novago ulozheniia* (St. Petersburg: Pri Imp. Akademii nauk, 1770), cited here and hereafter by chapter and item number. The Nakaz is available in a 1768 English translation in William Fiddian Reddaway (ed.), *Documents of Catherine the Great* (Cambridge: The University Press, 1931), which is unfortunately misleading at times. The translations here were made by the author.

It should be added that at least in the early years of her reign Catherine preferred to limit the state apparatus to overall supervision of the private economic scene and to the promotion of cooperation and mutuality of interest among private entrepreneurs, rather than to permit it to prohibit and prescribe. See especially Antonii Vasil'evich Florovskii, "K istorii ekonomicheskikh idei v Rossii v XVIII veke," *Nauchnye trudy Russkago narodnago universiteta v Prage,* I (1928), 90.

> [*k zavodam*]; ships, from her American settlements trading in Europe, must cast anchor in England. By these and similar [restrictions] she hinders the merchant, but all to the benefit [*pol'za*] of trade. [Ch. 13, No. 321]

The careful distinction between the freedom of enterprise and operation of the merchant on the one hand, and the prosperity of the whole national trade on the other, permitted Catherine to champion both "the liberty of trade" and proscriptions by her administration. Indeed in the next two sections of her *Nakaz* the only firm commercial principle accepted by Catherine becomes obvious—the benefits derived by the state are the only real measure of commercial prosperity and standard of commercial liberty:

> Where there is trade there are customhouses *(tamozhni)*. The purpose of trade is the export and import of goods to the benefit of the state *(gosudarstvo)*. The purpose of the customhouse is a fixed *(izvestnyi)* collection from these very imports and exports of goods to the benefit of that state; for this reason the state must guard the precise mean between the customhouse and trade, and make such regulations, that these two things will never be entangled one with the other: then the people will enjoy there liberty of trade. (Ch. 13, Nos. 322 & 323)

The other side of the coin of the merchants' liberty was the role of state commercial-industrial monopolies vis-à-vis private trade. On the state granting of exclusive monopolies to individuals or companies, Catherine stated flatly in the second supplement to the *Nakaz* dated 8 April 1768 that as a general rule a sensible monarch should "in all cases shun monopolies, that is, not give over to one [entrepreneur], excluding all others, [the right] to enterprise *(promyshliat')* in this or that" (Ch. 22, No. 590). To be sure she included this categorical advice in the chapter devoted to state finances and justified it on the ground that exclusive monopolies were likely to cause resentment among impost and tax payers not privy to the special dispensations given the monopolists. Still on many occasions the Empress declared her opposition to exclusive monopolies and concessions, both those reserved to the state and those granted to private persons. In an ukaz of 17 March 1775 she granted "to all and everyone" the privilege of freely engaging in any kind of handicraft without seeking permission from higher or lower authorities.[2] And again in 1788 she refused the Aleutian adventurers Golikov and Shelekhov an exclusive monopoly to trade in and colonize the North Pacific because "exclusive concession *(iskliuchitel'noe dozvolenie)* is not at all compatible with the principle of Her Majesty of the elimination of every kind of monopoly *(monopoliia)*."[3]

Finally as to the merchants themselves as individuals and as a group, Catherine expressed her concern for amelioration of their condition, but was not persuaded by their persistent requests to be given exclusive right to engage in trade, i.e., by excluding the peasantry and serfs on one hand and the gentry on the other. While she was unfavorable to the participation of Russia's gentry in the life of the marketplace and insisted when they did that they conform strictly to the rules and practices of trade, she refrained from withholding the privilege and granting it only to the registered merchants.[4]

The Empress thus was insistent that Russian merchants accept state regulation of their operations and in so far as they adhered to accepted rules and standards of commercial deportment they would experience Liberty, but beyond the willingness of Catherine to accept the successful big merchant within gentry society and ranks, the merchants were given to understand that they might not expect exclusivity of commercial privilege, others of nonmerchant rank would not be excluded from the right to trade.

Catherine, then, professed early in her reign a strong desire for the rational and reasonable organization of society and the nation. The main task of the administration was not to augment and insure the prerogatives and economic welfare of a single social group, the gentry, but to foster the regulation *(regulirovanie)* of all socioeconomic groups and classes to the ultimate benefit of *all* and thereby to the society as a whole. By accepting definition of its socioeconomic status and rights, each and every group received Liberty, gained the opportunity to pursue its own goals and to achieve its

2. *PSZ,* XX, No. 14275, 82-86, *Manifest* of 17 March 1775. See also Nikolai Nikolaevich Firsov, *Pravitel'stvo i obshchestvo v ikh otnosheniiakh k vneshnei torgovle Rossii v tsarstvovanie Imperatritsy Ekateriny II. Ocherki iz istorii torgovoi politiki* (Kazan': Tipo-litografiia Imperatorskago Universiteta, 1902), pp. 30-31.

3. *PSZ,* XXII, No. 16709, 1106, dated 12 September 1788.

4. See *Nakaz,* Ch. 13, Nos. 330 & 331.

own rewards. Clear distinctions among the several groups were consequently prerequisite; Catherine's well-known Charters to the Gentry and the Cities were intended to accomplish those distinctions in fact. There was not of course always a close fit between intent and actuality, between word and deed. Catherine and her administration stopped short of consistently carrying into practice even the most cherished of Catherine's economic notions. In a positive way the Catherinian period is not noted for concrete acts that implemented the Empress' ideas. The China trade functions as an instructive example of this. And it must always be remembered that some of the measures commonly associated with Catherine's reign and leadership came not so much from the attempt to apply theoretical predilections but from experiences accumulated in the decades before Catherine came to the throne. Her idea of free trade is one of these.

Broadly speaking Catherine's reign is and should be known by its devotion to easing the restrictions and prohibitions on private trade and encouraging its growth. In the weeks after her seizure of the throne on 28 June 1762, she approved the issuance of several decrees which essentially retained and broadened the liberal free trade measures of her unfortunate husband, Peter III, measures which of course he had no chance to implement. In an ukaz of 28 March Peter had declared the general principle of freedom of private trade in all spheres and in all goods.[5] And on 1 June another imperial decree to the procurator-general of the Senate permitted grain to be exported freely abroad, so long as the domestic price did not rise excessively.[6] Catherine's major pronouncement on free trade came quickly, in a Senate edict of 31 July 1762.[7] The burden of the twenty articles was that all commodities, except specifically enumerated items, were sanctioned for free private trade, with the payment of the proper customs duties as stipulated in the tariffs of the decade earlier. Grain, silks, salted meat, and even cattle were declared open for all to trade. Other goods, such as potash, pitch, tallow, and flax, were still forbidden

5. *PSZ,* XV, No. 11489, 959-66, Imperial decree to the Senate of 28 March 1762. See also the general discussion in *Ekonomicheskaia istoriia SSSR, Uchebnik dlia ekonomicheskikh vuzov,* ed. by I. S. Golubnichii, A. P. Pogrebinskii, and I. N. Shemiakin (Moscow: Sotsekgiz, 1963), pp. 114-30; and Firsov, *Pravitel'stvo,* pp. 193 ff.

6. *PSZ,* XV, No. 11557, 1028-29.

7. *Ibid.,* XVI, No. 11630, 31-38.

to private merchants either because long-term farms in them had been granted by Elizabeth or because the enterprises in Russia were still in need of special protection.

The China trade shared in the attention. Trade in rhubarb was for the nonce still reserved to the state, according to the 1762 decrees, but only until the stores of the root were sold. A flat guarantee was included in Catherine's decree that rhubarb would be opened up for private trade, with of course the payment of tariff duties, by a future decree. Tobacco was now freed, although it had been granted in 1759 to the since deceased Count Shuvalov and his heirs for a twenty-year period in return for which he paid the Treasury seventy thousand rubles annually. To insure a continued profit of at least seventy thousand rubles, the former duty of five kopeks per *pud* was quadrupled and was to be calculated in Russian money, not *efimki.* The edict was clear also on the Peking caravan. It was given over to private trade, i.e., now trade both at the border and in Peking itself was in the hands of private merchants. Any further caravans were required to conform to the provisions of the Treaty of Kiakhta and the general pattern of former caravans was to be followed. Captain-Lieutenant Kropotov was detailed to escort the first (if even one was organized) private caravan to Peking, although the director was to be chosen by the merchants themselves. More important than the caravan itself (for none ever travelled to Peking) was the striking down of the long-standing prohibitions on private trade in the best furs; all pelts were now freed for private trade either at the border or in Peking.

Were these liberties not broad enough, in a manifesto of 17 March 1775 all state economic monopolies were in theory ended, and the formation of industrial and commercial enterprises was thrown open to all, with no special permission needed.[8] Catherine persisted in denying her exclusive allegiance to the doctrine of free trade or, for that matter, to any other single socioeconomic doctrine, but she did continue to further the free trade tendencies already given a healthy nudge forward by Shuvalov in Elizabeth's reign. Particularly she opposed special monopolies, farms, and other privileges, and consequently abolished in 1779 the Manufacturing Collegium *(Manufaktur-kollegiia)* established under Peter I, in large part for the administration of the system of industrial

8. *Ibid.*, XX, No. 14275, 82-86, esp. Paragraph 11 (p. 84).

(and commercial) privileges.[9] In response to a 1763 request to the Senate from a merchant Sulov for a six-year farm in the trade of imported and Russian playing cards, Catherine marginally wrote: "The Devil take him with his farm: all of the merchants contend, he says, that in the Senate there is a disposition to farms."[10] And again in a half-dozen years later, "We, more than other lands, are unable to tolerate exclusive privileges *(iskliuchitel'nye privilegii).*"[11]

In spite of all these enactments which seem to reflect, at first glance, a new and liberal view of the Russian throne toward economic enterprise in general, Catherine never saw fit to instruct her *chinovniki* to loosen all of the restraints on private merchants and entrepreneurs. She persisted in balancing the requests of merchants against the needs and desires of the state. It must be said in all justice that her *Nakaz* strongly suggests this as a fundamental operating principle. Consequently many commodities were not freed for foreign trade. Some were prohibited to private merchants for security reasons, others for protectionist reasons, and still others (including rhubarb) were reserved to the state or leased to private persons simply and plainly because they proved financially too valuable to the Treasury to be set free. In spite of the promise made in 1762 to end the state monopoly in the rhubarb trade within two years, the prospect of continued large profits dampened Catherine's affection for unhampered private carriage in this item of commercial exotica. Some merchants of Novorossiisk *guberniia* announced to the state their desire to purchase all of the remaining stocks of rhubarb in St. Petersburg and Moscow and all imported in the next two years at St. Petersburg or Riga, at sixty rubles with the *brak* or fifty without.[12] The head of the Commerce Collegium

9. *Ibid.*, XX, No. 14947, 882-83, dated 22 November 1779.

10. Solov'ev, *Istoriia,* V. 1483.

11. *Sbornik RIO*, X (1872), 358-59.

12. If the rhubarb was received in St. Petersburg, these merchants wished to pay the customs duties on it in copper coin, and if in Riga, in silver; the duties they thought should be the same as in the previous year.

These were not the only merchants interested in rhubarb; they were simply the highest bidders. In 1763, the Senate, on report of the Commerce Collegium, arranged "to sell for overseas export" several *pud* of rhubarb at fifty rubles per *pud*; Chulkov, *Istoricheskoe opisanie.* VI, 330. Then the following year the Senate tried again. This time sale for foreign export had been requested by several English, Dutch, and Berlin merchants. As was usual with foreign firms, the initial bargaining was performed by the Commerce Collegium, which then reported to the Senate the amounts and prices agreed upon. The final

Ernst Minikh concluded a contract in 1764 with these monopolists and Her Majesty instructed the Senate to secretly admonish border commandant Iakobi to purchase at Kiakhta the very best rhubarb at the earlier usual price—sixteen rubles per *pud*—up to a maximum of five hundred *pud* annually.[13] Evidently the arrangement was a satisfactory one, for in June of 1765 the Commerce Collegium reported that the Novorossiisk merchants had purchased in St. Petersburg for overseas shipment more than 563 *pud* the preceding month at the stipulated price.[14] Rather than give up the monopoly, the Senate determined to strengthen it. In 1765 it established a crown apothecary in Selenginsk and appointed Brant to brack and generally oversee the purchases. The Siberian governor Chicherin was ordered to see to the raising of new detached buildings to properly store rhubarb and other medicinal roots and herbs.[15] Only in the early 1780's was rhubarb at last given up as a state monopoly, and both internal and external trade in it permitted private merchants at a totally unregulated price.[16]

Another instance of Catherinian trade monopoly in the China sector is that of Chinese damasks taken by the Treasury for use of the court. In 1763 an imperial ukaz issued from the Senate took note of sixty-three bundles of damasks taken into the Treasury of the Foreign Chamber *(Nemetskaia palata)* under an Elizabethan decree of 1752 and now stored in the Siberian Prikaz.[17] Catherine instructed that these bundles be handed over to the Court Treasurer Simonov, and that any other similar damasks purchased at the border by private merchants from the Chinese in that year be

(second) offering or auctioning *(peretorzhka)* of the rhubarb took place in the Senate itself. On this occasion the Senate and the bidders found it difficult to come to terms, and only four boxes were sold at the top price of fifty-four rubles to the agent of three English merchants, Daniel, Watson, and Southerland. Others came to buy at fifty-three rubles or even at fifty-two (the English merchant William Glen). The Senate instructed the Collegium on 28 April 1764 that all who would take at least one hundred *pud* should be granted the low price of fifty-two rubles; any who purchased less than one hundred must not pay less than fifty-three. The Senate ordered this information kept secret; *PSZ*, XVI, No. 12144, 729-30.

13. *Senatskii arkhiv,* XIII, 13-14, imperial ukaz of 28 May 1764. See also *ibid.*, XIII, 35-39, 39-40, 67-69, and 70-71; *PSZ*, XVI, No. 12082, 625-26; and Firsov, *Pravitel'stvo*, pp. 203-4.

14. *Senatskii arkhiv,* XIII, 70-71.

15. *PSZ*, XVII, No. 12477, 340-41, dated 21 September 1765.

16. *Ibid.*, XXI, No. 15169, 133; at this time (1780) potash and pitch were also freed.

17. *Ibid.*, XVI, No. 11922, 373-74, dated 17 September 1763.

delivered to the Imperial Treasury in exchange for a fair price. In the future these fine damasks were not to be privately traded at Kiakhta. Those already in Moscow were to be delivered to Lieutenant-General Betskoi for sale for support of the Foundling Home.

It is not surprising that Catherine and her administrators did not perfectly carry into practice the fine sentiments of her *Nakaz*. It is somewhat more unexpected that she seems to have developed no general criteria for deciding between the interests of her private merchants and the needs and desires of the state. Actual policy decision was not dictated by any prior theoretical predilection. Each matter was settled on its own merits and without any obvious reference to a general rule, except as rationalization after the fact. The state's experiences in the decades before 1762 did repeatedly relate to the Russian state's decisions and activities after that date. The history of state monopolies and private farms in the China trade suggests that their record of failure or inconsistent success, at least as far as the State Treasury was concerned, accounted for their abolition by Catherine rather than did her lofty philosophical view of the proper organization of society. As we have noted, those that still promised benefit to the Treasury and the state lived on.

Nothing said thus far should be taken to suggest that the Catherinian state withdrew from the private commercial sector of the economy, leaving it to regulate itself and to achieve prosperity wholly on its own. Catherine did show her willingness to expend some monies to improve the condition of private trade at Kiakhta. And a variety of edicts were issued which aided the Kiakhta merchants materially. Overall it must be said that Catherinian enactments and policies with regard to the China trade provided a more favorable climate for private commerce than had those of any of her predecessors.

The blue-ribbon conference which the Tsaritsa assembled in October, 1764 to consider the military dangers apparent then at the border took recognition of the close relationship of trade with the Chinese and the threatening hostilities. The notables proposed several measures for tightening the organization and discipline of the border merchants.[18] In spite of the disposition in

18. *Sbornik RIO*, LVII (1887), 37-47. Several members of Catherine's Commission on Commerce, reestablished in December of 1763, commented in the spring of 1764 on the utility of company organization for the Kiakhta merchants. Count G. N. Teplov, although strongly opposed to commercial monopolies in general, thought that in certain avenues of foreign trade, espe-

many circles, including the court, against economic monopolies and special privilege, these men were of one mind that the finest arrangement for improved bargaining with the Chinese was a private commercial company which would assume the prerogatives previously enjoyed by the state caravans. It was assumed, incorrectly, that Russian merchants would continue to travel to Urga, some 180 miles from Kiakhta. The conference members were under no illusions that the creation of a company was likely; the report to the Tsaritsa made blunt reference to the fact that Russian merchants "unite always with difficulty" and that the probabilities were very much against getting the Kiakhta traders to come to agreement on a single company in which all could and would participate.

Nonetheless, some form of business organization had to displace the disordered bands of competing traders, the conference members concluded. Private merchants had to be prevented, both for their own welfare and for the benefit of the state treasury, from bidding against one another, thereby lowering the asking prices of Russian goods (and reducing the customs intake). Chinese "domination" of the market had to end. Contraband trade had to be controlled. The Commission report proposed the halting of all merchants at Selenginsk; from among those who arrived soonest after the reopening of trade, three or four "directors" or "better to say brokers" should be selected by the merchants themselves. Their main task was to extract from all merchants who intended to go to Kiakhta precise declarations of their goods and prices, and then in general to arrange the sale of these goods at the declared prices. The teeth in this suggestion was that any merchant entering individually and directly into a sales agreement with a Chinese merchant would be fined by the brokers to the extent of 50 per cent of his goods, which would be distributed among the other merchants. Thereafter the offender would be excluded from trade with the Chinese at the border. An obvious

---

cially in the China trade, "commercial societies" *(obshchestva torgovye)* or companies might prove of great benefit. State Councillor Timofei Klingshtet asked whether a "China Trading Company" *(Kitaiskaia torgovaia kompaniia)* might not be necessary to promote this important commerce (he included other "eastern" countries as well: Persia, Turkey, etc.). As so often earlier in the century, Klingshtet compared Russia's China trade with that of several Western European countries that had developed chartered companies for foreign trade.

danger inherent in this arrangement was that the wealthier merchants were likely to dominate because they could afford smaller margins of profit on their goods and because they were likely to be, or to be friends of, the brokers. To obviate this danger the larger traders should be required to leave half of their merchandise in Selenginsk to be forwarded to Kiakhta only after the first half was disposed of.

Catherine marginally noted her approval of the project on 19 October 1764. Unlike the great plan of Lange twenty-five years earlier and the more modest one of Kropotov, this one related only to the border trade and offered no false hopes that the Kiakhta merchants could be bound together in a lasting, exclusive, and disciplined company. Like those earlier proposals, this one failed, so far as we can gather. There is no extant documentation to establish that local Irkutsk authorities actually tried to organize such a company. Until very late in the century observers on the scene continued to comment on the striking absence of mercantile organization in Kiakhta in particular. Peter Simon Pallas, after visiting the town in 1772, attributed the weak bargaining position of the Russians to their forsaking of unity, which he felt to be lamentable.[19] Jean Benoit Scherer about the same time blamed the intellectual and moral backwardness of the Russian people and serfdom *(rabstvo)* for the lack of commercial unity.[20]

Despite the very large growth of the Kiakhta trade in the last half of the century and the evident prosperity of many merchants involved in it, the notion of a single "company" organization for all Kiakhta merchants died hard. In the last of the many proposals stretching back to Peter the Great's mention of it in 1711, Tsar Paul in 1800 issued full instructions for organizing the Kiakhta trade, appended to a new tariff for the China trade. Point 2 of a long set of regulations for the guidance of the Troitskosavsk customs authorities reads as follows:

> For the preservation of this trade, as much as possible, in a condition advantageous to Russia, [it is ordered] to gather from among the merchantry, from each of the existing companies [!], one partner [*kompan'on*] from among the leading merchants. The duty of these partners is to prepare in closest

19. Pallas, *Voyages*, IV, 178, and Firsov, *Pravitel'stvo*, Pt. 3, pp. 146-47.

20. Jean Benoit Scherer, *Histoire raisonnée du commerce de la Russie* (Paris: Cuchet, 1778), II, 19-20.

> conformity [to the aims] of the enunciation here a regulation [*pravilo*] stipulating for the Kiakhta trade what will adduce the best compared with the previous situation. And accordingly binding the company members to the utmost to deport themselves with that alone so that Russian goods, in reciprocal barter, as much as possible are raised in value and the Chinese are lowered.[21]

The new orders went on to condemn Russian merchants who "by their own arbitrariness in having in view only private advantage" exchanged goods with the Chinese at unnecessarily low prices, below the generally prevailing levels. Paul's instructions as to how the merchants were to be organized were detailed, but differed only in minor points from earlier suggestions.[22] They did draw attention to one great advantage of company organization: all merchants could more easily learn which Russian goods sold best and in what quantities, for at the end of each trading season all goods remaining unsold would be available for inspection in the Troitskosavsk warehouses. Every merchant could better judge what to carry to Kiakhta another year.

21. *PSZ*, XXVI, No. 19327, 74-75, and No. 19328, 75-79, both dated 15 March 1800. See also L. M. Samoilov, "Istoricheskiia i statisticheskiia svedeniia o kiakhtinskoi torgovle," *Sbornik statisticheskikh svedenii o Rossii* ("Trudy Imperatorskago Russkago Geograficheskago Obshchestva"), Knizhka 2, Otdel 2 (1854), 18-19, and Gagemeister, *Statisticheskoe obozrenie Sibiri*, II, 594-95. Gagemeister accepted the existence of four of the six trading "companies," an error repeated widely by subsequent generations of historians.

22. All of the selected partners were, in a general gathering, to set prices on all Russian and Chinese merchandise in the market, before any bargaining or exchanging actually began. The bargaining was to be done by these select merchants personally inspecting all Russian goods as they arrived in Troitskosavsk, sorting the items by kind and quality, and then listing the prices in a register made up in three copies, one of which went to the individual merchant, one to the custom house, and the third retained by these merchants' representatives. Since the Chinese goods could not be inspected before the merchants looked them over and made bargains, they also were to be inspected after import in Troitskosavsk, rather than in Kiakhta, and sorted by quality. Fair market prices were to be established, and goods and prices listed in two copies, one for Customs and one for the selected merchants. Presumably this would have meant that the merchants themselves in their exchanges at Kiakhta would utilize price lists developed on similar goods previously traded, lists kept by the "companies." Divergence from these prices, once established, was to be punishable by reasonably heavy hand: a fifty-ruble fine for the first offense, double that for the second, and flat exclusion from the trade for the third. All fine monies were to revert to the Customs officials who were enjoined to use them for the benefit of the trade at large.

As had happened earlier, Paul's sanguine plans changed nothing. Now, as so often before, the hopes of St. Petersburg to bind these merchants together and to legislate a commercial discipline, not to speak of acumen, were based on ignorance of the actual state of Russia's merchants and an impractical devotion to neat social organization. There is no evidence that this effort had any more impact on merchant organization than did the many attempts of the preceding three-quarters of a century.

Catherine's famed decree of 1775 laid down an organizational scheme for Russia's merchants, which if operative in eastern Siberia would have gone a long way toward structuring and disciplining the Kiakhta traders. Three merchant guilds *(gil'dy)*, it will be recalled, were decreed, the members of which were to be called the merchantry proper *(kupechestvo)*, as distinguished from the lesser *meshchane*.[23] The first guild was to include all those with "turnover capital" *(oborotnyi kapital)* exceeding ten thousand rubles, and the second and third guilds, those merchants with capital ranging down to five hundred rubles. The business and personal rights and obligations of both the *kupets* and the *meshchanin* were carefully and quite exactly identified. Later decrees of 1758 and 1794 altered slightly the 1775 pronouncement, but mainly to raise the ruble figures of working capital required for admission to the several guilds.[24] These legal statements nowhere in Russia created *de novo* an organized, conscious, prideful, and cooperating merchant class. Indeed in nearly all of its details the act of 1775 was a dead letter. Aleksandr Radishchev who visited Kiakhta in 1792 recorded, as we earlier noted, that the guild organization did formally exist there, but did not operate successfully as a mechanism to organize commercial activities. During the trade suspension of 1785-92, some Irkutsk merchants attempted to gather together all of their first-guild colleagues, but many lowly third-guild merchants maneuvered their way into the guild, not only in their own names, but even five, six, or more camouflaged under the name of a single larger merchant.[25] Catherine's guilds had no impact on Russia's eighteenth-century trade with China.

23. *PSZ*, XX, No. 14327, 145-47, dated 25 May 1775.

24. *Ibid.*, XXII, No. 16188, Articles 102, 108, and 114, dated 21 April 1785. The first guild was to have capital of 10-50,000 rubles; the second, 5-10,000 rubles; and the third, 1-5,000 rubles. In 1794 (*ibid.*, XXII, No. 17223, 531-32, dated 23 June 1794), the figures were raised to 16-50,000 rubles for the first guild, 8-16,000 rubles for the second, and 2-8,000 rubles for the third.

25. Radishchev, *Polnoe sobranie sochinenii*, II, 21.

In other less dramatic ways the state apparatus did strive to support Kiakhta merchants and the trade, of which by far the most consequential both to the merchants and to the development of a sound commercial mechanism was the expansion of the system of promissory notes. The *veksel'* regulations of 1729, confirmed by Elizabeth, permitted only European Russian merchants to defer customs payments for a reasonable period of time during which they would have marketed their goods and have the cash to pay; Siberian merchants, presumably carrying shorter distances, were excluded from this important concession. Not until 1769, some forty years after the *veksel'* system began in Russia, were local Siberian merchants permitted to submit promissory notes in lieu of cash for their customs dues.[26] Especially for such a distant place as Irkutsk, the problem of proof of solvency immediately arose. In May of 1770 Irkutsk Governor A. I. Bril' requested that the Commerce Collegium require the magistracies and town-halls of the towns of origin of merchants and their agents to provide them with a statement or certificate (*attestat* or *odobrenie*) of their capital resources, in the absence of which a cash deposit was absolutely required.[27] The Collegium concurred and approved Bril' 's suggestion. All merchants were circularized to secure notes from the magistracy nearest them. The bills or notes were required to be discharged at the Petropavlovsk customhouse no later than six months after the merchants departure from the border, a somewhat stringent requirement in view of the distances involved in travel to European Russia, although reasonable where the goods turned over in one of the Siberian markets. Also under this arrangement the merchant must return to the border to pay his obligation; there was no other thoroughly secure way of transferring cash.

Eventually—in 1781—Russian merchants from west of the Urals could redeem their pledges by cash payments in either Moscow

26. *PSZ,* XVIII, No. 13380, 1014-15, dated 11 November 1769. The 1769 Senate decree permitted *veksel'* only for a six-month period and payment in cash had to be made in Moscow or St. Petersburg. The *veksel'* had to be effected in triplicate in the Commerce Collegium, one copy directed to the *Shtats-Kontora* in Moscow, the second to the Chancellery of the Siberian governor, and the third to the Irkutsk Military Paymaster (*Krigs-tsalmeistr*). In addition to the document itself, every merchant or his agent had to provide a separate guarantee that the note was serviceable. See also Chulkov, *Istoricheskoe opisanie,* III, Bk. 2, 331-32, 339.

27. Silin, *Kiakhta,* p. 94. This was a major step forward; under the original regulations (see Chapter 6), cash or goods had to be deposited as collateral.

or St. Petersburg within a full year with a surcharge of 6 per cent.[28] Alternatively the obligations now could be paid at either Tobol'sk or Irkutsk within nine months with the lower charge of 4 per cent. The advantages of utilizing the Siberian towns were great. Tobol'sk was, in addition to being the capital city of Siberia, adjacent to the important market fair of Irbit; and Irkutsk also had a market after 1768. The Siberian merchants were still discriminatively treated. Not until 1794 did an imperial edict allow merchants registered in Siberian towns and trading at Kiakhta to pay their duties at the border in cash or to transfer them by *veksel'* to any of the four cities available to European Russian merchants; the *veksel'* period was nine months and the interest a favorable 5 per cent.[29] By this time also the Russian or Siberian merchant could pay his duties either in foreign specie, favored of course by the Treasury, or in Russian currency.[30] Whenever it could, the Senate insisted on foreign gold and silver, but merchants throughout the empire, including Kiakhta, were notoriously unable to pay in other than the relatively cheap Russian copper money or assignats. To encourage the presentation of Chinese silver and gold, favorable conversion rates with Russian money were granted in 1800: 2 rubles 75 kopeks per *zolotnik* of pure gold and 19.5 kopeks per *zolotnik* of pure silver.[31]

It seems that the *veksel'* privilege found heavier use during the Catherinian period than earlier. It was a boon to all small merchants in particular, and especially after 1794 to Siberian traders, for it permitted them to turn over goods two or three times in less than a year. It did create some problems, particularly in the bureaucratic mechanism for registering the certificates, accepting the promissory notes, and forwarding them to the other cities at which payment was accepted. In a word, Irkutsk and eastern Siberia needed a banking system, absent from all of Siberia until

28. *Ibid.*, pp. 94-95.

29. *PSZ*, XXIII, No. 17251, 553-54, dated 13 September 1794. For the State Council approval in July, see Gosudarstvennyi Sovet, *Arkhiv Gosudarstvennago soveta* (St. Petersburg: Tip. Vtorago Otdeleniia Sobstvennoi E. I. Kantseliarii, 1869-1904), I, Pt. 2, 285.

30. *PSZ*, XIII, No. 17115, 420-21, dated 15 April 1793; XXIV, No. 17739, 286, dated 16 January 1797; XXIV, No. 17842, 499, dated 26 February 1797; XXVII, No. 20174, 68-69, dated 8 March 1802; and XXVII, No. 20715, 543, dated 17 April 1803.

31. *Ibid.*, XXVI, No. 19327, 74-75, dated 15 March 1800, active date 1 January 1801. The conversion rates varied considerably as paper assignats rose and fell in the market.

1776. The immediate cause of the establishment of a bank office in Tobol'sk in that year was the creation of the Assignation Bank only seven years before.[32] The Tobol'sk Bank Office began with a capital of one million rubles assignat, and of course its main function was the issuance of that paper currency in exchange for copper coin especially. In 1779 eastern Siberia received its first state bank with the establishment of a similar office in Irkutsk with no more than five hundred thousand rubles assignat in capital.[33] Neither of these offices survived long, apparently because of the comparatively light use of both paper and coin in Siberia; the Tobol'sk office closed after a dozen years of operation and the Irkutsk office after ten, although the latter had actually been inoperative since the beginning of the long trade suspension by the Chinese in 1785 and therefore maintained operations only a half dozen years.[34] Since of course these branches of the Assignation Bank were charged only with the emission of paper money and were not authorized to perform the other critical banking functions, especially short- and long-term loans, they seem not to have any significant impact on the China trade.

The *veksel'* system produced a second unpredicted shortcoming. Governor-General Iakobi complained in 1786 of the fiscal difficulties of his Irkutsk lieutenancy, partly attributable to the transfer to Moscow by *veksel'* of some of the customs revenues.[35] On total customs revenues of 500,000 rubles (actually they were considerably smaller than in 1785, although after trade picked up again in 1792 they rose to over that figure), Iakobi calculated an increment of 30,000 rubles from the 6 per cent *veksel'* charge, all of which presumably funnelled to Moscow. To service this system the Irkutsk administration was put to considerable expense for which it had inadequate non-customs revenues; Iakobi claimed annual expenses of 700,000 rubles and income from local taxes and other sources of 500,000 rubles. The Senate's solution to this difficulty was not, as might be expected, to transfer a portion of the customs revenues

32. *Ibid.*, XX, No. 14483, 397-98, dated 12 July 1776. For the edict on the creation of the Assignation Bank in 1768, see *ibid.*, XVIII, No. 13219, 787-92, dated 29 February 1768, printed 1 February 1769. The main offices were in St. Petersburg and Moscow.

33. *Ibid.*, XX, No. 14861, 810-11, dated 10 April 1779.

34. *Ibid.*, XXII, No. 16612, 1020-21, Imperial ukaz given to Chief Director of the State Assignation Bank Count Shuvalov on 21 January 1788.

35. *Ibid.*, XXII, No 16402, 607-11, dated 3 June 1786.

from Moscow, but to authorize the establishment in Irkutsk of a mint *(Monetnyi dvor)* for the conversion into coin of silver mined in the Nerchinsk region. To Muscovite administrators this made sense, for the carriage of this silver to the St. Petersburg mint for conversion had cost some 6321 rubles over the preceding three years, which was not a great sum when contrasted with the profits of silver mining and coining to the state.[36]

The state contributed in other small ways to the improvement of the Kiakhta private trade during the Catherinian period. For example, the very active governor Soimonov petitioned in 1763, even before the renewed interest in the China trade reflected in Catherine's special committee of the following year, for the improvement of the difficult Baikal passage.[37] To illumine the way on warm summer nights, a lighthouse was to be raised on a narrow peninsula known as Prorvaia or on a spit known as Korga. Also three boats, two largish seaworthy craft and one small boat, were to be built for use on the lake for either crown or private goods. In neither case did the government willingly accept the costs of construction or maintenance; rather it authorized Kiakhta Customs to levy a new assessment on all merchants trading there. The Senate stipulated that the treasury must suffer not the "slightest" loss in this project, since the merchants themselves would gain most from it.

More important though was the establishment, as noted above, of market fairs in Irkutsk, Iakutsk, and Udinsk a few years later.[38] The Russian merchants themselves originally proposed in 1766 a *iarmarka* in Irkutsk, and were supported by Governors Frauendorf and Bril', and various service personnel stationed there, including men of the Selenginsk regiment and some Polish deportees who found the cost of wearing apparel excessively high when it had to be procured from such a distance. Before his death in 1767 Frauendorf received permission to hold two fairs annually in

36. This loss was sustained on the three-year production in both state and private mines of 430 *pud* 23 *funt* 62 *zolotnik* of silver, estimated to net 367,437 rubles. The use of Nerchinsk silver for the need of the Irkutsk administration was only fair, for in 1762 Kiakhta customs administration was ordered by the Governing Senate to dispatch some of its revenues for the maintenance and expansion of the Nerchinsk smelting works; *ibid.*, XVI, No. 11676, 75, dated 3 October 1762.

37. *Ibid.*, XVI, No. 11840, 268, dated 2 June 1763. See also Cilin, *Kiakhta*, p. 86.

38. See Chapter 6, and *PSZ,* XVIII, No. 13139, 693-95, dated 25 June 1768.

Irkutsk, one lasting from November 15 to the first of January and the second from March 15 to the first of May, in which all "foreign" (i.e. non-Irkutsk) merchants might trade goods brought from elsewhere in Russia in addition to Chinese imports. The other two fairs were to be shorter of duration, two months in the newly designated provincial town Udinsk in Selenginsk *uezd* and a summer fair of two months, plus a winter one of the month of December, in northerly Iakutsk. The Irkutsk fair, shortly to become one of the famed ones of Siberia, ultimately served many purposes: it cheapened the acquisition of necessities by inhabitants of Irkutsk and all neighboring towns including Kiakhta; it provided a very convenient outlet for important Chinese goods carried by small merchants financially incapable of transferring them to markets further west, not to speak of Moscow or St. Petersburg; and it served as a good source of some Russian and Siberian goods intended for carriage to the Chinese. Once again the generosity of the Russian court, in the name of Procuror-General Aleksandr A. Viazemskii, did not go so far as to include the commitment of funds to build warehouses, display rooms, and other edifices necessary for the market, although by 1775 a Senate ukaz granted permission for the building of a stone "merchants' court" in Irkutsk to replace the cramped and deteriorating wooden buildings already there.[39]

And, finally, it might be added that by the end of the century the comfort of merchants, as well as all local inhabitants, was improved in two other ways. On request of Lieutenant-General Pil' the Senate authorized in 1788 the erection of some sixty-two taverns in Irkutsk *guberniia*, establishments that Pil' held to be an "urgent need."[40] Each received a state grant of 200 rubles, and an additional 195 rubles was spent for the purchase of two inns already in Selenginsk. Even though the State Council expected to have annual profits of nearly 100,000 rubles returned to the State Treasury, Pil' was instructed to use the 12,595 rubles authorized him only if absolutely necessary to build these taverns which would obviously be sincerely appreciated by the wandering merchants.

Then an apothecary was maintained in Irkutsk to supply not only the town but especially the state serving people in Irkutsk *guberniia* and much of eastern Siberia with medicants, an im-

39. Chulkov, *Istoricheskoe opisanie*, III, Bk. 2, 339.
40. *Arkhiv Gosudarstvennago soveta*, I, Pt. 2, 291-92.

portant detail in the modernizing of the region.[41] The *apteka* obtained fiscal support of 14,300 rubles in its first year of operation (1798) and 5000 rubles annually thereafter. These funds came from the State Treasury by way of the Medical Chancellery.

By this time it should be obvious that the interest of St. Petersburg in eastern Siberia and the China trade was singular. Projects that were revenue producing or enhancing usually won respect of the state councillors, the senators, and the throne. Even those that promised great return seldom merited the expenditure of substantial state funds seed money, although the St. Petersburg officials often objected not the slightest to the use of local governmental funds, always in short supply. The ceaseless efforts to organize and structure Russia's private merchants can be seen in this same light. "Company" discipline over disorderly traders not only fitted Catherinian penchant for organizing society and its classes and groups, but worked to prevent disputes with the Chinese, to keep commerce open, and to maximize customs revenues.

Several Catherinian measures which restructured the administrative organization of eastern Siberia contributed greatly, if indirectly, to improving the Kiakhta trade. Siberia had always been a Muscovite colony, separately administered and discriminatively treated. Not until the famed Speranskii reform of 1822 was its separate status abrogated and the great land brought into the Empire as an integral and regularly administered part. In many ways, however, Catherinian Siberia (and by extension the Kiakhta trade) was subjected increasingly to the regular administrative structure of the Empire. This was symbolized by the dismantling of the Siberian Prikaz in December of 1763, much of its function having disappeared with the abolition of many of the state's commercial monopolies, including the Peking caravan. Now the central administrative organs in St. Petersburg assumed general responsibility for Siberia and, particularly, for the gathering of the state treasury's share of Siberian furs.[42] In tariffs' and duties' collection Siberia (and Kiakhta) continued to be treated separately, although even in this the Ural customs posts, outmoded since the abolition of internal customs duties and almost totally inactive

41. *PSZ*, XXV, No. 18805, 505-6, Imperial edict of 31 December 1798.

42. Slovtsov, *Istoricheskoe obozrenie*, II, 309-10, n. 16; *PSZ*, XVI, No. 11989, 462-68, dated 15 December 1763.

since the Chinese suspension of trade in 1759, were closed early in 1764.

Siberia received a new governor in April, 1763, coinciding closely with the demise of the Prikaz.[43] Denis Ivanovich Chicherin, Major of the Bodyguards and descendant of Italian immigrants, arrived in Tobol'sk barely in time to preside over the diminution of his empire, i.e., to witness the splitting of Siberia into two independent *gubernii,* a move long in the making and as long needed.[44] Irkutsk became a fully constituted guberniia, decreed on 19 October 1764 and made effective on 15 March of the next year. It included the four southerly towns of Irkutsk, Ilimsk, Selenginsk, and Nerchinsk, and their adjacent regions; these were the jumping-off-places for the China trade. Kamchatka and the North Pacific explorations and settlements were administered by the two governors in Irkutsk and Tobol'sk. Irkutsk, long the cultural and commercial center of the east, was now a major administrative center a century and a decade after its first fort was built. The new governor, destined to serve Siberia until his death a little less than three years later, was Major General Karl Frauendorf, formerly commander of the Siberian Line.[45] He found, as we have seen, a developed town of nearly 150 houses, mostly of wood, straight and wide if unpaved streets, and an active commercial life.[46]

The separation of Irkutsk from Tobol'sk and its promotion in the imperial structure signified the recognition in the capital of the continuing and rising importance of the China trade and the remembrance of the enormous distance from St. Petersburg ("In consideration of the great expanse of Our Siberian *Tsarstvo* . . ."). Frauendorf and his three immediate successors were all high-ranking military men, and although one proved to be a man of

43. *Senatskii arkhiv,* XII, 361.

44. *PSZ,* XVI, No. 12269, 944, dated 19 October 1764.

45. He died on 2 January 1767 and was immediately succeeded by Major-General Adam Ivanovich Bril' (1769-74), Brigadier Fedor Glevovich Nemtsov (1775–79), and Frants Nikolaevich Klichka (1779-82). Bril' later became President of the Moscow Manufacturing Collegium; Klichka in 1783 assumed the office of governor of Kursk; and Nemtsov has survived in history mainly as one too devoted to self-enrichment. Consult, among others, Sukachev, *Irkutsk,* pp. 13-15, and Erik Amburger, *Geschichte der Behördenorganisation Russlands von Peter dem Grossen bis 1917* ("Studien zur Geschichte Osteuropas," 10 [Leiden: E. J. Brill, 1966]), pp. 405-6.

46. Le Clerc wrote that "le commerce d'Irkoutzk est le plus considérable de la Sibérie," and "les habitans sont nombreux, & la plupart commerçans; . . ." Clerc, *Histoire,* III, 384.

questionable ethics (Brigadier Fedor G. Nemtsov), all four were higher placed men than was typical of office holders of an earlier day in eastern Siberia. As time went by, both wealth and population of the Irkutsk region grew until by the early 1780's Irkutsk itself was said to have twenty thousand inhabitants, a dozen churches (including a Lutheran one), several schools, a library, a theater, and a banking office.

At this point Irkutsk itself was made the seat of a governor-general, it became a "vice-regency" *(namestnichestvo)*; Lieutenant-General Ivan V. Iakobi, of whom we shall hear a great deal more, assumed governor-generalship of Irkutsk and Kolyvan', an arrangement that survived in radically changed form until Speranskii.[47] Irkutsk *guberniia* was then (1783) expanded to include the North-east, Iakutsk and Okhotsk, a total of four *oblasti* and seventeen *uezdy*. Iakobi arrived to open "triumphantly" his "Viceregal Administration" *(Namestnicheskoe pravlenie)* in February of 1784, and within the year he arranged for the opening of a town *duma*, which began actual meetings on the first day of 1787. The first mayor *(gradskoi golova)* was significantly the first-guild merchant Mikhail Vasil'evich Sibiriakov, a member of probably the most distinguished and wealthy eastern Siberian mercantile family.[48] Still later the administration of Irkutsk was further developed and defined. In a decree of 1797 Irkutsk region became simply fifteen *uezdy* (no *oblast'*), which were reduced in number to seven some eight years later.[49] A full list of ranks *(shtaty)* accompanied the change.

The border posts through which the China trade funnelled did not escape St. Petersburg's tinkering. Stimulated of course by deteriorating relations with the Chinese, Elizabeth had instructed the Siberian governor in 1760 to see to the augmentation of the population in Transbaikalia.[50] All landowners might dispatch to Siberia any peasant not over forty-five years of age and in good muscle for field work, which contribution to Siberian development

47. *PSZ*, XXI, No. 15675, 873, dated 2 March 1783. See also *ibid.*, XIX, No. 13684, 359, dated 20 October 1771; XX, No. 14242, 21-42, dated 31 January 1775; XXI, No. 15680, 875-76, dated 6 March 1783; and XXII, No. 15921, 18, dated 4 February 1784.

48. Sukachev, *Irkutsk*, p. 16.

49. *PSZ*, XXIV, No. 17864, 508, dated 4 March 1797.

50. *Ibid.*, XV, No. 11166, 582-84, dated 13 December 1760. See also Andrievich, *Kratkii ocherk*, p. 191. Special regulations were also set down for monastery, church, and in general all ecclesiastical peasants.

could be counted against the owner's recruit quota. Children sent earned the landowner a state monetary reward: ten rubles for those under five; twenty rubles for those between five and fifteen; those over fifteen earned nothing but being counted in the recruit quota, which was quite enough. Female children counted for only one-half. The landlord had to provide the immigrant's clothing and a certain small sum of travelling funds, the latter used to defray the costs of maintenance of soldiers and officers who accompanied these settlers on the march. To ease the burden of the journey, these peasants should be sent in the summer only, that they might use navigable streams. And local authorities were enjoined to refrain from unkindnesses and brutalities toward them, employing instead cajolery which was hoped would reduce the number of runaways. Earlier in the same year (1760) the Siberian governor received instructions to undertake the organization and development of arable lands in the Nerchinsk and Selenginsk regions, particularly seeing to it that new settlers and long-time inhabitants would have the means to support themselves.[51] This was the latest of many efforts to bolster the populace along the border, an effort which succeeded, partly of course because of the comparative economic affluence given the territory by the prosperous China trade.

Kiakhta itself shared in these attentions. In 1774, on representation from the Irkutsk chief magistrate *(Glavnyi magistrat)*, the Senate authorized the creation of a magistracy or town hall *(Ratusha)* and the designation of magistrates as necessary.[52] The problem was that Kiakhta registered an exceptionally large number of merchants for that sector of the Empire—488 merchants plus 908 artel artisans—yet had no established office to handle their affairs. No notary was available, compelling the merchants to turn to the respected Kiakhta merchant Semen Avramov to perform those functions, primary of which was to handle the promissory notes brought by merchants. Kiakhta now had something of a regularized town administration, long overdue for the vastly important entrepôt.

Nine years later (1783), Iakobi received authorization for further

51. Andrievich, *Kratkii ocherk*, p. 188. Also *PSZ*, XV, No. 11101, 509-10, dated 12 September 1760.

52. *PSZ*, XIX, No. 14179, 1003-4, dated 21 August 1774. Based on the 1721 Regulation.

improvement of the frontier.[53] Irkutsk was too far from the frontier for the governor-general to exercise constant surveillance over the trade; he needed a local officer to whom to delegate responsibility for the conduct of all affairs with the Chinese. Issued as a supplementary provision to the earlier decree on the organization of Irkutsk, this order appointed a commandant in Troitskosavsk, who was supplied with a civil list to appoint a staff and was made responsible for the continued neighborly relations with the Chinese empire, suppression of border altercations, and supervision of the Russian merchants. This improvement completed, in a manner of speaking, the administrative structure of the border. Earlier (1766) the main customs collection point of the border was transferred from Kiakhta, where it will be recalled it had caused great resentment on the part of the Chinese, to Petropavlovsk to the north. And ten years later it was finally settled in Troitskosavsk, when the Troitskosavsk Commercial Mission *(Troitskaia kommercheskaia ekspeditsiia)* was organized under the supervision of the Irkutsk Commercial Commissariat *(Kommercheskii komissariat)*.[54] This latter body assumed general responsibility for customs tax collection. Thus existed for the remainder of the century and far into the next one the basic administrative structure of the border region. Irkutsk received the recognition it had to have as a major commercial center, and Kiakhta and the border towns were upgraded and simultaneously linked more directly to the responsible officials and offices in Irkutsk.

Continuing Relations with the Middle Kingdom

The last third of the eighteenth century was by no means placid for Russian-Chinese relations. Although it is quite common to emphasize the altercations, disputes, and even threats of violence of

53. *Ibid.*, XXI, No. 15683, 876-88, dated 6 March 1783; also Martens, *Revue de droit international et de législation comparée*, XII, Bks. 5-6 (1880), 539.

54. Kurts, *Russko-kitaiskie snosheniia*, p. 101; Silin, *Kiakhta*, pp. 87-88; Chulkov, *Istoricheskoe opisanie*, III, Bk. 2, 338-39; and Sychevskii, *Chteniia OIDR*, Bk. 2 (April-June, 1875), 291-92. The commandant of the Kiakhta post, a Major Kopylov, recommended this in 1769. It was the able governor Adam Bril' who carried it through and had the major warehouses as well as the customs mission moved to Troitskosavsk, adjacent to Kiakhta yet not in the border city, in order that the Chinese might be given full run of the border town. Bril' 's report was dated 9 August 1770; the Senate and Catherine granted approval. *PSZ*, XX, No. 14277, 87-97 (incorrectly paginated), dated 18 March 1775.

the pre-Nerchinsk period, of the 1720's, and for that matter, as we have done, of the 1760's when the prospect for armed hostilities loomed larger than ever before or since, the Catherinian period after 1768 gave witness to yet unsettled problems of pacific intercourse. To be sure the truly critical problems were settled: the Dzhungar war was over and Ch'ien-lung had defeated and divided the long-time Chinese antagonists, the borders along the entire length of Russian and Manchu dominions were at least fairly closely set and generally respected, and a somewhat more satisfactory handling of defectors and border violators was evolved in the 1768 agreement. The cessation of Russian caravans to Peking removed many of the small, yet cumulative, causes of dispute between Moscow and Peking, which had in the past provoked the Chinese to sever all trade, the most telling weapon against the Russians. And during the last half of the century some of the Russian aggressiveness and acquisitiveness came to be directed elsewhere than in Dauriia, Mongolia, or Central Asia; the North Pacific and its fur seal, Kamchatka, the Komandorskis, the Aleutians, and Russian America siphoned off much of the Russian fervor directed earlier toward regions wherein conflict with the Chinese was likely. After 1768 no spectre of war appeared. In spite of several long severances of commercial relations, the issues were in the main of secondary or tertiary consequence when contrasted with the first three quarters of the century. It was an era of good feeling of sorts and, as we shall see, of general commercial prosperity.

The first decade after the reopening of normal trade in 1768 was unmarred by serious event. The sole threat to tranquillity was the Turgut affair. The Turguts of the middle and lower Volga were courted, as noted earlier, by Manchu missions in 1714-15 and 1729-33, but resisted their blandishments to return to the Ili region and to join the fray against the Dzhungarian enemies. Late in 1770 a large number of these "Russian" Turguts embarked on what turned out to be a very long and very costly trek back to their homeland.[55] The numbers involved have long been a

55. See, among many other items, C. D. Barkman, "The Return of the Torghuts from Russia to China," *Journal of Oriental Studies*, II (January, 1955), 89-115; Thomas De Quincey, "Revolt of the Tartars, Or, Flight of the Kalmuck Khan and His People from the Russian Territories to the Frontiers of China," *Historical Essays and Researches*. Vol. VII of *The Collected Writings of Thomas De Quincey*, ed. David Masson (London: A. & C. Black, 1897), pp. 368-426; Bantysh-Kamenskii, *Diplomaticheskoe sobranie*, pp. 279ff.; Howarth, *History of the Mongols*, I, 574-80.

matter of scholarly dispute and will undoubtedly continue to be. The *Shuo-fang pei-ch'eng* records that four hundred thousand began the journey and somewhat fewer than three hundred thousand reached the Ili region.[56] These figures seem as reasonable as any; in any event the numbers were large in the beginning and the ravages of the road took a heavy toll.

The explanations for the trek are multiple. Chinese sources prefer to emphasize the distress caused the Turguts by a burdensome Russian military conscription, among other oppressions and it is true that the Russian official in charge of the Turguts was ordered to have them provide twenty thousand men at the outbreak of the Russo-Turkish War.[57] As early as July 1770, Catherine referred to the intent of these Mongols to cross the Iaik River and to migrate to Dzhungaria, in a rescript to the Astrakhan governor Beketov. Then too the Turguts had long maintained close ties with their Central Asian brothers and with Peking as well. Many years earlier, for example, the Dzhungarian Kontaisha Tsewang Araptan married the daughter of Turgut chieftain Ayuki. In more recent years (1756) a Turgut mission visited Peking and subsequently also the Dalai Lama in Tibet.[58] Finally She-leng and other Dzhungar fugitives among the Turguts apparently helped persuade them to return.

Russian troops pursued the now fleeting Turguts, several battles were fought, villages and settlements were pillaged, and Turgut ranks were decimated. On arriving in the Ili region, the Turgut leaders chose to surrender to the Chinese general of the region, I-le-tu, and their chief, Wo-pa-hsi, and She-leng were conducted to Peking. The survivors settled along the Ili with the aid of two hundred thousand *liang* of imperial silver.[59]

Had the migration occurred a decade earlier it is highly likely that bitter recriminations, threats of hostility, and possibly even overt Russian efforts to secure the return of these subjects would have resulted, but in 1770 and 1771 Russia had her hands full with the costly and disappointing war against Turkey, not concluded until July 1774. St. Petersburg consequently contented itself with pursuing the rebels to the border, not so much to force

56. *SFPC*, 38.10a. Also Baddeley, *Russia, Mongolia, China*, II, 439-40, n. J.

57. *Sbornik RIO*, XCVII, (1896), 113-23. For an alternate explanation see De Quincey, *Historical Essays*, pp. 370-75.

58. *SFPC*, 38.8-11.

59. *Ibid.*, Chuan shou, 2.21b-23b.

their return as to punish them for sacking Russian towns in their path, and protesting to Peking, especially for the return of the renegade She-leng.[60] Ch'ien-lung flatly rejected Russian demands; he stressed that the Turguts had voluntarily requested Chinese sanctuary, mainly because of hunger. Catherine did order Irkutsk governor Bril' and the commandant of the Siberian Line to accept any of the Turguts who attempted to re-enter Russia, to keep them in safety, and to report to the capital.[61] Beyond that some Cossacks were settled along the Selenginsk-Nerchinsk Line in 1773, but plans for these reinforcements were laid during the long trade suspension of 1764-68 and do not seem to relate directly to the Turgut affairs. On occasion thereafter Russian officials took the Manchus to task for having failed to convince the Turguts to return to the Volga, but seemed not to have meant the complaint to be taken seriously.

In 1775 there was a short trade interruption of three days caused by dispute over the interpretation of the agreements seven years before on customs collection and on the handling of fugitives.[62] Save for this, no suspensions interfered with trade for a full decade after 1768. In 1778 the issue of fugitives across the border once again roiled the waters and led the Chinese to break off all legal trade for a total of two years and thirteen days.[63] Dzhungars had fallen on a Russian caravan, plundered it, and retreated back into Manchu territory. Russian demands for their extradition and punishment were countered with Manchu requests for a number of deserters, including some who had absconded prior to 1768. Also the long standing issue of customs collection at Kiakhta complicated the situation, even though Grigorii Fedorovich Sharin, a

60. *Sbornik RIO,* CXVIII (1904), 1, 31-35.

61. *Ibid.,* CXVIII, 30-31.

62. The English envoy in Russia in 1773, Sir Robert Gunning, reported to Whitehall that the Pugachev rebellion spread so widely in the Kazan' and Orenburg regions as to cause "an entire stop" to the China trade; *Sbornik RIO,* XIX (1876) 392-93. The envoy was obviously speaking of the trade at the Orenburg border line which had been carried on primarily with Kazakhs, for there was no cessation of the Kiakhta trade at that time.

In 1775 the Russians argued that the relevant provisions of the 1768 accord were in a direct sense impossible to fulfill since they intended to collect duties internally, if not at the border, just as it was claimed the Chinese did at Kalgan. See Kurts, *Russko-Kitaiskie snoshennia,* p. 101, and Slovtsov, *Istoricheskoe obozrenie,* II, 310, n. 17. Cf. Fu, *A Documentary Chronicle,* I, 281-91.

63. Kurts, *Russko-kitaiskie snoshennia,* p. 102; Fu, *A Documentary Chronicle,* I, 281.

Russian student of Mongol who had been permitted to cross the border in the month before the cessation of trade in April, assured Manchu officials that the only charges now levied at Kiakhta were small local impositions laid on military serving people and merchants for the support of the local officials and the military establishment.[64] Chinese sources also mention the procrastination and high handedness of the Kiakhta chief in his conduct in the late spring of 1778 (May-June) of the joint investigation of an incident of a Russian illicitly entering Mongolian lands in search of horses to purchase.[65] Apparently trade was actually suspended in July of 1778, although the Peking Court through its representative in Urga, So-lin, Member of the Manchu Plain Blue Banner, delivered the cessation orders in the next month. Chinese sources, again, suggest that the set of Peking was on the side of peaceful negotiation of the differences, provided that the parleys took place between persons of equivalent rank and status and were carried on in a spirit of accord.[66] So-lin, judged to have been precipitous in his initial handling of the affair, was at first sternly upbraided and stripped of his rank, and then in September, 1778, removed from his office. His successor, Po-ch'ing-e, vice-president of the *Li-fan-yuan*, and the Tushetu Khan, Ch'e-teng To-erh-chi, quickly went to the border to negotiate the differences, i.e. to assure themselves that the Russians had repented their arrogance and reformed their conduct. All issues settled, trade was reopened in late April, 1780.

This suspension of a bit over two years caused some considerable damage to the trade. According to E. P. Silin, the Irkutsk archives contain many declarations of local merchants grumbling about the losses they had sustained.[67] The leading Irkutsk merchant, Aleksei Sibiriakov, reported an estimated loss of eight hundred rubles during the half-year of 1778 alone. Some of the slack was taken up by the Argun town of Tsurukhaitu; Siberian merchants, especially

64. Silin, *Kiakhta,* p. 95.

65. *SFPC,* 37.26a-26b. The Chinese sources are not clear on the name of the Russian; he is repeatedly referred to as Ma-yu-erh, which probably signifies major *(maior),* although it could be the personal name Mayer; see, e.g., Fu, *A Documentary Chronicle,* I, 281. General Zeddeler reported that the Chinese persisted into the nineteenth century in referring to the Russian border *nachal'nik* as major because that had been the rank held by early occupants of the office; Liudvig Ivanovich Zeddeler, "Kiakhta i Maimachen (Iz putevago zhurnala General-Leitenanta Barona Zeddelera)," *Severnaia pchela,* No. 286 (19 December 1845), 1144.

66. Fu, *A Documentary Chronicle,* I, 282-83, and *SFPC,* 37.26b, 46.6a.

67. Silin, *Kiakhta,* p. 81.

those from Selenginsk, Verkhneudinsk, and Irkutsk itself, began to send goods there, but most of these traders were the small operators and Tsurukhaitu never threatened to replace Kiakhta, even temporarily. After exchanges resumed at Kiakhta, Tsurukhaitu returned to its usual obscurity.

The next five years were comparatively quiescent, a lull between showers. Both sides manipulated the administration of border affairs in order to tighten control of the frontier, the merchants using it, and the natives living there, without drastically altering the structure derived from the Treaty of Kiakhta and the protocol of 1768. In 1779 and 1780 several imperial decrees from the court of Ch'ien-lung peremptorily instructed all border officers and all superior officials in the northwestern region of China to employ extreme zeal in apprehending any foreigners who crossed the border, whether for purposes of banditry or not.[68] All those seized were expected to be immediately arrested and reported to higher authorities for disposition. Execution should be expected by all officers who accept bribes to overlook intruders. Chinese and Mongol merchants travelling to the border must be intercepted and their carts, camels, and goods inspected at outposts *(k'a-lun)* presumably at considerable distance from Mai-mai-ch'eng. If all were in order, they were to be given passports which would be reinspected at the border. Under no circumstances could a merchant reaching the border without a properly issued passport be permitted to trade. These several orders merely renewed and reinforced the mechanism of border surveillance long since established.

The only major irritant between 1780 and 1785 was the affair of the Old Believers.[69] These Schismatics came voluntarily to southern Siberia in the 1760's, sponsored by the throne and granted state support in the form of land allotments and tax and service exemptions. Like the Dukhobory in Western Canada, they were an industrious lot and turned their bleak lands into a productive granary renowned in all of Siberia. Some fifty-nine of them attempted in 1783 to cross over in the region of Kobdo far to the west of Kiakhta. Peking officials chose to refuse asylum to the dissidents and extended to them the choice of voluntarily returning before their absence became an issue between the two governments or

68. *SFPC*, 37.26b-27a, and Fu, *A Documentary Chronicle*, I, 287-91.

69. *SFPC*, Chuan Shou 2.24b-26b; Fu, *A Documentary Chronicle*, I, 293-94; and Raeff, *Siberia*, p. 17.

being forcibly turned over to Russian border authorities. The reasons given were that these people were so different in modes and manners from the western Mongols among whom they would have to reside that they could not expect to integrate successfully and, as the clincher, asylum for them could well cause great perturbation among the Russians and consequently distress the now amicable relations. The Kobdo official Hai-ning was instructed to provide them with travel monies and to see them back to the border. The final disposition of the affair is unclear, but it seems not to have interrupted Russo-Chinese commercial relations at all.

In the very next year however, still another of those trivial border incidents took place which was to have far-reaching repercussions—it led to the longest, although by no measure the most critical, trade suspension of the entire eighteenth century. This last of the significant interruptions of regularized Russo-Chinese commerce lasted in all six years, eleven months, and twenty-three days.

A band of Russian Buriats led by one Ulaldzai (Uladzai) waylaid and robbed a Chinese merchant from Urga, Chin Ming, while the latter traded among the Mongols of the Uriankhai (Wu-liang-hai) region.[70] At the request of Urga officials, the governor of Irkutsk *guberniia*, Ivan Varfolomeevich Lamb, and the ranking officer at the border, Major Kalina Nalabardin, arrested the brigands, fined them ten-fold, and had them caned and branded on the ears and nose.[71] Then apparently Nalabardin determined on his own authority to transport them to the barren wilds of northeastern Siberia. The ranking Chinese agent at Urga, Lao (or Le) Pao, together with two Mongol leaders, the vice-general of Khalkha, Yun-tun To-erh-ch'i, and the Fourth-rank Prince Sun-tun To-erh-ch'i, met with Nalabardin to protest the Russian handling of the affair on the grounds that the 1768 Protocol called for public execution on the border of the men. Precisely speaking the Proto-

70. Among other things, see Bantysh-Kamenskii, *Diplomaticheskoe sobranie*, pp. 326-27; *SFPC*, 37.27a-27b; Uspenskii, *Russkaia mysl'*, XXV (November, 1904) 85; and Kurts, *Russko-kitaiskie snosheniia*, pp. 102ff. Ulaldzai was usually rendered Wo-lo-lao-tsa or Wu-la-erh-chai in Chinese texts.

71. Lamb came to Irkutsk in the year that Iakobi returned (1783). He was the son of Varfolomei Andreevich, a Briton who entered Russian service under Peter I. Ivan Lamb entered service in 1749 and ultimately rose to vice-president of the Military Collegium, general-of-infantry, and member of the State Council. The family name died out in Russia with his death in 1801, at which time he was administrator *(pravitel')* of Kostroma vice-regency.

Nalabardin began service in 1739 and spent most of his career as collector of customs at Kiakhta and Troitskosavsk.

col did not stipulate the execution of first offenders and, as far as can be deduced from the documentation, the Chinese negotiators did not establish these felons as three-time offenders, although they did claim in the midst of negotiations that Ulaldzai had returned to the border and perpetrated an attack on a Chinese guardhouse. The upshot was a strong note from the *Li-fan-yuan* to the Russian Senate of 27 November 1785, which sharply reprimanded the Russian border major for illegitimately taking upon himself the decision to dispose of the case and the Irkutsk governor for supporting his subordinate by declaring the case closed.[72] The *Li-fan-yuan* demanded the punishment of the "stupid" governor and the execution of Ulaldzai.

The Senate's reply argued that the case was for all intents and purposes closed; for Ulaldzai to be executed would constitute double jeopardy and would consequently be grossly unfair.[73] The Russian state had long refrained from use of the death penalty for offenses committed on the border, which the Irkutsk governor had been instructed to inform Peking. Nalabardin, the Senate insisted, had hoped originally to consult with the dzarguchei but unsure whether he would arrive for negotiations, determined to go ahead with the corporal punishment. The note concluded that Russia remained firmly interested in continued trade, abjured war as a solution to this misunderstanding, and was prepared to entertain a Chinese plenipotentiary to negotiate the outstanding differences. Dissatisfied with the Senate's explanation, Peking ordered trade at Kiakhta suspended on 26 March 1785.

The next note of the *Li-fan-yuan*, sent in the late spring of 1786, rejected the Russian logic, and acceded to the prospect of negotiation only for the purpose of renewing the existing treaty arrangements rather than for drafting a new treaty.[74] To punish a man twice for the same offense was certainly unjust, but the Chinese demand was nonetheless completely legitimate. The nub of the dispute was, then, that until Ulaldzai and his cohorts were returned to the border for disposition, no plenipotentiary would be forthcoming and the border would remain sealed, in spite of the Russian request that Russians still be permitted to cross over into Mongol territory. And thus matters stood for years.

72. Bantysh-Kamenskii, *Diplomaticheskoe sobranie*, p. 326.
73. *Ibid.*, pp. 327-28, summarized in Kurts, *Russko-kitaiskie snosheniia*, p. 103.
74. Bantysh-Kamenskii, *Diplomaticheskoe sobranie*, pp. 327-28.

Throughout this suspension of trade the spectre of military confrontation repeatedly presented itself, although in contrast to the altercation two decades earlier neither side indulged in significant military preparations or maneuvers and both forswore a military solution.[75] Catherine did issue on 26 June 1785 a secret rescript to the president of the Military Collegium, Field Marshall Grigorii A. Potemkin:

> You know the occurrences happening on the Chinese border, the closing of customs trade, and the present situation of that region. It is not less than our desire to place this on such a standing that in any circumstance of affairs with our neighbors, the borders of the Siberian *guberniia* are without danger. The fulfilment of this intent of ours we confer to your care, trusting to you the composition of the necessary regular and irregular troops, the supply of that region with adequate artillery and other arms and supplies, the instruction of the principles for the strengthening of the border or important places near to the border, the gathering and delivery there of the requisite people for carrying of all this into actuality; and in a word all arrangements necessary to the security of the designated regions. Your great zeal with regard to us and to the welfare of the state and your skill sufficiently assure us of the success of such arrangements, concerning which we anticipate a favorable report from you, our Imperial grace remains with you always affectionately.[76]

In spite of the seeming earnestness of these instructions, no major effort was undertaken to augment the troops already garrisoned on the Siberian-Mongolian border. Until 1787 one of Russia's perennial wars against the Turks absorbed Catherine's strength and attention, and by then it was quite obvious that neither side was inclined to carry this dispute to the field of Mars.

War talk and sentiment were not totally absent from Siberia and Russia. Aleksandr Radishchev, travelling then in Siberia, com-

75. Foreigners in Russia commented on the war talk; Alphonse Toussaint Joseph Fortia de Piles, *Voyage de deux Français en Allemagne, Danemarck, Suède, Russie et Pologne, fait en 1790-1792* (Paris: Chez Desenne, imprimeur-Libraire, 1796), IV, 336.

76. "Podpisannyi Imp. Ekaterinoiu II reskript Kn. G. A. Potemkinu ob umnozhenii voennykh sil na kitaiskoi granitse," *Sbornik RIO*, XXVII (1880), 352.

mented that in Tobol'sk and Irkutsk people talked not of trade, but of war.[77] Iakobi himself was dismissed in 1789 as governor-general of Irkutsk and Kolyvan', allegedly for actively promoting the prospect of hostilities in hopes of profiting personally from his position as governor of a region at war.[78] Catherine, it is said, was swayed by his arguments but calmer heads in the Senate balked and he was deposed. The Emperor Paul exonerated Iakobi, as he did so many who had been dropped from Catherine's grace, and promoted him to lieutenant-general, which leaves some doubt as to the authenticity of the allegation of combativeness brought against him.

On the Chinese side, the picture is little different. A Russian merchant, Pen'evskii, trading in the Ili region reported in 1785 that a Chinese army of twenty thousand was stationed in Kuldja in preparation for war. This army purportedly assembled after the summer of 1785 when a "Turkish ambassador" filled Ch'ien-lung's ear full of stories of Russian perfidy.[79] The force supposedly was stationed that far from Kiakhta-Mai-mai-ch'eng to avoid giving the Russians cause for military reaction. Pen'evskii professed to have received this intelligence from the ex-Volga Turguts among whom he traded. The entire tale is unsubstantiated and on the surface is of questionable credence, for the merchant also reported that on inquiring into the loyalties of the Turguts he was told that they had no weapons except pikes and bows and arrows, but even if they received less aid from the Russians than from the Chinese they would still not fight Russia. These judgments need not be

77. Radishchev, *Polnoe sobranie sochinenii*, II, 5-35.

78. Iakobi, born in 1726, returned to Selenginsk in 1747 after military training. During the next fifteen years, he was several times sent by his father as courier to Peking. On the death of his father in 1769 after twenty-nine years service in Selenginsk, the son left Siberia with the rank of colonel. He served in the active military forces, then as governor of Astrakhan *guberniia* and governor-general of Ifimsk and Simbirsk. In 1783 he returned once again to the border; *RBS*, vol. Iablonovski-Fomin, 56-57. Among other infractions, Iakobi was held responsible for delaying correspondence with the Chinese; *Arkhiv Gosudarstvennago soveta*, I, Pt. 2, 641. The Decembrist Baron Vladimir Ivanovich Shteingel, who also did service in Siberia, wrote of Iakobi in 1834 (apparently based on current local remembrance and lore) that he "was a satrap-sybarite. One thing remains of him in the memory of the Irkutskian: he lived sumptuously, gaily. His end we know: almost a decade's languor under indictment"; Vladimir Ivanovich Shteingel, "Sibirskie satrapy, 1765-1819 (Pis'mo barona V. I. Shteingelia k A. P. Ermolovu)," *Istoricheskii vestnik*, XVII (August, 1884), 370.

79. Uspenskii, *Russkaia mysl'*, XXV (November, 1904), 91-92.

taken too seriously for they are uncorroborated and smack of the exaggeration of a fanciful trader.

Both governments retreated from circumstances or incidents that could easily have been permitted to exacerbate the affair. The Adam Laksman expedition preparing to visit Japan was cautioned in 1791 to avoid any provocation in its investigation of the Amur river way so as to prevent the rise of new disputes.[80] In the same year, an incident involving a Turgut lama of the Tarbagatai pasturage threatened to disrupt relations even more; both sides willingly accepted the least entangling interpretation. The lama, Sa-ma-lin, wandered into Russian Kirgiz Kazakh territory around Omsk and brought back to China a letter or document indicating Russian intrique among the Turguts.[81] The Senate, responding in July to the *Li-fan-yuan,* flatly repudiated the document, claimed it a forgery since it was sealed improperly—an ordinary ruble coin had been used to make the impression—and in any event was composed "very stupidly" and was "almost impossible to understand." A Ch'ien-lung decree of 31 October 1791 accepted the Russian explanation and promised the speedy restoration of normal trade.[82] And even before the provocation, several trivial cases on the border involving homicide, horse thievery, etc. were handled amicably and with dispatch by the border officials on both sides.[83] Suspended trade did not lead to suspension of all intercourse.

The courts of both Peking and St. Petersburg also realized that the entire Ulaldzai affair had been bungled by the incumbent officers at and responsible for the border, and significantly both replaced key men among them. Soon after the closing of trade,

80. *Arkhiv Gosudarstvennago soveta,* I, Pt. 2, 671-74; *PSZ,* XXIII, No. 16985, 249-50, Imperial edict to Pil' dated 13 September 1791. By the same token, the Senate wrote to the Irkutsk lieutenancy in September, 1788 that it insist that all promyshlenniki operating in the Kuriles shun all "territorial quarrels" with Chinese subjects and "not touch on islands under the authority of other Powers [China and Japan]"; *PSZ,* XXIII, No. 16709, 1105-7, Senate decree dated 12 September 1788.

And the State Council in June of 1791 instructed Pil' to inform General Shtrandman commanding the Siberian Corps in Omsk to exercise "the greatest caution" in matters relating to the Chinese, to follow Pil' 's instructions, and to undertake nothing without the latter's knowledge and approval. Shtrandman must correspond with his counterparts across the border only when absolutely necessary and then orally, committing nothing to paper; *Arkhiv Gosudarstvennago soveta,* I, Pt. 2, 649-50.

81. *SFPC,* Chuan shou 2.27a-28a; Fu, *A Documentary Chronicle,* I, 309-11.

82. *Ibid.,* I, 315-16.

83. *Arkhiv Gosudarstvennago soveta,* I, Pt. 2, 643-44.

Sung-yun, a Mongol of the Plain Blue Banner and a grand secretary, was ordered out to investigate and report on the affair.[84] Sung-yun began his distinguished career as an interpreter in the *Li-fan-yuan* in 1772 and concluded it in 1834 having held most important administrative posts in the capital and in the provinces. George Macartney, whose embassy he accompanied in 1793, held him "a young man of high quality."[85] His first task was to enforce the trade suspension, to suppress smuggling, to see that Chinese subjects in the vicinity of the border were supplied with necessities formerly obtained from the Russians, to regulate all merchants who approached the border, and especially to interdict the export of rhubarb. But in the end he proved to be the man capable of skillfully negotiating with the Russians and settling the business.

In addition to Iakobi, who we have noted was removed in 1789 and replaced by Lieutenant-General Ivan Alfer'evich Pil', Lamb was also relieved of his duties in 1787 and replaced by Major-General Mikhail Mikhailovich Arsen'ev, who died in office five years later and was succeeded by another major general, Larion Timofeevich Nagel.[86] The persistent Chinese criticisms of Lamb in particular came to be accepted in St. Petersburg and he was held to have mismanaged the entire Ulaldzai affair. The departure

84. *Ibid.*, I, Pt. 2, 643-44; *SFPC*, 37.33; Fu, *A Documentary Chronicle*, I, 300, 302. For Sung-yun's biography consult Hummel, *Eminent Chinese*, II, 691-92, and *SFPC*, 46.1a.

85. Sir George Macartney, *An Embassy to China, Being the Journal Kept by Lord Macartney During His Embassy to the Emperor Ch'ien-lung, 1793-1794*, ed. by J. L. Cranmer-Byng (Hamden, Conn.: Archon Books, 1963), p. 127.

86. See *Arkhiv Gosudarstvennago soveta*, I, Pt. 2, 646-48, wherein Lamb is held responsible for blunders.

Arsen'ev, born 1730, attended the Naval Cadets Corps and was commissioned midshipman *(michman)* on 1 January 1755. He participated in the Seven Years' War and in the Archipelago Expedition, 1769-74. Subsequently his career was both naval and civil, and distinguished. He reached the rank of major-general in 1783 and received the Order of St. Vladimir, Third Rank. While governor of Irkutsk his promotion to lieutenant-general came through (5 February 1790.) He died in this last office. Consult *RBS*, vol. Aleksinskii–Bestuzhev-Riumen, pp. 321-22.

Nagel's early years are unknown, except that he served in the army. He was governor-general of Lifland and Estland for a time, and achieved the rank of major-general in 1789. He left Irkutsk in 1797 and died ten years later. He is variously referred to in the materials as Ludwig von Nagel and the semi-Russianized Liudvig Nagil. In Chinese materials he seems to have be referred to as Se-le-pai-t'e (or, after Hummel, Serabate), which forbids explanation. Consult *RBS*, vol. Naake-Nakenskii–Nikolai Nikolaevich Starshii, 10-11; Hummel, *Eminent Chinese*, II, 691; and Ch'en Po-wen, *Chung-O wai-chiao shih*, p. 19.

of both Iakobi and Lamb created probably more than any other factor the conditions in which the Chinese might be persuaded of Russian good intentions.[87] Only one other departure may have been more significant—Ulaldzai at long last contributed to the ending of the affair by conveniently dying in 1788.

By early 1788 Catherine and her court, burdened by the Turkish war which began in August of the previous year, concerned themselves with ending the Chinese dispute just as soon as possible, and came quickly to the opinion that concessions of whatever kind should be employed to restore the most valuable trade. The great losses to both the State Treasury and to private merchants were noted, which in mid-1790 were estimated to be in the neighborhood of six hundred thousand rubles annually for the state and five times that for private traders.[88] As early as July of 1788 the State Council accepted the necessity of concluding a new agreement *(soglashenie)* with the Chinese with regard to runaways and border depradations. The new Irkutsk governor Arsen'ev reported in September of that year the decided proclivity of the Chinese border commandant to come to agreement on the issues, and two months later he concluded that the Chinese waited only for a note from the Senate showing a willingness to mutually consider a change in the agreement on the punishment of border trespassers.[89] Arsen'ev asked for authorization to negotiate on the issue; the State Council agreed that he should have such.

Still in 1789 Ulaldzai's name continued to burden the otherwise maturing border negotiations. The local councillor Dolgopolov reported several conversations, all "pleasant and friendly," in which the Chinese duly noted the death of Ulaldzai but persisted in inquiring of the fate of his fellow culprits.[90] They waited for a decisive note from the Senate, although new depradations across the border by Buriats of Russian sovereignty kept the business muddied.[91] Mai-mai-ch'eng and Urga officials suspected that these

87. See, e.g., *Arkhiv Gosudarstvennago soveta*, II, Pt. 2, 642. It is not certain whether Nalabardin also was relieved, but the local negotiations seem to have been conducted by others, the councillor Dolgopolov and the director of the Troitskosavsk Commercial Mission Vonifat'ev.

88. *Ibid.*, I, Pt. 2, 646, see also p. 641.

89. *Ibid.*, I, Pt. 2, 642-43.

90. Uspenskii, *Russkaia mysl'*, XXV (November, 1904), 86; Silin, *Kiakhta*, p. 97.

91. *Arkhiv Gosudarstvennago soveta*, I, Pt. 2, 643-44. See also "Translation of a Chinese Dispatch sent to Russia, the 21st January, 1789," in George Thomas Staunton, *Miscellaneous Notices Relating to China, and Our Com-*

new incidents may well have been caused by Ulaldzai's compatriots. In December of 1789 the State Council ordered Governor-General Pil' to conduct a thorough investigation. A formal meeting of border commissars was held the next April with both sides turning to their capitals for further and more precise instructions.[92] Pil' asked specific instructions concerning the altering of Article 10 of the Treaty of Kiakhta, on which the disposition of the State Council was to prefer punishment of border violators according to the laws of their own country. If the Chinese strenuously insisted on death, then it must be made clear than the supreme penalty was to apply equally to each side. Also the Council desired inclusion of an article that would forbid the unilateral severance of trade prior to preliminary negotiation which revealed the actual impossibility of mutual agreement. In late 1790 Pil' persuaded the Senate to dispatch yet another note to the *Li-fan-yuan,* which was done and to which a favorable reply was received. But the spring of 1791 brought another snag in the form of the lama, Sa-ma-lin, and the spurious letter, described earlier. The Senate's explanation was immediately accepted in Peking, the way was finally clear to renew trade, and by September of 1791 the State Council communicated to Pil' that he should see to all necessary preparations for the opening of the border.[93]

It took until early February, 1792, before officials of equivalent rank empowered to attach their signatures to a new agreement could be assembled. On the eighth they were: Pil', Nagel, and the border commandant met Sung-yun, P'u-fu, a Mongol of the Blue Bordered Banner, and the Tushetu Khan, Ch'e teng To-erh-ch'i. Nagel and his three counterparts signed a protocol exchanged in Manchu, Mongol, and Russian.

The accord of 1792 has been called an international protocol, an international act, and even a full-blown treaty. It was in essence and in form an amendment to the Kiakhta Treaty of 1727, as already amended in 1768.[94] Trade was to be restored as it had

mercial Intercourse with That Country, Including a Few Translations from the Chinese Language (2d ed.; London: John Murray, 1822), pp. 89-94.

92. *Arkhiv Gosudarstvennago soveta,* I, Pt. 2, 645-46.

93. *Ibid.,* I, Pt. 2, 651.

94. Kurts (*Russko-kitaiskie snosheniia,* p. 103) includes a copy of the Russian text. An official Russian translation from the Manchu is in *Treaties, Conventions. Etc. between China and Foreign States,* I, 67-69. A Chinese paraphrase translation may be found in *SFPC,* 37.36-38. In Chinese the agreement is usually called the "Kiakhta Market Treaty" *(Chia-k'e-t'u hu-shih chi-lueh).*

existed seven years before, with the exception that debts incurred between merchants should be settled by a specified date annually. Both sides promised to appoint capable officers to handle border affairs. The Russians obligated themselves to restrain the Buriats and other Russian subjects near the border from pillaging across the frontier. Both the Treaty of Kiakhta and its supplement of 1768 were reaffirmed and, once again, the negotiators reiterated the extradition of the subjects of the other and the joint inquiry into incidents of homicide, robbery, etc. All such offenders were to be tried by their own laws, the only significant alteration of the Treaty as it stood, for earlier agreements did not specify this. As before fines were to be levied for the theft of goods across the border. Finally three Russian subjects held in Urga several years for depradations across the border were to be returned to Siberia.

Like the 1768 protocol, this agreement confirmed the Treaty of Kiakhta and reinforced the accords reached in it by defining somewhat more closely the knotty matter of punishment of border violators. The solution found was the best possible under the circumstances; it did leave each side to deal with its subjects by its own norms. The Russians could now avoid public execution and display of corpses on the border. The significance of this agreement lies primarily in the fact that it was reached amicably, without serious threat of resort to arms, and at the end of a long period of trade interruption that both sides throughout genuinely considered to be temporary. Similar to the earlier agreements and accords this one was between equals; unlike the Treaty of Kiakhta not even a show of physical force nor serious threat of it marred the proceedings. The settling here of the punishment issue which had vexed Sino-Russian relations for nearly three-quarters of a century removed one of the major impediments to unobstructed trade. Notably the first half of the nineteenth century a steadily increasing commerce between the empires developed without blemish of long trade suspension.

Aftermath

Commercial exchanges commenced again at the end of April, 1792.[95] In both Kiakhta and Mai-mai-ch'eng merchants gathered for some

95. *Arkhiv Gosudarstvennago soveta,* I, Pt. 2, 655. A Senate decree of 22 April 1792, based on a report from Pil' which recited the 8 February accord,

weeks prior to that; both local administrations published invitations to merchants to come again to the border on the heels of learning officially from St. Petersburg and Peking of their acceptance of the Nagel-Sung-yun agreement. The Russian border councillor and the dzarguchei met between the twenty-first and twenty-fourth of April and arranged all minor problems in the resumption of trade.

The trade itself picked up where it had left off seven years before. By mid-July Russian traders had conveyed to the border goods valued by the Troitskosavsk customs house director, Vonifat'ev, at 1,189,301 rubles, of which a quarter were already disposed of.[96] By the twenty-eighth of that month Pil' was able to report that over half of the Russian goods (600,000 rubles) were exchanged, and he added on the fifth of September that customs duties amounting to 182,383 rubles had already accumulated, the most important consideration for the *chinovniki* in St. Petersburg. Vonifat'ev did such a fine job that Pil' recommended him to the grace and benevolence of Her Majesty and for the knightly Order of St. Vladimir.

---

ordered the news of the reopening of trade announced "in all government offices, *guberniia* and vice-regal administrations, and in Moscow in the Departments and in the Holy Synod"; *PSZ*, XXIII, No. 17037, 323.

96. *Arkhiv Gosudarstvennago soveta,* I, Pt. 2, 656-58. Vonifat'ev was sometimes spelt Vanifant'ev.

The archive of the State Council includes a *Vedomost'* on the state of trade in the period 24 April 1792 to 12 August:

Total exports:	
Russian goods	607,496 rubles
Foreign goods	74,450 rubles
Total imports:	681,945 rubles
Customs duties collected on imports and exports:	136,564 rubles
Goods held by the "companies" but not yet inventoried and reported to the Mission:	
Export goods (Russian)	118,642 rubles
Export goods (Foreign)	1,948 rubles
Imported goods	120,590 rubles
Unexchanged goods stored in the merchants' court of Kiakhta:	
Russian goods	524,096 rubles
Foreign goods	384,762 rubles
Goods stored in Troitskosavsk warehouses not yet inspected or stamped, or inventory of them not yet given by the merchants to the Mission:	900,000 rubles
Goods for export or already imported for which merchants' associates *(kompan'ony)* had not given the Mission a preliminary accounting *(zapiska)*:	360,000 rubles

Note: all figures rounded to the nearest ruble.

In the last years of the eighteenth century, the total volume of trade at the border hovered around five million rubles annually. Not until the year 1800 did it exceed the peak year of 1781. Certainly this longest suspension of trade inflicted damage on the Kiakhta trade, which prior to 1785 showed every sign of strong, prosperous expansion. Nonetheless the damage was not permanent, for the early years of the next century saw this commercial avenue expand steadily in an atmosphere almost completely devoid of perilous threats to this mercantile idyl. Small ripples were smoothed at the border or in Irkutsk and Urga, and both sides seem to have diverted precipitous and heavy-handed administrators elsewhere. At other times a minor matter such as the erection of pickets by the Russians along the border in the vicinity of the Narym River, a tributary of the Irtysh above Bukhtarminsk, would have ended in affront, threats, suspension of trade, and long and sticky negotiations.[97] Several meetings in the autumn of 1794 between General Gustav von Shtrandman of Omsk and Chinese officials persuaded the State Council that, in spite of the usefulness of these fences in preventing Russian subjects from straying in Chinese territories, Chinese objections should prevail. Shtrandman had part of them pulled down.

All of which does not mean to suggest that things continued as before and that placidity and tranquillity completely supplanted occasional confrontation and constant irritant. Rather the trade and its setting changed significantly in a number of new ways at the very end of the eighteenth century and in the beginning of the nineteenth. These changes qualitatively altered the general milieu of Sino-Russian commerce.

The most striking alteration was the growth and expansion of Russian commercial interests in the Pacific area. The hunt for the disappearing fur-bearing animals largely accounts for this. Kamchatka, the Komandorskis, the Aleutians, and continental America were just the next source of pelts and the sea otter alone drew many in search of quick and great profits. Trapper-traders individually and in small groups had braved the treacherous northern seas since the 1740's, although the fickle weather, the lack of charts, and the very considerable investment required over a long period kept the returns small and the attractions dimmed. By the 1770's

97. Uspenskii, *Russkaia mysl'*, XXV (November, 1904), 80; *Arkhiv Gosudarstvennago soveta*, I, Pt. 2, 659-60.

and 1780's, the increasing prospects for fabulous profits caused much heavier financial backing and finer efforts at organization. Grigorii Ivanovich Shelekhov, for example, began as a minor but imaginative trader who made his first voyage to Alaska only in 1783-86.[98] Within a very few years he fashioned himself into one of the wealthiest men of Siberia. In partnership with Ivan Larionovich Golikov, a merchant from Kursk, he managed by the end of the century to build one of the most influential Russian companies with outposts in Alaska. Business acumen and shrewdness, highly placed political connections, and fierce personal drive were combined in Shelikhov, but he died before he completed the task. His son-in-law, Nikolai Petrovich Rezanov, and Golikov finished the job: an imperial ukaz of 8 July 1799 granted their company an exclusive monopoly to exploit the resources of the Aleutians and Russian America.[99] The Russian-American Company was the first joint-stock, limited liability, imperially-sanctioned company in Russian history, and its main office was in Irkutsk.

The proclamation of the monopoly solved only the smallest part of the enormous problems in taming and exploiting Russia's new empire. Outposts needed supplies, markets for pelts had to be opened or expanded, and growing foreign competition must be successfully met before the Company might boast sure profits. Supplying the Russian colonies proved to be a Herculean task, never completely done. Hauling of supplies over the Stanovoi Mountains from Iakutsk to Okhotsk was outrageously expensive, and the sea voyage from Okhotsk was dangerous and unsatis-

98. For Shelekhov's first voyage of "discovery," he and Golikov were awarded gold medals and silver swords, but no monopoly; *PSZ*, XXII, No. 16709, 1105–7, dated 12 September 1788. On the North Pacific expeditions and the Russian American Company, see among other things Mary E. Wheeler, "The Origins of the Russian-American Company," *Jahrbücher für Geschichte Osteuropas*, New Series, XIV (December, 1966), 485-94, and her "The Origins and Formation of the Russian American Company" (Ph.D. dissertation, The University of North Carolina, 1965). Also *Arkhiv Gosudarstvennago soveta*, I, Pt. 2, 661-68.

99. *PSZ*, XXV, No. 19030, 699-718, dated 8 July 1799; Okun', *The Russian-American Company*, pp. 22-44. Shelikhov and Golikov had long petitioned Catherine for such a monopoly, but were as often rebuffed; Aleksandr Ignat'evich Andreev (ed.), *Russian Discoveries in the Pacific and in North America in the Eighteenth and Nineteenth Centuries; A Collection of Materials*, trans. by Carl Ginsburg ("American Council of Learned Societies, Russian Translation Project," 13 [Ann Arbor: Published for the ACLS by J. W. Edwards, 1952]), pp. 70ff. Also *PSZ*, XXIV, No. 18076, 670, dated 5 August 1797; No. 18131, 725, dated 8 September 1797; XXVI, No. 19611, 348, dated 19 October 1800; and XXVIII, No. 21705, 972-75, dated 6 April 1805.

factory.[100] The solution was two-fold: finer ships and accumulated nautical experience for crews and masters; and another avenue of carriage of supplies from central Siberia to the Pacific. The Amur again recommended itself, and Japan might also prove to be a source of supplies, although Lieutenant Adam Laksman failed to persuade the Japanese to grant permit for regular trade in Nagasaki.[101]

The other side of the coin of colony was, of course, the disposal of its yield, especially the pelts. China was the closest and best market for American furs, as it had been for Siberian ones. Since the time of the earliest adventurers in the North Pacific the largest quantity of their pelts were returned to Kiakhta via Okhotsk.[102] But European and American merchants offered stiff competition. English and especially American bottoms transported furs from Northwest America and the Hudson Bay region to Canton, and even began to procure them from the Russian colonies in Alaska and from Kamchatka in exchange for badly needed provisions. The famed Russian naval captain Ivan Fedorovich Kruzenshtern witnessed the arrival of a small ship commanded by an Englishman and with a cargo of furs from Russian American when he visited Canton in 1798-99.[103] What astonished him was that the ship was at sea only five months, whereas the transport of Alaskan furs to Kiakhta by way of Okhotsk-Iakutsk often took two years or a bit more. The conclusion seemed obvious to Kruzenshtern: if Chinese markets were to be dominated by Russian-sold pelts, English and American competition had to be challenged on the coasts of China, as well as in Siberia. Russian ships must open Chinese ports, and Russian merchants must get to the interior of China both by land and by sea. If Russian mercantile horizons were not expanded beyond the Kiakhta system, Europeans and American would kill the Kiakhta trade which depended very heavily on fur

100. Ivan Fedorovich Kruzenshtern [Adam Johann von Krusenstern], *Voyage Round the World, in the Years 1803, 1804, 1805, and 1806, by Order of His Imperial Majesty Alexander the First, on Board the Ships "Nadezhda" and "Neva," under the Command of Captain A. J. von Krusenstern, of the Imperial Navy*, tr. from the German by Richard Belgrave Hoppner (London: John Murray, 1813), I, xxiii.

101. George Alexander Lensen, "Early Russo-Japanese Relations," *Far Eastern Quarterly*, X (November, 1950), 20, 28.

102. See, e.g., *PSZ*, XIX, No. 14129, 920-23, dated 24 February 1774.

103. Kruzenshtern, *Voyage*, I, xxvi. As early as 1787, Shelekhov and Golikov brought to the attention of the throne the increasing English, Dutch, and French trade in the Pacific; *Sbornik RIO*, XXVII (1880), 430-32.

sales. Such reasoning provoked Kruzenshtern to submit a memoir to the short-time Naval Minister, Admiral Nikolai Semenovich Mordvinov, in January of 1802 proposing the strengthening of the Pacific merchant marine and a direct assault on the China coast.[104] Small investment for enormous issue:

> In this manner it would no longer be necessary to pay each year large sums to England, Sweden and Denmark for East Indian and Chinese goods, and Russia would soon be in a condition to supply the north of Germany with them at a lower rate than either of those nations, as their preparations are much more expensive than ours, and they for the most part can only carry on this trade with specie. The Russian American Company could not fail to become in time of so much importance that the smaller East Indian Companies of Europe would not be able to stand in competition with it.[105]

This sanguine scheme lay on the desk of Count Nikolai Petrovich Rumiantsev, chancellor and minister of commerce, in the spring of 1802. He was not slow to realize its immense potentialities. The shaky colonies of the Russian American Company could be given a sound economic foundation; the fur trade to China, long monopolized by Russians, might be salvaged; English and American competition could be overcome.[106]

104. Kruzenshtern, *Voyage*, I, xxvi-xxviii. This was not the first serious suggestion of an officially-dispatched Russian ship to breach the sea wall of China. In an undated memoir of Catherine (probably of the late 1760's), she noted that Count Redern proposed that a ship under Imperial Russian flag be sent, well armed (equivalent to a 50-gun man-of-war) to fend off corsairs in the Indian Ocean, and laden with Russian manufactured goods: copper, bar iron, manufactured iron such as cannon, cordage, sail cloth, etc. Redern proposed that the ship put in first on the Coromandel coast, thence to Canton for teas, porcelains, silks, cottons, drugs, etc. So obvious were the advantages if the voyage were successful that the memoir declined to detail them. To which Catherine appended in her own hand—"C'est aux marchands à trafiquer, où bon leur semble; pour moi je ne fournirai ni hommes, ni navires, ni argent, et je renonce à perpétuité à toutes terres et possessions aux Indes orientales et en Amérique"; *Sbornik RIO*, X (1872), 384-86.

Murav'ev, a half century later, was quoted as having written to his Tsar: "Our destiny is down the Amur and into the Pacific. The English, by forcing trade concessions with China, are drying up our overland trade, and the merchants of Kiakhta will starve. Our settlements on the Pacific must be fostered"; Daniel Henderson, *From the Volga to the Yukon, The Story of the Russian March to Alaska and California, Paralleling Our Own Westward Trek to the Pacific* (New York: Hastings House, 1944), p. 195.

105. Kruzenshtern, *Voyage*, I, xxix.

106. Okun', *The Russian American Company*, pp. 50-52.

Kruzenshtern assumed command of a naval expedition on 7 August 1802. His instructions identified his primary mission: to open both China and Japan to Russian sea trade.[107] Rezanov himself, director of the Russian American Company and now court chamberlain, took passage to persuade the Japanese. Two ships were purchased in London early in 1803 for 17,000 pounds sterling, a three-year old 450 tonner, the *Nadezhda,* and a smaller one of 370 tons and somewhat newer, the *Neva.* Kruzenshtern and Iurii Fedorovich Lisianskii, who like Kruzenshtern had served in the Royal Navy, took command of the respective crafts. The squadron, as it turned out the first Russian ships to circumnavigate the world, moved slowly out of Kronshtadt road before calm south-southwest breezes on the morning of 26 July 1803. The Tsar personally sped them on with his felicitations.

The plan was to coast Brazil, double Cape Horn, and split up at the Sandwich Islands, the *Nadezhda* with Kruzenshtern and Rezanov pointing to Japan and the *Neva* under Lisianskii striking north to Kodiak to pick up a cargo of pelts. They were to rendezvous at Canton to dispose of the furs, take on a cargo of Chinese wares, and then return to Russia. All went well in the beginning. The Cape was rounded in early March of 1804 and the ships separated. *Nadezhda* was refurbished in Petropavlovsk, the largest settlement on Kamchatka, and put in at Nagasaki on 6 October. The Japanese welcomed the Russians pleasantly but not with open arms ("the time of our stay here was literally a confinement, from which the ambassador [Rezanov] was no more exempted than the meanest sailor on the ship").[108] Rezanov never did visit Edo as he hoped, and the Shogun's word given him was that Russian ships must in the future avoid Japan, the gifts offered were refused, and the Russians had to leave at their earliest convenience. In short, this part of the great expedition ended in complete failure. *Nadezhda*

107. This was the second time a round-the-world cruise had been proposed with these specific aims. On 22 December 1786, Catherine, on Iakobi's advice, ordered the outfitting of an expedition to protect Russian settlements in the Aleutians and Alaska. The tasks of the mission were to investigate the activities of foreigners in Russian American possessions, to carry out geographical inquiries, to initiate relations with Japan, and to bring nautical and military supplies to Siberia's Pacific ports. Five ships were earmarked for the expedition under the command of Captain Mulovskii; departure was scheduled for December, 1787, from England. War with Turkey and the break in diplomatic relations with Sweden forced cancellation of the voyage on 28 October 1787. Consult Lensen, *Far Eastern Quarterly,* X (November, 1950), 17-18.

108. Kruzenshtern, *Voyage,* I, 253.

put to sea on 17 April without Rezanov, who took passage on the *Maria* bound for Kodiak. Kruzenshtern explored briefly in the vicinity of Sakhalin and Kamchatka, then took the *Nadezhda* south to await Lisianskii at Canton.

When Kruzenshtern reached Macao in early November, 1805, he feared for the loss of *Neva* which was tardy. What he did not know was that Lisianskii found Sitka and the Russian colony in a desperate state.[109] Ravaged by Kolosh Indians three years earlier, the Russian settlement in the Alaskan panhandle barely held its own against the natives and the severity of the desolate environment. Lisianskii did not arrive in Macao until 21 November 1805. The English commercial house of Beale, Shank and Magniac (later the famed Jardine, Matheson firm) served as intermediary (Kruzenshtern met Beale and Shank on his earlier voyage to China) and the ships' cargoes sold for more than 190,000 Spanish piasters, 178,000 for the *Neva's* pelts and 12,000 for those brought from Kamchatka in the *Nadezhda*.[110] The Russians bought goods for 117,000 piasters, including 80,000 worth of the best teas. The unloading and reloading of the ships were nearly completed in mid-January, when "a sudden report was circulated that the Chinese government would not allow our ships to sail until special orders were received with regard to us from Peking."[111]

This distressing turn of events threatened foundering of the entire expedition. A Chinese guard took post over the ships and the last goods intended for carriage remained in the warehouses. Kruzenshtern remonstrated with the hoppo, the Chinese customs director, and with the viceroy of Canton, but in the end only the intercession of James Drummond, the factor of the English East India Company, prevented a dire fate. Drummond summoned a meeting at his residence of all hong merchants and the select committee of the English factory, Sir George Staunton, who had ac-

109. Iurii Fedorovich Lisianskii, *Puteshestvie vokrug sveta v 1803, 4, 5, i 1806 godakh, po poveleniiu ego Imperatorskogo velichestva Aleksandra Pervago, na korable Neve* (Moscow: OGIZ, Geografgiz, 1947), pp. 147-216.

110. This included 132,200 sealskins, 15,720 other fine furs, and 2,300 rabbit pelts, a total of 150,220 pelts. In this same year (1805), American ships brought a total of 247,922 furs, and English craft some 180; Hosea Ballou Morse (ed.), *The Chronicles of the East India Company, Trading to China, 1635-1834* (Oxford: The Clarendon Press, 1926-29), III, 3. See also Earl Hampton Pritchard, *The Crucial Years of Early Anglo-Chinese Relations, 1750-1800* ("Research Studies of the State College of Washington," 4, Nos. 3-4 [Pullman, 1936]), p. 179, n. 16, and Andreev, *Russian Discoveries*, pp. 186-88.

111. Kruzenshtern, *Voyage*, II, 290.

companied Macartney in 1793, and Messrs. Roberts and Pattle. The hong merchants persuaded the hoppo to allow the loading to continue, and no sooner was it done that the Russian ships left Canton (28 January 1806). Only when Kruzenshtern dropped anchor in Kronshtadt seven months later did he learn that an edict from Peking had been received in Canton shortly after the Russians' departure which directed detention of the ships and refused permission for any others to visit the Chinese coast in the future. The Russians, Peking made clear, were expected to confine their trade with the Middle Kingdom to the overland commerce through Kiakhta-Mai-mai-ch'eng![112]

There was a second front of the assault on the commercial isolation of East Asia; the embassy of Count Iurii Aleksandrovich Golovkin. It was Rumiantsev who first proposed in February, 1803, sending a dignitary to China, although Golovkin's final instructions were not published until 29 June 1805.[113] Formally and

112. This is of course exactly what Ch'ien-lung is reputed to have addressed to George III through Lord Macartney: ". . . your Ambassador requested that in the same Manner it was done for the Russians, A Place should be appointed for your trade at Pekin. . . . I acknowledge that the Russians had a Place assigned them for their Trade at Peking; but this was only for a Time, —untill a Place had been appointed for them at Keach-tou [Kiakhta] [which as we have seen was incorrect]. As soon as this was done, they were all sent thither and none permitted to remain at Peking. This Transaction took Place many years ago, and the Russians have ever since traded at Keach-tou, as your people do now at Canton"; Morse, *Chronicles*, II, 249.

113. Early in 1803 Rumiantsev suggested a courier only to meet with the amban, but noted he should stress "the necessity of Canton trade" for Russia; Ministerstvo Inostrannykh Del SSSR, *Vneshniaia politika Rossii XIX i nachala XX veka, Dokumenty rossiiskogo Ministerstva inostrannykh del,* Series 1: *1801-1815 gg.* (Moscow: Gospolitizdat, 1960–), I, 386, Document 157; Rumiantsev's memorandum to Alexander dated 20 February 1803. By late in the year, his thinking had progressed to the notion of an envoy *(poslannik)* sent directly to Peking, rather than merely a courier to exchange views at the border; *ibid.*, II, 544-45, Document 229: Rumiantsev to Minister of Foreign Affairs A. R. Vorontsov dated 3 November 1803. For the *doklad* of Rumiantsev to Alexander of 16 January 1805 which laid out Golovkin's tasks, see *ibid.*, II, 297-301, Document 95, and for Golovkin's patent as Ambassador Extraordinary and Minister Plenipotentiary signed by the Tsar on 29 June 1805 and countersigned by Czartoryski, see *ibid.*, II, 472, Document 142.

By the autumn of 1803 the *Li-fan-yuan* had been informed of the Russian desire for some sort of diplomatic representation, the *Yuan* agreed, and Alexander through the Senate affirmed the Chinese acceptance on 16 November 1803; *ibid.*, I, 553-56, Document 232. For further diplomatic correspondence, see *ibid.*, I, 555-56, Document 232; II, 127-28, Document 47. For full reproduction of Golovkin's final instructions, see Vasilii N. Basnin (ed.), "O posol'stve v Kitai grafa Golovkina," *Chteniia OIDR*, Bk. 4, Pt. 5 (October-December, 1875).

ostensibly he carried announcement of the accession of Alexander I; his real and substantive mission was to secure the "opening" of China, as Rezanov was to "open" Japan. His lengthy instructions are fascinating in their expectations.

Golovkin was to express to the Chinese the interest of St. Petersburg in expanding trade on the Irtysh Line, near the Bukhtarma River, virtually nil since the conquest of the Dzhungars. If the Chinese desired, a market town similar to Kiakhta could be established where the Mongols of Central Asia could barter and haggle.[114] The Amur issue again appeared; Golovkin was to ask for permission for the passage of several boats annually on the river.

Certainly a major reason for the Russian diplomatic penetration of China at this time was the full knowledge in St. Petersburg of the Cathcart-Macartney effort of 1793, reported from Siberia by Pil' and from London by Count Semen Romanovich Vorontsov. In spite of its failure, Russian authorities were concerned, especially prior to the Nagel-Sung-yun agreement, lest English success in China prejudice the Kiakhta trade. The State Council instructed the Governor of Irkutsk to bend his efforts to further Russia's case with the Urga amban to the end that he be persuaded to represent to Peking the value in receiving a "special agent" there. Even Rumiantsev referred directly to Macartney as late as 1805. Consult *Vneshniaia politika,* II, 297-301, Document 95, Point 1; *Arkhiv Gosudarstvennago soveta,* I, Pt. 1, 518, 658-59, 904, 915, 917; Andreev, *Russian Discoveries,* p. 110.

Golovkin, born in 1749, found his career mainly in Russian diplomatic service, in spite of (or because of) his notoriously bad knowledge of Russian. After his mission to China, he served as envoy to Stuttgart (1813-18), to Karlsruhe (1817-18), and in Vienna (1818-22). He died on 21 January 1846. Consult Ministerstvo Inostrannykh Del, *Ocherk istorii Ministerstva inostrannykh del, 1802-1902* (St. Petersburg: Tovarishchestvo R. Golike i A. Vil'borg, 1902), p. 28, and Shteingel, *Istoricheskii vestnik,* XVII (August, 1884), 376.

114. A lively trade in the Irtysh, Siberian Line region had been largely cut off after the completion of the conquest of the Dzhungars in 1757; illicit and unsponsored trade continued at a modest level carried on by local Mongol peoples and even by some Russian merchants disguised as natives of Kokand; Batrakov, *Trudy* Sredneasiatskogo Gosudarstvennogo Universiteta, New Series, Vyp. 78; Istoricheskie nauki, Kniga 11 (1956), p. 18. Early in 1797, General Shtrandman proposed expansion of the trade, in response to which Paul noted the importance of the region and especially of Ust'-Kamenogorsk *krepost' "because the Selenginsk regiment is located there"* (emphasis in original). The Tsar ordered Shtrandman to expedite any projects for increasing the commerce and added that two additional grenadier companies of the Selenginsk infantry regiment could be stationed there, if it would help; *PSZ,* XXIV, No. 17089, 515-16, dated 25 March 1797. Two years later the Senate ordered customs houses built on the line and the Orenburg tariff applied, rather than the one for Kiakhta as earlier; *PSZ,* XXV, No.19141, 802-5, dated 7 October 1799. Rumiantsev contributed that Bukhtarminsk *krepost'* was 2000 versta closer to Moscow than was Kiakhta; *Vneshniaia politika,* II, 297-301, Document 95. See also Kurts, *Russko-kitaiskie snosheniia,* p. 111, and *Arkhiv Gosudarstvennago soveta,* I, Pt. 2, 131ff, 659-60.

The explanation was to be the great need to supply the Kamchatka and American colonies. Next he was to press for trading rights for Russians at Canton similar to those enjoyed by several Western European companies, and beyond that for exclusive commercial rights at Nanking, an important source, it was felt, of cotton goods. The argument he was to use was that mutual trade with the Russian American Company would relieve China of dependence on European merchants and companies, and would counter mounting European and American competition with the Kiakhta trade, which as we noted, did not recover from the cutoff of 1785-92 as the Russians hoped. If these requests for coastal trade failed, Golovkin's fallback line was the demand for unrestricted entry of caravans from Siberia into all border and hinterland cities of China, or, if this also failed, at least Peking, Naun, and Urga should be open, as they had been before the Treaty of Kiakhta. With the prospect of renewed overland commerce to the interior of China, the Chinese were to be asked for routes more favorable than the one across the Gobi via Urga.

In the unlikely prospect that Peking acceded to the request for coastal trade, Golovkin was to seek the stationing of Russian commercial agents at the mouth of the Amur and in Canton, and a diplomatic agent in Peking itself. If a diplomatically credentialed person were refused for Peking, the archimandrite of the Orthodox ecclesiastical mission should serve as agent in matters of merchants' affairs; Golovkin should provide the cleric with whatever knowledge and aid he needed and to instruct him to dispatch reports to the Ministry of Foreign Affairs at least quarterly. These in summary were Golovkin's tasks in the realm of commerce.

Further the ambassador was to investigate the relations of the Manchu court with Persia, particularly ferreting out what he could concerning the knowledge the Chinese had of Russian military activity in the Persian area. He was to gather precise information on China's relations with Manchuria and Mongolia, and with the Dalai Lama and the Hutukhtu. He must inquire of the possibility of Russian trade with India through Tibet and find out what he could of English machinations in that mountain kingdom.[115] If

115. Consult Schuyler Cammann, *Trade through the Himalayas; The Early British Attempts to Open Tibet* (Princeton: Princeton University Press, 1951).

Several years earlier, the penetration of England in particular into Southern Asia caused a flurry of activity in St. Petersburg. A Special Department (or *Ekspeditsiia*) was established in the Collegium of Foreign Affairs to handle

permitted, Golovkin was to dispatch several officers of his embassy to travel across Chinese lands to Kabul bearing gifts for the local ruler. And to cap this intelligence operation, Golovkin must make a general survey of all of Eastern Asia, geographically, commercially, and politically.

His job with regard to China ended there. The instructions concluded with admonitions on the proper organization and conduct of an embassy and orders on several unrelated matters. The Spanish galleon *Ferrolegna* had foundered on the coast north of Canton and the Spanish merchants lost over 650,000 piasters in goods and money taken by the local inhabitants.[116] The Spanish ambassador in St. Petersburg was promised that Golovkin would intervene to try to recover the losses of this ship carrying silver from Manila to Canton and to secure release of the crew. We can assume that the Russian would in fact discharge this duty for he could keep 10 per cent of all he succeeded in recovering.

Golovkin's mission was then almost entirely commercial in nature. In many different ways and areas the Russian bureaucracy was determined to solicit a broad expansion of Russo-Chinese trade, renewing many old demands such as trade in the Irtysh-Kuld'ja region and transport down the Amur, and initiating an equal number of new ones. The old demands were intimately related to new conditions. By far the most influential was the commitment to develop and make productive Kamchatka and Russian America, which accounts for the concern for Russian sea trade at Canton and Nanking and passage of the Amur. Emerging English competition accounted for other demands on the Chinese—travel of a small group across Tibet to India and Kabul—and for much of Golovkin's intelligence function. Deepening British influence and power in India, Persia, Tibet, Bhutan, and Nepal, as well as the now nearly supreme position of their East India Company in the Canton trade, could not but provoke imperial Russia to counter these efforts. And carriage of Nootka Sound and Char-

---

the direction of affairs with all Asian peoples, both those within the Russian Empire and those outside with whom Russia had trade and intercourse. Acting State Councillor Lashkarev became its head at a salary of 2250 r. annually; *PSZ*, XXIV, No. 17844, 499-500, dated 26 February 1797. Shortly thereafter the Collegium committed 3000 rubles annually for the training of students in Asian languages: Chinese, Manchu, Persian, Turk, and Tatar; *PSZ*, XXV, No. 18599, 312, dated 24 July 1798.

116. Divers from the English ship "Coromandel" had already found 66,957 piasters of a total of 718,637 carried.

lotte Island pelts in British and American ships to the coasts of China obviously constituted a threat to destroy the entire structure of valuable trade the Russians had steadily built at Kiakhta. As it turned out in the second quarter of the nineteenth century the advisers of Paul and Alexander were quite correct; the danger of competition in Asian markets was not only real, it was fulfilled.

Golovkin failed abysmally to accomplish his several tasks. The large embassy (over two hundred men) gathered at Irkutsk toward the end of September, 1805, and moved down to Troitskosavsk in mid-October. On 8 October the ambassador informed Urga of his arrival of the border.[117] The usual diplomatic preliminaries and amenities were accomplished smoothly, the points of disagreement minor. The Manchus insisted that the tribute gifts precede the suite and that the complement not exceed one hundred. Golovkin objected only to the latter point on the grounds that for Russia at least there was no precedent for the demand. Both issues of small consequence, they were passed over, but in November there arose a matter that was ultimately disastrous. The imperial agent at Urga requested that Golovkin and his main subordinates practice the traditional Chinese *k'ou-t'ou,* most commonly three genuflexions and nine prostrations, before a rude bench covered with a cloth of symbolic yellow.[118] Golovkin stormed; he and his colleagues would happily abnegate themselves before the august person of Chia-ch'ing himself, but never before a yellow-dyed snippet of cotton. The final indignity—the mock rehearsal was set for mid-January in the open air with temperatures hovering below zero. Plainly the Urga agent merely carried out his duties as he saw them, to rehearse these tribute-bearers that they not embarrass themselves, the Emperor, and the agent himself by bungling the ceremony; the practice was intended not to degrade the ambassador but was for his own "protection" *(bezopasnost').*[119] Convinced the agent would come to his senses, Golovkin and his embassy crossed over to Urga early in January of 1806, but both sides stood adamant. Golovkin's argument that Izmailov and Vladislavich many years earlier had not been subjected to such demeaning treatment

117. *Vneshniaia politilka,* II, 609-11, Document 192.

118. Basnin, *Chteniia OIDR,* Bk. 4, Pt. 5 (October-December, 1875), 42-43. Also *Vneshniaia politika,* II, 643-44, Document 205, the Golovkin note of 19 November 1805 to the border administrator.

119. *Vneshniaia politika,* III, 154, 175-79, 291-93, 299, 500-501, 682 (n. 124). See also John King Fairbank, "Tributary Trade and China's Relations with the West," *Far Eastern Quarterly,* I (February, 1942), 129-49.

thawed the Urga agent not in the slightest, which left him no alternative except to dash off a note of protest to the *Li-fan-yuan*, retrace his steps to the border (in early March), report on the impasse to the Governing Senate, and turn himself, while he waited, to the study of eastern Siberia, especially the Shilka and Argun Rivers. Golovkin imaginatively blamed European merchants in China for his troubles, for which there is no evidence except the growing Russian conviction that their European competitors were a real and present danger to this great trade. The *Li-fan-yuan* formally announced the affair to the Senate in a note of 2 February 1806, to which the Senate replied on 15 May, upbraiding the Chinese provincial officials for this needless request of the distinguished ambassador.[120] Had not all Russian diplomats from Spafarii through Vladislavich generously performed the three knockings-of-the-head, and had not Golovkin promised to do so in Peking? Was there any need or justification for a dry run?

Russian logic did not prevail over Oriental form. The Golovkin mission was undone before it properly began. All that was left of the grand plans to open Japan and China, thwart the English and Americans in the North Pacific and on the China coast, turn away the English from Persia and Tibet, and insinuate Russian *kuptsy* in every Chinese hamlet, was a load of tea on St. Petersburg's wharves. And even that was symbolic of change of the Kiakhta system in the nineteenth century. Cottons and silks gave way among Chinese imports to tea, as the Russian adopted it as his national beverage or at least as his national nonalcoholic drink.

From the foregoing, it is reasonable to conclude that the Catherinian period was one of generally amicable relations with the Chinese, in spite of the unprecedentedly long trade suspension of 1785-92. The reason would seem to be that the patterns of intercourse, commercial and otherwise, were, by that time, stabilized. Old irritants, many of which sprang from the colonial expansion of both of the empires, were largely forgotten. The new matters of dispute were handled more easily and smoothly, partly because of improvements in border administration.

The stabilization and accommodations achieved made the possibility of armed conflict between Russia and China remote by the end of the century. In a sense this is symbolized by the complete failure of the Russians between 1803 and 1806 to persuade the

120. *Vneshniaia politika*, III, 177.

Peking court to alter the patterns of intercourse and trade that had developed since the Treaty of Kiakhta.

On the Russian side, we have also seen many improvements in the condition of the Kiakhta merchants. While none was drastic or dramatic, together they provided for the private merchant at the border a much more favorable circumstance for prosperous exchanges with the Chinese and for the state treasury steadily increasing customs revenues. To be sure, these private merchants were never brought together in a "modern" commercial company or companies which might exercise effective control over the entire trade and, perhaps, improve the bargaining positions of the Russians with the Chinese. But the central fact remains that this avenue of Russian trade grew many times over in the Catherinian period. It kept pace with Russia's total foreign trade and returned regularly to the Treasury a major portion of the Treasury's revenues.

Chapter IX. Rubles and Goods

This chapter is devoted to a reconstruction of the volume of Russian trade with China, particularly in the last half of the eighteenth century, and to a recitation and description of the items of exchange moving in both directions. For those whose passions are not aroused by tables of the ruble values of licit trade or by the differences in quality and price of the pelts of Arctic fox and the grey-necked variety it is recommended that they abjure these niceties and conclude with the next chapter.

The Kiakhta Trade in Figures

Dependable and fairly full reportage of the monetary value of Russia's exports and imports is not available for the eighteenth century; not until the ministry of Count Nikolai Petrovich Rumiantsev in 1802 did publication begin of annual statistical abstracts of the foreign trade of Russia across both "European and Asiatic borders."[1] For the second quarter of the eighteenth century, there has survived no body of data of the ruble values of the trade at Kiakhta nor has any researcher succeeded in reconstructing them beyond what has been suggested in earlier chapters. But beginning with 1755, which it will be recalled marked the final crown caravan to Peking, figures of trade have come to us, figures ostensibly for the silver ("stable") ruble values of the export of both Russian and foreign goods, and for the import of Chinese goods, plus the total customs duties collected each year on these exchanges.

Two sources, it turns out, are crucial in establishing these commercial statistics. The later of the publications is the compilation titled "Newest, Curious and Most Reliable Account about Eastern

1. Ministerstvo Kommertsii, *Gosudarstvennaia torgovlia 1802 goda v raznykh eia vidakh* (St. Petersburg: Pri Imperatorskoi Tipografii, 1802). Prefaces for 1802 following signed by Minister of Commerce Nikolai P. Rumiantsev. Title and publisher vary for subsequent years. In time the title stabilized as *Obzor vneshnei torgovli Rossii po evropeiskoi i aziatskoi granitsam.* The tables for 1802-5 were translated into French by Fr. Pfeiffer: *Tableaux du commerce de l'Empire de Russie, Années 1802, 1803, 1804, 1805,* Publiés par Nic. de Romantzof (St. Petersburg: F. Drechsler, 1808). Both Russian and French editions have been used.

Siberia, Much of Which Has Not, Until Now, Been Known."[2] This charming volume was published in 1817 by the Military Typographer of His Majesty's General Staff, its preface signed by Nikolai V. Semivskii, erstwhile vice-governor of Irkutsk and collegiate councillor, and its imprimatur granted by the censor Timkovskii on 21 February 1816. It survives as the "official" statement. *Table 1* is based largely on Semivskii's data, which as will be seen from the discussion appended to the figure, was repeated by a variety of nineteenth- and twentieth-century historians and general writers, particularly Korsak, Trusevich, and Samoilov. The other source is the monumental and indispensible survey of Russian trade done in the 1780's by Mikhail D. Chulkov.[3] Chulkov, a merchant himself, compiled and published his volumes privately, although he succeeded in giving us the standard reference work for Russian trade from earliest times through the first three quarters of the eighteenth century. Chulkov included ruble values for the Kiakhta trade covering only the five years from 1768 to 1772, but he did provide a breakdown of Russian exports into native Russian and foreign merchandise, as will be seen in *Table 2*, based on his figures. Semivskii on the other hand provided annual figures for the entire period after 1755, making no distinction between goods of Russian and non-Russian origin until after the year 1800.

Cursory comparison of Semivskii and Chulkov would seem to suffice, until it is noted that the *export* and *import* figures for the years 1769–72 are reversed, which is to say that the export figures of Semivskii are the import figures of Chulkov, and vice versa! A baffling case of switched statistics. The mystery is deepened when one recalls that the major nineteenth-century writers on the Kiakhta trade—Samoilov, Korsak, and Trusevich—all consulted both sources, yet accepted Semivskii without bothering to acknowledge the divergence between the two.

A reasonable initial suspicion is that a careless typographer or editor somehow switched the export and import columns in one or the other of these sources; were this to be true, the case could then be closed with a charge no more serious than misdemeanor. Semivskii's typographer or editor would appear to be the culprit, for Chulkov's figures for Russian and foreign exports sum properly to the figures he provides for the total ruble value of exports, and

2. Semivskii, *Noveishiia. . .povestvovaniia.*
3. Chulkov, *Istoricheskoe opisanie.*

Table 1. Volume of Russian-Chinese Trade at Kiakhta, 1755-1805 (Ruble value)

Year	Export of Russian and Foreign Goods	Import of Chinese Goods	Total Volume	Total Duties Collected
1755	606,084	230,982	837,066	193,173
1756	450,768	241,253	692,021	157,184
1757	421,879	418,811	840,689	147,216
1758	526,000	511,071	1,037,071	178,877
1759	718,145	698,985	1,417,130	230,482
1760	699,940	658,331	1,358,272	238,156
1761	391,469	619,598	1,011,067	230,840
1762	522,417	553,186	1,075,633	199,671
1763	302,798	401,607	704,405	179,066
1764	137,493	158,236	295,730	59,525
1765	149,875	244,478	394,353	90,472
1766	28,489	15,715	44,205	ca. 10,000
1767	. . .	. . .	. . .	. . .
1768	50,095	45,300	95,395	11,025
1769	1,074,651	928,984	2,003,636	401,708
1770	1,351,978	1,271,739	2,623,715	495,291
1771	1,246,410	1,142,511	2,388,921	451,343
1772	1,002,519	934,121	1,936,640	389,270
1773	1,140,183	1,153,992	2,294,175	397,420
1774	1,227,760	1,120,870	2,348,630	444,998
1775	1,365,826	1,278,584	2,644,410	453,279
1776	1,638,791	1,401,916	3,040,707	500,460
1777	1,440,546	1,342,127	2,782,674	479,061
1778	794,540	667,253	1,461,793	277,600
1779	. . .	. . .	. . .	. . .
1780	2,700,187	2,700,187	5,400,375	545,979
1781	3,735,312	3,735,312	7,470,624	706,219
1782	3,520,343	3,520,343	7,040,686	662,850
1783	2,789,177	2,789,177	5,578,354	509,148
1784	2,413,357	2,413,357	4,826,713	431,601
1785	1,805,926	1,805,926	3,611,852	347,579
1786-91	. . .	. . .	. . .	. . .
1792	2,467,280	2,467,280	4,934,559	509,830
1793	3,549,432	3,549,432	7,098,864	515,581
1794	2,522,942	2,522,942	5,045,884	527,070
1795	2,720,286	2,720,286	5,440,571	532,394
1796	2,551,764	2,551,764	5,103,529	488,320
1797	2,378,750	2,378,750	4,757,501	414,278
1798	2,783,943	2,783,943	5,567,885	509,685
1799	3,677,824	3,677,824	7,355,647	698,487
1800	4,191,923	4,191,923	8,383,846	715,365

Table 1, Continued

Year	*Export of Russian and Foreign Goods*	*Import of Chinese Goods*	*Total Volume*	*Total Duties Collected*
1801	1,855,160[a]			
	2,224,628[b]	4,079,788	8,159,577	839,292
	4,079,788[c]			
1802	2,015,584[a]			
	2,474,988[b]	4,490,572	8,981,144	902,243
	4,490,572[c]			
1803	1,704,407[a]			
	2,114,267[b]	3,818,674	7,637,349	778,027
	3,818,674[c]			
1804	1,955,366[a]			
	2,797,872[b]	4,753,238	9,506,477	950,510
	4,753,238[c]			
1805	2,376,959[a]			
	3,365,370[b]	5,742,328	11,484,657	1,090,213
	5,742,328[c]			

[a]Russian exports [b]Foreign exports [c]Total exports

Notes: The figures of *Table 1* were taken largely from Semivskii, *Noveishiia. . .povestvovaniia,* Primechaniia, pp. 169-79, except for those of the years 1762-66 which are from Trusevich, *Posol'skiia i torgovliia snosheniia,* pp. 163-64. All figures have been rounded off to the nearest ruble.

Trusevich's figures are precisely the same as Semivskii's, with the exception of those for the years noted above and several variants mentioned below. Trusevich, who published in 1882 credited Semivskii, the Archives of the Ministry of Foreign Affairs, and Semenov, *Izuchenie,* III, 199-200. Korsak, who published a quarter of a century earlier, also reproduced the figures as in Semivskii (*Istoriko-statisticheskoe obozrenie,* pp. 67, 73, 97, 105), although he failed to cite Semivskii as the source; Korsak elsewhere repeatedly used Semivskii as a source of information. Finally, Samoilov in 1854 repeated some, although not all, of Semivskii's statistics, i.e. those for the years 1755-62, 1768-85, and 1792 on (*Sbornik statisticheskikh svedenii,* pp. 7, 9, 16-17, 21). Samoilov credited no source.

Although Samoilov, Korsak, and Trusevich all repeated substantially the official figures of Semivskii, notable variants do appear (disregarding numerous errors of typography). Korsak (following Semivskii or Samoilov) gave no figures for the years of trade suspension from 1763 to 1766 and offered the figure of 139,315 rubles for the total volume of trade for 1762 (101,643 rubles in exports 37,672 rubles in imports), and 50,952 rubles and 7,309 rubles for the total volume and the duties collected respectively for the year 1768. Semivskii had offered no explanation for the rather extraordinary figures he inscribed for 1762: a total trade turnover of 139,315 rubles on which was extracted 199,671 rubles in duties! Korsak solved the puzzle by the simple expedient of neglecting to reproduce Semivskii's customs duties figure for that year. Trusevich, on the other hand, varied from Semivskii-Korsak at this juncture, and included the figures for 1762-68 incorporated into *Table 1.* Trusevich unfortunately does not identify the source of his contribution. These figures are used here because they present a more credible picture of the trend of trade during this period

Table 1, Continued

than do the figures of Semivskii, which show trade completely halted during the entire period from 1762-67. On the basis of what little is known, it is more reasonable to conclude that licit trade was greatly diminished, but *not* completely cut off. Trusevich's figure for 1768 must, nonetheless, be questioned. Chulkov (*Istoricheskoe opisanie,* III, Bk. 2, Table between pp. 340 and 341; see Table 2) accepted the same figure for the total ruble value of exports as did Trusevich, but provided the figure of 50,095 rubles for the value of Russian *and* foreign exports, *including* 15,517 rubles for foreign exports. Trusevich apparently added Chulkov's figure for foreign exports to the figure for the total volume of trade, hence including the value of foreign exports twice. Trusevich's figures for Russian and foreign exports and for the total trade turnover for the year 1768 must be rejected in favor of those of Chulkov. If these nineteenth-century scholars experienced some difficulties in rectifying figures from several sources, twentieth-century ones fare no better. M. I. Sladkovskii (*Ocherki ekonomicheskikh otnoshenii SSSR s Kitaem* [Moscow: Vneshtorgizdat, 1957], pp. 64, 71, 76, 81) follows Semivskii-Samoilov-Korsak for most of the eighteenth century, but in the tradition of Korsak does not explain the Semivskii discrepancy in 1762 customs duties.

How do these figures assembled from Semivskii-Korsak-Trusevich compare with scattered and incomplete figures given in other eighteenth-and nineteenth-century sources? Peter Simon Pallas (*Voyages,* IV, 215) provided a figure of 2,780,118 rubles for the total volume of trade for 1777. This compares closely to Semivskii's statistic. Pallas did include 11,215 rubles in imported gold and silver in his calculation (we have excluded it in the figure given above), but even if it is added, there remains only a small statistical difference between Pallas and Semivskii.

Robert Montgomery Martin in his *China: Political, Commerical and Social* (London: James Madden, 1847), pp. 417-18, furnished figures for the total volume for 1764 and 1765 strangely at variance with the figures of Trusevich. For 1764, Martin's figure is exactly that of Trusevich (although the figure he gives for customs duties collected is 9,230 rubles less). For the next year, Martin contributed the figure of 478,139 rubles total trade compared with Trusevich's 394,353 rubles. Most of the difference lies in the exports. Martin is notoriously inaccurate in many details and must here be discarded; see Earl H. Pritchard, *The Crucial Years of Early Anglo-Chinese Relations, 1750-1800* ("Research Studies of the State College of Washington," IV, Nos. 3-4 [Pullman, 1936]), p. 429.

Benedict F. J. von Herman (*Statistische Schilderung von Russland, in Rücksicht auf Bevölkerung, Landesbeschaffenheit, Naturprodukte, Landwirthschaft, Bergbau, Manufakturen und Handel* [St. Petersburg: Christian Tornow & Co.] 1790, Table opposite p. 445), combining both Kiakhta and Tsurukhaitu trade for the year 1775, gave Russian imports of 1,429,937 rubles and exports of 1,295,610 rubles, or a total volume of 2,725,547 r. If it is assumed that Hermann's figures for Kiakhta should agree generally with those of Semivskii, subtraction of the latter's from Hermann's should result in a figure for Tsurukhaitu trade (a rarity indeed). However, the result is exceptionally large: 81,137 rubles. This does not square with the few figures available which purport to represent Tsurukhaitu trade (see Table 3 below). Hermann's figures must be taken to be substantially higher than those of Semivskii. Hermann cited no source.

The fine compiler Heinrich Friedrich von Storch in his *Statistische Übersicht der Statthalterschafter des Russischen Reichs nach ihren Merkwürdigsten Kulturverhältnissen* (Riga: Johann Friedrich Hartknoch, 1795) included export and import figures for 1775, plus duties collected on them: 1,429,936 rubles in imports, 1,295,610 rubles in exports, and duties of 463,390 rubles. These are in the general range of Semivskii's figures, but notably show an adverse balance of trade, which Semivskii's do not.

Table 1, Continued

Although Trusevich accepted scattered figures for the period prior to 1755 from Semenov (*Izuchenie istoricheskikh svedenii,* III, 199-200) he obviously rejected those for years thereafter. Semenov combined the years 1759-61, 1775-81 (except for 1778 and 1779), and 1802-4. The resultant totals are incompatible with figures from any other source. They are of the magnitude of a single year, not several, e.g. for 1759-61 he gave a figure of 1,642,602 rubles, whereas Semivskii's figure for 1759 alone is 1,417,130 rubles. It would seem that Semenov's figures are some sort of arithmetic average, but even as such they are out of line with Semivskii. The average of Semivskii's figures for 1759-61 is 1,262,156 rubles. Only for 1792 did Semenov include a figure for a single year, and his total trade volume is over 30 per cent less than that of Semivskii. Semenov listed no sources for his figures. We are compelled to discard them.

Finally, there is the official compilation sponsored by Rumiantsev in the early nineteenth century (Ministerstvo Kommertsii, *Gosudarstvennaia torgovlia*). A prefatory note tells us that the statistics therein were taken from the documents of the Ministry of Commerce. Although the figures for 1802-5 embrace both Kiakhta and Tsurukhaitu, allowing for the trifling barter on the Argun (ca. 400 to 1000 rubles annually), they closely approximate Semivskii's figures except in one respect. Rumiantsev's export figures are close to Semivskii's for native Russian exports alone, not for total exports. Examination of the specific items of export listed by Rumiantsev supports the conclusion that he did not, in fact, include foreign items ;the usual European fabrics are conspicuously absent. Rumiantsev's figures are summarized below (in rubles):

Year	*Russian Exports*	*Total Imports*
1802	2,016,320	4,491,307
1803	1,704,802	3,819,129
1804	1,955,740	4,473,635
1805	2,377,384	5,742,814

If it is assumed that after 1780, the ruble values of total exports and imports must balance in Rumiantsev no less than they do in all other seemingly reliable sources, and that the difference between his figures for total exports and total imports lies in the export of goods of foreign origin, then Semivskii and Rumiantsev are in general agreement on the quantity of foreign exports to China during the first years of the nineteenth century, i.e. 2,100,000—3,300,000 rubles per year.

Semivskii's figures, as amended by Trusevich, stand then not only the test of historical reasonableness, but comparison with scattered notices of the day and of a later day. The generally more dependable Pallas and Rumiantsev correlate closely with Semivskii; the casual Martin and the unsubstantiated Hermann and Semenov are to be ignored.

Table 2. Volume of Russian-Chinese Trade at Kiakhta, 1768-72 (Ruble value)

Year	Native Russian Exports	Exports of Foreign Origin	Total Exports	Imports
1768	34,578	15,517	50,095	45,300
1769	634,241	294,744	928,984	1,074,651
1770	724,195	546,544	1,271,739	1,351,978
1771	663,601	478,910	1,142,511	1,246,410
1772	645,899	288,222	934,121	1,002,419

Note: Ruble values have been rounded off to the nearest whole ruble. Taken from Chulkov, *Istoricheskoe opisanie,* III, Bk. 2, Table between pp. 340-41. The export figures for 1770 do not sum properly, but they cannot be rectified.

besides he published earlier. The solution then is simply to reverse Semivskii's columns and press on undeterred. But how many of the annual figures should be switched? For the years 1769-72 alone? Or for the entire period after 1755? This is still a simple matter until the years 1801-5 are considered. Since Semivskii furnished, for these years, export figures divided into Russian and foreign items, it is a bit difficult to transfer these gross figures to the import column. And there arises reasonable doubt as to the advisability of switching the figures for any of the years.

Now, the best solution would be to employ the common source of both of our informants. Although they obviously used the same source, neither, unfortunately, has been good enough to indicate it. A simpler way out is to ignore the entire affair, dismiss Chulkov peremptorily, and adopt Semivskii, as Korsak, Trusevich, and Samoilov patently have done. This is equally an impossible solution, not only because all of Semivskii's export and import figures must now be suspected, but because a more consequential problem impinges on the little mystery—the question of the balance of trade and payments.

In 1780 the Commerce Collegium issued a *prikaz* commanding that in the future the ruble values of exports and imports in the Kiakhta trade must be reported as exactly the same, exports must equal imports.[4] The effect of this on the trade figures is quickly seen in *Table 1.* The ostensible reason for the measure was that

4. Semivskii, *Noveishiia . . . povestvovaniia,* Primechaniia, p. 172, n; Semenov, *Izuchenie,* III, 206; Samoilov, *Sbornik statisticheskikh svedenii,* p. 9, n.

exports and imports must necessarily balance and be shown to balance since, by treaty definition and Russian state fiat, all exchanges had to be barter *(menovaia torgovlia)*, involving neither merchants' credits in either direction across the border nor coin of the realms. The border administrators of both sides did in fact try repeatedly to discourage the use of precious metals in the balance of payments and the use of credit, at least beyond a single trading season.[5]

Merchants used both credit and precious metals at Kiakhta-Maimai-ch'eng in spite of the 1780 order and crackdowns both before and after that year on both sides. The issue of the nonpayment of debts, especially those incurred by Chinese merchants, repeatedly and throughout most of the century, disquieted border relations, as we have seen. As for the passage of precious metals between private merchants, scattered evidence suggests that Chinese gold and silver reached private Russian merchants, prohibitions from Peking and strong admonitions from St. Petersburg notwithstanding. Skal'kovskii remarked that in the second half of the century silver came to Siberia "in large amounts up to 500 *pud* (18,055 pounds avoirdupois)."[6] Pallas recorded the import of 11,215 rubles in gold and silver for the year 1777, and Radishchev mentioned it in the last decade of the century.[7] Rumiantsev listed among imports in 1805 bar silver worth forty-four rubles.[8] Although we can presume that much of this metal did not remain in private hands, some most assuredly did. No mention is found of the export of Russian precious metals to Chinese merchants, but if such was the case, the state interdiction would have prevented it from mention in official sources based on customhouse records. Illicit exports seem to have been primarily dearer furs, provisions, etc.; the Russian valuables appear to have been in sufficient demand that coin and metals were not needed even for illegal exchanges.

The spotty evidence suggests, then, that the balance of trade was in favor of Russia.[9] Yet Trusevich argued that a growing concern

5. See, e.g., Pallas, *Voyages*, IV, 181.

6. Konstantin Apollonovich Skal'kovskii, *Russkaia torgovlia v Tikhom okeane, Ekonomicheskoe izsledovanie russkoi torgovli i morekhodstva v Primorskoi oblasti Vostochnoi Sibiri, Koree, Kitae, Iaponii i Kalifornii* (St. Petersburg: Tipografiia A. S. Suvorina, 1883), p. 548.

7. Pallas, *Voyages*, IV, 215; Radishchev, *Polnoe sobranie sochinenii*, II, 12.

8. Ministerstvo Kommertsii, *Gosudarstvennaia torgovlia 1805 goda*, No. 10.

9. Tooke (*View*, III, 460) suggests the opposite, although he may not be taken as very well informed on this sort of thing.

in St. Petersburg over an unfavorable balance provoked the 1780 *prikaz.* Semivskii's figures (used by Trusevich) seem not to corroborate the contention. As is evident from *Table 1,* Russian imports exceeded exports for only a single year in the decade 1768-78 immediately preceding the *prikaz,* and then by the trivial sum of 13,807 rubles of a total volume of trade of over two million. Chulkov's table, on the other hand, shows an unfavorable balance for 1769-72. If Trusevich wished to clinch his argument and if he had seen Chulkov's table (which we must presume he did, since he cited Chulkov many times), why did he choose to use Semivskii's figures rather than Chulkov's? Trusevich fails to provide us with an obvious answer to this perplexing question. We might dare where Trusevich did not: reverse all of Semivskii's export and import figures for the years prior to 1780, retaining those after that year as Semivskii has them. Russia then has an unfavorable balance for the years 1755-60 and 1769-78 (except for 1773), but the only justification for this manipulation is weak indeed, i.e., giving credence to Chulkov's figures.

Another possible explanation for the issuance of the 1780 *prikaz* may have been the desire of the Commerce Collegium to conceal the increasing role played by goods of European origins in the total exports. Chulkov's figures (1769-72) give the ruble value of foreign items as 30 to 43 per cent of the total value of exports, an undeniably significant portion. Non-Russian pelts (especially beaver, otter, muskrat, and fox from North America) and fabrics did begin to make themselves felt in Russo-Chinese trade during the last quarter of the eighteenth century, as we saw in the last chapter. Whether or not the balance of trade favored Russia, the balance of payments was slight compared to the value of foreign items in this trade. Hence it may be reasoned that the sale of non-Russian peltries and fabrics maintained the value of total Russian exports at a level commensurate with the value of imports. After the end of the century, the importance of foreign items is immediately apparent in Rumiantsev's figures *(Table 2)*; they exceeded native Russian exports by 360,000 to 990,000 rubles annually for the half-decade 1801-5. And finally observation of the customs duties collected in the last half of the century tends to bear out the increasing importance of European goods. Comparison of the figures of customs revenues with the total volume of trade reveals that they did not rise proportionally to the volume of trade during the last two decades of the century. The new tariff of 1761 may account in large part for this, for foreign goods could be exported to the Chinese without added payments at Kiakhta, since duties had been collected on them already upon entry into European Russia.[10] All of which leaves us only with the question as to why the St. Petersburg bureaucracy might have felt the need to obscure for themselves and/or for others the large amounts of European merchandise transshipped to China. For that question there is not a reasonable answer, at least not readily at hand.

Yet another explanation of the enigmatic *prikaz* might lie in the desire of the Commerce Collegium to maximize customs revenues. If it is assumed that Russo-Chinese trade actually was barter in large part, that any transfers of specie or bullion (particularly from Russia to China) were reported in the unrevealing figures available to us, and that the extensive use of credit beyond a single trading season can be discounted, then the border trade may well have been balanced by the transfer of nondutiable items, e.g. horses, cattle, and provisions from Siberia or a variety of locally produced goods from Mongolia. If such was the case, it could be argued that in reality the trade did regularly balance or nearly so. The real intent of the *prikaz* could thus have been an effort to levy duties on all items exchanged, including those nondutiable prior to 1780. The result would have meant an increase, albeit small, in total customs revenues. This is an appealing hypothesis, but one that cannot be substantiated or disproved on the basis of available extant documentation. One of its assumptions is, however, worth emphasizing, that this trade was actually barter in large part and did balance for most practical purposes. If we resist the temptation to overemphasize the lack of a monetary balance of trade in any one year or succession of years prior to 1780, the salient fact is that the actual rubles value of the difference between exports and imports was always statistically very small. Although at times there seemed to be a flow of silver out of China, no consistent pattern can be drawn. Treaty requirements, Russian state edict, and testimony of Russian and foreign visitors at the border agree on the pervasive barter character of the business of Kiakhta-Mai-mai-ch'eng.

The mystery of the reversed statistics remains unsolved, at least until local Siberian archives turn up hitherto unused evidence.

10. Semenov, *Izuchenie,* III, 205.

Were the situation uncomplicated by considerations of balance of trade and payment, and gold and silver flow, Semivskii's figures could well be tampered with to include Chulkov's contribution, but Chulkov's adverse balance of trade is not entirely in accord with other scraps of evidence. Rumiantsev remarked in reference to Russia's commercial statistics prior to 1802 that the activities and records of the Commerce Collegium were "enveloped in a kind of mysterious cloak," of which this entire matter is but a small and distant example.

The total volume of Russian trade through Kiakhta can now be approximated without worrying the Semivskii-Chulkov mystery further. From *Tables 1* and *2*, it is readily seen that the total volume of trade falls logically into four periods, the interstices comprising the periods of trade suspension (1764-68, 1778-80, and 1785-92). Exports and imports both grew slowly and unspectacularly between 1755 and 1765. Thereafter, as seen in Chapter 8, they dropped swiftly to almost nothing in 1766 as a result of the enforcement of the trade cutoff. If we consider only the years before 1762 as a time of relatively uninfringed commerce, the average annual turnover totaled 1,032,000 rubles, between 7 and 8 per cent of the total turnover of Russia's foreign trade for that period.[11] Notably, the Kiakhta trade generated almost exactly the same proportion of customs revenues as did the total foreign trade of Russia, slightly less than 8 per cent.[12]

After the border reopened in 1768, exchanges spurted to heights previously unexperienced. In all probability, two factors operated: the maintenance of much of the mechanism of trade in surreptitious carriages across the closed border, and the accumulation of stocks of goods ready for sale on both sides.[13] In 1770 the total turnover reached a figure 85 per cent higher than the previous peak of 1759, over two and one-half million rubles. As soon as the warehoused goods were unloaded however, the total volume dropped back to less than two million in 1772, and then renewed its climb more slowly to a new high of over three million rubles in 1776. Disputes at the border during the following two years and the eventual suspension of trade by the Chinese in 1778 ac-

11. Consult Innokentii Iustinovich Patlaevskii, *Denezhnyi rynok v Rossii ot 1700 do 1762 goda* ("Zapiski Imperatorskogo Novorossiiskogo Universiteta," 2 [Odessa, 1868]), p. 464, and Lodyzhenskii, *Istoriia*, p. 95.

12. Consult Patlaevskii, *Denezhnyi rynok*, p. 169.

13. Sychevskii, *Chteniia OIDR*, Bk. 2 (April-June, 1875), p. 259.

count for a decline after this peak year until, between 1778 and 1780, legal exchanges were nil.

Once again, following the reinstitution of regular trade in 1780, the total volume leapt to a phenomenal new high of over seven and one-half million rubles in the next full trading year, and maintained a high level in 1782. The early 1780's were boom years, exchanges two and one-half times the highest peak prior to the suspension. The local reasons were similar to those for the spurt of the late 1770's, after the earlier suspension of trade—a build-up of warehoused merchandise awaiting exchange and, in all likelihood, a thriving contraband trade. But it must be recalled that the foreign trade of Russia in all directions increased steadily and rapidly during most of the Catherinian period. These were days of comparative maturity, freedom from bureaucratic manipulation, and state encouragement for Russia's larger private traders. Russia's general European trade, for example, registered a growth of almost one-third between 1776 and 1781, the peak years for Kiakhta trade.[14] And over the three decades, 1762-92, Russian trade westward increased in ruble value more than three and one-half times, which works out to nearly 12 per cent annually!

In the years leading up to 1785, a persistent decline in the Kiakhta trade set in. Still the average annual turnover for the six years 1780–85 was 5,654,000 rubles, almost four and one-half times the average for the period 1755-61 and nearly double that of 1769-78.

After Governor Nagel and Imperial Agent Sung-yun signed the agreement in 1792 that permitted the restoration of border trade, the trade did not register a new record, as it did after earlier long suspensions. Contraband seems to have been suppressed more effectively this time, and both Russian and Chinese merchants withdrew their merchandise from the border region and disposed of it elsewhere, at Tsurukhaitu for example. In spite of the somewhat slower beginning, total turnover achieved the high level of over seven million rubles in 1793, then dropped to an average of 5,970,000 rubles per years between 1792 and 1800 (a modest 5.5 per cent higher than the average of 1780-85). Still this means an average annual turnover of more than 300,000 rubles higher than in 1780-85 and over 4,300,000 rubles above that of 1755-61. And by 1800 the total volume reached over eight million, remaining

14. Calculated from Lodyzhenskii, *Istoriia*, p. 142.

after the turn of the century at a level exceeding even the peak year 1781.

Russian trade with China at Kiakhta-Mai-mai-ch'eng grew greatly and steadily in the forty-five years of the eighteenth century for which trade statistics of sorts are available, especially when it is recalled that fifteen of them were years of either complete suspension of legal exchanges or of sufficiently disruptive border relations as to hinder trading operations. Kurts accepted the great absolute increase in the volume of trade, but argued that it could not be regarded as significant if the population growths of both Russia and China were considered.[15] He has a point, but it is not one relevant to this eighteenth-century commerce. Most of the goods that crossed the border in either direction were destined for the carriage trade, not for wide distribution among the populace at large in either Russia or China. Kurts also overlooked the impact of the China trade on the general economy of Eastern Siberia, which, as we have seen, was considerable indeed in many ways.

A Note on the Tsurukhaitu Trade

Tsurukhaitu on the Argun, that other "treaty port," has been neglected here as it was in the eighteenth century. Its trade volume was always slight, momentarily invigorated in periods of suspension at Kiakhta-Mai-mai-ch'eng. Mainly it was just too far from Irkutsk, and the highroads and waterways were tortuous. That marvelous traveller and reporter Pallas, who visited Tsurukhaitu in 1772, observed that the items traded in small quantities were much the same as those traded at Kiakhta, but with greater emphasis on local goods.[16] The Russians brought the usual furs, but particularly those of the region: Dauriian fox pelts, ordinary sable pelts, and Lena weasel. Live animals—bulls, horses, and sheep—and animal skins—sheepskins, goatskins, lambskins, *iuft'*, and Morocco—were of equal importance, most of them probably from Dauriia. Pallas mentions Russian and Dutch fabrics and small mirrors, all in small

15. Kurts, *Russko-kitaiskie snosheniia*, pp. 110, n. 2, 112.

16. Pallas, *Voyages*, IV, 622-24. Cf. Trusevich, *Posol'skiia i torgovliia snosheniia*, pp. 157-58, and Wilhelm Christian Friebe, *Über Russlands Handel, Landwirthschaftliche Kultur, Industrie und Produkte; Nebst einigen Physischen und Statistischen Bemerkungen* (Gotha: Gerstenberg und Dittmar, 1796-98), III, 216-17.

Table 3. Volume of Trade at Tsurukhaitu, 1766, 1768-72, 1775, 1802-5 (Ruble value)

Year	*Russian Imports*	*Russian Exports*	*Total Volume of Trade*
1766	1,078	621	1,699
1768	7,372	2,845	10,217
1769	2,634	830	3,463
1770	1,282	884	2,166
1771	1,241	1,004	2,245
1772	1,012	776	1,788
1775	2,486	1,029	3,515
1802	735	736	1,471
1803	455	395	850
1804	397	374	771
1805	486	425	911

Note: All figures rounded to the nearest whole ruble. The figures for 1766 and 1768-72 are taken from Chulkov, *Istoricheskoe opisanie*, III, Bk. 2, Table between pp. 340-41; cf. Trusevich, *Posol'skiia i torgovliia snosheniia*, pp. 161-62. M. I. Sladkovskii, *Ocherki razvitiia*, p. 18, reproduced Chulkov's figures, but erred in presenting them in thousands of rubles (*v tys. rub.*). Tooke, *View*, III, 463, gave the figures for 1775, but added that 8,330 rubles duty was collected on the total turnover of 3,500 rubles! The figures for 1802 to 1805 were calculated from a comparison of Semivskii, *Noveishiia. . .povestvovaniia*, Primechaniia, pp. 169-70, and Ministerstvo Kommertsii, *Gosudarstvennaia torgovlia.* As explained in the note to *Table 1*, Rumiantsev's figures lump together Kiakhta and Tsurukhaitu, whereas Semivskii's list Kiakhta alone. Since Rumiantsev's figures of Russian exports apparently include only native Russian items, the actual total of Russian exports at Tsurukhaitu may be somewhat higher than indicated here, but it seems sensible to assume that the quantity of foreign goods exported through Tsurukhaitu was minuscule. These figures are at best approximate, but are of the right magnitude.

quantities. The Chinese border parties brought brick tea for Siberian consumption, fabrics (*kitaika* and *daba* cottons, damasks, foulard), yellow tobacco, brown sugar, sugar candy, and "Asiami" or Chinese dressing gowns for the souvenir trade.

Useful figures for the total trade turnover are available for only a few years. Lange noted in his 1736 account that very little trade was carried on in this outpost, as far as he could observe.[17] He assured St. Petersburg that it was certainly "less than 10,000 rubles per year," and probably much less, around 1000 rubles. *Table 3* reproduces figures for the later eighteenth-and early-nineteenth centuries. In all likelihood they are only suggestive, but they do indicate the small scale of the exchanges. In fact so small was it

17. Lange, *Akademicheskiia izvestiia na 1781 god*, Ch. 7 (April, 1781), 466-67.

that the inhabitants of Tsurukhaitu normally were compelled to repair on occasion to Nerchinsk and Irkutsk for many of the necessities of life. Even during the suspension of 1785-92, the indications are that most Siberian merchants transferred there only fractions of the goods they normally carried to Kiakhta-Mai-mai-ch'eng.

Russian Exports to China

Furs

Furs completely dominated Russia's exports to China through Kiakhta in the last three quarters of the eighteenth century. Korsak generalized for the years 1768 to 1785 that "the value of peltry . . . constituted about 85 per cent of the value of all exports, and the remaining 15 per cent went, for a long time, to leather and manufactured goods."[18] Trusevich claimed that peltry constituted 84 per cent of the total value of exports in 1792 (some 1,601,263 rubles in furs).[19] For the longer period 1792-1800, Korsak believed 70 per cent to be roughly accurate.[20] The considerably more careful and reflective historian, Andreev, is somewhat less grand in his figures; although the absolute exports continued to grow steadily throughout the century, he calculates that the proportion of furs to the total ruble value of exports tended to decline (1700-81 per cent, 1755—69.8 per cent, 1781—65 per cent, 1850—33 per cent).[21] Rumiantsev's compliation tends to confirm Andreev.[22] Furs con-

18. Korsak, *Istoriko-statisticheskoe obozrenie*, p. 74.

19. Trusevich, *Posol'skiia i torgovliia snosheniia*, Prilozhenie, Table 2, pp. 272-75. Cf. Semenov, *Izuchenie*, III, Prilozheniia, 470-71, and Semivskii, *Noveishiia . . . povestvovaniia*, pp. 169-70.

20. Korsak, *Istoriko-statisticheskoe obozrenie*, p. 98. Cf. Silin, *Kiakhta*, p. 119.

21. Andreev, *Severnaia Aziia, obshchestvenno-nauchnyi zhurnal*, Bks. 5-6 (1925), 66.

Year	*Total Exports*	*Furs*
1700	47,000 rubles	38,000 rubles
1755	606,000 rubles	423,000 rubles
1781	1,806,000 rubles	1,175,000 rubles
1800	6,164,000 rubles	2,047,000 rubles

22. Ministerstvo Kommertsii, *Tableaux du commerce*, Dixième Tableau.

Year	*Furs*	*Per Cent of Russian Exports*
1802	1,476,289 rubles	73
1803	1,244,508 rubles	71
1804	1,455,030 rubles	74
1805	1,623,747 rubles	68

tinued in the early nineteenth century to be the predominant item of Russian-produced goods, but the greatly increasing quantity of European goods carried to Kiakhta dropped the proportion of pelts in total exports to 32, 32, 30.5, and 28 per cent in the years 1802-5.

A wide variety of pelts were sold to the Chinese, either in Peking by the caravans or on the border. The attempt to identify, classify, and price them compared one with the other is complicated by the practice of packaging pelts of different species (and hence of value) in differing quantities. Some went as whole pelts (in forties, hundreds, or thousands) and others were dismembered into backs, bellies, throats, chests, paws, necks, tails, and heads. There was no standardized classification of varieties of pelts within any given species; few of the contemporary observers were skilled taxonomists. And there is little agreement among our sources as to the respective values of specific pelts. Cahen distinguishes four general criteria he suggests were likely used then: the species of the fur and its condition, its color, its visual beauty, and, above all, its authenticity, i.e., that it was in fact the species and variety it purported to be.[23] Dyeing and other imaginative techniques of fraud were rife, especially with dismembered pelts. The Chinese usually made their inspections on bright days, with clear skies and without direct sun, in order to detect the evidences of Russian skill. And lastly there is the consideration of the comparative value of pelts as reported in ruble prices. We have good cause to take lightly the precise prices inscribed in customs books, for as K. V. Bazilevich has happily pointed out, Russian customs duties of the eighteenth century were, at times, based on the "real," i.e. market, value of an item and, at other times, on "customs value," the average market price, or even an entirely arbitrary price, which sometimes did not change "in the course of several decades."[24] Bazilevich concluded that it was not and is not always possible to balance the sums of different items of exchange and the total monetary value of trade. He could well have added that it is equally impossible to believe the recorded prices of commodities. In spite of all of these con-

23. Cahen distinguished three types of furs: (1) *podsad*, a type of nap which is next to the skin; (2) *podos*, the intermediate fur; and (3) *os*, the long hair over and above the first two.

24. Konstantin Vasil'evich Bazilevich, "Tamozhennye knigi kak istochnik ekonomicheskoi istorii Rossii," *Problemy istochnikovedeniia*, Sbornik 1 (1933), 112. See also the pointed remark by Radishchev, *Polnoe sobranie sochinenii*, II, 9.

siderations, the values we have attempted to suggest below, both for the volume of sale of specific sorts of pelts and for their prices, may be taken as valid within broad and undefinable limits.

In total value and quantity, the most important pelts in the crown caravans of 1727-28 and 1735-36, about which we know something, were squirrel, ermine, certain varieties of fox, sable, lynx, otter and beaver.[25] Most of these pelts held their own in the second half of the century, except lynx and otter, and others rose to share the top places: skunk, muskrat, and cat.

Squirrel *(belka)* held first place throughout the century in total quantity of individual pelts carried through Kiakhta, typically two to four million pieces annually.[26] Of the many different varieties, *Teleutskii,* trapped on the Upper Ob' near Kuznetsk, was clearly the dearest.[27] Silver in color with a white belly, full pelts reportedly brought sixty to sixty-five rubles per thousand on or west of the Ob'. The next most popular was *Iletskii,* trapped in the Iletsk forest on the west of the Tobol River.[28] It brought somewhat less than *Teleutskii,* forty rubles per thousand. Squirrel of the Nerchinsk region or of the Ob' sold in larger quantities and for lower prices: twenty to thirty-five rubles.[29] The grey or north-

25. The following description of Russia's pelts was taken mainly from P. G., "Nachalo rossiiskoi torgovli s Kitaem," *Zhurnal manufaktur i torgovli,* Chast' 4, No. 11 (1836), 37-43; Lange, *Le livre de comptes,* pp. 85-102; Samoilov, *Sbornik statisticheskikh svedenii,* pp. 10-17; Strahlenberg, *An Historico-Geographical Description,* pp. 358, 369-71, 435, 446-47, 454; Pallas, *Voyages,* IV, 185-92 (Pallas recorded that the list he presents was given him by the erstwhile border commandant, Colonel Kropotov; IV, 184); Korsak, *Istoriko-statisticheskoe obozrenie,* pp. 75-99; Trusevich, *Posol'skiia i torgovliia snosheniia,* pp. 272-97; Silin, *Kiakhta,* pp. 119-30; and Coxe, *Account of Russian Discoveries,* p. 235.

26. The caravan of 1727-28 sold 1,376,380 pieces (*shtuka*: from the German *Stück*); Lange, *Le livre de comptes,* p. 85. According to Trusevich (*Posol'skiia i torgovliia snosheniia,* pp. 272-75), the caravan of 1735-36 disposed of 413,339 squirrel pelts. In the Kiakhta trade, squirrel exchanged at the rate of two to four million pelts annually in the sixteen years 1757-61, 1769-73, and 1780-84, according to Korsak (*Istoriko-statisticheskoe obozrenie,* p. 75). Although this very large rate declined in 1784 to 1,233,124 pelts, squirrel rose to over seven million after 1792; Samoilov, *Sbornik statisticheskikh svedenii,* p. 10. Radishchev (*Polnoe sobranie sochinenii,* II, 9) gave the sale of squirrel for a single year early in the last decade of the century as 11,937 rubles, the largest item among the furs.

27. This is the *Teleoute* of Cahen. In the caravan of 1727-28, it sold 760 pieces at eight *liang* each, compared to the remaining 1,375,620 squirrel pelts which went for thirty-five to forty *liang* per thousand; Lange *Le livre de comptes,* p. 85. Eight *liang* was approximately 112 rubles.

28. The Iletsk forest was in Ialutorovsk *uezd* which gave its name also to a variety of ermine.

29. Ob', 30-35; Nerchinsk and Barguzinsk, 30-35; Iakutsk, 20-22.

ern squirrel probably went in largest quantities, perhaps because it was taken in large amounts in Baikaliia, and in the Nerchinsk and Iakutsk areas. Pallas and Strahlenberg also mention the flying squirrel *(letiaga)*, shorter than the ordinary kind, at two to six kopeks per pelt. Pallas and others add a striped squirrel *(burunduk)*, smaller and thinner than the related European species, the pelt marked throughout with black stripes on a fawn-colored ground.[30] A short, smooth haired animal, prized because it had an appearance closer to the ermine than the usual squirrel, it sold for two to three kopeks.

Ermine or winter weasel *(gornostai)* came directly after squirrel in popularity. One hundred forty thousand to four hundred thousand pieces were exported annually. Among the finest of the qualities were *Iletskii, Ishinskii,* and *Barabinskii,* after the regions in which they were caught. Of less value was the ermine trapped in the forests between Tomsk and Krasnoiarsk, and in several places between Krasnoiarsk and Irkutsk. The prices on ermine pelts fluctuated widely, which Pallas preferred to attribute to a fraud of the Russians in the earlier days of this trade—sewing lead in the paws when they were sold by weight.[31] Closely related to ermine was "white weasel" *(lastka)*, a small ermine, half as expensive as the usual and exported almost exclusively to China.[32] It brought two to ten rubles per hundred.

Fox (*lisa*; dim. *lisitsa* or *lisichka*) came in many kinds, qualities, and prices. Arctic fox *(pesets)*, also known as blue fox *(golubaia lisitsa)*, especially to Germans, produced a light and very warm fur, excellent for wearing apparel and heavily in demand in China; it came from Iakutsk or other northernly regions—through which also were transshipped Kamchatka and American Arctic fox—and the Mangazeia territory, which supplied Europe as well as China.[33]

30. Erman, *Travels*, II, 239.

31. Pallas, *Voyages*, IV, 191. Korsak (*Istoriko-statisticheskoe obozrenie*, p. 76) noted that the best ermine were sold in Siberian cities for ten to fifteen rubles per hundred and by the trappers for six to eight rubles. Cahen (Lange, *Le livre de comptes*, p. 85) wrote that the finest ermine of the Ob' brought twelve rubles sixty kopeks to sixteen rubles eighty kopeks, although they did return as little as nine and as much as twenty-two per hundred. Trusevich (*Posol'skiia i torgovliia snosheniia*, pp. 290-97) gave prices for the years from 1735 to 1788 ranging from two rubles seventy-five kopeks to twenty rubles per forty.

32. This is evidently the *lastitsa* of Cahen, or as it was known to contemporaries in the diminutive, *lasochka*; Pallas also mentioned a "yellow weasel" ("Koulonki") of fiery color, selling for twenty-five to twenty-seven kopeks each.

33. Erman, *Travels*, II, 283.

The fur could show considerable variation in coloring, depending on the age of the animal and the season in which it was trapped, although most commonly it was white or bluish-white; this last was especially rare and dear. Total annual export of all varieties was fifteen to fifty thousand pieces in 1768-85, with a high of 72,084 pelts in 1777. Pallas priced the pelt at fifty kopeks to ten rubles seventy-five kopeks.[34]

A second major variety of fox was that known in Russia as *korsak*, a small grey animal mostly from the Kalmyk steppes, hence sometimes known as the steppe fox, or in Arkhangel'sk, as Kirgiz or kaisak. Approximately ten to twenty-five thousand pelts were disposed of annually, and after 1792 export rose to seventy thousand. *Korsaki* brought 125 kopeks to two rubles per full pelt.

"Red" fox, in several varieties, ran the gamut of coloring from deep red, through brownish-red, brown, and brownish-black, to black and grey. The brownish-black and black brought the highest prices, as high as six hundred to one thousand rubles for a perfect pelt, but more commonly four to 180 rubles.[35] Siberian trappers caught the majority of the black fox in Berezov, Surgut, Mangazeia, and Iakutsk *uzedy*, of which the Iakutsk sold poorest and Berezov best.[36] Excellent pelts also came from Kamchatka. Not surprisingly black fox, rare and highly sought, sold in comparatively small lots, 300-1,200 annually between 1768 and 1785, while greyish-black went at the rate of 2,000-4,000 per year. Equally distinctive as the black fox, but not as dear, was *ognevka*, the flame-red fox. Prior to 1773, 300 to 700 were sold yearly, but then sales diminished to almost nothing between 1780 and 1785. Flame-red priced at eighty kopeks to nine rubles per pelt.

The fourth and final general variety of fox was that distinguished by distinctive neck and breast coloration that was normally different from belly coloring. White-necked *(belodushki)* brought three and one-half rubles per pelt typically; the grey-necked *(sivodushki)*, one and one-half to ten rubles; black-necked *(cherno-*

34. Korsak (*Istoriko-statisticheskoe obozrenie*, p. 78) placed the value of Arctic fox in Mangazeia and in Irkutsk in the 1780's at forty to fifty rubles per hundred.

35. Pallas, *Voyages*, IV, 188. The caravan of 1727-28 disposed of six brownish-black fox pelts at twenty-two *liang* each, the single highest price obtained; Lange, *Le livre de comptes*, p. 85.

36. Korsak, *Istoriko-statisticheskoe obozrenie*, p. 77. Those of Iakutsk sold for five to ten rubles per pelt; Mangazeia ones for fifteen to thirty; Surgut, forty to one hundred; Berezov, 600 to 1,000.

dushki), in the same range. White-necked normally sold most heavily (6,000-12,000 pelts annually), and the grey-necked, 2,000-4,000.[37]

Sable *(sobol')*, individually, was one of the most expensive pelts in the Kiakhta trade. The very best were secured in eastern Siberia. In the Iakutsk, Nerchinsk, and Amur regions, and especially Kamchatka, Siberian prices ranged from twenty-five to fifty rubles per pelt, with the best (Iakutsk) bringing sixty to seventy rubles! Those of poorer quality and condition sold at Kiakhta for two and one-half to ten rubles each. During the 1770's, 6,000 to 16,000 sable pelts passed through Kiakhta annually; sable paws, usually separated, went in quantities of 50,000 to 100,000.

Domesticated cat (*koshachaia shkura* or *koshka*), although uncommon in early Russo-Chinese trade, was heavily exported by the last quarter of the century. In 1769, no more than 20,000 pelts moved by a decade later, the figure was 132,000, in 1785, 300,000, and after 1792, 387,000. The price was low.

Muskrat or desman *(vykhukhol)* also came to constitute a significant portion of fur exports.[38] Between 1768 and 1785, 80,000 to 200,000 pelts went through Kiakhta each year, with a typical value of thirty kopeks each.

Beaver *(bober)* in the same period was listed at 32,000 to 54,000 annually. The finest black beaver came from the basin of the river Taz, through Mangazeia in northern Siberia; Kamchatka produced large pelts. Ordinary beaver, without bellies, brought four to six and one-half rubles per pelt, and young river beaver *(kochlik)*, one-half to four rubles.

Ferret *(khorek)* reached 20,000 to 50,000 pelts at fifteen to twenty-five kopeks each.

The export of rabbit skins *(krolik)* did not begin until the early 1770's. Soon thereafter it increased to very great proportions. Between 1771 and 1778, 8,000 to 16,000 pelts sold each season, and later between 1780 and 1785, up to 40,000. They were always a most inexpensive fur; even on the border rarely brought more

37. In addition to whole fox pelts, large quantities of backs, paws, tails, bellies, and necks sold separately at widely varying prices. Samoilov *(Sbornik statisticheskikh svedenii,* p. 10) claimed that the annual sale between 1768 and 1785 of white-necked paws was 120,000 to 250,000 and of the grey-necked, 50,000 to 150,000.

38. Strahlenberg *(An Historico-Geographical Description,* p. 454) recorded that dried muskrat was an effective preservative against moths when laid among clothing. The Volga and especially the banks around Kazan', he says, literally swarmed with them.

than two kopeks per pelt. A small variety of rabbit, the white hare *(zaiats)*, entered the trade in quantity after 1792 only. Three years later 39,740 pieces were exchanged, and in 1796, 21,724. Many other species and sorts were exported at times in smallish quantities: lynx *(rysii)*, otter *(vydra)*, marten *(kunitsa)*, sea otter *(morskaia vydra)*, also known as sea or Kamchatka beaver (*morskii* or *kamchatskii bober)*, wolf *(volk)*, bear *(medved')*, glutton or wolverine *(rossomakha)*, mink *(norka)*, marmot *(syrok)*, dog *(sobaka)*, and musk deer *(kabarga)*.

So insatiable was the Chinese demand for furs that New World furs also figured predominantly in the Kiakhta market long before American and English sails brought them to Canton at the end of the century. Until the last two decades of the century, the Dutch dominated this trade through Amsterdam, to Arkhangel'sk and St. Petersburg.[39] Already well established in the Baltic trade, they increased their fleet to sixty to eighty ships a year to handle the furs. Beaver, otter, and fox from Northwest American passed through London to St. Petersburg and thence to Kiakhta, although the French failed to take full advantage of Canada and Hudson Bay because of the necessity of moving the furs through a glutted market in France before reaching Holland. Some Norweigan furs via Arkhangel'sk also entered the trade. As the North Pacific submitted to Russian conquest and settlement, from there was shipped especially the famed sea otter.

The eighteenth-century Russian informant, P. G., described as a bookkeeper of the Russian caravans, claimed that in 1775 the total value of all New World furs that found their way from east or west to Kiakhta was 500,000 rubles, a figure somewhat beyond credibility, for that was more than one-third of the total Russian exports in that year.[40] Tooke records that for the same year St. Petersburg imported 45,460 American beaver pelts and 7,143 otter, and Samoilov adds that 30,000-50,000 beaver pelts passed through Kiakhta annually in the years 1768-85, with a high in 1782—64,000.[41] The total quantity of this foreign item was probably upwards of 50,000 and in the very best years reached nearly one hundred

39. Rich, *Economic History Review*, 2d Series, VII (1955), 311-16; P. G., *Zhurnal manufaktur i torgovli*, Ch. 4, No. 11 (1836), 37-39; Samoilov, *Sbornik statisticheskikh svedenii*, p. 11; *Istoriia Moskvy*, II, 291.

40. P. G., *Zhurnal manufaktur i torgovli*, Ch. 4, No. 11 (1836), 39.

41. Samoilov, *Sbornik statisticheskikh svedenii*, p. 11. Also Tooke, *View*, III, 436.

thousand. Beaver generally held first place, a fact Rich attributes to a well-kept Russian processing secret "whereby they combed out the beaver wool from the undercoat of the beaver skin, leaving only the long fine guard hairs on the skin. This combed beaver was a fur which was more highly prized for trimming garments and for wearing as a 'natural' fur than was the original uncombed beaver from Canada."[42] Many of these returned to Hamburg, one of the great fur marts of the times, but those that reached Kiakhta brought seven to twenty rubles per pelt. Rabbit, otter, muskrat, lynx, and fox came next in order of quantities normally handled.

The extraordinary observation emerging from this recital of the quantities, kinds, and sources of furs exchanged with the Chinese at Kiakhta-Mai-mai-ch'eng is the apparent insatiable appetite of the Chinese-Manchus for furs of almost all qualities and species, unattractive and plain ones equally with the most magnificent and expensive. So great was the demand–it steadily increased throughout the century–that the prices at the border were far higher than elsewhere in Siberia, European Russia, or most places in western Europe. The very finest Siberian pelts naturally satisfied first the Russian court and the affluent gentry, but of the remainder the vast majority went to China. Prices on nearly all kinds generally rose in the eighteenth century, as in the case of the sea otter which sextupled.[43] In 1770 the best quality sold in Kiakhta for 100-140 rubles, whereas ten years earlier it brought sixty and eighty. And in Irkutsk the same pelt went for thirty or forty rubles; in Kamchatka for not more than ten to fifteen. What Baddeley remarked long ago for the seventeenth century, was no less true of the eighteenth: furs were the golden fleece that drew Russians on, but it was the Chinese who made it all worth the day.

Leathers

After peltry, the leading exports were tanned hides and leathers, often casually listed together with furs and pelts. *Iuft'*, that peculiarly "Russian leather" distinctive for its odor, sold most extensively. Under this rubric were classified the many qualities and sorts of tanned and processed leathers in black and red produced in almost every Russian town. For the China trade, the Siberian towns of Tobol'sk, Tiumen', Tomsk, and Irkutsk processed the

42. Rich, *Economic History Review*, 2d Series, VII (1955), 312.
43. P. G., *Zhurnal manufaktur i torgovli*, Ch. 4, No. 11 (1836), 37.

bulk. *Iuft'* increased greatly in export throughout the century until, between 1762 and 1785, normal export was 50,000 to 80,000 pieces annually. In 1792, 58,317 went through customs valued at 150,000 rubles.[44]

Lambskin *(merlushka)* and sheepskin *(ovchina)* came next, ordinarily listed together although very different in value and appearance. Strahlenberg reported the best as the Bukharan skins of slinks with hair or wool that lay flat or in broad waves, in contrast to the skins with small and tight curls.[45] Of all sorts, 600,000 to 1,000,000 pieces exchanged annually between 1768 and 1785, and after 1792 the figure went as high as 1,200,000. Radishchev reported the sale in one year of lambskins worth 123,337 rubles, the largest single item of Russian export for that year.[46] Prices ranged widely from thirty-five kopeks to one ruble per piece. Calf leather (*opoek*) and goatskins (*kozel*) contributed another 50,000 skins or somewhat less in a usual year. The best calfskins brought from six kopeks to one and one-half rubles each. Of all the leathers and skins, an especially popular Russian product was morocco (*saf'ian*), the most favored manufactured in Astrakhan in reds, yellows, and blacks of the skins of bucks and goats. It ran somewhat higher in price, ninety kopeks to two rubles per piece.[47]

Russian Cloth

Russian cloth and fabrics, linen, cottons, and woolens played a large role in the exports, although the quantities and values are impossible to pinpoint. Linens and woolens apparently outstripped cottons. Fabrics of flax, both plain and printed or striped, began to be sold in the 1770's and sales built up to between 2,300 and 11,500 yards annually. Rumiantsev gives the total value of all linens for 1802-5 as varying between 27,300 and 44,700 rubles.[48]

Russian woolens were, in the main, coarse, heavy fabrics, and generally brought lower prices than equivalent European goods. *Ordinarnoe* priced at forty kopeks to one ruble five kopeks and

44. Samoilov, *Sbornik statisticheskikh svedenii*, p. 12; Tooke, *View*, III, 387-94; Strahlenberg, *An Historico-Geographical Description*, p. 388.

45. Strahlenberg, *An Historico-Geographical Description*, pp. 410-11.

46. Radishchev, *Polnoe sobranie sochinenii*, II, 10. See also Samoilov, *Sbornik statisticheskikh svedenii*, p. 12, and Pallas, *Voyages*, IV, 194.

47. Pallas, *Voyages*, IV, 195. For a description of the processing of Morocco, see Tooke, *View*, III, 394-403.

48. Ministerstvo Kommertsii, *Tableaux du commerce*, Dixième Tableau.

soldatskoe at one ruble, while foreign woolens brought two to four per arshin (.77 yards). Even the names of the woolens imply their simple quality: common cloth (*sermiazhnoe sukhno*), peasant cloth (*muzhitskoe*), homespun (*kolomianka*), and Siberian felt (*voilok*). Prior to the suspension of trade in 1785, the usual export was 38,500 to 77,000 yards (50,000 to 100,000 arshins) of "common" cloth, in addition to over 6,000 yards of "ordinary" and less than 100 to over 300 of woolen carpets *(kover)* and mats. After 1792, export decreased.

Foreign Cloth

European fabrics enjoyed a sale to the Chinese at least equal to Russian fabrics, and by the end of the century appear to have outdistanced them. Something of the magnitude of 75,000 yards annually were exchanged prior to 1785; the growth continued until far into the nineteenth century. Prussian merchants purveyed to Russia the bulk of these fabrics, although German, Dutch, English, French, and Spanish merchants are also mentioned. The largest group of European fabrics were apparently coarse woolens: camlets, calmandes, druggets, and flannels. Pallas recorded that they sold for two to four rubles per arshin, many for much less.[49]

Miscellany

All of the goods recited above comprised probably 85 per cent or so of the usual exports at Kiakhta. All are either natural products or the issue of rude and ordinary technique. There were many manufactured goods representative of more advanced craft skills, but they were always traded in small quantities. Various ferrous products sold steadily: axes, knives, shears, scythes, and locks taken together were disposed of at the rate of 2,000 to 3,000 pieces annually. *Mishura*—imitation gold or brass foil—went at the rate of 8,000 spools (*tsevka*) each year, and rarely up to 1,600 skeins (*motok*). White sheet iron, apparently of Russian manufacture, ranged between 1,000 and 5,000 sheets (*listy*). Mirrors (some of them European ones), bottles and vases produced in Irkutsk glassworks, glass (*sliuda*) from Moscow, writing paper, glue, isinglass, watches, Portuguese snuff in Chinese form, and even Bengal and Turkish opium, were common enough to be

49. Pallas, *Voyages*, IV, 198.

mentioned in passing by various witnesses. As we have remarked, live animals—horned cattle, sheep, horses, camels, and hunting dogs—were most important to local trade in Baikalia, and some meats and provisions also sold. Sladkovskii claimed that between 1759 and 1761 horses valued at 44,500 rubles were marketed.[50]

One item of exotica, the precise nature and use of which have baffled historians, was repeatedly mentioned: *rog saigachii*. As an item of trade, this was a transparent or semitransparent horn of some considerable size, reportedly useful to convert into lanterns and, when powdered, had or was thought to have certain medicinal qualities—at least by Tibetans. The origin of the horns is the curious matter. Pallas understood them to be from giraffes, which he could not have meant precisely.[51] Sladkovskii is willing to agree provided the giraffe becomes a steppe antelope indigenous to Central Asia.[52] Chappe d'Auteroche identified the "sayga" as "a kind of wild goat, which is chiefly found . . . in the southern part of Siberia, near the origins of the rivers Irtysz, Jenissea, and the Oby."[53] Part of the confusion here was really dispelled by Strahlenberg: Siberia produced transparent horns useful as lamps or for ingestion in such quantity and of so many kinds that they could hardly be distinguished one from the other.[54] Swedish prisoners like himself "made there a sort of Tobacco-Horns, (or Boxes) as transparent almost as Glass itself." Reindeers, swordfish, and walrus all reportedly contributed to the horn supply, and prehistoric animals even unknowingly gave their tusks. Tupper is prepared to believe that some were the tusks of long-frozen hairy mammoths, among the largest land animals hunted by man.[55] There is no record of the pharmacological efficacy of any of these.

50. Sladkovskii, *Ocherki ekonomicheskikh otnoshenii*, p. 63.

51. Pallas, *Voyages*, IV, 194.

52. Sladkovskii, *Ocherki ekonomicheskikh otnoshenii*, p. 69, n. 3.

53. Jean Chappe d'Auteroche, *A Journey into Siberia, by Order of the King of France. Containing an Account of the Manners and Customs of the Russians, the Present State of Their Empire, with the Natural History, and Geographical Description of Their Country, and Level of the Road from Paris to Tobolsky* (London: T. Jefferys, 1770), p. 233.

54. Strahlenberg, *An Historico-Geographical Description*, p. 380. Samoilov (*Sbornik statisticheskikh svedenii*, p. 12) gives the export for the years 1780-85 as 200,000-370,000 pieces annually!

55. Harmon Tupper, *To the Great Ocean, Siberia and the Trans-Siberian Railway* (Boston: Little, Brown & Company, 1965), p. 116, n. See also Erman, *Travels*, II, 287-89. Erman suggests they may be mammoths' teeth. He also lists whale bone, walrus, and rhinoceros.

Chinese Exports to Russia

Cottons

It comes as something of a surprise that Chinese cottons led the list of China's exports to Russia throughout the eighteenth century. In 1751, for example, 257,940 rubles worth were declared by Russian merchants, representing nearly 60 per cent of the total value of Russian imports of that year. By 1759-61, the figures had gone over 500,000 rubles and 66 per cent, and by 1792 the ruble value reached 1,601,263.[56] The climb continued after the turn of the century. As Cahen put it, "Chinese cottons were indispensible to the peoples of Siberia and also of European Russia."[57] Eastern Siberians continued to use more Bukharan and Chinese cotton than Russian until the end of the nineteenth century.

There were, in general, two sorts of Chinese cottons in the trade, *kitaika* and *daba*. Kitaika, the dearer and choicer, was a lustrous fabric, strong and durable, and came in many colors, the best in blue or azure. Actually kitaika was a generic label; the Russian merchant distinguished among many varieties, qualities, and sorts, of which two main types were known for reporting purposes by the size of bales in which they were sold: *tiunevaia*, or kitaika sold by the normal *tiun'* or bale, and *odnoportichnaia*, marketed by the single *portische*, a bale larger and longer than the *tiun'*.[58] Between 1768 and 1785, more than 300,000 normal

56. Semenov, *Izuchenie*, III, 471.

57. Lange, *Le livre de comptes*, p. 139.

58. *Kitaika* was known to the English at Canton as Nankeen or Nanking. The Russians used various adjectives to describe and distinguish the many sorts; most of these are not now completely identifiable: *semilannaia* and *piatlannaia*, literally seven *liang* and five *liang* from the original price range; *skladnaia*, folded or plaited; *torgovaia* or Peking, sometimes designated the finest kitaika characterized by a high gloss; *torgovaia val'kova*, literally commercial wholesale, an ordinary, heavier kitaika, possibly from Central China and the Shanghai region; *samtsovaia* (of Mongol origins?); and "schanchai" (Shanghai?).

Cahen (Lange, *Le livre de comptes*, pp. 115-16, 123) calculated a *tiun'* to have been about 35.6 meters (38.9 yards) in length; a *konets* (an end), one-tenth of a tiun; and an *aune* (ell), one-hundredth of a tiun. These measures were usually used only for cottons; others for silks. There was also considerable variation in widths, the wider usually the finer. A letter of 1805 from the Russian-American Company agent then in Canton, F. I. Shemelin, noted that the better kitaika imported through Kiakhta usually measured eight vershok and one poldiuim (one twenty-fourth of a foot, i.e., about fifteen inches), in width, while that he found in Canton was always narrow, *viz.* pieces eight arshin (18.6 ft.) in length were six and one-fourth vershok (almost eleven inches) wide and the long pieces (ten arshins or 23.3 ft.) were six and one-

bales of all varieties were imported, at prices ranging from three to twelve rubles. Kitaika outsold daba probably ten to one.

Harry Parkes described daba as a "calico of a strong description, and generally dyed blue, red, or some bright color."[59] It was a coarse cloth akin to and sometimes confused with Bukharan cottons. Between 1768 and 1785, daba entered Russia in quantities of over 150,000 to nearly 300,000 yards each year.[60] The price ranged from one ruble per piece fifteen to twenty arshins in length down to fifty kopeks for somewhat smaller pieces.

These and other cotton goods either entered Siberian fairs or were sent on from Moscow to St. Petersburg and other cities of Russia. The majority of the cottons which reached European Russia were transshipped to Poland or distributed in Belorussia, Ukraine, Cossackdom, or the *gubernii* around Azov and Novorossiisk.[61]

Silks

After cottons came silks, raw, semiprocessed, and finished fabric. The unfinished forms constituted a large proportion of the silk imported, probably about one-third, either raw (*syrets*), twisted (*sychennyi*), or in skeins (*motok*). One hundred to 250 *pud* of raw silk, 250 of twisted, and 500 skeins were imported annually between 1755 and 1762. In the half-decade 1780-85, raw and twisted held their own; silk in skeins rose to the range of 800 to 3000. Silks prices are almost impossible to fix exactly, although Pallas gave a figure for unbleached silk of seventy-five to 150 rubles per *pud*, which permits some notion of the value.[62] By the

half vershok (11.4 inches) wide. Shemelin found an azure blue kitaika of tight weave *(lozhenaia)* not more than seven vershok (12.25 inches) wide, and a black kitaika of very different appearance thirteen arshin in length and 1.8 feet in width, which sold for two and three-fifths piasters per konets; *Vneshniaia politika Rossii,* Series 1, III, 20. See also Samoilov, *Sbornik statisticheskikh svedenii,* p. 13.

59. Harry Parkes, "Report on the Russian Caravan Trade with China," *Journal of the Royal Geographical Society,* XXIV (1854), 310. Cahen (Lange, *Le livre de comptes,* p. 106) accepted G. F. Müller's derivation of the word *daba* as from the Chinese *ta-pou* (*ta-pu* ?), describing it as a substantial and coarse cotton fabric usually red in color. It was close in quality to the Bukharan cotton known as Chaldar and many writers classed the two as one; see, e.g., Korsak, *Istoriko-statisticheskoe obozrenie,* p. 91.

60. Samoilov, *Sbornik statisticheskikh svedenii,* p. 13.

61. *Istoriia Moskvy,* II, 291, 298.

62. Pallas, *Voyages,* IV, 200.

early nineteenth century, the amount of unfinished silks seems to have declined until it did not exceed 15 per cent of the total value imported, i.e. 11,200 to 25,500 rubles per year.[63]

Fabric silk came in many kinds and price ranges. The main sorts seem to have been the damasks (*kamka*), imported by Peter the Great for his flags and standards, the satins (*atlas*), and the velvets (*barkhat*).[64] Lesser quantities were purchased of paper muslin or gauze (*fler*), foulard (*fanza*), brocade (*parcha*), crepe (*krep*), *solemenka, baiberek, svistun, lanza,* and Gros de Tours (*grosdetur*). Nearly all were exchanged in varying units and lengths and fell in the price range of ten to forty-five rubles for a piece of one *postav* in length (a little more than thirteen yards).[65] Silk fabrics of all sorts increased in volume of sales until the suspension of 1785-92, thereafter decreasing in absolute and relative importance. In 1751, they comprised over 23 per cent of the total ruble value of Chinese exports (103,050 rubles) and in 1761, 20.5 per cent (172,933 rubles). The ruble value rose to over 200,000 prior to 1781, but after 1792 declined (in that year silk fabric composed only 6.6 per cent of Chinese exports) and in the early nineteenth century continued to drop (74,000 to 150,000 rubles).

The explanation for the decline in finished silks is not obvious. Trusevich and others argued that the quality of Chinese silk fabrics deteriorated and China grew increasingly wary of exporting raw or semiprocessed forms.[66] Russian cottage industry developed silk fabricating early in the century and the decline

63. Ministerstvo Kommertsii, *Tableaux du commerce,* Dixième Tableau.

64. Agnes Geijer, "Chinese Silks Exported to Russia in the 17th Century," *Bulletin of the Museum of Far Eastern Antiquities,* XXV (1953), 4.

Satins were divided into three groups: (1) *us,* from the Russian *uzkii,* tight or narrow, a thin, slight fabric of average cost; (2) ordinary satins; and (3) *kanfa,* a thick, stout sort and the most expensive. Damasks were reported in several varieties, none now definable: *gol,* perhaps a Bukharan silk; *polugol,* half-*gol; piatilannyi,* a fabric which in the beginning sold for five *liang.* Two general varieties of velvets are mentioned: pile velvet, a looped or "terry" pile when the loops are left uncut; and cut *(rytyi),* when the loops are cut so that the pile is of single threads.

65. Pallas, *Voyages,* IV, 200-204. Cahen (Lange, *Le livre de comptes,* p. 123) concluded that the silks acquired by the 1727-28 caravan were of a close price range: two to twelve *liang* per *postav.* A *postav* was a silk measure of 12.1 meters (13.2 yards) on the average; hence the price above translates to approximately five to thirty rubles per fifteen to sixteen arshins.

66. Trusevich, *Posol'skiia i torgovliia snosheniia,* pp. 169-72, and Silin, *Kiakhta,* pp. 143-45.

of China as a supplier of raw silk, intensified by the long suspension before 1792, compelled it to turn elsewhere for supply, Persia for example.

Tea

Russians adopted tea as the national nonalcoholic beverage only at the end of the eighteenth century, although teas in smallish quantities entered the country throughout that century. The leading sort was *kirpichnyi* or "brick" tea, from the Russian word *kirpich*.[67] Brick or tile tea, as it was known in Europe, was consumed almost exclusively by native Siberian peoples, who infused it with rye-meal, mutton fat, and salt. Since the bricks were packed solid and resisted deterioration in the dry climate of Mongolia and Baikalia, they were often employed as units of value in the Kiakhta trade. Seventeen thousand *pud* came in annually between 1762 and 1785, as compared with 12,500 *pud* of leaves in other forms, and the amount had not increased strikingly by the end of the century (1799: 24,095 *pud*).

In the last decade of the century, loose leaf tea overtook brick. In 1800, for example, 38,400 *pud* of the former compared with 31,450 of the latter. Both green and black teas entered Russia, in that order of importance. The best green was *dzhulan*, sold by the *tsibik* of two and one-half *pud* at the rate of eighty to one-hundred rubles. Between 1768 and 1785 it amounted to 4000 *pud* annually. *Monikho* or *moni-kou*, described as an inferior variety of *dzhulan* scented with jasmine, was priced at thirty to forty kopeks per *bakcha* of one *funt*. Other greens included *modzhan* or *mad-khan*, poorer than the above and cheaper, packaged in small boxes (*tsybiki*) which sold for around four rubles, a *bakcha* from thirty-five kopeks to one ruble. *Lugan* or *lougan*, a still poorer sort, was used largely by Mongols, Buriats, and other border peoples; it cost ten kopeks per *pud*. And there were still others in smaller quantities.

Only after 1792 did tea rival cottons among the imports. In that year all varieties of tea totaled in value 540,236 rubles and accounted for over 22 per cent of the total trade. Ten years later

67. Parkes (*Journal of the Royal Geographical Society*, XXIV [1854], 310) reported that the bricks weighed about three to three and one-half *funt* each, and were packed in chests normally containing twenty-one bricks.

a dramatic change, the ruble value rose to 1,872,604 or over 40 per cent, and tea continued to climb.[68]

Tobacco and Other Things

Cottons, silks, and teas together amounted to over 90 per cent of Russian imports at all times in the eighteenth century. Other goods had a larger measure of exotic value. Tobacco, predominately in ball form or "Chinese tobacco" (*kitaiskii shar*), came into Siberia between 1762 and 1768 at the rate of 1,000 to 2,000 *pud* annually, at a price of ten to twenty rubles per *pud*. This trade held fairly steady, for by 1805 the total value of tobacco was still only 21,283 rubles. And most of these exotica which have always typified China to the foreigner were imported in commercially inconsiderable amounts: porcelains (*farfor*), earthenware, enamelware (*finift*), lacquerware, ivory, copper porringers and ladles, iron ladles, horn and paper lanterns, scrolls, ink, incense, rouge, fans, tobacco pouches, a Chinese smoking pipe known as a *ganza*, magnifying glasses, telescopes, glass lamps, sewing needles, coral, artificial and precious stones (primarily pearls), artificial flowers, live monkeys, tiger and panther skins, pepper, anise, preserved and jellied fruits (watermelon, pear, and apple), sugar candy, medicinal herbs (quinine), musk (a base for perfumes), and of course Chinese silver.

China, not Russia, exported the manufactured or finely processed goods in the eighteenth century. With the exception of some leathers and coarse woolens, and other items in small quantities, the single item with which the Russians succeeded in interesting the Chinese and upon which the entire trade was built was Siberian and New World furs. The Russian woolens and cottons were mainly the coarser and poorer fabrics not intended for fine wearing apparel. It was not for lack of trying that Russian manufacturers did not do well; we noted earlier that on a number of occasions St. Petersburg authorities stimulated local Siberian officials and caravan officers to inquire into new kinds of Russian products that might entice the Chinese, but to little avail. On the other hand, Chinese silks and cottons were, as far as may be discerned now, mainly fine luxury fabrics, the products of a well-developed and advanced textile industry.

68. Samoilov, *Sbornik statisticheskikh svedenii*, pp. 17-18; Semenov, *Izuchenie*, III, 471; Ministerstvo Kommertsii, *Tableaux du commerce*, Dixième Tableau.

Only at the end of the century did a "natural" product—tea—begin to reduce the sway held by these lovely cloths. Cahen's remark for the first quarter of the century applies no less to the last three quarters: "a cette époque en effet c'est la Chine le pays manufacturier."[69]

69. Lange, *Le livre de comptes*, p. 140.

Chapter X: Conclusion

The China trade was an important sector of economic entrepreneurial activity and experience for eighteenth-century Russia. For the Russian state it was, throughout the last three quarters of the century, a major source of revenue, as suggested by Sergei M. Troitskii. Although, as has been shown, the state caravans to Peking after the Treaty of Kiakhta did not return large profits in terms of the size of the investment, they did, nonetheless, probably operate in the black. As one caravan succeeded another, the difficulties and disadvantages of these expensive enterprises seemed to far outweigh the dwindling benefits to the state treasury and to some of the state's officers and institutions. The Siberian Prikaz did attempt on several occasions to investigate more thoroughly the Chinese market so that only products in great demand in Peking were carried, but, as far as may be gathered, it did not succeed in significantly altering the kinds of merchandise taken to the Chinese capital. It may well be that the main stimulus to continue sending the caravans as long as they were sent was the great hope of obtaining Chinese gold and silver badly needed to help retire the large amounts of debased coin issued prior to the 1730's. In another sense the state had no choice. As we have argued, the state was not irrevocably wedded to maintenance of this monopoly (nor of others, for that matter); the most important fact is that the most ambitious and well-prepared project for turning the Peking trade over to a private company failed signally to elicit response from Russia's private merchants and investors. After the early 1740's the state had to direct its own caravans to Peking or give up entirely the capital trade permitted and prescribed by the Treaty of Kiakhta.

As private trade at Kiakhta came to return large customs revenues to the Treasury, it became increasingly obvious that the more advantageous policy for St. Petersburg was to cease the caravans and to array and to support the private merchants at the border so as to maximize customs revenues derived from their considerable and growing trade. From the point of view of the state the ideal was the organization of all of the Kiakhta merchants into some form of company or society which could exercise commercial discipline over them, regulate sales and purchases, suppress contraband, and guarantee customs revenues. Throughout the last half of the century repeated suggestions were made to create such a company, but they fell on barren ground. Russia's China merchants never gave indication of any interest in participating in any organized operation so exposed to interference by the state. Certainly partnerships and other simple forms of organization were to be found engaging in trading at Kiakhta, but they were, it seems apparent, mostly if not entirely temporary associations rarely extending beyond a single trading season or employing sophisticated business methods. In such situations, all the state's officers could do was to try to improve the conditions of trade for these private merchants. Especially after the 1740's, by which time the failings of the caravan system were obvious and known, the administrative structure of eastern Siberia was distinctly improved. By and large the officials dispatched there in the last half of the century seem to have been men of calibre and rectitude compared with those of the first quarter of the century: a Governor Nagel contrasted with a Prince Gagarin. Although one is not struck by the large amounts of monies the state used to build better facilities in eastern Siberia, it is true that a number of measures it took did have at least some improving effect on the private trade of Kiakhta: the abolition of internal customs, the extension of the *veksel'* system, the establishment of swifter and surer means of communication, etc. Notably most of these improvements were underway before Catherine's reign. It seems fair to point out that her vaunted administration merely carried out or carried forward proposals or activities begun earlier. In this regard it might be recalled that the striking down of state monopolies and farms came finally in 1762 by which time all of those in the China trade had proven to be liabilities. It was not Catherinian economic theory or predilection in the main, but concrete experience in the several decades before that accounts for the end of these economic privileges.

It is far more difficult to observe closely the private merchants in the China trade and to identify their attitudes than it is the state and its officialdom. We do know that the China merchants were a large group and included, eventually, a wide range of persons, from a few wealthy big traders, such as Sibiriakov, to peasants and foreigners. In spite of the persistent wail of the Russian government and of unofficial observers that their "lack of organization" severely handicapped them in barter with the Chinese, large and small merchant alike held back from submitting themselves to the discipline of a company. In all likelihood the successful traders felt they had no need for a company; all that one could accomplish would be to interfere with their activities and to expose their funds and goods to observation and perhaps seizure by state officials. Small merchants, on the other hand, certainly harbored apprehensions of complete domination by the merchants with large amounts of capital; they probably had good reason to believe that they were better off competing against the big merchants than in making common cause with them. It would seem that by the end of the century all of the Kiakhta merchants had accepted a measure of common cause and action. At least all were compelled by the state to list their inventories, to trade only at specific times and places, and to reach those places only via prescribed routes. Certain habits and practices came thus to be shared. Some merchants must also have felt mutuality of interest existed in merchants working together to outflank the state's officers and customs functionaries.

In the first decade or so after the Treaty of Kiakhta, trade at the border seems to have grown slowly. There can be little doubt that the many state monopolies hindered significantly the trade of private merchants. The carriage by the caravans of fine merchandise directly to Peking, the monopolization by the state of the best pelts, rhubarb, and other things most desired by the Chinese, the absence of aids to prosperous trade such as well-built warehouses, adequate boats for Lake Baikal and the rivers, well developed market-fairs nearby, etc.—all of these made the Kiakhta trade in the early years a risky and difficult enterprise. As state monopolies died or were relinquished and as the conditions of trade improved, so too did the fortunes of the Kiakhta merchants. By the end of the 1740's private trade at Kiakhta had clearly outstripped the state's activities. It is likely that those merchants involved in the Kiakhta trade from early years sharpened their business skills and accomplished more favorable bargains with the Chinese. And Kiakhta also increasingly attracted merchants or their agents from elsewhere in Siberia, from European Russia, and even from abroad. Already by the mid-1740's there were large and highly successful merchants in the China trade and as the century went by there were many more.

At all times in the last three quarters of the eighteenth century, the Russian state involved itself deeply in the China trade, whether in the role of monopolist or of encourager of private trade. It had known long before, certainly by the beginning of the century, that this was a channel of commerce of great potential for large state revenues. Hence it repeatedly drew back from acts or words that might threaten the continuation and prosperity of that trade and, on the positive side, anxiously accommodated to Chinese demands and patterns to insure access to Peking and maintenance of border trading posts. In getting along with the Chinese, the Russians proved themselves willing to adapt to the strange ways of the East much more successfully than did the Europeans and Americans who traded in these times on the China coast. Several times the Chinese threatened to cut off permanently all intercourse, but each time the Russians chose to negotiate the differences patiently, undeterred by their failure to obtain an enormous extension of the rights and privileges already agreed upon. Thus, all in all, the setting for this trade between the two great empires was surprisingly amicable, even if often difficult to keep on an even keel. And it should not be overlooked that the problems faced by the Russians and Chinese—the Dzhungar wars, the deserters and runaways, the navigation of the Amur, the large Russian caravans trading in the middle of China's capital—were far more ticklish and dangerous than the issues faced by western nations trading at Macao and Canton.

If there is any general utility to this lengthy discourse on the China trade and its milieu, it lies in the contribution it makes to the very poorly understood historical trough between the luminescent Peter I and late eighteenth-century Russia of young, although sedate manhood. In the China trade at least, there was no hiatus, no break in economic (and adminstrative) development between Peter's "hothouse" burst of building and Catherine's maternal stewardship over a prosperous and ordered society and economy. Rather the contrary is true; it was precisely in the second and third quarters of the eighteenth century that the China trade and Baikalia achieved a measure of affluence. By the end of the century mandarin and Muscovite overcame most of the hurdles to stable and mutually advantageous trade.

Finally, the institutions and patterns of the China trade were fashioned in the very process of commerce and communication with the Chinese. Economic theory or predilection are quite absent from the picture. The state's monopolies were abolished not because of the influence of economic theory on Elizabeth, Peter, or Catherine, but because they were shown to be outmoded, to have exceeded their usefulness. This has been established here for the China trade.

Appendix I. Weights, Measures, and Currencies

Russian Weights

1 Berkovets	equals	10 Pud	equals	3.61 Quintals
1 Pud	equals	40 Funt	equals	36.11 Lbs. Avoirdupois
1 Funt	equals	32 Lot	equals	0.90 Lbs. Avoirdupois
1 Lot	equals	3 Zolotnik	equals	0.45 Ounces
1 Zolotnik			equals	4.25 Grams

Russian Measures

1 Versta	equals	500 Sazhen'	equals	0.6641 Miles
1 Sazhen'	equals	3 Arshin	equals	7.0 Feet (2.13 m.)
1 Arshin	equals	16 Vershok	equals	2.33 Feet (71.1 cm.)
1 Vershok	equals	1.75 Dium (Diuim)	equals	1.75 Inches
1 Fut	equals	12 Dium (Diuim)	equals	1 Foot
1 Dium (Diuim)	equals	10 Liniia	equals	1 Inch

Chinese Weights

1 Long Ton	equals	16.8 Piculs (Tan)		
1 Metric Ton	equals	16.54 Piculs		
1 Short Ton	equals	15 Piculs		
1 Picul	equals	100 Catties (Chin)	equals	133.3 Lbs. Avoirdupois
1 Catty (Chin)	equals	16 Ounces (Liang)	equals	1.3 Lbs. Avoirdupois
1 Catty	equals	1 Funt 44 Zolotnik		
1 Ounce (Liang)	equals	8 Zolotnik	equals	slightly more than one ounce Avoirdupois

Currencies

1 Ruble	equals	10 Grivennik	equals	100 Kopeks
1 Liang (Tael)	equals	10 Ch'ien	equals	100 Fen
1 Liang	equals	approximately 1.3 to 1.7 Rubles[1]		
1 Fen	equals	approximately 1.3 to 1.7 Kopeks		
1 Lb. Sterling	equals	approximately 3 to 4.5 Rubles[2]		
1 Spanish Dollar	equals	approximately 1 to 1.5 Rubles		

1. These conversions are, of course, only rough approximations. Kurts, for example, gives the value of a *liang* as of 1729 as 1.4 rubles (*Gosudarstvennaia monopoliia*, p. 47). The Complete Collection of Laws of the Russian Empire notes the 1768 value of a *liang* as 1.7 rubles (*PSZ*, XVIII, No. 13060, 435, ukaz dated 17 January 1768). And P. G. accepts 1 ruble 66 ¾ kopek to 1 ruble 70 kopek without indicating a date (*Zhurnal manufaktur i torgovli*, Ch. 4, No. 11 [1836], 19-139).

2. A. L. Gal'perin equates one lb. sterling as of 1710 with 3 rubles and as of 1763 with 4 rubles 35 kopek ("Russko-kitaiskaia torgovlia v XVIII-pervoi polovine XIX veke [Opyt sravneniia kiakhtinskogo torga s torgovlei cherez Guanchzhou]," *Problemy Vostokovedeniia*, V (1959), 218, citing *Biblioteka dlia chteniia*, XXIII (1837), Smes', 72-73). See also Reading, *The Anglo-Russian Commercial Treaty*, p. 25, n. 26; p. 247, n. 53.

Appendix II. Account of the Tret'iakov-Molokov Caravan on its Departure for Peking, September 1727

General Caravan Account Summarized[a]

Credit (*Prikhod*)	*rubles*	*kopeks*		
Treasury money for various articles	139,857	69 3/4		
Iasak goods	194,351	71 1/2		
	334,209	41 1/4		
Debit (*Raskhod*)			*rubles*	*kopeks*
Purchased and *iasak* goods of the state taken to China from the above noted sums:			268,036	62 3/4
Goods and chattels from Commissar Tret'iakov's widow:			6,869	70
Total of Goods			274,906	32 3/4
Money of the treasury (of which 234 rubles 96 1/4 kopeks belonged to Tret'iakova) for the purchase of goods:			9,830	19 1/2
Chinese silver (4,766 *zolotnik*, at 14 kopeks per *zolotnik*, probably for expenses):			667	24
Total of Money:			10,497	43 1/2
Total of Goods and Money Taken to China:			285,403	76 1/4
Monetary Expenses borne by the treasury:	44,056	40		
For forty horses taken by the Commissar in payment:	210			
Goods Expenses borne by the treasury:	4,539	25		
Total Expenses for the caravan:	48,805	65		
TOTAL OUTLAY FOR THE CARAVAN:			334,209	41 1/4

[a]From Kurts, *Gosudarstvennaia monopoliia,* p. 42, n., taken from Moskovskii Glavnyi Arkhiv, Ministerstvo Inostrannykh Del, Kitaiskie knigi 1687-1742 g., "Vypiska o poslannykh (1648-1742 g.) v Kitai ros. karavanakh, uchinennaia iz arkhivnykh kitaiskogo dvora bumag v 1776 g.", *l.* 40, and Moskovskii Glavnyi Arkhiv, Ministerstvo Inostrannykh Del, Snosheniia Rossii s Kitaem, *karton* 21, *delo* 1727 g., *No.* 16. This is in substance the account submitted by Lange to the Collegium of Foreign Affairs from "Chikoiskaia Strelka" on 13 September 1727.

Merchandise of the Tret'iakov-Molokov Caravan (Excluding Sales after Caravan's Return)[b]

Russian Merchandise Carried to Peking

Item	*Total Carried*	*Amount Sold*	*Price*	*Unsold and Returned*
Furs				
Squirrel pelts	1,416,112	1,376,380	35-40 *liang*/1000	39,732
Ermine pelts	512,279	228,020	7-12 *liang*/100 (young ermine at 10 *liang* & 13 *liang* 50 *fen*/1000)	284,259
Fox pelts	144,644	99,587	360-500 *liang*/1000 (the rarest sold individually)	45,057
Fox paws, pairs	45,255	45,250	Most at 3-6 *fen*/pair	5
Sable pelts	51,794	27,550	Most at 75 *fen*-1 *liang* each	24,244
Sable paws, individual	46,425	46,425	Most at 8 *liang*/1000	
Sable backs	14,025	4,600	Most at 400 *liang*/1000	9,425
Sable tails	3,253	3,253	Most at 14 *liang*/100	
Lynx pelts	3,583	3,421	Most at 2 *liang* 50 *fen* each	162
Lynx paws, pairs	3,040	3,040	40 *fen*/pair	
Otter pelts	2,006	2,006	1 *liang* 50 *fen* & 2 *liang* each	
Sea Otter pelts	582	581	11 *liang* 50 *fen* each	
Various furs[1]	681	35	1 *liang* 87 1/2 *fen* to 40 *liang* each	646

[b]Taken from Lange, *Le livre de comptes*, pp. 85-95, and Kurts, *Gosudarstvennaia monopoliia*, pp. 45-47; consult Appendix I for table of weights, measures, and currencies, and Chapter 9 for a discussion of the various items of trade.

Total of furs carried: 2,148, 959 pelts (i.e. whole pelts, backs, and tails) and 71,508 pairs of paws

Total of furs sold: 1,745,433 pelts and 71,503 pairs of paws

Total of furs unsold and returned to border: 403,525 pelts and five pairs of paws

Walrus tusks (*kosti morzhovogo zuba*)[2]	214 *pud* 31 *funt*	31 *p.* 18 *f.*	12 *liang*/*pud*	176 *p.* 13 *f.*
Seal skins	2,300	2,300	16 *fen*/each	
Sea Otter blankets	3	1	55 *liang*	2

1. Included marten, steppe cat, sea bear, Arctic fox bellies, etc.

2. There is a discrepancy of seven rubles in these figures for walrus tusks than cannot be rectified.

luft', red	47 1/2	12	5 *liang* 60 *fen* & 6 *liang* 45 *fen*/ each; 1 red piece at 2 *liang* 50 *fen*	35 1/2
Dutch cloth (*Galanskoe sukhno*), arshins	477 1/2	5	3 *liang*/arshin	472 1/2
Clocks with chimes	2	1	70 *liang*	1
Mirrors	1,192	1	40 *fen*	1,191
Korolek	6 *funt* 30 *zolotnik*			6 f. 30 z.

Chinese Merchandise Imported from Peking

Silks: Satins

Us (a thin fabric of average cost): 2,504 postavs[3] at 2 *liang* 50 *fen* to 4 *liang* 50 *fen* per postav

Atlas (ordinary satin): 216 postavs and 3 portishches at 1 *liang* 33 *fen* to 6 *liang* 10 *fen* per postav

Kanfa (a thick satin): 1,370 postavs and 39 portishches at 4 to 12 *liang* per postav

Total of Satins: 4,090 postavs and 42 portishches (54,165 yards)

Silks: Damasks (Kamka)

Piatilannaia (5 *liang*): 724 postavs, 3 portishches at 1 *liang* 20 *fen* to 5 *liang* per postav

Shestilannaia (6 *liang*): 59 postavs at 2 *liang* 50 *fen* to 6 *liang* per postav

Semilannaia (7 *liang*): 2,365 postavs at 3 *liang* 50 *fen* to 7 *liang* 50 *fen* per postav

Total of Damasks: 3,578 postavs and 69 portishches at 1 *liang* 20 *fen* to 12 *liang* per postav (i.e., 47,685 yards)

Silks: Diverse

Baiberek: 854 postavs, 3 portishches at 5 *liang* per postav

Gros de Tours: 360 postavs, 3 portishches, first quality at 8 *liang* and second at 7 *liang* 10 *fen* per postav

Svistun: 193 postavs, 2 portishches, 13 pieces (*kusok*) at 4 *liang* to 6 *liang* 50 *fen* per postav

Brocade (*Parcha*): 110 postavs, 22 portishches, 27 pieces at about 12 *liang* per postav

Crepe (*Krep*): 100 postavs, 525 pieces at about 3 *liang* per postav

Solomenka: 76 postavs, 2 portishches, 8 pieces at about 5 *liang*

Velvet (*Barkhat*): 20 pieces with gold threads and flowers at 9 *liang* 20 *fen* per piece

Velvet: 4 pieces with gold threads at 25 *liang* per piece

Velvet, Striped: 10 arshins at 40 *fen* per arshin

Watered Silk (*Moire*): 9 3/4 arshins at 15 *fen* per arshin

Lenza: 3 pieces at 66 *fen* per piece

Total of All Silks: 9,361 postavs, 143 portishches, 600 pieces, plus 19 3/4 arshins of velvets and watered silk, i.e. approximately 125,000 yards of silk fabrics

3. Determining with precision the value of the measures used by the Russians for Chinese textiles is extremely difficult. In spite of the fine effort by Gaston Cahen he was compelled to concede that his conclusions must be regarded as only approximate at best; Lange, *Le livre de comptes*, pp. 111-17. Silks were usually measured in *postav* and *portishche*. Cahen calculated the postav to be on the average seventeen arshins or some 13.2 yards, and the portishche to be about one-half of a postav. Some silks were also measured in pieces (*kuski*, sing. *kusok*), the value of which is impossible to fix.

Cottons: Kitaika (Nanking)

14,705 bales (*tiun'*)[4], 42 ends (*konets*), most at 3 *liang* per bale

Total Cottons: Approximately 572,200 yards of cotton fabrics

Gold: Bullion

2,186 *liang* 61 1/2 *fen*,[5] each *liang* valued at 10 *liang* of commercial silver

Gold: Vessels and Other Objects

76 *liang* 91 *fen*

Total, Gold (by weight): 2,946 *liang* 61 1/2 *fen*, valued at 22,626 *liang* of commercial silver

Silver: Bullion

23,961 *liang* 28 *fen*

Silver: Objects

295 *liang* 80 *fen*

Total, Silver (by value): 24,257 *liang* 8 *fen*

Tea: Dzhulan (Green Tea of First Quality)

2,619 *chin*[6] at 60 *fen* per *chin*

Tea: Lan-hoa (A Second Quality Green Tea)

21,902 *chin* at 40 *fen* per *chin*

Tea: Black

582 *chin* at 50 *fen* per *chin*

Total of Teas: 25,103 chin of green and black (33,387 lbs. avoirdupois)

Star Anise (Badian)

1,140 *chin* at 27 *fen* per *chin*

360 *chin* at 26 *fen* per *chin*

Total of Anise: 1,500 chin (1,995 lbs. avoirdupois)

Tobacco Balls

751 *bakcha*[7] at 8 *fen* per *bakcha*

Various Medicants

1,002 *liang* (Mexican baum, quinine [?])

Miscellaneous

Silk Curtains and Tapestries: 70 at 2 *liang* 40 *fen* to 50 *liang* each

Silk Counterpanes: 4 at 1 *liang* 50 *fen* to 4 *liang* each

Cushions: 2 at 2 and 3 *liang*

Silk Jackets (*Kaftan*): 3 at 1 to 2 liang each

Untanned Ox-Skins: 205 at 1 *liang* each

Pearls: 31 *liang* (i.e. Chinese ounces here, 1/16th of a *chin*) at 3 *liang* 50 *fen*, 3.88 and 3.89 *liang* per Chinese ounce, and 350,000 pearls at 30 *fen* per 1,000

4. Russian measures for Chinese cottons were usually three: the bale *(tiun')*, the end *(konets)*, and the aune *(ell)*. A *tiun'* was on the average seventeen arshins or 38.0 yards; a *konets*, one-tenth of a *tiun'*; and an *ell*, one-hundredth of a *tiun'*; *ibid.*, pp. 115-16.

5. The Chinese *liang* was basically a unit of weight, and by extension the weight of gold or silver. The unit used throughout this account—except here in the weight of gold—is the silver *liang* which was employed in commerce at the time (otherwise known as "khanish silver" and minted by the Manchu imperial treasury; it was worth one-tenth more than "commercial silver"). The ratio between silver and gold was ten or twelve and one-half to one.

6. A *chin* or "Chinese pound," also a catty, was considered to be one and one-third pounds avoidupois for tariff purposes.

7. A *bakcha* was about one Russian pound, 0.90 pounds avoirdupois.

Total Value of Russian and Chinese Goods Exchanged

In Peking markets	152,534	*liang*	49	*fen*
In Mongolia on the road	7,462	liang	90	*fen*

Taking 1 *liang* as roughly equal to I ruble 40 kopeks at this time, the total value of goods and precious metals exchanged was 221,325 rubles 31 kopeks, plus 145,120 rubles 74 kopeks in sales and exchanges at Kiakhta (through the year 1729 when Lange was ordered to Moscow with the caravan account books), or a grand total of 366,446 rubles 5 kopeks.

Bibliography

Bibliography

Primary Sources

Manuscripts

Gosudarstvennyi Arkhiv Irkutskoi Oblasti (GAIO), *fond* 67, *op.* 1, *ed. khr.* 2, *l.* 75, Spisok s ukaza Senata o razreshenii oberinspektoru Shemiakinu . . . , 24 January 1761.

——. *fond* 67, *op.* 1, *ed. khr.* 5, *l.* 131, Ukaz sibirskogo gubernatora general-maiora Iakobi . . . , 1766.

——. *fond* 67, *op.* 1, *ed. khr.* 9, *ll.* 558-566, Delo po kontraktu ustiugskogo kuptsa Nikolaia Strogova . . . , 1768.

——. *fond* 67, *op.* 1, *ed. khr.* 10, *ll.* 107-108, Ukaz gubernatora Irkutskoi gubernii A. D. Brilia o poriadke ukladki kitaiskikh tovarov . . . , 1769.

——. *fond* 67, *op.* 1, *d.* 25, *l.* 158, Ukaz irkutskogo gubernskogo magistrata irkutskikh zemskikh del starostam . . . , 1780.

Tsentral'nyi Gosudarstvennyi Arkhiv Drevnikh Aktov (TsGADA), Selenginskaia gorodovaia ratusha, *fond* 1801, *ed. khr.* 8, *ll.* 1-1a, Ukaz Selenginskoi voevodskoi kantseliarii o vydache deneg . . . , 8 January 1735.

——. *fond* 1801, *ed. khr.* 8, *ll.* 7-7a, Donoshenie Selenginskogo distrikta v Selenginskuiu zemskuiu izbu o vydache deneg . . . , 7 February 1735.

——. *fond* 1801, *ed. khr.* 8, *ll.* 115-115a, Ukaz Irkutskoi ratushi Selenginskoi zemskoi izbe o zapreshchenii prodazhi za granitsu porokha i svintsa, 27 February 1725.

——. *fond* 1801, *ed. khr.* 8, *l.* 102, Postanovlenie Selenginskoi zemskoi uzby o predostavlenii podvod dlia perevozki kitaiskikh torvarov, 27 March 1735.

——. *fond* 1801, *ed. khr.* 8, *l.* 103a, Vedenie A. Parshevnikova v Selenginskuiu zemskuiu izbu ob otpravke 30 podvod . . . , 28 March 1735.

——. *fond* 1801, *ed. khr.* 8, *l* 104, Donoshenie iz Selenginskoi zemskoi izby v Selenginskuiu voevodskuiu kantseliariiu ob otpravke 30 podvod dlia perevozki kitaiskikh tovarov, 29 March 1735.

——. *fond* 1801, *ed. khr.* 8, *ll.* 125-125a, Ukaz Irkutskoi ratushi Selenginskoi izbe o vydache deneg . . . , March, 1735.

——. *fond* 1801, *ed. khr.* 8, *ll.* 229-229a, Ukaz Irkutskoi ratushi

Selenginskoi zemskoi izbe o zapreshchenii vyvoza russkikh mekhov v Kitai . . . , 29 April 1735.

——. *fond* 1801, *ed. khr.* 8, *ll.* 210-210a, Ukaz Selenginskoi voevodskoi kantseliarii Selenginskoi ratushe o predostavlenii deneg na zakupku loshadei i verbliudov . . . , 3 June 1735.

——. *fond* 1801, *ed. khr.* 8, *l.* 211, Prigovor Selenginskoi zemskoi izby o predostavlenii deneg . . . , 3 June 1735.

——. *fond* 1801, *ed. khr.* 8, *ll.* 212-212a, Donoshenie Selenginskoi ratushi v Selenginskuiu voevodskuiu kantseliariiu o predostavlenii deneg na zakupku loshadei i verbliudov . . . , 9 June 1735.

——. *fond* 1801, *ed. khr.* 8, *ll.* 290-end, Perepiska mezhdu Selenginskoi voevodskoi kantseliariei i Selenginskoi zemskoi izboi o zakupke loshadei i verbliudov . . . , 25 July 1735.

——. *fond* 1801, *ed. khr.* 16, *ll.* 3-3a, Ukaz Selenginskoi voevodskoi kantseliarii o vydache zhalovan'ia litsam . . . , January, 1740.

——. *fond* 1801, *ed. khr.* 16, *ll.* 65-65a, Donoshenie Selenginskoi zemskoi izby o vydache deneg . . . , 8 February 1740.

——. *fond* 1801, *ed. khr.* 16, *ll.* 65a, Donoshenie Selenginskogo distrikta o vydache deneg P. Sizovu . . . , 22 February 1740.

—— *fond* 1801, *ed. khr.* 8, *ll.* 229-300a, 318-318a, Ukazy Irkutskoi ratushi i Selenginskoi voevodskoi kantseliarii ob organizatsii kompanii . . . , 9 August 1740.

——. *fond* 1801, *ed. khr.* 8, *l.* 185, Ukaz Pogranichnoi ekspeditsii po promemorii direktora kitaiskogo karavana Vladykina . . . , 17 May 1754.

——. *fond* 1801, *ed. khr.* 37, *ll.* 424-425, Ukaz irkutskogo magistrata Selenginskoi ratushe ob izmenenii razmera poshliny . . . , 30 September 1754.

——. *fond* 1801, *ed. khr.* 37, *l.* 169a, Ukaz irkutskogo magistrata Selenginskoi ratushe ob obiazatel'nom proezde kuptsov . . . , 22 March 1755.

——. *fond* 1801, *ed. khr.* 89, *l.* 448a, Ukaz irkutskogo gubernskogo magistrata Selenginskoi ratushe o sobliudenii ustanovlennykh druzhestvennykh otnoshenii, 27 August 1769.

——. *fond* 1801, *ed. khr.* 84, *ll.* 146-148a, Vypiska iz postanovleniia Selenginskoi ratushi ob uchastii zhitelei goroda . . . , 14 October 1768.

Printed Sources

Archives diplomatiques, recueil mensuel de diplomatie, d'histoire et de droit internationale. 54 vols. in 144. Paris: Amyot, 1861-1914.

Bantysh-Kamenskii, Nikolai Nikolaevich. *Diplomaticheskoe sobranie del mezhdu rossiiskim i kitaiskim gosudarstvami s 1619 po 1792-oi god, Sostavlennoe po dokumentam, khraniashchimsia v Moskovskom arkhive Gosudarstvennoi kollegii inostrannykh del, v 1792-1803 godu.* Kazan': Tipografiia Imperatorskago Universiteta, 1882. Bantysh-Kamenskii, a protégé of G. F. Müller, succeeded him as Head Archivist of these Archives.

Bell, John, of Antermony. *Travels from St. Petersburg in Russia, to divers Parts of Asia.* 2 vols. Glasgow: Robert & Andrew Foulis, 1763. Many later editions, including that in John Pinkerton's *A General Collection,* VII, 271-516, which incorporates the account of Lange (see below). Also available in a new edition, with an introduction by J. L. Stevenson (Edinburgh: The University Press, 1965).

Bol'shakov, Anton Mikhailovich and Nikolai Aleksandrovich Rozhkov. *Istoriia khoziaistva Rossii v materialakh i dokumentakh.* 2d ed., rev. and enl., 3 vols. Leningrad: Gosudarstvennoe Izd., 1925.

Buckinghamshire, John Hobart, Second Earl of. *The Despatches and Correspondence of John Hobart, Second Earl of Buckinghamshire, Ambassador to the Court of Catherine II. of Russia 1762-1765.* Edited for the Royal Historical Society by Adelaide D'Arcy Collyer. ("Royal Historical Society, Camden Series," 3rd series, 1 & 2.) 2 vols. London: Offices of the Society, 1900-1902.

Catherine II. *Bumagi imperatritsy Ekateriny II, khraniashchikhsia v Gosudarstvennom arkhive Ministerstva inostrannykh del.* Comp. and ed. Petr Pekarskii. 3 vols. in 2. St. Petersburg: Tip. I. Akademii Nauk, 1871-74. Reprinted from *Sbornik RIO,* vols. 7, 10, 13, 27, 42.

———. *Nakaz Eia imperatorskago velichestva Ekateriny vtoryia, samoderzhitsy vserossiiskiia, dannyi Komissii o sochinenii proekta novago ulozheniia.* St. Petersburg: Pri Imperatorskoi Akademii Nauk, 1770. Added title pages in Latin, German, and French; text in all four languages. An English translation done in 1768 by "Michael Tatischeff" may be found in *Documents of Catherine the Great, The Correspondence with Voltaire and the* Instruction *of 1767 in the English Text of 1768.* Ed. William Fiddian Reddaway. Cambridge: The University Press, 1931. Pp. 215-309.

Chappe d'Auteroche, Jean. *A Journey into Siberia, by Order of the King of France. Containing an Account of the manners and Customs of the Russians, the Present State of Their Empire, with the Natural History, and Geographical Description of Their Country, and Level of the Road from Paris to Tobolsky.* Trans. from the French. London: T. Jefferys, 1770.

Original: *Voyage en Sibérie, fait par ordre du roi en 1761. . . .* 2 vols. in 3, plus atlas. Paris: Debure, père, 1768.

China, Inspectorate General of Customs at Shanghai, Statistical Department. *Treaties, Conventions, Etc., Between China and Foreign States.* 2d ed. Shanghai: Customs, 1917. First edition published in 1908 in 2 vols.

Cook, John. *Voyages and Travels Through the Russian Empire, Tartary, and Part of the Kingdom of Persia.* 2 vols. Edinburgh: Printed for the author, 1770.

Diplomaticheskaia perepiska angliiskikh poslov i poslannikov pri russkom dvore. . . . Soobshcheno iz angliiskago Gosudarstvennago arkhiva i Arkhiva Ministerstva inostrannykh del. Title varies. In *Sbornik RIO,* vols. 12, 19, 39, 50, 61, 66, 76, 80, 85, 91, 99, 102, 103, 110.

Diplomaticheskaia perepiska frantsuzskikh predstavitelei pri dvore Ekateriny II. . . . In *Sbornik RIO,* vols. 140, 141, 143.

Diplomaticheskaia perepiska Imperatritsy Ekateriny II. . . . In *Sbornik RIO,* vols. 48, 51, 57, 67, 87, 97, 118, 135.

Dobell, Peter. *Travels in Kamtchatka and Siberia; With a Narrative of a Residence in China.* 2 vols. London: Henry Colburn & Richard Bentley, 1830.

Doneseniia frantsuzskago poverennago po delam pri russkom dvore. . . . In *Sbornik RIO,* vols. 34, 40, 49, 52, 58, 64, 75, 81, 86, 92, 96, 100, 105.

Dvorianskaia imperiia XVIII veka (osnovnye zakonodatel'nye akty), Sbornik dokumentov. Comp. Mikhail Timofeevich Beliavskii. Moscow: Izdatel'stvo Moskovskogo Universiteta, 1960.

Firsov, Nikolai Nikolaevich (comp.). *Chteniia po istorii Sibiri.* 2 vols. Moscow: Izd. Russkogo Bibliograficheskogo Instituta Br. A. i I. Granat i Ko., 1920-21. *Vypusk* 1 originally published in 1915.

Fortia de Piles, Alphonse Toussaint Joseph André Marie Marseille, comte de. *Voyage de deux Français en Allemagne, Danemarck, Suède, Russie et Pologne, fait en 1790-1792.* 5 vols. Paris: Chez Desenne, Imprimeur-Libraire, 1796. Vols. 3 and 4 are devoted to Russia. Also in Pinkerton's *A General Collection,* VI, 373-569.

Fries, Jakob. *Eine Reise durch Sibirien im XVIII Jahrhundert. Die Fahrt des Schweizer Doktors Jakob Fries.* Eingeleitet, herausgegeben und mit bibliographischen Anmerkungen versehen von Walther Kirchner. Munich: Isar Verlag, 1955.

Fu Lo-shu (comp. and trans.). *A Documentry Chronicle of Sino-Western Relations (1644-1820).* 2 vols. ("The Association for

Asian Studies: Monographs and Papers," 22.) Tucson: The University of Arizona Press, 1966. See also the same author's *A Documentary Chronicle of the Celestial Empire; Sino-Western Relations as Revealed in Chinese Sources.* 8 vols. N.p., 1962-63. Typescript. The latter is particularly useful for the many illustrations.

Georgi, Johann Gottlieb. *Russia: or, A Compleat Historical Account of all the Nations which compose that Empire.* Trans. from the German by the Rev. William Tooke. 4 vols. London: Printed for J. Nichols, 1780-83.

Gmelin, Johann Georg. "Voyage au Kamtschatka par la Siberie. Journal de M. Gmelin, traduit de l'Allemand," *Histoire génèrale des voyages.* Ed. Antoine François Prevost. 20 vols. Paris: Rozet, 1746-91. Vol. XVIII, 72-483. Originally published in Göttingen, 1751-52, in 4 vols. in 2. English trans. published in Haarlem, 1752-57, in 4 vols.

Ides, Evert Ysbrandszoon. *Three Years Travels from Moscow Over-land to China: Thro' Great Ustiga, Siriania, Permia, Sibiria, Daour, Great Tartary, &c. to Peking. Containing, An Exact and Particular Description of the Extent and Limits of those Countries. . . .* London: Printed for W. Freeman, J. Walthoe, T. Newborough, J. Nicholson, and R. Parker, 1706. First Dutch edition published in Amsterdam in 1704.

Iuzefovich. T. *Dogovory Rossii s Vostokom, politicheskie torgovye.* St. Petersburg: Tip. O. I. Baksta, 1869.

Krasheninnikov, Stepan Petrovich. *Opisanie zemli Kamchatki, s prilozheniem raportov, donesenii i drugikh neopublikovannykh materialov.* Moscow: Izdatel'stvo Glavsevmorputi, 1949. Originally published in St. Petersburg in 1755. Abridged English translation by James Grieve printed in Gloucester in 1764; reissued by Quadrangle Books in 1962.

Kruzenshtern, Ivan Fedorovich (Adam Johann von Krusenstern). *Voyage Round the World, in the Years 1803, 1804, 1805, and 1806, by Order of His Imperial Majesty Alexander the First, on Board the Ships "Nadezhda" and "Neva," under the command of Captain A. J. von Krusenstern, of the Imperial Navy.* Trans. Richard Belgrave Hoppner, 2 vols. in 1. London: John Murray, 1813. Original German edition published in St. Petersburg, 1810-14, in 3 vols. plus atlas.

Ku-kung O-wen shih-liao, Ch'ing-K'ang ch'ien-chien E-kuo lai-wen yuan-tang. Trans. Wang Chih-hsiang; comp. Liu Tse-jung. Peiping: National Palace Museum, 1936. Added Russian title: *Arkhivnye materialy na russkom iazyke iz byvshego pekinskogo imperatorskogo dvortsa, Pis'ma, poluchennye iz Rossii v gody tsarstvovanii Kan-si i Tsian-lun.* Added English title: *Documents in Russian Preserved in the National Palace Museum of Peiping, Kanghsi-Chienlung Period.*

Kurdiukov, I. F. (comp.). "Iz istorii russko-kitaiskikh otnoshenii (1695-1720 gg.)," *Istoricheskii arkhiv,* No. 3 (May-June, 1957), 174-84.

Lange, Lorents. "Dnevnyia zapiski karavannomu puti chrez naunskuiu dorogu ot Tsurukhaitu do Pekina, 1736 godu," *Akademicheskiia izvestiia na 1781 god,* Chast' 7 (April, 1781), 466-505; Chast' 8 (June, 1781), 602-31.

———. "A Journal from St. Petersburg in Russia, to Pekin in China, with an Embassy from His Imperial Majesty, Peter the First, to Kamhi Emperor of China, in the year 1719," and "Journal of the Residence of Mr. de Lange, Agent of His Imperial Majesty of All the Russias, Peter the First, at the Court of Pekin, During the Years 1721 and 1722," in John Bell of Antermony. "Travels from St. Petersburg in Russia, To Various Parts of Asia, in 1716, 1719, 1722 &c.," in John Pinkerton. *A General Collection of the Best and Most Interesting Voyages and Travels in All Parts of the World.* 7 vols. London: Longman, Hurst, Rees, Orme, and Brown, and Cadell and Davies, 1811. Vol. VII, 318-434, 435-84. This version of Lange's accounts translated by John Bell and published in Glasgow in 1763. It is presumably Lange's corrected and revised version intended to replace that published in Friedrich Christian Weber. *The Present State of Russia.* Trans. from the High Dutch. 2 vols. London: W. Taylor, 1723. Vol. II, 3-35. Published in Russian in *Severnyi arkhiv* in 1822.

———. *Le livre de comptes de la caravane Russe à Pékin en 1727-1728.* Trans. and commentary by Gaston Cahen. Paris: Félix Alcan, 1911.

Ledyard, John. *John Ledyard's Journey Through Russia and Siberia, 1787-1788; The Journal and Selected Letters.* Ed. with an introduction by Stephen D. Watrous. Madison: The University of Wisconsin Press, 1966.

Lisianskii, Iurii Fedorovich. *Puteshestvie vokrug sveta v 1803, 4, 5, i 1806 godakh, po poveleniiu ego Imperatorskogo velichestva Aleksandra Pervago, na korable Neve.* 2 vols. St. Petersburg: F. Drekhsler, 1812. Reprinted in Moscow (OGIZ, Geografgiz) in one volume in 1947.

Macartney, Sir George. *An Embassy to China, Being the Journal Kept by Lord Macartney During His Embassy to the Emperor Ch'ien-lung, 1793-1794.* Ed. J. L. Cranmer-Byng. Hamden, Conn.: Archon Books, 1963.

Maki, John M. (comp.). *Selected Documents, Far Eastern International Relations (1689-1951)*. Seattle: University of Washington, 1951. Photolithographic edition.

Martens, Fedor Fedorovich (ed.). *Recueil des traites et conventions conclus par la Russie avec les puissances étrangères*. 15 vols. in 8. St. Petersburg: Impr. du Ministère des Voies de Communication (A. Böhnke), 1874-1905.

Mavor, William. *An Historical Account of the Most Celebrated Voyages, Travels, and Discoveries, From the Time of Columbus to the Present Period*. 24 vols. Philadelphia: Samuel F. Bradford, 1803.

Mayers, William Frederick (ed.). *Treaties Between the Empire of China and Foreign Powers, Together with Regulations for the Conduct of Foreign Trade, Conventions, Agreements, Regulations Etc.* 5th ed. Shanghai: North-China Herald, Ltd., 1906.

Messerschmidt, Daniel Gottlieb. *Forschungsreise durch Sibirien, 1720-1727*. Ed. E. Winter, G. Uschmann and G. Jarosch. 4 vols. to date. ("Quellen und Studien zur Geschichte Osteuropas," Bd. 8, Teil 1-4). Berlin: Akademie-Verlag, 1962–.

Morse, Hosea Ballou (ed.). *The Chronicles of the East India Company, Trading to China, 1635-1834*. 5 vols. Oxford: The Clarendon Press, 1926-29.

"Neskol'ko svedenii o Fedore Ivanoviche Soimonove, byvshem sibirskim gubernatore," ed. Nikolai Abramov, *Chteniia OIDR*, Bk. 3 (1865).

"O posol'stve v Kitai grafa Golovkina," ed. Vasilii Nikolaevich Basnin, *Chteniia OIDR*, Bk. 4 (October-December, 1875), 1-103.

Ogloblin, Nikolai Nikolaevich. *Obozrenie stolbtsov i knig sibirskago prikaza (1592-1768 gg.)*. 4 vols. Moscow: Universitetskaia Tipografiia, 1895-1900.

Pallas, Peter Simon. *A Naturalist in Russia, Letters from Peter Simon Pallas to Thomas Pennant*. Ed. Carol Urness. Minneapolis: The University of Minnesota Press, 1967.

———. *Voyages de M. P. S. Pallas, en différentes provinces de l'empire de Russie, et dans l'Asie septentrionale*. Trans. Gauthier de la Peyronie. 5 vols. plus atlas. Paris: Maradan, 1788-93. Original German edition published in St. Petersburg in 3 vols., 1771-76.

Paul, Robert (ed.). "Letters and Documents Relating to Robert Erskine, Physician to Peter the Great, Czar of Russia, 1677-1720," *Publications of the Scottish History Society*, 44; Mis-

cellany (Second Volume) of the Society (February, 1904), 371-430.
"Perevod s dvukh kitaiskikh listov, prislannyi pri donosheniiakh v Kollegiiu inostrannykh del ot sibirskogo gubernatora ot 1758 g.," ed. and trans. Nikolai Abramov, *Chteniia OIDR,* Bk. 4 (1868), Pt. 5, Smes', 6-14.
Pinkerton, John. *A General Collection of the Best and Most Interesting Voyages and Travels in All Parts of the World; Many of Which are Now First Translated into English.* 17 vols. London: Longman, Hurst, Rees, Orme, and Brown, 1808-14.
Pososhkov, Ivan Tikhonovich. *Kniga o skudosti i bogatstve, i drugie sochineniia.* Edited with a commentary by B. B. Kafengauz. Moscow: Izd. Akademii Nauk SSSR, 1951.
Radishchev, Aleksandr Nikolaevich. "Pis'ma Aleksandra Nikolaevicha Radishcheva k grafu A. R. Vorontsovu, 1782-1800," *Arkhiv kniazia Vorontsova.* Kniga 5: *Bumagi grafa Aleksandra Romanovicha Vorontsova.* Moscow: Tip. V. Got'e, 1872. Chast' 1, pp. 284-374.
———. *Polnoe sobranie sochinenii.* 3 vols. Moscow: Izd. Akademii Nauk SSSR, 1938-52.
Ripa, Matteo. *Memoirs of Father Ripa, During Thirteen Years' Residence at the Court of Peking in the Service of the Emperor of China.* Selected and translated from the Italian by Fortunato Prando. New ed. London: John Murray, 1855.
Russia. Arkheograficheskaia Komissiia. *Pamiatniki sibirskoi istorii XVIII veka.* 2 vols. St. Petersburg: Tip. Ministerstva Vnutrennykh Del, 1882-85.
———. Departament Tamozhennykh Sborov. *Sbornik svedenii po istorii i statistike vneshnei torgovli Rossii.* Ed. V. I. Pokrovskii. Vol. I: *Ocherk istorii vneshnei torgovli Rossii.—Otpusk i privoz tovarov v XIX stoletii.—Tablitsy otpuska, privoza i tamozhennykh dokhodov.* St. Petersburg: Tipo-litografiia M. P. Frolovoi, 1902.
———. Departament Tamozhennykh Sborov. Statisticheskoe Otdelenie. *Statisticheskiia svedeniia o torgovle Rossii s Kitaem.* St. Petersburg: Tipo-litografiia M. P. Frolovoi, 1909.
———. Gosudarstvennyi Sovet. *Arkhiv Gosudarstvennago soveta.* 5 vols. in 16. St. Petersburg: Tip. Vtorago Otdeleniia Sobstvennoi E. I. V. Kantseliarii, 1869-1904.
———. Imperatorskaia Kantseliariia. *Polnoe sobranie zakonov rossiiskoi imperii s 1649 goda,* First Series: 1649-1825. 46 vols. in 48, plus 3 Appendices. St. Petersburg: Pechatano v Tipografii II Otdeleniia Sobstvennoi Ego Imperatorskago Velichestva Kantseliarii, 1830. Cited as *PSZ.*

———. Imperatorskoe Russkoe Istoricheskoe Obshchestvo. *Sbornik Imperatorskago russkago istoricheskago obshchestva.* 148 vols. St. Petersburg, 1867-1916. Cited as *Sbornik RIO.*

———. Imperatorskoe Russkoe Geograficheskoe Obshchestvo. Statisticheskoe Otdelenie. *Sbornik statisticheskikh svedenii o Rossii.* (*Trudy* of the Society.) 3 vols. St. Petersburg, 1851-58.

———. Kabinet Ministrov. *Bumagi Kabineta ministrov imperatritsy Anny Ioannovny, 1731-1740 gg.* Comp. and ed. A. N. Filippov. In *Sbornik RIO,* vols. 104, 106, 108, 111, 114, 117, 120, 124, 126, 130, 138.

———. Ministerstvo Inostrannykh Del. *Sbornik dogovorov Rossii s Kitaem, 1689–1881 gg.* St. Petersburg: Tip. I. Akademii Nauk, 1889.

———. Ministerstvo Inostrannykh Del SSSR. *Vneshniaia politika Rossii XIX i nachala XX veka, Dokumenty rossiiskogo Ministerstva inostrannykh del.* Series I: *1801-1815 gg.* Vol. I: *Mart 1801 g.—aprel' 1804 g.* (1960). Vol. II: *Aprel' 1804 g.—dekabr' 1805 g.* (1961). Moscow: Gospolitizdat, 1960–.

———. Ministerstvo Kommertsii. *Gosudarstvennaia torgovlia . . . goda v raznykh eia vidakh.* St. Petersburg: Pri Imperatorskoi Tipografii, 1802–. Title and publisher vary for subsequent years. In time the title stabilized as *Obzor vneshnei torgovli Rossii po evropeiskoi i aziatskoi granitsam.* Also *Tableaux du commerce de l'Empire de Russie. Années 1802, 1803, 1804, 1805.* Trans. Fr. Pfeiffer. St. Petersburg: F. Drechsler, 1808.

———. Ministerstvo Vnutrennykh Del. *Statisticheskoe obozrenie Sibiri, sostavlennoe na osnovanii svedenii pocherpnutnykh iz aktov pravitel'stva i drugikh dostovernykh istochnikov.* St. Petersburg: Tipografiia Shnora, 1810.

———. Ministerstvo Inostrannykh Del. *Svod mezhdunarodnykh postanovlenii, opredeliaiushchikh vzaimnyia otnosheniia mezhdu Rossieiu i Kitaem, 1689-1897.* St. Petersburg: Tip. V. F. Kirshbauma, 1900.

———. Ministerstvo Torgovli i Promyshlennosti. *Sbornik torgovykh dogovorov zakliuchennykh Rossieiu s inostrannymi gosudarstvami.* Ed. Nikolai Vladimirovich Verkhovskii. St. Petersburg: Izd. Otdela Torgovli, Tip. V. F. Kirshbauma, 1912.

———. Moskovskii Universitet. Obshchestvo Istorii i Drevnostei Rossiiskikh. *Chteniia v Imperatorskom Obshchestve istorii i drevnostei rossiiskikh pri Moskovskom universitete.* Title varies. 264 vols. Moscow, 1846-1918. Cited as *Chteniia OIDR.*

———. Pravitel'stvuiushchii Senat. *Senatskii arkhiv.* 15 vols. St. Petersburg: Senatskaia Tip., 1888-1913.

———. Verkhovnyi Tainyi Sovet. *Protokoly, zhurnaly i ukazy Verk-*

hovnago tainago soveta, 1726-1730. Ed. N. F. Dubrovin. In *Sbornik RIO*, vols. 55, 56, 63, 69, 79, 84, 94, 101.

Russian Discoveries in the Pacific and in North America in the Eighteenth and Nineteenth Centuries; A Collection of Materials. Ed. Aleksandr Ignat'evich Andreev. Trans. Carl Ginsburg. Ann Arbor: Published for the American Council of Learned Societies by J. W. Edwards, 1952. A translation of *Russkie otkrytiia v Tikhom okeane i Severnoi Amerike v XVIII–XIX vekakh, Sbornik materialov.* Moscow: Izd. Akademii Nauk SSSR, 1944. A second edition bears the slightly altered title *Russkie otkrytiia v Tikhom okeane i Severnoi Amerike v XVIII veke.* Moscow: OGIZ, Gos. Izd. Geograficheskoi Literatury, 1948.

Russko-kitaiskie otnosheniia, 1689-1916, Ofitsial'nye dokumenty. Comp. Petr Emil'ianovich Skachkov and Vladimir Stepanovich Miasnikov. Moscow: Izd. Vostochno Literatury, 1958.

Sarychev, Gavrila Andreevich. *Account of a Voyage of Discovery to the North-East of Siberia, The Frozen Ocean, & the North-East Sea.* 2 vols. in 1. London: Printed for Richard Phillips by J. G. Barnard, 1806-7. Most recent Russian edition is *Puteshestvie po severo-vostochnoi chasti Sibiri, Ledovitomu moriu i Vostochnomu okeanu.* Moscow: Gos. Izd. Geograficheskoi Literatury, 1952.

Sauer, Martin. *An Account of a Geographical and Astronomical Expedition to the Northern Parts of Russia for Ascertaining the Degree of Latitude and Longitude of the Mouth of the River Lena. . . . Performed by Command of Her Imperial Majesty Catherine II, by J. Billings in the Years 1785-1794.* London: T. Cadell, jun., 1800.

Sbornik pogranichnykh dogovorov, zakliuchennykh Rossiei s sosednimi gosudarstvami. St. Petersburg: Tip. Trenke i Fiusno, 1891.

Sbornik ukazov po monetnomu i medal'nomu delu v Rossii pomeshchennykh v Polnom sobranii zakonov s 1649 po 1881 g. Comp. M. Demmeni. Published by Grand Duke Georgii Mikhailovich. 3 vols. St. Petersburg, 1887.

Staunton, Sir George Thomas (trans.). *Narrative of the Chinese Embassy to the Khan of the Tourgouth Tartars, in the Years 1712, 13, 14, & 15; by the Chinese Ambassador, and Published, by the Emperor's Authority, at Pekin.* London: John Murray, 1821.

Strahlenberg, Philip Johan Tabbert von. *An Historico-Geographical Description of the North and Eastern Parts of Europe and Asia; but more Particularly of Russia, Siberia, and Great Tar-*

tary; Both in their Ancient and Modern State: Together with an Entire New Polyglot-Table of the Dialects of 32 Tartarian Nations. . . . Trans. from the German. London: W. Innys and R. Manby, 1738. Originally published in 2 vols. in Stockholm in 1730.

Sychevskii. "Istoricheskaia zapiska o kitaiskoi granitse, Sostavlennaia sovetnikom Troitsko-Savskogo pogranichnogo pravleniia Sychevskim v 1846 g.," ed. V. N. Basnin, *Chteniia OIDR*, Bk. 2 (April-June, 1875), 1-292.

Timkowski, George. *Travels of the Russian Mission Through Mongolia to China, and Residence in Peking, in the Years 1820-21.* With corrections and notes by Julius von Klaproth. Trans. H. E. Lloyd. 2 vols. London: Longman, Rees, Orme, Brown, and Green, 1827.

Vockerodt, Johann G. *Rossiia pri Petre Velikom, po rukopisnomu izvestiiu Ioanna Gottgil'fa Fokkerodta.* Trans. from the German by A. N. Shemiakin. In *Chteniia OIDR*, Bk. 2 (April-June, 1874), Pt. IV (Materialy inostrannye), 1-120. Excerpted in Bol'shakov and Rozhkov, *Istoriia khoziaistva*, II, 32-37.

"Zhurnal druzheskago svidaniia irkutskago grazhdanskago gubernatora, deistvitel'nago statskago sovetnika Treskina, s kitaiskimi pogranichnymi praviteliami, vanom i ambanem, s 19-go fevralia po 13 marta 1810 goda," *Chteniia OIDR*, Bk. 1 (1860), 167-250.

Vladislavich-Raguzinskii, Sava Lukich. "Sila advantazha rossiiskago imperiia vo vruchennoi mne komissii pri dvore kitaiskom," part of "Protokoly, zhurnaly i ukazy Verkhovnago tainago soveta," VII (January-June, 1729), in *Sbornik RIO*, XCIV (1894), 424-26.

———. "Graf Vladislavich o Kitae v XVIII veke," *Russkii arkhiv*, XXXVIII, Pt. (1900), 572-80. Notes composed in 1730.

Secondary Works

Books

Akademicheskiia izvestiia, Soderzhashchiia v sebe istoriiu nauk i noveishiia otkrytiia onykh. 8 chasti in 31 books. St. Petersburg: Pri S. Peterburgskoi Imp. Akademii Nauk, 1779-81.

Amburger, Erik. *Geschichte der Behördenorganisation Russlands von Peter dem Grossen bis 1917.* ("Studien zur Geschichte Osteuropas," 10.) Leiden: E. J. Brill, 1966.

Anderson, Adam. *An Historical and Chronological Deduction of the Origin of Commerce, From the Earliest Accounts.* Revised ed. 4 vols. London: Printed for J. White, 1801.

Andreev, Aleksandr Ignat'evich. *Ocherki po istochnikovedeniiu Sibiri.* Vypusk I: *XVII vek.* 2d ed. rev. and enl. Leningrad: Izd. Akademii Nauk SSSR, Leningradskoe Otdelenie, 1960. Vypusk 2: *XVIII vek (pervaia polovina).* Moscow-Leningrad: Izd. "Nauka," 1965.

Andrievich, Vladimir Kalistratovich. *Istoriia Sibiri.* 2 vols. St. Petersburg: Tip. V. V. Komarova, 1889.

———. *Kratkii ocherk istorii Zabaikal'ia ot drevneishikh vremen do 1762 goda.* St. Petersburg: Voennaia Tipografiia, 1887.

Armstrong, Terence E. *Russian Settlement in the North.* ("Scott Polar Research Institute, Special Publication," 3.) Cambridge: The University Press, 1965.

Arsen'ev, Vladimir Klavdievich. *Russen und Chinesen in Ostsibirien.* Trans. Franz Daniel. Berlin: August Scherl, 1926.

Atkinson, Lucy. *Recollections of the Tartar Steppes and Their Inhabitants.* London: John Murray, 1863.

Baburin, Dmitrii. *Ocherki po istorii Manufaktur kollegii.* ("Trudy Istoriko-arkhivnogo Instituta," 1.) Moscow: Glavnoe Arkhivnoe Upravlenie NKVD SSSR, 1939.

Baddeley, John F. *Russia, Mongolia, China. Being Some Record of the Relations Between Them from the Beginning of the XVIIth Century to the Death of the Tsar Alexei Mikhailovich, AD. 1602-1676, Rendered Mainly in the Form of Narratives Dictated or Written by the Envoys Sent by the Russian Tsar, or Their Voevodas in Siberia to the Kalmuk and Mongol Khans & Princes; and to the Emperors of China. . . .* 2 vols. London: Macmillan & Co., Ltd., 1919. Reprinted by Burt Franklin in 1963 in 2 vols.

Bantysh-Kamenskii, Dmitrii Nikolaevich. *Biografii rossiiskikh generalissimusov i general-fel'dmarshalov, s 48 portretami.* 2 vols. St. Petersburg: V Tipografii Tret'iago Departamenta Ministerstva Gosudarstvennykh Imushchestv, 1840-41.

———. *Deianiia znamenitykh polkovodtsev i ministrov, sluzhivshikh v tsarstvovanie gosudaria imperatora Petra Velikago.* 2 vols. in 1. Moscow: Tip. N. S. Vsevolozhskago, 1812-13. English translation issued in London in 1851 by T. C. Newby.

———. *Istoricheskoe sobranie spiskov kavaleram chetyrekh rossiiskikh imperatorskikh ordenov.* Moscow: V Tip. N. S. Vsevolozhskago, 1814.

———. *Slovar' dostopamiatnykh liudei russkoi zemli. . . .* 5 vols. plus 3 vols of supplements. Moscow, 1836–47.

Bantysh-Kamenskii, Nikolai Nikolaevich. *Obzor vneshnikh sno-*

shenii Rossii (po 1800 god). 4 pts. Moscow: Tipografiia E. Lissnera i Iu. Romana, 1894-1902.

Bartol'd, Vasilii Vladimirovich. *Four Studies on the History of Central Asia.* Trans. V. and T. Minorsky. Vol. 1: *A Short History of Turkestan* and *A History of the Semirechyé.* Leiden: E. J. Brill, 1956.

——. *Ocherk istorii Semirech'ia.* 2d ed. Frunze: Kirgizgosizdat, 1943.

——. *La découverte de l'Asie, Historie de l'orientalisme en Europe et en Russie.* Trans. and annotated by B. Nikitin. Paris: Payot, 1947.

Bates, Lindon Wallace. *The Russian Road to China.* Boston: Houghton Mifflin Co. 1910.

Belikov, Trofim Ivanovich. *Kalmyki v bor'be za nezavisimost' nashei rodiny (XVII–nachalo XIX vv.).* Elista: Kalmgosizdat, 1965.

Ber, Adol'f (Adolph Beer). *Istoriia vsemirnoi torgovli.* Trans. E. Tsimmerman. 3 vol. Moscow: Izdanie K. T. Soldatenkova, 1876.

Bobovicha, Irina Mikhailovna. *Lektsii po istorii narodnogo khoziaistva SSSR (epokha feodalizma).* Leningrad: Izd. Leningradskogo Universiteta, 1959.

Blinov, Iv. *Gubernatory, istoriko-iuridicheskii ocherk.* St. Petersburg: Tipo-litografiia K. L. Pentkovskago, 1905.

Bodnarskii, Mitrofan Stefanovich. *Slovar' geograficheskikh nazvanii,* 2d ed., rev. and enl. Moscow: Gos. Uchebno-Pedagogicheskoe Izd. Ministerstva Prosveshcheniia RSFSR, 1958.

Bol'shaia sovetskaia entsiklopediia. 2d ed. 51 vols. plus 2 vols. of index and annuals since 1957. Moscow: Gosudarstvennoe Nauchnoe Izdatel'stvo "Bol'shaia Sovetskaia Entsiklopediia," 1949-58.

Bolshakoff, Serge. *The Foreign Missions of the Russian Orthodox Church.* London: Society for Promoting Christian Knowledge, 1943.

Bray, William G. *Russian Frontiers: From Muscovy to Krushchev.* Indianapolis: The Bobbs-Merrill Co., Inc., 1963.

Brunnert, Hippolit Semenovich and V. V. Hagelstrom. *Present Day Political Organization of China.* Rev. N. Th. Kolessoff. Trans. A. Beltchenko and E. E. Moran. Shanghai: Kelly & Walsh, Ltd., 1912.

Bulgarin, Faddei Venediktovich. *Rossiia v istoricheskom, statisticheskom, geograficheskom i literaturnom otnosheniiakh.* 2 chasti. St. Petersburg: V Tipografii A. Pliusheva, 1837.

Cahen, Gaston. *Histoire des relations de la Russie avec la Chine sous Pierre le Grand, 1689-1730.* Paris: Félix Alcan, 1912. A partial English translation was made by W. Sheldon Ridge and published in *The National Review* (Shanghai) in 1913-14, under the title *Some Early Russo-Chinese Relations.* Photographically reprinted in 1967 by University Prints + Reprints.

———. "Les cartes de la Sibérie au XVIIIe siècle, Essai de bibliographie critique," *Nouvelles Archives des Missions scientifiques et litteraires, choix de rapports et instructions publié sous les auspices du Ministère de l'instruction publique et des beaux-arts.* New Series, Fascicule 1. Paris: Imprimerie Nationale, 1911.

Cammann, Schuyler. *Trade through the Himalayas; The Early British Attempts to Open Tibet.* Princeton: Princeton University Press, 1951.

Chen, Vincent. *Sino-Russian Relations in the Seventeenth Century.* The Hague: Martinus Nijhoff, 1966.

Ch'en Po-wen. *Chung-O wai-chiao shih.* Shanghai: Commercial Press, 1929-32.

Cheng Tien-fong. *A History of Sino-Russian Relations.* Washington: Public Affairs Press, 1957.

Chernevskii, Petr Osipovich (comp.). *Ukazatel' materialov dlia istorii torgovli, promyshlennosti i finansov, v predelakh rossiiskoi imperii. Ot drevneishikh vremen do kontsa XVIII stoletiia.* St. Petersburg: Tip. Imperatorskoi Akademii Nauk, 1883.

Chevnigny, Hector. *Russian America, The Great Alaskan Venture, 1741-1867.* New York: The Viking Press, 1965.

Ch'ing shih-kao. Ed. Chao Erh-hsun *et al.* 131 ts'e, 536 chuan, 20 han. Peking: Ch'ing-shih-kuan, 1928. Photo-reprint in 2 vols. (Hong Kong, 1960).

Chulkov, Mikhail Dimitrievich. *Istoricheskoe opisanie rossiiskoi kommertsii pri vsekh portakh i granitsakh ot drevnikh vremen do nyne nastoiashchego i vsekh preimushchestvennykh uzakonenii po onoi gosudaria imperatora Petra Velikago i nyne blagopoluchno tsarstvuiushchei gosudaryni imperatritsy Ekateriny Velikiia.* 21 vols. in 7. St. Petersburg: Pri Imp. Akademii Nauk, 1781-88.

———. *Slovar' uchrezhdennykh v Rossii iarmarok, izdannyi dlia obrashchaiushchikhsia v torgovle.* Moscow: V Tip. Ponamareva, 1778.

Clerc, Nicholas Gabriel (Le Clerc). *Histoire physique, morale, civile et politique de la Russie moderne par MM. Le Clerc pere [and] . . . Le Clerc fils.* 3 vols. (Paris: Froullé, 1783-94.

Cochrane, John Dundas. *Narrative of a Pedestrian Journey through*

Russia and Siberian Tartary, From the Frontiers of China to the Frozen Sea and Kamchatka; Performed During the Years 1820, 1821, 1822, and 1823. London: J. Murray, 1824.

Courant, Maurice Auguste Louis Marie. *L'Asie centrale aux XVIIe et XVIIIe siècles; Empire Kalmouk ou empire Mantchou?* Lyon: A. Rey, 1912.

Coxe, William. *Account of Russian Discoveries Between Asia and America, To Which are Added, The Conquest of Siberia, and the History of the Transactions and Commerce Between Russia and China.* London: T. Cadell, 1780. Also published in Pinkerton's *A General Collection,* IV, 215ff.

The Cyclopedia of Medicine, Surgery and Specialties. Ed. George Morris Piersol and others. 15 vols. plus index. Philadelphia: F. A. Davis Co., 1948.

Davidson-Houston, J. V. *Russia and China, From the Huns to Mao Tse-tung.* London: Robert Hale, Ltd., 1960.

Demidova, Natal'ia Fedorovna and Vladimir Stepanovich Miasnikov. *Pervye russkie diplomaty v Kitae ("Rospis'" I. Petlina i stateinyi spisok F. I. Baikova).* Moscow: Izd. "Nauka," 1966.

De Quincey, Thomas. "Revolt of the Tartars, Or, Flight of the Kalmuck Khan and His People from the Russian Territories to the Frontiers of China," in *Historical Essays and Researches.* Vol. VII of *The Collected Writings of Thomas De Quincey.* Ed. David Masson. London: A. & C. Black, 1897. Pp. 368-426.

Donner, Kai. *La Sibérie. La vie en Sibérie. Les temps anciens.* Trans. from the Finnish by Léon Froman. 2d ed. Paris: Gallimard, 1956.

Drew, Ronald Farinton. "Siberia: An Experiment in Colonialism, A Study of Economic Growth under Peter I." Unpublished Ph.D. dissertation, Stanford University, 1957.

Dučić, Jovan. *Jedan Srbin diplomat na dvoru Petra Velikog i Katarine I, grof Sava Vladislavich.* ("Sabrana dela", Bk. 10.) Beograd-Pittsburg, 1942.

Dukes, Paul. *Catherine the Great and the Russian Nobility, A Study Based on the Materials of the Legislative Commission of 1767.* Cambridge: The University Press, 1967.

Efimov, A. V. *Iz istorii velikikh russkikh geograficheskikh otkrytii v Severnom Ledovitom i Tikhom okeanakh XVII-i—pervaia polovina XVIII v.* Moscow: Gosudarstvennoe Izdatel'stvo Geograficheskoi Literatury, 1950. An earlier edition published in 1948 under the title *Iz istorii russkikh ekspeditsii na Tikhom okeane.*

Ekonomicheskaia istoriia SSSR, Uchebnik dlia ekonomicheskikh vuzov. Ed. I. S. Golubnichii, A. P. Pogrebinskii, and I. N.

Shemiakin. Moscow: Sotsekgiz, 1963. Chapters on the eighteenth century written by F. Ia. Polianskii and L. Ia. Fridberg.

Entsiklopedicheskii slovar'. 41 vols. St. Petersburg: Semenovskaia Tipo-Litografiia (I. A. Efrona), 1890-1904.

Erman, Adolph. *Travels in Siberia: Including Excursions Northwards, Down the Obi, to the Polar Circle, and, Southwards, to the Chinese Frontier.* Trans. from the German by William Desborough Cooley. 2 vols. Philadelphia: Lea & Blanchard, 1850.

Eroshkin, Nikolai Petrovich. *Ocherki istorii gosudarstvennykh uchrezhdenii dorevoliutsionnoi Rossii. Posobie dlia uchitelia.* Moscow: Gos. Uchebno-pedagogicheskoe Izdatel'stvo Ministerstva Prosveshcheniia RSFSR, 1960.

Fedorov, Aleksandr Fedorovich. *Istoriia vekselia, istoriko-iuridicheskoe izsledovanie.* ("Zapiski Imp. Novorossiiskogo Universiteta," 66.) Odessa: Tip. Shtaba Okruga, 1895.

Firsov, Nikolai Nikolaevich. *Pravitel'stvo i obshchestvo v ikh otnosheniiakh k vneshnei torgovle Rossii v tsarstvovanie imperatritsy Ekateriny II. Ocherki iz istorii torgovoi politiki.* Kazan': Tipo-litografiia Imperatorskago Universiteta, 1902.

———. *Russkiia torgovo-promyshlenyia kompanii v l-iu polovinu XVIII stoletiia (Ocherki iz istorii torgovo-promyshlennoi politiki i sootvetstvuiushchikh obshchestvennykh otnoshenii).* Kazan': Tipo-litografiia Imperaticheskago Universiteta, 1896.

Fisher, Raymond Henry. *The Russian Fur Trade, 1550-1700.* ("University of California Publications in History," 31.) Berkeley: University of California Press, 1943.

Formozov, Aleksandr Nikolaevich. *Sputnik sledopyta.* 7th ed. Moscow: Gos. Izd. Detskoi Literatury Ministerstva Prosveshcheniia RSFSR, 1959. An earlier edition was translated into French as *Manuel du trappeur, La faune des steppes et des forêts de Russie.* Paris, n.d.

Friebe, Wilhelm Christian. *Über Russlands Handel, Landwirthschaftliche Kultur, Industrie und Produkte; Nebst einigen Psysischen und Statistischen Bemerkungen.* 3 vols. Gotha: Gerstenberg und Dittmar, 1796-98.

Fu Lo-shu. "Sino-Western Relations During the K'ang-hsi Period, 1661-1722." Unpublished Ph.D. dissertation, University of Chicago, June, 1952.

Gagemeister, Iulii Andreevich (Julius Heinrich von Hagemeister). *Statisticheskoe obozrenie Sibiri,* Sostavlennoe po vysochaishemu ego imperatorskago velichestva poveleniiu, pri Sibirskom komitete, 3 vols. St. Petersburg: V Tipografii II Otdeleniia Sobstvennoi Ego Imperatorskago Velichestva Kantseliarii, 1854.

Giles, Herbert A. *A Chinese Biographical Dictionary.* London: Bernard Quaritch, 1898.

Gille, Bertrand. *Histoire économique et sociale de la Russie du moyen-âge au XXe siècle.* Paris: Payot, 1949.

Gilmour, James. *Among the Mongols.* New York: The American Tract Society, n.d.

Golovachev, Petr Mikhailovich. *Sibir' v ekaterinskoi komissii. Etiud po istorii Sibiri XVIII veka.* Moscow: Tip. V. F. Rikhter, 1889.

Gosudarstvennye uchrezhdeniia Rossii v XVIII veke (zakonodatel'nye materialy), Spravochnoe posobie, ed. Nikolai Petrovich Eroshkin. Issued by the Ministerstvo Vysshego i Srednego Spetsial'nogo Obrazovaniia RSRSR and the Moskovskii Gosudarstvennyi Istoriko-Arkhivnyi Institut. Prepared for publication by A. V. Chernov. Moscow, 1960.

Grumm-Grzhimailo, Grigorii Efimovich. *Zapadnaia Mongoliia i uriankhaiskii krai.* Leningrad: Izdanie Uchebnogo Komiteta Mongol'skoi Narodnoi Respubliki, 1926.

Henderson, Daniel. *From the Volga to the Yukon, The Story of the Russian March to Alaska and California, Paralleling Our Own Westward Trek to the Pacific.* New York: Hastings House, 1944.

Hermann, Benedict Franz Johann von. *Statistische Schilderung von Russland, in Rucksicht auf Bevolkerung, Landesbeschaffenheit, Naturprodkte, Landwirthschaft, Bergbau, Manufakturen und Handel.* St. Petersburg: Christian Tornow & Co., 1790.

Hill, S. S. *Travels in Siberia.* 2 vols. London: Longman, Brown, Green, and Longmans, 1854.

Hoo Chi-tsai. *Les bases conventionnelles des relations modernes entre la Chine et la Russie.* Paris: Jouve & ĉie, 1918.

Howarth, Sir Henry Hoyle. *History of the Mongols, From the 9th to the 19th Century.* 4 vols. in 5. London: Longmans, Green, and Co., 1876-1927.

Hsieh Pao-chao. *The Government of China, 1644-1911.* Baltimore: Johns Hopkins Press, 1925.

Hsü, Immanuel C. Y. *The Ili Crisis, A Study of Sino-Russian Diplomacy.* Oxford: The Clarendon Press, 1965.

Hummel, Arthur W. (ed.). *Eminent Chinese of the Ch'ing Period (1644-1912).* 2 vols. Washington: U.S. Government Printing Office, 1943.

Istoriia Buriat-Mongol'skoi ASSR. 2d ed. rev. and enl. (vol. 1 only). 2 vols. Ulan-Ude: Buriat-Mongol'skoe Knizhnoe Izd., 1954-59. First ed. of vol. 1 published in 1951.

Istoriia Kazakhskoi SSR. 2 vols. Alma-Ata: Izd. Akademii Nauk Kazakhskoi SSR, 1957-59.

Istoriia Kirgizii. 2 vols. Frunze: Kirgizskoe Gosudarstvennoe Izdatel'stvo, 1963.

Istoriia Moskvy. 7 vols. Moscow: Izd. Akademii Nauk SSSR, 1953-64.

Istoriia Sibiri s drevneishikh vremen do nashikh dnei v piati tomakh. Vol. 2: *Sibir' v sostave feodal'noi Rossii.* Leningrad: Izdatel'stvo "Nauka," Leningradskoe Otdelenie, 1968. Editorial college of this volume: V. I. Shunkov and others.

Kabanov, Petr Ivanovich. *Amurskii vopros.* Blagoveshchensk: Amurskoe Knizhnoe Izdatel'stvo, 1959.

Kafengauz, Boris Borisovich. *Vneshniaia politika Rossii pri Petre I.* Moscow: OGIZ, Gos. Izd. Politicheskoi Literatury, 1942.

Kaidanov, Nikolai Ivanovich. *Sistematicheskii katalog delam Komissii o kommertsii i o poshlinakh, khraniashchimsia v Arkhive departamenta tamozhennykh sborov.* St. Petersburg: Tip. V. Kirshbauma, 1887.

———. *Sistematicheskii katalog delam Sibirskago prikaza, Moskovskago kommisarstva i drugikh, byvshikh, uchrezhdenii po chasti promyshlennosti i torgovli, khraniashchimsia v Arkhive departamenta tamozhennykh sborov.* St. Petersburg: Tip. V. Kirshbauma, 1888.

Kennan, George. *Siberia and the Exile System.* 2 vols. New York: The Century Co., 1891.

Kerner, Robert Joseph. *The Urge to the Sea, The Course of Russian History, The Role of Rivers, Portages, Ostrogs, Monasteries and Furs.* Berkeley: University of California Press, 1942.

Khromov, Pavel Alekseevich. *Ekonomicheskoe razvitie Rossii, Ocherki ekonomiki Rossii s drevneishikh vremen do Velikoi oktiabr'skoi revoliutsii.* Moscow: Izd. "Nauka," 1967.

———. *Ocherki ekonomiki feodalizma v Rossii.* Moscow: Gospolitizdat, 1957.

Kirchner, Walther. *Commercial Relations Between Russia and Europe, 1400 to 1800; Collected Essays.* ("Indiana University Publications, Russian and East European Series," 33.) Bloomington: Indiana University, 1966.

Kiuner, Nikolai Vasil'evich. *Snosheniia Rossii s Dal'nim Vostokom na protiazhenii tsarstvovaniia doma Romanovykh; rech' proizneshennaia na torzhestvennom akt v Vostochnom institute 22 fevr. 1913 g. po sluchaiu trekhsotletiia tsarstvovaniia doma Romanovykh.* 2d ed., enl. Vladivostok: Izdanie i pechat Vostochnago Instituta, 1914.

Klaproth, Julius Heinrich von. *Mémoires relatifs à l'Asie, con-*

tenant des recherches historiques, géographiques et philologiques sur les peuples de l'Orient. 3 vols. Paris: Librairie Orientale de Dondey-Dupré Père et Fils, 1824-28. Russian translation of the first part published in *Moskovskii telegraf,* Pt. 7 (1826), 145-58.

Korsak, Aleksandr Kazimirovich. *Istoriko-statisticheskoe obozrenie torgovykh snoshenii Rossii s Kitaem.* Kazan': I. Dubrovin, 1857.

Kostarev, S. P. *Istoricheskie pamiatniki Buriatii (Kratkii spravochnik).* Ulan-Ude: Buriatskoe Knizhnoe Izd., 1959.

Krandievskii, Semen Ivanovich. *Ocherki po istoriografii ekonomicheskoi istorii (XVII-XIX vv.).* Khar'kov: Izd. Khar'kovskogo Ordena Trudovogo Krasnogo Znameni Gos. Universiteta imeni A. M. Gor'kogo, 1964.

Kratkii ocherk o pushnoi promyshlennosti v Sibiri. Moscow: Tip. Obshchestva Rasprostraneniia Poleznykh Knig, 1896.

Kratkoe pokazanie o byvshikh kak v Tobol'skie, tak i vo vsekh sibirskikh gorodakh i ostrogakh s nachala vziatiia sibirskago gosudarstva, voevodakh i gubernatorakh, i prochikh chinakh; i kto oni imianno, i v kakikh gorodakh byli; i kto kakoi gorod stroil, i kogda. Tobol'sk: V Tipografii u Vasil'ia Kornil'eva, 1792.

Krausse, Alexis Sidney. *Russia in Asia, A Record and a Study, 1558-1899.* New York: Henry Holt and Co., 1899.

Krieger, Bogdan. *Die ersten hundert Jahre Russisch-Chinesischer Politik.* Berlin: Carl Heymann, 1904.

Kudriavtsev, Fedor Aleksandrovich and V. I. Dulov. *Boevye traditsii sibiriakov.* Irkutsk: OGIZ, Irkutskoe Oblastnoe Izdatel'stvo, 1942.

Kudriavtsev, Fedor Aleksandrovich and German Aleksandrovich Vendrikh. *Irkutsk, ocherki po istorii goroda.* Irkutsk: Irkutskoe Knizhnoe Izdatel'stvo, 1958.

Kulisher, Iosif Mikhailovich. *Ocherk istorii russkoi torgovli.* Peterburg: Izdatel'stvo "Atenei," 1923.

Kurts, Boris Grigor'evich. *Gosudarstvennaia monopoliia v torgovle Rossii s Kitaem v pervoi polovine XVIII st.* ("Naukovi Zapiski Kiivs'kogo Institutu Narodn'ogo Gosudarstva," 9). Kiev, 1928.

———. *Russko-kitaiskie snosheniia v XVI, XVII i XVIII stoletiiakh.* Issued by the Vseukrainskaia Nauchnaia Assotsiatsiia Vostokovedeniia. Khar'kov: Gosudarstvennoe Izdatel'stvo Ukrainy, 1929.

Lang, David Marshall. *The First Russian Radical, Alexander Radishchev, 1749-1802.* London: George Allen & Unwin, Ltd., 1959.

Lantzeff, George V. *Siberia in the Seventeenth Century, A Study of Colonial Administration.* ("University of California Publications in History," 30.) Berkeley: University of California Press, 1943.

Lattimore, Owen. *Inner Asian Frontiers of China.* "American Geographical Society Research Series," No. 21. New York: American Geographical Society, 1940.

Laufer, Berthold. *Tobacco and Its Use in Asia.* ("Anthropology Leaflet," 18). Chicago: Field Museum of Natural History, 1924.

Lebedev, D. M. *Geografiia v Rossii petrovskogo vremeni.* Moscow: Izd. Akademii Nauk SSSR, 1950.

Lappo-Danilevskii, Aleksandr S. *Russkiia promyshlennyia i torgovyia kompanii v pervoi polovine XVIII veke.* St. Petersburg: Tipografiia V. S. Balasheva i Ko., 1899.

Liudi russkoi nauki, Ocherki o vydaiushchikhsia deiateliakh estestvoznaniia i tekhniki: Geologiia, geografiia. Ed. I. V. Kuznetsov. Moscow: Gosudarstvennoe Izdatel'stvo Fiziko-Matematicheskoi Literatury, 1962.

Lobanov-Rostovsky, Andrei. *Russia and Asia.* New York: Macmillan, 1933.

Lodyzhenskii, Konstantin Nikolaevich. *Istoriia russkago tamozhennago tarifa.* St. Petersburg: Tip. V. S. Balasheva, 1886.

Makarova, Raisa Vsevolodovna. *Russkie na Tikhom okeane vo vtoroi polovine XVIII v.* Moscow: Izd. "Nauka," 1968.

Mal'gin, Timofei Semenovich. *Opyt istoricheskago izsledovaniia i opisaniia starinnykh sudebnykh mest rossiiskago gosudarstva i o kachestve lits i del v onykh.* St. Petersburg: Pri Imperatorskoi Akademii Nauk, 1803.

Marbault. *Essai sur le commerce de Russie, avec l'histoire de ses découvertes.* Amsterdam, 1777.

Martin, Robert Montgomery. *China, Political, Commercial and Social.* 2 vols. in 1. London: James Madden, 1847.

Marx, Karl and Friedrich Engels. *Sochineniia.* 2d ed. 39 vols. in 42. Moscow: Gospolitizdat, 1955-66.

Masterson, James Raymond and Helen Brower. *Bering's Successors, 1745-1780; Contributions of Peter Simon Pallas to the History of Russian Exploration toward Alaska.* Seattle: University of Washington Press, 1948.

Mayers, William Frederick. *The Chinese Government. A Manual of Chinese Titles, Categorically Arranged and Explained, with an Appendix.* 3rd ed., revised by G. M. H. Playfair. Shanghai: Kelly & Walsh, Ltd., 1897.

Mel'gunov, Petr P. *Ocherki po istorii russkoi torgovli IX-XVIII vv.* Moscow: Izdanie Magazina "Sotrudnik Shkol" A. K. Zalesskoi, 1905.

Mets, Nonna Dmitrievna. *Nash rubl', Istoricheskii ocherk.* Moscow: Sotsekgiz, 1960.

Ministerstvo Inostrannykh Del. *Ocherk istorii Ministerstva inostrannykh del, 1802-1902.* St. Petersburg: Tovarishchestvo R. Golike i A. Vil'borg, 1902.

Morse, Hosea Ballou. *The International Relations of the Chinese Empire.* 3 vols. London: Longmans, Green & Co., 1910-18.

Müller, Gerhard Friedrich (Fedor Ivanovich Miller). *Istoriia Sibiri.* 2 vols. Moscow-Leningrad: Izd. Akademii Nauk SSSR, 1937-41.

Müller, Gerhard Friedrich and Peter Simon Pallas. *Conquest of Siberia, and the History of the Transactions, Wars, Commerce, &c. &c., carried on between Russia and China, From the Earliest Period.* London: Smith, Elder, and Co., 1842.

Murray, Hugh. *Historical Account of Discoveries and Travels in Asia, From the Earliest Ages to the Present Time.* 3 vols. Edinburgh: Archibald Constable and Co., and London: Longman, Hurst, Rees, Orme, and Brown, 1820.

Murzaev, Ed. M. *Mongol'skaia narodnaia respublika, Fiziko-geoficheskoe opisanie.* Moscow: OGIZ, Gosudarstvennoe Izdatel'stvo Geograficheskoi Literatury, 1948. A second edition published in 1952.

Nebol'sin, Grigorii P. *Statisticheskiia zapiski o vneshnei torgovle Rossii.* Chast' 2. St. Petersburg: V Tipografii Departamenta Vneshnei Torgovli, 1835.

———. *Statisticheskoe obozrenie vneshnei torgovli Rossii.* 2 vols. in 1. St. Petersburg: V Tipografii Departamenta Vneshnei Torgovli, 1850.

Nevskii, V. V. *Pervoe puteshestvie Rossiian vokrug sveta.* Moscow: Gos. Izd. Geograficheskoi Literatury, 1951.

Nikolai Mikhailovich, *Velikii kniaz'. Moskovskii nekropol'.* 3 vols. St. Petersburg: Tip. M. M. Stasiulevicha, 1907-8.

———. *Peterburgskii nekropol'.* 4 vols. St. Petersburg: Tip. M. M. Stasiulevicha, 1912-13.

Novyi i polnyi geograficheskii slovar' rossiiskago gosudarstva ili leksikon. 6 vols. Moscow: V Universitetskoi Tipografii, u N. Novikova, 1788.

Nozikov, Nikolai Nikolaevich. *Russkie krugosvetnye moreplavateli.* Ed. M. A. Sergeeva. 2d ed. Moscow: Voennoe Izd. Ministerstva Vooruzhennykh Sil Soiuza SSR, 1947. Translated as *Russian Voyages Round the World* by Ernst and Mira Lesser. London: Hutchinson & Co., Ltd., 1945.

Ocherki istorii kalmytskoi ASSR, Dooktiabr'skii period. Moscow: Izd. "Nauka," 1967.

Ocherki istorii SSSR. Vol. VII: *Period feodalizma, Rossiia v pervoi chetverti XVIII v., Preobrazovaniia Petra I* (1954). Ed. B. B. Kafengauz and N. I. Pavlenko. Vol. VIII: *Period feodalizma, Rossiia vo vtoroi chetverti XVIII v., Narody SSSR v pervoi polovine XVIII v.* (1957). Ed. A. I. Baranovich, L. G. Beskrovnyi, E. I. Zaozerskaia, and E. I. Indova. Vol. IX: *Period feodalizma, Rossiia vo vtoroi polovine XVIII v.* (1956). Ed. A. I. Baranovich, B. B. Kafengauz, P. K. Alefirenko, Iu. R. Klokman, and E. N. Kushevaia. Moscow: Izd. Akademii Nauk SSSR.

Ogden, Adele. *The California Set Otter Trade, 1784-1848.* Berkeley: University of California Press, 1941.

Okun', Semen Bentsionovich. *Rossiisko-amerikanskaia kompaniia.* Ed. Boris D. Grekov. Moscow: Sotsekgiz, 1939. Translated as *The Russian American Company.* Preface by Robert Joseph Kerner. Cambridge: Harvard University Press, 1951.

Parry, Albert. "Russian (Greek Orthodox) Missionaries in China, 1689-1917: Their Cultural, Political and Economic Role." Unpublished Ph.D. dissertation, University of Chicago, June, 1938.

Pashkov, A. I. (ed.). *Istoriia russkoi ekonomicheskoi mysli.* Vol. I: *Epokha feodalizma.* Chast' 1: *IX-XVIII vv.* Moscow: Gos. Izd. Politicheskoi Literatury, 1955. This volume translated as *A History of Russian Economic Thought: Ninth Through Eighteenth Centuries.* Ed. John M. Letiche. Trans. John M. Letiche, with the collaboration of Basil Dmytryshyn and Richard A. Pierce. Berkeley: University of California Press, 1964.

Patlaevskii, Innokentii Iustinovich. *Denezhnyi rynok v Rossii ot 1700 do 1762 goda.* ("Zapiski Imperatorskogo Novorossiiskogo Universiteta," 2.) Odessa, 1868.

Pavlenko, Nikolai Ivanovich. *Istoriia metallurgii v Rossii XVIII veka, Zavody i zavodovladel'tsy.* Moscow: Izd. Akademii Nauk SSSR, 1962.

Pavlovsky, Michel N. *Chinese-Russian Relations.* New York: Philosophical Library, 1949.

Petech, Luciano. *China and Tibet in the Early 18th Century, History of the Establishment of Chinese Protectorate in Tibet.* ("Monographies du T'oung Pao," 1.) Leiden: E. J. Brill, 1950.

Petrov, V. P. *Albazintsy v Kitae.* Washington: Izdanie Knizhnogo Magazina Victor Kamkin, Inc., 1956.

Piasetskii, Pavel Iakovlevich. *Russian Travellers in Mongolia and*

China. Trans. J. Gordon-Cumming. 2 vols. London: Chapman & Hall, 1884.

Playfair, George MacDonald Home. *The Cities and Towns of China, A Geographical Dictionary*. 2d ed. Shanghai: Kelly & Walsh, Ltd., 1910.

Pleshcheev, Sergei. *Survey of the Russian Empire, According to Its Present Newly Regulated State, Divided into Different Governments*. Trans. with additions by James Smirnove. 3rd ed. London: Printed for J. Debrett, 1792.

Pokrovskii, Serafim Aleksandrovich. *Vneshniaia torgovlia i vneshniaia torgovlaia politika Rossii*. Moscow: "Mezhdunarodnaia Kniga," 1947.

Pokshishevskii, Vadim Viacheslavovich. *Zaselenie Sibiri (istoriko-geograficheskoe ocherki)*. Irkutsk: Irkutskoe Oblastnoe Gosudarstvennoe Izd., 1951.

Potanin, Grigorii Nikolaevich. "Materialy dlia istorii Sibiri," *Chteniia OIDR*, No. 4 (October-December, 1866), 1-128; No. 1 (January-March, 1867), 129-230; No. 2 (April-June, 1867), 231-324.

———. "O karavannoi torgovle s dzhungarskoi Bukhariei v XVIII stoletii," *Chteniia OIDR*, Bk. 2 (1868), 21-113.

Price, Jacob M. *The Tobacco Adventure to Russia; Enterprise, Politics, and Diplomacy in the Quest for a Northern Market for English Colonial Tobacco, 1676-1722*. ("Transactions of the American Philosophical Society," New Series, 51, Pt. 1.) Philadelphia, 1961.

Pritchard, Earl Hampton. *Anglo-Chinese Relations during the Seventeenth and Eighteenth Centuries*. ("University of Illinois Studies in the Social Sciences," 17, Nos. 1-2.) Urbana: University of Illinois Press, 1929.

———. *The Crucial Years of Early Anglo-Chinese Relations, 1750-1800*. ("Research Studies of the State College of Washington," 4, Nos. 3-4.) Pullman, Washington, 1936.

Ptitsyn, Vladimir Vasil'evich. *Selenginskaia Dauriia. Ocherki zabaikal'skago kraia*. St. Petersburg: Ekonomicheskaia Tipo-Litografiia, B. Vul'fova, 1896.

Pushkin, Aleksandr Sergeevich. *Eugene Onegin, A Novel in Verse*. Trans. with a commentary by Vladimir Nabokov. 4 vols. ("Bollingen Series," LXXII.) New York: Pantheon Books, 1964.

Raeff, Marc. *Michael Speransky, Statesman of Imperial Russia, 1772-1839*. The Hague: Martinus Nijhoff, 1957.

———. *Siberia and the Reforms of 1822*. Seattle: University of Washington Press, 1956.

Reading, Douglas K. *The Anglo-Russian Commercial Treaty of 1734.* ("Yale Historical Publications, Miscellany," 32.) New Haven: Yale University Press, 1938.

Riazanovskii, Valentin Aleksandrovich. *Customary Law of the Mongol Tribes (Mongols, Buriats, Kalmucks).* Harbin: "Artistic Printing House," 1929.

——. *Fundamental Principles of Mongol Law.* Tientsin, 1937. Reprinted in 1965: "Indiana University Publications, Uralic and Altaic Series," 43. Bloomington: Indiana University.

Richard, Louis. *Comprehensive Geography of the Chinese Empire and Dependencies.* Trans., rev. and enl. by M. Kennelly, S. J. Shanghai: T'usewei Press, 1908.

Rubel, Paula G. *The Kalmyk Mongols, A Study in Continuity and Change.* ("Indiana University Publications, Uralic and Altaic Studies," 64.) Bloomington: Indiana University, 1967.

Rubinshtein, Nikolai Leonidovich. *Russkaia istoriografiia.* Moscow: OGIZ, Gospolitizat, 1941.

Russia. Ministerstvo Inostrannykh Del. *Ocherk istorii Ministerstva inostrannykh del, 1802-1902.* St. Petersburg: Tovarishchestvo R. Golike i A. Vil'borg, 1902.

——. Upravlenie Imperatorskimi Zavodami. *Imperatorskii farforovyi zavod, 1744-1904.* St. Petersburg: Izdanie Upravleniia Imperatorskimi Zavodami, 1906.

Russkii biograficheskii slovar'. Ed. A. Polovtsov. 25 vols., incompleted. St. Petersburg: Izdanie Imp. Russkago Istoricheskago Obshchestva, 1896-1918. Cited as *RBS.* When volumes are missing consult *Azbuchnyi ukazatel' imen russkikh deiatelei dlia Russkago biograficheskago slovaria,* published as vols. LX and LXII (1887-88) of *Sbornik RIO.*

Savary des Bruslons, Jacques. *Dictionnaire universel de commerce. . . .* 3 vols. Paris: J. Estienne, 1723-30. Trans. as *The Universal Dictionary of Trade and Commerce. . . .* Trans. Malachy Postlethwayt. 2 vols. London: J & P. Knapton, 1751-55. The edition used here is the 4th (1774) issued in two volumes: London: Printed for W. Strahan *et alia.*

Savvin, V. P. *Vzaimootnosheniia tsarskoi Rossii i SSSR s Kitaem.* Moscow: Gosudarstvennoe Izd., 1930.

Scherer, Jean Benoit. *Histoire raisonnée du commerce de la Russie.* 2 vols. Paris: Cuchet, 1778.

Schnitzler, Johann Heinrich. *Essai d'une statistique générale de l'Empire de Russie, accompagnée d'apercus historiques.* St. Petersburg: J. Brieff, 1829.

Schuyler, Eugene. *Peter the Great, Emperor of Russia, A Study of*

Historical Biography. 2 vols. New York: C. Scribner's Sons, 1884.

Schwartz, Harry. *Tsars, Mandarins, and Commissars, A History of Chinese-Russian Relations.* Philadelphia: J. B. Lippincott Co., 1964.

Sebes, Joseph, S. J. *The Jesuits and the Sino-Russian Treaty of Nerchinsk (1689). The Diary of Thomas Pereira, S. J.* ("Bibliotheca Instituti Historici Societatis Iesu," 18.) Rome: Institutum Historicum S. I., 1961.

Semenov, Aleksei V. *Izuchenie istoricheskikh svedenii o rossiiskoi vneshnei torgovle i promyshlennosti s poloviny XVII-go stoletiia po 1858 god.* 3 vols. St. Petersburg: Tip. I. I. Glazunova i Ko., 1859.

Semenov, Iurii Nikolaevich. *Siberia: Its Conquest and Development.* Trans. J. R. Foster. London: Hollis & Carter, 1963. An earlier edition published under the title *The Conquest of Siberia, An Epic of Human Passions.* Trans. E. W. Dickes. London: George Routledge & Sons, Ltd., 1944. Originally published in Berlin in 1937 as *Die Eroberung Sibiriens: Ein Epos menschlicher Leidenschaften.*

Semenov-Tian-Shanskii, Petr Petrovich. *Geografichesko-statisticheskii slovar' rossiiskoi imperii.* 5 vols. St. Petersburg, 1863-85.

Semivskii, Nikolai Vasil'evich. *Noveishiia, liubopytnyia i dostovernyia povestvovaniia o vostochnoi Sibiri, iz chego mnogoe donyne ne bylo izvestno.* St. Petersburg: Voennaia Tipografiia Glavnago Shtaba Ego Imperatorskago Velichestva, 1817.

Shuo-fang pei-ch'eng. Ed. Ho Ch'iu-t'ao. 68 chuan, 4 han. 1881. Cited as *SFPC.*

Sibir' XVII-XVIII vv. Vypusk 1 of *Sibir' perioda feodalizma, Materialy po istorii Sibiri.* Novosibirsk: Izd. Sibirskogo Otdeleniia Akademii Nauk SSSR, 1962.

Sibirskaia sovetskaia entsiklopediia. Ed. M. K. Azadovskii and others. 3 vols. incompleted. Novosibirsk: Sibirskoe Kraevoe Izdatel'stvo, 1929-32.

Sibirskie goroda, Materialy dlia ikh istorii XVII i XVIII stoletii: Nerchinsk, Selenginsk, Iakutsk. Moscow: Tip. M. G. Volchaninova, 1886.

Silin, E. P. *Kiakhta v XVIII veke, iz istorii russko-kitaiskoi torgovli.* Irkutsk: OGIZ, Irkutskoe Oblastnoe Izdatel'stvo, 1947.

Skal'kovskii, Konstantin Apollonovich. *Russkaia torgovlia v Tikhom okeana, ekonomicheskoe izsledovanie russkoi torgovli i morekhodstva v Primorskoi oblasti Vostochnoi Sibiri, Koree, Kitae, Iaponii i Kalifornii.* St. Petersburg: Tip. A. S. Suvorina, 1883.

———. *Vneshniaia politika Rossii i polozhenie inostrannykh derzhav.* 2d ed. St. Petersburg: Tip. A. S. Suvorina, 1901. First ed. published in 1897.

Sladkovskii, M. I. *Ocherki ekonomicheskikh otnoshenii SSSR s Kitaem.* Moscow: Vneshtorgizdat, 1957. Trans. into English as "Russian-Chinese Trade, 1618–1956" by the U.S. Joint Publications Research Service (23 March 1959, JPRS: 1385-N), distributed by Research and Microfilm Publication (Annapolis).

———. *Ocherki razvitiia vneshneekonomicheskikh otnoshenii Kitaia.* Moscow: Vneshtorgizdat, 1953.

Slovtsov, Petr Andreevich. *Istoricheskoe obozrenie Sibiri.* 2 vols. in 1. St. Petersburg: Izd. I. M. Skorokhodova, 1886.

Solov'ev, Sergei Mikhailovich. *Istoriia Rossii s drevneishikh vremen.* 2d ed. 29 books in 6 vols., plus a volume of index. St. Petersburg: "Obshchestvennaia Pol'za," 1894-95.

Spiridonakis, Basile G. (comp.). *Mémoires et documents du Ministère des Affaires Etrangères de France sur la Russie.* Sherbrooke, Canada: Faculte des Arts, Universite de Sherbrooke, 196?. Photolithographic reproduction of typescript.

Spiridonova, E. V. *Ekonomicheskaia politika i ekonomicheskie vzgliady Petra I.* Moscow: Gosudarstvennoe Izd. Politicheskoi Literatury, 1952.

Staunton, Sir George Thomas. *Miscellaneous Notices Relating to China, and Our Commercial Intercourse with That Country, Including a Few Translations from the Chinese Language.* 2d ed. London: John Murray, 1822.

Stejneger, Leonhard Hess. *George Wilhelm Steller, The Pioneer of Alaskan Natural History.* Cambridge: Harvard University Press, 1936.

Steuart, Archibald Francis. *Scottish Influences in Russian History From the End of the 16th Century to the Beginning of the 19th Century.* Glasgow: James Maclehose and Sons. 1913.

Storch, Heinrich Friedrich von. *Statistische Übersicht der Statthalterschaften des Russischen Reichs nach ihren Merkwürdigsten Kulturverhältnissen.* Riga: Johann Friedrich Hartknoch, 1795.

Studenski, Paul. *The Income of Nations.* Part 1: *History.* Washington Square: New York University Press, 1961.

Sukachev, Vladimir P. (ed.). *Irkutsk. Ego mesto i znachenie v istorii i kul'turnom razvitii vostochnoi Sibiri. Ocherk.* Moscow: Tipolitografiia I. N. Kushnerev i Ko., 1891.

———. *Pervoe stoletie Irkutska. Sbornik materialov dlia istorii goroda s "Vvedeniem" i zakliuchitel'noi stat'ei priv.-dots. P. M. Golovacheva.* St. Petersburg: Tip. I. N. Kushnereva i Ko., 1902.

Sumner, Benedict H. *Peter the Great and the Emergence of Russia.* London: The English Universities Press, Ltd., 1951.

Sviatlovskii, Vladimir Vladimirovich. *Istoriia ekonomicheskikh idei v Rossii.* Vol. I: *Merkantilizm, fiziokratizm, klassicheskaia shkola i ee razvetvleniia.* Petrograd: "Nachatki Znanii," 1923.

Syromiatnikov, B. I. *"Reguliarnoe" gosudarstvo Petra Pervogo i ego ideologiia.* Chast' 1. Moscow-Leningrad: Izd. Akademii Nauk SSSR, 1943.

Tarasov, Georgii L'vovich. *Vostochnaia Sibir'.* Moscow: Izd. "Prosveshchenie," 1964.

Tikhomirov, Mikhail Nikolaevich (ed.). *Ocherki istorii istoricheskoi nauki v SSSR.* Vol. 1. Moscow: Izdatel'stvo Akademii Nauk SSSR, 1955.

Tolstoi, Dmitrii Andreevich. *Istoriia finansovykh uchrezhdenii Rossii so vremeni osnovaniia gosudarstva do konchiny imperatritsy Ekateriny II.* St. Petersburg: V Tipografii Konstantina Zhernakova, 1848.

Tooke, William. *The Life of Catherine II, Empress of Russia.* 3rd ed. 3 vols. London: Printed for T. N. Longman and O. Rees, and J. Debrett, 1799.

———. *View of the Russian Empire, During the Reign of Catherine the Second, and to the Close of the Eighteenth Century.* 2d ed. 3 vols. London: Printed by G. Woodfall, for T. N. Longman and O. Rees, 1800.

Travels in Northern Asia, compiled from Authentic Sources. Dublin: Christopher Bentham, 1823.

Troitskii, Sergei Martinovich. *Finansovaia politika russkogo absoliutizma v XVIII veke.* Moscow: Izd. "Nauka," 1966.

Trusevich, Kh. *Posol'skiia i torgovliia snosheniia Rossii s Kitaem (do XIX veka).* Moscow: T. Malinskago Moroseika, Chelovekoliubivago Obshchestva, 1882.

Tugan-Baranovskii, Mikhail Ivanovich. *Russkaia fabrika v proshlom i nastoiashchem.* 7th ed. Moscow: Sotsekgiz, 1938. Originally published in 1898.

Tupper, Harmon. *To the Great Ocean, Siberia and the Trans-Siberian Railway.* Boston: Little, Brown & Company, 1965.

Ulianitskii, Vladimir Antonovich. *Russkiia konsul'stva za granitseiu v XVIII veke.* 2 vols. Moscow: Tip. G. Lissnera i A. Geshelia, 1899.

U. S. War Department. *Siberia and Eastern Russia.* 3 vols. Washington: Government Printing Office, 1918.

Van der Sprenkel, Sybille. *Legal Institutions in Manchu China, A Sociological Analysis.* ("London School of Economics, Monographs on Social Anthropology," 24.) London: University of London, The Athlone Press, 1962.

Vernadskii, Georgii V. *Ocherki istorii prava russkago gosudarstva XVIII-XIX vv. (Period imperii).* Prague: Izd. "Plamia," 1924.

Vsevolzhskii, Nikolai Sergeevich. *Dictionaire géographique-historique de l'Empire de Russie. . . .* 2 vols. Moscow: Imprimerie de l'Auteur, 1813.

Wang Sun. "Sino-Russian Relations in the Eighteenth Century." Unpublished Master's thesis, University of Chicago, 1948.

Weigh, Ken Shen. *Russo-Chinese Diplomacy.* Shanghai: Commercial Press, 1928.

Wheeler, Mary Elizabeth. "The Origins and Formation of the Russian American Company." Unpublished Ph.D. dissertation, University of North Carolina, 1965.

———. "Russian Discovery and Colonization of America, 1741-1818, Its Bibliographical Foundations." Unpublished Master's thesis, University of North Carolina, 1962.

Wright, George Frederick. *Asiatic Russia.* 2 vols. New York: McClure, Phillips, & Co., 1902.

Wu, Aitchen K. (Wu Ai-ch'en). *China and the Soviet Union, A Study of Sino-Soviet Relations.* New York: John Day, 1950.

Wu Ch'i-yu. "China, Russia and Central Asia; A Study of the Political and Diplomatic Relations Between (I) China and Central Asia; (II) Russia and Central Asia; (III) Russia and China in regard to Their Respective Interests in Central Asia Beginning Roughly from the Commencement (1644) of the Ching Dynasty to the Year 1895." Unpublished Ph.D. dissertation, Princeton University, 1933.

Zinchenko, Nikolai Eliseevich. *Russo-kitaiskaia torgovlia (Doklad, chitannyi 17 aprelia 1898 g. v Obshchem sobranie Obshchestva dlia sodeistviia russkoi promyshlennosti i torgovli).* St. Petersburg: Tipografiia A. Porokhovshchikova, 1898.

Zinner, Ervin Petrovich. *Sibir' v izvestiiakh zapadnoevropeiskikh puteshestvennikov i uchenykh XVIII veka.* N.p.: Vostochno-Sibirskoe Knizhnoe Izdatel'stvo, 1968.

Zlatkin, Il'ia Iakovlevich. *Istoriia dzhungarskogo khanstva (1635-1758).* Moscow: Izdatel'stvo "Nauka," 1964.

Zorin, V. A. and others (eds.). *Istoriia diplomatii.* 2d ed., rev. and enl. Vol. 1. Moscow: Gospolitizdat, 1959.

Articles

Andreev, M. "Iz istorii snoshenii Rossii s Kitaem (XVII-XX vv.)," *Severnaia Aziia, obshchestvenno-nauchnyi zhurnal,* Bks. 5-6 (1925), 53-84.

Barkman, C. D. "The Return of the Torghuts from Russia to China," *Journal of Oriental Studies,* II (January, 1955), 89-115.

Batrakov, V. S. "K istorii torgovykh sviazei Kazakhstana s Rossiei v XVIII–XIX vv.," *Trudy* Sredneasiatskogo Gosudarstvennogo Universiteta im. V. I. Lenina, New Series, Vypusk 78; Istoricheskie nauki, Book 11 (Tashkent, 1956), 3-39.

Bazilevich, Konstantin Vasil'evich. "K voprosu ob izuchenii tamozhennykh knig XVII v.," *Problemy istochnikovedeniia, Sbornik* II (1936), 71-90.

———. "Tamozhennye knigi kak istochnik ekonomicheskoi istorii Rossii," *Problemy istochnikovedeniia, Sbornik* I (1933), 110-29.

Boardman, Eugene Powers. "Chinese Mandarins and Western Traders," *Social Education,* XX (April-May, 1956), 150-52, 197-200.

Borovoi, Saul Iakovlevich. "Voprosy kreditovaniia torgovli i promyshlennosti v ekonomicheskoi politike Rossii XVIII veke," *Istoricheskie zapiski,* XXXIII (1950), 92-122.

Bryce, James. "Western Siberia and the Altai Mountains, With Some Speculations on the Future of Siberia," *National Geographic Magazine,* XXXIX (May, 1921), 469-507.

Cahen, Gaston. "Deux ambassades chinoises en Russie au commencement du XVIIIe siècle," *Revue historique,* CXXXIII (January-February, 1920), 82-89.

———. "Les relations de la Russie avec la Chine et les peuplades limitrophes à la fin du XVIIe siècle et dans le premier quart du XVIIIe," *Revue historique,* XCIV (May-August, 1907), 45-62.

Chang Te-ch'ang. "Ming-tai kuang-chou chih hai-po mao-i," *Tsinghua Journal* VII, No. 2 (June, 1932), 1-18. An English version published as "Maritime Trade at Canton during the Ming Dynasty," *Chinese Social and Political Science Review,* XVII (1933), 264-82.

Ch'en, Agnes Fang-chih. "China's Northern Frontiers: Historical Background," *Yenching Journal of Social Studies,* IV (August, 1948), 15-87.

———. "Chinese Frontier Diplomacy: Kiakhta Boundary Treaties and Agreements," *Yenching Journal of Social Studies,* IV (February, 1949), 151-205.

———. "Chinese Frontier Diplomacy: The Coming of the Russians and the Treaty of Nerchinsk," *Yenching Journal of Social Studies,* IV (February, 1949), 99–149.

——. "Chinese Frontier Diplomacy: The Eclipse of Manchuria," *Yenching Journal of Social Studies,* V (July, 1950), 69-141.

——. "Ch'ing-tai pien-chih shu lueh," *Yenching Journal of Chinese Studies,* No. 34 (June, 1948), 133-64.

Ch'en Fu-kuang. "Sino-Russian Diplomatic Relations Since 1689," *Chinese Social and Political Science Review,* X (1926), 120ff., 476ff., 711ff., 933ff.; XI (1927), 155-66.

Constantin, G. I. "The Transbaikalian Routes to China as Known to or Explored by Nicolaie Milescu (Spathary)—1675," *Studia et Acta Orientalia* (Bucarest), I (1957), 83-119.

Culin, Stewart (ed.). "Across Siberia in the Dragon Year of 1796," *Asia,* XX (June, 1920), 505-12.

——. "The Wreck of the Wakamija Maru," *Asia,* XX (May, 1920), 365-372, 436.

Drew, Ronald Farinton. "The Siberian Fair: 1600-1750," *The Slavonic and East European Review,* XXXIX, No. 93 (June, 1961), 423-39.

Dudgeon, John. "Russian Ecclesiastical Mission," *The Chinese Recorder and Missionary Journal,* III (November, 1870), 143-46; III (March, 1871), 273-80; III (April, 1871), 319-22; III (May, 1871), 337-45; IV (June, 1871), 10-17.

——. "Sketch of Russian Ecclesiastical Intercourse with, and the Greek Church in, China," *The Chinese Recorder and Missionary Journal,* IV (July, 1871), 35-40; IV (August, 1871), 68-74; IV (September, 1871), 96-99; IV (November, 1871); 186-92; IV (January, 1872), 206-14.

——. "Preface to the Papers on the Russian Ecclesiastical Mission," *The Chinese Recorder and Missionary Journal,* IV (February, 1872), 227-31.

Fairbank, John King. "Tributary Trade and China's Relations with the West," *Far Eastern Quarterly,* I (February, 1942), 129-49.

Fairbank, John King and Teng Ssu-yu. "On the Ch'ing Tributary System," *Harvard Journal of Asiatic Studies,* VI (June, 1941), 135-246.

——. "On the Types and Uses of Ch'ing Documents," *Harvard Journal of Asiatic Studies,* V (1940), 1-71.

——. "On the Transmission of Ch'ing Documents," *Harvard Journal of Asiatic Studies,* IV (1939), 12-46.

Field, Daniel. Review of M. T. Beliavskii, *Krest'ianskii vopros v Rossii nakanune vosstaniia E. I. Pugacheva* (Moscow: Izd. Moskovskogo Universiteta, 1965), in *Kritika, A Review of Cur-*

rent Soviet Books on Russian History, II, No. 3 (Spring, 1966), 29-43.

Florovskii, Antonii Vasil'evich. "K istorii ekonomicheskikh idei v Rossii v XVIII veke," *Nauchnye trudy Russkago narodnago universiteta v Prage,* I (1928), 81-93.

Foust, Clifford M. "Russian Expansion to the East through the Eighteenth Century," *Journal of Economic History,* XXI (December, 1961), 469-82.

———. "Russia's Peking Caravan, 1689-1762," *South Atlantic Quarterly,* LXVII, No. 1 (Winter, 1968), 108-24.

Frank, V. S. "The Territorial Terms of the Sino-Russian Treaty of Nerchinsk, 1689," *Pacific Historical Review,* XVI (August, 1947), 265-70.

G., P. "Ukazatel' neposredstvennoi torgovli chrez Moskvu s Kitaem," *Zhurnal manufaktur i torgovli,* Chast' 4, No. 11 (1836), 19-139; Chast' 1, No. 4 (1837), 1-36.

———. "Sravnenie torgovli, proizvodimoi v Kantone s proizvodimoiu na Kiakhte; preimushchestva poslednei pred pervoiu, v tom sluchae kogda ona budet proizvodst'sia posredstvom khorosho ustroennago sotovarishchestva," *Zhurnal manufaktur i torgovli,* Chast' 1, No. 4 (1837), 1-36.

Gal'perin, A. I. "Russko-kitaiskaia torgovlia v XVIII-pervoi polovine XIX veke (Opyt sravneniia kiakhtinskogo torga s torgovlei cherez Guanchzhou)," *Problemy Vostokovedeniia,* V (1959), 215-27.

Geijer, Agnes. "Chinese Silks Exported to Russia in the 17th Century," *Bulletin of the Museum of Far Eastern Antiquities,* XXV (1953), 1-18.

Greisbach, Adolf. "Early Russo-Chinese Relations," *The National Review* (Shanghai), (23 August 1913), p. 177; (30 August 1913), pp. 205-6; (6 September 1913), p. 235; (20 September 1913), pp. 299-300; (4 October 1913), p. 376; (11 October 1913), pp. 393-409; (18 October 1913), pp. 427-29; (25 October 1913), pp. 459-60; (8 November 1913), pp. 518-19; (15 November 1913), pp. 545-47.

Hsü, Immanuel C. Y. "Russia's Special Position in China During the Early Ch'ing Period," *Slavic Review,* XXIII, No. 4 (December, 1964), 688-700.

Iakovleva, P. T. "Russko-kitaiskaia torgovlia cherez Nerchinsk nakanune i posle zakliucheniia nerchinskogo dogovora (1689 g.)," in *Mezhdunarodnye sviazi Rossii v XVII-XVIII vv. (Ekonomika, politika i kul'tura), Sbornik statei,* ed. L. G. Beskrovnyi, M. M. Shtrange, and P. T. Iakovleva (Moscow: Izd. "Nauka," 1966), pp. 122-51.

"Izvestie o torgakh sibirskikh," *Ezhemesiachnyia sochineniia, k pol'ze i uveseleniiu sluzhashchie,* No. 2 (September and December, 1755), 195-250, 525-37; No. 1 (February, March, April and May, 1756), 180-91, 195-226, 339-60, 387-421.

Kahan, Arcadius. "Continuity in Economic Activity and Policy during the Post-Petrine Period in Russia," *The Journal of Economic History,* XXV (March, 1965), 61-85.

———. "Entrepreneurship in the Early Development of Iron Manufacturing in Russia," *Economic Development and Cultural Change,* X (July, 1962), 395-422.

Kerner, Robert Joseph. "The Russian Eastward Movement: Some Observations on Its Historical Significance," *Pacific Historical Review,* XVII (May, 1948), 135-48.

Kirchner, Walther. "Relations économiques entre la France et la Russie au XVIIIe siècle," *Revue d'histoire économique et sociale,* XXXIX, No. 2 (1961), 158-97.

———. "Samuel Bentham and Siberia," *The Slavonic and East European Review,* XXXVI (June, 1958), 471-80.

Kliuchevskii, Vasilii Osipovich. "Russkii rubl' XVI-XVII v. v ego otnoshenii k nyneshnemu. Opyt opredeleniia menovoi stoimosti starinnago rublia po khlebnym tsenam," *Chteniia OIDR,* No. 1 (1884), 1-72.

Kurts, Boris Grigor'evich. "Kolonial'naia politika Rossii i Kitaia v XVII–XVIII v.v.," *Novyi Vostok,* Bk. 19 (1927), 194-206.

Laufer, Berthold. "Supplementary Notes on Walrus and Narwhal Ivory," *T'oung Pao,* 2d Series, XVII (1916), 348-89.

Lensen, George Alexander. "Early Russo-Japanese Relations," *Far Eastern Quarterly,* X (November, 1950), 3-37.

Lin, T. C. "Manchuria Trade and Tribute in the Ming Dynasty: A Study of Chinese Theories and Methods of Control over Border Peoples," *Nankai Social & Economic Quarterly,* IX, No. 4 (January, 1937), 855-92.

Liu Hsuan-min. "Chung o ts'ao ch'i mou-i k'ao," *Yen-ching hsueh-pao,* XXV (June, 1939), 153-212. Abstracted in English, pp. 266-67.

Longinov, Mikhail. "Abram Petrovich Gannibal," *Russkii arkhiv,* II (1864), 218-32.

Manassein, V. S. "Irkutskii ostrog (Istoriko-arkheologicheskii ocherk)," *Izvestiia Obshchestva izucheniia vostochnosibirskogo kraia,* I (LVI) (1936), 6-25.

Mancall, Mark. "China's First Missions to Russia, 1729-1731," *Papers on China from the East Asia Regional Studies Seminar* (East Asia Program, Committee on Regional Studies, Harvard University), IX (August, 1955), 75-110.

———. "The Kiakhta Trade," in Charles Donald Cowan (ed.), *The Economic Development of China and Japan, Studies in Economic History and Political Economy* (New York: F. A. Praeger, 1964), pp. 19-48.

———. "The Kiakhta Trade," Mimeographed report given at the School of Oriental and African Studies, Study Group on the Economic History of East and South-East Asia, 21 pp.

Marsh, Cody. "Glimpses of Siberia, The Russian 'Wild East,' " *National Geographic Magazine,* XXXVIII (December, 1920), 513-36.

Martens, Fedor Fedorovich. "Le conflict entre la Russie et la Chine, ses origines, son développement, et sa portée universelle," *Revue de droit international et de législation comparée* (Ghent), XII, Bks. 5-6 (1880), 513-45, 582-620. Translated into Russian and published in St. Petersburg in 1881.

Meng Ssu-ming. "The E-lo-ssu Kuan (Russian Hostel) in Peking," *Harvard Journal of Asiatic Studies,* XXIII (1961), 19-46.

Modzalevskii, B. (ed.). "K istorii Sibiri v kontse XVIII veke, Vospominanie T. P. Kalashnikova," *Russkii arkhiv,* XLVII, Pt. 3 (1904), 145-83.

Müller, Gerhard Friedrich (Fedor Ivanovich Miller). "O pervykh rossiiskikh puteshestviiakh i posol'stvakh v Kitai," *Ezhemesiachnyia sochineniia, k pol'ze i uveseleniiu sluzhashchie* (10 vols. in 20; St. Petersburg: Imp. Akademiia Nauk, 1755-64), I (July, 1755), 15-57.

Mushkin, P. "Osnovanie goroda Kiakhty i nachalo torgovli s Kitaem," *Severnaia pchela,* No. 120 (31 May 1851), 479-80.

Nidershteter, G. "O torgovykh snosheniiakh mezhdu Evropoiu i Kitaem, i v osobennosti o torgovle suknami," *Zhurnal manufaktur i torgovli,* No. 8 (1827), 96-119.

Nieh Ch'ung-ch'i. "Man-kuan han-shih," *Yen-ching hsueh-pao,* No. 32 (June, 1947), 97-115.

Nolde, J. J. "Chinese-Russian Relations Since the Seventeenth Century," *Contemporary China,* I (1955), 1-17.

O'Brien, C. Bickford. "Ivan Pososhkov: Russian Critic of Mercantilist Principles," *The American Slavic and East European Review,* XIV (December, 1955), 503-11.

Obruchev, Vladimir Afanas'evich. "Kratkii geologicheskii ocherk karavannago puti ot Kiakhtu do Kalgana," *Izvestiia Imperatorskago russkago geograficheskago obshchestva,* XXIX, Vypusk 5 (1893), 347-90.

Ogorodnikov. "Neskol'ko slov o kiakhtinskoi torgovle," *Severnaia pchela,* No. 199 (9 September 1856), 1013-16; No. 200 (11 September 1856), 1019-20.

Parker, Edward Harper. "Campaigns of K'ang-hi, Yung-cheng, and K'ien-lung," *China Review,* XVI (1887-1888), 105-18.

——. "Manchu Relations with Mongolia," *China Review,* XV (1886-87), 319-28.

——. "Manchu Relations with Russia," *China Review,* XVI (1887-88), 41-46.

Parkes, Harry. "Report on the Russian Caravan Trade with China," *Journal of the Royal Geographical Society,* XXIV (1854), 306-12.

Parry, Albert. "Russian (Greek Orthodox) Missionaries in China, 1689-1917; Their Cultural, Political, and Economic Role," *Pacific Historical Review,* IX (December, 1940), 401-24.

Pritchard, Earl Hampton. "Private Trade Between England and China in the Eighteenth Century (1680-1833)," *Journal of Economic and Social History of the Orient,* I, No. 1 (August, 1957), 108-37; I, No. 2 (April, 1958), 221-56.

——. "The Struggle for Control of the China Trade during the Eighteenth Century," *Pacific Historical Review,* III (September, 1934), 280-95.

Radovskii, M. I. "Pervaia vekha v istorii russko-kitaiskikh nauchnykh sviazei," *Vestnik Akademii nauk SSSR,* No. 9 (September, 1959), 95-97.

Raeff, Marc. "State and Nobility in the Ideology of M. M. Shcherbatov," *The American Slavic and East European Review,* XIX (October, 1960), 363-79.

Rich, E. E. "Russia and the Colonial Fur Trade," *Economic History Review,* 2d Series, VII (1955), 307-28.

Rubinshtein, Nikolai Leonidovich. "Ulozhennaia komissiia 1754-1766 gg. i ee proekt novogo ulozheniia 'O sostoianii poddannykh voobshche' (K istorii sotsial'noi politiki 20-kh—nachala 60-kh godov XVIII v.," *Istoricheskie zapiski,* XXXVIII (1951), 208-51.

"Russko-kitaiskie traktaty," *Severnaia pchela,* No. 52 (23 February 1862), 205-7; No. 53 (24 February 1862), 209-10; No. 54 (25 February 1862), 213-14.

"Russo-Chinese Relations (112-1912)," *Edinburgh Review,* CCXV (January, 1912), 190–212.

Sakharov, I. P. "O kitaiskoi torgovle," *Zhurnal manufaktur i torgovli,* Chast' 3, No. 4 (1837), 15-42, 43-71.

Samoilov, L. M. "Istoricheskiia i statisticheskiia svedeniia o kiakhtinskoi torgovle," *Sbornik statisticheskikh svedenii o Rossii* ("Trudy Imperatorskago Russkago Geograficheskago Obshchestva"), Knizhka 2, Otdel 2 (1854), 3-38.

Shastina, N. P. "Istoriia izucheniia Mongol'skoi narodnoi respubliki (Kratkii ocherk)," in *Mongol'skaia narodnaia respublika, sbornik statei.* Ed. Il'ia Ia. Zlatkin (Moscow: Izdatel'stvo Akademii Nauk SSSR, 1952), pp. 15-55.

Shmurlo, E. "Abram Petrovich Gannibal," *Entsiklopedicheskii slovar'* (Brokgauz i Efron), VIII, 87-88.

Shteingel, Vladimir Ivanovich. "Sibirskie satrapy, 1765-1819 (Pis'-mo barona V. I. Shteingelia k A. P. Ermolovu)," *Istoricheskii vestnik,* XVII (August, 1884), 366–86.

Shumakher, Petr B. "Nashi snosheniia s Kitaem (s 1567 po 1805)," *Russkii arkhiv,* XVII, Bk. 2 (1879), 145-83.

Skachkov, Petr E. "Istoriia izucheniia Kitaia v Rossii v XVII i XVIII vv. (Kratkii ocherk)," in *Mezhdunarodnye sviazi Rossii v XVII-XVIII vv. (Ekonomika, politika i kul'tura), Sbornik statei,* ed. L. G. Beskrovnyi, M. M. Shtrange, and P. T. Iakovleva (Moscow: Izd. "Nauka," 1966), pp. 122-51.

Stanton, John W. "Russian Embassies to Peking during the Eighteenth Century," *University of Michigan Historical Essays,* ed. Arthur E. R. Boak (Ann Arbor: University of Michigan Press, 1937), 97-112.

"Torgovlia shelkom v Kitae," *Zhurnal manufaktur i torgovli,* No. 3 (1854), 340-47.

Treadgold, Donald W. "Russian Expansion in the Light of Turner's Study of the American Frontier," *Agricultural History,* XXVI, No. 4 (October, 1952), 147–52.

Tsiang Ting-fu. "Tsui-chin san-pai-nien tung-pei wai-huan-shih," *Tsing-hua Journal,* VIII (1932), 1-70.

Uspenskii, D. I. "Iz istorii russkikh snoshenii s narodami Vostoka (Russko-kitaiskiia nedorazumeniia)," *Russkaia mysl',* XXV (November, 1904), 75-96.

Vernadsky, George. "The Expansion of Russia," *Transactions of the Connecticut Academy of Sciences,* XXXI (July, 1933), 393-425.

Wheeler, Mary Elizabeth. "The Origins of the Russian-American Company," *Jahrbücher für Geschichte Osteuropas,* New Series, XIV (December, 1966), 485-94.

Williams, Frederick Wells. "A Sketch of Russo-Chinese Intercourse," *New Englander and Yale Review,* XVIII (New Series), LIV (Complete Series) (May, 1891), 403-30.

Wylie, Alexander. "The Overland Journey from St. Petersburg to Pekin," *Journal of the North China Branch of the Royal Asiatic Society,* New Series, No. 1 (December, 1864), 1-20.

Zeddeler, Liudvig Ivanovich, "Kiakhta i Maimachen (Iz putevago zhurnala General-Leitenanta Barona Zeddelera," *Severnaia pchela,* No. 286 (19 December 1845), 1143-44; No. 287 (20 December 1845), 1147-48.

Zlatkin, Il'ia Iakovlevich. "O roli Rossii v bor'be Mongolov za nezavisimost protiv man'chzurskikh zavoevatelei vo vtoroi polovine XVII-pervoi polovine XVIII v.," *Kratkie soobshcheniia Instituta vostokovedeniia,* VI (1952), 46-52.

Index